R. Gupta's®

POPULAR MASTER GUIDE

Madhya Pradesh
High School Teacher
Eligibility Test

PART–A (COMPULSORY FOR ALL)

• Pedagogy • सामान्य हिन्दी • General English • Reasoning Ability
• Numerical Ability • General Knowledge • Madhya Pradesh General Knowledge

Conducted by
Professional Examination Board, Bhopal

by
RPH Editorial Board

2019
E D I T I O N

Ramesh Publishing House, New Delhi

Published by
O.P. Gupta *for* Ramesh Publishing House

Admin. Office
12-H, New Daryaganj Road, Opp. Officers' Mess,
New Delhi-110002 ✆ 23261567, 23275224, 23275124

E-mail: info@rameshpublishinghouse.com
Website: www.rameshpublishinghouse.com

Showroom
● Balaji Market, Nai Sarak, Delhi-6 ✆ 23253720, 23282525
● 4457, Nai Sarak, Delhi-6, ✆ 23918938

© Reserved with the Publisher

No Part of this book may be reproduced or transmitted in any form or by any means, electronic or mechanical including photocopying, recording or by any transformation storage and retrieval system without written permission from the Publisher.

Indemnification Clause: *This book is being sold/distributed subject to the exclusive condition that neither the author nor the publishers, individually or collectively, shall be responsible to indemnify the buyer/user/possessor of this book beyond the selling price of this book for any reason under any circumstances. If you do not agree to it, please do not buy/accept/use/possess this book.*

Book Code: R-1993

ISBN: 978-93-87918-74-0

HSN Code: 49011010

- There will be one Question paper for this exam of 150 marks. There will be a total of 150 Multiple Choice Questions (MCQs) in this paper.

- There will be two parts of the Question Paper—**Part-'A'** and **Part-'B'.** Part-A will be compulsory for all. Candidate must have to select one subject from the subject list included in **Part-'B'.**

- There will be Five Sections in Part-'A' in which weightages of marks are as follows—

Sr. No.	Subject	No. of Questions	Full Marks
1.	General Hindi	10	10
2.	General English	08	08
3.	General Knowledge & Current Affairs	10	10
4.	Reasoning and Numerical Abiltiy	07	07
5.	Pedagogy	15	15
	Total	**50**	**50**

- Part-B will be of 100 marks and there are 100 Multiple Choice Questions (MCQs) in this Question Paper asked from Candidate's subject.

❏❏❏

CONTENTS

Model Paper

Pedagogy

सामान्य हिन्दी

General English

Reasoning Ability

Numerical Ability

General Knowledge & Current Affairs

Madhya Pradesh General Knowledge

R. Gupta's® Useful Books for this Exam

Book Name	Book-Code	Price	Book Name	Book-Code	Price
● Objective Botany	R-1212	₹ 140	● Objective History	R-681	₹ 210
● Objective Agricultural Science	R-1157	₹ 195	● Objective Public Administration	R-679	₹ 130
● Objective Physics	R-755	₹ 190	● Objective Geography	R-712	₹ 190
● Objective Chemistry	R-658	₹ 150	● Objective Economics	R-720	₹ 180
● Objective Biology	R-663	₹ 150	● Objective Commerce	R-809	₹ 230
● Objective Mathematics	R-66 2	₹ 180	● Objective Sociology	R-802	₹ 180
● Objective Home Science	R-898	₹ 170	● Objective Political Science	R-786	₹ 160
● Objective Science	R-1014	₹ 160	● Objective General English	R-229	₹ 140

Ramesh Publishing House

12-H, New Daryaganj Road, Opp. Officers' Mess, Delhi-110002
For Online Shopping: www.rameshpublishinghouse.com

1810

Model Paper (Solved)
MADHYA PRADESH HIGH SCHOOL TEACHER
Eligibility Test

PART-A

सामान्य हिन्दी

निर्देश : *निम्नलिखित विकल्प में से शुद्ध वर्तनी वाला शब्द छाँटिए—*

1. A. मातृभूमि   B. मात्रभूमि
   C. मातरभूमि   D. मातभूमि

निर्देश : *निम्नलिखित वाक्यांश के लिए एक उपयुक्त शब्द चुनिए—*

2. जो व्याकरण का ज्ञाता हो—
   A. ज्ञानी   B. बुद्धिमान
   C. वैयाकरण   D. भाषाविद्

निर्देश : *दिए गए शब्द के विभिन्न विकल्पों में से एक शब्द पर्यायवाची (समानार्थक) नहीं है, उसे छाँटिए—*

3. अद्वितीय
   A. अपूर्व   B. अनुपम
   C. श्रेष्ठ   D. निरुपम

निर्देश : *दिए गए शब्द का सही विलोम (विपरीतार्थक) चुनिए—*

4. नैसर्गिक
   A. कृत्रिम   B. बुटिल
   C. सिक्त   D. पुरातन

निर्देश : *निम्नलिखित में से किस समूह के तीनों शब्द समान लिंग के हैं—*

5. तीनों पुल्लिंग शब्द—
   A. रजनी, सरिता, अमेरिका   B. बाजरा, डिबिया, नर्मदा
   C. भारत, पत्थर, वर्ष   D. अध्यापिका, मास्टर, नागिन

निर्देश : *निम्नलिखित शब्द का सही सन्धि-विच्छेद होगा।*

6. विषम
   A. विः + सम   B. वि + शम
   C. वि + सम   D. वि + षर्म

निर्देश : *पदक्रम की दृष्टि से निम्नलिखित विकल्पों में से कौन-सा असंगत है?*

7. A. सौ-पचास   B. हीरे-जवाहरात
   C. यहाँ-वहाँ   D. नाले-नदी

8. निम्नलिखित विकल्पों में से उस विकल्प की पहचान करो जिसमें केवल संज्ञा शब्द हों—
   A. हिमालय, कागज, राम   B. सुन्दर, शरीफ, ऊँचा
   C. चलना, उड़ना, पीना   D. आप, मैं, कौन

9. अल्पविराम (,) के सही प्रयोग की दृष्टि से इनमें से कौन-सा विकल्प सही है?
   A. महोदय निवेदन है, कि मैं आगे पढ़ना चाहता हूँ
   B. महोदय, निवेदन है कि मैं आगे पढ़ना चाहता हूँ
   C. महोदय निवेदन है कि मैं, आगे पढ़ना चाहता हूँ
   D. महोदय निवेदन है कि मैं आगे, पढ़ना चाहता हूँ

निर्देश : *नीचे दिए गए मुहावरे का सही अर्थ छाँटिए—*

10. चिकनी-चुपड़ी बातें करना—
   A. सुन्दर बातें करना   B. घी खाकर बातें करना
   C. खुशामद करना   D. अर्थ स्पष्ट नहीं है

GENERAL ENGLISH

Directions (Qs. 11 & 12): *Choose the word which best expresses the meaning of the underlined word in the sentence.*

11. He spent his whole life caught up in <u>mundane</u> matters.
   A. worldly   B. foolish
   C. inconsequential   D. criminal

12. Smart people are often good at <u>camouflaging</u> their real character.
   A. projecting
   B. displaying
   C. hiding
   D. revealing

Directions (Qs. 13 & 14): *Choose the word which is closest to the opposite in meaning of the underlined word in the sentence.*

13. We had a <u>delectable</u> meal yesterday.
A. nice
B. tasty
C. heavy
D. unsavory

14. Never adopt a <u>callous</u> attitude towards your duties.
A. cooperative
B. considerate
C. cautious
D. courteous

Directions: *Choose the option which best expresses the meaning of the underlined idiom/phrase in the sentence.*

15. Our politicians are often <u>in a Catch-22 situation.</u>
A. absurd
B. dangerous
C. hopeful
D. depressive

Directions (Qs. 16 & 17): *A word has been written in four different ways out of which only one is correctly spelt. Choose the correctly spelt word.*

16. A. Etiquete
B. Ettiquete
C. Etiquette
D. Ettiquette

17. A. Diarhoea
B. Diarheoa
C. Diarrheoa
D. Diarrhoea

Directions: *Following question has a group of sentences marked (1), (2), (3), (4) and (5). Arrange these to form a logical sequence.*

18.
1. According to well known management gurus, these team activities can have unintended consequences for certain employees.
2. I humbly suggest you think again about it.
3. So you believe that office parties are the ultimate team building exercise?
4. Finally, recent research reveals that while social events help homogenous teams form close bonds, they do not have the same benefits for racially diverse groups of co-workers.
5. Research points out otherwise.
A. 5 1 4 3 2
B. 3 2 5 1 4
C. 4 1 3 5 2
D. 2 5 1 4 3

GENERAL KNOWLEDGE & CURRENT AFFAIRS

19. Which of the following Indian rivers flows into the Arabian Sea?
A. Narmada
B. Brahmaputra
C. Ravi
D. Subarnarekha

20. Which one of the following is NOT a pair of North Eastern states of India?
A. Assam and Bhutan
B. Arunachal Pradesh and Manipur
C. Tripura and Assam
D. Meghalaya and Mizoram

21. Who wins FIFA World Cup-2018?
A. France
B. Croatia
C. England
D. Belgium

22. Which one of the following was NOT a Moghul emperor?
A. Safdarjang
B. Humayun
C. Jahangir
D. Bahadur Shah II

23. Novak Djokovic, the winner of multiple Grand Slam Tennis tournaments, is from :
A. Serbia
B. Croatia
C. France
D. England

24. The first World War ended in the year:
A. 1945
B. 1857
C. 1706
D. 1918

25. Who developed the Oral Polio Vaccine?
A. Edward Jenner
B. Albert Sabin
C. Michiaki Takahashi
D. Louis Pasteur

26. Which is the apex banking institution for providing finance for agriculture and rural development in India?
A. RBI
B. SEBI
C. IBRD
D. NABARD

27. The number of Lok Sabha seats from Madhya Pradesh is:
A. 29
B. 30
C. 31
D. 32

28. Where is 'Bharat Bhavan' situated in Madhya Pradesh?
A. Bhopal
B. Jabalpur
C. Indore
D. Sagar

REASONING ABILITY & NUMERICAL ABILITY

29. Select the related letters from the given alternatives.
FHJL : USQO :: PRTV : ?
A. QSUW
B. KIGE
C. MJGD
D. EGIL

30. Select the related numbers from the given alternatives.
23 : 34 :: 47 : ?
A. 56
B. 60
C. 62
D. 69

31. Six friends J, K, L, M, N and O are sitting around a circle facing towards the centre. J is not adjacent to K or L; M is not adjacent to L or N; K and L are adjacent. O is in the middle of M and L. If one neighbour of J is M, who is the other one?

A. K

B. L

C. N

D. O

32. From the given alternatives, select the word which can be formed using the letters of the given word. You can use a letter only as many times as it appears in the word below.

DISPROPORTIONATE

A. PERSONAL

B. DISPOSE

C. PROPONENT

D. STATION

33. Select the diagram that best represents the relationship among classes given below.

Red, Shirts, Flowers

34. What is the smallest 4-digit number which is divisible by 18, 24 and 32?

A. 1112

B. 1152

C. 1440

D. 1584

35. Two containers contain 850 litres and 680 litres of oil respectively. What is the maximum capacity of a container which can measure the oil of both containers an exact number of times?

A. 10

B. 17

C. 85

D. 170

PEDAGOGY

36. Inclusion of children with special needs:
A. is an unrealistic goal
B. is detrimental to children without disabilities
C. will increase the burden on schools
D. requires a change in attitude, content and approach to teaching

37. "Having a diverse classroom with children from varied social, economic and cultural backgrounds enriches the learning experiences of all students." This statement is:
A. incorrect, because it can confuse the children and they may feel lost
B. correct, because children learn many skills from their peers
C. correct, because it makes the classroom more hierarchical
D. incorrect, because it leads to unnecessary competition

38. A child with hearing impairment:
A. should be sent only to a school for the hearing impaired and not to a regular school
B. will not benefit from academic education only and should be given vocational training instead
C. can do very well in a regular school if suitable facilitation and resources are provided
D. will never be able to perform on a par with classmates in a regular school

39. Which of the following is a characteristic of a gifted learner?
A. He gets aggressive and frustrated.
B. He can feel understimulated and bored if the class activities are not challenging enough.
C. He is highly temperamental.
D. He engages in ritualistic behaviour like hand flapping, rocking, etc.

40. A teacher can enhance effective learning in her elementary classroom by:
A. offering rewards for small steps in learning
B. drill and practice
C. encouraging competition amongst her students
D. connecting the content to the lives of the students

41. Which of the following statements about children are **correct**?
1. Children are passive recipients of knowledge.
2. Children are problem solvers.
3. Children are scientific investigators.
4. Children are active explorers of the environment.
A. 1, 2 and 4
B. 2, 3 and 4
C. 1, 2, 3 and 4
D. 1, 2 and 3

42. Which of the following are secondary agents of socialization?
A. Family and neighbourhood
B. School and neighbourhood
C. School and immediate family members
D. Family and relatives

43. According to Lev Vygotsky, the primary cause of cognitive development is:
A. equilibration
B. social interaction
C. adjustment of mental schemas
D. stimulus-response pairing

44. In the context of Kohlberg's stages of moral reasoning, under which stage would the given typical response of a child fall?

"Your parents will be proud of you if you are honest. So you should be honest."
A. Punishment-obedience orientation
B. Social contract orientation
C. Good girl-good boy orientation
D. Law and order orientation

45. According to Jean Piaget, which of the following is necessary for learning?
A. Active exploration of the environment by the learner
B. Observing the behaviour of adults
C. Belief in immanent justice
D. Reinforcement by teachers and parents

46. According to Jean Piaget, schema building occurs as a result of modifying new information to fit existing schemes and by modifying old schemes as per new information. These two processes are known as:
A. accommodation and adaptation
B. assimilation and adaptation
C. equilibration and modification
D. assimilation and accommodation

47. In a progressive classroom setup, the teacher facilitates learning by providing an environment that:
A. promotes discovery
B. is restrictive
C. discourages inclusion
D. encourages repetition

48. Howard Gardner's theory of Multiple Intelligence (MI) suggests that:
A. every child should be taught every subject in eight different ways in order to develop all of the intelligences
B. intelligence is solely determined by IQ tests
C. teachers should use MI as a framework for devising alternative ways to teach the subject matter
D. ability is destiny and does not change over a period of time

49. Which of the following is the most effective method to encourage conceptual development in students?
A. New concepts need to be understood on their own without any reference to the old ones.
B. Replace the students' incorrect ideas with correct ones by asking them to memorize.
C. Give students multiple examples and encourage them to use reasoning.
D. Use punishment till students have made the required conceptual changes.

50. 'Gender' is a/an:
A. biological entity
B. physiological construct
C. innate quality
D. social construct

ANSWERS

1	2	3	4	5	6	7	8	9	10
A	C	C	A	C	A	D	A	B	C

11	12	13	14	15	16	17	18	19	20
A	C	D	D	A	C	D	B	A	A

21	22	23	24	25	26	27	28	29	30
A	A	A	D	B	D	A	A	B	C

31	32	33	34	35	36	37	38	39	40
C	D	D	B	D	D	B	C	A	D

41	42	43	44	45	46	47	48	49	50
B	B	B	C	A	D	A	C	C	D

1810

Note: *In addition to these 50 Questions of Part-A, 100 Questions of Part-B will be asked from Concerned Subjects.*

Child Development & Pedagogy

CHILD DEVELOPMENT

SECTION a

CONCEPT OF DEVELOPMENT AND ITS RELATIONSHIP WITH LEARNING

The discipline of Child Development is concerned with the changes in the behaviour of children over time and explains why and how they occur. It aims to describe and explain development in the areas of physical, social, emotional, language and cognitive functioning.

Development and Growth

The term 'development' is used for changes in a person's physical and behavioural traits that emerge in orderly ways and last for a reasonable period of time. The three main characteristics of these changes are progressive, orderly and long lasting. Development refers to both quantitative as well as qualitative changes. It includes changes not only in structure but also in function.

'Growth' refers to physical increase in the size of the body. Increase in weight, height and internal organs is growth. Growth refers to a quantitative change, that is, a change that can be measured.

Growth is only one aspect of the larger process of development. Development continues even when physical changes are not visible. Physical growth slows down considerably after adolescence but development does not.

Stages of Development

The human life span has been divided into the stages of infancy, childhood, adolescence and adulthood.

The period from birth to two years of age is referred to as the period of infancy. In this period the child is totally dependent on the caregiver for the fulfilment of his needs. After birth, this is the period of most rapid growth and development. The child's skills and abilities increase. By the end of infancy he is able to walk, run, communicate his needs verbally, feed himself, identify family members, recognise himself and venture confidently in familiar surroundings.

The period of childhood is from two to twelve years of age. Development at this stage is not as rapid as during infancy. During this period the child refines the skills he has acquired during infancy and learns new skill as well. During childhood he also learns the ways of behaviour that are considered appropriate by the society. The child meets many people outside the family and forms attachments with more people. As the child grows and his thinking capacities mature, he realises that he can do many things. This gives him a feeling of confidence. During this period he becomes more independent though adult guidance is constantly needed. The period of childhood is divided into two stages : the period of early childhood (2–6 years) and middle childhood (6–12 years). The period of early childhood is also referred to as the preschool age because at this age the child is learning skills that will help him to do tasks associated with schooling. The preschooler has mastered the words to ask questions about things and people. He learns about numbers, colours, shapes and the reasons for everyday events. All these concepts develop from actually seeing things and doing various activities. The child in the age group 6–12 years has matured a great deal and is expected to behave more responsibly than the preschooler.

The next stage is referred to as the period of adolescence (12–18 years). The beginning of this period is marked by puberty. Puberty refers to the stage around 11–14 years of the age, when there is a spurt in physical growth. This results in a rapid increase in height and weight and the emergence of secondary sexual characteristics. These rapid physical changes lead to a need for emotional readjustment.

At this age the peer group becomes very important and the adolescent follows the rules and the codes of her group. Feelings of loyalty and pride for the group are very strong. At times the values of the peer group may become more important than those of the family. During adolescence thinking develops further and becomes more complex. The individual can understand and deal with varied situations. He can think of abstract problems and work out their solutions. All this helps him to prepare for the roles and responsibilities, which he will be expected to carry out as an adult.

After the age of 18 years the person is referred to as an adult. Physical changes are completed in this stage and person becomes mature.

Areas of Development

The various developments that take place during the life span of an individual can be classified thus: physical and motor development, social development, emotional development, cognitive and language development.

Physical development refers to the physical changes in the size, structure and proportion of the parts of the body that take place from the moment of conception.

Motor development means the development of control over body movements. This results in increasing coordination between various parts of the body. As a result of physical and motor development the child acquires many abilities. These developments will bring about the change from an infant who at the time of birth is capable of only lying on his back to one who learns to roll over, hold his head, sit, walk, run and climb stairs. The improving coordination between the eye and the hand movements will help him to eat food without smearing it on his face. Gradually he will learn to clothe himself, draw, skip, paint, ride a bicycle and type. As he grows he will refine the skills already acquired as well as develop new ones.

Language development refers to those changes that make it possible for an infant, who in the early months uses crying for communication, to learn words and then sentences to converse fluently. How the child learns to speak grammatically correct sentences is amazing! At first the child indicates his need for water through crying. Then he learns to say "water". A little later he says, "Mummy water" and finally he speaks a complete sentence, "Mummy, I want to drink water". He will be about three years by this time.

Cognitive development concerns the emergence of thinking capabilities in the individual. We can see how the child's thinking develops and changes from one age to the next. The infant is not born with the reasoning and thinking, abilities of adults. In fact, the infant acts as if an object that is removed from his sight has ceased to exist. Gradually he learns that objects and people are permanent and they exist even if he cannot see them. Around five years of age he can understand concepts such as heavy and light, fast and slow, colours and sizes which he did not comprehend earlier. Exploration of the surroundings and the questions regarding the 'why' and 'how' of things result in an increasing store of information. His thought develops but he is still unable to see a situation from another person's point of view. For example, he is unable to understand why another child cannot climb the tree when he can do so. He thinks that everybody else should be able to do what he can and feel the way he does. He believes that all things have life and feelings like him including the sun, stone, pencil and table. A ten year old has learnt to reason and analyze but this ability is limited to real life concrete situations. He cannot usually think in abstract terms or predict future event. The capacity for abstruct thinking develops fully during the period of adolescence. He can now handle complex situations. Thus at each stage of a person's life, the ability to think is qualitatively different and more developed compared to the earlier stage.

Cognitive development is the process of mental development from infancy to adulthood. Cognition refers to the process of 'coming to know', which is accomplished through the gathering and processing of information. It includes perceiving, learning, remembering, problem solving, and thinking about the world. Intelligence is a term difficult to define. Nevertheless, according to a well known definition, it refers to the individual's ability to "act purposefully, think rationally and deal effectively with the environment".

Social development refers to the development of those abilities that enable the individual to behave in accordance with the expectations of the society. It is concerned with the child's relationships with people and his ways of interaction with them. The infant instinctively reaches out to the person who approaches him with love and affection. Gradually he learns to recognize his mother and other caregivers and forms attachment to them.

Emotional development refers to the emergence of emotions like anger, joy, delight, happiness, fear, anxiety and sorrow and the socially acceptable ways of expressing them. As the child grows up and becomes aware of acceptable ways of behaviour, a variety of emotions also emerge. As an infant he expresses only discomfort and delight. As he grows older, expressions of joy, happiness, fear, anger and disappointment appear. He learns to express these emotions in a healthy manner. For example, initially the child hits out when angry. Gradually he learns to control this and expresses anger in other ways.

Theories of Child Development and Learning

Maturationist Theory

The maturationist theory was advanced by the work of Arnold Gessell. Maturationists believe that development is a biological process that occurs automatically in predictable, sequential stages over time. This perspective leads many educators and families to assume that young children will acquire knowledge naturally and automatically as they grow physically and become older, provided that they are healthy.

School readiness, according to maturationists, is a state at which all healthy young children arrive when they can perform tasks such as reciting the alphabet and counting; these tasks are required for learning more complex tasks such as reading and arithmetic. Because development and school readiness occur naturally and automatically, maturationists believe the best practices are for parents to teach young children to recite the alphabet and count while being patient and waiting for children to become ready for kindergarten. If a child is developmentally unready for school, maturationists might suggest referrals to transitional kindergartens, retention, or holding children out of school for an additional year. These practices are sometimes used by schools, educators, and parents when a young child developmentally lags behind his or her peers. The young child's underperformance is interpreted as the child needing more time to acquire the knowledge and skills needed to perform at the level of his or her peers.

Environmentalist Theory

Theorists such as John Watson, B.F. Skinner, and Albert Bandura contributed greatly to the environmentalist perspective of development. Environmentalists believe the child's environment shapes learning and behaviour in fact, human behaviour, development, and learning are thought of as reactions to the environment. This perspective leads many families, schools, and educators to assume that young children develop and acquire new knowledge by reacting to their surroundings.

Kindergarten readiness, according to the environmentalists, is the age or stage when young children can respond appropriately to the environment of the school and the classroom (*e.g.*, rules and regulations, curriculum activities, positive behaviour in group settings, and directions and instructions from teachers and other adults in the school). The ability to respond appropriately to this environment is necessary for young children to participate in teacher-initiated learning activities. Success is dependent on the child following instructions from the teacher or the adult in the classroom. Many environmentalist-influenced educators and parents believe that young children learn best by rote activities, such as reciting the alphabet over and over, copying letters, and tracing numbers. This viewpoint is evident in kindergarten classrooms where young children are expected to sit at desks arranged in rows and listen attentively to their teachers. At home, parents may provide their young children with workbooks containing such activities as colouring or tracing letters and numbers—activities that require little interaction between parent and child. When young children are unable to respond appropriately to the classroom and school environment, they often are labelled as having some form of learning disabilities and are tracked in classrooms with curriculum designed to control their behaviours and responses.

Constructivist Theory

The constructivist perspective of readiness and development was advanced by theorists such as Jean Piaget, Maria Montessori, and Lev Vygotsky. Although their work varies greatly, each articulates a similar context of learning and development. They are consistent in their belief that learning and development occur when young children interact with the environment and people around them. Constructivists view young children as active participants in the learning process. In addition, constructivists believe young children initiate most of the activities required for learning and development. Because active interaction with the environment and people are necessary for learning and development, constructivists believe that children are ready for school when they can initiate many of the interactions they have with the environment and people around them.

Constructivist-influenced schools and educators pay a lot of attention to the physical environment and the curriculum of the early childhood classroom. Kindergarten classrooms often are divided into different **learning centers** and are equipped with developmentally appropriate materials for young children to play with and manipulate. Teachers and adults have direct conversations with children, children move actively from one center to another, and daily activities are made meaningful through the incorporation of children's experiences into the curriculum. At home, parents engage their young children in reading and storytelling activities and encourage children's participation in daily household activities in a way that introduces such concepts as counting and language use. In addition, parents may provide young children with picture books containing very large print, and toys that stimulate interaction (such as building blocks and large puzzles). When a young child encounters difficulties in the learning process, the constructivist approach is neither to lable the child nor to retain him or her; instead, constructivists give the child some individualized attention and customize the classroom curriculum to help the child address his or her difficulties.

Today, most researchers have come to understand child development and the learning process as articulated by the constructivists. However, this view has not been widely translated into practice. Many kindergarten teachers and parents still believe that young children are not ready for school unless they can recite the alphabet, count, and have the ability to follow instructions from adults.

PRINCIPLES AND THEORIES OF CHILD DEVELOPMENT

Studying and understanding child growth and development are important parts of teaching young children. No two children are alike. Children differ in physical, cognitive, social and emotional growth patterns. Even identical twins, who have the same genetic makeup, are not exactly alike. They may differ in the way they respond to play, affection, objects and people in their environment.

Knowledge of the areas of child development is basic to guiding young children. Linked to this is the understanding of healthy brain development. These stimuli begin at birth. Therefore, it is vital for children to have loving caregivers. Young children need dependable, trusting relationships. They thrive in environments that are predictable and nurturing. Understanding theories about how people develop helps form your knowledge base in caring for young children.

Child Development

Development refers to change or growth that occurs in children. It starts with infancy and continues to adulthood. By studying child development, you will form a profile of what children can do at various ages.

Different names are used to describe young children at different ages. From birth through the first year, children are called **infants. Toddlers** are children from age one up to the third birthday (Because of an awkward style of walking, the name toddler describes this age group). The term **preschooler** is often used to describe children ages three to six years of age.

Areas of Development

The study of child development is often divided into three main areas. These include physical, cognitive and social-emotional development. Dividing development into these areas makes it easier to study.

Physical development refers to physical body changes. It occurs in a relatively stable, predictable sequence. It is orderly, not random. Changes in size and weight are also part of physical development.

Physical skills, such as crawling, walking and writing, are the result of physical development. These skills fall into two main categories:

1. **Grossmotor development :** It involves improvement of skills using the large muscles in the legs and arms. Such activities as running, skipping and bike riding fall into this category.

2. **Fine-motor development :** It involves the small muscles of the hands and fingers. Grasping, holding, cutting and drawing are some activities that require fine-motor development.

Environmental factors also affect what children can do physically. These factors include proper nutrition and appropriate toys and activities.

Cognitive development, sometimes called **intellectual development,** refers to processes people use to gain knowledge. Language, thought, reasoning and imagination are all included. Identifying colours and knowing the difference between one and many are examples of cognitive tasks.

Language and thought are a result of cognitive development. These two skills are closely related. Both are needed for planning, remembering and problem solving. As children mature and gain experience with their world, these skills develop.

The third area of development is called social-emotional development. These two areas are grouped together because they are so interrelated. Learning to relate to others is social development. Emotional development, on the other hand, involves feelings and expression of feelings. Trust, fear, confidence, pride, friendship and humor are all part of social-emotional development. Other emotional traits include timidity, interest and pleasure.

Learning to express emotions in appropriate ways begins early. Caregivers promote this learning when they positively model these skills. A person's self-concept and self-esteem are also part of this area. As children have success with all skills confidence flourishes. This leads to a healthy self-concept and sense of worth.

The physical, cognitive and social-emotional areas of development are linked to one another. Development in one area can strongly influence another area. For instance, writing words requires fine-motor skills. It also requires cognitive development. Language, a part of cognitive development, is needed to communicate with others. It is also necessary for growing socially and emotionally.

Principles of Development

Although each child is unique, the basic patterns or principles of growth and development are universal, predictable and orderly. Through careful observation and interaction with children, researchers and those who work with children understand the characteristics of the principles that follow:

1. Development tends to proceed from the head downward. This is called the **cephalocaudal principle.** According to this principle, the child first gains control of the head, then the arms, then the legs. Infants gain control of head and face movements within the first two months after birth. In the next few months, they are able to lift themselves up using their arms. By 6 to 12 months of age, infant start to gain leg control and may be able to crawl, stand or walk.

2. Development also proceeds from the center of the body outward according to the **proximodistal principle**. Accordingly, the spinal cord develops before other parts of the body. The child's arms develop before the hands and the hands and feet develop before the fingers and toes. Fingers and toes are the last to develop.

3. Development also depends on maturation. **Maturation** refers to the sequence of biological changes in children. These orderly changes give children new abilities. Much of the maturation depends on changes in the brain and the nervous system. These changes assist children to improve their thinking abilities and motor skills. A rich learning environment helps children develop to their potential.

Children must mature to a certain point before they can gain some skills. For instance, the brain of a four-month-old has not matured enough to allow the child to use words. A four-month-old will babble and coo. However, by two years of age, with the help of others, the child will be able to say and understand many words. This is an example of how cognitive development occurs from simple tasks to more complex tasks. Likewise, physical skills develop from general to specific movements. For example, think about the way an infant waves its arms and legs. In a young infant, these movements are random. In several months, the infant will likely be able to grab a block with his or her whole hand. In a little more time, the same infant will grasp a block with the thumb and fore finger.

INFLUENCE OF HEREDITY AND ENVIRONMENT

Heredity and environment greatly influence the growth, development and behaviour of a child. Each child inherits certain capacities for growth. The way in which these capacities develop is influenced by the opportunities afforded by the environment, for example, the height to which the individual is capable of growing is determined by heredity. The environment cannot change the limits imposed by heredity. Whereas a poor environment *i.e.*, lack of exposure will slow down a child who is genetically clever, a rich environment which provides and exposes a child to a lot of educational facilities will not change a child who is genetically born not clever to become clever. A good environment will enable the individual to reach these limits. The environment influences the speed with which the child develops. The environment shapes the individual's development in the sense that it promotes the growth of certain capacities and neglects the growth of others. For instance, if the child experiences more emphasis on academic and no attachment to physical education, the child's capacity to develop certain skills will be neglected.

Effects of Heredity and Environment on Development of Personality

Before discussing the contribution of hereditary factors let us see what is meant by heredity when we talk of heredity we usually have biological heredity in mind. The term 'heredity' may also be used in another sense, for example, if a child is brought up in a particular social environment say of a tribe, the value of that tribe and the norms of that tribe are inculcated in him through other members of that social group and we call it **social heredity.** In the same way, a student in a classroom situation brings with him a specific cultural heredity also. Here our discussion will be focused on the influence of only biological heredity on individual differences. Each individual has a specific set of potentials which are developed through the environment. These potentialities and characteristics possessed by the individual are the result of his biological heredity. The influence of heredity is so strong that twins brought up in drastically different environment show very much similarity in terms of their mental abilities and other traits. This shows that even drastically different environments are not capable of overcoming hereditary influences.

Hereditary, or the genetic transmission of characteristics from parents to offspring, determine personality to a certain extent. Hereditary characteristics manifest at birth such as hair and eye colour, skin colour and body type. Hereditary also includes aptitude or the capacity to learn a skill or inclination for a particular body of knowledge. It establishes the limits of one's personality traits that can be developed. This aptitude creates the desire for a person to learn something. For instance, the son of a sports hero like a boxer superstar is expected to inherit the genes of his father. His capacity for growth in the boxing arena is immense because he is born with the ability.

Behavioural geneticists, Dr. David Reiss and colleagues from George Washington University, conducted a thorough and long-term study on the effects of genetics to a person's personality. The result of their study revealed that 'it seems that genetic influences are largely responsible for how 'adjusted' kids are : how well they do in school, how they get along with their peers, whether they engage in dangerous or delinquent behaviour'.

Effect of Environment on Personality Development

Apart from heredity, environment also effects the child development. The concept of environment needs little clarification when we say the environment of the child is not good, sometimes we mean that he is living in a locality which does not have desirable people or we mean that he is living in the rural area where he does not have access to many things which an urban environment may provide. As has rightly been said, the psychological environment consists of the sum total of the stimulation the individual receives from conception till death. This is an active concept of environment *i.e.*, the physical presence of objects does not in itself constitute environment unless the objects serve as stimuli for the individual.

The role of the prenatal environment on the development of the child is well known and has been demonstrated through various experiments. The diet a mother takes at the time of pregnancy, her mental status, glandular secretions and even the thinking process influence the development of the child. Environmentalists firmly believe that, under favourable circumstances, every individual is almost infinitely improvable.

Newman, Freeman and Holzinger conducted thorough research on nineteen pairs of identical twins reared in different environments. Initially they found that the pairs reared apart show mere differences in I.Q. But Woodworth (1941) in his analysis of the results pointed out a factor called error of measurement that is always involved in intelligence testing. When this factor was taken into account and results interpreted, Woodworth concluded that environmental differences do operate to produce I.Q. differences in persons with exactly the same hereditary potentialities. But the magnitude of these differences is not as large as those found among children whose heredity is not alike.

Environment and its Interaction with Hereditary Factors

Nature refers to what a child has inherited genetically, from the parents (*e.g.* eye colour, appearance, etc). The influence of environment on the development of the child (*e.g.* liking for a type of music) is referred to as nurture. The earlier view of child development focused either entirely on nature or nurture. Many favoured heredity, and believed that we are born with certain talents and personalities. These determine who we are and what we become.

In the other view, the focus was on the role of environment. We learn to do things for which we get rewards (or praises) and do not do things for which we are punished (including disapproval from elders). Both views contained some truth but neither is complete. To understand the development of a person, we have to study the complex interaction between nature and nurture (or heredity and environment).

Let us consider an example. A child is born with a talent for music. In the child's family, this talent for music is expressed by the child at an early age, through his activities of singing and listening to music. The parents notice the child's interest in music and expose the child to more music and give him a toy musical instrument (*e.g.* ek tara or flute). The child's interest in music grows further and his talent develops and this make the parents offer even more musical experiences (*e.g.* playing music on stage, attending music concerts etc.). This has a further positive effect on the child's talent and his desire to play music.

It is thus clear that both the child's inherited talent and environment shaped his/her development. The child had the talent for music, but this led to a change in the environment by making her parents provide more musical experiences at home. Now these experiences in the environment further developed the child's talent and motivation and made the parents introduce more musical experiences to the child. The process goes on and on like this in a form of transaction. This approach to understanding development is called a transactional model (TA).

The TA model is able to explain why brothers and sisters, though physically in the same environment, always grow up in 'different' ways. This simply means that the environment of family life is always changing in the process of adjusting to the personalities of its members. A first born child grows up with very different experiences than a middle born or youngest child. A child who displays temper tantrums (getting angry easily, without sufficient cause) has a very different experience with her parents as compared to her easy going brother.

Let us take another example to make the point more clear. Suppose you as a parent (if not today, then in the future) are facing difficulty with your argumentative 12-year-old. The TA model reminds you that you must first think about the factor which has brought your child to this point. Is it a personality trait that is troubling you? Is she stubborn (does not listen to others) all the time and is thus part of her nature? Does she resist any change in her usual routine? Does she lack the ability to talk to you about what's troubling her, and could that be upsetting her? The child represents one part of the puzzle or problem which has to be solved.

The next questions you have to ask are : What is my role in all this? Am I somehow rewarding the very behaviours? Am I trying to stop by paying too much attention to them? Am I having too much expectation from a 12-year old? Am I reminded of my younger sister with whom I had faced a similar problem, and could be causing irritation in me now? The environment which includes you forms the other-part of the picture.

Finally, you need to put the two together to obtain a full picture of what is going on and how to bring about a positive change. In which way my behaviour is affecting my child? And most importantly, what do I need to change to break this pattern of behaviour (argumentation in the child) located in its transactions with nurture? How can I better understand the forces behind my child's behaviour so as to improve my response to it?

This may sound very theoretical to some of you but it's exactly the questions which many parents are always asking themselves, even if they are not aware of it. By understanding the TA-model you will be in a better position to understand the interaction between nature and nurture which is responsible for your child's behaviour and development. This will help you in deciding which role you can play for effective development and improve the child's behaviour.

In summary according to the transactional model of development, the child changes the environment which in turn changes the child. The child's development is like a complex dance in which nature and nurture both lead, and are led.

SOCIALISATION PROCESS

As a child grows up, there is a deliberate and conscious effort made through active training to make the child learn the values and expectations of the society he or she lives in. The child has to learn to adjust and accommodate her behaviour according to the rules for appropriate behaviour in the society. Parents, teachers, elders as well as the peers (same age group children) all influence and control the behaviour of a child.

According to the Indian view, a child comes to this world with certain behavioural tendencies which carry over from previous birth. The role of the family is to bring up the child in such a way that her positive capacities are developed fully and negative tendencies are controlled. Apart from the family, there are also other influences on the child from the outside environment. The important agents of socialisation include media, day-care centers, peer group, school and religion.

Parents have the most direct effect on the socialisation of the child. They are role models for children. Their responses to child behaviour, giving approval or disapproval etc. mould the personality of child and plays a very important role in acquiring rules. In addition, parents arrange the environment of a children in different ways. They take the child outside in specific settings like museum, church, temple, mosque, hill station, sea beach. The grand parents and aunts and uncles of the child also contribute in the socialisation process. Children learn manners and skills by observing parents. During the life span of a person, at different ages, specific rituals are performed. These rituals represent the changes in the child from one stage to another. They contribute in forming the identity of the child.

The influence of the **peer group** of the child, particularly during middle childhood is very important. In the interactions with the children of the same age group, a child learns the importance of team work, sharing and trust. One of the significant effects of this is that the child learns to adjust and accommodate to the view point of the others.

The school which the child attends is another very important socializing agent. The child learns different types of social, intellectual and physical skills in school. The school provides the child with a miniature society where he or she has to learnt the right values and rules and follow them. Values such as honesty, democracy and fairness etc. are learnt in the school setting.

Now-a-days, children search and know the world through TV, magazines, books, comics, radio and films. This media influences the socialisation of the child in significant ways. A positive influence can be learning the importance of family values by watching good and informative programmes. Watching aggressive programmes and programmes based on violence can influence the child negatively.

In the present way of life, when both parents are doing jobs, very young children have to be left at day-care centers. These centers, therefore, play an important role in the socialisation of the child because the child will learn many things about appropriate behaviour in the society. For children from poor background the Aganwadis under the programme of Integrated Child Developments (ICDs) help children to learn about appropriate social behaviour and the importance of community life.

Theories of Development

Psychologists continue to study human development. They are learning more about what people are like and how they develop. Over the past century, many psychologists have provided theories that are considered practical guides. A theory is a principle or idea that is proposed, researched and generally accepted as an explanation. Developmental theories provide insights into how children grow and learn. Theories are helpful for understanding and guiding developmental processes.

Theories can be useful decision-making tools. Since a variety of theories exists, teachers need to understand these different approaches for working with children. Theories will help you understand strategies for promoting children's development. Four major theories about how children learn are important. These include theories of mid-twentieth century psychologists Erik Erikson, Jean Piaget and Lev Vygotsky. The final theorist, Howard Gardner, is a twenty first century developmental psychologist. These theories are based on observation and experiences with children.

Erikson's Psychosocial Theory

Erik Erikson proposed a theory of psychosocial development. He believed development occurs throughout the life span. His theory provided new insights into the formation of a healthy personality. It emphasizes the social and emotional aspects of growth. Children's personalities develop in response to their social environment. The same is true of their skills for social interaction.

Erikson's theory includes eight stages. At each stage, a social conflict or crisis occurs. These are not generally tragic situations; however, they require solutions that are satisfying both personally and socially. Erikson believed that each stage must be resolved before children can ascend to the next stage.

Maturity and social forces help in the resolution of the crisis or conflict. Therefore, teachers and parents play a powerful role in recognizing each stage. By providing social opportunity and support, teachers and parents can help children overcome each crisis. Following table contains the first four stages of Erikson's theory. These stages occur during the early

childhood years. The paragraphs that follow give a brief overview of these early stages.

Erikson's Stages of Development During Early Childhood		
Stage	Approximate Age	Psychosocial Crisis
I	Birth–18 months	Trust versus mistrust
II	18 months–3 years	Autonomy versus shame and doubt
III	3–5 years	Initiative versus guilt
IV	6–12 years	Industry versus inferiority

Note : *The first four stages of Erikson's theory concern children from birth to twelve years.*

Stage 1 : Trust Versus Mistrust

During the first eighteen months of life, children learn to trust or mistrust their environment. To develop trust, they need to have warm, consistent, predictable, and attentive care. They need caregivers who will accurately read and respond to their signals. When infants are distressed, they need to be comforted. They also need loving physical contact, nourishment, cleanliness, and warmth. Then they will develop a sense of confidence and trust that the world is safe and dependable. Mistrust will occur if an infant experiences an unpredictable world and is handled harshly.

Stage 2 : Autonomy Versus Shame and Doubt

This second stage occurs between eighteen months and three years of age. During this stage, toddlers use their new motor and mental skills. They want to be independent and do things for themselves. They are in the process of discovering their own bodies and practicing their developing locomotor (physical movement) and language skills.

The objective of this stage is to gain self-control without a loss of self-esteem. Fostering independence in children is important. At this age, toddlers start to become self-sufficient. They need to learn to choose and decide for themselves. To do this, toddlers need a loving, supportive environment. Positive opportunities for self-feeding, toileting, dressing and exploration will result in *autonomy,* or independence. On the other hand, overprotection or lack of adequate activities results in self-doubt, poor achievement, and shame.

Stage 3 : Initiative Versus Guilt

Between three and five years of age, the third stage occurs. According to Erikson, it emerges as a result of the many skills children have developed. Now children have the capacity and are ready to learn constructive ways of dealing with people and things. They are learning how to take initiative without being hurtful to others. They are also busy discovering how the world works. Children begin to realize that what they do can have an effect on the world, too. Challenged by the environment, children are constantly attempting and mastering new tasks. Aided by strong initiative, they are able to move ahead energetically and quickly forget failures. This gives them a sense of accomplishment.

Children at this stage need to develop a sense of purpose. This happens when adults direct children's urges toward acceptable social practices. If children are discouraged by criticism, feelings of incompetence are likely to emerge. This can also occur if parents demand too much control.

Stage 4 : Industry Versus Inferiority

The major crisis of this stage occurs between six and twelve years of age. At this time, children enjoy planning and carrying out projects. This helps them learn society's rules and expectations. During this stage, children gain approval by developing intellectual skills such as reading, writing, and math.

The way family, neighbours, teachers, and friends respond to children affects their future development. Realistic goals and expectations enrich children's sense of self. Children can become frustrated by criticism or discouragement, or if parents demand too much control. Feelings of incompetence and insecurity will emerge.

PIAGET'S COGNITIVE DEVELOPMENT THEORY

Jean Piaget's thinking has challenged teachers to focus on the *ways* children come to know as opposed to *what* they know. His theory of cognitive development focuses on predictable cognitive (thinking) stages. Piaget believed that thinking was different during each stage of development. His theory explained mental operations. This includes how children perceive, think, understand and learn about their world.

Piaget believed that children naturally attempt to understand what they do not know. Knowledge is gathered gradually during active involvement in real-life experience. By physically handling objects, young children discover that relationships exist between them. Terms Piaget used to describe these processes were *schemata, adaptation, assimilation* and *accommodation*. These processes occur during each stage of development.

Schemata are mental representations or concepts. As children receive new information, they are constantly creating, modifying, organizing and reorganizing schemata.

Adaptation is a term Piaget used for children mentally organizing what they preceive in their environment. When new information or experiences occur, children must adapt to include this information in their thinking. If this new information does not fit with what children already know, a state of imbalance occurs. To return to balance, adaptation occurs through either assimilation or accommodation.

Assimilation is the process of taking in new information and adding it to what the child already knows.

Accommodation is adjusting what is already known to fit the new information. This process is how people organize their thoughts and develop intellectual structures.

Piaget's stages of cognitive development are the same for all children. Most children proceed through the stages in order. Each stage builds on a previous stage. However, the age at which a child progresses through these stages is variable due to differences in maturation.

Although Piaget did not apply his theory directly to education, he did strongly influence children's early education. Many teaching strategies have evolved from his work. Caregivers and teachers now know that learning is an active process. Providing children with stimulating, hands-on activities helps them build knowledge. Piaget's theory includes four stages: sensorimotor, preoperational concrete, and formal operations. The first three stages occur during early childhood and the early school-age years. The following paragraphs describe these stages.

Piaget's Stages of Development

The **sensorimotor stage** takes place between birth and two years of age. Infants use all their senses to explore and learn. In this way, sensory experiences and motor development promote cognitive development. Babies' physical actions, such as sucking, grasping and hitting, help them learn about their surroundings. Movements are random at first. Gradually they become intentional as behaviours are repeated. Children begin to learn that objects still exist even when they are out of sight. This is known as *object permanence*. Through exploration and exposure to new experiences, new concepts are learned.

The **preoperational stage** takes place between ages two and seven. Children during this stage are very *egocentric*. This means that they assume others see the world the same way they do. Children do not yet have the ability to see others' points of view. During this time, representation skills are learned. These skills include language, symbolic play, and drawing. Children learn to use symbols and internal images, but their thinking is illogical. It is very different from that of adults. Children begin to understand that changing the physical appearance of something does not change the amount of it. They are able to recognize the difference between size and volume. For example, a ball of clay can be stretched into a long rope. Even if the physical appearance changes, the amount of the object does not change. This skill is called *conservation*. At this stage, children can also classify groups of objects and put objects in a series in order.

During the ages of seven to eleven years, **concrete operations** begin. Children develop the capacity to think systematically, but only when they can refer to actual objects and use hands-on activities. Then they begin to internalize some tasks. This means they no longer need to depend on what is seen. They become capable of reversing operations. For example, they understand that 3 + 1 is the same as 1 + 3. When real situations are presented, they are beginning to understand others' points of view.

The fourth stage, *formal operations,* takes place from eleven years of age to adulthood (the age range you are in right now). According to Piaget, young people develop the capacity to think in purely abstract ways. They no longer need concrete examples. Problem solving and reasoning are key skills developed during this stage.

VYGOTSKY'S SOCIOCULTURAL THEORY

Both Jean Piaget and Lev Vygotsky believed that children build knowledge through experiences. Piaget believed this happened through exploration with hands-on activities. Vygotsky, on the other hand, believed that children learn through social and cultural experiences. Interactions with peers and adults help children in this process. While interacting with others, children learn the customs, values, beliefs, and language of their culture. For this reason, families and teachers should provide plently of social interaction for young children.

Vygotsky believed language is an important tool for thought and plays a key role in cognitive development. He introduced the term *private speech,* or self-talk. This refers to when children "think out loud". After learning language, children engage in this self-talk to help guide their activity and develop their thinking. Generally, self-talk continues until children reach school age.

One of Vygotsky's most important contributions was the *zone of **proximal development*** (ZPD). This concept presents learning as a scale. One end of the scale or "zone" includes the tasks that are within the child's current development level. The other end of the scale includes tasks too difficult for children to accomplish, even with help. In the middle are the tasks children cannot accomplish alone. These are achieved with help from another knowledgeable peer or adult. The term used for this assistance is *scaffolding*. Just as a painter needs a structure on which to stand and point a building, scaffolding provides the structure for learning to occur. For example, a teacher could scaffold a child's learning while constructing a puzzle. The teacher might demonstrate how a piece fits or provide clues regarding colour, shape or size. The "zone" is constantly changing. In contrast to Piaget, Vygotsky believed that learning was not limited by stage or maturation. Children move forward in their cognitive development with the right social interaction and guided learning.

KOHLBERG'S THEORY OF DEVELOPMENT

According to him moral development of the child proceeds in sequential but distinctive stages. These stages are given below:

(a) **Stage-I :** In the early years of a child's life (from zero-four years) the physical consequences of an action determines its goodness or badness. If fire burns the child, he does not touch it. The child is ego-centric and standards of morality are external here.

(b) **Stage-II :** The child gives importance to his own point of view, (his self) and is able to take account of other's roles insofar as he can use them in his own way. This is a period of make belief. Right action is what which satisfies the needs of the child. The role of others is also important in the sense that a child does only what can bring approval of others. Thus, only that behaviour is moral which can satisfy not only self needs of the child but it must please others also.

(c) **Stage-III :** At this stage the child adopts the view pints of others on the basis of their consequences. He does not question the views of others. The child considers only that thing as right which are considered as right by others. Thus, the child is totally conformist to the standard of the society.

(d) **Stage-IV:** At this stage, the child is able to make any moral decision on his own without caring for the thinking of others. Though he considers laws and regulations set by the society as the essence of morality, yet he develops his own principles of morality on various occasions. Thus, he is a non-conformist to the norms of the society to a great extent.

(e) **Stage-V :** Standards and norms are more internalized here. The adolescents examine various view points prepared by different societies and recognize them. They think that the laws prepared by their own society are correct. Other societies may have good moral principles that must be adopted after careful appraisal.

(f) **Stage-VI :** This is the last stage of moral development according to Kohlberg. Here the universality of the view points of the individual is seen. He formulates his own universal moral principles which he thinks that all societies should adhere to it. True understanding of right and wrong is developed at this stage.

Gardner's Multiple Intelligences Theory

Howard Gardner has helped teachers rethink how they work with young children. Traditional intelligence tests mainly focus on language and math/logic skills. In contrast, Gardner's theory of **multiple intelligences** emphasizes that there are different kinds of intelligences used by the human brain. Gardner believes intelligence is the result of complex interactions between children's heredity and experiences. This theory focuses on how cultures shape human potential.

Gardner claims that children learn and express themselves in many different ways. In the process, they are using several types of intelligence. Each intelligence functions separately, but all are closely linked. According to Gardner, a potential intelligence will not develop unless it is nurtured. Learning can best be achieved by using a child's strongest intelligence. Gardner claims, however, that all children need opportunities to develop all areas of intelligence.

The multiple intelligence theory allows teachers to see the positive attributes of all children. Teachers also view Gardner's theory as a meaningful guide for making curriculum decisions. It gives them a chance to assess children's learning strengths. From this data, teachers can plan a wide variety of learning experiences. Following chart lists Gardner's eight intelligences. The paragraphs that follow explain these intelligences in detail.

(i) Bodily-Kinesthetic Intelligence

Bodily-kinesthetic intelligence involves the ability to control body movements. This includes using parts of the body to solve problems, handle objects, and express emotions. People with this type of intelligence typically enjoy sports, dance or creative drama. They are able to express themselves with their entire bodies.

Children will benefit from creative-movement experiences and role-playing.

Children with this type of intelligence process knowledge through sensation. They enjoy touch and creating with their hands. Therefore, daily opportunities should be provided for hands-on activities. Clay, sand, dough, feely boxes and other sensory activities help them develop fine-motor skills. Movement is also needed for gross-motor skills and coordination. It is important for caregivers and teachers to provide activities involving physical challenges. These may include playing kickball, jumping rope, and moving to music.

(ii) Musical-Rhythmic Intelligence

Musical-rhythmic intelligence involve the ability to recognize musical patterns. It also includes the ability to produce and appreciate music. Since music evokes emotion, this is one of the earliest intelligences to emerge. Composers and musicians are examples of people with this type of intelligence.

Children with this type of intelligence love listening to music. They are drawn to the art of sound and appreciate all forms of musical expression. They have a well-developed auditory sense and can discriminate tone, pitch and rhythmic patterns. As a result, they often cannot get songs out of their minds. You will hear them repeatedly singing or humming. This helps them understand concepts and remember information.

Activities to support musical intelligence can be included throughout the day. Offer opportunities for sound exploration through listening and singing. Use songs for directions and moving children from one activity to another. Play background music during self-selected play. Include songs during large and small group activities. Record the children creating their own music while singing or chanting. Explore rhythm by moving to recorded music. Use different instruments and instruments from other cultures to add variety.

(iii) Logical-Mathematical Intelligence

Logical-mathematical intelligence is more than just the ability to use math. It is the ability to use logic and reason to solve problems. Math experts have this form of intelligence. Scientists and composers may also have it. This intelligence involves the ability to explore categories, patterns and other relationships. It includes applying the principle of cause and effect. It also involves the skill to make predictions about patterns.

Children with this type of intelligence take pleasure in finding patterns and relationships. They enjoy discovering similarities and differences. Manipulatives for matching, measuring, and counting should be provided. Blocks can encourage the children's problem-solving and reasoning skills. Storybooks that show a sequence of events hold appeal for this type of intelligence. Water and sand activities with different-size containers help teach the concept of volume.

(iv) Verbal-Linguistic Intelligence

Verbal-linguistic intelligence involves the ability to use language for expression. People with this type of intelligence have well-developed language skills. They demonstrate sensitivity to the meaning, sound and rhythm of words. Lawyers, poets, public speakers and language translators have this type of intelligence.

Young children with this intelligence learn best by talking, listening, reading and writing. These children quickly learn the words to new stories, songs and finger plays. They enjoy talking to other people and are able to speak in an interesting and engaging manner. They are also able to learn a second language with ease.

This intelligence can be nurtured by environments rich with language opportunities. Children learn language in setting where it is used. Teachers need to follow the children's interests. They can then use these interests to engage children in meaningful conversations. Children's storybooks, songs, poetry, chants, and rhymes can serve as means for learning new vocabulary words. Listening to and telling stories can also promote language development.

(v) Interpersonal Intelligence

People with *interpersonal intelligence* display excellent communication and social skills. These people have a gift for understanding the feelings, behaviours, moods and motives of others. They make friends easily. They use language to develop trust and bonds with others. They are also skilled in supporting others and empathizing with them. These skills are important for teachers, politicians, salespeople and people working in the service industry.

These skills are nurtured in young children when caring behaviours are modeled for them. Teachers should keep this in mind. They can share experiences and provide the children with chances for verbal interaction. Books focusing on emotions can be acted out.

(vi) Intrapersonal Intelligence

Intrapersonal intelligence is the ability to understand the inner self. This is also known as *self-awareness*. It involves knowing your skills, limits, and feelings. It includes understanding your desires and motives. The ability to organize groups of people is part of

this strength. Communicating needs clearly is another aspect. Psychologists, social workers, religious leaders, and counsellors are examples of people with this type of intelligence.

How can you foster this type of intelligence? In the classroom, share emotions that all children experience. These include joy, sadness, regret and disappointment. Classroom examples should be shared as well as storybooks that contain emotional concepts.

(vii) Visual-Spatial Intelligence

Visual-spatial intelligence allows people to use their vision to develop mental images. People who have this type of intelligence show a preference for pictures and images. Photographers and artists are some examples. Architects, engineers, and surgeons also need this ability. They use it to see the relationship of objects in space.

Teachers can foster this intelligence by providing children with unstructured materials. Building blocks and puzzles strengthen this type of intelligence, 4-18. Make and use visual aids wherever possible. For example, classroom schedules, recipes, and stories can all be displayed on charts. Shelving units can be labelled with pictures cut from equipment catalogs.

(viii) Naturalistic Intelligence

Naturalistic intelligence is developed from the need to survive. This is the ability to classify objects in nature such as animals and plants. It depends on a type of pattern recognition. This strength also includes the ability to distinguish among types and brands of objects. Sailors, gardeners, chefs, and farmers are people who have this intelligence.

To build on this intelligence, provide cooking activities and nature walks. These help develop use of the senses to gather information. Planting and growing a garden helps the children observe cycles. Rocks, seashells, flowers, leaves, seeds, and coins can also be collected. In the classroom, they can be sorted and classified. Post picture collections and share books about natural events.

CONCEPTS OF CHILD-CENTERED AND PROGRESSIVE EDUCATION

Child-Centered Education

Child-centered education is the idea that the needs and desires of the child should take precedence in structuring the learning day. The whole idea is that learning should be fun and engaging for the child, and is most likely to be that way if the child is incharge of the learning experience, rather than the adult parent or teacher.

Child-centered education is most characterised by learning 'centers' in a classroom that promote

14

hands-on, active participation by the child. There may be magnifying glasses and bug slides in the science center, books and puppets that could be used to re-tell the stories in the language arts center, and wood blocks and shapes in the math center. The children are free to manipulate the objects in these centers. It is the process, the activity, the experience, that is valuable, not the facts, ideas, concepts or skills.

It is a relatively new approach to education. For centuries past, adults defined what education should be and children were the ones who did the adjusting. Education was considered work, not play.

Then came the softening influences of child psychologist Jean-Jacques Rousseau, as well as Dr. Marria Montessori, John Dewey, Jean Piaget and Lev Vygotsky, who all contended that a child's self-esteem and self-concept should be built up in order to create a better learner. Soon, the colleges of education were promoting child-centered education instead of instructionally centered education.

Role of Learner in Child-Centered Education

Learners are active as opposed to passive recipients of knowledge. Learners may assume a decision-making role in the classroom. Learners often decide what is to be learned, through which activities and at what pace. Learners can also produce materials and provide activities for the classroom.

Role of Teacher in Child-Centered Education

To put this approach into practice, teachers need to help students set achievable goals; they encourage students to assess themselves and their peers; help them to work co-operatively in groups and ensure that they know how to make use of all the available resources for learning.

Progressive Education

During most of the twentieth century, the term 'progressive education' has been used to describe ideas and practices that aim to make schools more effective agencies of a democratic society. Although there are numerous differences of style and emphasis among progressive educators, they share the conviction that democracy means active participation by all citizens in social, political and economic decisions that will affect their lives. The education of engaged citizens, according to this perspective, involves two essential elements: (1) respect for diversity, meaning that each individual should be recognised for his or her own abilities, interests, ideas, needs, and cultural identity, and (2) the development of critical, socially engaged intelligence, which enables individuals to understand and participate effectively in the affairs of their community in a collaborative effort to achieve a common good. These elements of progressive education have been termed 'child-centered' and 'social reconstruction' approaches, and while in extreme forms they have sometimes been separated, in the thought of John Dewey and other major theorists they are seen as being necessarily related to each other.

The term 'progressive' arose from a period (roughly 1890–1920) during which many Americans took a more careful look at the political and social effects of vast concentrations of corporate power and private wealth. Dewey, in particular, saw that with the decline of local community life and small scale enterprise, young people were losing valuable opportunities to learn the arts of democratic participation, and he concluded that education would need to make up for this loss. In his Laboratory School at the University of Chicago, where he worked between 1896 and 1904, Dewey tested ideas he shared with leading school reformers such as Francis W. Parker and Ella Flagg Young. Between 1899 and 1916 he circulated his ideas in works such as The School and Society, The Child and the Curriculum, Schools of Tomorrow, and Democracy and Education, and through numerous lectures and articles. During these years other experimental schools were established around the country, and in 1919 the Progressive Education Association was founded, aiming at "reforming the entire school system of America".

Therefore, progressive education is a reaction against the traditional style of teaching which teaches facts largely at the expense of understanding what is being taught. According to **John French,** "The progressive school teaches the child to think for himself instead of passively accepting stereotyped ideas. It keeps always in mind that each child is different from every other, and that what makes an educated person useful in his particular walk of life, what makes him interesting, what makes him an individual, is not his resemblance to other people, but his differences".

Philosophies and Practices of Progressive Education

1. Curriculum is strongly influenced by what the children are interested in, and is child-centered rather than adult driven.

2. Learning is 'hands-on', experiential and the emphasis is on process rather than product children are 'learning to learn'.

3. Children learn through integrated, theme-based units or inquiry projects and the 'theme' often emerges from the children.

4. Assessment is authentic and holistic. Children are well known by their teachers and peers.

There are no tests or letter grades. Instead, narrative reports are written about children that cover all aspects of their development: social, emotional, personal, physical and intellectual level.

5. Classes are usually of mixed ages and no ability grouping is used. Children are able to work at their own pace and cross-age friendships are encouraged.

6. Progressive education practices a developmental approach which holds that each child is a unique being unfolding and developing at their own pace according to a specific pattern. At each stage of development there are things that can be learned and things that should not be learned. Respecting a child's development is central to progressive education.

Types of Progressive Education

1. **Humanistic :** The humanistic form of progressive education focuses on the humanities, arts and social sciences. Its emphasis is on the individual child and not the curriculum. This type of progressivism aims to build a well-rounded individual with highly developed critical thinking and reasoning skills. The children learn think for themselves instead of accepting everything teachers tell them. Social development and interaction among the students are seen as valuable learning techniques.

2. **Constructivism :** Constructivism is a type of child-centered progressivism. It focuses on the child's creativity and learning abilities. Teachers should build the curriculum around the requirements and interests of the child. It maintains that education should consider children's developmental stages. Swiss psychologist **Jean Piaget** influenced the theories of constructivist education. Experiential learning, or learning by doing, allows students to construct their own knowledge.

3. **Montessori :** Italian doctor Marria Montessori started the Montessori progressive educational system. She developed her teaching theories by clinical observation and analysis of how children learn. Her method of education focused on how children naturally learn, all by themselves, without the help of adults. Maria Montessori concluded that children teach themselves, and it's the job of teachers to facilitate this process, not dominate it. Montessori teachers provide a sensory-rich environment and hands-on activities.

CRITICAL PERSPECTIVE OF THE CONSTRUCT OF INTELLIGENCE

Introduction

The most important variable that affects schooling or performance on a job is intelligence. Psychologists have interpreted the term intelligence in different ways and there is no consensus among them on the term even so far. In psychology this term is treated as a construct whose structure is different in different individuals.

The vagueness of the term arises due to the fact that intelligence is not a concrete material. It is rather abstraction from the behaviour of the individual which is indirectly inferred and elaborated as an adjective.

The dictionary meaning of term "intelligence" is the capacity to acquire and apply knowledge. **Boring** defines intelligence as intelligence is what an intelligence test measures.

Definitions of Intelligence

Several psychologists have classified and defined intelligence in several ways. Some of them are given below:

1. Vernon's Classification of Intelligence

(a) *Biological Approach:* Man is an organism among millions living on earth. Environment works as a foe for him. Intelligence is the capacity to adapt to the environment or new situations of life at every moment.

This definition of intelligence can be criticized on the ground that there have been many intelligent and renowned persons who were ill adapted to their social and physical environment. Besides, if we want to study individual differences in a society, this definition serves no practical purpose.

(b) *Psychological Approach :* According to psychologists intelligence is the relative effects of heredity and environment both. An English psychologist, **C. Burt** defined intelligence as the innate general cognitive ability.

In support of psychological definitions of intelligence **Hebb** and **R.B. Catell** distinguished two kinds of intelligence. The first is intelligence "A" which is Fluid intelligence and which is related to genetic potentialities or innate qualities of the individual's nervous system. Second is intelligence "B" which is crystalised "intelligence" and which is related to experiences, learning and environmental factors. These two types of intelligence in normal circumstances so much overlap on each other that they are practically indistinguishable.

(c) *Operational Approach :* These definitions help us to understand the concept of intelligence in clear and definite terms. In this approach scientific terms are first of all defined operationally and then observations are conducted with reference to these terms. For example, in order to determine a child's IQ, we first administer a test of a specific kind. Then we observe his performance on the test and finally draw certain conclusions in the context of the pre-determined objectives.

2. Freeman's Classification

(a) *Ability of adjustment :* An individual is intelligent to the extent to which he is able to adjust to new situations and problems of life. The more a person is intelligent, the more he is able to adapt to his environment in antagonistic conditions. The person who is low in intelligence has less capacity to adjust to the new situations of life.

(b) *Ability of learning :* Learning ability is also an index of intelligence. The more a person is intelligent, the more he will be able to learn new things.

(c) *Ability to carry on abstract thinking :* This category of definitions of intelligence is related to the effective use of concepts and symbols in dealing with situations and solving the problems through the use of verbal and numerical symbols. According to **Terman**, an individual is intelligent to the extent he is able to carry on abstract thinking.

3. E.L. Thorndike's Classification

(a) *Concrete intelligence :* The intellectual ability in relation to concrete materials is called concrete intelligence. It is the ability of a person to comprehend the actual situations and react to them adequately. This kind of intelligence is measured by using performance tests or picture tests in which the subject manipulates the concrete materials.

(b) *Abstract intelligence :* It is the ability to respond to words, letters, numbers or symbols. This type of intelligence is required in all academic activities in schools or outside the schools. The highest level of abstract intelligence is manifested in the thoughts of philosophers or in the inventions of scientists and mathematicians.

(c) *Social intelligence :* It is the ability of an individual to react to social situations of life.

It is the ability to understand others and to react to them in such a manner that they may not feel unjust attitude regarding them.

4. Intelligence as a Global Capacity

A comprehensive definitions of intelligence : **Stoddard** (1943) and **Wechsler** (1944) have defined intelligence in the following words :

"Intelligence is the aggregate or the global capacity of the individual to act purposefully, to think rationally and to deal with the environment effectively".

Stoddard further elaborated that intelligence is the capacity of a person to undertake such activities which are: (*i*) difficult (*ii*) complex (*iii*) abstract (*iv*) economical (*v*) goal directed (*vi*) valuable from social view points (*vii*) original. These activities demand concentration of energy and a resistance to emotional forces.

Characteristics of Intelligence

From the above definitions of intelligence, we can draw the following characteristics of intelligence:

(i) Intelligence is the composite of several intellectual skills, such as thinking, doing, reasoning, dealing, learning etc.

(ii) Intelligence is displayed by the behaviour of the individual as a whole and intelligent behaviour is always goal directed.

(iii) Intelligence is the ability to adjust to abnormal and challenging situations of life.

(iv) Intelligence is not related to ordinary tasks of life. It is always related to extra ordinary manipulation.

(v) Wechsler has included the concepts of drive and incentive which are implied in his statement. "To act purposefully" and "to deal effectively". But many psychologists are of the view that drive and incentive are non-intellectual traits of personality and if they are included in a test of mental ability, more confusions will be created thereof.

(vi) There are seven fundamental elements of intelligence according to **Stoddard.** Intelligent person can undertake difficult and abstract tasks with ease. He can manipulate and deal the abstract ideas and concepts efficiently. Similarly, economy refers to the rate at which a mental task is done or a problem is solved. If "A" solves a problem sooner than 'B' then 'A' will be considered more intelligent than 'B'. The term social value indicates whether a mental task performed by a person is in accordance with the socially desirable and acceptable norms or not. The last term original refers to a person's, ability to discover something new and different, *i.e.*, this term is directly related to creative potential of a person. Discovery of some new facts and principles and inventions of new concrete materials by the scientists are few examples of originality.

Stoddard's definition of intelligence has been criticized on two grounds :

(a) It includes social values in intelligence, *i.e.*, intelligent task must be socially desirable. Psychologists criticize this point by saying that social value is a subjective phenomenon, *i.e.*, what is desirable for me, may not be necessarily desirable for others. So, there is no scope of subjectivity in an objective intelligence test.

(b) He has included two conditions of intelligent behaviour in his definition. First is concentration of energy and second is resistance to emotional forces. Psychologists say that these elements are non-intellectual traits and hence they should not be included in mental abilities at any cost.

Theories of Intelligence

1. Faculty theory of intelligence:

This is the oldest theory of intelligence given during the period of pre-experimental psychology. According to this theory mind is made up of different faculties like reasoning, logic, memory, imagination and discrimination. These faculties are independent of each other and can be developed by rigorous mental exercises of the difficult subject-matter.

This theory does not take the hereditary factors of intelligence into account and thus this theory was discarded by the later psychologists who believed that we can never improve the intellectual capacity of a person if he is mentally slow by birth.

2. Unifactor theory:

According to Alfred Binet (1916) intelligence is a general intellectual ability which is made up of several discrete abilities. These abilities include

(i) to reason well with abstract material

(ii) to comprehend well

(iii) to have a clear direction of thoughts

(iv) to relate thinking with the attainment of a desirable end and

(v) to be self-critical.

All these abilities combined together is called general mental ability. Thus, intelligence is a single but complex mental process which can be measured by different kinds of materials designed for the purpose.

3. Two factors theory:

This theory was developed by an English psychologist, **Charles Spearman** in 1904. According to him, intellectual abilities consist of two factors, general ability known as 'G' factors and specific abilities known as 'S' factors.

Characteristics of G factors

(i) It is universal inborn ability.

(ii) It is general mental energy.

(iii) It is constant, *i.e.*, it remains the same in all the individuals and does not change with time.

(iv) The amount of G differs from person to person depending on his genes.

(v) It is used in every life activity.

(vi) Greater the amount of G in an individual, larger is the chance of his success in life.

Characteristics of 'S' factors

(i) It is learnt and hence acquired in the environment.

(ii) It varies from activity to activity in the same individual.

(iii) The amount of S also differs from person to person due to his accessibility to learning situations.

(iv) 'S' factors are related to the specific activity. A low correlation between two or more functions or activities indicates the presence of 'S' factor involved in the activity. A person can be expert only in one or few activities because of the specific factors involved in the activity.

According to Spearman, out of these two factors 'G' factor is more important and thus it is an important measure of intelligence. So, any intelligence test should measure only 'G' factor because it provides most important basis of predicting a person's behaviour in different situations. Raven's Progressive Matrices and Catell's Culture Fair Test both measure 'G' factor.

Spearman has explained his theory with the help of a tetrad equation which is given below :

$$rap \times rbq - raq \times rbp = 0$$

Here,

a = opposites
b = discrimination
p = completion
q = cancellation

Thus, rap means correlation between opposites and completions, rbq means correlation between cancellation and discrimination, raq means correlation between opposite and cancellation and rbp means correlation between discrimination and completion. This theory can also be explained with the help of a diagram given below :

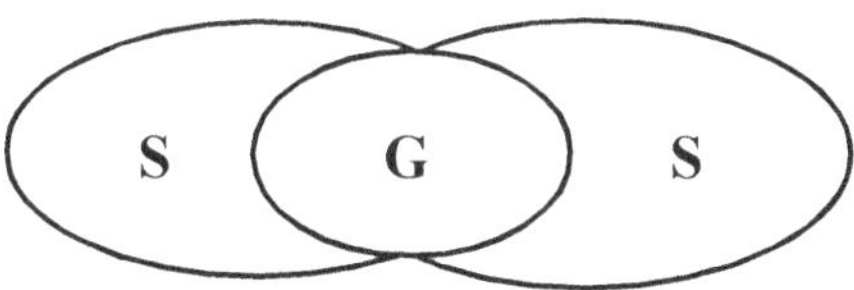

4. Multi-factors theory :

This theory was developed by an American psychologist, **E.L. Thorndike.** He opposed the theory of general intelligence by saying that there are specific stimuli and specific mental responses. Intelligence is nothing more than a potential specific connections between these stimuli and responses. Differences of intelligence among people are due to the different number of such connections in the neurological system. This theory is also called **atomistic theory** of intelligence. There are **four attributes of intelligence** according to him:

(a) Level : It refers to the difficulty of a task that can be removed by using intelligence. If different tasks are arranged in increasing difficulty order, then the height that a person can attain determines his level of intelligence. It is a kind of power test.

(b) Range : It refers to the number of tasks of the same difficulty value that a person can do in a certain period of time. Theoretically, an individual possessing a certain level of intelligence should be able to solve the whole range of tasks at a given level. It is a kind of speed test.

Range and level can not be completely isolated from each other. We can not measure range without altitude (level) and vice versa.

(c) Area : It refers to the total numbers of situations at each level to which the individual is able to respond. Area is the summation of all ranges at each level of intelligence. Area = Level × Range.

(d) Speed : It refers to the rapidity with which an individual can respond to a test items. Speed and level are positively correlated. It is different from range in the sense that no specific time is given here to complete a task.

Every intelligence test should consist of these four attributes.

5. Group factor structure of intelligence (PMA Test) :

This theory was developed by **L.L. Thurstone.** According to him, intelligence is not an expression of general factor but a combination of group of traits. They are intermediate factors, *i.e.,* they are not so universal as 'G' factor and they are not so specific as 'S' factor. This primary group of factors give the common mental abilities, a functional cohesiveness and then constitute a group. Another group of common mental abilities is said to have another primary factor and so on. In this way, there are a number of groups of mental abilities each of which has its own primary factors. On the basis of factor analysis of these groups, Thurstone identified the following seven group factors which are termed as primary mental abilities (PMA).

1. Number factor (N) : It is the ability to do numerical calculations rapidly and accurately.

2. Verbal factor (V) : They are related to the operations involving verbal comprehension.

3. Space factor (S) : It is related to the tasks in which subject manipulates an object imaginary in space.

4. Word fluency factor (W) : It is involved to the situation when the subject is asked to think of isolated words at a fast rate.

5. Reasoning factors (R) : It is used in those tasks that require the subject to discover a rule or principles involved in series or groups of letters.

6. Rote memory (M) : It is the ability to memorize a fact quickly.

7. Perceptual speed (P) : It is the ability to note perceptual (visual) details rapidly.

   The point to be noted here is that these seven abilities are significantly correlated with each other.

6. Structure of intelligence (SI) model :

This model was given by **J.P. Guilford** in 1966 in the University of California on the basis of factor analysis of many tests. According to him human mind is composed of at least three dimensions—operations, contents and products, and each dimension of intellect is sufficiently distinct which can be detected by factor analysis. These three dimensions of mind are given below:

(A) Operations : Operations can be divided into five major groups of intellectual abilities.

- **Cognition :** It includes discovery, recognition of informations and new understanding of the facts.

- **Memory :** It is the ability to recognize or recall previously learnt material.

- **Divergent thinking :** This operation is closely associated with creative potential.

It refers to the ability to search out and think in a novel out of track way.

- **Convergent thinking :** It refers to the generation of information from given information and drawing conclusion from the given facts.

- **Evaluation :** It is the ability to make judgement on the basis of merits and demerits of a phenomenon. Here, value judgement on knowledge and thoughts is placed after critically examining them.

(B) Contents : Five kinds of contents are involved here. Operations are performed on these contents.

- **Figural content :** It is the concrete material perceived through the senses. Visual materials have three properties, size, form and colour.

- **Auditory content :** It includes nature and characteristics of sound perceived.

- **Symbolic content :** It includes letters, digits and other conventional signs usually organised in general pattern.

- **Semantic content :** It refers to those verbal meanings, ideas and concepts for which no examples are necessary.

- **Behavioural content :** It includes knowledge regarding other persons.

(C) Products : When five operations are applied to five types of contents, six kinds of products are made.

- **Units :** It refers to the production of a single word, definition or isolated bits of informations.

- **Classes :** It refers to the production of a concept.

- **Relations :** It refers to the production of any form of relationship, such as, analogy, opposite or similar ones.

- **System :** It refers to the production of internally consistent set of classification of various forms.

- **Transformation :** It refers to the production of changes in meaning, organisation or some other arrangement.

- **Implication :** It refers to the production of such information which is beyond the data given.

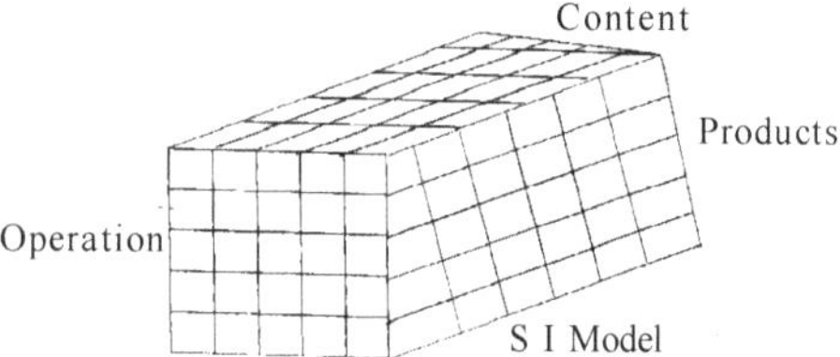

On the basis of the model given above it can be stated that there are $5 \times 5 \times 6 = 150$ factors involved in intelligent acts.

Educational Implication of the Model

(a) In psychology : This model is very much helpful for constructing various types of intelligence tests suitable to different age groups. These tests will help us to study individual differences in the society. This model is taxonomic in nature and has discovered many abilities which were not known before. If test maker has included items representing contents and operations, he can see whether products are same or different. Conversely, if products are shown by the subject through the test, the test maker can find out the content and operation and match them with the items given in the test.

(b) In vocational testing : This model shows that there are 150 intellectual abilities. This model predicts five kinds of mental abilities classified as content. This means that different kinds of test items are needed in vocational testing. Six types of products are also tested on the basis of items representing the products. For example, if a person is able to deal with items of figural contents, he can deal with machines, operators, engineers etc. and any or all of the six types of products can be made by him, such as, he can define a machine or any operator. He can give clear concept about how a machine is operated and so on.

(c) In the field of education : Conventionally, learner was considered to be a kind of stimulus response device. Once the stimulus is given to him, he will respond but the new conception of the learner in the light of SI model is that of electronic computer which not only stores information but uses that information to generate new information either by divergent or convergent thinking.

Thus, this model gives the idea that learning is not merely the association of informations but it is the discovery of information as well. Model suggests that in order to understand human learning and higher mental processes of thinking, some drastic modifications are to be made in our theory of curriculum construction and pedagogy of instruction. Similarly, education is no longer considered to be the training of mind. Now, main emphasis on education is given to the learning of specific skills and modification of behaviour and all these materials are not taught merely for the purpose of training the mind of humans.

7. Two Level Process Theory of Intelligence :

This theory was developed by **Jensen** in 1968. According to him intelligence is a combination of two levels of processes. One is associative intelligence and the other is abstract intelligence. Associative intelligence includes those kinds of tests that depend upon memory and simple verbal association. Abstract intelligence includes those factors as concept learning, thinking, problem solving skills, multiple discrimination, principle learning etc.

8. Burt and Vernon's hierarchy theory :

Burt (1940) separated four factors of intelligence by using statistical techniques :

- General factors (common to all traits)
- Group factors (common to some of the traits)
- Specific factors (limited to few traits)
- Error factors (limited to a particular trait when it is measured)

When human mind is put at the top, there will be 5 level hierarchical model of intelligence where general factors will come next to intelligence and error factors will come in the last.

Vernon, on the other hand, suggested that intelligence tests measure an overall factor G as well as two other mental abilities. First are related to verbal, numerical and educational. Second are related to practical, mechanical, spatial and physical. These two major factors can be divided into minor group factors. These minor factors can further be divided into various specific factors and so on.

MEASUREMENT OF INTELLIGENCE

Historical development of mental testing can be divided into three periods for the purpose of convenience.

(A) Pre-Binet Period :

In the 19th century, there was a good deal of interest in the field of psychophysics in which attempts were made to develop general rule of sensory judgement. The functioning of sensory reactions of the typical individuals is actually studied in psycho-physics. Method of limits procedure was used here to measure the extent to which people were able to differentiate between stimuli. But the limitation of these experiments was that accurate generalization of the result was not possible.

Francis Galton was the first psychologist who took interest in studying whether individual characteristics are acquired or inherited. For this purpose, he studied the lives of prominent English men and in his book "Hereditary Genius" he demonstrated that personal characteristics, (mental and physical) of men are inherited. He developed a series of tests to measure these characteristics. It was the starting point of mental measurement.

The first laboratory of experimental psychology was established by **Wundt** in 1879 in Leiping. He employed two methods to test vision, hearing, reaction time and psychosomatic problems— *(i)* psycho-physical method *(ii)* Introspection method. He also developed mental tests which could measure the keenness of vision and hearing, muscular strength, reaction time and other sensory motor functions of body.

Many of **Galton's** ideas were brought to USA by an American psychologist **J.M. Catell.** Like **Galton** he also believed that intellectual functions can best be measured by the reaction time and sensory discrimination tests.

In the last quarter of the 19th century, many psychological laboratories came into existence and studies of individual differences in mental abilities started.

The word "**Mental Test**" was first used by Catell in 1890 but his tests were actually tests of sensory discrimination, speed of motor responses and the like.

Thus, upto this period mental ability was identified as sensory acuity of an individual. The correlation between mental abilities and academic achievements was not known at the time.

Drawbacks of this period:

- Psychologists were unable to identify and define the nature of intelligence. Keenness of sensory motor reactions were related to intelligence.
- They were unable to measure the complex functions of the body.
- Intelligence tests developed during this period were measuring other than intelligence.

(B) Binet Period :

An important incident led the people to think about mental measurement during this period. In the beginning of the 20th century in France, a large number of students failed in the examination. For this teachers and students blamed each other. Seeing this, superintendent of public instruction appointed a committee to device some techniques to screen out slow learners in the schools. Binet and Simon were among members of the committee. They developed a variety of paper pencil tests in their psychological laboratory established in 1889, to administer them on children of different ages. Through these tests Binet tried to measure more complex mental functions such as power of judgement and reasoning, memory, arithmetic ability, etc.

An important contribution of Binet and Simon is that they categorised their tests in terms of age levels by administering their test items to children of different ages. In this way, an age scale of intelligence was also developed. For example, if an item was correctly answered by majority of seven years old children but only few six years old children could respond it correctly, then this item was reserved for seven years old children. In this way, Binet and Simon developed separate tests for different ages.

Similarly, if an item suited to eight years old child was correctly answered by a child of 6 years and if the same trend was shown by the six years old child in most of the cases of a test, then the mental age of the child was considered to be eight years not six years, though his chronological age is six years only. Thus, the concept of mental age was also introduced by Binet and Simon for the first time in the history of mental testing and with the help of this concept we could assess the intellectual ability of a person. Some of the tests developed during this period are given below:

Binet-Simon Scale

The first scale of Binet-Simon was published in 1905. This scale consisted of 30 items arranged in increasing order of difficulty. This scale was a crude measure of intelligence of school going children.

In order to remove some of its defects they revised their scale in 1908. It was the first age based scale and it created a lot of interest among the psychologists across the world. The items in the tests were grouped according to the appropriate age levels from 3 to 13 years.

Some items for three years age

- Point to your nose, eyes and mouth.
- Repeat two digits 3, 5.
- Repeat sentences of six syllables.
- Enumerate objects in a picture.
- Give family names.

Some items of eight years age

- Read a passage and remember two lines.
- Add up the value of five coins.
- Name four colours.
- Count reverse from 20 to zero.
- Give differences between two objects.

1908 revision of Binet-Simon Scale was adopted by many psychologists of America, Switzerland and Germany and many suggestions were given by them for the improvement of the scale. Binet-Simon accepted their suggestions and revised their scale again in 1911.

Some sample items of 1911 scale are given below:

(A) Age = 8 years

- Gives difference between two objects.

- Counts reverse from 20 to zero.
- Points out omissions from unfinished pictures.
- Tells the dates correctly.
- Repeats the digits.

(B) Age = 10 years

- Arranges five blocks in order of increasing weights.
- Reproduces two geometric designs by using memory.
- Criticizes absurd statements.
- Comprehends and answers difficult questions.
- Uses three given words in two sentences.

Main Features of Binet-Simon Scale

(i) They are really scales, *i.e.*, items of the tests are arranged in the increasing difficulty order. Easiest items are put in the beginning and the most difficult item is put in the last. Thus, these scales measure the level or aptitude of an examinee and not their speed.

(ii) These tests measure the general abilities of intelligence instead of specific abilities.

(iii) They can also measure the mental growth of the subject because they are arranged according to different ages from 3 to 14 years.

(iv) They are administered on subjects individually.

(v) Their system of scoring is tied to age norms. A child's performance on the scale will be compared to that of children of his own age.

L.M. Terman's revision of Binet–Simon Scale: L.M. Terman of **Stanford** University revised this scale in 1916 to adapt to American situations. He introduced one new concept which was intelligence Quotient (IQ) in his revision. His scale consisted of 90 items ranging from 3 to 14 years of age. Some items of this scale are given below:

Age = 7 years

- Knows number of fingers on both hands.
- Describes pictures.
- Repeats five digits.
- Gives differences between paired objects.
- Ties a bowknot.

1937 Revision of Binet-Simon Scale : Terman along with his associate Merill revised 1916 scale again in 1937. This revision had two equivalent forms L and M. The number of items in the test was raised to 129 in each L M. forms. A new change was also introduced in the test which was the calculation of chronological age. Upto 13 years CA was taken to be as original but after 13 years CA was computed in the following manner.

At 14 years = 13 yrs+2/3 of 14th year = 13 2/3 years.

At 15 years = 13+2/3 of 2 years = 14 1/3 years.

At 16 years = 13+2/3 of 3 years = 15 years.

Besides, 16 years was taken to be the last age for calculation of IQ. After that, CA was taken to be constant.

LM form revision of 1960 : Binet-Simon scale was last revised in 1960 in which items of both L and M forms were included in the scale. This revision has a range of 2 years of mental age scores to 22 years and 11 months of mental age score. This form of the test measures abilities from 7 categories namely, language, memory, reasoning, social intelligence, conceptual phenomenon, numerical, reasoning and visual motor. Test items are in the form of words, objects and pictures and the responses given by the examinees are in the form of drawing, calculating, writing and speaking. Administration of the test requires one full hour. In this revision intelligence is expressed in terms of standard scores of the deviation IQ.

Wechsler Scale : This scale may be considered an improvement over Binet-Simon scale as it can measure the intelligence of adults very effectively. David Wechsler developed this scale in 1939. This scale was developed in two equivalent forms, each form consisted of ten subtests of which five tests were verbal and five were non-verbal or performance type. This scale was revised in 1955 and was renamed as Wechsler Adult Intelligence Scale (WAIS). It comprised of 11 sub tests of which six were verbal and five were non-verbal. This scale is used on persons above 16 years of age upto 64 and administration time of the scale is one hour. The detail of these 11 subtests are given below:

(a) Verbal subtests :

1. *Information* : 29 questions are given here to test the recall of knowledge concerning wide varieties of information.

2. *Comprehension* : 14 questions are given here to test understanding of knowledge concerning a particular subject or event.

3. *Arithmetic* : 14 questions are given here to test numerical ability. These questions are solved orally without using paper and pencil at all.

4. *Similarity* : 13 questions are given here to measure abstract verbal reasoning. Examinees are required here to compare two objects and find out the relationship between them.

5. *Digit span* : Memory for digits are measured here. In the first half, the examinee is asked to repeat in the same order, three to nine digits presented in the forward directions and in the second half, the digits are repeated in a backward direction.

6. *Vocabulary* : 40 words of increasing difficulty value are presented before the examinees here and they are asked to tell the meaning of these words.

(b) Non-verbal or performance subtests:

1. *Digit symbol* : Nine digits each with different digit symbols are given to the examinees here and they are asked to give the right code for each digits or symbols.

2. *Picture completion* : This subtest measures the ability of the examinees to analyse the parts from the whole. Examinees are given 21 cards containing incomplete pictures and they are asked to fill the missing part of each picture.

3. *Block design* : Its purpose is to measure the ability to analyse the complex whole. There are only 7 designs in these blocks which have red, white and red-white sides. Examinees are asked to produce a given design with the help of these blocks.

4. *Picture arrangement* : Its purpose is to measure the ability to identify the whole from the parts. Here six set of pictures are given to the examinees and they are asked to arrange them in an order which tells a meaningful story.

5. *Object assembly* : Its purpose is to measure the ability to synthesise the whole with the help of parts. Here examinees are given some puzzle pictures each representing some parts of the human body and they are asked to assemble them in the form of a complete man.

Speed and accuracy factors are also scored in Arithmetic, digit symbol, block design, picture arrangement and object assembly. Raw scores of each subject are converted into normalized standard scores with a mean of 10 and SD of 3. This makes the scores of each sub tests comparable. Separate IQ for verbal and non-verbal subtest forms is calculated by adding up the respective subtests of the two forms and if we add up scores on all the 11 subtests, we obtain total scale score. These standard scores are expressed in the form of deviation IQ with a mean of 100 and SD of 15.

Wechsler developed another scale known as Wechsler intelligence Scale for Children in 1949 to test the intelligence of children from 5 to 15 years of age. It also takes one hour to administer, though there are 12 subtests in this scale. Maze test is the only test which is extra in WISC. Maze subtest has eight mazes to be traced by the examinee with a pencil. These mazes are given in increasing order of difficulty.

The scoring system of both the tests WAIS and WISC are the same. Here also the total scores are converted into deviation IQ with a mean of 100 and SD of 15.

Advantages of Wechsler Scales

(i) Though Binet's scale and Wechsler's scale both are individual scales, yet the later can be administered on small groups of children and adults.

(ii) Wechsler's scale is easier to administer than Binet's Scale and its scoring is also less complex than the former.

(iii) Wechsler has prepared separate scales for children and adults Binet's scale does not possess this advantage.

Other differences of Wechsler Scales and Stanford Binet Scale

(i) In Wechsler scale, items are not grouped in terms of mental age as is the case of Stanford-Binet scale. Points are given here for all correct responses. Thus, WAIS or WISC is a point scale.

(ii) In Stanford-Binet scale items are interpreted in terms of different age levels of the examinees but in WAIS or WISC similar types of items are grouped together to form subtests.

(iii) WAIS has separate age norms for adults but in SB Scale all the individuals above 18 are treated in a similar manner as far as computation of IQ is concerned. Thus, people of all age levels are treated as 18 years of age after 18.

(iv) In SB tests items are varied, unrelated and upgraded but in WAIS and WISC tests, items are graded according to various range of ages.

(v) SB scale is internally standardized and rigid but WAIS is externally standardized and flexible.

(vi) SB scale refers to qualitative evaluation while WAIS refers to quantitative evaluation.

(vii) Slight chance of statistical treatment is possible in SB scale but WAIS is fully subject to all statistical analysis.

(c) Post Binet period :

This period is particularly known for testing intelligence in groups and thus group test of intelligence became popular during this periods.

A group test is one that can be given to a number of subjects at a time by a single examiner. This type of test came into being during first World War for the purpose of classifying soldiers for various jobs in accordance with their mental abilities. Army Alpha and Army Beta, two tests were developed during this period. Army Alpha is a verbal group test of intelligence meant for literate people. Army beta is a non-verbal group test of intelligence meant for illiterate persons.

We will discuss here some more group test of intelligence :

1. **Catell's Culture Fair Test :** This test was developed by RB Catell and was published by IPAT (Institute for Personality and Ability Testing) in 1961. The test has three scales and can be administered on children and adults both.

Scale I   meant for 4-8 years

Scale II   meant for 8-15 years

Scale III   meant for 15 years and above

This test measures the general intelligence factor and takes 30-60 minutes to administer. The test has been prepared in such a manner that previously learnt skill or knowledge does not help the examinee to score more on this test. That is why, it is said to be independent of school achievement, social advantages and environmental influences.

2. **Large Thorndike's Intelligence Test :** This test is meant for primary and secondary school children graded into five different levels. The purpose of the test is to measure verbal comprehension, numerical skill and reasoning abilities. Test has verbal as well as non-verbal items. Only non-verbals items are, however, included at the lower levels. The administration of the test takes 30 minutes in all.

3. **Raven Progressive Matrices Test :** This test was developed in England. It consists of geometric figures and designs. The subjects find out the relationship between figures and select appropriate parts for completion of each pattern of relations.

Classification of Intelligence Test

(A) Classification from the point of view of administration

1. **Individual intelligence test :** An individual intelligence test is one which is administered to only one person at a time. Binet-Simon is an example.

2. **Group intelligence test :** A group intelligence test is one which can be administered to more than one persons at a time. Army Alpha and Army Beta are two examples of such tests.

Some general characteristics of group intelligence tests are as follows :

(i) They have been developed on the assumption that intelligence is a general capacity and can be measured by sampling a variety of mental activities.

(ii) In group tests the similar types of items are pooled together in different subtests.

(iii) Every group test is standardized for a special range of ages or school grades.

(iv) Construction of individual test is also very difficult and costly as compared to group tests. Their scoring and standardization is also time consuming process.

(v) It is very difficult to establish rapport between the examiner and the examinees and hence examinees can not be motivated properly in group tests of intelligence. These two limitations are not seen in individual tests.

(vi) Group tests are superior to individual tests in the sense that norms established here are more dependable than that of individual tests. It is because these norms are calculated on the basis of a very large sample.

(vii) Individual test provides qualitative performance of the individual while group tests are mostly point scale and express the performance in quantities.

(B) Classification from the point of view of nature of items of the test

1. **Verbal test :** Verbal test of intelligence is one in which instructions and items are produced before the examinees through the written language. So, examinees must be literate to take these tests. Mohsin's General intelligence Test, Joshi's General Mental Ability test and Jalota's Group General Mental Ability Test are some examples of verbal tests of intelligence of Indian origin.

2. **Non-verbal test :** A non-verbal test is one which requires the use of language only to impart instructions. The examinees are asked to manipulate the test materials in their own way. Since language is not needed to respond to items here, it can be administered to illiterate persons as well. They are also culturally free and hence they can be applied to any situation representing any culture. Test items are usually of figured relation type. Army Beta is a good example of non-language test.

3. **Performance test :** A performance test is one in which a subject has to perform some thing or to manipulate some concrete materials without much use of the language ability. Non-verbal and performance tests are useful for the following groups of people:

   (a) Deaf and Dumb : Those children who cannot hear or speak can be tested with the help of performance test.

   (b) Illiterates : Verbal test of intelligence is useless for those who cannot read or write. Performance test is useful for them.

   (c) Shy children : Many withdrawn children are hesitant to express before others. Performance and non-verbal test of intelligence will suit them very much.

   (d) Educationally deficient children : Verbal test of intelligence generally measure learning along with intelligence. If children are educationally poor, they will perform poorly on intelligence test too and thus they will be wrongly declared as children of below average intelligence. Such a problem can be overcome by using performance test or non-verbal intelligence test.

   (e) Useful for children of other culture : A particular culture dominates in every verbal intelligence test and thus the test can not be adopted by other cultures. Due to free from culture, performance test is suitable for these foreign students.

Some performance tests of intelligence are given below :

(a) Pintner Paterson Scale : This is the first systematic performance test. This scale was standardized in 1917. It consists of 15 subtests.

(b) Goodenough Drawing Test : This scale was developed by Florence Goodenough in 1926. Here child is asked to draw the picture of a man as best as possible without any time limit. This is especially useful for those children who are suspected to be mentally retarted.

Weaknesses of performance test :

- Here the subject can score high due to practice effect and chance success is more frequent than verbal tests. Because of this reason, reliability coefficient is very low.

- They fail to distinguish between gifted and average children due to limited scope of these tests.

- These scales fail to test fine mental abilities such as, ability to make abstraction or concept formation or evaluation abilities of mind.

Interpretation of Intelligence Test Scores : Intelligence test scores can be interpreted in the following three ways:

1. **Mental age :** This concept was first introduced by **Afred Binet** of France in 1908. It refers to a score that is determined by comparing a child's score with the scores obtained by younger or older children in the norming group. Here a child's score is compared with the average score of his own age. For example, if a 9-year-old child scores 60 on an

intelligence test and suppose mental age norms for that scale are as follows:

Mental age of 8 years = 60

Mental age of 9 years = 70

Mental age of 10 years = 80

Then, in that case, mental age of the child will be considered as 8 years instead of 9 though his chronological age is 9 years.

Similarly, if another child of 8 years obtains a score of 80, then his mental age will be 10 years, though his chronological age is 8 years only.

Thus, we can say that the mean performance of each age level becomes the mental age for that age level.

2. **Intelligent Quotient (IQ) :** IQ is also based on the concept of mental age. It is the ratio of mental age to the chronological age multiplied by 100.

$$IQ = \frac{MA}{CA} \times 100.$$

Suppose, the mental age of a 10-year-old child is 12 years on the basis of his scores on an intelligence test, his IQ will be

$$\frac{12}{10} \times 100 = 120.$$

Similarly, if mental age of a person is nine years two months and his age is 12 years 6 months, then his IQ will be

$$\frac{110}{150} \times 100 = 73.3.$$

General classification of persons in terms of IQ

IQ	Classification
140 and above	Genius
130-140	Very superior
120-130	Superior
110-120	Bright
90-110	Average
80-90	Dull
70-80	Borderline
Below 70	Mentally retarded.

Shortcomings of IQ: Some of the main short comings of IQ are as follows:

(i) It is a well-known fact that after 18 years, the mental age of a person tends to stabilize. Thus, if IQ is calculated after this age, the result will be misleading, *i.e.,* a person will be less intelligent if he grows in age.

(ii) Variability of IQ scores from one test to another is not the same. As a result IQ scores for different tests would not be directly comparable.

(iii) It has also been found that variability in IQ scores for the different age levels on the same test is not the same. In that case IQ scores would be a misleading index because it would indicate that a person's IQ may increase or decrease as he grows in age. An example will illustrate this point.

Age	IQ	SD
9 years old child	120	12
7 years old child	120	9

Here IQ of 120 of both the children is not the same due to difference in SD.

3. **Deviation IQ :** Now-a-days IQ ratio is converted into a normalized standard score with a fixed mean of 100 and SD of 15. This is known as DIQ. This fixed mean and SD remain constant through all the age levels. It means that if a child's score is 1 SD above the mean his DIQ will be 100 + 15 = 115. Similarly, if his score is 1 SD below the mean his DIQ will be 100 – 15 = 85 and so on. Thus, with the help of these **DIQ** scores inter age comparison is also possible.

Uses of Intelligence Test

Intelligence tests can be applied in the following situations.

1. **Measurement of general learning abilities:** Intelligence and achievement in schools are highly correlated. If a person is high on an intelligence test, he is expected to score high on school achievements also. Conversely if a person scores high on an intelligence test and still his school achievement is very poor, we can find out other reasons for his educational backwardness.

2. **Assessment of individual differences and categorization :** With the help of intelligence tests we can categories a particular class into several convenient groups and plan our instructional strategies accordingly. Thus, intelligence testing is very useful for educational guidance.

3. **Exact definition of mental retardation is possible :** It is said that those who are below 70 in IQ are retarded but to what extent they are mentally retarded can further be studied with the help of higher screening. We may define the three groups of mentally retarted in the following ways.

Category	IQ level
Morons	45-69
Imbeciles	25-45
Idiots	Below 25

4. **Identification of gifted children :** Gifted children are the treasure of the society. They must be identified in the earlier stages of their lives so that they can be fully guided and helped for their better advancement which is directly related to the advancement of the society as well. Intelligence testing will help the concerned organisations to chalk out plans in the desired manner.

5. **Vocational guidance :** Some children are very forward in verbal abilities and some are superior in non-verbal abilities. This identification is possible only with the help of intelligence tests. Since academic subjects need verbal intelligence and technical subjects need non-verbal or performing abilities, hence children may be guided accordingly.

6. **Screening :** In today's age of competition and rush, screening has become a necessity. Every school has limited seats of admission and it has to select only those students who can raise the academic level of the school high and get name for it. Same is the case with appointments in jobs. For all these purposes, intelligence testing is a must.

7. **Study of mental growth :** Mental abilities develop in a sequential order onward. We can use intelligence tests for studying the trends of mental development of individuals. Intelligence tests have made it clear that mental development of children is a steady consistent process from year-to-year till the age of 25. Intelligence tests show that mind does not develop rapidly in the period of adolescence like the physical and emotional development, but in childhood, it develops rapidly.

Limitations of Intelligence Tests

1. Generally intelligence test shows what a person can do at a certain point of time. These abilities are tested on the basis of certain items included in the test. In order to make the results dependable, a proper size of the sample must be selected for standardization of the test.

2. Some people may be fatigued earlier than others when take a test. This extent of fatigue may reduce their scores and hence intelligence testing will not be accurate. So scores should be taken with caution.

3. No intelligence test is fully free from cultural influences. So, home or school background may affect the intelligence test scores of subjects.

4. Administration of the test also affects the scores of subjects. If proper rapport is there between the examiner and the examinee. IQ scores may be high. On the other hand, if children are frightened with the testing situation as is case of slow learners they will perform poorly on the test.

5. Taking intelligence scores in absolute form is misleading. Intelligence tests do not reveal all the mental abilities in most of the cases. So, intelligence test must be supplemented with clinical setting and case history method to collect detailed information about a subject as is done in clinics by physician who does not entirely believe in physical investigations. He rather takes the help of clinical diagnosis before giving remedial treatment to the patients.

THOUGHT AND LANGUAGE

In this section we examines the relationship between language and thought: that language determines thought, that thought determines language, and that thought and language have different origins. Let us examine these three viewpoints in some detail.

Language as Determinant of Thought

In Hindi and other Indian languages we use a number of different words for various kinship relationships. We have different terms for mother's brother, father's elder brother, father's younger brother, mother's sister's husband, father's sister's husband and so on. An English person uses just one word *uncle* to describe all these kinship relationships. In the English language there are dozens of words for colours whereas some tribal languages have only two to four colour terms. Do such differences matter for how we think? Does an Indian child find it easier to think about and differentiate between various kinship relationships compared to her English-speaking counterpart? Does our thinking process depend on how we describe it in our language?

Benjamin Lee Whorf was of the view that language determines the contents of thought. This view is known as **linguistic relativity hypothesis**. In its strong version, this hypothesis holds what and how individuals can possibly think is determined by the language and linguistic categories they use **(linguistic determinism).** Experimental evidence, however, maintains that it is possible to have the same level or quality of thoughts in all languages depending upon the availability of linguistic categories and structures. Some thoughts may be easier in one language compared to another.

Thought as Determinant of Language

The noted Swiss psychologist, Jean Piaget believed that thought not only determines language, but also precedes it. Piaget argued that children form an internal representation of the world through thinking. For example, when children see something and later copy it (a process called imitation), thinking does take place, which does not involve language. A child's observation of other's behaviour and imitation of the same behaviour, no doubt involves thinking but not language. Language is just one of the vehicles of thinking. As actions become internalised, language may affect children's range of symbolic thinking but is not necessary for the origins of thought. Piaget believed that though language can be taught to children, understanding of the words require knowledge of the underlying concepts (*i.e.* thinking). Thus, thought is basic, and necessary if language is to be understood.

Different Origins of Language and Thought

The Russian psychologist, Lev Vyogotsky, argued that thoughts and language develop in a child separately until about two years of age, when they merge. Before two years thought is preverbal and is experienced more in action (Piaget's sensory motor stage). The child's utterances are more automotic reflexes—crying when uncomfortable—than thought-based. Around two years of age, the child expresses thought verbally and her/his speech reflects rationality. Now children are able to manipulate thoughts using soundless speech. He believed that during this period the development of language and thinking become interdependent; the development of conceptual thinking depends upon the quality of inner speech and vice versa. Thought is used without language when the vehicle of thinking is non-verbal such as visual or movement-related. Language is used without thought when expressing feelings or exchanging pleasantries, for example "Good morning! How are you?" "Very well, I am fine". When the two functions overlap, they can be used together to produce verbal thought and rational speech.

Development of Language

Language is a complex system and unique to human beings. Psychologists have tried to teach sign language, use of symbols to chimpanzees, dolphins, parrots, etc. But it is observed that, human language is more complex, creative, and spontaneous than the system of communication other animals can learn. There is also a great deal of **regularity** with which children all over the world seem to be learning the language or languages to which they are exposed. When we compare individual children, we find that they differ a great deal in the rate of their language development as well as in how they go about it. But when we take a general view of children's acquisition of language all over the world we find some *predictable pattern* in which children proceed from almost no use of language to the point of becoming competent language users. Language develops through some of the stages discussed below.

Newborn babies and young infants make a variety of sounds, which gradually get modified to resemble words. The first sound produced by babies is crying. Initial crying is undifferentiated and similar across various situations. Gradually, the pattern of crying varies in its pitch and intensity to signify different states such as hunger, pain, and sleepiness, etc. These differentiated crying sounds gradually become more meaningful *cooing sounds* (like 'aaa', 'uuu', etc). usually to express happiness.

At around six months of age children enter the *babbling* stage. Babbling involves prolonged repetition of a variety of consonants and vowel sounds (for example, da—, aa—, ba—). By about nine months of age these sounds get elaborated to strings of some sound combinations, such as 'dadadadadada' into repetitive patterns called *echolalia*. While the early babblings are random or accidental in nature, the later babblings seem to be imitative of adult voices. Children show some understanding of a few words by the time they are six months old. Around the first birthday (the exact age varies from child-to-child) most children enter the *one-word-stage*. Their first word usually contains one syllable—*ma or da*, for instance. Gradually they move to one or more words which are combined to form whole sentences or phrases. So they are called *holophrases*. When they are 18 to 20 months of age, children enter a *two-word stage* and begin to use two words together. The two-word stage exemplifies *telegraphic speech*. Like telegrams (got admission, send money) it contains mostly nouns and verbs. Close to their third birthday, *i.e.* beyond two-and-a-half years, children's language development gets focused on rules of the language they hear.

How is language acquired? You must be wondering: "How do we learn to speak?" As with many other topics in psychology, the questions of whether a behaviour develops as a result of inherited characteristics (nature) or from the effects of learning (nurture) has been raised with regard to language. Most psychologists accept that both nature and nurture are important in language acquisition.

Behaviourist B.F. Skinner believed we learn language the same way as animals learn to pick keys or press bars. Language development, for the behaviourists follow the learning principles, such as association (the sight of bottle with the word 'bottle'), imitation (adults use of word ''bottle''), and reinforcement (smiles and hugs when the child says something right). There is also evidence that children produce sounds that are appropriate to a language of the parent or care-giver and are reinforced for having done so. The principle of shaping leads to successive approximation of the desired responses so that the child eventually speaks as well as the adult. Regional differences in pronunciation and phrasing illustrate how different patterns are reinforced in different areas.

Linguist Noam Chomsky put forth the innate proposition of development of language. For him the *rate at which children acquire words and grammar* without being taught can not be explained only by learning principles. Children also *create all sorts of sentences* they have never heard and, therefore, could not be imitating. Children throughout the world seem to have a *critical period*—a period when learning must occur if it is to occur successfully—for learning language. Children across the world also go through the same stages of language development. Chomsky believes language development is just like physical maturation given adequate care, it "just happens to the child". Children are born with "universal grammar". They readily learn the grammar of whatever language they hear.

Skinner's emphasis on learning explains why infants acquire the language they hear and how they add new words to their vocabularies. Chomsky's emphasis on our built-in readiness to learn grammar helps explain why children acquire language so readily without direct teaching.

GENDER AS A SOCIAL CONSTRUCT; GENDER ROLES, GENDER-BIAS AND EDUCATIONAL PRACTICE

Gender refers to the social distinctions between boys and girls and men and women that are socially constructed rather than biologically determined. These distinctions are reflected in the roles that boys and girls play in society and the status that they occupy within it. Gender roles tend to be dynamic. They vary from one culture and time period to another and are characterized by unequal power relationships.

Ending gender bias and discrimination is crucial to the empowerment of women and girls and to the achievement of gender equality in education. Applying a gender perspective helps to make differences in power relations visible. It also helps us to see more clearly the needs and rights of girls and boys in particular geographical, cultural and economic contexts.

The ultimate goal is to eliminate gender biases and discriminatory practices and policies, both overt and covert. This is at the heart of gender analysis. Gender analysis should therefore be a prerequisite for identifying and understanding problems as they relate to education, and especially to the continued exclusion of girls from quality schooling. Gender analysis guides the process of finding viable and sustainable solutions to the problems of access, quality and learning achievement.

Gender analysis of what learners bring to education (including early childhood socialization, feeding and health access, cultural heritage and language), the content of education, teaching and learning processes, learning environments and learning outcomes help to highlight bad (and good) educational practices and policies. This analysis, in turn, should form the basis for educational interventions that are sensitive to both gender and human rights.

Gender Bias in Teaching

A common response from teachers when asked about gender inequity in classrooms is that they treat all their students the same. There are two problems with this statement. First, students are diverse and have different learning issues, thus treating all students in the same way means that some students will have a better learning experience than their peers. Second, teachers may be ignoring their unconscious gender biases towards their students, their schools and themselves. If ignored, these gender biases, which may have developed from cultural norms, may lead to bias in the classroom.

Gender bias occurs when people make assumptions regarding behaviours, abilities or preferences of others based upon their gender. Because there are strong gender role stereotypes for masculinity and femininity, students who do not match them can encounter problems with teachers and with their peers. For example, the expectation is that boys naturally exhibit boisterous, unruly behaviour, are academically able, rational, and socially uncommunicative, whereas girls are quiet, polite, and studious. Girls are also expected to possess better social skills than boys and to excel at reading and the language arts. So girls who present discipline problems for teachers, or quiet, studious boys, may encounter a lack of understanding from peers and teachers. Within the classroom, these biases unfold in students' practices and teachers' acceptance of certain behaviours from one student or another based upon the students' gender. Also, bias due to a person's gender is not mutually exclusive of other social categories such as race, ethnicity, class, religion, and language. For example, some teachers may perceive African American or other Black girls as loud and uncontrollable because the girls do not exhibit the feminine behaviours associated with White women, such as quiet, self-effacing and malleable.

Gender bias can occur within subject areas and school activities. For example, in subjects such as mathematics and the sciences, there are different participation patterns for girls and boys. Gender bias promulgates a myth that boys are naturally better at mathematics and science than girls. The implications are that if girls succeed in these subjects it is due to their hard work, not their intelligence, whereas boys' success is credited to their natural talent. There are some signs that gender bias in schools may be decreasing in some areas. The percentage of girls participating in science has increased and achieved parity with boys in biology, chemistry and algebra. However, subjects that are prerequisites for college majors such as engineering or physics remain dominated by men. Only 25% of high school students enrolled in physics are female. Moreover, there has been little increase in the percentage of women in engineering programs.

Males are also more likely than females to be in remedial programs and students' race also impacts these patterns. For example, African American males are more likely than White or female peers to enroll in remedial reading and mathematics courses. And non-White students have a higher representation in vocational and noncollege preparatory courses than their White peers. Teachers are critical components in challenging gender bias in schooling, but they also can be major contributors to it as well, through their pedagogical practices, curriculum choices, and assessment strategies.

Gender Bias in Teachers

Teachers' unconscious gender biases can produce stereo-typic expectations for students' success and participation in the classroom. Teachers view male students' domination of the classroom and their time as typical masculine behaviour. However, these biases have consequences for the students and the classroom climate. More than two decades ago, researchers identified and named groups of students who dominated the teacher's time and the classroom resources as ''target students'' (Tobin & Gallagher, 1987). Target students were typically white and male. They answered most of the teacher's questions and also asked most of the questions. This behaviour pattern was particularly insidious in mathematics and science classrooms because teachers did not expect girls to have competent knowledge in these subject areas. Classroom observations documented that target

students typically called out answers to the teacher's questions, thus denying other students the opportunity to engage in dialogue with the teacher or get to grips with the subject matter. Furthermore, because boys are perceived as having natural talent in science, teachers asked boys harder and more complicated questions than girls. If girls attempted to answer more difficult questions than boys and faltered, teachers often repeated the question and asked that another student, typically a boy, provide the answer. However, if a boy failed to answer correctly, teachers reframed the question or broke it into a series of simpler questions that could help the student find the answer. Teachers' unconscious stereotyped gender bias that boys are smarter than girls, especially in mathematics and the sciences, meant they were willing to work with boys to reach the answer because they perceived boys were capable of achieving that goal but girls were not. Conversely, teachers of subjects perceived as feminine will spend more time engaged with girls.

Teachers' gendered perceptions of students' ability is also reflected in the type of praise and expectations they have of their students. Teachers often give girls less meaningful and less critical praise than boys. Boys' work is described as unique or brilliant, while girls' work is often undervalued, critically ignored and praised for its appearance. This aspect of teachers' behaviour is particularly detrimental to girls because it means they do not receive feedback on their work that could help them develop deeper understandings of concepts (Liu, 2006).

Teachers also use target students to maintain the tempo and pace of classroom instruction. For example, in a lecture or whole class discussion when a teacher is posing questions to the class, he or she may encourage target students to call out answers in order to keep the lesson moving, rather than wait for the other students to process the question and provide an answer. This short ''wait time'' may be detrimental to learning. More than three decades ago, researchers found that if teachers waited three to five seconds before accepting a student's answer, more students became engaged in the classroom and also improved their understanding of the content. Moreover, the longer wait time meant that teachers began to ask more cognitively challenging questions. However, the existence of target students in classes who often call out answers without direction from teachers meant that fewer students, especially girls, engaged in the lessons. In the absence of proactive teacher intervention, these patterns in which males dominate classroom interactions also occur in mixed-gender, small groups.

Target students dominate classroom interactions and exchanges at all education levels. In the early

2000s, researchers identified these same patterns of engagement in a professional development program for science teachers. When alerted to the invasive behaviours of the male teachers in the cohort, faculty began using overt breaching strategies to stop the target students calling out answers, dominating the human and materials resources of the classroom, and showing disrespect to their peers (Martin Milne & Scantlebury, 2006).

Teachers' gender bias towards students can also extend to their response to students who challenge their authority. Such risk-taking behaviour in boys is expected and at times praised, but assertiveness in girls is viewed negatively and labelled unfeminine. Similarly, boys who do not exhibit stereotypic masculine behaviours may be ridiculed (Renold, 2006).

Teachers use gender expectations as a means of maintaining classroom control. For example, teachers will seat undisciplined boys next to girls as a classroom management strategy. Further, teachers use the gendered expectation that girls' nurturing characteristics will lead them to place others' needs before their own. In other words, teachers often ask girls to assume mothering roles towards students who have fallen behind with learning because of inattentiveness, absenteeism through truancy, or in-school disciplinary procedures, and often those students are male.

Effects of Gender Bias

Gender bias can impact students' attitudes towards learning and their engagement with the subject. If affected by gender bias, girls will tend to believe that any success they have is due to hard work rather than any innate talent or intelligence. Boys may be encouraged to believe that success in science and mathematics should come easily to them because of their gender. Some males report dropping out of college science and mathematics programs because they no longer perceive these subjects as easy. Overall, teachers have lower expectations for girls' academic success compared to boys, and their attitudes are shown through the type and quality of the student-teacher interaction. The type and quality of critique teachers give their students can also have an impact. Teachers' comments on girls' work focuses on its appearance but with boys' work teachers focus on the content. Girls often do not receive substantive comments or criticism from teachers from which they could improve their ability to learn. During the many hours spent in classrooms, girls receive less time and attention from teachers than their male peers. Teachers usually ask girls easier questions than they ask boys. Typically, girls receive fewer opportunities to engage in classroom discourse, use equipment and assert their knowledge in classrooms.

Reducing Gender Bias

Gender bias in education is a series of microinequities whose impact is cumulative and often ignored. Girls are rewarded and praised for compliant behaviour. Teachers do not challenge girls with questions and rarely offer criticisms of their works. Teachers can reduce and challenge gender bias through an examination of their pedagogical practices and by posing simple questions about their practices. For example, which students do they frequently interact with? Are target students evident in their classroom? If so, how does the teacher deal with those students? What questioning techniques does the teacher use to engage students? Does the teacher ask complicated questions to girls as well as boys? Does the teacher use a variety of pedagogical and assessment practices? Which students are engaged with the curriculum?

Another way of reducing gender bias would be for teachers to videotape their classes and review their interactions with the students. Or they could invite a colleague to watch their teaching and record which students are being asked questions and what type of questions. However, teachers must also prepare for the consequences of changing their practices. Girls are conditioned to receiving less of the teacher's attention, and they do not usually cause discipline problems if they are not receiving their fair share, but boys can react negatively to losing the teacher's attention, causing disruption to lessons and becoming discipline problems. Moreover, research has also shown that boys avoid written work and often have poor communication skills when asked to work in singlesex groups.

However, the gains in reducing gender bias in education may disappear with the requirements of high-stakes testing required by No Child Left Behind (NCLB). NCLB requires that states report academic achievement data in most social categories, except gender (Kahle, 2004). This may result in less attention being placed on gender bias and less data that might reveal it. Continued monitoring of gender bias is necessary to minimize its impact on students' opportunities for learning and achievement.

INDIVIDUAL DIFFERENCES AMONG LEARNERS

It is not unusual to find a wide range of differences among students in a class or a group. These differences are invariably identified in terms of student's characteristics such as physical (appearance, height, size, sex, colour, etc.), demographic (age, caste, socio-economic status, etc.) and cognitive behaviour (thinking, remembering, problem solving, creating idea, etc.). The differences that exist among students due to physical, demographic, affective behaviour and cognitive behaviour characteristics are referred to as individual differences.

Differences due to physical and demographic characteristics are conspicuous and easy to identify. However, the differences that exist in the way they solve problem in Mathematics or in their ability to interpret and explain ideas are not easily visible but are identified through their performance. Let us examine, for instance, the answers given by Bitto and Neha, two students of the same class to the following proverb.

Interpret the saying, "Pen is mighter than the sword".

Bitto's Interpretation

It means that writing had always been able to influence mankind more than any amount of sheer physical strength; writing undoubtedly makes a more lasting impact in the minds of the people than any form of physical demonstration. In the case of the latter the impact might be forceful though less lasting. Great thinkers, writers and philosophers have from time immemovial been able to hold sway over the minds of the people by means of their profound knowledge through their writings. For example, Socrates won the wrath of a powerful state, because of his great ability to hold spellbound the young through his discourses. Similarly, the writing of Voltaire and Rousseau inspired the French to rise up in revolt.

Neha's Interpretation

It is a common proverb which simply means that through writing it is possible to win more victories than by using physical force and weapons. When any good book is read it is possible to retain in our memory the message it contains. On the other hand, success achieved through physical might is not for mankind.

The above illustration reflects the differences between Bitto and Neha in their interpretation of the proverb. While Bitto delves deep in her interpretation, Neha states only the meaning.

According to Skinner, individual differences in learner behaviours are the result of the organism's genetic endowment and reinforcement. Thus, Skinner believed that defective genetic endowment and/or defective reinforcement contingencies in an individual's experience result in a failure to acquire a variety of learned behaviours.

The process of an individual's mental activities such as remembering, analysing, interpreting, reasoning, problem solving and thinking are cognitive domain behaviours and are essential for learning and achievement. How we think, what and how we remember, how we solve problem and how we create ideas are cognitive domain behaviours and individuals differ by these behaviours. Such differences are often identified by psychologists in terms of intelligence, aptitude, creating and academic achievement.

Individual differences are crucial for teachers who are responsible for guiding all forms of learning. In fact, many educators would suggest that the primary role of teachers is to provide education to meet the individual differences and to develop student cognitive process.

Do Individuals Differ in Intelligence?

Well, they do differ. But how? Differences are due to the differences in the level of general intellectual ability and the underlying cognitive process among individuals.

How do we identify differences in intelligence?

Using suitable intelligence tests we can measure and identify the difference. An intelligence test may contain sub-tests (sub-sections) and each sub-test represents a different set of ability. The scores obtained in all sub-tests are added up to obtain a single score to represent the general ability of the student. Thus, the single score obtained for each individual in a test is expressed in terms of **intelligence quotient** (IQ). IQ is a measure of intelligence and is defined as the ratio of mental age (average age of children who give correct responses/answers in an intelligence test) to the chronological age (actual age) multiplied by 100 (to avoid fraction). Thus mental age is:

$$IQ = \frac{\text{Mental age}}{\text{Chronological age}} \times 100$$

IQ scores help us estimate individual differences by categorising individuals on the basis of their IQs. These differences have important consequences for learning and performance. Let us examine the different categories of students based on their intelligence level.

Gifted : Those students who possess IQs of 130 or above are called gifted students. They are superior in intelligence and have high ability to reason. As compared to other children, they can perform academic activities grasping concepts, memorising, perceiving, seeing relationships, generalising, dealing with abstract ideas, critical thinking and solving problems more effectively and quickly. They have a broad attention span that permits concentration and the ability for a high level of academic performance. They take initiative in intellectual work and follow complex directions. Such individuals are small in number as compared to normal or average children. Normal groups have those children whose IQs range from 90 to 110 and they are able to profit from regular school programmes with varying degrees of effort.

Disabled : There are children with **disability** due to low level to intellectual functioning or specific learning deficits. Children with low level or below-average intellectual functioning are called mentally retarded. The children with inadequate level of intelligence are impaired in their ability to learn and to adapt to the demands of society. Mentally retarded children are of different categories. They can be:

- **Border line** (IQ ranges 90-70) and **educable mentally retarded** (IQ ranges 70-50) children can perform academic activities but are slow in their learning. Special instructional strategies can help them to profit from learning activities. They can take care of themselves and live independently as adults.

- **Trainable mentally retarded** (IQ ranges 50-35) are capable of learning only certain rudimentary literacy materials and simple occupational skills. They possess some ability to take care of their personal needs and can be trained in daily living skills. Such children require special classes or schools to study in.

- **Severely retarded** (IQ below 35) have quite limited adaptive behaviour and are never found in school. They are dependent on their families for their personal needs.

Children with specific learning defects are called learning disabled group. They are normal to above-average on intelligence but have difficulties in one or more psychological processes involved in understanding or in using language or numbers (written or spoken). The difficulties manifest in their ability to listen, think, speak, read, write, spell or do mathematical calculations. These difficulties are identified as **aphasia** (difficulty in grasping spoken language), **dylesia** (difficulty in reading), **hyperlexia** (little or no comprehension), **dyscalculia** (difficulty in doing arithmetic) and **dysgraphia** (difficulty in writing). Some are hyperactive in the sense that they are excessively active inattentive and behave impulsively. They follow instructions poorly and do not often complete the assigned tasks.

Instructional Strategies for Handling Individual Differences

- Organise instruction for the development of cognitive process.
- Use existing cognitive level as base.
- Strengthen memory.
- Formulate level specific instructional strategy.
- Use individual meeting.

- Provide instructions to overcome learning disability.

Do Individuals Differ in Aptitude?

Yes, they do differ. An individual may have a mechanical aptitude, another may have an aptitude for mathematics or yet another may have an aptitude for language, music or athletics. Such differences are due to the differences in the combination of abilities related to the cognitive processes, and the sensory and psychomotor components. For instance, when we talk of mechanical aptitude, we may deal with ability for spatial relations, ability to acquire information on mechanical matters and ability to comprehend mechanical relations, besides sensory and psychomotor abilities. Similarly, when we discuss aptitude in music, we may identify ability for musical memory, pitch discrimination, loudness discrimination, time discrimination and judgement of rhythm. Likewise, abilities required for science or mathematics are different and each requires a separate set of abilities.

The differences in aptitude can be identified using aptitude tests. Aptitude tests for areas such as mechanical skills, mathematics, science, language, music and graphic art can be used to identify the aptitude of students in each area of performance. You might have heard of the use of aptitude tests in medicine, engineering, business management, law or teacher training for selection of students for studies in the respective fields. The aptitude test, in fact, provides a measure of the candidates promise or teachability in a field of study, say, medicine. In other words, the test would tell whether the candidate possesses the required aptitude or readiness to profit from studies in the concerned field of study.

Instructional Strategy for Handling Individual Differences

The suggested approach for handling individual differences is **adaptive instructional system**. In this approach at least two alternative instructional treatments are needed to ensure academic success. Which is the most appropriate instructional treatment for the student depends upon his or her existing level of aptitude (learning readiness). Students with high aptitude may choose unstructured instructional strategy. With minimum guidance from teacher, they may be encouraged to learn through the discovery oriented approach. You may use the inductive process but instructional treatment is essentially learner-centered.

In contrast, highly structured instructional treatment for low aptitude learners is designed in small units through sequential steps and feedback. Frequent summary and review with simplified illustration, analogy and precise explanation of concepts and principles to be learned will facilitate progressive learning. Periodic achievement and aptitude assessments and comparison of these scores with the aptitude scores obtained at the start of instruction would tell the degree to which each learner in the specific treatment group has achieved.

However, for those who are unable to profit from either of the alternative treatments presented above, **compensatory aptitude training** is suggested. This consists of directed reading skill, study habits, self-learning skills, note taking and related activities. The main aim of compensatory aptitude training is to develop readiness for entry into structured treatment. Periodic monitoring should be formulated to identify the students who reach the required level for entry into alternative treatment.

Do Learners Differ in their Academic Achievements?

They do differ, but how? We have seen that those who possess appropriate pre-requisite knowledge learn more effectively than those who lack such knowledge. Differences in pre-requisite knowledge possessed by students create differences in the attainment of knowledge. Further, knowledge is attained progressively. Progressive differences in knowledge attainment leads to cumulative differences in knowledge attainment and this form of differences is often called **Mathew Effect.** It means that academically rich get richer and those who are poor continue to be poor. Thus, differences in pre-requisites and cumulative knowledge lead to differences in the knowledge possessed by the students likewise, they also differ in their capabilities to manipulate the knowledge in a given situation and the differences are identified in terms of the abilities to apply, analyse, synthesise and evaluate knowledge. In fact, ability is an essential condition for learning and the abilities related to intelligence, aptitude and creativity are important for academic achievement. We have seen the instructional strategies for meeting the differences in intelligence, aptitude and creativity through classroom situations. It means that differences in intelligence, aptitude and creativity do create differences in academic achievement.

The differences in academic achievement can be identified using an achievement test in the concerned subject. However, if the achievement test contains only knowledge level items (questions), it tells only knowledge level differences. On the other hand, if it contains items (questions) on knowledge and capabilities—comprehension, application, analysis, synthesis and evaluation—the various levels of differences can be identified. Besides, the total marks, each level-wise total is needed to identify the strengths and weaknesses of every student as well as the differences among students. As a teacher, if you know the strengths and weaknesses of your students in a subject, you may be able to adopt appropriate instructional strategies to suit their strenghts and weaknesses in that subject.

Apart from these achievement differences are quite often identified in terms of categories of achievers by classifying students as high, average and low achievers. Though there is no strict cut-off points, these categories can be created using marks. High achievers are those who possess higher level of knowledge and capabilities (say, with marks 66% and above) than the rest and those who possess average level of knowledge and capabilities (say, with marks 36% to 65%) are called average achievers. On the other extreme, you may find learners with low level knowledge and capabilities (with 35% and below marks). They are called low achievers. If you are interested in identifying the high, average and low achievers in a subject, say Science or language, the categories are created using the marks obtained in the concerned subject. However, categories can also be created based on the overall achievement in a class.

As a teacher, you may be curious to know the strategies for meeting the achievement differences in your classroom or the challenges posed by the strengths and weaknesses of the students in teaching-learning situations. Let us discuss important instructional strategies.

What are Instructional Strategies?

Let us discuss the major strategies to cope up with the differences in academic achievement.

- Provide appropriate pre-requisites to organise and learn new information.
- Use visual aids.
- Use analogy, example and illustration.
- Ensure learner's active involvement in learning.
- Periodic assessment.

EVALUATION AND ASSESSMENT

Evaluation

Evaluation, particularly educational evaluation is a series of activities designed to measure the effectiveness of the teaching-learning systems as a whole. According to Mary Thorpe (1980), ''Evaluation is the collection, analysis and interpretation of information about any aspect of a programme of education.'' Teaching-learning process is a continuous activity. It needs to be evaluated from beginning to end. Evaluation during the learning process (continuous assessment), often termed as "formative evaluation", is important for learners and teachers alike.

The bases of evaluation are learning objectives, performance standards and achievement tests on the one hand, and learners' and experts' opinions on the other. Evaluation helps to build an educational programme, assess its achievement and improve upon its effectiveness. It also provides valuable feedback on the design, development and implementation of the programme. It is, of course, an important component of the teaching-learning process. It helps in making the value judgement, determining educational status, or measuring achievement of learners.

The scope of evaluation in schools extents to almost all the areas of learner's personality development. It includes both scholastic and non-scholastic areas. It reveals the strengths and weaknesses of the learners, so that the learners have better opportunity to understand and improve themselves.

Evaluation is helpful to teachers also. It provides feedback to them to reshape their teaching strategies according to the needs of the learners. Evaluation in education in general and in distance education in particular becomes imperative to know as to what extent the goals of education have been achieved.

Thus, evaluation is not merely assigning grades to learners. It is a continuous process of acquiring and processing information in order to improve one's learning and to assess decisions made in designing an instructional system. If we analyse the above statement we easily notice that it has three important implications for the entire teaching-learning system. They are as follows:

1. Evaluation is a continuous process and not a one time performance measurement, effected at the end of a course/programme. It starts at the stage of curriculum development and continues until the instruction ends.

2. Evaluation process is goal-directed. It is aimed at finding ways and means to improve learning and thereby to achieve learning objectives more effectively and more efficiently.

3. Evaluation requires the use of accurate and appropriate measuring instructions to collect information for taking decisions about the quality and operation of education.

It is clear that in designing an effective learning system, one of the earliest steps we need to take is to prepare a comprehensive evaluation plan, which should be developed soon after the learning objectives have been formulated. This practice will help us to:

- determine whether the objectives are attainable or need revisions before we start designing the instructional system;

- collect data/information in a form that suits our purposes adequately and at a time when it is available, otherwise the opportunity to collect specific information may be lost; and

- have sufficient time to test the effectiveness of a design.

Continuous and Comprehensive Evaluation (CCE)

Continuous and Comprehensive Evaluation (CCE) refers to a system of school based evaluation of a student that covers all aspects of a student development. It is a developmental process of student which emphasizes on two fold objectives. These objectives are continuity in evaluation and assessment of broad based learning and behaviourial outcomes on the other.

The term **'continuous'** is meant to emphasise that evaluation of identified aspects of students **'growth and development'** is a continuous process rather than an event, built into the total teaching-learning process and spread over the entire span of academic session. It means regularity of assessment, frequency of unit testing, diagnosis of learning gaps, use of corrective measures, retesting and feedback of evidence to teachers and students for their self evaluation.

The second term **'comprehensive'** means that the scheme attempts to cover both the scholastic and the co-scholastic aspects of the students' growth and development. Since abilities, attitudes and aptitudes can manifest themselves in forms other than the written word, the term refers to application of variety of tools and techniques (both testing and non-testing) and aims at assessing a learner's development in areas of learning, like:

- Knowledge
- Understanding
- Applying
- Analyzing
- Evaluating
- Creating

Objectives of CCE

- To help develop cognitive, psychomotor and affective skills.

- To lay emphasis on thought process and de-emphasise memorization.

- To make evaluation an integral part of teaching-learning process.

- To use evaluation for improvement of students achievement and teaching-learning strategies on the basis of regular diagnosis followed by remedial instructions.

- To use evaluation as a quality control device to maintain desired standard of performance.
- To determine social utility, desirability or effectiveness of a programme and take appropriate decisions about the learner, the process of learning and the learning environment.
- To make the process of teaching and learning a learner-centered activity.

Features of CCE

- The **'continuous'** aspect of CCE takes care of **'continual'** and **'periodicity'** aspect of evaluation.
- Continual means assessment of students in the beginning of instructions (placement evaluation) and assessment during the instructional process (**formative evaluation**) done informally using multiple techniques of evaluation.
- Periodicity means assessment of performance done frequently at the end of unit/term (**summative evaluation**).
- The **'comprehensive'** component of CCE takes care of assessment of all round development of the child's personality. It includes assessment in **Scholastic as well as Co-Scholastic** aspects of the pupil's growth.
- Scholastic aspects include curricular areas or subject specific areas, whereas Co-Scholastic aspects include Life Skills, Co-Curricular Activities, Attitudes and Values.
- Assessment in Scholastic areas is done informally and formally using multiple techniques of evaluation continually and periodically. The diagnostic evaluation takes place at the end of unit/term test. The causes of poor performance in some units are diagnosed using diagnostic tests. These are followed with appropriate interventions followed by retesting.
- Assessment in Co-Scholastic areas is done using multiple techniques on the basis of identified criteria, while assessment in Life Skills is done on the basis of Indicators of Assessment and Checklists.

Functions of CCE

- It helps the teacher to organize effective teaching strategies.
- Continuous evaluation helps in regular assessment to the extent and degree of Learner's progress (ability and achievement with reference to specific Scholastic and Co-Scholastic areas).
- Continuous evaluation serves to diagnose weaknesses and permits the teacher to ascertain an individual learner's strengths and weaknesses and her needs. It provides immediate feedback to the teacher, who can then decide whether a particular unit or concept needs a discussion again in the whole class or whether a few individuals are in need of remedial instruction.
- By continuous evaluation, children can know their strengths and weaknesses. It provides the child a realistic self assessment of how he/she studies. It can motivate children to develop good study habits, to correct errors, and to direct their activities towards the achievement of desired goals. It helps a learner to determine the areas of instruction in where more emphasis is required.
- Continuous and comprehensive evaluation identifies areas of aptitude and interest. It helps in identifying changes in attitudes and value systems.
- It helps in making decisions for the future, regarding choice of subjects, courses and careers.
- It provides information/reports on the progress of students in Scholastic and Co-Scholastic areas and thus helps in predicting the future success of the learner.

Continuous evaluation helps in bringing awareness of the achievement to the child, teachers and parents from time-to-time. They can look into the probable cause of the fall in performance if any, and may take remedial measures of instruction in which more emphasis is required. Many times, because of some personal reasons, family problems or adjustment problems, the children start neglecting their studies, resulting in sudden drop in their performance. If the teacher, child and parents do not notice the sudden drop in the performance of the child in academics, it could result in a permanent deficiency in the childs' learning.

The major emphasis of CCE is on the continuous growth of students ensuring their intellectual, emotional, physical, cultural and social development and therefore, it will not be merely limited to assessment of learner's scholastic attainments. CCE uses assessment as a means of motivating learners to provide feedback and follow up work to improve upon the learning in the classroom and to present a comprehensive picture of a learner's profile. It is this that has led to the emergence of the concept of **School Based Continuous and Comprehensive Evaluation.**

Scholastic and Co-Scholastic Assessment

In order to have Continuous and Comprehensive Evaluation, both Scholastic and Co-Scholastic aspects need to be given due recognition. Such a holistic assessment requires maintaining an ongoing and comprehensive profile for each learner that is honest, encouraging and discreet. While teachers frequently reflect, plan and implement remedial strategies, the child's ability to retain and articulate what has been learned over a period of time also requires periodic assessment. These assessments can take many forms but all of them should be as comprehensive and discreet as possible. **Weekly, fortnightly,** or **quarterly** reviews (depending on the learning area), that do not openly compare one learner with another are generally recommended. The objective is to promote and enhance not just learning and retention among children, but their soft skills as well.

Scholastic Assessment

The objectives of the Scholastic domain are:-

- Desirable behaviour related to the learner's knowledge, understanding, application, evaluation, analysis and the ability to apply it in an unfamiliar situation.
- To improve the teaching learning process.
- Assessment should be both **Formative** and **Summative**.

Summative and Formative Assessment

Assessment is often divided into formative and summative categories for the purpose of considering different objectives for assessment practices.

Summative Assessment

Summative assessment is intended to measure learning outcomes and report those outcomes to students, parents and administrators. In an educational setting, it generally occurs at the conclusion of a class, course, semester or academic year. In the context of a course summative assessments are typically used to assign students a course grade. It is also referred to in a learning context as **"assessment of learning"**. **Performance-based assessment** is similar to summative assessment, as it focuses on achievement. A well-defined task is identified and students are asked to create, produce, or do something, often in settings that involve real-world application of knowledge and skills. Proficiency is demonstrated by providing an extended response. Performance formats are further differentiated into products and performances. The performance may result in a product, such as a painting, portfolio, paper, or exhibition, or it may consist of a performance, such as a speech, athletic skill, musical recital, or reading.

Definitions of Summative Assessment

- "Good summative assessments—tests and other graded evaluations—must be demonstrably reliable, valid, and free of bias" (Angelo and Cross, 1993).
- '...assessment (that) has increasingly been used to sum up learning' (Black and William, 1999).
- '...looks at past achievements ... adds procedures or tests to existing work ... involves only marking and feedback grades to student ... is separated from teaching ... is carried out at intervals when achievement has to be summarized and reported.' (Harlen, 1998).

Features of Summative Assessment

- Assessment of learning.
- Generally taken by students at the end of a unit or semester to demonstrate the **"sum"** of what they have or have not learned.
- Summative assessment methods are the most traditional way of evaluating student work.

Formative Assessment

Formative assessment is generally carried out throughout a course or project. In an educational setting, formative assessment is used by teachers to consider approaches to teaching and next steps for individual learners and the class, and would not necessarily be used for grading purposes. Formative assessment, also referred to as **"educative assessment"** or **"assessment for learning"**, is used to aid learning. Assessment for learning is defined as "all those activities undertaken by teachers and/or students, which provide information to be used as feedback to modify the teaching and learning activities in which they are engaged" (Black and William 2004).

Definitions of Formative Assessment

- '... often means no more than that the assessment is carried out frequently and is planned at the same time as teaching'. (Black and William, 1999)
- '... provides feedback which leads to students recognizing the (learning) gap and closing it ... it is forward looking ...' (Harlen, 1998).
- '... includes both feedback and self-monitoring'. (Sadler, 1989)
- '... is used essentially to get a feedback into the teaching and learning process.' (Tunstall and Gipps, 1996)

Features of Formative Assessment

- Is diagnostic and remedial.
- Makes provision for effective feedback.

- Provides a platform for the active involvement of students in their own learning.
- Enables teachers to adjust teaching to take account of the results of assessment.
- Recognizes the profound influence assessment has on the motivation and self-esteem of students, both of which are crucial influences on learning.
- Recognizes the need for students to be able to assess themselves and understand how to improve.
- Builds on students' prior knowledge and experience in designing what is taught.
- Incorporates varied learning styles to decide how and what to teach.
- Encourages students to understand the criteria that will be used to judge their work.
- Offers an opportunity to students to improve their work after they get the feedback.
- Helps student to support their peer group and vice-versa.

A common form of formative assessment is **"diagnostic assessment"**. Diagnostic assessment measures a student's current knowledge and skills for the purpose of identifying a suitable program of learning. **"Self-assessment"** is a form of diagnostic assessment which involves students assessing themselves. **"Forward-looking assessment"** asks those being assessed to consider themselves in hypothetical future situations.

Co-Scholastic Assessment

The desirable behaviour related to learner's life skills, attitudes, interests, values, co-curricular activities and physical health are described as skills to be acquired in co-scholastic domain.

The process of assessing the students' progress in achieving objectives related to scholastic and co-scholastic domain is called comprehensive evaluation. It has been observed that usually under the scholastic domain such as knowledge and understanding of the facts, concepts, principles etc. of a subject are assessed. The Co-Scholastic elements are either altogether excluded from the evaluation process or they are not given adequate attention. For making the evaluation comprehensive, both Scholastic and Co-Scholastic aspects should be given importance. Simple and manageable means of assessment of Co-Scholastic aspects of growth must be included in the comprehensive evaluation scheme.

Comprehensive evaluation would necessitate the use of a variety of tools and techniques. This will be so because both different and specific areas of learner's growth can be evaluated through certain special techniques.

School Based CCE

School based Evaluation is held at school level unlike external examination conducted by the Boards of School Education. This is done by the teachers according to the schedule developed by the school and guidelines given by the Board. Though this evaluation has been done at school level all along, certain shortcomings have crept into this system. These shortcomings can be attributed to various factors. The basic factor is the misconception of teachers regarding the place of evaluation and its importance in the educational process. The other factor has been the imitation of the practice of external examination which is generally held at the end of the session.

In the School Based System of evaluation, the focus on the purpose of assessment has changed. Now, it includes readiness testing, screening of development, evaluation of performance in cognitive, affective and psychomotor domains more frequently, systematically and effectively.

In other words, School Based Evaluation is child-centred, school-centred and multidimensional evaluation. Hence, in its true spirit, it triggers an all round development of the learner. It encourages all kinds of learning in life both inside the school as well as outside it. It is child-centered as it attempts to consider the learner as a unique entity for its individual pattern of development. It builds on individual child's abilities, progress and development in achieving already set goals and objectives of education as an individual and not just his/her position in relation to other learners.

Further, this evaluation helps a learner to use his/her potential in a better manner and also provides insight to the teachers to discover the methods which may be helpful to the individual learner in resolving his/her problems and difficulties.

Besides being *child-centred,* this evaluation is *school-centred* as well. It means that no outside agency interferes in this evaluation process. It is entirely school based and done by the teacher. The teacher is trusted and given full responsibility of evaluating students with the brief that the teacher knows best about his/her students.

School Based Evaluation is *multidimensional.* Its multidimensional nature is reflected in recognizing and taking care of learners' social, emotional, physical, intellectual and other areas of development which are interrelated and cannot be considered in isolation. It also calls for the use of multiple techniques and tools of evaluation.

Aim of School Based CCE

- Elimination of chance element and subjectivity (as far as possible), de-emphasis on memorization, encouraging comprehensive evaluation incorporating both Scholastic and Co-Scholastic aspects of learners development.

- Continuous evaluation spread over the total span of the instructional time as an integral built-in aspect of the total teaching-learning process.

- Functional and meaningful declaration of results for effective use by teachers, students, parents and the society.

- Wider uses of test results for purposes not merely of the assessment of levels of pupils' achievements and proficiencies, but mainly for their improvement, thorough diagnosis and remedial/enrichment programmes.

- Improvement in the mechanics of conducting examinations for realizing a number of other allied purposes.

- Introduction of concomitant changes in instructional materials and methodology.

- Introduction of the semester system.

- The use of grades in place of marks in determining and declaring the level of pupil performance and proficiency.

Its Characteristics

School Based Evaluation has the following characteristics:

- Is broader, more comprehensive and continuous than traditional system.

- Aims primarily to help learners for systematic learning and development.

- Takes care of the needs of the learner as responsible citizens of the future.

- Is more transparent, futuristic and provides more scope for association among learners, teachers and parents.

School based evaluation provides opportunities to teachers to **know the following about their learners:**

- What they learn?

- How they learn?

- What type of difficulties/limitations they face in working in tandem?

- What do the children think?

- What do the children feel?

- What are their interests and dispositions?

The focus has shifted to developing a deep learning environment. There is a paradigm shift in the pedagogy and competencies from 'controlling' to 'enriching' to 'empowering' schools.

Traditional Schooling	Enriching Schooling	Empowering Schooling
• Teacher centred	• Student centred	• Experience centred
• Subjects and classes-teacher directed	• Self directed	• Virtual authenticity
• Sorting and ranking individuals	• Continuous assessment	• Multi literacies
Competency:	**Competency:**	**Competency:**
• Memory	• Critical thinking	• Risk taking
• Competitive	• Collaborative	• Ethical
	• Creative	• Interactive

Implementing School Based Assessment would mean:

- Elimination of chance element and subjectivity (as far as possible), de-emphasis of memorization, encouraging Comprehensive evaluation incorporating both scholastic and co-scholastic aspects of learners development.

- Continuous evaluation spread over the total span of the instructional time as an integral built-in aspect of the total teaching-learning process.

- Functional and meaningful declaration of results for effective use by teachers, students, parents and the society.

- Wider uses of test results for purposes not merely of the assessment of levels of pupils' achievements and proficiencies, but mainly for its improvement, through diagnosis and remedial/enrichment programmes.

- Improvements in the mechanics of conducting examinations for realizing a number of other allied purposes.

- Introduction of concomitant changes in instructional materials and methodology.

- Introduction of the semester system from the secondary stage onwards.
- The use of grades in place of marks in determining and declaring the level of pupil performance and proficiency.

The above goals are relevant for both external examination and evaluation in schools.

Shortcoming of Traditional External Examination

- It is a one shot examination at the end of a year at the terminal stage of schooling.
- It mainly evaluates only the scholastic aspects of learning of the students.
- It does not evaluate all the abilities of the children. On the basis of marks obtained in written examination the students are declared pass or fail and further classified into predetermined divisions.
- Pass and fail system causes frustration and is inhumane because the failed candidates come to feel that they are good for nothing.
- Co-scholastic areas are almost totally ignored and have no place in the currently prevalent scheme of education and evaluation.
- The practice of testing of untaught content also reflects poor learning achievement.
- Only limited techniques of evaluation without potential for judging a student are being used.
- The aim of evaluation is to improve learner's quality which is not served by external examination.
- The current practice of awarding marks suffers from many discrepancies due to variety of errors.
- The varied ranges of obtained scores of students in different subjects create the problem in declaring reliable results.
- Analysis and interpretation of test results is not done in a scientific way.

School Based Continuous and Comprehensive Evaluation System should be Established to:

- reduce stress on children.
- make evaluation comprehensive and regular.
- provide space for the teacher for creative teaching.
- provide a tool of diagnosis and remediation.
- produce learners with greater skills.

Four Assessment Paradigms

Assessment *of* Learning

The 'assessment **of** learning' is defined as a process whereby someone attempts to describe and quantify the knowledge, attitudes or skills possessed by another. Teacher direction is paramount and the student has little involvement in the design or implementation of the assessment process in these circumstances.

- Teacher designs learning
- Teacher collects evidence
- Teacher judges what has been learnt (and what has not been learnt)

Assessment *for* Learning

The 'assessment **for** learning' involves increased level of student autonomy, but not without teacher guidance and collaboration. The assessment **for** learning is sometimes seen as being akin to 'formative assessment'. There is more emphasis towards giving useful advice to the student and less emphasis on the giving of marks and the grading function.

- Teacher designs learning
- Teacher designs assessment with feedback to student
- Teacher judges what has been learnt (student develops insight into what has not)

Assessment *as* Learning

The 'assessment **as** learning' is perhaps more connected with diagnostic assessment and can be constructed with more of an emphasis on peer learning. Assessment **as** learning generates opportunities for self assessment and peer assessment. Students take on increased responsibility to generate quality information about their learning and that of others.

- Teacher and student co-construct learning
- Teacher and student co-construct assessment
- Teacher and student co-construct learning progress map

Assessment **for** learning and assessment **as** learning activities should be deeply embedded in teaching and learning and be the source of interactive feedback, allowing students to adjust, re-think and re-learn.

Assessment *in* Learning

The 'assessment **in** learning' places the question at the centre of teaching and learning. It deflects the teaching from its focus on a 'correct answer' to a focus on 'a fertile question'. Through enquiry students engage in processes that generates feedback about their learning, which come from multiple sources and activities. It contributes to the construction of other learning activities, line of enquiry and the generation of other questions.

- Student as the centre of learning

- Student monitors, assesses and reflects on learning
- Student initiates demonstration of learning (to self and others)
- Teacher as coach and mentor.

Teachers and students need to understand the purpose of each assessment strategy. The overall assessment 'package' being used by learners and teachers should accurately capture, generate and use meaningful learning information to generate deep learning and understanding.

ASSESSING LEARNERS

Any meaningful report on the quality and extent of a child's learning needs to be comprehensive. We need a curriculum whose creativity, innovativeness, and development of the whole being, the hallmark of a good education makes uniform tests that assess memorised facts and textbook-based learning obsolete. We need to redefine and seek new parameters for and ways of evaluation and feedback. In addition to the learner's achievements in specific subject areas that lend themselves to testing easily, assessment would need to encompass attitudes to learning, interest, and the ability to learn independently.

ASSESSMENT IN THE COURSE OF TEACHING

Preparing report cards is a way for the teacher to think about each individual child and review what she/he has learnt during the term, and what she/he needs to work on and improve. To be able to write such report cards, teachers would need to think about each individual child, and hence pay attention to them during their everyday teaching and interaction. One does not need special tests for this; learning activities themselves provide the basis for such ongoing observational and qualitative assessments of children. Maintaining a daily diary based on observation helps in continuous and comprehensive evaluation. An extract from the diary of a teacher for a week notes the following: "Kiran enjoyed his work. He took an instant liking to the books that were informative and brief. He says that he likes simple and clear language. In noting down facts, he goes for short answers. He says that it helps him understand things easily. He favours a practical approach." Similarly, keeping samples and notes of the child's work at different stages provides both the teacher and the learner herself or himself with a systematic record of his/her learning progress.

The belief that assessment must lead to finding learning difficulties to then be remediated is often very impractical and not founded on a sound understanding of pedagogic practice. Problems regarding conceptual development cannot and do not wait for formal tests in order to be detected. A teacher can, in the course of teaching itself, come to know of such problems by asking questions that make children think or by giving them small assignments. She can then attend to them in the process of teaching—by ensuring that her planning is flexible and responsive to the learners and their learning.

CURRICULAR AREAS THAT CANNOT BE 'TESTED FOR MARKS'

Each area of the curriculum may not lend itself to being 'tested'; it may even be antithetical to the nature of learning in the curricular area. This includes areas such as work, health, yoga, physical education, music and art. While the skill-based component of physical education and yoga could be tested, the health aspect needs continuous and qualitative assessments. Currently, this has the effect of making these subjects and activities 'less important' in the curriculum; these areas are inadequately provided for in terms of material resources and curricular planning, and marked by a lack of seriousness. Further, the time allocated for them is also frequently sacrificed to accommodate special classes. This is a serious compromise with parts of the curriculum that have deep educational significance and potential.

Even if 'marks' cannot be given, children can be assessed for their development in these areas. Participation, interest, and level of involvement, and the extent to which abilities and skills have been honed, are some markers that can help teachers to gauge the benefits of what children learn and gain through such activities. Asking children to self-report on their learning can also provide teachers with insight into children's educational progress and give them feedback on improving curriculum or pedagogy.

DESIGN AND CONDUCT OF ASSESSMENT

Assessments and examinations must be credible, and based on valid ways of gauging learning.

As long as examinations and tests assess children's ability to remember and recall textbook knowledge, all attempts to redirect the curriculum towards learning will be thwarted. First, tests in knowledge-based subject areas must be able to gauge what children have learnt, and their ability to use this knowledge for problem solving and application in the real world. In addition, they must also be able to test the processes of thinking to gauge if the learner has also learnt where to find information, how to use new information, and to analyse and evaluate the same.

The types of questions that are set for assessment need to go beyond what is given in the book. Often children's learning is restricted as teachers do not accept their answers if they are different from what is presented in the guidebooks.

Questions that are open-ended and challenging could also be used. Designing good test items and questions is an art, and teachers should spend time thinking about and devising such questions. The interest and ability of teachers to design good questions can be promoted through district—or state-level competitions. All question papers must be designed graded for difficulty in order to permit all children to experience a level of success, and to gain confidence in their ability to answer and solve problems.

Trying to devise a good and effective open-book examination can be a challenge that we must try to take up in our curricular efforts at all levels of school. This would require teachers and examination setters to emphasise the interpretation and application of learning over the arguments and facts that can be located in the book. There have been successful demonstrations that such examinations can be carried out on a large scale, and that teachers can themselves be trusted with moderating the results of such examinations. In this way, the assessment of projects and lab work can also be made credible and sound.

It is important that after receiving their corrected papers, children rewrite the answers and that these are again reviewed by teachers to ensure that children have learnt and gained something out of the ordeal.

Competition is motivating, but it is an extrinsic rather than intrinsic form of motivation. It is, of course, much easier to establish and to manipulate, and therefore frequently resorted to by teachers and school systems as a way creating and nurturing the drive for excellence. Schools begin 'ranking' children as early as their pre-primary years as a way of inculcating in them a competitive spirit. Such a competitive drive has several negative side effects on learning, often superficial learning is sufficient to create and maintain impressions, and over time students lose their ability to take initiative or do things for the fulfilment of one's own interest; hence, areas that cannot be 'marked' are neglected. This has unhealthy consequences for classroom culture, making children individualistic and unsuited to team work. There is an absurd and unnecessary importance given to term examinations, often accompanied by extreme arrangements of invigilation and secrecy. While the physical and psychological effects of this may not be readily visible until middle school, they frequently lead to high levels of stress in children, and cause early burnout. Schools and teachers need to ask themselves whether there is really much to be gained

out of such practices and to what extent learning requires such systems of marking and ranking.

SELF-ASSESSMENT AND FEEDBACK

The role of assessment is to gauge the progress that both learner and teacher have made towards achieving the aims that have been set and appraising how this could be done better. Opportunity for feedback, leading to revision and improvement of performance, should constantly be available, without exams and evaluations being used as a threat to study.

Grading and correction carried out in the presence of students and providing feedback on the answers they get right and wrong, and why. Asking children about why they answered what they did assists teachers in going beyond the written answer to engage with children's thinking. Such processes also take away the frightening judgemental quality of marks obtained in a test, and enable children to understand and focus on their mistakes and learn through these mistakes. Sometimes head teachers object, claiming that correction in the presence of the child reduces 'objectivity'. This is a misplaced concern for 'objectivity', stemming from a competitive system that believes in judging children. Such a concern for 'objectivity' is misplaced in evaluation, which is consistent with educational goals.

Not only learning outcomes but also learning experiences themselves must be evaluated. Learners happily comment on the totality of their experience. Exercises, both individual and collective, can be designed to enable them to reflect on and assess their learning experiences. Such experiences also provide them with self-regulatory capabilities essential for 'learning to learn'. Such information is also valuable feedback to the teacher, and can be used to modify the learning system as a whole.

Every classroom interaction with children requires their evaluation of their own work, and a discussion with them about what should be tested and the ways of finding out whether the competencies are being developed or not. Even very young children are able to give correct assessments of what they can or cannot do well. The role of teaching is to provide an opportunity to each child to learn to the best of his or her ability and provide learning experiences that develop cognitive qualities, physical well-being and athletic qualities, as also affective and aesthetic qualities.

Report cards need to present to children and parents a comprehensive and holistic view of the child's development in many fields. Teachers must be able to say things about each child/student, that conveys to them a sense of individualised attention, reaffirms a positive self-image, and communicates personal goals for them to work towards. Whether it is marks or grades that are reported, a qualitative statement by the teacher is necessary to support the assessment. Only through such a relationship with each child can any teacher succeed in influencing him/her, and contributing to his/her learning. Along with the teacher assessing each child, each student could also assess himself or herself and include this self-assessment in the report card.

Currently, many report cards carry information on subject areas and have nothing to say about other aspects of the child's development, including health, physical fitness and abilities in games, social skills, and abilities in art and craft. Qualitative statements about these aspects of children's education and development would provide a more holistic assessment of educational concerns.

AREAS THAT REQUIRE FRESH THINKING

There are many areas of the curriculum that can be assessed but for which we still do not have reliable and efficient instruments. This includes assessing learning that is carried out in groups, and learning in areas such as theatre, work and craft where skills and competencies develop over longer time scales and require careful observation.

Continuous and comprehensive evaluation has frequently been cited as the only meaningful kind of evaluation. This also requires much more careful thinking through about when it is to be employed in a system effectively. Such evaluation places a lot of demand on teachers' time and ability to maintain meticulous records if it is to be meaningfully executed and if it is to have any reliability as an assessment. If this simply increases stress on children by reducing all their activities into items for assessment, or making them experience the teacher's 'power', then it defeats the purpose of education. Unless a system is adequately geared for such assessment, it is better for teachers to engage in more limited forms of evaluation, but incorporating into them more features that will make the assessment a meaningful record of learning.

Finally, there is a need to evolve and maintain credibility in assessment so that they perform their function of providing feedback in a meaningful way.

ASSESSMENT AT DIFFERENT STAGES

ECCE and Classes I and II of the Elementary Stage: At this stage, assessment must be purely qualitative judgements of children's activities in various domains and an assessment of the status of their health and physical development, based on observations through everyday interactions. On no account should they be made to take any form of test, oral or written.

Class III to Class VIII of the Elementary Stage: A variety of methods may be used, including oral and written tests and observations. Children should be aware that they are being assessed, but this must be seen by them as a part of the teaching process and not as a fearful constant threat. Grades or marks along with qualitative judgements of achievement and areas requiring attention are essential at this stage. Children's own self-evaluation can also be a part of the report card from Class V onwards. Rather than examinations, there could be short tests from time-to-time, which are criterion based. Term-wise examinations could be commenced from Class VII onwards when children are more psychologically ready to study large chunks of material and, to spend a few hours in an examination room, working at answering questions. Again, the progress card must indicate general observations on health and nutrition, specific observations on the overall progress of the learner, and information and advice for the parents.

Class IX to Class XII of the Secondary and Higher Secondary Stages: Assessment may be based more on tests, examinations and project reports for the knowledge-based areas of the curriculum, along with self-assessment. Other areas would be assessed through observation and also through self-evaluation.

Reports could include much more analysis about the students, various skill/knowledge areas and percentiles, etc. This would assist them by pointing out the areas of study that they need to focus on, and also help them by providing a basis for further choices that they make regarding what to study thereafter.

CONCEPT OF INCLUSIVE EDUCATION & UNDERSTANDING CHILDREN WITH SPECIAL NEEDS

SECTION

INCLUSIVE EDUCATION: DEFINITION AND CONCEPT

Inclusive Education denotes that all children irrespective of their strengths and weaknesses will be part of the mainstream education. Thus, inclusive education means, "the act of ensuring that all children despite their differences, receive the opportunity of being part of the same classroom as other children of their age, and in the process get the opportunity to being exposed to the curriculum to their optimal potential."

Every child is special for his/her parent and, every child has a special need for love, acceptance and a feeling of belongingness. Here, we call **children with special needs** to those who are "different" from their cohorts. They are born equal with some limitations and with the help of inclusion be able to actively participate as equal citizens in all aspects of society and community life. Thus, children with special needs refer to "all those children who require adaptations to the normal process of education due to problems of vision, hearing, movement, learning and intellect." In other words, these children have some kind of **disability**.

Disability: Definitions

Disability refers to any limitations experienced by the disabled in comparisons to able persons of similar age, sex and culture. The UN Declaration on the Rights of Disabled Persons has defined disabled person as "any person unable to ensure by himself or herself, wholly or partly, the necessities of a normal individual and/or social life, as a result of a deficiency, either congenital or not, in his or her physical or mental capabilities".

DISTINCTIONS AMONG IMPAIRMENT, DISABILITY AND HANDICAP

The World Health Organisation (WHO) has made distinctions between the definitions of impairment, disability and handicap as follows:

- Impairment is any loss or abnormality of psychological, physiological or anatomical structure or function generally taken to be at organ level. Impairment is a damage to tissue due to disease or trauma.
- A disability is any restriction or lack of ability (resulting from an impairment) to perform an activity in the manner or within the range considered normal for a human being.
- A handicap is a disadvantage for an individual, resulting from impairment or disability that limits or prevents fulfilment of a role that is normal (depending on age, sex and social cultural factors) for that individual. Handicap is a condition or burden, which is imposed on the person confronted with the disability.

Types of Disability According to PWD Act, 1995

The PWD Act, 1995 has given the following seven types of disability as:

1. Blindness
2. Low Vision
3. Leprosy-cured
4. Hearing impairment
5. Locomotor disabilities
6. Mental retardation
7. Mental illness

EDUCATIONAL PROVISIONS FOR CHILDREN WITH SPECIAL NEEDS

The last two decades of the 19th century has witnessed the knowledge and processes of educating the disabled children through Christian Missionaries. The first school for the deaf was established in Mumbai in 1883 and the first school for the blind in Amritsar in 1887. At that time, it was believed that children with disabilities could not be educated alongwith normal children. Therefore, education to disabled children was offered through special school. This trend continued early sixties of the last century with the help of some international agencies who developed programme of integrated education. Here, children disabilities were placed in regular school so that they could study alongwith their non-disabled 'peers". The integrated education adopts various models for service deliver. Presently the emphasis is on the need to provide education for all in appropriate environment with inclusive philosophy through inclusive education.

Integrated Education for the Disabled Children (IEDC)

With the development of science and technology and improvement in Medical Services and Aggressive neo-natal intervention has ensured that a large number of babies who would earlier have not survived but often with different abilities. The number of differently abled children is on the increasing trend but it is not possible to create the required number of special schools throughout the country to meet this challenge due to the high cost and also due to the fact that the population is so scattered. The best alternative under these situations is to make use of the infrastructural facilities already present in terms of regular schools and integrate children into the mainstream of education.

Consequent on the success of international institutions in introducing differently abled children in regular schools, the planning commission, Govt. of India, in 1971 includes in its plan a programme for integrated education. In 1974, the Union Government introduced a scheme called "Integrated Schools" to do just this. This scheme was later revised and a plan of action formulated. The important aims of IEDC includes:

- Provide educational opportunity to differently abled children in regular schools.

- Facilitate retention of differently abled in the school system.

- Integrate children from special school to common schools.

The scope of the scheme of IEDC includes pre-school training, counselling for the parents, and special training in skills for all kinds of differently abled children. It provides facilities in the form of books, stationary, uniforms and allowances for transport, reader and escort etc.

Project Integrated Education for the Disabled (PIED)

This scheme was launched by MHRD Govt. of India in collaboration with UNICEF in 1987 to strengthen the integration of differently abled into regular schools. Under this scheme, a cluster instead of individual school is given importance. This scheme is an improvement over the special schools in one or many ways and provides a way towards universalisation of elementary education and Education for All including for differently abled children.

ASSUMPTION ABOUT INTEGRATED EDUCATION

Integrated education assumes a process of bringing disabled children into mainstream schools, where the system remains the same. As per the system, the child is the problem. So, it is essential to change the child where the resources are focused on the individual child. The failure is due to the child's problem; he is not able, not ready, not good enough to cope up with the system.

In integrated education; it is the children with disabilities who are seen as the problem, who must be "fixed", "changed" & "adapted" to suit the existing regular, mainstream school. It is the disabled child who is seen as a square peg in a round table. The system remains the same. The onus for successful integration therefore, is on the disabled child.

ASSUMPTION ABOUT INCLUSIVE EDUCATION

Assumptions of inclusive education is opposite to integrated education. Inclusive education assumes that changes the system to fit the child. It is essential to addresses all types of individual needs, not just disability. Teachers and schools are held responsible for children's learning. It focuses on flexibility of curriculum, teacher training and change in environmental. Failure is the problem with the system not with the child. It is quite essential to assumes that all children can learn and that all children need their learning to be supported in diverse ways.

In this model of inclusive education, it is not the child, but the education system, which is seen as a problem. Therefore, it is the system (with all its components) with should be changed, modified & made flexible enough to accommodate the diverse needs of all learners, including children with disabilities. The onus for success is therefore on the flexibility of the system. It focuses on the environment, as the "disabling" cause because it fails to provide appropriate access to equal opportunities for all persons to participate fully in social life.

Though integrated education of differently abled children has gained momentum all over the country since 1974, there are some other possibilities too for these children to get education. For example, the NIOS (National Institute of Open Schooling) offers education which have the advantage of being specially adopted to the needs of every child as well as aimed at giving the child every opportunity to progress at his/her pace. Another example is alternative schooling and community-based rehabilitation programmes.

EDUCATION FOR A COHESIVE SOCIETY

Despite more than half a century of independence, India is struggling for freedom from various kinds of biases and imbalances such as rural/urban, rich/poor, and differences on the basis of caste, religion, ideology, gender etc. Education can play a very significant role in minimising and finally eliminating these differences by providing equality of access to quality education and opportunity.

Equality of opportunity means ensuring that every individual receives suitable education at a pace and through methods suited to his/her being. Children of the disadvantaged, and socially discriminated groups and also those suffering from specific challenges must be paid special attention.

Provision for equal opportunity to all not only in access, but also in the conditions for success is a precondition for the promotion of equality. The curriculum must create an awareness of the inherent equality of all with a view to removing prejudices and complexes transmitted through the social environment and the factor of birth.

EDUCATION OF GIRLS

Equality among sexes is a fundamental right under the constitution of India. The state, however, also has the right to exercise positive protective discrimination in favour of the disadvantaged population groups including women. Emphasis in education has moved from 'Equality of Educational Opportunity' (NPE, 1968) to 'Education for Women's Equality and Empowerment' (1986). As a result, the curricular and training strategies for the education of girls now demand more attention. Besides, making education accessible to more and more girls, especially rural girls, removing all gender discrimination and gender bias in school curriculum, textbooks and the process of transaction is absolutely necessary. There is a need to develop and implement gender inclusive and gender sensitive curricular strategies to nurture a generation of girls and boys who are equally competent and are

sensitive to one another, and grow up in a caring and sharing mode as equals, and not as adversaries.

EDUCATION OF LEARNERS FROM DISADVANTAGED GROUPS

For achieving a cohesive society it would be essential to respond to specific educational needs of learners from different sections of the society with special emphasis on the Scheduled Castes, the Scheduled Tribes and the other socially and economically disadvantaged groups. In order to do so, there is a need for integrating the socio-cultural perspectives partly by showing concern for their linguistic specificities and pedagogic requirements. Implications of the multilingual and multicultural environment shall have to be taken care of through specifically devised methodology. Contextualisation of curriculum shall have to be effected through curricular materials. The fundamental rights of the disadvantaged groups have to be consciously incorporated in the curriculum. Even the problem of educating the migrating population shall have to be handled through specific condensed educational programmes based on the main ingredients of the national curriculum.

EDUCATION OF THE GIFTED AND TALENTED

An educational system has the dual role of promoting equality as well as excellence. Education is increasingly called upon to liberate all the creative potentialities of human consciousness. Man essentially fulfils himself in and through creation. It is in the context of this, that education of gifted and talented children assumes great importance. A curricular programme while on the one hand should identify such children, on the other it should also nurture their diverse creative abilities by paying them special attention. It is also important that the identification and nurturance begins right from the earliest stage of education. Moreover, the task of identifying the gifted and talented must be accomplished on the basis of a broad conceptualisation of the process from multiple perspectives rather than as a search for a unitary human attribute. Not only their IQ (Intelligence Quotient) but also their EQ (Emotional Quotient) and SQ (Spiritual Quotient) ought to be assessed.

NATIONAL LEVEL POLICY AND LEGISLATION

Kothari Commission (1964-66)

The Kothari Commission first suggested that the education of handicapped children has to be organised not merely on humanitarian grounds, but also an aspects of utility. The commission emphasised that the education of children with disability should be "an inseparable part of the general education system. The commission also specifically emphasised that the education of children with disability should be "an inseparable part of the general education system. The commission also specifically emphasised. the importance of integrated education in meeting this target as it is cost effective and useful in developing mutual understanding between children with and without disabilities.

National Policy on Education (1986)

The National Policy on Education was adopted by Indian Parliament in 1986. The policy emphasized the removal of disparities, and ensuring equalisation of educational opportunity under its para education of the disabled.

National Policies for Persons with Disabilities (2006)

This recognises that persons with disabilities are valuable human resources for the country and seek to create an environment that provides them equal opportunities, protection of their rights and full participation in society.

Persons with Disabilities (Equal Opportunities, Protection of Rights & Full Participation) Act, 1995

Landmark legislation in the history of special education in India is the persons with Disabilities Act, 1995. This comprehensive Act covers seven disabilities, namely blindness, low vision, hearing impaired, loco-motor impaired, mental retardation, leprosy cured and mental illness.

The Rehabilitation Council of India (RCI) Act, 1992

This Act was passed in 1992 for the purpose of constituting the Rehabilitation Professionals and for maintenance of a Central Rehabilitation Register. It was amended by Rehabilitation Council of India (Amendment) Act, 2000 to provide for monitoring the training of rehabilitation professionals and personal, promoting research in rehabilitation and special education as additional objectives of the council.

SECTION 4 | LEARNING AND PEDAGOGY

HOW CHILDREN THINK AND LEARN

Children learn from anything and everything they see and act upon. They have learnt a lot before they join school, and they continue to learn outside the school hours. If we believe that children learn only in school, it is because of what we wrongly regard as learning. When a child spends hours on trying to solve a Jigsaw puzzle (say), he/she is often reprimanded by adults for wasting study time. Little do the grown-ups realise that it is through such interesting games that this child may be increasing his/her understanding of shapes and size. And, this learning is taking place outside the school hours, without formal instruction. A curriculum built upon assumptions about children's learning, that ignore this aspect, is also responsible for children losing interest in mathematics or in any formal learning.

From the time a child is born, his/her interaction with the world around his/her starts. He/she perceives things around his/her, and gradually makes sense of them. He/she slowly begins to recognise people and objects, relate more and more to the environment, and observe things through the senses of touch, sight, taste, smell and sound. There are **four different stages** of learning or development that each child goes through.

Sensorimotor

This is from the ages of birth to about two years old. During this time the child's primary mode of learning occurs through the five senses. He/she learns to experience environment. The child touches things, holds, looks, listens, tastes, feels, bangs, and shakes everything in sight. When the child adds motor skills such as creeping, crawling and walking, his/her environment expands by leaps and bounds. The child is now exploring their environment with both senses and the ability to get around.

Preoperational

This is the stages between ages two and seven. During this stage the child is busy gathering information or learning, and then trying to figure out ways that they can used what they have learned to begin solving problems.

During this stage of his/her life child will be thinking in specifics and will find it very difficult to get generalise anything. This is the time when a child learns by asking questions. The child generally will not want a real answer to his question at this point. When he asks why do we have grass .... He simply wants to know that it is for him to play in. No technical answers for know. The child in this age group judges everything on the 'me' basis—How does it affect me? Do I like it?

Concrete Operations Period

This is the period of time when child is between the ages of seven to ten. This is a wonderful age as this is when children begin to manipulate data mentally. They take the information at hand and begin to define, compare and contrast it. They, however, still think concretely.

The concrete operational child is capable of logical thought. This child still learns through their senses, but no longer relies on only them to teach him. He now thinks as well. A good teacher for this age group would start each lesson at a concrete level and then more toward a generalised level. The child, during this period, is very literal in their thinking.

Formal Operations Period

The period begins at about age eleven. At this time the child will break through the barrier of literalism and more on to thinking in more abstract terms. He no longer restricts thinking to time and space. This child now starts to reflect, hypothesize and theorize.

In the formal operation period, children need to develop cognitive abilities. The following is a list of six simple categories of cognitive abilities. The following is a list of six simple categories of cognitive abilities:

1. **Knowledge of facts and principals:** This is the direct recall of facts and principals. **Examples:** memorisation of dates, name, definition, vocabulary words.

2. **Comprehension:** Understanding of facts and ideas.

3. **Application:** Needs to know, rules, principles, and procedures and how to use them.

4. **Analysis:** Breaking down concepts into parts.

5. **Synthesis:** Putting together information or ideas.

6. **Evaluation:** Judging the value of information.

BASIC PROCESSES OF TEACHING AND LEARNING

Teaching-learning process is the heart of education. On it depends the fulfilment of the aims & objectives of education. It is the most powerful instrument of education to bring about desired changes in the students. Teaching learning are related terms. In teaching-learning process, the teacher, the learner, the curriculum & other variables are organised in a systematic way to attain some pre-determined goal.

Essential Aspects of the Teaching-learning Process

According to Diana Laurillard, there are four aspects of the teaching-learning process:

1. **Discussion**—between the teacher and learner.

2. **Interaction**—between the learner and some aspect of the world defined by the teacher.

3. **Adaptation**—of the world by the teacher and action by the learner.

4. **Reflection**—on the learner's performance by both teacher and learner.

According to **Burton** in the figure above

1. Teaching can become effective only by relating it to process of learning.

2. Teaching objective cannot be realised without being related to learning situation.

3. We may create and use teaching aids to create some appropriate learning situation.

4. The strategies and devices of teaching may be selected in such a manner that the optimal objectives of learning area achieved.

5. To understand principles, goals, objectives of education in right perspective.

6. Appropriate learning situation condition may be created for congenial and effective teaching.

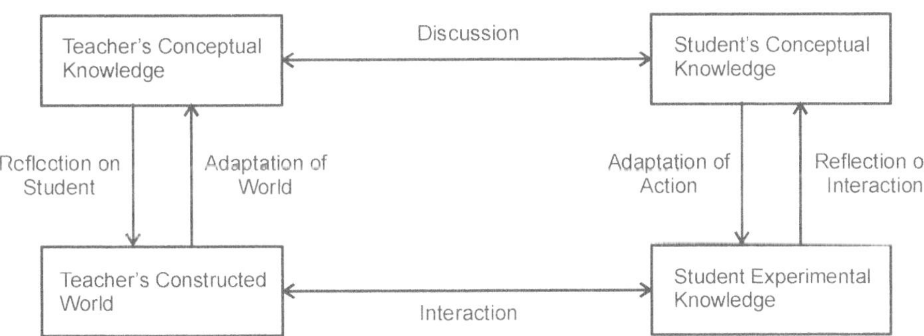

Fig. 1: *Essential aspects of the ideal teaching-learning process*

Approaches to Learning Theories

Aspect	Behaviourist	Cognitivist	Humanist
Learning theorists	Thorndike, Pavlov, Watson, Guthrie, Hull, Tolman, Skinner	Koffka, Kohler, Lewin, Piaget, Ausubel, Bruner, Gagne	Maslow, Rogers
View of the learning process	Change in behaviour	Internal mental process (including insight, information processing, memory, perception)	A personal act to fulfil potential
Locus of learning	Stimuli in external environment	Internal cognitive structuring	Affective and cognitive needs

Aspect	Behaviourist	Cognitivist	Humanist
Purpose in education	Produce behavioural change in desired direction	Develop capacity and skills to learn better	Become self-actualized autonomous
Educator's role	Arranges environment to elicit desired response	Structures content of learning activity	Facilitates development of the whole person
Manifestations in adult learning	Behavioural objectives	Cognitive development	Andragogy
	Competency-based education	Intelligence, learning and memory as function of age	Self-directed learning
	Skill development and training	Learning how to learn	

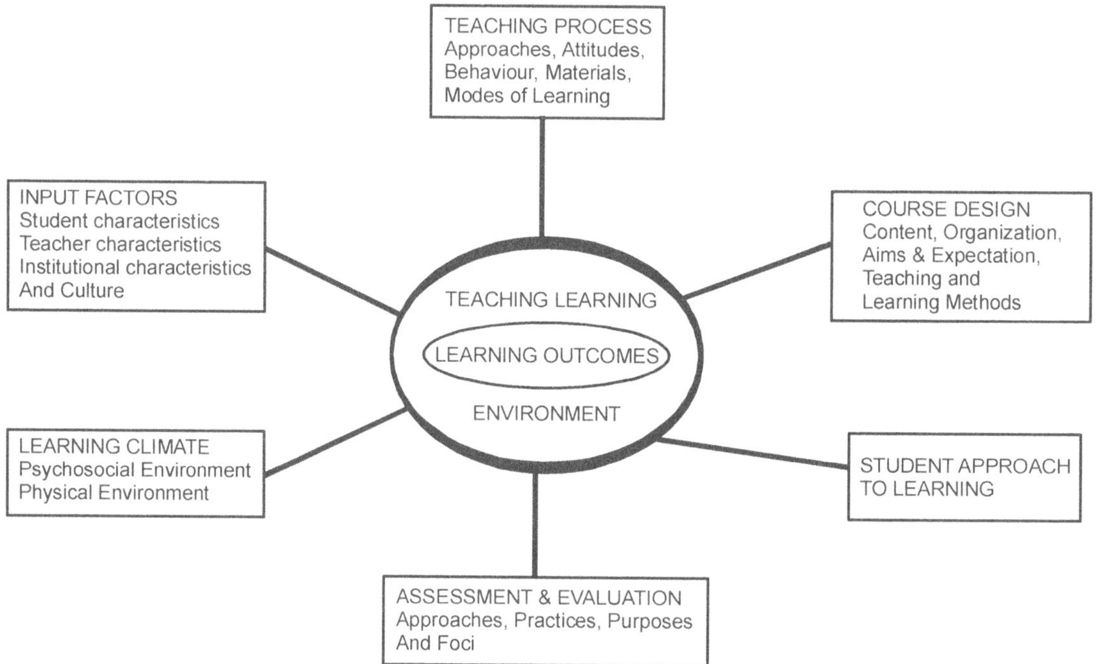

Fig. 2: *Teaching-Learning Environment*

PARADIGMS OF LEARNING

Learning takes place in many ways. There are some methods that are used in acquisition of simple responses while other methods are used in the acquisition of complex responses. The simplest kind of learning is called conditioning. Two types of conditioning have been identified. The first one is called classical conditioning and the second instrumental/operant conditioning. In addition, we have observational learning, cognitive learning, verbal learning, concept learning and skill learning.

Classical Conditioning

This type of learning was first investigated by Ivan P. Pavlov. Like many great scientific advances, classical conditioning was discovered accidentally.

The nineteenth-century Russian physiologist Ivan Pavlov was looking at salivation in dogs in response to being fed, when he noticed that his dogs would begin to salivate whenever he entered the room, even when he was not bringing them food. However, when Pavlov discovered that any object or event which the dogs learnt to associate with food (such as the food bowl) would trigger the same response, he realised that he had made an important scientific discovery, and he devoted the rest of his career to studying this type of learning.

Classical conditioning is 'classical' in that it is the first systematic study of basic laws of learning. Classical conditioning involves learning to associate an unconditioned stimulus that already brings about a particular response (*i.e.* a reflex) with a new (conditioned) stimulus, so that the new stimulus brings about the same response. The unconditioned stimulus (or UCS) is the object or event that originally produces the reflexive/natural response.

Once the neutral stimulus has become associated with the unconditioned stimulus, it becomes a conditioned stimulus (CS). The conditioned response (CR) is the response to the conditioned stimulus. Thus, learning situation in classical conditioning is one of S-S learning in which one stimulus becomes a signal of another stimulus.

Determinants of Classical Conditioning

How quickly and strongly acquisition of a response occurs in classical conditioning depends on several factors. Some of the major factors influencing learning a CR are described below:

1. Time Relations between Stimuli: The classical conditioning procedures, discussed below, are basically of four types based on the time relations between the onset of conditioned stimulus (CS) and unconditioned stimulus (US). The first three are called forward conditioning procedures, and the fourth one is called backward conditioning procedure. The basic experimental arrangements of these procedures are as follows:

(*a*) When the CS and US are presented together, it is called simultaneous conditioning.

(*b*) In delayed conditioning, the onset of CS precedes the onset of US. The CS ends before the end of the US.

(*c*) In trace conditioning, the onset and end of the CS precedes the onset of US with some time gap between the two.

(*d*) In backward conditioning, the US precedes the onset of CS.

It is now well established that delayed conditioning procedure is the most effective way of acquiring a CR. Simultaneous and trace conditioning procedures do lead to acquisition of a CR, but they require greater number of acquisition trials in comparison to the delayed conditioning procedure. It may be noted that the acquisition of response under backward conditioning procedure is very rare.

2. Type of Unconditioned Stimuli: The unconditioned stimuli used in studies of classical conditioning are basically of two types, *i.e.* appetitive and aversive. Appetitive unconditioned stimuli automatically elicits approach responses, such as eating, drinking, caressing, etc. These responses give satisfaction and pleasure. On the other hand, aversive US, such as noise, bitter taste, electric shock, painful injections, etc. are painful, harmful, and elicit avoidance and escape responses. It has been found that appetitive classical conditioning is slower and requires greater number of acquisition trials, but aversive classical conditioning is established in one, two or three trials depending on the intensity of the aversive US.

3. Intensity of Conditioned Stimuli: This influences the course of both appetitive and aversive classical conditioning. More intense conditioned stimuli are more effective in accelerating the acquisition of conditioned responses. It means that the more intense the conditioned stimulus, the fewer are the number of acquisition trials needed for conditioning.

Operant/Instrumental Conditioning

B.F. Skinner is regarded as the father of operant conditioning, but his work was based on **Thorndike's law of effect.** In the late nineteenth century, psychologist Edward Thorndike proposed the law of effect. The law of effect states that any behaviour that has good consequences will tend to be repeated, and any behaviour that has bad consequences will tend to be avoided. In the 1930s, B.F. Skinner, extended this idea and began to study operant conditioning. Operant conditioning is a type of learning in which responses come to be controlled by their consequences.

Operants are those behaviours or responses, which are emitted by animals and human beings voluntarily and are under their control. The term operant is used because the organism operates on the environment. Conditioning of operant behaviour is called operant conditioning. Skinner conducted his studies on rats and pigeons in specially made boxes, called the Skinner Box.

Determinants of Operant Conditioning

The operant or instrumental conditioning is a form of learning in which behaviour is learned, maintained or changed through its consequences. Such consequences are called **reinforcers**. A reinforcer is defined as any stimulus or event, which increases the probability of the occurrence of a (desired) response. A reinforcer has numerous features, which affect the course and strength of a response. They include its type—positive or negative, number or frequency, quality—superior or inferior, and schedule—continuous or intermittent (partial).

Reinforcement may be positive or negative. Positive reinforcement involves stimuli that have pleasant consequences. They strengthen and maintain the responses that have caused them to occur. Positive reinforcers satisfy needs, which include food, water, medals, praise, money, status, information, etc. Negative reinforcers involve unpleasant and painful stimuli. Responses that lead organisms to get rid of painful stimuli or avoid and escape from them provide negative reinforcement. Thus, negative reinforcement leads to learning of avoidance and escape responses. For instance, one learns to put on woollen clothes, burn firewood or use electric heaters to avoid the unpleasant cold weather. One learns to move away from dangerous stimuli because they provide negative reinforcement. It may be noted that negative reinforcement is not punishment. Use of punishment reduces or suppresses the response while a negative reinforcer increases the probability of avoidance or escape response. For instance, drivers and co-drivers wear their seat belts to avoid getting injured in case of an accident or to avoid being fined by the traffic police.

Classical and Operant Conditioning : Differences

1. In classical conditioning, the responses are under the control of some stimulus because they are reflexes, automatically elicited by the appropriate stimuli. Such stimuli are selected as US and responses elicited by them as UR. Thus Pavlovian conditioning, in which US elicits responses, is often called respondent conditioning.

   In instrumental conditioning, responses are under the control of the organism and are voluntary responses or 'operants'. Thus, in the two forms of conditioning different types of responses are conditioned.

2. In classical conditioning, the CS and US are well-defined, but in operant conditioning CS is not defined. It can be inferred but is not directly known.

3. In classical conditioning, the experimenter controls the occurrence of US, while in operant conditioning the occurrence of the reinforcer is under the control of the organism that is learning. Thus, for US in classical conditioning the organism remains passive, while in operant conditioning the subject has to be active in order to be reinforced.

4. In the two forms of conditioning, the technical terms used to characterise the experimental proceedings are different. Moreover what is called reinforcer in operant conditioning is called US in classical conditioning. An US has two functions. In the beginning, it elicits the response and also reinforces the response to be associated and elicited later on by the CS.

OBSERVATIONAL LEARNING

The other form of learning takes place by observing others. Earlier this form of learning was called **imitation**. Bandura and his colleagues in a series of experimental studies investigated observational learning in detail. In this kind of learning, human beings learn social behaviours, therefore, it is sometimes called **social learning**. In many situations individuals do not know how to behave. They observe others and emulate their behaviour. This form of learning is called **modelling**.

Examples of observational learning abound in our social life. Fashion designers employ tall, pretty, and gracious young girls and tall, smart, and well-built young boys for popularising clothes of different designs and fabrics. People observe them on televised fashion shows and advertisements in magazines and newspapers. They imitate these models. Observing superiors and likeable persons and then emulating their behaviour in a novel social situation is a common experience.

The children observe adults' behaviours, at home and during social ceremonies and functions. They enact adults in their plays and games. For instance, young children play games of marriage ceremonies, birthday parties, thief and policeman, house keeping, etc. Actually they enact in their games what they observe in society, on television, and read in books.

Children learn most of the social behaviours by observing and emulating adults. The way to put on clothes, dress one's hair, and conduct oneself in society are learned through observing others. It has also been shown that children learn and develop various personality characteristics through observational learning. Aggressiveness, prosocial behaviour, courtesy, politeness, diligence, and indolence are acquired by this method of learning.

COGNITIVE LEARNING

Some psychologists view learning in terms of cognitive processes that underlie it. They have developed approaches that focus on such processes that occur during learning rather than concentrating solely on S-R and S-S connections. Thus, in cognitive learning, there is a change in what the learner knows rather than what he/she does. This form of learning shows up in insight learning and latent learning.

Insight Learning

Kohler demonstrated a model of learning which could not be readily explained by conditioning. He performed a series of experiments with chimpanzees that involved solving complex problems. Kohler placed chimpanzees in an enclosed play area where food was kept out of their reach. Tools such as poles and boxes were placed in the enclosure. The chimpanzees rapidly learned how to use a box to stand on or a pole to move the food in their direction. In this experiment, learning did not occur as a result of trial and error and reinforcement, but came about in sudden flashes of insight. The chimpanzees would roam about the enclosure for some time and then suddenly would stand on a box, grab a pole and strike a banana, which was out of normal reach above the enclosure. The chimpanzee exhibited what Kohler called insight learning—the process by which the solution to a problem suddenly becomes clear.

In a normal experiment on insight learning, a problem is presented, followed by a period of time when no apparent progress is made and finally a solution suddenly emerges. In insight learning, sudden solution is the rule. Once the solution has appeared, it can be repeated immediately the next time the problem is confronted. Thus, it is clear that what is learned is not a specific set of conditioned associations between stimuli and responses but a cognitive relationship between a means and an end. As a result, insight learning can be generalised to other similar problem situations.

Latent Learning

Another type of cognitive learning is known as latent learning. In latent learning, a new behaviour is learned but not demonstrated until reinforcement is provided for displaying it. Tolman made an early contribution to the concept of latent learning. To have an idea of latent learning, we may briefly understand his experiment. Tolman put two groups of rats in a maze and gave them an opportunity to explore. In one group, rats found food at the end of the maze and soon learned to make their way rapidly through the maze. On the other hand, rats in the second group were not rewarded and showed no apparent signs of learning. But later, when these rats were reinforced, they ran through the maze as efficiently as the rewarded group.

Tolman contended that the unrewarded rats had learned the layout of the maze early in their explorations. They just never displayed their latent learning until the reinforcement was provided. Instead, the rats developed a cognitive map of the maze, *i.e.* a mental representation of the spatial locations and directions, which they needed to reach their goal.

LEARNING AS A SOCIAL ACTIVITY

Learning is a social activity. Our learning is intimately associated with our connection with other human beings, our teachers, our peers, our family as well as casual acquaintances, including the people before us or next to us. We are more likely to be successful in our efforts to educate, if we recognise this principle rather than try to avoid it. Much of traditional education, as Dewey pointed out, is directed towards isolating the learner from all social interaction, and towards seeing education as a one-on-one relationship between the learner and the objective material to be learned. In contrast, progressive education (to continue to use Dewey's formulation) recognizes the social aspect of learning and uses conversations interaction with others, and the application of knowledge as an integral aspect of learning.

SOCIAL CONTEXT OF LEARNING

Social Learning theory

Social learning theory focuses on the learning that occurs within a social context. It considers that people learn from one another, including such concepts as observational learning, imitation, and modelling. Among others **Albert Bandura** is considered the leading proponent of this theory.

General Principles of Social Learning Theory Follows:

1. People can learn by observing the behaviour is of others and the outcomes of those behaviours.

2. Learning can occur without a change in behaviour. Behaviourists say that learning has to be represented by a permanent change in behaviour, in contrast social learning theorists say that because people can learn through observation alone, their learning may not necessarily be shown in their performance. Learning may or may not result in a behaviour change.

3. Cognition plays a role in learning. Over the last 40 years social learning theory has become increasingly cognitive in its interpretation of human learning. Awareness and expectations of future reinforcements or punishments can have a major effect on the behaviours that people exhibit.

4. Social learning theory can be considered a bridge or a transition between behaviourist learning theories and cognitive learning theories.

How the Environment Reinforces and Punishes Modelling:

People are often reinforced for modelling the behaviour of others. Bandura suggested that the environment also reinforces modelling. This is in several possible ways:

1. The observer is reinforced by the model. For example, a student who changes dress to fit in with a certain group of students has a strong likelihood of being accepted and thus reinforced by that group.
2. The observer is reinforced by a third person. The observer might be modelling the actions of someone else, for example, an outstanding class leader or student. The teacher notices this and compliments and praises the observer for modelling such behaviour thus reinforcing that behaviour.
3. The imitated behaviour itself leads to reinforcing consequences. Many behaviours that we learn from others produce satisfying or reinforcing results. For example, a student in my multimedia class could observe how the extra work a classmate does is fun. This student in turn would do the same extra work and also receive enjoyment.
4. Consequences of the model's behaviour affect the observers behaviour vicariously. This is known as vicarious reinforcement. This is where in the model is reinforced for a response and then the observer shows an increase in that same response. Bandura illustrated this by having students watch a film of a model hitting a inflated clown doll. One group of children saw the model being praised for such action. Without being reinforced, the group of children began to also hit the doll.

Contemporary Social Learning Perspective of Reinforcement and Punishment

1. Contemporary theory proposes that both reinforcement and punishment have indirect effects on learning. They are not the sole or main cause.
2. Reinforcement and punishment influence the extent to which an individual exhibits a behaviour that has been learned.
3. The expectation of reinforcement influences cognitive processes that promote learning. Therefore, attention pays a critical role in learning. And attention is influenced by the expectation of reinforcement. An example would be, where the teacher tells a group of students that what they will study next is not on the test. Students will not pay attention, because they do not expect to know the information for a test.

Cognitive Factors in Social Learning

Social learning theory has cognitive factors as well as behaviourist factors (actually operant factors).

1. **Learning without performance:** Bandura makes a distinction between learning through observation and the actual imitation of what has been learned.
2. **Cognitive processing during learning:** Social learning theorists contend that attention is a critical factor in learning.
3. **Expectations:** As a result of being reinforced, people form expectations about the consequences that future behaviours are likely to bring. They expect certain behaviours to bring reinforcements and others to bring punishment. The learner needs to be aware however, of the response reinforcements and response punishment. Reinforcement increases a response only when the learner is aware of that connection.
4. **Reciprocal causation:** Bandura proposed that behaviour can influence both the environment and the person. In fact each of these three variables, the person, the behaviour, and the environment can have an influence on each other.
5. **Modelling:** There are different types of models. There is the live model, and actual person demonstrating the behaviour. There can also be a symbolic model, which can be a person or action portrayed in some other medium, such as television, videotape, computer programs.

Behaviours that can be learned through modelling:

Many behaviours can be learned, at least partly, through modelling. Examples that can be cited are, students can watch parents read, students can watch the demonstrations of mathematics problems, or seen someone acting bravely and a fearful situation. Aggression can be learned through models. Much research indicate that children become more aggressive when they observed aggressive or violent models. Moral thinking and moral behaviour are influenced by observation and modelling. This includes moral judgments regarding right and wrong which can in part, develop through modelling.

Conditions Necessary for Effective Modelling to Occur:

Bandura mentions four conditions that are necessary before an individual can successfully model the behaviour of someone else:

1. **Attention:** the person must first pay attention to the model.
2. **Retention:** the observer must be able to remember the behaviour that has been

observed. One way of increasing this is using the technique of rehearsal.

3. **Motor reproduction:** the third condition is the ability to replicate the behaviour that the model has just demonstrated. This means that the observer has to be able to replicate the action, which could be a problem with a learner who is not ready developmentally to replicate the action. For example, little children have difficulty doing complex physical motion.

4. **Motivation:** the final necessary ingredient for modelling to occur is motivation, learners must want to demonstrate what they have learned. Remember that since these four conditions vary among individuals, different people will reproduce the same behaviour differently.

Effects of Modelling on Behaviour:

Modelling teaches new behaviours.

Modelling influences the frequency of previously learned behaviours.

Modelling may encourage previously forbidden behaviours.

Modelling increases the frequency of similar behaviours. For example, a student might see a friend excel in basketball and he tries to excel in football because he is not tall enough for basketball.

Educational implications of social learning theory:

Social learning theory has numerous implications for classroom use.

1. Students often learn a great deal simply by observing other people.

2. Describing the consequences of behaviour is can effectively increase the appropriate behaviours and decrease inappropriate ones. This can involve discussing with learners about the rewards and consequences of various behaviours.

3. Modelling provides an alternative to shaping for teaching new behaviours. Instead of using shaping, which is operant conditioning, modelling can provide a faster, more efficient means for teaching new behaviour. To promote effective modelling a teacher must make sure that the four essential conditions exist; attention, retention, motor reproduction, and motivation.

4. Teachers and parents must model appropriate behaviours and take care that they do not model inappropriate behaviours.

5. Teachers should expose students to a variety of other models. This technique is especially important to break down traditional stereotypes.

6. Students must believe that they are capable of accomplishing school tasks. Thus, it is very important to develop a sense of self-efficacy for students. Teachers can promote such self-efficacy by having students receive confidence-building messages, watch others be successful, and experience success on their own.

7. Teachers should help students set realistic expectations for their academic accomplishments. In general in my class that means making sure that expectations are not set too low. I want to realistically challenge my students. However, sometimes the task is beyond a student's ability, example would be the cancer group.

8. Self-regulation techniques provide an effective method for improving student behaviour.

CHILD AS A PROBLEM SOLVER AND A SCIENTIFIC INVESTIGATOR

Problem solving is the foundation of a young child's learning. It must be valued, promoted, provided for and sustained in the early childhood classroom. Opportunities for problem solving occur in the everyday context of a child's life. By observing the child closely, teachers can use the child's social, cognitive, movement and emotional experiences to facilitate problem solving and promote strategies useful in the lifelong process of learning.

Problem solving is thinking that is goal-directed. Almost all our day-to-day activities are directed towards a goal. Here, it is important to know that problems are not always in the form of obstacles or hurdles that one faces. It could be any simple activity that you perform to reach a defined goal, for example, preparing a quick snack for your friend who has just arrived at your place. In problem solving there is an initial state (*i.e.* the problem) and there is an end state (the goal). These two anchors are connected by means of several steps or mental operations. Following table would clarify our understanding of various steps through which one solves a problem.

Table: Mental Operations Involved in Solving a Problem

Let us look at the problem of organising a play in school on the occasion of Teachers' Day. Problem solving would involve the following sequence.

Mental operation	Nature of problem
1. Identify the problem	A week is left for teachers' day and you are given the task of organising a play.
2. Represent the problem	Organising a play would involve identification of an appropriate theme, screening of actors, actresses, arranging money, etc.
3. Plan the solution: Set sub-goals	Search and survey various available themes for a play, and consult teachers and friends who have the expertise. The play to be decided, based on such considerations as cost, duration, suitability for the occasion, etc.
4. Evaluate all solutions (plays)	Collect all the information/stage rehearsal.
5. Select one solution and execute it	Compare and verify the various options to get the best solution (the play).
6. Evaluate the outcome	If the play (solution) is appreciated, think about the steps you have followed for future reference for yourself as well as for your friends.
7. Rethink and redefine problems and solutions	After this special occasion you can still think about ways to plan a better play in future.

Learning Through Problem Solving

By exploring social relationships, manipulating objects, and interacting with people, children are able to formulate ideas, try these ideas out, and accept or reject what they learn. Constructing knowledge by making mistakes is part of the natural process of problem solving. Through exploring, then experimenting, trying out a hypothesis, and finally, solving problems, children make learning personal and meaningful. Piaget states that children understand only what they discover or invent themselves. It is this discovery within the problem solving process that is the vehicle for children's learning. Children are encouraged to construct their own knowledge when the teacher plans for problem solving; bases the framework for learning in problem solving; and provides time, space, and materials.

Teacher's Role

Changing through problem solving is modelled by adults and facilitated by the teacher in the classroom environment. When teachers articulate the problems they face and discuss solutions with children, children become more aware of the significance of the problem-solving process. Being a problem solver is modelled by the teacher and emulated by the children. The teacher's role is two-fold: first, to value the process and be willing to trust the learner, and second, to establish and maintain a classroom environment that encourages problem solving. It is the attitude of the teacher that must change first in the problem-solving classroom. Values and goals must be clearly defined to include a child-centered curriculum, the development of communication skills, promotion of cooperative learning, and inclusion of diverse ideas.

The teacher must be willing to become a learner, too. By being curious, observing, listening, and questioning, the teacher shares and models the qualities that are valued and promoted by the problem-solving process.

Planning for Problem Solving

A curriculum that accommodates a variety of developmental levels as well as individual differences in young children sets the stage for problem solving. Choices, decision-making, and a curriculum framework that integrates learning, such as Katz and Chard's project method, are especially appropriate for young learners. The project approach facilitates cooperative learning and promotes diverse ideas. Donna Ogle's K-W-L (what you KNOW, what you WANT to know, and what you have LEARNED) is another method of organizing work that promotes problem solving. Themes, units, webbing, and the KWL method are all ways of organizing curriculum that can support problem solving. Beginning with the needs and interests of the children, problem solving develops from meaningful experiences important to the children. The teacher-designed curriculum provides the classroom basis for these experiences.

For example, a second grade investigation of waste materials from a classroom led one group of young children to explore the topic in an integrated way. Reading, writing, counting, measuring, interviews of community people, and science experiments were planned, initiated and reported. Solutions to many problems posed during the investigation were tried out and some were found to be successful. Through group work, individuals were able to participate and communicate as cognitive and social needs were met. Each child, at individual levels and in individual ways, was successful within the group experience. Problem solving empowers children.

Providing for Problem Solving

Problem solving is a skill that can be learned and must be practiced. It is facilitated by a classroom schedule that provides for integrated learning in large blocks of time, space for ongoing group projects, and many open-ended materials. The teacher provides the time, space, and materials necessary for in-depth learning.

1. Time: Teachers can provide for problem solving by enlarging blocks of learning time during the school day. Because making choices, discussing decisions, and evaluating mistakes takes time, large time blocks best suit the problem-solving process. It is important that children know they have time to identify and solve problems.

2. Space: Projects and group meetings may require an assessment of classroom space. Moving desks and tables together facilitates communication and cooperation in the classroom. Once the teacher has observed the patterns of traffic in the classroom, equipment can be moved or eliminated to promote problem solving.

3. Materials: The open-ended materials that are needed for the construction and concrete solving of problems should be safe, durable, and varied. Well-marked storage units should be easily accessible to children, and materials should be available for ongoing exploration and manipulation. Access to a variety of materials encourages children to use materials in new and diverse ways. This freedom promotes problem solving.

The Problem-Solving Model

Individuals or groups can solve problems. Group problem solving is important to young children because many diverse ideas are generated. Both individual and group processes should be included in the early childhood classroom. Becoming skillful at problem solving is based on the understanding and use of sequenced steps. These steps are:

1. Identifying the problem,
2. Brainstorming a variety of solutions,
3. Choosing one solution and trying it out, and
4. Evaluating what has happened.

Choosing Good Problems

Goffin provides teachers with guiding questions that will help them identify appropriate problems for young children. Some of these are:

1. Is the problem meaningful and interesting?
2. Can the problem be solved at a variety of levels?
3. Must a new decision be made?
4. Can the actions be evaluated?

Problem solving is a way to make sense of the environment and, in fact, control it. The process allows children in an increasingly diverse world to be active participants and to implement changes. By including problem solving in the early childhood classroom, we equip children with a life-long skill that is useful in all areas of learning.

Obstacles to Solving Problems

Two major obstacles to solving a problem are mental set and lack of motivation.

Mental Set

Mental set is a tendency of a person to solve problems by following already tried mental operations or steps. Prior success with a particular strategy would sometimes help in solving a new problem. However, this tendency also creates a mental rigidity that obstructs the problem solver to think of any new rules or strategies. Thus, while in some situations mental set can enhance the quality and speed of problem solving, in other situations it hinders problem solving. You might have experienced this while solving mathematical problems. After completing a couple of questions, you form an idea of the steps that are required to solve these questions and subsequently you go on following the same steps, until a point where you fail. At this point you may experience difficulty in avoiding the already used steps. Those steps would interfere in your thought for new strategies. However, in day-to-day activities we often rely on past experiences with similar or related problems.

Like mental set, **functional fixedness** in problem solving occurs when people fail to solve a problem because they are fixed on a thing's usual function. If you have ever used a hardbound book to hammer a nail, then you have overcome functional fixedness.

Lack of Motivation

People might be great at solving problems, but all their skills and talents are of no use if they are not motivated. Sometimes people give up easily when they encounter a problem or failure in implementing the first step. Therefore, there is a need to persist in their effort to find a solution.

ALTERNATIVE CONCEPTIONS OF LEARNING

When teachers provide instruction on concepts in various subjects, they are teaching students who already have some pre-instructional knowledge about the topic. Student knowledge, however, can be erroneous, illogical or misinformed. These erroneous understandings are termed alternative conceptions or misconceptions (or intuitive theories). Alternative conceptions (misconceptions) are not unusual. In fact, they are a normal part of the learning process. We quite naturally form ideas from our everyday experience, but obviously not all the ideas we develop are correct with respect to the most current evidence and scholarship in a given discipline. Moreover, some concepts in different content areas are simply very difficult to grasp. They may be very abstract, counterintuitive or quite complex. Hence, our understanding of them is flawed. In addition, things we have already learned are sometimes unhelpful in learning new concepts/theories. This occurs when the new concept or theory is inconsistent with previously learned material. Accordingly, as noted, it is very typical for students (and adults) to have misconceptions in different domains (content knowledge areas). Indeed, researchers have found that there is a common set of alternative conceptions (misconceptions) that most students typically exhibit. There is one class of alternative theories (or misconceptions) that is very deeply entrenched. These are "ontological misconceptions," which relate to ontological beliefs (*i.e.*, beliefs about the fundamental categories and properties of the world).

Alternative conceptions (misconceptions) can impede learning for several reasons. First, students generally are unaware that the knowledge they have is wrong. Moreover, misconceptions can be very entrenched in student thinking. In addition, new experiences are interpreted through these erroneous understandings, thereby interfering with being able to correctly grasp new information. Also, alternative conceptions (misconceptions) tend to be very resistant to instruction because learning entails replacing or radically reorganizing student knowledge. Hence, conceptual change has to occur for learning to happen. This puts teachers in the very challenging position of needing to bring about significant conceptual change in student knowledge. Generally, ordinary forms of instruction, such as lectures, labs, discovery learning, or simply reading texts, are not very successful at overcoming student misconceptions. For all these reasons, misconceptions can be hard nuts for teachers to crack. However, several instructional strategies have been found to be effective in achieving conceptual change and helping students leave their alternative conceptions behind and learn correct concepts or theories.

Instructional strategies that can lead to change in students' alternative conceptions (misconceptions) and to learning of new concepts and theories

1. Present new concepts or theories that you are teaching in such a way that students see as plausible, high-quality, intelligible and generative.

2. Use students' correct conceptions and build on those by creating a bridge of examples to the new concept or theory that students are having trouble learning due to misconceptions they hold.

3. Use model-ased reasoning, which helps students construct new representations that vary from their intuitive theories.

4. Use diverse instruction, wherein you present a few examples that challenge multiple assumptions, rather than a larger number of examples that challenge just one assumption.

5. Help students become aware of (raise student metacognition about) their own alternative conceptions (misconceptions).

6. Present students with experiences that cause cognitive conflict in students' minds. Experiences (as in strategy 3 above) that can cause cognitive conflict are ones that get students to consider their erroneous (misconception) knowledge side-by-side with, or at the same time as, the correct concept or theory.

7. Engage in Interactive Conceptual Instruction (ICI).

8. Develop students' epistemological thinking, which incorporates beliefs and theories about the nature of knowledge and the nature of learning, in ways that will facilitate conceptual change. The more naive students' beliefs are about knowledge and learning, the less likely they are to revise their misconceptions.

9. Help students "self-repair" their misconceptions.

10. Once students have overcome their alternative conceptions (misconceptions).

Presenting new concepts or theories

In presenting new concepts or theories, teachers should be sure to show these theories or concepts as:

1. Plausible: The new information should be shown to be consistent with other knowledge and able to explain the available data. Learners must see how the new conception (theory) is consistent with other knowledge and a good explanation of the data.

2. High quality: Of course, the theory/concept to be taught is of high quality from a scientific point of view, since it is a correct theory. However, the presented theory should take a better account of the data than what students currently have available to them. For example, the instructor should deal with the problem from the perspective of the students (*e.g.*, students for whom a "flat earth" theory provides a better account of the data available than does a "spherical earth" theory). Hence, the quality of the new theory must be considered along with the kind of data that students know about.

3. Intelligible: Teachers should do what they can to increase the intelligibility of the new theory. Learners must be able to grasp how the new conception works. To increase intelligibility, teachers can use methods such as use of:

(*a*) analogies,

(*b*) models, and

(*c*) direct exposition.

4. Generative/fruitful: Teachers should show that the new concept/theory can be extended to open up new areas of inquiry. Learners must be able to extend the new conception to new areas of inquiry. Teachers might accomplish this by illustrating the application of the new concept/theory to a range of problems. These problems can include familiar ones and new ones.

UNDERSTANDING CHILDREN'S 'ERRORS' AS SIGNIFICANT STEPS IN THE LEARNING PROCESS

The legacy of Jean Piaget to the world of early childhood education is that he fundamentally altered the view of how a child learns. And a teacher, he believed, was more than a transmitter of knowledge she was also an essential observer and guide to helping children build their own knowledge.

As a university graduate, Swiss-born Piaget got a routine job in Paris standardizing Binet-Simon IQ tests, where the emphasis was on children getting the right answers. Piaget observed that many children of the same ages gave the same kinds of incorrect answers. What could be learned from this?

Piaget interviewed many hundreds of children and concluded that children who are allowed to make mistakes often go on to discover their errors and correct them, or find new solutions. In this process, children build their own way of learning. From children's errors, teachers can obtain insights into the child's view of the world and can tell where guidance is needed. They can provide appropriate materials, ask encouraging questions, and allow the child to construct his own knowledge.

Piaget's continued interactions with young children became part of his life-long research. After reading about a child who thought that the sun and moon followed him wherever he went, Piaget wanted to find out if all young children had a similar belief. He found that many did indeed believe this. Piaget went on to explore children's countless "why" questions, such as, "Why is the sun round?" or "Why is grass green?" He concluded that children do not think like adults. Their thought processes have their own distinct order and special logic. Children are not "empty vessels to be filled with knowledge" (as traditional pedagogical theory had it). They are "active builders of knowledge-little scientists who construct their own theories of the world."

COGNITION & EMOTIONS

What is Cognition?

Cognition is the ability to preceive, memorise, reason and understand. These abilities change with age. As the child grows, her thinking becomes more mature and efficient. Therefore, cognition can simply be defined as the process of acquiring, processing, organising and using knowledge. The development of cognition means development of all these abilities. A child's thinking changes as result of both age (maturation) and increased experiences.

Major Cognitive Characteristics of Children

Infancy

It is interesting to see the number of changes that take place in the first two years. Children at this stage are very active learners. Even when it seems the child is only lying and looking at nothing (e.g. 2 month old) she is actually looking at and trying to understand the things around her.

The first two years children begin by exploring their own bodies and move to the outside objects. Children at 2/3 months discover their thumb or hand or occasionally their own foot. These fascinate them they try to play with them. For a two month old a toy is not as satisfying as her/his own thumb in her/his mouth. Gradually, by about six months, children begin to play with objects outside the body. This could be the toy, the sheet, the bottle, etc. Later, by two years they can even indulge in pretend play [example doctor-doctor, house-house, etc.].

What children also achieve by two years is the understanding of object permanence. **Object**

permanance is the understanding that things exist even if you can not see them. Let us take an example. If you show a five month old a toy she gets excited. If you hide the toy the child soon forgets that any toy even existed. This is because she thinks out of sight is out of mind. Do the same thing with a 1½ year old and you will find the child is either looking for it or asks you to find it. This is because she knows the toy exists even if she can not see it. This understanding, that things exist even if you can not see them, is called object permanance.

The other major development that happens by two years is that children begin to learn the symbols. What are symbols? A two year old can convey her thoughts and desires through language. All these are essential processes of cognition.

Early Childhood

This is a period when the childs mastery in use of symbols increases. We can observe this in the everyday behaviour and activities of the child, *i.e.* in what she plays, her language etc. Gradually her representations of objects become more flexible and less self centred. A one year old while playing does not need a toy phone to pretend speaking on the phone. She can use any object. This is indicative of flexibility in thinking. Gradually, children also start directing play between dolls, *e.g.,* one doll is the mother and the other doll the child. This is indicative of the child moving away from self to becoming less self centred.

Children at this stage also believe that all objects have feelings like human beings. That is why you will often see the child feeding her teddy bear.

Children at this stage can also focus on only one aspect of a situation and can not go back. Let us now take an example. You offer cola to a 4 yr old in a tall glass. You then change your mind and pour the coke from the tall glass to a short glass and give it to the child. You will find the child will say I want the big glass. This is because she can only focus on one aspect (height) at a time. Also, she is not able to go back mentally and realise that in the process of pouring from big to small glass, no cola was taken away.

Similarly, take two plates and put in one 6 pieces of chocolate spreadout and in the other make a tower of 6 pieces of chocolate. You will find the child thinking the spread out chocolate is more. This is because the child can only focus on one aspect at a time. This limitation seriously restricts the problem solving and logical thinking abilities of the child.

It also indicates the child's inability to understand that another point of view different from her own can exist, *e.g.,* you often find children responding to your question by nodding their heads, even if they are not in the same room as you. This is because they do not see another's point of view.

Middle Childhood

During this period, children begin to understand that another view point can exist. They are also able to focus on more than one aspect of a situation and go back and forth on their thinking. This makes their thinking more logical and efficient. However, children are only comfortable with concrete ideas/objects. It means, something that is real for them, *i.e.,* either something they have seen, *e.g.,* a house or something is in front of them, a plant or something linked to what they know, *e.g.,* blue like the sky. They are not able to think about abstract ideas, *e.g.,* what would happen if everyone could fly?

Emotion

Emotions, put simply, are feelings. In infants we can see these very clearly in the form of joy, anger and fear. These are similar to the emotions that adults have.

1. **The variety of emotions increases with age:** The basic emotions of joy, fear, anger are visible in infants. Gradually, as a sense of self develops; children begin to relate with people around them and value their opinions. Then we can see the emotion like pride, shame, sympathy, guilt also developing in them.

2. **The expression of emotion also changes with age:** Emotions are both innate and learnt. The instinctive response to a stimulus is innate but how to express that feeling is learnt, *e.g.* taking away of a toy makes the child angry (innate) but instead crying she is encouraged to ask for it back (learnt). Frustration tolerance increases with age. As children grow older, their responses change in both as well as instinctive method of expression, *e.g.,* when 2 year old falls downs she cries loudly and later forgets quickly. A 6 year old on the other hand, may not cry but forgets far less easily.

3. **The triggers or cause of emotions change with age:** The stimuli that elicit emotion also change with age, *e.g.,* an infant may cry on hearing the loud explosion of a cracker but a middle childhood child may laugh. Sucking a thumb may give great joy to an infant but provides no pleasure to a child is middle childhood.

4. **The coping techniques change with age:** Methods of coping with frustration and stress change with age. While a younger child may cry, or cling to the adult, an older child is likely to suppress the emotion.

Factors Affecting Emotional Development

If we look round in our environment, we will find that people differ in the emotions they experience and express. Some are happy, some are angry, some moody, some helpful. What then affects our emotional development?

1. **Parenting style:** Democratic parenting where induction is used as a method of disciplining allows for more mature emotional development and also for development of personal behaviour.

2. **Role model:** There are two factors which influence what a child ultimately learns:

   (i) How adults and others in the child's environment handle their emotions.

   (ii) How successful is the emotional expression in achieving their needs.

3. **Violence in the child's environment:** The kind of behaviour the child see in the community (*e.g.* during riots) or on TV will affect her expressions of emotions.

4. **Cultural norms:** Emotional expressions are learnt from the environment. It is the environment that tells us how to react in a situation (*e.g.* some people feel the emotion of fear when a black cat crosses their path). It is also the environment that tells us the acceptable way of expressing ones emotions (*e.g.* in many families it is unacceptable for boys to express their distress by crying). Therefore, our cultural beliefs and values also influence our emotional development.

MOTIVATION AND LEARNING

Motivation

Motivation is the heart of the learning process. It generates the will in an individual to do something. Adequate motivation not only engages the student in an activity which results in learning, but also sustains and directs learning. Two types of motivation are commonly recognised. These are: intrinsic and extrinsic motivation.

Intrinsic motivation arises when the resolution of tension is to be found in mastering the learning task itself; the material learned provides its own reward. For example, the student who studies the construction of model aeroplanes diligently so that he can make a model, is experiencing a kind of intrinsic motivation.

Extrinsic motivation occurs when a student pursues a learning task, but for reasons which are external. If a student engages in construction of model aeroplanes because he thinks it will please his father, who is an ex-pilot, rather than because of intrinsic motivation. We should remember that in most learning situations motivation can not be dichotomised so neatly. It is the function of the total learning situation and hinges on some blend of personal concern for the work itself and the concern for some extrinsic factors as well. As a working principle, motivation is probably a function of an interactive situation where reward to a particular action acts as an incentive. Some of the common forms of extrinsic motivation are:

- **Purposive striving, goals and ideals:** The goal and purposes of learning clearly perceived by the individual, provide strong motivation for better action and learning.

- **Knowledge of results:** Knowledge of results in terms of success and failure provides incentive for greater efforts on the part of the student. If a student practices a task without knowing the accuracy or inaccuracy of his performance, he may practise wrong task. In such a case, all learning will be futile. Therefore, if results of performance are known to the student, he learns better as compared to when he does not know about the results. Mere repetition of a task without knowledge of its results fails to bring about learning. Knowledge of results serves two purposes: (i) it enables the subject to evaluate his efficiency and to change his responses in the direction of greater accuracy, and (ii) it adds to the satisfaction in reaching a goal, one tends of repeat rewarded responses.

- **Punishment and rewards:** Punishment can be understood as an act of inflicting pain deliberately with the purpose of affecting the future conduct of an individual being punished. Punishment is based on fear of physical pain, embarrassment and loss of status. Thus, punishment of fear of being punished is one of the common and obvious methods of keeping under control and guiding the students. Punishment or fear is a very strong stimuli, a negative incentive to learning especially when errors occur. Thorndike showed that generally punishment speeds up learning and reduces the number of errors as it produces emotional excitement which tends to fix at punished response. But it does not mean that punishment under all the circumstances and with all the students is equally effective. For example, it may prove disastrous and destructive when task is very difficult.

Contrary to punishment, rewards are certainly better and positive incentives to learning. They are responsible for initiative, energy, competition, self-expression and creative ability. According to law of effect, reward is satisfying and pleasant, thus reward strengthens learning. Rewards may in the form of gifts, prizes, money, badges, cups, certificates of merit, or other objects of some value. Motivation through such objects feeds the natural drive in all the human beings. But, when these rewards are too much strived for, they degenerate the whole learning.

- **Praise and blame:** These are also strong incentives for effective learning. Praise stimulates average and inferior children, but has less effect on those of superior intelligence. Reproof is felt most by superior children, but girls seem more susceptible to praise than do boys. Regardless of age sex, or initial ability, praise is the most effective of the incentives. Reproof seems to be less effective for all students. Chase (1932) reported praise to be less effective than blame with young children, but Hurlock (1920) generalised, still accepted by contemporary investigators, that praise is more effective stimulus in motivating both immediate and long-continued tasks.

- **Rivalry:** The rivalry between students which leads to resentment, jealousy, etc., or rivalry between groups of students which creates hatred, is the least desirable type of incentive to be encouraged in the schools. Self-rivalry or rivalry in the form of healthy competition is the most valuable type. This tendency should be developed in the student. Though experimental researchers have shown rivalry to be a powerful motivation influence, the emotional and social consequences of rivalry must be considered by the teacher.

Functions of Motivation

The major functions of motivation in learning are as follows:

- To energies the students in learning
- To direct behaviour
- To select behaviour
- To help capture the attention
- To help in acquiring knowledge
- To help in character formation
- To develop social qualities

Attention in Relation to Motivation

Attention is the basic pre-requisite of all learning in the classroom. Learning is possible only if students concentrate their attention on the object or stimuli to be learnt. Attention increases the amount and rate of learning, and also the efficiency of work.

Attention is closely related to motivation. Attention is motivated behaviour, in which the student makes a variety of efforts for achieving the goal. Thus motivation helps in capturing attention. You can help your students by motivating them to concentrate their attention on the tasks to be learnt by them.

Between the two types of motivation, intrinsic motivation should be preferred to extrinsic motivation. It produces better learning because it is related to interest. The learner pursues the activity in which he has interest without waiting for any external pressure. When the learner does not show any intrinsic motivation or interest in learning we have to resort to extrinsic motivation by the use of 'incentives'—whether financial or non-financial (monetary or non-monetary)—such as rewards, awards, prizes, competitions, praise, etc.

In-built Motivation

Another type of motivation is called in-built motivation. Whatever may be the type of motivation, it should be an in-built component of the whole programme of education/training. Right type of trainers, attractive and need-based reading materials, supportive training methodologies, constant awareness of the new dimensions of the programme will facilitate motivation in an in-built manner.

Theories of Motivation

The main theories of motivation are: (a) Psycho-analytic Theory, (b) Maslow's Theory of Self-actualisation, (c) Physiological Theory and (d) Achievement-Motivation Theory.

Psycho-Analytic Theory

According to this theory, motivation gives the vital life forces which are the prime mover of life and its activities. 'It is will power that motivates a person', *i.e.,* 'no will power—no activity'. All these versions agree on one point *i.e.,* 'building ego of man'.

Maslow's Theory of Self-Actualisation

This theory is based on human needs and their satisfaction. Maslow (1998) has arranged man's basic needs in a hierarchy, *i.e.,* some needs are strong or more important than others. According to him the five basic needs, progressing from physiological needs through safety needs, love, esteem needs and the need for self-actualisation. These basic needs are described here under:

- **Physiological needs:** Maslow states that physiological needs are undoubtedly the most powerful of all needs. Examples are the needs for food, sleep or rest. Until the biological needs are met, an individual may lack awareness of other needs. When a person is gratified he/she is released and higher needs can emerge. Some potential adult learners from low-economic background actually have unmet physiological needs, such as hunger, which prevent them from learning. An old person may not be able to see or hear well and he might not be open to satisfying other needs.

- **Safety Needs:** When physiological needs are satisfied, safety needs emerge, such as need for security, for physical safety, for stability in one's life. Safety needs are seen when a person prefers the familiar over the unfamiliar. An adult would rather go to a meeting in a building with which he is familiar than in a building new to him.

- **Love or Belongingness:** If both the physiological and safety needs are gratified, the needs for love, affection and belongingness emerge. Love needs involve both giving and receiving love. They involve the feeling of being wanted. The person who does not feel he belongs, no matter what the reason, probably will not continue with the group and discontinue his participation in adult education programme. The teacher should be affectionate towards adult learners and develop a group spirit among learners.

- **Esteem:** All people in our society have a need, a desire, for self-respect or self-esteem and for the esteem of others. There are two types: The desire for achievement and the desire for prestige or recognition from others. Satisfaction of the need for self-esteem leads to feelings of self-confidence and of being useful to the society. Thwarting of these needs produce feelings of inferiority or weakness. Fear or failure or lack of self-esteem might prevent an adult from participating in educational activities.

- **Self-Actualisation:** Even after the earlier needs are satisfied a person might still feel restless unless he becomes everything he is capable of becoming. This is called self-fulfilment or self-actualisation. The specific form of this needs varies from person-to-person. One person might desire to be an ideal mother or an ideal leader.

- **Implications for Adult Learning:** Before starting the adult education class, the basic needs of the learners should be studied. It may be possible that due to poverty and less per capita income, the basic biological needs of the learners may not be fulfilled. Then the main aim of adult education should be to provide regular income to the learners. This can be done by starting various income generating projects. The educators should also help by marketing of such products produced by the learners. The officials connected with adult education should take steps to start such programmes. This will make the classes more interesting to the learners. The teacher needs to strengthen the group spirit among learners and should identify himself/herself with the group. The learning experiences in the centres should promote the talents, attitudes capacities and potentialities of adults.

Physiological Theory of Motivation

This theory has been developed by Clifford Morgan and William James. According to this theory of the body determines attitudes and interests and explains activities and behaviour of people.

Implications for Adult Education: Participa-tion in physical activities decrease with age so also interests change as a person becomes older. Many physical limitations affect the amount of time an adult has for educational activities. After working all day at a job, some adults are too tired to participate in educational activity, such people can be motivated giving them work which gives them relaxation. Hearing and vision also decrease with age. The ages of the group members will determine the size of letters that a teacher writes on a black board, the colour of the chalk used, the size of the articles he holds for the adults to see, and how loudly and distinctly he speaks. The size, type and quality of handout material are also important.

Achievement-Motivation Theory

This theory has been developed by McClelland (1985). According to this theory all human behaviour is intended to reduce tension and reach a state of physiological and psychological equilibrium. It is a desire to do better, to achieve unique accomplishment, to compete with a standard of excellence and to involve oneself with long term achievement goals. It can be identified on the basic of individual expectation of success. It applies only when the individual knows that his/her performance will be evaluated by himself or by others in terms of excellence, and that the consequences of his action will either succeed or fail.

FACTORS CONTRIBUTING TO LEARNING

Introduction

Learning, can be considered as the process by which skills, attitudes, knowledge and concepts are acquired, understood, applied and extended. All human beings, whether grown ups or children engage in the process of learning, either consciously, sub-consciously or subliminally. It is through learning that their competence and ability to function in their environment get enhanced. It is important to understand that while we learn some ideas and concepts through instruction or teaching, we also learn through our feelings and experiences. Feelings and experiences are a tangible part of our lives and these greatly influence what we learn, how we learn and why we learn.

Learning has been considered partly a cognitive process and partly a social and affective one. It qualifies as a cognitive process because it involves the functions of attention, perception, reasoning, analysis, drawing of conclusions, making interpretations and giving meaning to the observed phenomena. All of these are mental processes which relate to the intellectual functions of the individual. Learning is a social and affective process, as the societal and cultural context in which we function and the feelings and experiences which we have, greatly influence our ideas, concepts, images and understanding of the world. These constitute inner subjective interpretations and represent our own unique, personalized constructions of the specific universe of functioning. Our knowledge, ideas, concepts, attitudes, beliefs and the skills which we acquire are a consequence of these combined processes.

CLASSIFICATION OF FACTORS: PERSONAL & ENVIRONMENT

To understand how we categorise the factors affecting learning, let us begin by considering the following examples:

- Ravi is sixteen year old and wants to please his mother by getting good results in his board examinations. He is so eager to please her, that he spends long hours of concentrated time and energy on his studies. He consciously tries to control other sources of distraction in his life and reduces the time spent on watching television, playing games and chatting with his friends.

- Rita Williams wants to be a famous tennis player. To achieve her goal, she practices tennis whenever she can, even though she gets no encouragement from her family. She makes it a point to watch tennis matches and maintain a good rapport with her sports teacher.

- Yuvraj is a good student, but lately he has been scoring very low marks at school. He is not able to concentrate or pay attention and his class work and home assignments reflect

a very poor quality. Sources revealed that his parents fight a lot with each other and are about to get divorced.

- Arti and Kavita are two sisters. Arti is very good at art and craft and can sketch just about anything she sees. Kavita has a ear for music. She knows most songs and can sing them even if she has heard them only once. Both of them spend hours together pursuing their respective interest areas.

- Sayeeda is tall, attractive and has a very good figure. She wants to be a model or an air-hostess and nurtures this secretly as her dream. She is too scared to share her wishes with her family, since she belongs to an orthodox family, where girls at best can pursue teaching as a career. When she tries telling her mother what she wants, she is firmly told that she can only do her B.Ed and can go to the coaching classes for these.

The above cited examples illustrate that learning is a universal phenomenon mediated by a number of factors, both personal and environmental in nature. The dictum "everybody learns" is as true as its corollary, *i.e.*, everybody learns in accordance with his/her unique, individualized blend of personal and environmental factors. For example, in case of Ravi, the desire to please his mother, striving to do well in his board exams and managing his life situations appropriately constitute the key factors which influence him. For Rita Williams, it is her intrinsic desire to be a good tennis player which is paramount. She is not deterred by the lack of family support and continues to make efforts to promote her love for tennis on her own and fulfil her desire to be successful.

In case of Yuvraj, in spite of his innate capacity to study and perform well, his lack of achievement can be attributed to the emotional insecurity stemming from his parents' divorce. As far as Arti and Kavita are concerned, their special interests and talent in art and music respectively, seem to guide their activities.

For Sayeeda, the home environment and family culture and values determine her professional choice. Her own inner interests, desires and wishes are not to be taken into cognizance.

In all the examples cited, we can find evidence of both personal and environmental factors influencing the process of learning. Learning can thus be defined as a function of the interaction of personal and environmental factors.

$$L = f (EF \times PF)$$

L = learning; f = function; EF = environmental factors; PF = personal factors.

Personal factors are the intra individual factors like motivation, interests, abilities etc which predispose an individual towards learning as in the case of Rita Williams, Arti and Kavita. Environmental factors on the other hand, are those contextual factors which highlight the role of the environment in learning, such as the socio-emotional, societal and cultural factors as seen in the case of Yuvraj and Sayeeda. Although the two factors represent different categories, they operate in a common system. The environmental factors provide the context within which the personal factors, operate. The learner and the learning process can only be completely understood with reference to the interaction of both environmental and personal factors. This may be diagrammatically represented as follows:

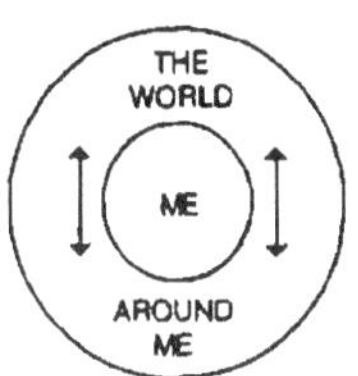
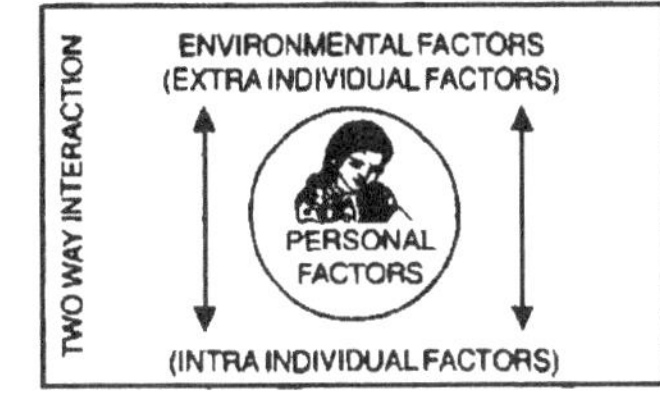

Fig: *Factors affecting learning*

Personal Factors Influencing Learning

The process of learning is influenced by a variety of personal factors. A thorough knowledge of these factors will prove very helpful for teachers and parents in understanding and guiding their children's learning. Some of the personal factors that influence the learning process may be classified as under : sensation and perception, fatigue and boredom, maturation, emotional condition, needs, interests, motivation, attention, intelligence, aptitude, attitude, etc. Let us discuss the important personal factors in the following sub-sections.

Sensation and Perception

Apart from the general health of the students, sensation and perception are the psychological factors which help in learning. Sensation is at the core of perception. There are five sense organs *i.e.*, skin, ears, tongue, eyes and nose. These sense organs are the gateways of knowledge and help in perception of various stimuli in the environment. Any defect in any of the sense organs will affect learning and hence acquisition of knowledge. For example, defects of vision such as myopia, hypermetropia, astigmatism, etc., cause headaches, nausia and general disinclination to study. A blind person depends upon the sense of touch or skin for learning and thus acquires knowledge and skills, as he can not visualise the objects. The stimuli are preceived and assimilated, and hence learnt through various sense organs. In this way we can say that sensation and perception is the bases of knowledge and learning.

Fatigue and Boredom

It is virtually boredom or lassitude rather than fatigue which bothers the students. The difference between the two is that fatigue is mental or physical tiredness which decreases in efficiency and competency to work. Boredom, on the other hand, is a lack of desire on an aversion to work. Such an aversion makes one feel fatigued without being actually fatigued. Studying seldom causes fatigue. It is mainly boredom which, besides causing the impression of fatigue, decreases student efficiency in learning.

Age and Maturation

Learning is directly dependent upon age and maturation. No learning can take place unless individual is matured enough to learn. Some children can learn better at earlier age while others take more time to learn the same content.

Mental age increases with the chronological age and ceases at about the age of sixteen years. Increase in age means intellectual maturation which helps in solving difficult problems. The principle of maturation warns us against enforcing learning on a child when he is not mature enough to learn the specific skills. Teachers should explain this principle to parents who are over ambitious or over enthusiastic in sending their children to school at the very early age.

Emotional Conditions

Desirable emotional conditions enhance the quality and speed of learning. Happiness, joy and satisfaction are always favourable for any type of learning. Adverse emotional conditons, on the other hand, hinder learning. Many studies have established the fact that emotional strain, stress, tensions, disturbances, etc., are extremely inimical to scholastic pursuits.

Needs

A need is the lack of something which, if provided, would facilitate child's usual behaviour. The lack of something is experienced by the child. The child then tries to perform that activity which culminates in the satisfaction of the need. Thus, the needs are associated with goals. Among human beings, the needs are realtively permanent tendencies which seek satisfaction in achieving certain specific goals. When these goals are achieved, the particular need is satisfied or met for the time being, but it recurs sooner or later and energises further activity. The needs in human beings can be physiological such as need for oxygen, food, water, etc. They may be social such as the need for affection, recognition, self-regard, etc. Social needs are however, quite different from physiological needs. Social needs might originate after physiological needs are satisfied. These needs have a complex structure and dominate the individual's behaviour.

There is not equal urgency in the satisfaction of all needs. Some have to be satisfied before others can manifest themselves.

In schools, children are not expected to do any intellectual thinking unless their physiological needs are satisfied. Poor, starved children may concentrate less on attainment of knowledge than on food. Similarly, very cold or hot classrooms or over-crowded seats will not be conducive to good learning. Likewise the need for safety, love and esteem, all act as powerful motives in the learning situations. If the child is afraid of the teacher or feels unsafe while in the school on account of too much beating or some other form of punishment, no learning can take place. Similarly, his needs for warmth and affection are very stimulating and hence results in effective learning.

Interests

Various types of interests of the students can be exploited to facilitate their learning. The interests during early infancy are mostly limited and short lived. As the child grows older his interests diversify and stabilize. You, a school teacher, should have thorough knowledge of children's interests. You can eliminate much drudgery, monotony and boredom from the school work if you make your instruction lively and stimulating and arouse student interest in it.

Once the students' interest is aroused in an activity you should expend more effort on it. No learning can be achieved without proper expenditure of effort on it. Students can even overcome distraction, fatigue and boredom if they feel interested in your instruction and class activities. It has often been found that, in most cases, fatigue in reality is loss of interest in the learning activity. Interest, should be exploited to yield results of greater quantity and quality learning in school.

Life is so exciting that many interesting things and activities often clamor to attract our attention. Children frequently face the dilemma of mutually conflicting interests. Immediate interests often seem to be clashing with the remoter ones. A student might be in a quandary at least for the time being when his interest in sports impels him towards the play-field and his interest in studies force him to concentrate on books.

In such cases of conflicting interests a lot of hesitancy, wastage, frustration and unhappiness is bound to follow. What is needed is education at home and school which helps/trains children to achieve a healthy balance in their interests. They should be trained to budget their time in such a manner as to pay a reasonable attention to various interests, scholastic, athletic, social etc., within the time at their disposal.

Motivation

Motivation is the heart of the learning process. It generates the will in an individual to do something. Adequate motivation not only engages the student in an activity which results in learning, but also sustains and directs learning. Two types of motivation are commonly recognised. These are: intrinsic and extrinsic motivation.

Intelligence

Intelligence as expressed by an I.Q. score on an intelligence test is positively related to learning. Generally, students with higher I.Q. learn rapidly. However, higher I.Q. in itself is no guarantee for rapid learning, since other factors such as needs, interest, motivation, etc., of the students and the methods used for learning are also important.

Aptitude

A student who possesses appropriate aptitude for a particular subject of study or skill, will learn better and retain it for a longer time. On the other hand, he will require relatively longer time to study a subject for which he lacks natural aptitude. He is liable to forget it soon besides feeling bored and unhappy all the time while learning it. Hence, it is extremely desirable to analyse the aptitude of students before prescribing courses of study for them.

Attitude

The learning process is also influenced considerably by the attitude of the student. If he is alert, attentive and interested in the material to be learnt, he is bound to have a favourable attitude towards it. Such an attitude will enable him to tackle the learning situation economically, pleasantly and effectively. Conversely, if he is inattentive and is uninterested in the material his attitude is bound to be unfavourable. This will hinder the smooth learning of the material in hand besides involving undue strain and tension in the learner.

Environmental Factors

Environmental influences begin since the time of the conception of the child in the womb of the mother. Mother's mental, physical and emotional conditions influence the development of foetus in the womb. The external environment starts from the time of birth of the child. It (external environment) refers to the surroundings which prevail in home, school and locality. At these places, the child interacts with members of the family, teachers, classmates or peers and neighbours and establishes relationship with them. The relationship with the members of the society, and the surroundings may affect the development of the child and also the way he learns. Some of the environmental factors are discussed as follows:

Surrounding : Natural, Social and Cultural

As the title of the sub-section indicates, we shall discuss here natural, social and cultural environment the child interacts with and get influenced.

Natural surrounding covers the climatic and atmospheric condition. These conditions affect learning directly. It has been found that high temperature and humidity reduces mental efficiency. For a limited time, humidity and high temperature can be tolerated but prolonged humidity and high temperature become unbearable and decrease mental efficiency. The intellectual productivity and creativeness of people living in hot regions are much low. Likewise, the morning time is always better for mastering difficult tasks. Mental efficiency decreases due to increased humidity and temperature. Studies on the academic progress of evening school students shows losses of efficiency varying from one to six per cent.

Social surrounding includes especially the environment of home, school and locality. Physical conditions at home such as large family, small family, (specific place of the study), insufficient ventilation, improper lighting, uncomfortable temperature, noisy home environment due to use of radio, TV, etc., noisy neighbourhood, constant visits by friends or relatives, etc., influence the intellectual learning of the student. The socio-emotional factors such as child rearing practices, reward and punishment, scope for freedom and independence in activities and decision making, play and study facilities, ambitions and aspirations of the parents, disorganisation and discord among birth positions such as eldest, youngest or single child have their definite influence on learning. For example, a student who comes from a very poor family and never had any intellectual stimulation at home remains dull and unresponsive in the class. In some societies there is a strong sex bias. Girls are directly or indirectly told that education is not meant for them. In the middle class families, on the other hand, parents are rather over-ambitious. They wish their children to make quick academic progress, grow-up and find a respectable vocation preferably a white collar job. Such children, therefore get sufficient incentive from their families. This, of course, is most favourable to scholastic learning, although an overdose of family emphasis on acquiring academic excellence might affect the child's mental and physical health adversely. Similarly, school activities, study facilities and teaching methods and behaviour of teachers, principals and non-teaching staff have an impact upon learning. If the school atmosphere is unconducive, it adversely affects the learning process. Locality also has an influence on a child. If the locality is bad, the learning will be ineffective to some extent.

Cultural demands and social expectations also influence learning. The spirit of culture is reflected in its social and educational institutions. Children's learning, therefore, is greatly determined by the demands and expectations of their culture. Thus, for instance, in an industrialized culture the emphasis mostly centres mechanical sciences and preparing children for highly mechanised vocations. In an agriculture based community, on the other hand, the educational process focusses on preparing its members for those skills which are suited to the needs of an agrarian community.

The philosophical elements of culture also influence the spirit of children's learning. Children in a democratic culture tend to acquire democrative and values and attitudes. A feudal, aristocratic or dictatorial culture, on the other hand, promotes autocratic modes of thought and behaviour.

Relationship with Teacher, Parents and Peers

The teacher is an important constituent in the instructional process. She/he plays an important role in shaping the behaviour of students. The way he teaches and manages the students has an affect on their learning. An authoritarian teacher will create an aggression and hostility among students while a democratic teacher will create a participatory climate for learning. The democratic environment leads students to constructive, thoughtful and cooperative behaviour. Generally, students learn better in a democratic set up because they like democratic procedures. The teacher is no more an instructor or the director of learning in a democratic set up. She/he helps his/her students in their learning. The teachers no more dominate the scene, they can get better results by decentralizing authority, increasing independence of students. They can attend to the comments and questions of the students. They can encourage students to participate in learning activities in and outside the class. There should be more emphasis on activity-centred classroom where student's active participation in the teaching-learning process is encouraged and the teacher acts as a guide to promote learning.

Relationship with parents plays a vital role in the learning process of the student. If the child-parents relationship is based on mutual respect and faith, it can provide the child a congenial atmosphere which in turn can facilitate his/her learning. A distorted and unhealthy environment, on the other hand, adversely affects the learning of the student. The upward mobility brings resistance on the part of the student to learn. Students in such families find themselves unable to cope up. A subtle but powerful influence on the growing child arises from his/her position among the children in the family. The parents of the first born expect the child to act like miniature adults and hence the first-born are found to encounter a variety of expectations and stresses. Whereas parents tend to be more relaxed in their do's and dont's with the last-born. Factors like traumatic events at home, separation or death can also precipitate learning problems in the normal child.

A healthy peer group relationship also plays an important role in learning. Student-student relationship in the classroom, school, society, etc., create a particular type of emotional climate. The climate solely depends upon their relationships. A sound relationships provides a tension free environment to the student to learn more and to compete in the class. If the relationship among peers is not good, it adversely affects their learning. Therefore, to improve the classroom learning climate, free discussion should be there. You should help your students understand each other in formal or informal meetings. They should be encouraged to meet each other and their teachers freely. If any misunderstanding is created or developed, it should be immediately clarified so as to maintain the healthy climate and cordial relationship among peers.

Media Influence on Learning

Media has been considered an important component of transmitting information. Media can be divided into two broad categories—print and non-print media. Print media refers to texts or printed materials. It is economical and has traditionally been used for pedagogical purposes.

But, it may not be the only or the perfect medium to impart education. Non-print media, also known as modern electronic media, have certain unique qualities which, in certain cases, facilitate learning much more faster than the print medium. These helps meet diverse learning objectives more efficiently than the printed matter.

Certain non-print media formats and delivery systems contribute well to student's learning actitivies, For example, audio tapes or computers can be used effectively to drill and practice in language and learning arithmatic. Electronic media can help promote the discovery approach to learning. For example, a film can be exploited for discovery teaching in the physical sciences. Students keep watching the various sections of the film until they perceive the relationships between the visuals. Then they are curious to find out the principles that explain those relationships. Likewise, in the social sciences various media can be used to present students with visual and auditory experiences that provide related inquiry. Films and stimulation are often used to present real-life or laboratory learning situations to students.

The role of the electronic media has proved effective for teaching students. These excite the student psychologically and prepare/motivate them to participate in teaching-learning activites. Non-print media perform following fuctions:

- direct attention,
- arouse motivation,
- increase student's concentration, and
- help them actively involve in the learning process.

PRACTICE PAPER

1. Mass media, cinema and library are passive agencies of education because
   (a) learner can not react to the feedback system of these agencies directly
   (b) they provide informal education
   (c) they can not come closer to the educant
   (d) all of these

2. Education of a child really begins
   (a) Once he takes birth
   (b) Once he attains the age of three
   (c) Once he is admitted to post nursery schools
   (d) Once he learns to speak

3. Family is the original social institution from which all other institutions emerged, who said this
   (a) Brown
   (b) Ballard
   (c) Machiver
   (d) None of them

4. Which of the following is not the primary function of schools
   (a) reorganization and reconstruction of Human experiences
   (b) all-round development of the child
   (c) to make the children self reliant
   (d) advancement of culture

5. In a democratic country, school should reflect
   (a) National aspirations
   (b) Community related local aspirations
   (c) Both of these
   (d) None of these

6. The best teacher in a village school is he who
   (a) carries community experiences to the class room
   (b) prepares instructional programmes in the interest of the community
   (c) carries classroom experiences to the community
   (d) all of these

7. Universalisation of education is the concept adopted by
   (a) modern state
   (b) democratic state
   (c) totalitarian state
   (d) religious state

8. Secular education in India means
   (a) an education opposed to religion
   (b) an education indifferent to religion
   (c) an education emphasizing equality of religions
   (d) none of these

9. School works as a social sub system for
   (a) transmission of culture
   (b) preservation of culture
   (c) advancement of culture
   (d) all of these

10. "Society is nothing but a process of interaction among people." Who said this?
    (a) Lapier
    (b) Cuber
    (c) Reuter
    (d) Payne

11. The best model of schooling is
    (a) Close interaction between education of society
    (b) Self reliant society by education
    (c) Reflection of openness by schools
    (d) All of these

12. Special provisions have been made for socially and educationally backward classes of the nation under article
    (a) 29
    (b) 31
    (c) 15
    (d) 19

13. Religious education is prohibited in government schools and colleges under Article
    (a) 29
    (b) 28 (1)
    (c) 39 (2)
    (d) 15 (a)

14. Religious and linguistic minorities shall have the right to establish and administer their own educational institutions under Article
    (a) 30(1)
    (b) 31(2)
    (c) 40
    (d) 41

15. Article 351 is about
    (a) education of tribals
    (b) promotion of Hindi
    (c) promotion of secularism
    (d) English as official language

16. Status of central university is given to any educational institution under union list of
    (a) Entry 65
    (b) Entry 63
    (c) Entry 66
    (d) None of these

17. Entry 25 of concurrent list states about
    (a) vocational and technical training of labour
    (b) the education of working class
    (c) the education of disabled
    (d) none of the above

18. Education in the mother tongue at primary stage to children belonging to linguistic minorities has been mentioned in Article
    (*a*) 250   (*b*) 350
    (*c*) 349   (*d*) 351

19. Educational and economic interests of SCs and STs have been safeguarded under Article
    (*a*) 46   (*b*) 45(a)
    (*c*) 351   (*d*) 52

20. Education of union territories is administered by the central government under Article
    (*a*) 350   (*b*) 229
    (*c*) 239   (*d*) 50

21. Education was transferred from state list of subjects to concurrent list in
    (*a*) 1976   (*b*) 1972
    (*c*) 1980   (*d*) 1950

22. Which of the following statements about growth and development is not correct?
    (*a*) Growth generally refers to quantitative changes while development refers to qualitative changes
    (*b*) Growth is a function of the environment
    (*c*) Growth is not possible without development and vice versa
    (*d*) Growth is determined by intrinsic and genetic factors of the organism

23. The limit of growth is fixed by
    (*a*) internal factors of the organism
    (*b*) nutrition and exercise
    (*c*) both of these
    (*d*) none of these

24. Development is
    (*a*) Maturation
    (*b*) Learning
    (*c*) Synthesis of abilities
    (*d*) All of these

25. Development takes place when
    (*a*) environmental forces work on the organism
    (*b*) environmental forces interact with the hereditary forces in an organism
    (*c*) both of these
    (*d*) none of these

26. Which of the following statements about development is correct?
    (*a*) Process of development can be improved by exercise and nutrition
    (*b*) Development may be positive and negative both
    (*c*) Development proceeds from general to specific
    (*d*) All of these

27. The son of a goldsmith becomes an expert goldsmith. It is an example of a
    (*a*) biological heredity
    (*b*) social heredity
    (*c*) transfer of instinct
    (*d*) none of these

28. All humans contain .... chromosomes.
    (*a*) 26   (*b*) 36
    (*c*) 46   (*d*) 42

29. DNA test helps us to know
    (*a*) the genetic traits of a person
    (*b*) nature of personality and its composition
    (*c*) both of these
    (*d*) none of these

30. The law of inheritance was discovered by Gregor Mendel in
    (*a*) 1866   (*b*) 1911
    (*c*) 1888   (*d*) 1920

31. Which of the following statements regarding personality traits is correct?
    (*a*) Traits of personality can not be developed in isolation without taking the help of environment
    (*b*) Subjective traits of the individual are determined by genetic factors
    (*c*) Bad environment can surpass good inheritance but good environment is not a substitute for poor heredity
    (*d*) All of these

32. Which of the following characteristics denote infancy period?
    (*a*) Physical growth is curvilinear
    (*b*) Physical growth is rapid
    (*c*) Head grows at relatively slower rate as compared to other parts of the body
    (*d*) All of these

33. Which of the following is not the characteristic of infancy period?
    (*a*) From bilateral to unilateral trend in motor organs
    (*b*) From general to specific trend in motor organs
    (*c*) Emotional/social development is not associated with motor development
    (*d*) Steady mental development

34. Which of the following illustrates conceptual development?
    (*a*) Perception is the beginning of concept formation
    (*b*) Concept changes with changes in experiences
    (*c*) Concept changes with age
    (*d*) All of these

35. There is one thing common in language and physical development what is that?
    (*a*) Spurts of development at different ages
    (*b*) Dependence on experience
    (*c*) Dependence on training
    (*d*) None of these

36. Which of the following characteristics is not associated with emotional development?
    (a) Emotion is accompanied by physiological changes
    (b) Emotions start immediately after birth
    (c) Intense form of emotions are seen during early childhood period
    (d) Emotions are unrelated to physical development

37. The child acquires about three fourth of the brain weight by the age of
    (a) 2½ years   (b) 2 years
    (c) 6 years   (d) 8 years

38. Social development of an infant depends on
    (a) his chance of interaction with others
    (b) love and affection shown to the child
    (c) the extent to which he is able to attract the attention of others
    (d) all of the above

39. In which of the following stages the child looks self centred?
    (a) Infancy   (b) Early childhood
    (c) Adolescence   (d) Adulthood

40. In the period of infancy, emotions are
    (a) intense, frequent and unstable
    (b) like an open book(overt)
    (c) need based
    (d) all of these

41. Which of the following organs of the body shows rapid growth in infancy?
    (a) growth of hands   (b) growth of head
    (c) growth of legs   (d) growth of fingers

42. In normal learning environment, forgetting is caused
    (a) due to back of practice for a long time
    (b) due to the interference of other learnt material
    (c) due to lack of consolidation of memory traces
    (d) all of these

43. Clear conception of size, weight, colour, time etc., is seen at the age of
    (a) six   (b) four
    (c) four and half   (d) five

44. Which of the following is not the characteristics of intellectual development of early childhood?
    (a) increased span of attention
    (b) exploration of the environment
    (c) ability to verbalize all known concepts
    (d) ability to distinguish past, present and future

45. Social development by the end of early childhood is marked by
    (a) the feeling of autonomy
    (b) the end of solitary plays
    (c) the temperament of co-operation and friendliness
    (d) all of these

46. Fictional world of the child starts at the age of
    (a) 5-6   (b) 6-8
    (c) 3-4   (d) 4-5

47. Girls are more dominating than boys in social situations in which of the following periods?
    (a) pre-adolescent period
    (b) early childhood period
    (c) both of these
    (d) none of these

48. In the period of early childhood, child is
    (a) helpless to hide his emotions
    (b) seen shifting his emotions very rapidly and frequently
    (c) guided by his innate tendencies and instincts
    (d) all of these

49. A nursery teacher should organize
    (a) group games in the school
    (b) those games which involve motor organs of the body
    (c) those games which help the child to manipulate the environment
    (d) all of these

50. Later childhood is called latency period because
    (a) creative potentials are dormant
    (b) sex remains dormant
    (c) it is a period of inactivity
    (d) all of these

51. Physical development of later childhood is marked by
    (a) Auscification of bones
    (b) Permanent teeth
    (c) Excessive motor activity
    (d) All of these

52. Girls surpass boys physically in
    (a) infancy
    (b) later childhood
    (c) early childhood
    (d) adolescence

53. The period of later childhood is marked by
    (a) intellectual maturity
    (b) high muscular energy
    (c) hero worship
    (d) all of these

54. Which of the following is not the characteristics of intellectual development of later childhood?
    (a) High interest in science fiction
    (b) Increased logical power
    (c) Careful for future
    (d) End of imaginary fears

55. Children are very much hateful or indifferent to opposite sex at the age of
    (a) 11-12   (b) 13-14
    (c) 10-11   (d) 15-16

56. Period of later childhood is marked by
   (a) slow and steady physical growth
   (b) stability in emotions
   (c) anger against injustice
   (d) all of these

57. At the end of later childhood period, the child
   (a) feels himself superior to girls
   (b) becomes independent of his family
   (c) wants to become hero
   (d) all of these

58. The best place of social development for a 12 years old child is
   (a) neighbourhood
   (b) family
   (c) playground
   (d) school

59. Group activities and group loyalties are at its peak at the age of
   (a) 10-12   (b) 13-15
   (c) 8-10   (d) 18-20

60. A teacher should not let a 12 years old child any time free because
   (a) child is always interested to get involve in physical or mental activities
   (b) spurts of creativity are seen at this age
   (c) child is frustrated
   (d) all of these

61. Elektra complex refers to
   (a) daughter comes closer to the father
   (b) son comes closer to the mother
   (c) inferiority complex in the presence of girls
   (d) none of these

62. According to Freud, super ego is properly developed during
   (a) latency period   (b) anal period
   (c) phallic period   (d) none of these

63. Development is a process of observable social interaction. This is the opinion of
   (a) Erikson   (b) Skinner
   (c) Robert Sears   (d) None of these

64. The secondary behaviour of the child according to Robert Sears starts with
   (a) reinforcement   (b) imitation
   (c) modelling   (d) none of these

65. The period of sensory motor adoptation of Piaget is
   (a) 0-2 years   (b) 1-3 years
   (c) 3-5 years   (d) 4-6 years

66. The child adopts the view points of others on the basis of consequences of these views in the
   (a) third stage of Kohlberg's theory
   (b) second stage of Kohlberg's theory
   (c) fourth stage of Kohlberg's theory
   (d) fifth stage of Kohlberg's theory

67. Which of the following is not the view point of cognitive theories of development?
   (a) moral principles are acquired automatically with age
   (b) super ego is formed during the period of adolescence
   (c) Moral values are determined by culture
   (d) Mural principles are universal

68. Organization of sensory experiences about a particular object is called
   (a) percepts   (b) reasoning
   (c) concept   (d) none of these

69. The concept building in a person depends on
   (a) the age and maturity of the person
   (b) past experiences of the learner
   (c) intelligence of the learner
   (d) all of these

70. Agreement on a concept is possible because
   (a) concepts are subjective
   (b) concepts are objective
   (c) concepts are hierarchical
   (d) b and c both

71. Which of the following statements about concepts is correct?
   (a) Some concepts are more powerful than others
   (b) All concepts are universal
   (c) Concepts are differentiated on the basis of their attributes
   (d) None of these

72. Which is the highest level of concept formation?
   (a) formal level   (b) sensory level
   (c) concrete level   (d) none of these

73. How many steps of problem solving has been given by Gates?
   (a) Six   (b) Seven
   (c) Five   (d) Ten

74. Freeman considers intelligence as an ability
   (a) to adjust in an adverse situation
   (b) to learn better and faster
   (c) to manipulate abstract materials
   (d) all of these

75. Single factor theory of intelligence was given by
   (a) Alfred Binet   (b) Thorndike
   (c) Freeman   (d) None of them

76. Which of the following is not the characteristics of 'S' factor according to Spearman ?
   (a) It is the acquired capacity of the individual
   (b) Specialization in only one trade is possible
   (c) It varies from activity to activity in the same individual
   (d) Individuals differ only in 'S' factor of intelligence

77. In multifactor theory, range is related to
   (a) Number of tasks that a person can do in a limited period of time

(*b*) Difficulty level of items
(*c*) General intelligence of learners
(*d*) None of these

78. SI model of intelligence was given by I P Guilford in
(*a*) 1911   (*b*) 1904
(*c*) 1966   (*d*) 1975

79. Hierarchy theory of intelligence was given by
(*a*) Jenson
(*b*) Thorndike
(*c*) Burt and Vernon
(*d*) None of them

80. In the pre-Binet period, intelligence was considered as
(*a*) Sensory acuity of the individual
(*b*) Verbal ability of the individual
(*c*) Associative ability of the individual
(*d*) All of these

81. An age scale of intelligence was first developed by
(*a*) Spearman   (*b*) Terman
(*c*) Binet-Simon   (*d*) None of them

82. Binet-Simon scale of intelligence measures
(*a*) General mental abilities not specific ones.
(*b*) Mental growth of the individual over a period of time
(*c*) The aptitude or level of an examinee not their speed
(*d*) All of these

83. WAIS came into being in
(*a*) 1939   (*b*) 1955
(*c*) 1960   (*d*) 1964

84. Wechsler developed an intelligence test for children in
(*a*) 1939   (*b*) 1949
(*c*) 1955   (*d*) 1956

85. Catell's culture fair test of intelligence was developed in
(*a*) 1960   (*b*) 1961
(*c*) 1965   (*d*) 1955

86. Non-verbal test of intelligence is suitable for
(*a*) deaf and dumb
(*b*) illiterates
(*c*) backward children
(*d*) all of these

87. Intelligence testing is useful for knowing
(*a*) individual difference
(*b*) mental retardation
(*c*) educational backwardness
(*d*) all of these

88. Scores on intelligence tests can not be fully relied on because
(*a*) fatigue level can influence the performance
(*b*) cultural factors can influence the score
(*c*) they generally do not reveal all the mental abilities of a person

(*d*) all of these

89. Who among the following psychologists is of the view that a learner can be motivated by satisfying his needs?
(*a*) Henry Murray   (*b*) Abraham Maslow
(*c*) Both of these   (*d*) None of these

90. Permanent change in behaviour brought about by experience or training is called.
(*a*) Learning   (*b*) Motivation
(*c*) Assimilation   (*d*) None of these

91. The book **"Theory of Motivation"** has been written by
(*a*) K B Madson   (*b*) Maslow
(*c*) Murray   (*d*) None of them

92. Motivated behaviour of a person is
(*a*) Well directed and well guided towards the goal
(*b*) Agitated until the goal is achieved
(*c*) Both of these
(*d*) None of these

93. Factors affecting motivations are
(*a*) Physiological factors only
(*b*) Psychological factors only
(*c*) Psycho-social factors
(*d*) All of these

94. Process of motivation is affected by all except
(*a*) Habits
(*b*) Mental sets and values
(*c*) Physical factors
(*d*) None of these

95. Which of the following does not come under the category of social motives?
(*a*) Prestige and Status
(*b*) Social approval
(*c*) Personal goal
(*d*) Money hoarding

96. Our action and behaviour is motivated by the desire for getting pleasure and avoiding pain. This is the opinion of
(*a*) Thomas Hobbes   (*b*) Descartes
(*c*) Kant   (*d*) John Locke

97. Fundamental instincts of humans are inherited rather than acquired. These instincts are the spring of human behaviour. The above opinion was held by
(*a*) Charles Darwin   (*b*) Mc Dougall
(*c*) Both of these   (*d*) None of these

98. Instinct theory of behaviour was rejected by psychologists on which of the following grounds?
(*a*) Adult behaviour is guided by experience and learning also. It is not always guided by instinct
(*b*) Human behaviour is affected by the cultural factors also

(c) Human being is a rational animal. He is not supposed to be directed by instincts only

(d) All of these

99. Central motive state was explained by

(a) Morgan

(b) Mc Dougall

(c) Murray

(d) None of them

100. Abraham Maslow was basically a

(a) Pragmatist   (b) Humanist

(c) Realist   (d) All of them

101. A self actualized person is one who

(a) Does not accept restrictions imposed by the society

(b) Always seeks perfection

(c) Is very good in inter personal relationship with others

(d) All of these

102. The theory of achievement motivation was developed by Mc Clelland of Harward University in

(a) 1949   (b) 1951

(c) 1965   (d) 1944

103. Achievement motive in a child can be developed by

(a) Proper guidance and high expectation from the child

(b) Telling the stories of great men to the child

(c) Setting a realistic goal for the child

(d) All of these

104. Which of the following is not a characteristic of learning?

(a) Learning is a relatively permanent change in behaviour

(b) Learning is a growth of the organism

(c) Learning is directly observed

(d) Learning is a goal directed process

105. In the beginning of life, the baby is guided by

(a) maturation

(b) instincts

(c) learning

(d) none of these

106. Accumulation of knowledge or facts becomes learning when

(a) It is applied in real life situation

(b) It is done by the learner himself

(c) It is provided by the teacher

(d) None of these

107. Dancing, driving, writing etc are the examples of

(a) Mechanical learning

(b) Perceptual motor learning

(c) Psychomotor learning

(d) both (b) and (c)

108. In Gagne's hierarchy, learning has been divided into

(a) eight parts   (b) nine parts

(c) seven parts   (d) none of the above

109. Match the following:

	(A)	**(B)**
(i)	Classical conditioning	1. Kohler
(ii)	Drive reduction	2. Hull
(iii)	Sign gestalt	3. Pavlov
(iv)	Learning by insight	4. Tolman

	(i)	(ii)	(iii)	(iv)
(a)	1	2	3	4
(b)	3	2	4	1
(c)	2	1	3	4
(d)	4	3	2	1

110. Reflexes are of two types according to Pavlov. They are physiological and

(a) Psychic   (b) Neural

(c) Mental   (d) None of these

111. In classical conditioning, extinction will take place when

(a) Organism is poor in generalization

(b) CS is given without UCS for a long time

(c) CS > UCS

(d) None of these

112. Backward conditioning will take place when

(a) UCS is presented prior to CS

(b) CS is presented prior to UCS

(c) Reward is not given to the organism

(d) None of these

113. When connection is not established between a CS and CR, due to any factor, that is called

(a) Spontaneous recovery

(b) Extinction

(c) Inhibition

(d) None of these

114. When a child responds to all women who wear black suit because of the black suit of her mother, it is the example of

(a) internal inhibition

(b) generalization

(c) assimilation

(d) all of these

115. Which of the following is not a behaviourist?

(a) Watson

(b) Skinner

(c) Pavlov

(d) Lewin

116. Learning according to Watson is

(a) the shifting of old responses to the new stimuli

(b) the result of connection between S-R formed in the brain

(c) both of these

(d) none of these

117. Which of the following points differentiates the theories of Watson and Guthrie?
    (a) law of contiguity
    (b) law of recency
    (c) generalization
    (d) law of frequency

118. In operant conditioning reward works as motives but in Guthrie's theory motives are
    (a) Stimuli given to the learner
    (b) Actions done by the learner
    (c) Both of these
    (d) None of these

119. We forget something not by disuse but by other learning. This is the theory of
    (a) contiguity
    (b) trial and error
    (c) learning by insight
    (d) perception

120. Which of the following is not an essential requirement for trial and error learning?
    (a) Drive
    (b) Barrier
    (c) Chance success
    (d) Selective movement of the organism

121. According to the law of trial and error, learning occurs when
    (a) it is satisfying for the learner
    (b) bond between S-R is strengthened by the repeated use
    (c) drive is there in the learner to act
    (d) all of these

122. Which of the following facilitates learning according to Thorndike?
    (a) Transfer of training
    (b) Mental set of the learner
    (c) Law of contiguity
    (d) All of these

123. In Hull's theory, for learning to occur, the S-R connection must be associated with the
    (a) cognitive field of the learner
    (b) diminution of the need
    (c) both of these
    (d) none of these

124. Reinforcement in Skinner's theory is similar to drive reduction in which theory
    (a) Hull's theory
    (b) Guthrie's theory
    (c) Lewin's theory
    (d) None of these

125. Which of the following theories is most quantitatively measurable?
    (a) Pavlov's
    (b) Skinner's
    (c) Hull's
    (d) None of these

126. In drive reduction theory, the effective stimulus in learning is the trace. It is formed
    (a) in the brain
    (b) by the bond of S-R
    (c) in the nervous system
    (d) none of these

127. In drive reduction theory, habit formation is a function of
    (a) stimulus potential
    (b) stimulus generalization
    (c) reaction potential
    (d) all of these

128. Hull may be considered superior to other S-R Theorists in the sense that he was able to measure
    (a) latency of response
    (b) reinforcement potential
    (c) both of these
    (d) none of these

129. Which of the following points differentiates Skinner from other S-R theorists?
    (a) His operant conditioning (type R learning)
    (b) His schedule of reinforcement
    (c) His way of shaping behaviour
    (d) All of these

130. Skinner's theory is more objective in nature than the others because
    (a) operant behaviour is external
    (b) reflexes never have zero strength
    (c) reinforcement is followed by responses
    (d) all of these

131. Aversive stimuli in operant conditioning means
    (a) individual will not do a particular act because of fear of such stimuli
    (b) individual will not do a particular act because of the disapproval from others
    (c) both of these
    (d) none of these

132. In Skinner's theory, reinforcement is given to the learner when
    (a) his response is 100% correct
    (b) his response is closer to the correct behaviour
    (c) both of these
    (d) none of these

133. Which of the following statements regarding S-R theories is not correct?
    (a) Man behaves like a machine
    (b) Behaviour is overt and can be objectively measured
    (c) Learning proceeds from simple to complex
    (d) Things are perceived in the context of figure ground *i.e.*, in relation to other things

134. Which of the following statements regarding field theories are correct?
    (a) Learning is not additive

(*b*) Molar approach of behaviour is followed here

(*c*) Interaction between organism and the environment is essential for learning

(*d*) All of these

135. Operant conditioning is different from respondent conditioning in which of the following points

(*a*) In OC reinforcement is given after the response is made

(*b*) In operant conditioning, behaviour is controlled by central nervous system

(*c*) A chain of responses is needed for shaping the behaviour (learning)

(*d*) All of these

136. Thorndike and Skinner do not differ at all in

(*a*) the law of effect

(*b*) law of readiness

(*c*) law of contiguity

(*d*) all of these

137. According to gestalt psychologists, behaviour can not be quantified because

(*a*) it is always changeable

(*b*) it is governed by the configuration produced in the mind

(*c*) it is rarely overt

(*d*) all of these

138. Law of pragnanz is the other name of the law of

(*a*) continuity

(*b*) closure

(*c*) contiguity

(*d*) none of these

139. How does the law of similarity work according to field theorists?

(*a*) Similar ideas and experiences get associated to form a whole

(*b*) Similar objects or experiences are easily learnt

(*c*) Both of these

(*d*) None of these

140. Learning by insight looks similar to some extent to which of the following theories?

(*a*) Need reduction theory

(*b*) R type of learning

(*c*) Trial and error theory

(*d*) None of the above

141. The other name of conditioned reflexes is

(*a*) psychic reflexes

(*b*) motor reflexes

(*c*) physiological reflexes

(*d*) none of the above

142. According to Renzuli, a gifted child is one

(*a*) Who possesses above average ability in almost every field

(*b*) Who is committed to task and highly motivated

(*c*) Who is definitely creative

(*d*) All of these

143. Gifted and talented children must be identified as early as possible because

(*a*) If their potentials are not developed by proper guidance of the teacher, it is a loss of the society

(*b*) They are likely to create problems for others, if they are not given work according to their ability

(*c*) Ordinary level of curriculum will not suit to these children

(*d*) All of these

144. Achievement test can be a good indicator of intellectual power if

(*a*) It is conducted immediately after the teaching is over

(*b*) A student shows good performance consistently on different achievement test

(*c*) Both of these

(*d*) None of these

145. Which of the following skills does not require high intellectual ability?

(*a*) Technical skills

(*b*) Mechanical skills

(*c*) Teaching skills

(*d*) Management skills

146. Cognitive abilities related to giftedness are all except

(*a*) High comprehensive and analytical abilities

(*b*) High level of verbal intelligence

(*c*) High retention power

(*d*) None of these

147. A superior child is advanced to a normal child by at least

(*a*) 2½ years

(*b*) Four years

(*c*) 1 years

(*d*) 1½ years

148. A gifted child is

(*a*) realistic in his approach

(*b*) highly interested in solving social problems

(*c*) more frequently chosen by his age mates and peers

(*d*) all of these

149. Which of the following enrichment programmes is suitable for gifted children in the school?

(*a*) Mathematics or Science Olympiad

(*b*) Challenging home assignments

(*c*) Map work during studies

(*d*) All of these

150. Which of the following does not come under the category of acceleration for gifted children?

(*a*) Skipping of classes

(*b*) Early admission

(*c*) Extra laboratory work

(*d*) Organizing summer camps

151. Under achievers are those who

(*a*) Score low on intelligence tests

(*b*) Achieve low in the class consistently despite their superior intelligence

(*c*) Are unable to correspond their achievement to the level of their innate abilities

(*d*) Both (*b*) and (*c*)

152. Which of the following conditions must be satisfied in order to designate a person mentally retarded?

(*a*) Sub-normal intellectual functioning

(*b*) Very poor adaptive ability

(*c*) Dependability on others

(*d*) All of these

153. The best measure of identifying mildly mentally retarded is

(*a*) Administration of standardized intelligence test

(*b*) Administration of behaviour test

(*c*) Administration of adjustment test

(*d*) A combination of all

154. Physical trauma during pregnancy may cause

(*a*) Mental retardation

(*b*) Blindness

(*c*) Deafness

(*d*) All of these

155. All of the following may cause mental retardation except

(*a*) Blood incompatibility

(*b*) Action of toxic agent

(*c*) Radio-activity

(*d*) None of these

156. Which of the following is an important postnatal cause of mental retardation?

(*a*) Brain injury

(*b*) Infection

(*c*) Severe malnutrition

(*d*) All of these

157. Dullers do not differ from normal children in

(*a*) Physical characteristics

(*b*) Level of social expectancy

(*c*) Both of these

(*d*) None of these

158. Which of the following things is not required for educating mildly mentally retarded children?

(*a*) Regular counseling

(*b*) Remedial teaching

(*c*) Modification in the curriculum

(*d*) Regular evaluation

159. Teaching of which of the following skills is not suitable to borderline cases?

(*a*) Electric fitting

(*b*) Repairing of electric or electronic equipments

(*c*) Oratory skills

(*d*) Activity based skills

160. IQ range of morons are in the range of

(*a*) 60-90   (*b*) 50-75

(*c*) 60-80   (*d*) 30-50

161. Morons are slow in

(*a*) Physical growth

(*b*) Thinking and planning

(*c*) Taking initiative

(*d*) All of these

162. Unsatisfactory relation of a mentally retarded child with the environment is technically called

(*a*) Autism

(*b*) Maladjustment

(*c*) Pseudo-dullness

(*d*) None of these

163. All of the following are characteristics of morons except

(*a*) They are restricted to unskilled or semi skilled occupations

(*b*) They are likely to be delinquent more easily

(*c*) They have stronger sex drives than the normals

(*d*) They are educable upto normal level but at a slower rate

164. Which of the following modifications in the curriculum is needed for morons?

(*a*) Activity based curriculum

(*b*) Skill dominated curriculum

(*c*) Emphasis on social training

(*d*) All of these

165. Which of the following things can not be taught to Imbeciles?

(*a*) Self help skills

(*b*) Unskilled job to be performed under supervision

(*c*) Writing skills

(*d*) Social skills

166. In which of the following cases divergent thinking is required?

(*a*) Attempting a multiple choice items

(*b*) Writing an essay

(*c*) Doing a research activity

(*d*) Both (*a*) and (*c*)

167. Which of the following tests is similar to Guilford's test of cognitive abilities?

(*a*) Word association test

(*b*) Things test

(*c*) Hidden shapes test

(*d*) None of these

168. In Hidden shapes test of creativity, which of the following things is used?

(*a*) Pictures

(*b*) Words

(*c*) Things

(*d*) None of them

169. A creative child in the class can not be satisfied unless

(*a*) He is given freedom to manipulate ideas or things

(*b*) He is allowed to ask questions in his own way

(*c*) Both of these

(*d*) None of these

170. A creative child is one who

(*a*) Is ideationally productive and unconventional

(*b*) Does not stick to social and religious norms in a hard manner

(*c*) Is all the time restless to do something uncommon and unique

(*d*) All of these

171. For the development of creative potential of a child, the teacher should

(*a*) Allow him to be critical to ideas and people

(*b*) Give them chance of problem solving

(*c*) Both of these

(*d*) None of these

172. New ideas (Eureka) suddenly comes in the minds of the creative children in the stage of

(*a*) Preparation

(*b*) Illumination

(*c*) Revision

(*d*) Incubation

173. The technique to foster creativity in children is

(*a*) Brain storming

(*b*) Problem solving

(*c*) Both of these

(*d*) None of these

174. A teacher can foster creativity in children by

(*a*) Developing confidence in them

(*b*) Giving them opportunity to express

(*c*) Both of these

(*d*) None of these

175. Learning disabled children are

(*a*) Deficient in using potentials

(*b*) Low in intelligence

(*c*) Slow in activity

(*d*) None of these

176. Learning disabled children perform very poorly in

(*a*) academic areas

(*b*) technical areas

(*c*) both of these

(*d*) none of these

177. Problem of learning disability is more complex than that of other disabilities because

(*a*) Its causes can not be easily ascertained by applying usual tests

(*b*) It is associated to behaviour problems

(*c*) Both of these

(*d*) None of these

178. Educationally, learning disabled look similar to

(*a*) dullers

(*b*) backward children

(*c*) both of these

(*d*) none of these

179. In which of the following physical characteristics learning disabled children differ from the normal ones?

(*a*) They are all the time clumsy and awkward

(*b*) Poor coordination of motor abilities

(*c*) Height, weight and health

(*d*) All of these

180. Which of the following methods is most suitable for learning disabled children?

(*a*) Behaviour guidance method

(*b*) Remedial teaching

(*c*) Brain storming

(*d*) None of them

181. In order to improve work habits of learning disabled what should be done?

(*a*) Unattending behaviour should be penalized

(*b*) Close monitoring of the behaviour is needed

(*c*) Cues and prompt should be given

(*d*) All of these

182. Those who are normal in intelligence but slow in academic achievement due to psycho-social reasons are called

(*a*) Backward children

(*b*) Gifted under achievers

(*c*) Both of these

(*d*) None of these

183. Consistent low achievement leads to low intelligence because

(*a*) 50% intellectual ability is expressed in verbal form

(*b*) Learning develops thinking and reasoning power

(*c*) Both of these

(*d*) None of these

184. Which of the following situations may lead to educational backwardness?

(*a*) Sensory impairment

(*b*) Motor disability

(*c*) Long diseases and health problems.

(*d*) All of these

185. Emotional disturbances may lead to educational backwardness because

(*a*) Proper emotional development is necessary for social interactions

(*b*) Emotions will develop intellectual power, *i.e.,* emotional intelligence (*c*) Both of these

(*d*) None of these

186. Which of the following factors will not lead to educational backwardness?

(*a*) Poor socio economic status of the family

(*b*) Poor educational environment of the school

(*c*) Occupation of the family

(*d*) Poor emotional climate of the family

187. Which of the following is an important cause of educational backwardness at primary level of education in India?

(*a*) Poor school organisation

(*b*) Lack of accountability

(*c*) Attitude of the masses towards education

(*d*) All of these

188. Which of the following measures should be adopted by the teacher to check educational backwardness?

(*a*) Continuous evaluation and regular feedback

(*b*) Remedial teaching

(*c*) Adjustment and behaviour training

(*d*) All of these

189. Teaching by small steps and frequent short assignment techniques are useful for

(*a*) Slow learners

(*b*) Learning disabled

(*c*) Educationally backward children

(*d*) Children of all types of disabilities

190. Special schools are required for backward children when

(*a*) Backwardness is due to any serious physical handicap

(*b*) The size of population of backward children in the society is very large as is the case of Gujarat where the achievement of students in mathematics is always seen very low

(*c*) Both of these

(*d*) None of these

191. Which of the following should be considered the most important quality of a teacher at primary level?

(*a*) Patience and perseverance

(*b*) Competence in methods of teaching and knowledge of subjects

(*c*) Competence to teach in highly standardised language

(*d*) Eagerness to teach

192. A teacher, because of his/her democratic nature, allows students to sit all over the class. Some sit together and discuss or do group reading. Some sit quietly and read themselves. A parent does not like it. Which of the following may be the best way to handle the situation?

(*a*) Parents should request the principal to change the section of their ward

(*b*) Parents should show trust in the teacher and discuss the problem with the teacher

(*c*) Parents should take away the child from that school

(*d*) Parents should complain against the teacher to the principal

193. The stage in which a child begins to think logically about objects and events is known as

(*a*) Formal operational stage

(*b*) Pre-operational stage

(*c*) Concrete operational stage

(*d*) Sensori-motor stage

194. 'Mind mapping' refers to

(*a*) a plan of action for an adventure

(*b*) drawing the picture of a mind

(*c*) researching the functioning of the mind

(*d*) a technique to enhance comprehension

195. The best way, specially at primary level, to address the learning difficulties of students is to use

(*a*) expensive and glossy support material

(*b*) easy and interesting textbooks

(*c*) story-telling method

(*d*) a variety of teaching methods suited to the disability

196. Which of the following will foster creativity among learners?

(*a*) Providing opportunities to question and to nurture the innate talents of every learner

(*b*) Emphasizing achievement goals from the beginning of school life

(*c*) Coaching students for good marks in examination

(*d*) Teaching the students the practical value of good education

197. According to Piaget, at which of the following stages does a child begin to think logically about abstract propositions?

(*a*) Formal operational stage (11 years and up)

(*b*) Sensori-motor stage (Birth–02 years)

(*c*) Pre-operational stage (02–07 years)

(*d*) Concrete operational stage (07–11 years)

198. Learning can be enriched if

(*a*) more and more teaching aids are used in the class

(*b*) teachers use different types of lectures and explanation

(*c*) due attention is paid to periodic tests in the class

(*d*) situations from the real world are brought into the class in which students interact with each other and the teahcer facilitates

199. Which of the following statements ***cannot*** be considered as a feature of the process of learning?

(*a*) Learning is a comprehensive process

(*b*) Learning is goal-oriented

(*c*) Unlearning is also a learning process

(*d*) Educational institutions are the only place where learning takes place

200. A student of V-grade with 'visual deficiency' should be
   (*a*) helped with his/her routine-work by parents and friends
   (*b*) treated normally in the classroom and provided support through Audio CDs
   (*c*) given special treatment in the classroom
   (*d*) excused to do a lower level of work

201. Which of the following is *not* related to the socio-psychological needs of the child?
   (*a*) Need for emotional security
   (*b*) Regular elimination of waste products from the body
   (*c*) Need for company
   (*d*) Need for appreciation or social approval

202. Which is the place where the child's 'cognitive' development is defined in the best way?
   (*a*) School and classroom environment
   (*b*) Auditorium
   (*c*) Home
   (*d*) Playground

203. .... is considered a sign of motivated teaching.
   (*a*) Remedial work given by the teacher
   (*b*) Questioning by students
   (*c*) Pin drop silence in the class
   (*d*) Maximum attendance in the class

204. Which of the following is *not* a sign of an intelligent young child?
   (*a*) One who has the ability to communicate fluently and appropriately
   (*b*) One who carries on thinking in an abstract manner
   (*c*) One who can adjust oneself in a new environment
   (*d*) One who has the ability to cram long essays very quickly

205. "Children actively construct their understanding of the world" is a statement attributed to
   (*a*) Pavlov   (*b*) Kohlberg
   (*c*) Skinner   (*d*) Piaget

206. Kritika who does *not* talk much at home, talks a lot at school. It shows that
   (*a*) teachers demand that children should talk a lot at school
   (*b*) she does not like her home at all
   (*c*) her thoughts get acknowledged at school
   (*d*) the school provides opportunities to children to talk a lot

207. A teacher should make an attempt to understand the potentialities of her/his students. Which of the following fields is related to this objective?
   (*a*) Social Philosophy
   (*b*) Media – Psychology
   (*c*) Educational Psychology
   (*d*) Educational Sociology

208. Motivation, in the process of learning,
   (*a*) differentiates new learning from old learning
   (*b*) makes learners think unidirectionally
   (*c*) creates interest for learning among young learners
   (*d*) sharpens the memory of learners

209. The term 'curriculum' in the field of education refers to
   (*a*) overall programme of the school which students experience on a day-to-day basis
   (*b*) evaluation process
   (*c*) text-material to be used in the class
   (*d*) methods of teaching and the content to be taught

210. At lower classes, play-way method of teaching is based on
   (*a*) principles of methods of teaching
   (*b*) psychological principles of development and growth
   (*c*) sociological principles of teaching
   (*d*) theory of physical education programmes

211. "A young child responds to a new situation on the basis of the response made by him/her in a similar situation as in the past." This is related to
   (*a*) 'Law of Effect' of learning
   (*b*) 'Law of Attitude' of learning process
   (*c*) 'Law of Readiness' of learning
   (*d*) 'Law of Analogy' of learning

212. .... is *not* considered a sign of 'being gifted'.
   (*a*) Fighting with others
   (*b*) Novelty in expression
   (*c*) Curiosity
   (*d*) Creative ideas

213. Education of children with special needs should be provided
   (*a*) by methods developed for special children in special schools
   (*b*) in special schools
   (*c*) by special teachers in special schools
   (*d*) along with other normal children

214. To make assessment a 'useful and interesting' process, one should be careful about
   (*a*) labelling students as intelligent or average learners
   (*b*) using a variety of ways to collect information about the student's learning across the scholastic and co-scholastic boundaries
   (*c*) using technical language to give feedback
   (*d*) making comparisons between different students

215. 'Dyslexia' is associated with
   (*a*) Mathematical disorder

(*b*) Reading disorder

(*c*) Behavioural disorder

(*d*) Mental disorder

216. Parents should play a .... role in the learning process of young children.

(*a*) proactive

(*b*) sympathetic

(*c*) neutral

(*d*) negative

217. "Development is a never ending process." This idea is associated with

(*a*) Principle of continuity

(*b*) Principle of integration

(*c*) Principle of interaction

(*d*) Principle of interrelation

218. The 'insight theory of learning' is promoted by

(*a*) Pavlov

(*b*) Jean Piaget

(*c*) Vygotsky

(*d*) 'Gestalt' theorists

219. In which of the following stages do children become active members of their peer group?

(*a*) Adulthood

(*b*) Early childhood

(*c*) Childhood

(*d*) Adolescence

220. Four distinct stages of children's intellectual development are identified by

(*a*) Erikson   (*b*) Skinner

(*c*) Piaget   (*d*) Kohlberg

CHILD DEVELOPMENT & PEDAGOGY

ANSWERS

1	2	3	4	5	6	7	8	9	10
(*a*)	(*a*)	(*b*)	(*d*)	(*c*)	(*d*)	(*a*)	(*c*)	(*d*)	(*c*)
11	12	13	14	15	16	17	18	19	20
(*a*)	(*c*)	(*b*)	(*a*)	(*b*)	(*b*)	(*a*)	(*b*)	(*a*)	(*c*)
21	22	23	24	25	26	27	28	29	30
(*a*)	(*b*)	(*a*)	(*d*)	(*c*)	(*d*)	(*b*)	(*c*)	(*c*)	(*a*)
31	32	33	34	35	36	37	38	39	40
(*d*)	(*d*)	(*c*)	(*d*)	(*a*)	(*d*)	(*b*)	(*d*)	(*a*)	(*d*)
41	42	43	44	45	46	47	48	49	50
(*c*)	(*d*)	(*a*)	(*c*)	(*d*)	(*a*)	(*c*)	(*d*)	(*d*)	(*b*)
51	52	53	54	55	56	57	58	59	60
(*d*)	(*b*)	(*d*)	(*c*)	(*a*)	(*d*)	(*d*)	(*c*)	(*a*)	(*a*)
61	62	63	64	65	66	67	68	69	70
(*a*)	(*a*)	(*c*)	(*b*)	(*a*)	(*a*)	(*c*)	(*a*)	(*d*)	(*d*)
71	72	73	74	75	76	77	78	79	80
(*b*)	(*a*)	(*c*)	(*d*)	(*a*)	(*d*)	(*a*)	(*c*)	(*c*)	(*a*)
81	82	83	84	85	86	87	88	89	90
(*c*)	(*d*)	(*b*)	(*b*)	(*b*)	(*d*)	(*d*)	(*d*)	(*c*)	(*a*)
91	92	93	94	95	96	97	98	99	100
(*a*)	(*c*)	(*d*)	(*d*)	(*c*)	(*a*)	(*c*)	(*d*)	(*a*)	(*b*)
101	102	103	104	105	106	107	108	109	110
(*d*)	(*b*)	(*d*)	(*c*)	(*b*)	(*a*)	(*d*)	(*a*)	(*b*)	(*a*)
111	112	113	114	115	116	117	118	119	120
(*b*)	(*a*)	(*c*)	(*b*)	(*d*)	(*c*)	(*d*)	(*a*)	(*a*)	(*d*)
121	122	123	124	125	126	127	128	129	130
(*d*)	(*d*)	(*b*)	(*a*)	(*c*)	(*c*)	(*a*)	(*a*)	(*d*)	(*a*)
131	132	133	134	135	136	137	138	139	140
(*a*)	(*c*)	(*d*)	(*d*)	(*d*)	(*a*)	(*b*)	(*b*)	(*a*)	(*c*)
141	142	143	144	145	146	147	148	149	150
(*a*)	(*d*)	(*d*)	(*c*)	(*a*)	(*d*)	(*a*)	(*d*)	(*d*)	(*c*)
151	152	153	154	155	156	157	158	159	160
(*d*)	(*d*)	(*d*)	(*d*)	(*d*)	(*d*)	(*c*)	(*c*)	(*c*)	(*b*)

161	162	163	164	165	166	167	168	169	170
(d)	(a)	(d)	(d)	(d)	(d)	(b)	(a)	(c)	(a)
171	172	173	174	175	176	177	178	179	180
(c)	(b)	(c)	(c)	(d)	(a)	(a)	(b)	(b)	(a)
181	182	183	184	185	186	187	188	189	190
(d)	(a)	(c)	(d)	(c)	(c)	(d)	(d)	(d)	(c)
191	192	193	194	195	196	197	198	199	200
(a)	(b)	(c)	(c)	(d)	(a)	(d)	(d)	(d)	(b)
201	202	203	204	205	206	207	208	209	210
(b)	(a)	(b)	(d)	(d)	(c)	(c)	(c)	(a)	(b)
211	212	213	214	215	216	217	218	219	220
(a)	(a)	(d)	(b)	(b)	(a)	(a)	(d)	(d)	(c)

———————

GLOSSARY

Accommodation : Piaget used this term for modification or reorganisation of existing cognitive structure (schemata) to deal with environmental demands. Accommodation is the adjustment the individual makes when incorporating external reality. Piaget uses this concept in conjunction with assimilation, which is the individual's response to the immediate and compelling environmental demands that have been and are being assimilated.

Advance organisers : Introductory information intended to facilitate a student's learning by providing a framework and organisation for the material to be learned.

Affective domain : One of the categories of educational objectives for students attitudes, values and emotional growth. The affective domain includes five basic categories: receiving, responding, valuing, organisation and characterisation by a value.

Assimilation : Assimilation is the process of taking within or internalising, one's environmental experience. The term is used by Piaget for the process of making sense of experiences and perceptions by fitting them into previously established cognitive structure (schemata). Assimilation is used by Piaget in conjunction with the concept of accommodation. Piaget believes that assimilation is a spontaneous process on the part of the child.

Attitudes : A learned predisposition to respond either positively or negatively to persons, situations, or things. Attitudes carry a strong emotional component and therefore can never be neutral.

Attribution theory : The term attribution refers to the explanation a person gives for his or her own or another person's actions or beliefs. An attribution based on internal factors is called a dispositional attribution, and one based on external factors is called a situational attribution.

Behaviourism : A school of thought in Psychology usually considered to have originated in the work and writings of John B. Watson in 1913. Watson argued against the use of introspection in gathering psychological data. He considered observable behaviour the only valid data in Psychology. According to Watson, any concepts, like mind or consciousness, that have mentalistic overtones must be purged from the field of psychology. The most famous current representative of this tradition is Harvard University's B.F. Skinner.

Classical conditioning : A procedure in which the conditioned stimulus after being paired with the unconditioned stimulus often enough, can then be substituted for it. It is often called "stimulus substitution."

Cognition : The process of faculties by which knowledge is acquired and manipulated (*e.g.*, thinking or remembering).

Cognitive domain : A part of Bloom's Taxonomy of educational objectives. Bloom divided the objectives in the cognitive domain into six categories: knowledge, comprehension, application, analysis, synthesis and evaluation.

Cognitive style : The consistent way in which an individual responds to a wide range of perceptual tasks.

Computer-assisted instruction (CAI) : The use of a computer as tutor to present information, give students opportunities to practice what they learn, evaluate student achievement, and provide additional instruction.

Concept learning : The acquisition of pattern-recognition knowledge involving the learning of a rule or rules for classifying a number of objects into mutually exclusive categories based on one or more salient characteristics of the objects.

Conditioned response : A response elicited by a conditioned stimulus. The response is similar but not identical to its associated unconditioned response.

Cognitive learning : The view that learning is based on a restructuring of perceptions and thoughts occurring within the organism is called cognitive learning. This restructuring allows the learner to perceive new relationships, solve new problems and gain understanding of a subject area. Cognitive learning theorists stress the reorganisation of one's perceptions in order to achieve understanding, as opposed to the behaviourist theorists, who stress the importance of associations formed between stimuli and responses.

Conditioned response : The term is used both in classical conditioning, and in operant conditioning. In classical conditioning, the conditioned response is the response being elicited by the conditioned stimulus. The stronger the conditioning, the greater the magnitude of the conditioned response and the shorter its latency. In Pavlov's experiment the conditioned response was the dog's salivation to the tone.

In operant conditioning, since the response must precede the reinforcer, the conditioned response is defined not in terms of magnitude or latency, but in terms of either the rate of response or its resistance to extinction. For example, a strongly conditioned operant will occur for more rapidly than one that has been only weakly conditioned. Also, a strongly conditioned operant will be far more difficult to extinguish.

Conditioned stimulus : In classical conditioning, the previously neutral stimulus takes on the power to elicit the response through association with an unconditioned stimulus. For this to occur, the conditioned stimulus must precede the unconditioned stimulus on enough occasions to cause the conditioned stimulus to serve as a signal that the unconditioned stimulus will follow. In Pavlov's experiment on conditioning the dog, the tone was used as the conditioned stimulus. The tone was consistently followed by the meat powder, until the dog began salivating to the tone alone.

Conditioning : Process of learning whereby stimuli and responses become associated through training. There are two general types of conditioning, classical and operant. In classical conditioning a conditioned stimulus is presented, followed by an unconditioned stimulus. Conditioning is exhibited when the organism learns to respond to the conditioned stimulus alone. In operant conditioning the operant is allowed to occur and then is followed by a reinforcing stimulus. Operant conditioning is exhibited when the rate of responding increases over the original, preconditioned rate.

Convergent thinking : A term used by Guilford to describe the type of thinking in which an individual produces a single response to a specific question or problem.

Creativity : The capacity of individuals to produce novel or original answers or products.

Culture : The ways in which a group of people think, feel, and react in order to solve problems of living in their environment.

Cumulative records : A file on a student that includes such information as family data, health, academic grades, standardized test scores, attendance and teacher comments.

Discovery learning : Term is used to describe a form of learning that results not from rote memorisation or conditioning but from the active exploration of alternatives on the part of the learner. This learning is largely a result of learner's own efforts. Learning attained through discovery is more meaningful and long-lasting than that from memorisation.

Divergent thinking : A term used by Guilford to describe the type of thinking wherein an individual produces multiple responses or solutions (often non-traditional) to a single question or problem. Divergent thinking is associated with creativity.

Egocentrism : Piaget's term for describing children in the preperational stage, who have difficulty in assuming the point of view of others.

Enactive : Bruner's first stage of cognitive development, in which children understand the environment through physical action on that environment.

Encoding : The short-term memory process of transforming incoming information into episodic or semantic form and associating it with old knowledge for storage in long-term memory.

Entry behaviour : The knowledge, skills, or attitudes that a learner brings into a new learning situation.

Formal-operations stage : This is a stage of cognitive development according to Jean Piaget, occurring during early adolescence. The period of formal operations (eleven to sixteen years) is the last of Piaget's stages and is characterised by the youth's ability to develop full, formal patterns of thinking based on abstract symbolism. The youth is able to reason things out logically at the abstract level, develop symbolic meanings, and generalize to other situations. This is the highest level of thinking and according to Piaget, must await the maturation of certain structures in the brain for its full development.

Equilibration : A motivation principle in Piaget's theory that identifies human beings as active and exploratory in attempting to impose order and meaningfulness on experiences. This order or balance occurs through the processes of assimilation and accommodation.

Evaluation : This is a process of obtaining information to form judgments so that educational decisions can be made.

External locus of control : A feeling that one has little control over one's and the failure to perceive a cause-and-effect relationship between actions and consequences.

Extrinsic motivation : Motivation influenced by external events such as grades, marks or money.

Gestalt psychology : A school of thought maintaining that the organised whole, configuration, or totality of psychological experience should be the proper object of study. Founded in Germany by Max Wertheimer in the early 1900s, gestalt psychology's first interest was in the field of perception. Later, under Wolfgang Kohler's direction, studies were done in the area of learning, and under Kurt Lewin's direction, in the area of motivation. Gestalt psychologists tend to emphasize cognitive processes in the study of learning. They stress that true understanding occurs only through the reorganisation of ideas and perceptions, not through memorisation or conditioning.

Information processing : Theory of learning and remembering that is based on the computer as a model. Information is seen as following into and within the organism. The sense organs respond to incoming information, and it is passed along and encoded in the memory and nervous system. The encoded information may then be stored and processed and finally retrieved and acted on. As with the computer, there is information input, storage and/or processing, and output.

Insight : A suddenly realised solution to a problem, sometimes called the ''a-ha! phenomenon''. Introduced by Wolfgang Kohler, the concept of insight is used to explain the apparently spontaneous appearance of a solution to a problem. Insight results from the reorganisation of ideas and perceptions rather than from simple trial-and-error behaviour. The concept of insight is used typically by gestalt psychologists.

Inquiry learning : A process that is similar to discovery learning. Students learn strategies to manipulate and process information, test hypothesis and apply their conclusions to new content or situations.

Intelligence : The capacity, or a set of capacities that allows an individual to learn, solve problems, and/or interact successfully with his or her environment. As hypothetical construct, intelligence has come to mean higher-level thought processes, or intellectual abilities. Statistical studies of intelligence utilise the concept of measured intelligence, which is the score received on a standardised intelligence test.

Intelligence Quotient (IQ) : Originally, a measure of intelligence calculated by dividing a student's mental age (MA) by the chronological age (CA) and multiplying by 100, that is, $IQ = MA/CA \times 100$. This is called the ratio method of obtaining an IQ.

More recently, IQ has been computed by the deviation method. One's deviation IQ is defined by one's relative standing among peers. The deviation IQ is computed on the basis of how far one's score deviates from the mean score obtained for the entire group of individuals of the same chronological age. This technique is based on the standard, or z-score concept and assumes a normal distribution for each age group.

Law of effect : This is one of E.L. Thorndike's main laws of learning. It states that when an association between a stimulus and response is followed by a satisfying state of affairs, the association (or connection) is strengthened. When the association is followed by an annoying state of affairs, it is weakened. In brief, reward strengthens and punishment weakens any connection between stimuli and responses. In a later version of the law, Thorndike soft-pedaled the importance of punishment of a weakening agent. Thorndike's law of effect is considered by many psychologists to be the cornerstone on which B.F. Skinner built his system of operant conditioning.

Law of exercise : One of E.L. Thorndike's three main laws of learning. It states that the more frequently a stimulus response connection occurs, the stronger the resulting association and hence, the stronger the learning. The repetition of a learned response strengthens the bond between stimulus situation and the response. The law was later amended to incorporate the importance of the consequences of the action; thus, practice without knowledge of results is not nearly as effective as when the consequences become known to the learner.

Law of readiness : One of E.L. Thorndike's three main laws of learning. It states that learning occurs when the student is mentally ready to learn. The reference here is to momentary readiness rather than maturational readiness.

Learning : Learning is a very general term refering to a process that leads to a relatively permanent change in behaviour resulting from experience. Thus, such activities as acquiring physical skills, memorizing poems, acquiring attitudes, etc., are all examples of learning. Learning may be conscious or unconscious, adaptive or maladaptive, overt or covert. Although the learning process is typically measured on the basis of a change in performance, most psychologists agree that an accompanying change occurs within the nervous system. Though there are a great many theories and explanations concerning learning, there is general agreement regarding its definition.

Locus of control : The concept identifies the type of personal control used by an individual. When the locus of control is internal, individual views himself as personally in charge of his own destinies. When the locus of control is external, the person feels he is at the mercy of external circumstances.

Long-term memory (LTM) : In the information-processing system, LTM is the second of the two main storage systems. Information that is in short-term memory may, under certain conditions, be passed along for processing and consolidation into a more permanent storage site, long-term memory. Long-term memory has the potential for holding encoded information for long periods.

Mental age : Term first used by Alfred Binet as the unit for measuring intelligence. Binet defined mental age in terms of the age at which a given number of test items are passed by an average child. If, for example, the average six-year-old could correctly answer a certain number of items, then any other child correctly answering the same number of items would be assigned at least a mental age of six.

Motivation : A general psychological term used to explain behaviour initiated by needs and directed towards a goal. Motives may be biogenic (that is stemming from tissue needs within the organism) or acquired (that is, learned through interaction with the environment, especially the social environment).

Among learning theorists, Jerome Bruner makes much of the principle of motivation, assuming that almost all children have a built-in "will to learn".

Nature-nurture controversy : Debate over which component, nature (heredity) or nurture (environment), is more influential in determining behaviour. In Psychology the behaviourists consistently argued on behalf of nurture, and the intelligence testers favoured nature. Educational Psychology has long been the battleground on which this issue has been fought, since the psychologists primarily concerned with this issue were the learning theorists (largely behaviourists).

Need hierarchy : Theory proposed by Abraham Maslow that suggests that human beings place their needs on the following universal, order-of-importance scale: (*i*) physiological needs, (*ii*) safety needs, (*iii*) love needs, (*iv*) esteem needs, and (*v*) self-actualising needs.

Needs : The part of the motivational cycle seen as deficits that lie within the individual. These may be physiological (*e.g.*, the needs for food) or psychological (*e.g.*, the need for approval).

Non-verbal behaviour : Body language. Based largely on the theroy of Charles Galloway and some research by Robert Rosenthal, the teacher's non-verbal behaviour represents an important avenue for the transmission of teacher expectations. Galloway has shown how non-verbal behaviour can promote or reduce student learning. Rosenthal has shown how his test (Profile of Non-verbal Sensitivity) can identify the channels for communicating how teachers really feel about their students.

Operants : Responses, according to B.F. Skinner, for which the original stimuli are either unidentified or non-existent are called operants. The consequences of operant behaviour can be observed even though the stimulus is not known. For example, if a rat presses the lever in a Skinner box and this results in reinforcement, an increase in operant rate will be observed despite the fact that no stimulus could be identified as initiating the original stimulus could be identified as initiating the original lever pressing. In operant conditioning, reinforcement is contingent on the operant's first being emitted. The organism must in some way "operate" on the environment in order that the reinforcement will follow. Operant responding at one time was called instrumental responding by some psychologists.

Operant conditioning : A type of learning that involves an increase in the probability that a response will occur as a function of reinforcement. This is a forn of conditioning, described by B.F. Skinner, in which the free operant is allowed to occur and is followed by a reinforcing stimulus that is, in turn, followed by an increased likelihood of the operant's occurring again. For optimum conditioning the reinforcing stimulus should follow the operant immediately. The rate of responding for a conditioned operant may jump dramatically over the preconditioned rate (operant level).

Operant level : The original, or preconditioned, rate of operant responding before any reinforcing stimuli have been introduced. If a rat happens to press the lever in a Skinner box four times an hour (without being reinforced), the operant level for that response is established at four per hour. Thus, the operant level is the rate at which the free operant is typically emitted prior to conditioning.

Positive reinforcement : A procedure that maintains or increases the rate of a response by presenting a stimulus (a positive reinforcer) following the response.

Preoperational stage : The second stage in Piaget's theory of cognitive development, in which the lack of logical operations forces children to make decisions bases on their perceptions.

Primary reinforcement : The process of using a stimulus that is reinforcing in the absence of any learning. Such stimuli as food and water are primary reinforcers.

Programmed instruction (PI) : PI is an arrangement of instructional material in a step-by-step sequence designed to lead the student to a specified goal. The material being presented is broken down into small steps called frames. There are two general approaches to programming: (*i*) linear programmes, in which all students go through the entire programme and the frames gradually increase in difficulty, and (*ii*) branched programmes, in which the student skips forward or backward in the programme (the order of the frame presentation varies) as a result of the success or failure experienced in responding.

PI can be in book form, or it can be presented through the use of a teaching machine and/or computer. The concept of programmed instruction is credited to B.F. Skinner.

Psychoanalytic theory : This reveals the theory/ method of studying and treating mental illness presented by Sigmund Freud. The theory attempts to give a rational explanation for irrational thoughts and responses. Psychoanalytic theory states (*i*) that all behaviour is determined by specific motives; (*ii*) that most human motives lie at the unconscious level, and therefore people are unaware of the reasons for most of their own behaviour; (*iii*) that neurotic symptoms result from an individual's inner conflicts; and (*iv*) that inner conflicts are a product of childhood trauma and anxiety. The technique is based on the therapist's revealing to the patient the source of his or her anxiety and helping the patient achieve insight and emotional release.

Puberty : The biological changes that lead to reproductive maturity. Its onset is identified by such factors as the growth of body hair, voice changes in males, and menstruation and breast development in females.

Punishment : A method for controlling behaviour through the use of aversive stimulation. In other words, punishment is a procedure in which an aversive stimulus is presented immediately following a response, resulting in a reduction in the rate of response. Punishment, though not itself causing the extinction of a conditioned response, does severely reduce the rate of responding while the punishment is in force. Punishment should not be confused with negative reinforcement.

Reinforcement : Any stimulus that increases the likelihood of a response's recurring. Reinforcement, as a Skinnerian concept, should not be confused with reward, feelings of pleasure, or any other concept with subjective of mentalistic overtones. Reinforcement may be used in either classical (respondent) or operant conditioning. In respondent condition the unconditioned stimulus serves as the reinforcement. In operant conditioning the presentation of any stimulus following the emitted response can be considered a reinforcement if it results in a higher response rate.

Schemata : Cognitive structures created through the abstraction of previous experience. Schemata function in the comprehension and recall of data and can aid learning or be responsible for many types distortion in recall.

Secondary reinforcement : A process that uses a stimulus that is not originally reinforcing but that acquires reinforcing properties when paired with a primary reinforcer. Money is a secondary reinforcer.

Self-actualization : Maslow's term for the psychological need to develop one's capabilities and potential in order to enhance personal growth. It refer to a person's constant striving to realise the potential within and to develop inherent talents and capabilities.

Self-concept : The total organisation of the perceptions individuals have of themselves.

Self-esteem : The value, or judgement, individuals place on their behaviour. Self-esteem and self-concept are often used interchangeably in educational literature.

Self-reinforcement : A procedure in which individuals reinforce their own behaviour.

Sensitive period : This is a time period when an organism is susceptible to a change in behaviour due to certain kinds of environmental stimulation. The sensitive periods typically occur early in the organism's life and tend to produce behaviour changes that are relatively long-lasting. The process of mother-infant bounding is said to occur only during the baby's first three days of life.

Short-term memory (STM) : In the information processing system, STM is the first of two main storage systems. Sometimes it is called working or active memory. Estimates of how long information may be retained in short-term memory vary from about twenty seconds to over a minute.

Social facilitation : The concept from the field of social psychology is used to explain the fact that in some circumstances individuals perform more quickly when in a group situation than when alone. Social facilitation is most pronounced in the case of fairly simple mechanical tasks. The more difficult and the more intellectual the task, the less the effect of social facilitation.

Social learning theory : Theory, proposed by Albert Bandura, suggests that a large part of what a person learns occurs through imitation or modelling. Bandura's major concern is with learning that takes place in the context of a social situation in which individuals come to modify behaviour as a result of how others in the group respond. Social learning does not require primary reinforcement.

Stimulus-response : A theory that stresses the importance of the build up of stimulus response associations in defining learning. Most behaviourists adhere to stimulus response learning theories, the major exception being E.C. Tolman. The leading stimulus response theorists are E.L. Thorndike, Ivan Pavlov, J.B. Watson, Edwin Guthrie, C.L. Hull, and B.F. Skinner. Stimulus response theorists stress the importance of nurture in the nature-nurture debate. Most theories of learning during the first half of the twentieth century were stimulus response theories. The cognitive-gestalt position, however, was not based on a stimulus-response theory.

Stimulus variety : Variation, at all sensroy modes, of stimulus inputs. Stimulus variety was seen by many early-experience theorists as the crucial ingredient in intellectual development. The more the child hears, sees, and touches, the more he or she will want to hear, see, and touch and the more intellectual growth will occur.

Teaching machine : A device used to present an instructional programme one step (or frame) at a time. The student either writes in answers or presses a button corresponding to the correct alternative. The advantages of the teaching machine are that (*i*) the student can proceed at his or her own pace; (*ii*) the student receives immediate feedback; (*iii*) for many students the machines are intrinsically motivating.

Unconditioned response : An unconditioned response is any response that can be elicited automatically by the presentation of a certain stimulus, without any training or learning. The term is used in classical conditioning and in Ivan Pavlov's original experiment the unconditioned response was salivation to the stimulus of meat powder being placed in the dog's mouth.

Unconditioned stimulus : Any stimulus that will elicit a given response automatically, without any training or learning. The term is used in classical conditioning and in the case of Ivan Pavlov's own experiment, the unconditioned stimulus was meat powder placed in the dog's mouth.

व्याकरण

व्याकरण वह शास्त्र है जिसके द्वारा किसी भी भाषा के शब्दों और वाक्यों के शुद्ध स्वरूपों एवं शुद्ध प्रयोगों का ज्ञान कराया जाता है।

व्याकरण के चार अंग हैं : (i) वर्ण विचार (ii) शब्द विचार (iii) पद विचार और (iv) वाक्य विचार

भाषा : भाषा अभिव्यक्ति का एक ऐसा साधन है जिसके द्वारा मनुष्य अपने विचारों को दूसरों पर प्रकट कर सकता है और दूसरों के विचार जान सकता है। भाषा के दो रूप हैं–(i) मौखिक और (ii) लिखित।

बोली : भाषा का क्षेत्रीय रूप बोली कहलाता है।

लिपि : किसी भी भाषा के लिखने की विधि को लिपि कहते हैं।

वर्ण : हिन्दी भाषा में प्रयुक्त सबसे छोटी ध्वनि वर्ण कहलाती है। जैसे–अ, आ, ई, क्, ख्, आदि

वर्णमाला : वर्णों के समुदाय को वर्णमाला कहते हैं। हिन्दी वर्णमाला में 44 वर्ण हैं। जिनमें 11 स्वर तथा 33 व्यंजन हैं।

स्वरवर्ण : उन वर्णों को कहते हैं, जिनका उच्चारण बिना किसी दूसरे वर्ण की सहायता से होता है। हिन्दी में 11 स्वर हैं–अ, आ, इ, ई, उ, ऊ, ए, ऐ, ओ, औ, ऋ।

व्यंजन वर्ण : उन वर्णों को कहते हैं, जिनका उच्चारण स्वर वर्णों की सहायता के बिना नहीं हो सकता है। इनकी संख्या 33 है–

क ख ग घ ङ च छ ज झ ञ ट ठ

ड ढ ण त थ द ध न प फ ब भ

म य र ल व श ष स ह।

वर्ण : एक या अधिक वर्णों से बनी हुई स्वतन्त्र सार्थक ध्वनि शब्द कहलाती है।

शब्दों को तत्सम, तद्भव, देशज और विदेशी भागों में बाँटा जाता है।

तत्सम : जो शब्द संस्कृत भाषा से हिन्दी में बिना किसी परिवर्तन के लिए जाते हैं वे तत्सम कहलाते हैं, जैसे– अग्नि, क्षेत्र, मित्र, नासिका आदि।

तद्भव : उन शब्दों को कहते हैं, जो संस्कृत से ही लिए गए हैं, परन्तु हिन्दी में आने पर जिनका रूप बदल गया है। जैसे–आग, खेत, रात आदि।

देशज : उन शब्दों को कहते हैं, जो बोलचाल तथा देश की अन्य भाषाओं से लिए गए हैं। जैसे–कटोरा, झंझत, डिबिया, लोटा आदि।

विदेशज या विदेशी : उन शब्दों को कहते हैं, जो किसी विदेशी भाषा से आए हैं। जैसे–स्कूल, कार, कमरा, खुदा, जोश, सरकार आदि।

शब्द सम्पदा

तत्सम शब्दों के तद्भव रूप

तत्सम	तद्भव	तत्सम	तद्भव	तत्सम	तद्भव	तत्सम	तद्भव
अग्नि	आग	अद्य	आज	पाद	पाँव	हस्त	हाथ
अष्ट	आठ	अक्षि	आँख	नासिका	नाक	कंटक	काँटा
अर्ध	आधा	अस्थि	हड्डी	दश	दस	दधि	दही
अश्रु	आँसू	आम्र	आम	दीप	दीया	निद्रा	नींद
ग्राम	गाँव	गर्दभ	गधा	नव	नौ	पत्र	पत्ता
गृध्र	गीध	गौर	गोरा	प्रस्तर	पत्थर	जिह्वा	जीभ
गृह	घर	घट	घड़ा	हस्ती	हाथी	दन्त	दाँत
धातु	धात	धृत	घी	क्षेत्र	खेत	नृत्य	नाच
लक्ष	लाख	सप्त	सात	सूचिका	सूई	स्वर्णकार	सुनार
त्वम्	तुम	दुग्ध	दूध	लोक	लोग	पर्यङ्क	पलंग
रत्न	रतन	वर्ष	बरस	स्वप्न	सपना	कातर	कायर
भक्त	भगत	मर्कट	बन्दर	पुत्र	पूत	मानव	मनुष्य
रात्रि	रात	उलूक	उल्लू	शत	सौ	पुष्प	फूल
अन्धकार	अन्धेरा	क्षीर	खीर	पक्व	पक्का	कृषक	किसान
निद्रा	नींद	पृष्ठ	पीठ	कर्म	कार्य	आम्र	आम
ज्येष्ठ	जेठ	स्वर्ण	सोना	कर्ण	कान	अष्ट	आठ
श्वास	साँस	काक	काग	घंटिका	घंटी	चन्द्र	चन्द
कार्य	काज	कर्ण	कान	यव	जौ	धूम्र	धुआँ

विराम चिह्न

विराम का अर्थ रुकना। अपने विचारों को ठीक ढंग से प्रकट करने के पढ़ते अथवा लिखते समय हमें कुछ रुकना पड़ता है। इस प्रकार के रुकने को विराम कहते हैं।

प्रत्येक-विराम के लिए अलग-अलग चिह्न हैं—

पूर्ण विराम	[।]
अल्प विराम	[,]
अर्ध विराम	[;]
प्रश्न बोधक	[?]
विस्मयादि बोधक	[!]
योजक	[–]
उद्धरण	[" "]

कारक

कारक शब्द उस रूप को कहते हैं, जिससे संज्ञा या सर्वनाम वाक्य के साथ सम्बन्ध जाना जाता है। जैसे—शीला कलम **से** लिखती है।

यह सीमा **की** पुस्तक है।

कारक के भेद विभक्ति चिह्नों सहित

कारक	विभक्ति
कर्त्ता	ने
कर्म	को
करण	से
सम्प्रदान	के लिए
अपादान	से
सम्बन्ध	का, के, की
अधिकरण	में, पर
सम्बोधन	हे, अरे!

पर्यायवाची शब्द

जिन शब्दों से एक समान अर्थ का बोध होता है, उन्हें पर्यायवाची या समानार्थी शब्द कहते हैं।

कुछ पर्यायवाची शब्दों के उदाहरण निम्नलिखित हैं—

आग	–	अग्नि, अनल, पावक, हुताशन, ज्वाला।
आकाश	–	नभ, आसमान, गगन, लोभ।
असुर	–	राक्षस, दानव, निशाचर, दैत्य।
अमृत	–	अभिय, पीयूष, सुधा, सोम।
अन्धकार	–	अन्धेरा, तिमिर, तम, तमिस्र।
आँख	–	नेत्र, नयन, लोचन, चक्षु, दृग।
कमल	–	जलज, पंकज, नीरज, राजीव।
इन्द्र	–	सुरपति, देवेन्द्र, सुरेन्द्र, देवेश।
ईश्वर	–	प्रभु, भगवान, जगदीश, दीनबन्धु।
पक्षी	–	खग, विहग, चिड़िया, नभचर।
बादल	–	घन, जलधर, वारिद, नीरद।
गंगा	–	सुरसरि, जाह्नवी, त्रिपथगा, देवनदी, विष्णुपदी।
चन्द्रमा	–	शशि, मयंक, निशाकर, सुधाकर, सुधांशु, सोम हिमांशु, राकेश।
जल	–	पानी, नीर, लोभ, अम्बु, सलिल, क्षीर, वारि।
फूल	–	पुष्प, कुसुम, सुमन, प्रसून, सारंग।
पृथ्वी	–	भू, भूमि, धरा, वसुन्धरा, वसुधा, धरती क्षमा, लोक।
कपड़ा	–	पट, वस्त्र, चीर, अम्बर, दुकूल।
घर	–	गृह, गेह, निकेतन, आलय, निलय, भवन, शाला, धाम, सदन।
जंगल	–	वन, कानन, अरण्य, विपिन।
तालाब	–	सरोवर, ताल, जलाशय, तड़ाग।
दिन	–	दिवस, वासर, वार।

पहाड़	–	गिरि, पर्वत, गूधर, नग, महीधर, मेरू।
पत्थर	–	पहाड़, प्रस्तर, पाहन।
पवन	–	वायु, समीर, हवा, मारुत, अनिल।
पुत्र	–	सुत, तनय, पूत, आत्मज।
बिजली	–	तड़ित, चपला, दामिनी।
वृक्ष	–	तरु, रूख, विटप, पेड़।
मनुष्य	–	नर, मानव, मनुज, आदमी।
हाथी	–	करि, हस्ती, गज।
मित्र	–	सखा, मीत, सहचर, दोस्त।
राजा	–	नरेश, नृप, महीप, भूप।
समुद्र	–	सागर, सिन्धु, जलधि, नीरधि।
सरस्वती	–	शारदा, वागेश्वरी, भारती, महाश्वेता।
साँप	–	पन्नग, सर्प, विषधर, अहि, व्याल।
सूर्य	–	दिनकर, दिवाकर, रवि, भानु, भास्कर।
स्त्री	–	नारी, महिला, दारा, वामा।
शरीर	–	देह, तन, काया, गात, बदन।
गणेश	–	गजानन, गणपति, विनायक, एकदन्त, गजवदन लम्बोदर, विघ्न नाशक।
घोड़ा	–	तुरंग, बाजि, हय, अश्व, घोटक।
युद्ध	–	समर, रण, संग्राम।
सिंह	–	केसरी, मृगराज, केहरी।
शत्रु	–	अरि, रिपु, बैरी।
विष्णु	–	हरि, कमलेश, रमापति, चक्रपाणि, केशव, माधव पीताम्बर।
कोष	–	खजाना, भण्डार, निधि।
धन	–	दौलत, द्रव्य, मुद्रा।

तलवार	– कृपाण, असि, खड्ग।	**मृत्यु**	– मौत, काल, देहान्त।
अंग	– भाग, हिस्सा, अवयव।	**रक्त**	– रुधिर, शोणित, खून, लहू।
चोर	– तस्कर, दस्यु, रजनीचर।	**विष**	– जहर, हलाहल, गरल।
पत्नी	– भार्या, दारा, गृहिणी।	**सोना**	– कंचन, स्वर्ण, कनक।
पुत्र	– तनय, सुत, लड़का, बेटा।	**हृदय**	– उर, छाती, वक्ष, वक्षस्थल, हिय, हिया।
पुत्री	– तनया, सुता, लड़की, बेटी।	**सभा**	– अधिवेशन, परिषद्, बैठक, महासभा, समागम, समिति, सम्मेलन।
माता	– जननी, अम्बा, अम्बिका, अम्मा, माँ, धात्री।		
मोर	– शिखी, नीलकण्ठ, मयूर।	**यमुना**	– कालिन्दी, कृष्णा, जमुना, रविसुता तरणि-तनुजा।

विलोम-शब्द

शब्दों के अपने निश्चित अर्थ होते हैं। उन अर्थों के विपरीत अर्थ देने वाले शब्द को विलोम-शब्द कहते हैं।

शब्द	विलोम	शब्द	विलोम
अमृत	विष	उदार	संकीर्ण
अनुकूल	प्रतिकूल	अनुराग	विराग
आदि	अन्त	उत्थान	पतन
इच्छा	अनिच्छा	उचित	अनुचित
अल्पायु	दीर्घायु	अनुज	अग्रज
उन्नति	अवनति	आकाश	पाताल
अधिक	न्यून	आयात	निर्यात
एक	अनेक	अन्धकार	प्रकाश
अर्थ	अनर्थ	उदय	अस्त
परकीया	स्वकीया	जड़	चेतन
जय	पराजय	अनिवार्य	वैकल्पिक
नकद	उधार	अपेक्षा	उपेक्षा
उपस्थित	अनुपस्थित	आदर	अनादर
अन्धेरा	उजाला	अपना	पराया
उत्तम	अधम	आय	व्यय
सुपुत्र	कुपुत्र	स्वाधीन	पराधीन
आहार	निराहार	कठोर	कोमल
दाता	याचक	दोषी	निर्दोषि
खेद	प्रसन्नता	धनी	निर्धन
निकट	दूर	चर	अचर
देव	दानव	खरा	खोटा
गरीब	अमीर	प्रेम	घृणा
जीवन	मृत्यु	बुरा	भला
सजीव	निर्जीव	मित्र	शत्रु
सुगन्ध	दुर्गन्ध	मौखिक	लिखित
संक्षेप	विस्तार	कटु	मधुर
आरम्भ	अन्त	कड़वा	मीठा
कृतज्ञ	कृतघ्न	दिन	रात
साक्षर	निरक्षर	पवित्र	अपवित्र
पाप	पुण्य	जल	थल
धीर	अधीर	निर्मल	मलिन

शब्द	विलोम	शब्द	विलोम
गुण	अवगुण	नश्वर	अनश्वर
निन्दा	स्तुति	भारी	हल्का
मनुष्यता	पशुता	सरस	नीरस
मान	अपमान	क्रय	विक्रय
धर्म	अधर्म	गहरा	उथला
गुरु	शिष्य	पक्ष	विपक्ष
जन्म	मृत्यु	बन्धन	मुक्ति
यश	अपयश	ज्ञान	अज्ञान
आदर	अनादर	पूर्ण	अपूर्ण
सफल	असफल	शान्त	अशान्त
कीर्ति	अपकीर्ति	वादी	प्रतिवादी
आस्तिक	नास्तिक	स्वदेश	परदेश
सज्जन	दुर्जन	राग	द्वेष
ऊसर	उर्वर	उदार	कृपण
अगला	पिछला	अगम	सुगम
अग्नि	जल	अति	अल्प
अर्थ	अनर्थ	अतल	वितल
अत्यधिक	स्वल्प	अधः	उपरि
अधिकतम	न्यूनतम	अतिवृष्टि	अनावृष्टि
अनाथ	सनाथ	ईश्वर	जीव
अनुलोम	विलोम	अर्पण	ग्रहण
अवनि	अम्बर	अस्त	उदय
आकर्षण	विकर्षण	आगे	पीछे
आजाद	गुलाम	आदान	प्रदान
आधुनिक	प्राचीन	आना	जाना
आय	व्यय	आयात	निर्यात
आवश्यक	अनावश्यक	आशा	निराशा
आस्था	अनास्था	इहलोक	परलोक
उच्च	निम्न	उत्थान	पतन
उपकार	अपकार	उपयोग	दुरुपयोग
एकता	अनेकता	कल	आज
कृत्रिम	प्राकृत	कृष्ण	शुक्ल
कपूत	सपूत	कोमल	कठोर
गगन	धरा	ज्ञान	अज्ञान

लिंग

लिंग का अर्थ है 'चिन्ह'। लिंग शब्द उस चिन्ह को कहते हैं जिससे वस्तु के पुरुष या स्त्री होने की कल्पना हो। लिंग दो प्रकार के होते हैं—
(1) पुल्लिंग (2) स्त्रीलिंग

पुल्लिंग—पुल्लिंग संज्ञा के उस रूप को कहते हैं जिससे उसके पुरुष होने का ज्ञान होता है। जैसे—राम, श्याम, घोड़ा, हाथी, कुत्ता आदि।

स्त्रीलिंग—स्त्रीलिंग संज्ञा के उस रूप को कहते हैं जिससे उसके स्त्री होने का ज्ञान हो। जैसे—भैंस, गाय, बकरी, सीता, रमा इत्यादि।

पुल्लिंग	स्त्रीलिंग	पुल्लिंग	स्त्रीलिंग
इन्द्र	इन्द्राणी	मेहतर	मेहतरानी
नौकर	नौकरानी	जेठ	जेठानी
देवर	देवरानी	सेठ	सेठानी
पण्डित	पण्डिताइन	ओझा	ओझाइन
बनिया	बनियाइन	दुबे	दुबाइन
हलवाई	हलवाइन	चौबे	चौबाइन
गुरु	गुरुआइन	लड़का	लड़की
दास	दासी	कबूतर	कबूतरी
हिरण	हिरणी	क्षत्रिय	क्षत्राणी
मुगल	मुगलानी	हिन्दू	हिन्दुआनी
चौधरी	चौधरानी	भव	भवानी
लाला	ललाइन	पण्डा	पण्डाइन
ठाकुर	ठकुराइन	बाबू	बबुआइन
घोड़ा	घोड़ी	गूँगा	गूँगी
बच्चा	बच्ची	चाचा	चाची
बकरा	बकरी	मामा	मामी
मुर्गा	मुर्गी	साला	साली
चींटा	चींटी	रस्सा	रस्सी
देव	देवी	ब्राह्मण	ब्राह्मणी
बेटा	बेटी	बूढ़ा	बुढ़िया
चूहा	चुहिया	डिब्बा	डिबिया
गुड्डा	गुड़िया	कुम्हार	कुम्हारिन
सुनार	सुनारिन	नाती	नातिन
जुलाहा	जुलाहिन	दर्जी	दर्जिन
पापी	पापिन	हाथी	हथिनी

पुल्लिंग	स्त्रीलिंग	पुल्लिंग	स्त्रीलिंग
पिता	माता	बैल	गाय
कवि	कवयित्री	विधुर	विधवा
बाप	माँ	बादशाह	बेगम
नर	मादा	मर्द	औरत
युवक	युवती	वर	वधू
सम्राट्	सम्राज्ञी	साढू	साली
फूफा	बुआ	पुत्र	पुत्री
पहाड़	पहाड़ी	गोप	गोपी
गधा	गधी	तरुण	तरुणी
नर्तक	नर्तकी	बेटा	बिटिया
बछड़ा	बछिया	चिड़ा	चिड़िया
बन्दर	बन्दरिया	कुत्ता	कुतिया
नाई	नाइन	धोबी	धोबिन
ग्वाला	ग्वालिन	भंगी	भंगिन
स्वामी	स्वामिनी	विद्वान्	विदुषी
साधु	साध्वी	पुरुष	स्त्री
पति	पत्नी	वीर	वीरांगना
साहब	मेम	सास	ससुर
मियाँ	बीबी	राजा	रानी
बिलाड़	बिल्ली	अनुज	अनुजा
छात्र	छात्रा	महोदय	महोदया
प्रिय	प्रिया	मामा	मामी
लोटा	लुटिया	मोर	मोरनी
शेर	शेरनी	जाट	जाटिन
डाक्टर	डाक्टरनी	मालिक	मालकिन
माली	मालिन	बाघ	बाघिन
हाथी	हथिनी	स्वामी	स्वामिनी
बालक	बालिका	धनवान	धनवती
धावक	धाविका	नेता	नेत्री
गुणवान	गुणवती	नर	मादा
अभिनेता	अभिनेत्री	प्राचार्य	प्राचार्या
प्रबन्धकर्ता	प्रबन्धकर्ती	दाता	दात्री
ननदोई	ननद	अध्यापक	अध्यापिका

वचन

शब्द के जिस रूप से उसके एक अथवा अनेक होने का बोध हो, उसे वचन कहते हैं।

हिन्दी में दो वचन होते हैं—

(1) एकवचन और (2) बहुवचन

एकवचन—शब्द के जिस रूप से एक ही वस्तु का बोध हो, उसे एकवचन कहते हैं। जैसे—लड़का, गाय, बकरी, घोड़ा, राम, सीता आदि।

बहुवचन—शब्द के जिस रूप से अनेकता का बोध हो उसे बहुवचन कहते हैं। जैसे—लड़के, कपड़े, गायें आदि।

एकवचन	बहुवचन	एकवचन	बहुवचन	एकवचन	बहुवचन	एकवचन	बहुवचन
लड़का	लड़के	कौवा	कौवे	डिबिया	डिबियाँ	नाक	नाकें
बेटा	बेटे	कमरा	कमरे	पूँछ	पूँछें	मूँछ	मूँछें
कपड़ा	कपड़े	बहन	बहनें	चिड़िया	चिड़ियाँ	सरिता	सरिताएँ
चीज	चीजें	गधा	गधे	बालिका	बालिकाएँ	चाभी	चाभियाँ
रुपया	रुपये	घोड़ा	घोड़े	कहानी	कहानियाँ	दरवाजा	दरवाजे
नहर	नहरें	रात	रातें	कलम	कलमें	कुटिया	कुटियाँ
बात	बातें	सड़क	सड़कें	रानी	रानियाँ	नाई	नाइयों
दाना	दाने	लोटा	लोटे	माता	माताएँ	बाल	बालों
पैसा	पैसे	पुस्तक	पुस्तकें	हाथ	हाथों	मुख	मुख
कन्या	कन्याएँ	वधू	वधुएँ	कोट	कोट	दाँत	दाँतों
नारी	नारियाँ	लड़की	लड़कियाँ	नाखून	नाखूनों	पैर	पैरों
मुर्गा	मुर्गे	घण्टा	घण्टे	बैल	बैलों	माली	मालियों
गद्दा	गद्दे	हीरा	हीरे	राजा	राजाओं	पिता	पिता
बच्चा	बच्चे	प्याला	प्याले	चन्द्रमा	चन्द्रमा	कवि	कवियों
छाता	छाते	गाय	गायें	मुनि	मुनियों	कौआ	कौए
कथा	कथाएँ	कविता	कविताएँ	छात्रा	छात्राएँ	सेना	सेनाएँ
बहू	बहुएँ	टोपी	टोपियाँ	दिशा	दिशाएँ	गुड़िया	गुड़ियाँ
नाली	नालियाँ	बेटा	बेटे	मेज	मेजें	भैंस	भैंसें
ताला	ताले	जूता	जूते	अंगूर	अंगूरों	समुद्र	समुद्र

अनेक शब्दों के लिए एक शब्द

जिसकी कोई उपमा न हो	: अनुपम	मछली की तरह आँखों वाली	: मीनाक्षी
तेज बुद्धि वाला	: कुशाग्रबुद्धि	मयूर की तरह आँखों वाली	: मयूराक्षी
कल्पना से परे हो	: कल्पनातीत	बच्चों के लिए काम की वस्तु	: बालोपयोगी
जो उपकार नहीं मानता है	: कृतघ्न	जिसकी बहुत अधिक चर्चा हो	: बहुचर्चित
जो उपकार मानता है	: कृतज्ञ	जिस स्त्री को कभी सन्तान न हुई हो	: बन्ध्या (बाँझ)
किसी की हँसी उड़ाना	: उपहारा	फेन से भरा हुआ	: फेनिल
ऊपर कहा हुआ	: उपर्युक्त	प्रिय बोलने वाली स्त्री	: प्रियम्वदा
ऊपर लिखा हुआ	: उपरलिखित	जिसकी उपमा न हो	: निरुपम
जिस पर उपकार किया गया हो	: उपकृत	जो थोड़ी देर पहले पैदा हुआ हो	: नवजात
इतिहास का ज्ञाता	: इतिहासज्ञ	जिसका कोई आधार न हो	: निराधार
आलोचना करने वाला	: आलोचक	नगर में वास करने वाला	: नागरिक
ईश्वर में आस्था रखने वाला	: आस्तिक	रात में घूमने वाला	: निशाचर
बिना वेतन का	: अवैतनिक	ईश्वर में विश्वास न रखने वाला	: नास्तिक
जो कहा न जा सके	: अकथनीय	माँस न खाने वाला	: निरामिष
जो गिना न जा सके	: अगणित	बिल्कुल बर्बाद हो गया	: ध्वस्त
जिसका कोई शत्रु ही न जन्मा हो	: अजातशत्रु	जिसकी धर्म में निष्ठा हो	: धर्मनिष्ठ
जिसके समान कोई दूसरा न हो	: अद्वितीय	देखने योग्य	: दर्शनीय
जो परिचित न हो	: अपरिचित	बहुत तेज चलने वाला	: द्रुतगामी
आकाश में उड़ने वाला	: नभचर	जो किसी पक्ष में न रहे	: तटस्थ
जो टुकड़े-टुकड़े हो गया हो	: खण्डित	तत्त्व को जानने वाला	: तत्त्वज्ञ

तप करने वाला	: तपस्वी	जहाँ अनाथ रहते हों	: अनाथालय
जिसे देखकर डर लगे	: डरावना	प्रत्येक मास होने वाला	: मासिक
जो जन्म से अन्ध हो	: जन्मान्ध	जहाँ पानी के जहाज आकर रुकते हैं	: बन्दरगाह
जीने की प्रबल इच्छा	: जिजीविषा	प्रत्येक सप्ताह होने वाला	: साप्ताहिक
जिसने इन्द्रियों को जीत लिया हो	: जितेन्द्रिय	प्रत्येक वर्ष होने वाला	: वार्षिक
चिन्ता में डूबा हुआ	: चिन्तित	जो कठिनाई से मिले	: दुर्लभ
जो बहुत समय तक ठहरे	: चिरस्थायी	जिसका आकार हो	: साकार
जिसकी चार भुजाएँ हों	: चतुर्भुज	जिसका आकार न हो	: निराकार
जिसके हाथ में चक्र हों	: चक्रपाणि	जो कभी बूढ़ा न हो	: अजर
जिससे घृणा की जाए	: घृणित	बहुत बोलने वाला	: वाचाल
जिसे गुप्त रखा जाए	: गोपनीय	पृथ्वी पर रहने वाला	: थलचर
गणित ज्ञाता	: गणितज्ञ	जल में रहने वाला	: जलचर
आकाश को चूमने वाला	: गगनचुम्बी	नभ में विचरण करने वाला	: नभचर
जिसका आदि न हो	: अनादि	जल-थल दोनों में रहने वाला	: उभयचर
जो कुछ न जानता हो	: अज्ञ	जिसमें रस न हो	: नीरस
जो अनुकरण करने योग्य हो	: अनुकरणीय	पढ़ने वाला	: पाठक
जिसका अन्त न हो	: अनन्त	जो भाषण देता हो	: वक्ता
जो कभी न मरे	: अमर	जो साथ में पढ़ता हो	: सहपाठी
जो कम बोलता हो	: अल्पभाषी	जिसके नीचे रेखा खींची हो	: रेखांकित
जिसका इलाज न हो	: लाइलाज	जानने की इच्छा रखने वाला	: जिज्ञासु
जिसका कोई नाथ न हो	: अनाथ	जिसकी कोई सन्तान न हो	: निःसन्तान
कम जानने वाला	: अल्पज्ञ	जिसका कोई मूल्य न हो	: अमूल्य
जहाँ जाना सम्भव न हो	: अगम	जो वन में घूमता हो	: वनचर
बड़ा भाई	: अग्रज	जो इस लोक के बाहर की बात हो	: अलौकिक
कम खाने वाला	: अल्पाहारी	जो इस लोक की बात हो	: लौकिक
जो बात पहले कभी न हुई हो	: अभूतपूर्व	जिसका सम्बन्ध पश्चिम से हो	: पाश्चात्य
दूसरों के पीछे चलने वाला	: अनुचर	जो स्थिर रहे	: स्थावर
जो पहले न पढ़ा हो	: अपठित	दुःखान्त नाटक	: त्रासदी
जिसके आर-पार दिखाई देता हो	: पारदर्शी	ज्ञान देने वाली	: ज्ञानदा
आज्ञा पालन करने वाला	: आज्ञाकारी	भूत, वर्तमान भविष्य को देखने वाला	: त्रिकालदर्शी
काम से जी चुराने वाला	: कामचोर	जो क्षमा के योग्य हो	: क्षम्य
प्रतिदिन होने वाला	: दैनिक	हिंसा करने वाला	: हिंसक
जिसका कोई अर्थ न हो	: निरर्थक	हित चाहने वाला	: हितैषी
हाथ से लिखा हुआ	: हस्तलिखित	सब कुछ जानने वाला	: सर्वज्ञ
आँखों के सामने होने वाला	: प्रत्यक्ष	जो स्वयं पैदा हुआ हो	: स्वयंभू
जिसका आचरण अच्छा हो	: सदाचारी	जो शरण में आया हो	: शरणागत
वह पुरुष जिसकी पत्नी मर गई हो	: विधुर	जिसका वर्णन न किया जा सके	: वर्णनातीत
वह स्त्री जिसका पति मर गया हो	: विधवा	व्याकरण जानने वाला	: वैयाकरण
जिसका रूप अच्छा न हो	: कुरूप	रचना करने वाला	: रचयिता
सदा सत्य बोलने वाला	: सत्यवादी	खून से रंगा हुआ	: रक्तरंजित
बड़ी इमारत के टूटे-फूटे भाग	: खण्डहर	अत्यन्त सुन्दर स्त्री	: रूपसी
प्रशंसा के योग्य	: प्रशंसनीय	कीर्तिमान पुरुष	: यशस्वी

महत्त्वपूर्ण शब्दों की भाववाचक संज्ञा

शब्द	भाववाचक संज्ञा	शब्द	भाववाचक संज्ञा	शब्द	भाववाचक संज्ञा	शब्द	भाववाचक संज्ञा
दास	दासता	क्षत्रिय	क्षत्रियत्व	अहं	अहंकार	अपना	अपनापन
पशु	पशुता	बालक	बालकपन	व्यक्ति	व्यक्तित्व	मीठा	मिठास
बन्धु	बन्धुत्व	मित्र	मित्रता	गरीब	गरीबी	सफल	सफलता
बूढ़ा	बुढ़ापा	सती	सतीत्व	बुरा	बुराई	स्वस्थ	स्वास्थ्य
सेवक	सेवा	शिशु	शैशव	सरल	सरलता	कंजुस	कंजुसी
अपना	अपनत्व	पराया	परायापन	कमजोर	कमजोरी	हरा	हरियाली
पण्डित	पाण्डित्य	पुरुष	पुरुषत्व	गर्म	गर्मी	मोटा	मोटाई
ब्राह्मण	ब्राह्मणत्व	बच्चा	बचपन	चालाक	चालाकी	गम्भीर	गम्भीरता
प्रभु	प्रभुता	नारी	नारीत्व	पढ़ना	पढ़ाई	लिखना	लिखाई
देव	देवत्व	लड़का	लड़कपन	थकना	थकावट	लिखना	लिखावट
मनुष्य	मनुष्यता	दानव	दानवता	लूटना	लूट	लड़ना	लड़ाई
निज	निजता	स्व	स्वत्व	हँसना	हँसी	आप	अपनत्व

महत्त्वपूर्ण शब्दों के विशेषण

शब्द	विशेषण	शब्द	विशेषण	शब्द	विशेषण	शब्द	विशेषण
अंक	अंकित	अर्थ	आर्थिक	वन	वन्य	विष्णु	वैष्णव
इतिहास	ऐतिहासिक	उदासी	उदास	शहर	शहरी	तप	तपस्वी
कलंक	कलंकित	कुसुम	कुसुमित	जापान	जापानी	तेज	तेजस्वी
जटा	जटिल	भार	भारी	तत्त्व	तात्त्विक	दया	दयालु
बनारस	बनारसी	बाजार	बाजारू	देव	दैविक	निंदा	निंदक
प्यास	प्यासा	पुराण	पौराणिक	नव	नवीन	पोषण	पोषक
पंक	पंकित	पक्ष	पाक्षिक	पेट	पेटू	पाप	पापी
धन	धनी	दो	दूसरा	पूजा	पूज्य	भूख	भूखा
तीन	तीसरा	झगड़ा	झगड़ालू	फेन	फेनिल	भारत	भारतीय
ठण्ड	ठण्डा	जाति	जातीय	माया	मायावी	रंग	रंगीन
काँटा	कँटीला	विदेश	विदेशी	विष	विषैला	श्री	श्रीमान
रोज	रोजाना	भूगोल	भौगोलिक	सुर	सुरीला	विवाह	वैवाहिक
पीड़ा	पीड़ित	पुत्र	पुत्रवान	आदर	आदरणीय	ऋण	ऋणी
आलस्य	आलसी	अंतर	आंतरिक	किताब	किताबी	क्रम	क्रमिक
ईर्ष्या	ईर्ष्यालु	कर्म	कर्मठ	ग्राम	ग्रामीण	घर	घरेलू
करुणा	कारुणिक	कृपा	कृपालु	चतुर	चतुरता	जहर	जहरीला
गुण	गुणी	जल	जलमय	सप्ताह	साप्ताहिक	अनुभव	अनुभवी
जीव	जैविक	तट	तटस्थ	ओज	ओजस्वी	कल्पना	काल्पनिक
तर्क	तार्किक	धर्म	धार्मिक	कुल	कुलीन	गाँव	गँवार
नमक	नमकीन	पत्थर	पथरीला	चमक	चमकीला	चाचा	चचेरा
पल्लव	पल्लवित	पान	पनवाड़ी	दीन	दीनता	नगर	नागरिक
मुख	मुखर	मिठास	मीठा	नागपुर	नागपुरी	परिवार	पारिवारिक
मास	मासिक	मद	मादक	पुष्प	पुष्पित	पिता	पैतृक
रक्त	रक्तिम	रस	रसीला	फ्रांस	फ्रांसीसी	बाहर	बाहरी

शब्द	विशेषण	शब्द	विशेषण	शब्द	विशेषण	शब्द	विशेषण
भय	भयभीत	मधु	मधुर	गाना	गायक	बेचना	बिकाऊ
मौन	मौनी	मन	मानसिक	भागना	भगोड़ा	वन्द	वन्दनीय
मानव	मानवीय	रक्षा	रक्षक	चलना	चलती	घूमना	घुमक्कड़
रघु	राघव	रोग	रोगी	चलना	चालू	मरना	मरियल
वर्ष	वार्षिक	शक्ति	शक्तिशाली	भूलना	भुलक्कड़	पीछे	पिछला
श्रम	श्रमिक	अंत	अंतिम	भीतर	भीतरी	नीचे	निम्न
कागज	कागजी	मर्म	मार्मिक	अणु	आणविक	अधिकार	आधिकारिक
शब्द	शाब्दिक	अज्ञान	अज्ञानी	अनुभव	अनुभवी	अन्याय	अन्यायी
गुलाब	गुलाबी	प्रकृति	प्राकृतिक	अपमान	अपमानित	अभ्यास	अभ्यासी
परिचय	परिचित	पूजा	पुजारी	अवश्य	आवश्यक	आदि	आदिम
रोग	रोगी	ग्राम	ग्रामीण	आयु	आयुष्मान्	उदय	उदित
सुगंध	सुगंधित	मैं	मेरा	उपज	उपजाऊ	एकता	एक
जो	जैसा	आप	आप-सा	अंत	अंतिम	कुल	कुलीन
तुम	तुम्हारा	कौन	कैसा	खर्च	खर्चीला	खून	खूनी
वह	वैसा	पढ़ना	पढ़ाकू	गुण	गुणी		

श्रुतिसम भिन्नार्थक शब्द

शब्द	अर्थ	शब्द	अर्थ	शब्द	अर्थ	शब्द	अर्थ
आदि	आरम्भ	आदी	अभ्यस्त	बन्द	खुला नहीं	बद	बुरा
कुल	वंश	कूल	किनारा	पथ	रास्ता	पथ्य	रोगी का भोजन
अरि	शत्रु	अरी	सम्बोधन	पुर	नगर	पूर	बाढ़
अगम	दुर्गम	आगम	शास्त्र	भवन	महल	भुवन	संसार
अयश	अपकीर्ति	अयस्क	लोहा	लक्ष्य	उद्देश्य	लक्ष	लाख
अपेक्षा	चाहना, तुलना में	उपेक्षा	निरादर	सर	तालाब	शर	बाण
अनिल	हवा	अनल	आग	सर्ग	अध्याय	स्वर्ग	एक लोक
अवधि	काल, समय	अवधी	अवध की भाषा	कर्म	कार्य	क्रम	सिलसिला
आयात	बाहर से आना	आयत	एक आकृति	चिता	शव जलाने के लिए लकड़ियों का ढेर	चीता	बाघ
चिर	पुराना	चीर	कपड़ा	शव	लाश	शब	रात
तनु	पतला	तनू	पुत्र, गाय	शस्त्र	हथियार	शास्त्र	ग्रन्थ
तरंग	लहर	तुरंग	घोड़ा	श्रवण	सुनना	श्रमण	बौद्ध संन्यासी
दारा	स्त्री	द्वार	दरवाजा	मत	विचार	मत्त	मस्त
दूत	संदेशवाहक	द्यूत	जुआ	शोक	दुःख	शौक	चाव
जलद	बादल	जलज	कमल	ग्रह	नक्षत्र	गृह	घर
प्रदीप	दीपक	प्रतीप	उल्टा	कपट	धोखा	कपाट	दरवाजा
प्रसाद	कृपा	प्रासाद	महल	उपयुक्त	ठीक	उपर्युक्त	ऊपर कहा गया
पास	निकट	पाश	बन्धन	सुत	बेटा	सूत	धागा
द्विप	हाथी	द्वीप	टापू	शूर	वीर	सूर	अंधा
देव	देवता	दैव	भाग्य	श्याम	कृष्ण	शाम	संध्या
नीर	जल	नीड़	घोंसला	दिन	वार	दीन	गरीब
पवन	वायु	पावन	पवित्र	कटिबद्ध	तैयार रहना	करबद्ध	हाथ जोड़ना

अनेकार्थक शब्द

शब्द	विभिन्न अर्थ	शब्द	विभिन्न अर्थ
अंक	संख्या, गोद	द्विज	पक्षी, ब्राह्मण
अक्षर	वर्ण, ईश्वर	तीर	किनारा, बाण
पानी	जल, प्रतिष्ठा	प्रकृति	स्वभाव, कुदरत
अचल	पर्वत, स्थिर	पत्र	चिट्ठी, पत्र
आम	फल, सामान्य	पद	पैर, उपाधि
अंबर	वस्त्र, आकाश	फल	परिणाम, फल
अवस्था	आयु, दशा	तनु	पतला, कोमल
उत्तर	दिशा, जबाव	वर्ण	रंग, जाति
विधि	तरीका, भाग्य	हल	समाधान, खेत जोतने का साधन
कर	हाथ, टैक्स	अशोक	राजा, वृक्ष
कनक	सोना, धतुरा	आभीर	अहीर, एक राग
गुरु	श्रेष्ठ, शिक्षक	एकाक्ष	काना, कौआ
घन	भारी हथौड़ा, बादल	खल	दुष्ट, खलिहान
जड़	मूर्ख, मूल	घट	घड़ा, हृदय
कल	मशीन, आनेवाला कल, चैन	जलज	कमल, मछली
सुर	देवता, स्वर	हेम	सोना, जल

सामान्य अशुद्धियाँ

अशुद्ध	शुद्ध	अशुद्ध	शुद्ध	अशुद्ध	शुद्ध	अशुद्ध	शुद्ध
दुनियां	दुनिया	श्रीमति	श्रीमती	अनुग्रहीत	अनुगृहीत	बृज	ब्रज
सामिग्री	सामग्री	वापिस	वापस	बनस्पति	वनस्पति	श्राप	शाप
प्रदर्शिनी	प्रदर्शनी	द्वारिका	द्वारका	सैना	सेना	सेनिक	सैनिक
ऊत्थान	उत्थान	दुसरा	दूसरा	इतिहासिक	ऐतिहासिक	प्रशक	पृथक
प्रशाद	प्रसाद	अमावश्या	अमावस्या	सम्पति	सम्पत्ति	कृतघन	कृतघ्न
बसंत	वसंत	बर्ष	वर्ष	बिमारी	बीमारी	व्यक्तिक	वैयक्तिक
विना	बिना	बन	वन	वितीत	व्यतीत	निस्वार्थ	निःस्वार्थ
दाइत्व	दायित्व	सम्वाद	संवाद	परिस्थित	परिस्थिति	रचियता	रचयिता
कुन्डली	कुण्डली	मॉसिक	मानसिक	मैथिलिशरण	मैथिलीशरण	आर्शिवाद	आशीर्वाद
कन्ठ	कण्ठ	अगामी	आगामी	निरिक्षण	निरीक्षण	पत्लि	पत्नी
सप्ताहिक	साप्ताहिक	संसारिक	सांसारिक	शताब्दि	शताब्दी	लड़ायी	लड़ाई
आधीन	अधीन	हस्ताक्षेप	हस्तक्षेप	स्थाई	स्थायी	लिखायी	लिखाई
बरात	बारात	क्षत्रीय	क्षत्रिय	अलोकिक	अलौकिक	कृप्या	कृपया
तिथी	तिथि	कालीदास	कालिदास	गंवार	गँवार	असोक	अशोक
पुर्ती	पूर्ति	अतिथी	अतिथि	दुस्कर	दुष्कर	मूल्यावान	मूल्यवान्
नीती	नीति	ग्रहणी	गृहिणी	नवमृ	नवम	क्षात्र	छात्र
क्यूँ	क्यों	साधू	साधु	छमा	क्षमा	प्रन्तु	परन्तु
वधु	वधू	रेणू	रेणु	प्रीक्षा	परीक्षा	मरयादा	मर्यादा
नुपुर	नूपुर	निर्वान	निर्वाण	दुदर्शा	दुर्दशा	विषेश	विशेष
जादु	जादू	द्रश्य	दृश्य	उज्वल	उज्ज्वल	आल्हाद	आह्लाद

अशुद्ध	शुद्ध	अशुद्ध	शुद्ध	अशुद्ध	शुद्ध	अशुद्ध	शुद्ध
महत्व	महत्त्व	उपलक्ष	उपलक्ष्य	प्रनाम	प्रणाम	प्रयाप्त	पर्याप्त
लीये	लिये	पिओ	पियो	प्रसंशा	प्रशंसा	प्रांगन	प्रांगण
हुये	हुए	कवित्री	कवयित्री	प्रान	प्राण	पृष्ट	पृष्ठ
प्रमात्मा	परमात्मा	घनिष्ट	घनिष्ठ	ब्रत	व्रत	भगीरथी	भागीरथी
यथेष्ठ	यथेष्ट	पियास	प्यास	भरथ	भरत	भष्म	भस्म
व्यस्क	वयस्क	त्यौहार	त्योहार	मंत्रीमंडल	मंत्रिमण्डल	रसायण	रसायन
मुसलिम	मुस्लिम	ऐनक	ऐनक	राज्यमहल	राजमहल	रामायन	रामायण
नोकरी	नौकरी	कल्यान	कल्याण	वनोवास	वनवास	वानी	वाणी
पाणी	पानी	आसा	आशा	वाल्मीकी	वाल्मीकि	वास्प	वाष्प
हुदय	हृदय	घ्रणा	घृणा	व्योहार	व्यवहार	सन्यासी	संन्यासी
श्रंगार	शृंगार	हिन्दुस्थान	हिन्दुस्तान	सम्राज	साम्राज्य	सविनयपूर्वक	सविनय
प्रशन	प्रश्न	ग्यान	ज्ञान	सिंदुर	सिंदूर	स्त्रवण	श्रवण
अन्धेरा	अँधेरा	पेड	पेड़	हरीश्चन्द्र	हरिश्चन्द्र	हिन्दु	हिन्दू
महयान्हन	मध्यान्ह	मेंहदी	मेहंदी	हिन्दूस्तान	हिन्दुस्तान	बुध्दिवान	बुद्धिमान्
शमशान	शमशान	चिन्ह	चिह्न	भाग्यमान	भाग्यवान	विद्धान	विद्वान्
कुंज	कुञ्ज	ग्रहस्थ	गृहस्थ	श्रीमान	श्रीमान्	आंख	आँख
अजोध्या	अयोध्या	अनधिकार	अनाधिकार	ऊंट	ऊँट	कंगना	कँगना
अनिष्ठा	अनिष्ट	अनुकुल	अनुकूल	गँगा	गंगा	गांधी	गाँधी
अनुसंगिक	आनुषंगिक	अनुशरण	अनुसरण	जांच	जाँच	तांगा	ताँगा
अभिसेक	अभिषेक	अरमाण	अरमान	दांत	दाँत	मंहगा	महँगा
अहिल्या	अहल्या	आदरनीय	आदरणीय	मांस	माँस	मुह	मुँह
आविस्कार	आविष्कार	उँचाई	ऊँचाई	सांप	साँप	सांस	साँस
उत्तरदाई	उत्तरदायी	उपर	ऊपर	हुँकार	हुंकार	निर्पेक्ष	निरपेक्ष
उपरोक्त	उपर्युक्त	उश्रृंखल	उच्छृंखल	भाष्कर	भास्कर	सन्मुख	सम्मुख
कलस	कलश	कल्यान	कल्याण	माताहीन	मातृहीन	विद्यार्थि	विद्यार्थी
गनित	गणित	जबाब	जवाब	गुणि	गुणी	दैवाषिक	द्विवार्षिक
तत्व	तत्त्व	तलाब	तालाब	पूज्यनीय	पूजनीय	अकाश	आकाश
तिरष्कार	तिरस्कार	त्रिवार्षिक	त्रैवार्षिक	इद	ईद	इसलाम	इस्लाम
दिपिका	दीपिका	देहिक	दैहिक	ऐसा	ऐसा	दोसरा	दूसरा
द्न्द	द्वन्द्व	नरायन	नारायण	पुत्रि	पुत्री	प्रस्तूत	प्रस्तुत
निरव	नीरव	निरोग	नीरोग	हरयाली	हरियाली	दिवाली	दीवाली
पुष्टी	पुष्टि	पुस्प	पुष्प	राष्ट्रिय	राष्ट्रीय	एकहरा	इकहरा
पेत्रिक	पैतृक	प्रनय	प्रणय	एतबार	इतबार		

<h2 align="center">वाक्यगत अशुद्धियाँ</h2>

अशुद्ध	शुद्ध	अशुद्ध	शुद्ध
हम अच्छी भाषण दिए थे।	हमने अच्छा भाषण दिया था।	राम रोटी खाया।	राम ने रोटी खायी।
आप खाए कि नहीं?	आपने खाया कि नहीं?	लड़की ने दही गिरा दी।	लड़की ने दही गिरा दिया।
वह मुझे देखा तो घबरा गया।	उसने मुझे देखा तो घबरा गया।	शुद्ध गाय की घी दो।	गाय का शुद्ध घी दो।
मैं किताब पढ़ा हूँ।	मैंने किताब पढ़ी है।	तुम, मैं और वह चलेगा।	तुम, वह और मैं चलूँगा।
मैं सारी पुस्तक पढ़ डाली।	मैंने सारी पुस्तक पढ़ डाली।	राम और सीता आयी थी।	राम और सीता आए थे।
सीता भात खायी।	सीता ने भात खाया।	भाई-बहन जा रही हैं।	भाई-बहन जा रहे हैं।

अशुद्ध	शुद्ध	अशुद्ध	शुद्ध
वह लड़की को बुलाओ।	उस लड़की को बुलाओ।	ये सब मेरा पुस्तक है।	ये सब मेरी पुस्तकें हैं।
मेरे लिए पढ़ता हूँ।	अपने लिए पढ़ता हूँ।	सूरज पूरब में उगते हैं।	सूरज पूर्व में उगता है।
सीता राम की आज्ञाकारी पत्नी थी।	सीता राम की आज्ञाकारिणी पत्नी थीं।	वह लौट आए।	वे लौट आए।
देरी न करना।	देर न करना।	वहाँ अनेकों लोग थे।	वहाँ अनेक लोग थे।
उसे मृत्युदण्ड की सजा मिली।	उसे मृत्युदण्ड मिला।	मेरे को मत मारो।	मुझे मत मारो।
हमारे शिक्षक प्रश्न पूछते हैं।	हमारे शिक्षक प्रश्न करते हैं।	मोहन ने पत्र को पढ़ा।	मोहन ने पत्र पढ़ा।
कै बजे? तीन बजा।	कितना बजा? तीन बजे।	पुस्तक पर नहीं लिखो।	पुस्तक पर मत लिखो।
उसका प्राण उड़ गया।	उसके प्राण उड़ गये।	वह सज्जन पुरुष है।	वह सज्जन है।
मैंने आँख से देखा।	मैंने आँखों से देखा।	आप हमारे घर आओ।	आप हमारे घर आइए।
अपन को पढ़ना है।	मुझे पढ़ना है।	हम आपसे कुछ कहे थे।	हमने आपसे कुछ कहा था।
पुस्तक फट गया।	पुस्तक फट गई है।	मकान की दायीं ओर सड़क है।	मकान के दायीं ओर सड़क है।
घोड़ी तेज दौड़ता है।	घोड़ी तेज दौड़ती है।	पिताजी घर नहीं हैं।	पिताजी घर पर नहीं हैं।
मेरा प्रणम स्वीकार करो।	मेरा प्रणाम स्वीकार करो।	घर पर सब कुशल हैं।	घर में सब कुशल हैं।
दो बालक खेलता है।	दो बालक खेलते हैं।	उसे भारी दुःख हुआ।	उसे बहुत दुःख हुआ।
		सड़क में मत खेलो।	सड़क पर मत खेलो।

मुहावरे तथा लोकोक्तियाँ

- अँगूठी का नगीना–अत्यन्त महत्त्वपूर्ण।
- अंधा दरबार–न्यायहीन स्थान।
- अंधेर नगरी–न्याय का अभाव।
- अक्ल का दुश्मन–मूर्ख।
- अक्ल का दुम–मूर्ख।
- आँख का तारा–अतिप्रिय।
- ईद का चाँद–बहुत दिनों के बाद दिखाई देना।
- कछुआ चाल–धीमी गति।
- काला नाग–दुष्ट आदमी।
- किताबी कीड़ा–सदैव कुछ-न-कुछ पढ़ना।
- किस्मत का मारा–भाग्य का मन्द।
- कोल्हू का बैल–बहुत कठिन परिश्रम करनेवाला।
- कोड़ी का तीन–तुच्छ।
- खाली हाथ–पैसे का अभाव।
- गाजर-मूली–अशक्त।
- गुलर का फूल–दुर्लभ वस्तु।
- गोबर-गणेश–निरामूर्ख।
- घर का उजाला–कुल-दीपक।
- घड़ियाली आँसू–बनावटी शोक।
- चलता-पुरजा–चालाक।
- चाँद का टुकड़ा–परम सुन्दर वस्तु या व्यक्ति।
- चाँदी का जूता–रिश्वत।

- चार दिन की चाँदनी–थोड़े समय का सुख।
- जलती आँख–क्रोधाभिभूत।
- जीभ का पतला–लालची।
- टेढ़ी खीर–विकट काम।
- ठिकाने की बात–न्यायसंगत बात।
- अढ़ाई दिन की हुकूमत–थोड़े समय का ऐश्वर्य।
- तकदीर का सिकन्दर–भाग्य का बलवान्।
- थाली का बैंगन–मत बदलते रहना।
- दाँत कटी रोटी–घनिष्ठता।
- दाहिना हाथ–सहायक।
- दिल का बादशाह–बहुत बड़ा उदार।
- दूध का दूध और पानी का पानी–उचित न्याय।
- दूध का धोआ–निर्दोष।
- दो दिन का मेहमान–बहुत थोड़े समय ठहरने वाला।
- धरती का फूल–ऐसा व्यक्ति जो हाल में अमीर हुआ है।
- धोबी का कुत्ता–निकम्मा।
- नसीब का मारा–बुरे दिन देखनेवाला।
- निन्यानबे का फेरा–धन बढ़ाने की चिन्ता।
- पत्थर का कलेजा–हर दुःख सहने की शक्ति।
- पत्थर की लकीर–चिरस्थायी सदा सत्य।
- फूलों की सेज–आनन्ददायक कार्य।
- बगुला-भगत–कपटी व्यक्ति।

- बच्चों का खेल–साधारण काम।
- बलि का बकरा–निःसहाय व्यक्ति।
- बरसाती बादल–अस्थायी।
- बात का पक्का–सत्यवादी।
- बायें हाथ का खेल–सरल काम।
- बिन बादल बरसात–असमय लाभ।
- बे-पेंदी का लोटा–बे ठिकाने का आदमी।
- भागीरथ प्रयत्न–अत्यधिक परिश्रम।
- भीष्म प्रतिज्ञा–दृढ़ संकल्प।
- मक्खी चूस–कंजूस।
- मिट्टी के मोल–बहुत सस्ता।
- मोटा असामी–मूर्ख मालदार।
- राम कहानी–आत्मवृत्तान्त।
- लँगोटिया यार– बचपन का मित्र।
- हवाई महल–कोरी कल्पना।
- आँख लगना–नींद आना।
- आँख खुलना–होश में आना।
- आँखें दिखाना–क्रोध से घूरना।
- आँसू पोंछना–धैर्य बँधाना।
- अन्धे की लकड़ी–एकमात्र सहारा।
- कान भरना–चुगली करना।
- कान पर जूँ न रेंगना–कोई असर न होना।
- नाक कटना–प्रतिष्ठा खत्म होना।
- नाक रगड़ना–दीनता दिखाना।
- नाकों चने चबवाना–खूब सताना।
- मुँह की खाना–बुरी तरह हारना।
- आस्तीन का साँप–विश्वासघाती मित्र।
- कन्धे से कन्धा मिलाना–पूरा सहयोग करना।
- ईंट से ईंट बजाना–पूरी तरह नष्ट कर देना।
- नौ दो ग्यारह होना–भाग जाना।
- दाँत खट्टे करना–बुरी तरह हराना।
- हाथ मलना–पछताना।
- खून का प्यासा–जानी दुश्मन।
- घी के दिए जलाना–खुशी मनाना।
- चार चाँद लगाना–प्रतिष्ठा बढ़ाना।
- तीन तेरह होना–अलग-अलग होना।
- पानी फेर देना–नाश कर देना।
- गाल बजाना–डींगे मारना।
- जान से हाथ धो बैठना–मारा जाना।

- पानी-पानी होना–बहुत लज्जित होना।
- फूला न समाना–बहुत प्रसन्न होना।
- अपना उल्लू सीधा करना–अपना मतलब निकालना।
- आँखें चुरा लेना–अनदेखा कर देना।
- अन्धे की लाठी–एकमात्र सहारा।
- आसमान पर चढ़ना–बहुत अभिमान करना।
- आँखें खुलना–होश आना।
- चोरी और सीना जोरी–दोषी होकर धमकाना।
- आग में घी डालना–क्रोध को भड़काना।
- अँगुली पर नचाना– अच्छी तरह वश में करना।
- एक आँख से देखना–समान दृष्टि से देखना।
- एक ही थैले के चट्टे-बट्टे–एक जैसे।
- ओखली में सिर देना–जान-बूझकर आपत्ति मोल लेना।
- कलेजा मुँह को आना–बहुत दुःखी होना।
- कफन बाँधकर चलना–मौत से न घबराना।
- काँटे बिछाना–बाधा डालना।
- कलेजा ठण्डा होना–सन्तोष होना।
- कमर कसना–तैयार होना।
- खून खौलना–जोश में आना।
- खाक छानना–मारे-मारे फिरना।
- गागर में सागर भरना–थोड़े शब्दों में बहुत कुछ कह देना।
- घाव पर नमक छिड़कना–दुखी को अधिक दुखी करना।
- घी के दिए जलाना–खुशी मनाना।
- घोड़े बेचकर सोना–गहरी नींद में सोना।
- चल बसना–परलोक सिधारना।
- छठी का दूध याद आना–भारी संकट में पड़ना।
- छाती पर साँप लोटना–बहुत ईर्ष्या होना।
- जमीन पर पैर न रखना–अधिक घमण्ड होना।
- झक मारना–व्यर्थ समय खोना।
- टेढ़ी खीर–कठिन काम।
- डींग मारना–अपनी झूठी प्रशंसा करना।
- डूब मरना–बहुत लज्जित होना।
- तलवे चाटना–चापलूसी करना।
- ताक में रहना–मौका ढूँढ़ते रहना।
- दंग रह जाना–आश्चर्य में पड़ जाना।
- दाल न गलना–वश न चलना।
- दाल में काला होना–संदेह होना।
- पीठ दिखाना–हारकर भागना।
- मुँह तोड़ उत्तर देना–खरा उत्तर देना।

वस्तुनिष्ठ प्रश्न

अभ्यास-1

निर्देशः नीचे प्रत्येक शुद्ध शब्द की वर्तनी के लिए चार विकल्प दिए गए हैं। आपको सही विकल्प का चयन करना है।

1. A. ऋषि   B. ऋष्री
   C. रिषी   D. ऋसि
2. A. विषेसन   B. विशेषण
   C. विसेशन   D. विशेशन
3. A. दुशासन   B. दुसाशन
   C. दूशाषण   D. दुःशासन
4. A. संस्कृति   B. संस्कृति
   C. संष्कृति   D. संस्कृती
5. A. दूनियां   B. दुनियां
   C. दुनिया   D. दूनिआ
6. A. टिपनी   B. टिप्पणि
   C. टिप्पणी   D. टिप्पनी
7. A. शाषण   B. साशन
   C. शासन   D. शाशन
8. A. किसमस   B. किरसमस
   C. क्रिसमस   D. कृसमस
9. A. अनुग्रहित   B. अनुग्रहीत
   C. अनुगृहीत   D. अनुग्रहित
10. A. पराकम   B. प्राक्रम
    C. पराक्रम   D. प्राकर्म
11. A. नायका   B. नाइका
    C. नाइक   D. नागिका
12. A. समरिधी   B. समद्धी
    C. समृद्धि   D. समरिद्धि
13. A. युधिष्ठर   B. युधिष्ठर
    C. युधिष्ठिर   D. युधिष्टर
14. A. वाल्मीकि   B. बाल्मीकि
    C. बालमीकि   D. बाल्मिक
15. A. परलोकिक   B. प्रलौकिक
    C. पारलौकिक   D. परलौकिक
16. A. त्रितीय   B. तर्तीय
    C. तृतीय   D. तिरतीय
17. A. व्योहार   B. व्यौहार
    C. व्यवहार   D. ब्यवहार
18. A. अहिल्या   B. अहल्या
    C. अहिलया   D. अहीलया
19. A. आदरनीय   B. आदरणीय
    C. आदरनीया   D. आदरणीया
20. A. आर्द   B. आद्र
    C. आर्द्र   D. आर्दृ
21. A. आधीन   B. अधिन
    C. अधीन   D. अधीम
22. A. आविस्कार   B. आविष्कार
    C. आवीस्कार   D. आविश्कार
23. A. आसा   B. आषा
    C. आशा   D. अशा
24. A. उज्वल   B. उजज्ज्वल
    C. उजज्वल   D. उज्ज्वल
25. A. उन्ती   B. उन्नित
    C. उन्नति   D. उन्नती
26. A. कलस   B. कलष
    C. कलश   D. कलशा
27. A. गनीत   B. गनित
    C. गणीत   D. गणित
28. A. तलाव   B. तालाव
    C. तलाब   D. तालाब
29. A. दुष्ट   B. दूष्ट
    C. दुस्त   D. दुश्त
30. A. निरोग   B. निररोग
    C. नीरोग   D. नीरोगी

उत्तरमाला

1. A	2. B	3. D	4. A	5. C
6. C	7. C	8. C	9. C	10. C
11. D	12. C	13. C	14. A	15. C
16. C	17. C	18. B	19. B	20. C
21. C	22. B	23. C	24. D	25. C
26. C	27. D	28. D	29. A	30. C

अभ्यास-2

निर्देशः नीचे कुछ शब्द दिए गए हैं। प्रत्येक के पर्यायवाची के चार विकल्प दिए गए हैं। इनमें से एक विकल्प सही पर्यायवाची है, उसका चयन कीजिए :

1. **अग्नि**
   A. अनिल   B. अनल
   C. गर्म   D. ताप
2. **अमृत**
   A. पीयूष   B. गरल
   C. सरस   D. जीवनदायनी

3. आँख
   A. लोचन B. आस्थि
   C. वदन D. जलज

4. आकाश
   A. अनन्त B. पाताल
   C. वितल D. तल

5. कपड़ा
   A. परिधान B. पटिका
   C. पीताम्बर D. लँहगा

6. कमल
   A. सरोज B. सरोवर
   C. पंक D. पुष्प

7. गंगा
   A. पाताल नदी B. हिमनदी
   C. भागीरथ D. त्रिपथगा

8. चाँद
   A. मयंक B. भानु
   C. दिनकर D. रवि

9. नदी
   A. सरिता B. प्रवाह
   C. धारा D. जलधर

10. पर्वत
    A. पत्थर B. चट्टान
    C. शिखर D. मेरू

11. पवन
    A. अनिल B. अनल
    C. अग D. विहग

12. पति
    A. साजन B. प्रिया
    C. भार्या D. दारा

13. पानी
    A. मही B. मेदिनी
    C. अम्बु D. तरणी

14. पुत्र
    A. आत्मज B. तनया
    C. सुता D. आत्मजा

15. पुत्री
    A. सुता B. सुत
    C. आत्मज D. नन्दन

16. फूल
    A. बहार B. मधु
    C. माधव D. सुमन

17. वृक्ष
    A. विटप B. अम्र
    C. प्रसून D. रसा

18. बादल
    A. अज B. व्यामोह
    C. नीरद D. मधुप

19. बिजली
    A. चंचला B. खटका
    C. त्रास D. संत्रास

20. माता
    A. धात्री B. धरणी
    C. धरित्री D. श्यामा

21. घोषणा
    A. आवाज B. पुकारना
    C. ऐलान D. ललकारना

22. उत्कर्ष
    A. आकर्षण B. विकर्षण
    C. उन्नति D. निष्कर्ष

23. उदय
    A. अन्त B. विकास
    C. प्रगट D. व्यस्त

24. दक्ष
    A. निपुण B. समर्थ
    C. कर्मठ D. मेहनती

25. संवाद
    A. विवाद B. झगड़ा
    C. सम्बोधन D. वार्तालाप

उत्तरमाला

1. B	2. A	3. A	4. A	5. A
6. A	7. D	8. A	9. A	10. D
11. A	12. A	13. C	14. A	15. A
16. D	17. A	18. C	19. A	20. A
21. C	22. C	23. C	24. A	25. D

अभ्यास-3

निर्देशः नीचे चार-चार शब्दों के समूह दिए गए हैं। प्रत्येक समूह में एक शब्द बेमेल है तथा शेष तीन शब्द पर्यायवाची हैं, आपको उस शब्द का चयन करना है, जो बेमेल है :

1. A. तम B. अंधकार
   C. तिमिर D. अंश

2. A. अनल B. आग
   C. दहन D. तमिस्रा

3. A. अतुल B. अद्वितीय
   C. अनुपम D. शुष्मा

4. A. अहं B. अहंकार
   C. दर्प D. निराला

5. A. पता   B. खोज
   C. जाँच   D. शोध

6. A. गरल   B. पीयूष
   C. सुधा   D. सोम

7. A. कानन   B. जंगल
   C. पादप   D. वन

8. A. अश्व   B. गज
   C. घोड़ा   D. तुरंग

9. A. दानव   B. मानव
   C. दैत्य   D. राक्षस

10. A. आँख   B. चक्षु
    C. नयन   D. मुख

11. A. अन्तरिक्ष   B. वसुन्धरा
    C. आसमान   D. गगन

12. A. इच्छा   B. अभिलाषा
    C. कामना   D. प्रयोजन

13. A. कपड़ा   B. चीर
    C. वसन   D. पोशाक

14. A. अब्ज   B. कमल
    C. राजीव   D. आम्र

15. A. कोयल   B. पिक
    C. काग   D. वनप्रिय

16. A. गंगा   B. देवनदी
    C. गोदावरी   D. भागीरथी

17. A. गणेश   B. एकदन्त
    C. देवराज   D. गणपति

18. A. घर   B. निलय
    C. निकेतन   D. झोपड़ी

19. A. चाँद   B. हिमांशु
    C. विनायक   D. सुधांशु

20. A. नदी   B. तरणी
    C. तटिनी   D. सरिता

21. A. पक्षी   B. चिड़िया
    C. सुमन   D. विहग

22. A. पवन   B. अचला
    C. वात   D. वायु

23. A. समीर   B. पृथ्वी
    C. भू   D. भूमि

24. A. पानी   B. समीर
    C. अम्बु   D. जल

25. A. पुत्र   B. तनया
    C. तनय   D. सुत

26. A. पुत्र   B. तनया
    C. सुता   D. कन्या

27. A. गृहिणी   B. आदमी
    C. पुरुष   D. नर

28. A. मधु   B. फूल
    C. पुष्प   D. सुमन

29. A. माधव   B. तरु
    C. पेड़   D. वृक्ष

30. A. माता   B. अम्बु
    C. अम्मा   D. जननी

उत्तरमाला

1. D	2. D	3. D	4. D	5. A
6. A	7. C	8. B	9. B	10. D
11. B	12. D	13. D	14. D	15. C
16. C	17. C	18. D	19. C	20. B
21. C	22. B	23. A	24. B	25. B
26. A	27. A	28. A	29. A	30. B

अभ्यास-4

निर्देश: *गहरे काले शब्द के विलोम शब्द का चयन कीजिए:*

1. उसे हर काम में **सफलता** मिल रही है।
   A. असफलता   B. सफल
   C. कुशलता   D. निपुणता

2. कभी किसी की **निन्दा** नहीं करनी चाहिए।
   A. गुणगान   B. स्तुति
   C. प्रशंसा   D. यशोगान

3. आलस्य व्यक्ति का सबसे बड़ा **दुश्मन** है।
   A. शत्रु   B. घातक
   C. मित्र   D. सहायक

4. वे बुढ़ापे से **दुखी** हैं।
   A. अप्रसन्न   B. सुखी
   C. खुश   D. नाराज

5. यहाँ उसकी **चतुराई** नहीं चली।
   A. चालाकी   B. बहादुरी
   C. निपुणता   D. मूर्खता

6. शहद की **मिठास** कम नहीं होती।
   A. मीठा   B. तीखा
   C. कड़ुवा   D. खहा

7. साहसी के **साहस** को देखकर मैं चकित रह गया।
   - A. हिम्मत
   - B. बहादुरी
   - C. निडर
   - D. भय

8. फिल्मोत्सव में सर्वश्रेष्ठ **अभिनेता** को पुरस्कार प्रदान किया गया।
   - A. हीरोइन
   - B. नेत्री
   - C. मीनाक्षी
   - D. अभिनेत्री

9. नाटक में नायक और **नायिका** की भूमिका महत्वपूर्ण होती है:
   - A. हीरो
   - B. नायक
   - C. नेत्र
   - D. नेता

10. कवि-सम्मेलन में एक कवि और एक **कवयित्री** को आमंत्रित किया गया था।
    - A. लेखक
    - B. सम्पादक
    - C. नेता
    - D. कवि

11. विद्यालय के वार्षिकोत्सव के लिए नेता और एक **नेत्री** को आमंत्रित किया गया।
    - A. अभिनेता
    - B. विद्वान्
    - C. विदुषी
    - D. नेता

12. मोहन बहुत **चतुर** है।
    - A. निपुण
    - B. तेज
    - C. सुस्त
    - D. मूर्ख

13. सोहन अब पूर्ण **स्वस्थ** है।
    - A. प्रसन्न
    - B. खुश
    - C. अस्वस्थ
    - D. अप्रसन्न

14. पक्षी **आकाश** में उड़ते हैं :
    - A. गगन
    - B. नम
    - C. धरती
    - D. पाताल

15. वह विद्यालय में देर से आया और **अनुपस्थित** हो गया।
    - A. पूर्व
    - B. उपस्थित
    - C. प्रवेश
    - D. समयपूर्व

16. **बालक** चाँद की ओर देख रहा है।
    - A. बालिका
    - B. लड़का
    - C. बच्चा
    - D. बच्ची

17. मैं उसके विचार से बिल्कुल **सहमत** नहीं हूँ।
    - A. समर्थन
    - B. सहमति
    - C. असहमत
    - D. प्रशंसक

18. उसकी हालत **अधिक** खराब है।
    - A. बहुत
    - B. कम
    - C. ठीक
    - D. कुशल

19. **धर्म** की सर्वत्र विजय होती है:
    - A. अधर्म
    - B. ज्ञान
    - C. भक्ति
    - D. ईमानदारी

20. अच्छे चरित्र के बिना जीवन **निर्थक** है:
    - A. व्यर्थ
    - B. अर्थपूर्ण
    - C. सार्थक
    - D. कुशल

21. **ईमानदारी** बड़ी दुर्लभ वस्तु है:
    - A. सच्चाई
    - B. भलाई
    - C. बेइमानी
    - D. परोपकारी

22. एवरेस्ट संसार का सबसे **ऊँचा** पर्वत है:
    - A. नीचा
    - B. वितल
    - C. पाताल
    - D. मध्यम

23. वह विश्वास के **योग्य** नहीं है:
    - A. काबिल
    - B. विश्वासी
    - C. अयोग्य
    - D. बेकार

24. क्या वह इतना **मूर्ख** है?
    - A. चालाक
    - B. विद्वान्
    - C. बुद्धिमान
    - D. धूर्त

25. कितना सुहावना **दृश्य** है!
    - A. अदृश्य
    - B. दर्शनीय
    - C. सुन्दर
    - D. व्यर्थ

उत्तरमाला

1. A	2. C	3. C	4. B	5. D
6. C	7. D	8. D	9. B	10. D
11. D	12. D	13. C	14. D	15. B
16. A	17. C	18. B	19. A	20. C
21. C	22. A	23. C	24. C	25. A

अभ्यास-5

निर्देशः नीचे प्रत्येक **काले गहरे शब्द** के चार विलोम दिए गए हैं। इनमें सही विलोम का चयन कीजिए :

1. **अग्नि**
   - A. आग
   - B. अनल
   - C. दहन
   - D. जल

2. **अग्रज**
   - A. अनुज
   - B. भ्राता
   - C. भाई
   - D. अम्बा

3. **अच्छा**
   - A. बुरा
   - B. खराब
   - C. गंदा
   - D. भ्रष्ट

4. **अंत**
   - A. प्रारम्भ
   - B. समाप्त
   - C. शेष
   - D. अल्प

5. **अचल**
   - A. विचल
   - B. वितल
   - C. सजल
   - D. चल

6. अति
   A. अधिक B. बहुत
   C. अल्प D. कम

7. अत्यधिक
   A. अल्प B. अधिक
   C. स्वल्प D. न्यूनतम

8. अंधकार
   A. अंधेरा B. प्रकाश
   C. रात्रि D. दिन

9. अतिवृष्टि
   A. अनावृष्टि B. वृष्टि
   C. वर्षा D. वर्षण

10. अनाथ
    A. नाथ B. स्वामी
    C. मासिक D. सनाथ

11. अनुकूल
    A. मनोकूल B. प्रतिकूल
    C. अनुकरण D. मनस्वी

12. अनुराग
    A. राग B. विराग
    C. विग्रह D. स्नेह

13. अन्त
    A. श्री गणेश B. आदि
    C. शुरुआत D. समाप्त

14. अपना
    A. अपनत्व B. पराया
    C. मित्र D. शत्रु

15. अपमान
    A. मान B. सम्मान
    C. वर्तमान D. स्वाभिमान

16. अपेक्षा
    A. इच्छा B. स्वेच्छा
    C. प्रविच्छा D. उपेक्षा

17. अमर
    A. मर्त्य B. मृत्यु
    C. सुधा D. गरल

18. अल्पायु
    A. चिरायु B. उमरदराज
    C. नश्वर D. सनातन

19. अस्त
    A. उदय B. विकास
    C. निर्माण D. सृष्टि

20. आकर्षण
    A. प्रतिकर्षण B. विकर्षण
    C. सम्मोहन D. विरत

21. आकाश
    A. गगन B. नभ
    C. वसुन्धरा D. पाताल

22. आगे
    A. पीछे B. पूर्व
    C. पृष्ट D. पृष्ठ

23. आजाद
    A. स्वतंत्र B. स्वतंत्रतता
    C. परतंत्र D. गुलाम

24. आदान
    A. आयात B. निर्यात
    C. प्रदान D. निदान

25. आधुनिक
    A. अर्वाचीन B. नूतन
    C. प्राचीन D. वर्तमान

उत्तरमाला

1. D	2. A	3. A	4. A	5. D
6. D	7. C	8. B	9. A	10. D
11. B	12. B	13. A	14. B	15. B
16. D	17. A	18. A	19. A	20. B
21. D	22. A	23. D	24. C	25. C

अभ्यास-6

निर्देशः *नीचे कुछ शब्द दिए गए हैं प्रत्येक शब्द के चार वैकल्पिक अर्थ दिए गए हैं। सही अर्थ का चयन कीजिए :*

1. सुरक्षित
   A. कुशल B. घटना
   C. दुर्घटना D. बचाव

2. प्रतिभाशाली
   A. सज्जन B. कुशाग्र
   C. विद्वान् D. वैभवशाली

3. आत्मसमर्पण
   A. अपने आप को सौंपना B. समर्पण
   C. अर्पण D. त्यागज

4. सिद्धहस्त
   A. निपुण B. कर्मठ
   C. मेहनती D. परिश्रमी

5. सुशोभित
   A. मजेदार B. सुस्वागतम्
   C. अच्छा D. शोभा पाना

6. स्वादिष्ट
   A. मजेदार B. बेकार
   C. मीठा D. तीखा

7. स्वावलम्बी
   A. निर्भर
   B. परालंबी
   C. आत्मनिर्भर
   D. अतिथि

8. उपकरण
   A. साधन
   B. युक्ति
   C. यंत्र
   D. मशीन

9. कीमत
   A. क्रय
   B. विक्रय
   C. मूल्य
   D. बिक्री

10. संगठन
    A. एकता
    B. अनेकता
    C. समूह
    D. संस्था

11. विपत्ति
    A. दुख
    B. विपदा
    C. मुसीबत
    D. सुख

12. तृण
    A. तिनका
    B. धूल
    C. धूप
    D. लकड़ी

13. आश्चर्य
    A. निरीक्षण
    B. दृष्टिगोचर
    C. हैरानी
    D. थकावट

14. हार्दिक
    A. हृदय से
    B. शरीर से
    C. मन से
    D. मस्तिष्क से

15. नियति
    A. भाग्य
    B. किनारा
    C. समय
    D. पवित्र

16. सुगन्धित
    A. दुर्गन्ध
    B. खुशबू वाला
    C. फूल
    D. कमल

17. उत्साह
    A. होश
    B. हवास
    C. जोश
    D. हिम्मत

18. सहयोग
    A. मिलन सार
    B. मेहनती
    C. परोपकारी
    D. आपसी सहायता

19. मुसीबत
    A. विपत्ति
    B. सुशोभित
    C. सहायता
    D. मदद

20. निरक्षर
    A. साक्षर
    B. दर्शनीय
    C. पठनीय
    D. अनपढ़

21. उपवन
    A. वन
    B. तीर
    C. जंगल
    D. बाग

22. मेघ
    A. बादल
    B. पंकज
    C. राजीव
    D. मेघनाद

23. आधुनिक
    A. प्राचीन
    B. पुरातन
    C. भूतकाल
    D. आज का

24. तीर
    A. वाण
    B. धनुष
    C. किनारा
    D. नदी

25. परीक्षण
    A. जाँच
    B. पड़ताल
    C. परीक्षा
    D. इम्तहान

26. अभिवादन
    A. नमस्ते
    B. प्रणाम
    C. बधाई
    D. शुभकामना

27. सर्वत्र
    A. नश्वर
    B. सजीव
    C. ईश्वर
    D. सभी जगह

28. हलवाहा
    A. चरवाहा
    B. किसान
    C. मजदूर
    D. हल चलाने वाला

29. शिखर
    A. पर्वत
    B. पहाड़
    C. टीला
    D. चोटी

30. भयानक
    A. डरावना
    B. भयभीत
    C. डरना
    D. खूँखार

उत्तरमाला

1. D	2. B	3. A	4. A	5. D
6. A	7. C	8. C	9. C	10. A
11. C	12. A	13. C	14. A	15. A
16. B	17. C	18. D	19. A	20. D
21. D	22. A	23. D	24. A	25. A
26. B	27. D	28. D	29. D	30. A

अभ्यास-7

निर्देशः नीचे कुछ शब्द दिए जा रहे हैं। प्रत्येक शब्द के **उपसर्ग** के सन्दर्भ में चार विकल्प दिए गए हैं। आपको सही विकल्प का चयन करना है :

1. अलबत्ता
   A. अ
   B. अल
   C. लब
   D. त्ता

2. अलगरज
   A. अल
   B. लग
   C. गर
   D. रज

3. कमसिन
 A. क B. कम
 C. सि D. सिन

4. अनमोल
 A. अ B. अन
 C. मो D. मोल

5. अनजान
 A. अ B. अन
 C. जा D. जान

6. अनपढ़
 A. अ B. पढ़
 C. प D. अन

7. अधखिला
 A. अ B. अध
 C. ला D. खिला

8. अधजला
 A. अ B. ज
 C. अध D. ला

9. अधपका
 A. अ B. अध
 C. पका D. का

10. अघखिला
 A. अ B. अघ
 C. खिला D. ला

11. उन्नीस
 A. उन B. उन्
 C. नीस D. स

12. उनसठ
 A. उ B. उन
 C. सठ D. ठ

13. दुकाल
 A. द B. दुक
 C. दु D. काल

14. दुबला
 A. दब B. दुब
 C. ला D. दु

15. निकम्मा
 A. नि B. निक
 C. कम्मा D. मा

16. निर्लज्ज
 A. निर B. निल
 C. नि D. लज्ज

17. बिनब्याहा
 A. बि B. बिन
 C. ब्याहा D. हा

18. भरपेट
 A. भर B. पेट
 C. पे D. ट

19. भरपाई
 A. भ B. र
 C. पा D. भर

20. कुपात्र
 A. कु B. कुप
 C. पा D. पात्र

21. सुजान
 A. सु B. सुज
 C. सुजा D. जान

22. गैर कानूनी
 A. गै B. गैर
 C. कानु D. नुनी

23. गैरसरकारी
 A. गैर B. सर
 C. का D. कारी

24. अपमान
 A. अ B. अप
 C. मा D. मान

25. अनुशासन
 A. अ B. शासन
 C. सन D. अनु

26. अविनीत
 A. अवि B. अ
 C. नी D. नीत

27. अभिमान
 A. अभि B. अ
 C. मा D. मान

28. अभियान
 A. अ B. मान
 C. यान D. अभि

29. अध्ययन
 A. अध् B. अधि
 C. यन D. न

30. निश्चल
 A. नि B. निर
 C. निस D. चल

उत्तरमाला				
1. B	2. A	3. B	4. B	5. B
6. D	7. B	8. C	9. B	10. B
11. A	12. B	13. C	14. D	15. B
16. A	17. B	18. A	19. D	20. A
21. A	22. B	23. A	24. B	25. D
26. B	27. A	28. D	29. B	30. A

अभ्यास-8

निर्देशः *निम्नलिखित शब्दों में प्रयुक्त प्रत्यय सम्बन्धी चार विकल्प दिए गए हैं, सही विकल्प का चयन कीजिए :*

1. भलाई
   - A. ई
   - B. लाई
   - C. आई
   - D. भला

2. चतुराई
   - A. चतु
   - B. रा
   - C. ई
   - D. आई

3. भूखा
   - A. भू
   - B. भूख
   - C. खा
   - D. आ

4. भिड़न्त
   - A. भिड़
   - B. भि
   - C. न्त
   - D. अन्त

5. प्यासा
   - A. आस
   - B. सा
   - C. आसा
   - D. सा

6. बिकाऊ
   - A. बिक
   - B. काऊ
   - C. आऊ
   - D. ऊ

7. तैराक
   - A. तै
   - B. तैर
   - C. राक
   - D. आक

8. सन्नाटा
   - A. सन्
   - B. सन्ना
   - C. नाटा
   - D. आटा

9. लोहार
   - A. लोह
   - B. आरा
   - C. आरी
   - D. आर

10. मिलान
    - A. आना
    - B. आने
    - C. आनी
    - D. आन

11. चढ़ाव
    - A. चढ़
    - B. चढ़ा
    - C. आव
    - D. व

12. लगाव
    - A. लग
    - B. अव
    - C. आव
    - D. गाव

13. लिखावट
    - A. लिख
    - B. लिखा
    - C. वट
    - D. आवट

14. मिलावट
    - A. मिल
    - B. वट
    - C. आवट
    - D. ट

15. मिठास
    - A. मिठ
    - B. ठास
    - C. आस
    - D. स

16. चिकनाहट
    - A. चिक
    - B. नाट
    - C. हट
    - D. आहट

17. सड़ियल
    - A. सड़
    - B. यल
    - C. ड़ियल
    - D. इयल

18. मरियल
    - A. मर
    - B. यल
    - C. मरि
    - D. इयल

19. गड़रिया
    - A. गड़
    - B. इया
    - C. रिया
    - D. या

20. सजीला
    - A. ईला
    - B. इला
    - C. ला
    - D. स

21. लुटेरा
    - A. लुट
    - B. एरा
    - C. ऐरा
    - D. रा

22. लठैत
    - A. ए
    - B. ऐ
    - C. ऐत
    - D. त

23. भगोड़ा
    - A. ओ
    - B. ओड़ा
    - C. ड़ा
    - D. भगो

24. खपत
    - A. ख
    - B. प
    - C. त
    - D. पत

25. जीवट
    - A. व
    - B. अट
    - C. जीव
    - D. जी

उत्तरमाला

1. C	2. D	3. D	4. D	5. D
6. C	7. D	8. D	9. D	10. D
11. C	12. C	13. D	14. C	15. C
16. D	17. D	18. D	19. B	20. A
21. B	22. C	23. B	24. C	25. B

अभ्यास-9

निर्देशः *नीचे कुछ मुहावरे दिए गए हैं। प्रत्येक के अर्थ के लिए चार विकल्प दिए गए हैं। आपको सही विकल्प का चयन करना है :*

1. **अक्ल पर पत्थर पड़ना**
   A. बुद्धि काम न करना   B. दुविधा होना
   C. संकट में होना   D. परेशान होना

2. **अपना उल्लू सीधा करना**
   A. अवसर देखना   B. काम निकालना
   C. मतलब साधना   D. मूर्ख बनाना

3. **अपने मुँह मियाँ-मिट्ठू बनना**
   A. मिठाई खाना   B. प्रशंसा करना
   C. निंदा करना   D. अपनी प्रशंसा स्वयं करना

4. **अपने पाँव पर आप कुल्हाड़ी मारना**
   A. हानि पहुँचाना   B. खेद होना
   C. अपना पैर काटना   D. अपनी हानि स्वयं करना

5. **आँखें चुरा लेना**
   A. भाग जाना   B. छिप जाना
   C. अनदेखा करना   D. मिल जाना

6. **अक्ल का दुश्मन**
   A. मित्र होना   B. शत्रु होना
   C. महामूर्ख   D. महाविद्वान्

7. **अंधे की लाठी**
   A. एक मात्र सहारा   B. मित्र होना
   C. शत्रु होना   D. दुख पहुँचाना

8. **आकाश-पाताल एक करना**
   A. भाग-दौड़ करना   B. परेशान होना
   C. थक जाना   D. कठिन परिश्रम करना

9. **घड़ों पानी पड़ना**
   A. लज्जित होना   B. तुच्छ समझना
   C. लाभ होना   D. थकावट

10. **अगर-मगर करना**
    A. नुकसान करना   B. बहाने बनाना
    C. बदनाम करना   D. कपट करना

11. **मुँह की खाना**
    A. गिर जाना   B. हार जाना
    C. भाग जाना   D. व्यर्थ होना

12. **आस्तीन का साँप होना**
    A. शत्रु   B. मित्र
    C. कपटी मित्र   D. दयालु

13. **एक आँख से देखना**
    A. बुरा व्यवहार   B. समान व्यवहार
    C. कपट करना   D. लज्जित होना

14. **बाल-बाँका न होना**
    A. घायल होना   B. साफ बच जाना
    C. क्रोधित होना   D. स्वस्थ होना

15. **दाँतों तले उँगली दबाना**
    A. उँगली काटना   B. चिंतित हो जाना
    C. चकित रह जाना   D. प्रसन्न हो जाना

16. **जान के लाले पड़ना**
    A. मरने का खतरा होना   B. भाग जाना
    C. हार जाना   D. मुश्किल में पड़ना

17. **बोली मारना**
    A. ताना देना   B. सताना
    C. मजाक करना   D. याद दिलाना

18. **अंधों में काना राजा**
    A. मूर्खों में अल्पज्ञ को विद्वान् माना जाना
    B. सबको मूर्ख समझना
    C. अत्यधिक महत्त्वपूर्ण
    D. काना राजा

19. **अक्ल के घोड़े दौड़ाना**
    A. बुद्धि लड़ाना
    B. कल्पना करना
    C. तरह-तरह के उपाय सोचना
    D. ज्ञान-प्राप्त करना

20. **पानी उतर जाना**
    A. शर्म करना   B. लज्जित न होना
    C. भाग जाना   D. इज्जत करना

21. **तीन-पाँच करना**
    A. तितर-बितर करना
    B. वचन देकर फिर जाना
    C. घुमा-फिरा कर बातें करना
    D. परेशान करना

22. **हथियार डाल देना**
    A. हार जाना   B. जीत जाना
    C. धोखा देना   D. विजय होना

23. **आँख खुलना**
    A. होश में आना   B. अत्यन्त प्यार होना
    C. उल्टा काम करना   D. क्रोध करना

24. **कमर सीधी करना**
    A. थक जाना   B. थकावट दूर करना
    C. काम करना   D. परिश्रम करना

25. **पगड़ी रखना**
    A. चैन की सांस लेना   B. अपमान करना
    C. दया की भीख माँगना   D. अपमान होना

26. **लोहा मानना**
    A. संघर्ष करना   B. विजय होना
    C. श्रेष्ठता स्वीकार करना   D. खुशामद करना

27. **काठ मार जाना**
    A. दुःखी होना   B. चुप होना
    C. सफल होना   D. मर जाना

28. **चाँद पर थूकना**
   A. अपमान करना
   B. बढ़कर बातें करना
   C. महान पुरुष पर लांछन लगाना
   D. महत्त्वाकांक्षी होना

29. **उगल देना**
   A. अपराध स्वीकार कर लेना
   B. सच बोलना
   C. उल्टी करना
   D. अनपच होना

30. **हाथ मलना**
   A. पश्चाताप करना   B. सर्दी मिटाना
   C. दुख करना   D. तैयार होना

उत्तरमाला

1. A	2. C	3. D	4. D	5. C
6. C	7. A	8. D	9. A	10. B
11. B	12. C	13. B	14. B	15. C
16. D	17. A	18. A	19. A	20. B
21. C	22. A	23. A	24. B	25. C
26. C	27. B	28. C	29. A	30. A

अभ्यास-10

निर्देशः *नीचे कुछ वाक्य खण्ड दिए गए हैं, पूरे वाक्य खण्ड के लिए एक शब्द का चयन कीजिए।*

1. जिसका आदि न हो
   A. अनंत   B. अमर
   C. शाश्वत   D. अनादि

2. जो कुछ न जानता हो
   A. मूर्ख   B. महामूर्ख
   C. ज्ञानी   D. अज्ञ

3. जो अनुकरण करने योग्य हो
   A. अनुकरणीय   B. अद्वितीय
   C. आदरणीय   D. अगम

4. जिसका अंत न हो
   A. अनंत   B. अनादि
   C. आदि   D. परलोक

5. जो कभी न मरे
   A. मर्त्य   B. मुर्त्त
   C. अमुर्त्त   D. अमर

6. जिसके समान दूसरा न हो
   A. अनुकूल   B. प्रतिकूल
   C. कृतज्ञ   D. अद्वितीय

7. जो कम बोलता हो
   A. मृदुभाषी   B. वाचाल
   C. अल्पभाषी   D. अल्पज्ञ

8. जिसका इलाज न हो
   A. मरणशील   B. अमरत्व
   C. बिमारी   D. लाइलाज

9. जिस का विश्वास न किया जा सके
   A. विश्वसनीय   B. अविश्वसनीय
   C. विश्वासी   D. धूर्त्त

10. जिसका कोई नाथ न हो
   A. सनाथ   B. स्वामी
   C. नाथ   D. अनाथ

11. कम जानने वाला
   A. अल्पज्ञ   B. अज्ञ
   C. विद्   D. विद्वान

12. जहाँ जाना संभव न हो
   A. दुर्गम   B. अगम
   C. तल   D. वितल

13. कम खाने वाला
   A. बहुभोजी   B. पेटु
   C. कंजूस   D. अल्पाहारी

14. जो बात पहले कभी न हुई हो
   A. भूतपूर्व   B. अभूतपूर्व
   C. प्राचीन   D. अर्वाचीन

15. जिस स्त्री के सन्तान न हों
   A. बाँझ   B. कुलटा
   C. पतिता   D. विधवा

16. जो कहा न जा सके
   A. अकथनीय   B. अकथ्य
   C. करणीय   D. सम्भव

17. एहसान न मानने वाला
   A. कृतज्ञ   B. कृतघ्न
   C. आस्तिक   D. विश्वासी

18. जिसने देश के साथ विश्वासघात किया हो
   A. विश्वासघाती   B. द्रोही
   C. आतंकवादी   D. देश द्रोही

19. जिसने राष्ट्र के हित में अपना जीवन बलिदान कर दिया हो
   A. देशभक्त   B. शहीद
   C. राष्ट्रभूत   D. भारतपुत्र

20. वह जमीन जिसमें कुछ भी पैदा न हो
   A. ऊसर   B. बंजर
   C. उर्वर   D. पथरीला

21. वह वस्तु जिसकी चाह हो
   A. श्रेष्ठ   B. आवश्यक
   C. इच्छित   D. अभीष्ट

22. दूसरों के पीछे चलने वाला
    A. अनुयायी   B. अनुज
    C. अनुचर   D. अनुकरणीय
23. जो पहले न पढ़ा हो
    A. पठित   B. अपठित
    C. पठनीय   D. अपठनीय
24. जिसके आर-पार दिखाई देता हो
    A. अपारदर्शी   B. गम्य
    C. अगम्य   D. पारदर्शी
25. आज्ञा पालन करने वाला
    A. शिष्य   B. शिष्या
    C. अनुचर   D. आज्ञाकारी
26. काम से जी चुराने वाला
    A. कामचोर   B. आलसी
    C. कर्मठ   D. परिश्रमी
27. प्रतिदिन होने वाला
    A. दैनिक   B. शाश्वत
    C. सनातन   D. अमर
28. जिसका कोई अर्थ न हो
    A. सार्थक   B. निरर्थक
    C. आर्थिक   D. अनार्थिक
29. उपकार मानने वाला
    A. कृतज्ञ   B. कृतघ्न
    C. विश्वासी   D. अनुयायी
30. हाथ से लिखा हुआ
    A. पठनीय   B. अपठनीय
    C. स्पष्ट   D. हस्तलिखित

उत्तरमाला

1. D	2. D	3. A	4. A	5. D
6. D	7. C	8. D	9. B	10. D
11. A	12. A	13. D	14. B	15. A
16. A	17. B	18. D	19. B	20. A
21. C	22. C	23. B	24. D	25. D
26. A	27. A	28. B	29. A	30. D

अभ्यास-11

निर्देशः *नीचे कुछ संज्ञा शब्द दिए जा रहे हैं। प्रत्येक के संज्ञा-भेद के लिए चार विकल्प दिए गये है। सही विकल्प का चयन कीजिए :*

1. तुलसीदास
   A. जातिवाचक   B. भाववाचक
   C. व्यक्तिवाचक   D. समूहवाचक
2. यमुना
   A. व्यक्तिवाचक   B. जातिवाचक
   C. समूहवाचक   D. भाववाचक
3. बच्चा
   A. जातिवाचक   B. समूहवाचक
   C. भाववाचक   D. व्यक्तिवाचक
4. मानवता
   A. भाववाचक   B. जातिवाचक
   C. द्रव्यवाचक   D. समूहवाचक
5. हिमालय
   A. व्यक्तिवाचक   B. जातिवाचक
   C. भाववाचक   D. समूहवाचक
6. भारत
   A. जातिवाचक   B. भाववाचक
   C. व्यक्तिवाचक   D. समूहवाचक
7. एशिया
   A. व्यक्तिवाचक   B. भाववाचक
   C. द्रव्यवाचक   D. समूहवाचक
8. महाराष्ट्र
   A. जातिवाचक   B. व्यक्तिवाचक
   C. समूहवाचक   D. द्रव्यवाचक
9. सूर सागर
   A. व्यक्तिवाचक   B. भाववाचक
   C. द्रव्यवाचक   D. समूहवाचक
10. सोमवार
    A. जातिवाचक   B. व्यक्तिवाचक
    C. द्रव्यवाचक   D. समूहवाचक
11. खटमल
    A. जातिवाचक   B. व्यक्तिवाचक
    C. द्रव्यवाचक   D. समूहवाचक
12. मैना
    A. जातिवाचक   B. व्यक्तिवाचक
    C. द्रव्यवाचक   D. समूहवाचक
13. चाँदी
    A. द्रव्यवाचक   B. समूहवाचक
    C. भाववाचक   D. व्यक्तिवाचक
14. अच्छाई
    A. भाववाचक   B. समूहवाचक
    C. जातिवाचक   D. व्यक्तिवाचक
15. पीतल
    A. द्रव्यवाचक   B. भाववाचक
    C. व्यक्तिवाचक   D. जातिवाचक
16. वीरता
    A. भाववाचक   B. जातिवाचक
    C. द्रव्यवाचक   D. समूहवाचक
17. रूस
    A. जातिवाचक   B. व्यक्तिवाचक
    C. भाववाचक   D. द्रव्यवाचक

18. लम्बाई
    A. भाववाचक
    B. समूहवाचक
    C. द्रव्यवाचक
    D. व्यक्तिवाचक

19. दल
    A. जातिवाचक
    B. व्यक्तिवाचक
    C. समूहवाचक
    D. द्रव्यवाचक

20. मार्च
    A. समूहवाचक
    B. व्यक्तिवाचक
    C. द्रव्यवाचक
    D. जातिवाचक

21. झुण्ड
    A. समूहवाचक
    B. जातिवाचक
    C. व्यक्तिवाचक
    D. द्रव्यवाचक

22. टोली
    A. जातिवाचक
    B. व्यक्तिवाचक
    C. समूहवाचक
    D. द्रव्यवाचक

23. सुभाष चौक
    A. जातिवाचक
    B. समूहवाचक
    C. व्यक्तिवाचक
    D. भाववाचक

24. संघ
    A. जातिवाचक
    B. द्रव्यवाचक
    C. समूहवाचक
    D. भाववाचक

25. गिरोह
    A. समूहवाचक
    B. द्रव्यवाचक
    C. जातिवाचक
    D. भाववाचक

उत्तरमाला

1. C	2. A	3. A	4. A	5. A
6. C	7. A	8. B	9. A	10. B
11. A	12. A	13. A	14. A	15. A
16. A	17. B	18. A	19. C	20. B
21. A	22. C	23. C	24. C	25. A

अभ्यास-12

निर्देशः *नीचे दिए गए वाक्य में रिक्त स्थान है। प्रत्येक वाक्य के नीचे कारक चिह्न दिए गए हैं। रिक्त स्थान की पूर्ति के लिए उपयुक्त कारक चिह्न का चयन कीजिए :*

1. निम्नलिखित शब्दों........अर्थ बताइए
   A. का
   B. के
   C. से
   D. पर

2. सरकार मुझे नौकरी........मत निकालिए
   A. पर
   B. में
   C. से
   D. को

3. इस कथन........पुष्टि कीजिए
   A. को
   B. से
   C. की
   D. ने

4. छात्र-छात्राएँ राष्ट्र........सम्पत्ति और उसके भावी कर्णधार होते हैं
   A. के
   B. की
   C. को
   D. में

5. प्रत्येक प्रश्न........चार सम्भावित उत्तर दिए गए हैं
   A. के लिए
   B. में
   C. के
   D. से

6. माता बच्चे........पढ़ाती है
   A. को
   B. के
   C. की
   D. से

7. गुरुजी........सबसे छोटे लड़के को एक नारंगी दी
   A. ने
   B. को
   C. से
   D. के लिए

8. मोहन सोहन से मिलने........गया है
   A. से
   B. के
   C. को
   D. के लिए

9. उसने कलम........लिखा
   A. के
   B. में
   C. पर
   D. से

10. मैं ड्राइवर........गाड़ी चलवाता हूँ
    A. के
    B. पर
    C. में
    D. से

11. शिक्षक छात्रों........पुस्तक पढ़वाते हैं
    A. के लिए
    B. में
    C. पर
    D. से

12. मैंने दाढ़ी........उसे मुसलमान समझ लिया
    A. से
    B. के
    C. को
    D. के लिए

13. श्याम अपने भाई हरि........आम लाया है
    A. के
    B. के लिए
    C. का
    D. पर

14. मोहन घर........आता है
    A. में
    B. पर
    C. से
    D. का

15. उसे पाँच दिनों........मूर्च्छा आया करती है
    A. पर
    B. से
    C. के
    D. को

16. मेधावी छात्र परीक्षा........चोरी नहीं करते
    A. में
    B. पर
    C. से
    D. के लिए

उत्तरमाला

1. A	2. C	3. C	4. B	5. C
6. A	7. A	8. D	9. D	10. D
11. D	12. A	13. B	14. C	15. B
16. D				

गद्यांश (अपठित-बोध)

गद्यांश 1

यदि हम निरन्तर प्रयत्न करेंगे तो निश्चय ही अपने सभी लक्ष्यों को प्राप्त कर लेंगे, किन्तु प्रायः देखा जाता है कि अधिक आशावादी लोग थोड़ा सा प्रयत्न करके अधिक फल की कामना करने लगते हैं और मनोवांछित फल प्राप्त न होने पर निराश हो जाते हैं। अतः जीवन में सफलता प्राप्त करने के लिए परिस्थितियों के समक्ष घुटने न टेकें, बल्कि दृढ़ता से उनका मुकाबला करें। याद रखें, जितना कठोर हमारा परिश्रम होगा उसका फल भी उतना ही मीठा होगा।

उपर्युक्त गद्यांश को ध्यानपूर्वक पढ़ें और निम्न प्रश्नों के उत्तर के लिए सही विकल्प को चुनें:

1. फल न मिलने पर कौन निराश हो जाते हैं?
   - A. आशावादी लोग
   - B. कम आशावादी लोग
   - C. अधिक आशावादी लोग
   - D. निराशावादी लोग

2. लक्ष्य प्राप्ति के लिए क्या किया जाना चाहिए?
   - A. फल की कामना
   - B. हिम्मत से मुकाबला
   - C. निरन्तर प्रयत्न
   - D. परिस्थितियों से मुकाबला

3. आशावादी शब्द का विलोम शब्द है:
   - A. निराश
   - B. निराशावादी
   - B. दुखी
   - D. अप्रसन्न

4. मनोवांछित शब्द का क्या अर्थ है?
   - A. इच्छित
   - B. परीक्षित
   - C. लाभदायक
   - D. मन को खुश करने वाले

5. परिश्रम शब्द का अर्थ है:
   - A. साहस
   - B. हिम्मत
   - C. काम
   - D. कठिन मेहनत

गद्यांश 2

पन्द्रह अगस्त 1947 को हमारा देश स्वतंत्र हुआ। स्वतन्त्रता प्राप्ति के बाद विश्व के दूसरे देशों के साथ भारत के राजनयिक एवं सांस्कृतिक सम्बन्ध जुड़े। पर्यटकों के साथ-साथ राजनीतिज्ञों और साहित्यकारों को भी विदेश यात्रा के पर्याप्त अवसर मिले। विभिन्न प्रकार की छात्रवृत्तियों के माध्यम से बहुत से लोग विदेशों में पढ़ने गए। बहुत से लोगों ने विदेशों में उपलब्ध आजीविका के अवसरों का लाभ उठाया। इन सबके परिणामस्वरूप प्रचुर मात्रा में यात्रावृत्तांत लिखे गए। विदेश-विषयक यात्रावृत्तांतों में रूस और स्वदेश-विषयक यात्रावृत्तांतों में लेखकों की दृष्टि कश्मीर से कन्याकुमारी तक व्याप्त हुई।

उपर्युक्त गद्यांश को ध्यानपूर्वक पढ़ें और निम्नलिखित प्रश्नों के उत्तर के लिए सही विकल्प को चुनें:

1. भारत कब स्वतंत्र हुआ?
   - A. 15 अगस्त 1947
   - B. 15 अगस्त 1946
   - C. 15 अगस्त 1948
   - D. 15 अगस्त 1949

2. स्वतंत्र भारत के अन्य देशों के साथ किस प्रकार के संबंध जुड़े?
   - A. राजनीतिक
   - B. राजनयिक
   - C. धार्मिक
   - D. राजनयिक एवं सांस्कृतिक

3. आजीविका का क्या अर्थ है?
   - A. उपार्जन
   - B. वेतन
   - C. मेहनत
   - D. रोजगार

4. यात्रा-वृत्तांत का क्या अर्थ है?
   - A. भ्रमण
   - B. पर्यटन
   - C. सफरनामा
   - D. विदेशभ्रमण

5. स्वतंत्र का विलोम शब्द है:
   - A. परतंत्र
   - B. आजाद
   - C. गुलामी
   - D. मुक्ति

गद्यांश 3

युवा वर्ग का मस्तिष्क नई-नई बातों की ओर ज्यादा तेज दौड़ता है। उसमें अन्य वर्ग के व्यक्तियों से अधिक आवेश और शक्ति होती है। इस अवस्था में यदि सही शिक्षा और उचित मार्ग-दर्शन न मिले तो यही शक्ति प्रेरणा और निर्माण के स्थान पर विनाश की ओर ले जाती है। बिगड़ने और बनने की यही आयु होती है। दुर्भाग्य से हमारे देश में शिक्षा पद्धति केवल उपाधि बाँटने का काम ही करती है। एक सम्पूर्ण व्यक्तित्वपूर्ण मनुष्य बनाना आज की शिक्षा पद्धति के लिए मुश्किल है।

उपर्युक्त गद्यांश को ध्यानपूर्वक पढ़ें और निम्नलिखित प्रश्नों के उत्तर के लिए सही विकल्प को चुनें।

1. निर्माण का विलोम शब्द क्या है?
   - A. रचना
   - B. बनावट
   - C. विनाश
   - D. सृजन

2. मार्ग-दर्शन का क्या अर्थ है?
   - A. उपाधि
   - B. रास्ता
   - C. उद्देश्य
   - D. रास्ता दिखलाना

3. शक्ति विनाश की ओर कब अग्रसर होती है?
   - A. अधिक आवेश और शक्ति के अभाव में
   - B. सही शिक्षा और उचित मार्ग दर्शन के अभाव में
   - C. दुर्भाग्यपूर्ण शिक्षा पद्धति के कारण
   - D. इनमें से कोई नहीं

4. हमारे देश की शिक्षा पद्धति क्या कार्य करती है?
   - A. मार्ग-दर्शन
   - B. शक्ति प्रेरणा
   - C. उपाधि देना
   - D. उपर्युक्त सभी

5. दुर्भाग्य का विपरीत शब्द है:
   - A. भाग्य
   - B. सौभाग्य
   - C. भाग्यशाली
   - D. भाग्यवान

गद्यांश 4

भिखारी की भाँति गिड़गिड़ाना प्रेम की भाषा नहीं है। यहाँ तक कि मुक्ति के लिए भगवान् की उपासना करना भी अधम उपासना में गिना जाता है। प्रेम कोई पुरस्कार नहीं चाहता। प्रेम सर्वथा प्रेम के लिए ही होता है। भक्त इसलिए प्रेम करता है कि बिना प्रेम किए वह रह ही नहीं सकता। जब तुम किसी मनोहर प्राकृतिक दृश्य को देखकर उस पर मोहित हो जाते हो तो तुम किसी फल की याचना नहीं करते और न वह दृश्य ही तुमसे कुछ माँगता है। फिर भी उस दृश्य का दर्शन तुम्हारे मन को आनंद से भर देता है।

उपर्युक्त गद्यांश को ध्यानपूर्वक पढ़ें और निम्नलिखित प्रश्नों के उत्तर के लिए सही विकल्प का चयन करें:

1. प्रेम का उद्देश्य क्या होता है?
   - A. मुक्ति
   - B. उपासना
   - C. भक्ति
   - D. प्रेम

2. मुक्ति का अर्थ है:
   - A. आजादी
   - B. स्वतंत्रता
   - C. परतंत्र
   - D. निर्वाण

3. कैसी उपासना अधम मानी गई है?
   - A. प्रेम की उपासना
   - B. भगवान की उपासना
   - C. मुक्ति की उपासना
   - D. भक्ति की उपासना

4. मनोहर शब्द हैं:
   - A. विशेषण
   - B. संज्ञा
   - C. सर्वनाम
   - D. अव्यय

5. प्राकृतिक शब्द का अर्थ है:
   - A. ईश्वरीय
   - B. मानव संबंधी
   - C. प्रकृति संबंधी
   - D. प्रेम संबंधी

गद्यांश 5

कुछ लोग भाग्यवादी होते हैं और सब-कुछ भाग्य के सहारे छोड़कर कर्म से विरत हो जाते हैं। ऐसे लोग समाज के लिए बोझ हैं। वे कभी कोई बड़ा काम नहीं कर पाते। बड़ी-बड़ी खोज, बड़े-बड़े आविष्कार और बड़े-बड़े निर्माण कार्य कर्मशील लोगों के द्वारा ही संभव हो सके हैं। हम अपनी बुद्धि और प्रतिभा तथा कार्य-क्षमता के बल पर सही मार्ग पर चल सकते हैं, किन्तु बिना कठिन श्रम के अपने लक्ष्य तक नहीं पहुँच सकते। कठिन परिश्रम करने के बाद पाई गई सफलता हमारे मन को अलौकिक आनंद से भर देती है। यदि हम अपने कार्य में अपेक्षित श्रम नहीं करते तो हमारा मन ग्लानि का अनुभव करता है।

उपर्युक्त गद्यांश को ध्यानपूर्वक पढ़ें और निम्नलिखित प्रश्नों के उत्तर के लिए सही विकल्प चुनें:

1. ''आविष्कार'' शब्द का अर्थ है :
   - A. अनुसंधान
   - B. खोज
   - C. निर्माण
   - D. विनाश

2. **अलौकिक** शब्द का क्या अर्थ है?
   - A. संसारिक
   - B. भौतिक
   - C. अमानुषी
   - D. प्राकृतिक

3. सफलता का विलोम क्या है?
   - A. सफल
   - B. असफल
   - C. सफलतापूर्वक
   - D. असफलता

4. परिश्रम करने और न करने से हमारे जीवन पर क्या प्रभाव पड़ता है?
   - A. लोग भाग्यवादी बन जाते हैं
   - B. कर्म से विरत हो जाते हैं
   - C. मन में ग्लानि का अनुभव होता है
   - D. इनमें से कोई नहीं

5. किस प्रकार के लोग समाज के लिए बोझ हैं?
   - A. भाग्यवादी
   - B. कर्मठ
   - C. परिश्रमी
   - D. प्रतिभाशाली

गद्यांश 6

वैदिक काल से हिमालय के पहाड़ बहुत पवित्र माने जाते हैं। इसमें कोई सन्देह नहीं कि हिमालय के पहाड़ों का दृश्य अति सुन्दर है। उसकी विशालता को देखकर मन में आनन्द और कृतज्ञता की लहर उठती है। ऐसा लगता है कि यह विशाल सृष्टि प्रभु की अनुपम देन है। सारी सृष्टि के प्रति समभाव जाग्रत होता है। वस्तुतः यह दृष्टि कोरी कल्पनात्मक या आध्यात्मिक नहीं है। देखा जाए तो सारे भारत की जलवायु का समतोल करने वाले यह हिमालय के पहाड़ हैं, विशेषकर उत्तरी भारत को वर्षा और पानी देने वाले ये ही हैं। गंगोत्री, यमुनोत्री, बद्री, केदार को तीर्थ माना जाता है, जो व्यर्थ कल्पना नहीं है। उन स्थानों से निकलने वाली पवित्र नदियाँ ही वास्तव में हमारी प्राणदात्री रही हैं।

उपर्युक्त गद्यांश को ध्यानपूर्वक पढ़ें और निम्नलिखित प्रश्नों के उत्तर के लिए सही विकल्प चुनें :

1. हिमालय के पर्वत बहुत पवित्र कब से माने जाते हैं?
   - A. पाषाण काल से
   - B. वैदिक काल से
   - C. प्राचीन काल से
   - D. आधुनिक काल से

2. विशालता शब्द है :
   - A. जातिवाचक
   - B. भाववाचक
   - C. विशेषण
   - D. सर्वनाम

3. भारत की जलवायु को समतोल कौन करता है?
   - A. गंगोत्री
   - B. यमुनोत्री
   - C. केदार
   - D. हिमालय

4. सृष्टि का समानार्थक शब्द है :
   - A. सृजन
   - B. रचना
   - C. प्रकृति
   - D. संसार

5. प्राणदात्री का क्या अर्थ है?
   - A. गंगोत्री
   - B. यमुनोत्री
   - C. प्राणसंचार करने वाली
   - D. समभाव जाग्रत करने वाली

गद्यांश 7

सच्चा मित्र एक शिक्षक की भाँति होता है। जिस प्रकार शिक्षक अपने छात्र को सन्मार्ग की ही ओर अग्रसर करता है, उसी प्रकार एक सच्चा मित्र अपने मित्र को पाप के गर्त में गिरने से बचाता है। मानव-जीवन अधिक रहस्यपूर्ण है। कभी-कभी जीवन में ऐसे अवसर उपस्थित हो जाते हैं, जब मनुष्य की धर्मबुद्धि नष्ट हो जाती है और उसका मन द्रुत गति से पाप की ओर दौड़ता है। ऐसे समय में मित्र का ही उपदेश अधिक कल्याणकारी सिद्ध होता है। मित्र के उपदेश का जितना प्रभाव हृदय पर पड़ता है, उतना और किसी का नहीं पड़ता है।

उपर्युक्त गद्यांश को ध्यानपूर्वक पढ़ें और निम्नलिखित प्रश्नों के उत्तर के लिए सही विकल्प चुनें :

1. सच्चा मित्र किस प्रकार का होता है?
   A. विपत्ति में सहायता देने वाला
   B. गलत मार्ग पर चलने से रोकने वाला
   C. शिक्षक के भाँति
   D. धार्मिक गुरु की तरह

2. सन्मार्ग शब्द का विपरीत शब्द है :
   A. अग्रसर
   B. कुमार्ग
   C. सुमार्ग
   D. मार्गदर्शक

3. व्यक्ति को पाप के गर्त में गिरने से कौन बचाता है?
   A. शिक्षक
   B. भाई
   C. पिता
   D. सच्चा मित्र

4. मानव पाप की ओर कब दौड़ता है?
   A. जब स्वार्थी बन जाता है
   B. जब धर्म-बुद्धि नष्ट हो जाती है
   C. जब सच्चामित्र साथ छोड़ देता है
   D. जब धनवान बन जाता है

5. उपदेश में कौन-सा उपसर्ग है?
   A. उ
   B. उप
   C. दे
   D. देश

गद्यांश 8

सब तरह के भावों को प्रकट करने की योग्यता रखने वाली और निर्दोष होने पर भी यदि कोई भाषा अपना निज का साहित्य नहीं रखती, तो वह रूपवती भिखारिन की तरह कदापि आदरणीय नहीं हो सकती। उनकी शोभा, उसकी बड़ी सम्पन्नता, उसकी मान-मर्यादा उसके साहित्य पर ही अवलम्बित रहती है। उसके विचारों और राजनैतिक स्थितियों का प्रतिबिम्ब देखने को यदि कहीं मिल सकता है, तो उसके ग्रन्थ साहित्य में मिल सकता है। सामाजिक शक्ति या सजीवता, सामाजिक अशक्ति या निर्जीवता और सामाजिक सभ्यता तथा असभ्यता का निर्णायक एकमात्र साहित्य है।

उपर्युक्त गद्यांश को ध्यानपूर्वक पढ़ें और निम्नलिखित प्रश्नों के उत्तर के लिए सही विकल्प चुनें :

1. साहित्य विहीन भाषा किस प्रकार की होती है?
   A. आदरणीय
   B. भिखारिन
   C. रूपवती
   D. रूपवती भिखारिन

2. रूपवती का पुल्लिंग रूप है:
   A. रूपवान
   B. सुन्दर
   C. सुन्दरी
   D. रूपवत

3. भाषा की मान मर्यादा किस पर निर्भर करती है?
   A. लिपि पर
   B. साहित्यकार पर
   C. भक्ति पर
   D. साहित्य पर

4. "सम्पन्नता" शब्द का विपरीत शब्द है:
   A. गरीबी
   B. विपन्न
   C. अमीर
   D. विपन्नता

5. राजनैतिक, सामाजिक शक्ति का दर्शन हमें किसमें मिलता है?
   A. समाज
   B. राज्य
   C. नेता
   D. साहित्य

गद्यांश 9

स्वतंत्र भारत का सम्पूर्ण दायित्व आज विद्यार्थियों के ही ऊपर है, क्योंकि आज जो विद्यार्थी हैं, वे ही कल स्वतंत्र भारत के नागरिक होंगे। भारत की उन्नति, उसका उत्थान उन्हीं की उन्नति और उत्थान पर निर्भर करता है। अतः विद्यार्थियों को चाहिए कि वे अपने भावी जीवन का निर्माण बड़ी सतर्कता और सावधानी के साथ करें। उन्हें प्रत्येक क्षण अपने राष्ट्र, अपने समाज, अपने धर्म, अपनी संस्कृति को अपनी आँखों के सामने रखना चाहिए, जिससे उनके जीवन से राष्ट्र को कुछ बल प्राप्त हो सके। जो विद्यार्थी राष्ट्रीय दृष्टिकोण से अपने जीवन का निर्माण नहीं करते, वे राष्ट्र और समाज के लिए भार-स्वरूप हैं।

उपर्युक्त गद्यांश को ध्यानपूर्वक पढ़ें और निम्नलिखित प्रश्नों के उत्तर के लिए सही विकल्प चुनें :

1. भारत की उन्नति किस पर निर्भर करती है?
   A. युवाओं पर
   B. नेताओं पर
   C. साहित्यकारों पर
   D. विद्यार्थियों पर

2. **उन्नति** का समानार्थक शब्द है :
   A. पतन
   B. उत्थान
   C. विकास
   D. उदय

3. **उत्थान** का विपरीत शब्द है :
   A. उदय
   B. पतन
   C. पराजय
   D. हार

4. किसे अपने जीवन का निर्माण सतर्कता और सावधानी से करना चाहिए?
   A. युवाओं को
   B. नेताओं को
   C. बच्चों को
   D. विद्यार्थियों को

5. धर्म, संस्कृति तथा समाज का रक्षक कौन है?
   A. नागरिक
   B. ग्रामीण
   C. विद्यार्थी
   D. युवा

गद्यांश 10

हास्य एक ऐसा माध्यम है, जो नीरस-जीवन को भी सुखद बना देता है। हास्य का जादू इतना प्रभावशाली होता है कि वह छूत के रोग की तरह चारों ओर फैल जाता है। जिसने कभी हँसना नहीं सीखा, सचमुच उसने जीना नहीं सीखा। सामान्यतः मनुष्य को जीवन में इतनी मुसीबतें झेलनी पड़ती हैं कि वह अपने जीवन को पहाड़ समझने लगता है। ऐसे दूभर जीवन को यदि जीने योग्य बनाना हो तो उसके लिए आवश्यक है कि जीवन में हँसने की गुंजाइश हो। हँसी के सहारे मनुष्य अपने कष्टों को भुलाने का प्रयत्न करता है। संघर्ष, तनाव, व्यस्तता, घुटन यदि आज के जीवन की सहज देन हैं, तो इनसे बचने के लिए यह आवश्यक है कि हम हँसना सीखें।

उपर्युक्त गद्यांश को ध्यानपूर्वक पढ़ें और निम्नलिखित प्रश्नों के उत्तर के लिए सही विकल्प चुनें :

1. नीरस जीवन को कौन सुखद बना देता है?
   A. संगीत B. गीत
   C. आमोद प्रमोद D. हास्य

2. नीरस का संधि विच्छेद है :
   A. नी + रस B. नि + रस
   C. निः + रस D. नीः + रस

3. किसका जीवन व्यर्थ है?
   A. जिसने रोना नहीं सीखा
   B. जिसने हँसना नहीं सीखा
   C. जिसने गाना नहीं सीखा
   D. इनमें से कोई नहीं

4. हँसना शब्द है :
   A. संज्ञा B. विशेषण
   C. क्रिया विशेषण D. क्रिया

5. तनाव और घुटन से बचने के लिए क्या करना चाहिए?
   A. रोना चाहिए B. गाना चाहिए
   C. हँसना चाहिए D. काम करना चाहिए

गद्यांश 11

किसी पुस्तक को पढ़ने में जल्दी नहीं करनी चाहिए, जो कुछ लेखक कहता है, उसे समझने की चेष्टा करनी चाहिए। प्रत्येक शब्द का अर्थ समझने की चेष्टा करनी चाहिए। यदि लेखक योग्य है, तो दूसरी बार वह पुस्तक और अधिक आनन्द देगी और तीसरी बार और अधिक। प्रत्येक बार अध्ययन करने पर आपको नवीन सुन्दर और नए विचार मिलेंगे और उसे आप जितना ही पढ़ेंगे, उतना ही स्नेह करने लगेंगे। सहस्रों व्यक्तियों ने गीता और रामायण तथा कुरान और बाइबिल को बार-बार पढ़ा है। उनका अनुभव है कि प्रत्येक बार उन्हें नई सूझ और नए विचार मिलते गए। कुछ लोग तो इस बात पर गर्व करते हैं कि उन्होंने अमुक पुस्तक को अनेक बार पढ़ा है, उन्हें कंठस्थ हो गई है।

उपर्युक्त गद्यांश को ध्यानपूर्वक पढ़ें और निम्नलिखित प्रश्नों के उत्तर के लिए सही विकल्प चुनें :

1. किसे समझने की चेष्टा करनी चाहिए?
   A. पुस्तक B. रामायण
   C. महाभारत D. गीता

2. पुस्तक की सजीवता किस पर निर्भर करती है?
   A. लेखक B. प्रकाशक
   C. पाठक D. चिन्तक

3. आनन्द का विपरीत शब्द है :
   A. शोक B. दुख
   C. संताप D. खुशी

4. नवीन, सुन्दर और नए विचार हमें कहाँ से प्राप्त होता हैं?
   A. पुस्तक को बार-बार पढ़कर
   B. सुनकर
   C. भाषण से
   D. अच्छे व्यक्तियों से मिलने पर

5. कंठस्थ शब्द का शब्दार्थ है :
   A. कंठ में स्थित B. सुंदर कंठ
   C. जबानी याद D. पंडित जी

गद्यांश 12

अहिंसा परम धर्म है और हिंसा आपद् धर्म। मनुष्य बराबर अहिंसा की ओर चलना चाहता है, किन्तु परिस्थितियाँ उससे हिंसा कराती है, अर्थात् परमधर्म की रक्षा के लिए आदमी बराबर आपद्धर्म से काम लेता रहा है। भारत अपनी सेनाओं को विघटित कर दे, तब भी उसका अपमान उससे अधिक होने वाला नहीं, जितना नेफा में हुआ। किन्तु परमधर्म पर टिकने की सामर्थ्य अगर भारत में नहीं है, तो आपद्धर्म पर उसे आना चाहिए। व्यवहारतः आपद्धर्म परमधर्म का विरोधी नहीं, उसका रक्षक है।

उपर्युक्त गद्यांश को ध्यानपूर्वक पढ़ें और निम्नलिखित प्रश्नों के उत्तर के लिए सही विकल्प चुनें :

1. परमधर्म का विपरीत शब्द है :
   A. महान धर्म B. आपद्धर्म
   C. सच्चाधर्म D. इनमें से कोई नहीं

2. आपद्धर्म किसे कहा जाता है?
   A. अहिंसा B. सत्याग्रह
   C. विपत्ति D. हिंसा

3. मानव से हिंसा कौन करवाती है?
   A. लोभ B. स्वार्थ
   C. द्वेष D. परिस्थितियाँ

4. सामर्थ्य का शब्दार्थ है :
   A. संघर्ष B. परिश्रम
   C. शक्ति D. पराक्रम

5. परमधर्म की रक्षा कौन करता है?
   A. अहिंसा B. हिंसा
   C. आपदधर्म D. युद्ध

गद्यांश 13

वर्तमान काल विज्ञापन का युग माना जाता है। समाचार-पत्रों के अतिरिक्त रेडियो और टेलीविजन भी विज्ञापन के सफल साधन हैं। विज्ञापन का मूल उद्देश्य उत्पादक और भोक्ता में सीधा सम्पर्क स्थापित करना होता है। जितना अधिक विज्ञापन किसी पदार्थ का होगा, उतनी ही उसकी लोकप्रियता बढ़ेगी। इन विज्ञापनों पर धन तो अधिक व्यय होता है, पर इनसे बिक्री बढ़ जाती है। ग्राहक जब इन आकर्षक विज्ञापनों को देखता है तो वह उस वस्तु-विशेष के प्रति आकृष्ट होकर उसे खरीदने को बाध्य हो जाता है।

उपर्युक्त गद्यांश को ध्यानपूर्वक पढ़ें और निम्नलिखित प्रश्नों के उत्तर के लिए सही विकल्प चुनें :

1. वर्तमान को किसका युग माना जाता है?
   - A. फैशन
   - B. विज्ञापन
   - C. संगीत
   - D. धन

2. उत्पादक तथा भोक्ता के बीच कौन संबंध स्थापित करता है?
   - A. टेलीविजन
   - B. समाचार-पत्र
   - C. रेडियो
   - D. विज्ञापन

3. **वर्तमान** शब्द का विपरीत शब्द है :
   - A. अर्वाचीन
   - B. आधुनिक
   - C. आजकल
   - D. प्राचीन

4. **आकर्षक** का शब्दार्थ है :
   - A. विकर्षक
   - B. सुन्दर
   - C. मनमोहक
   - D. आश्चर्यजनक

5. भोक्ता किस कारण वस्तुओं को खरीदने के लिए बाध्य हो जाता है?
   - A. विज्ञापन
   - B. आकर्षक विज्ञापन
   - C. लोकप्रियता के कारण
   - D. आसानी से उपलब्ध होना

गद्यांश 14

लगभग दो सौ वर्ष की गुलामी ने भारत के राष्ट्रीय स्वाभिमान को पैरों से रौंद डाला, हमारी संस्कृति को समाप्त कर दिया, हमारे विश्वासों को हिला दिया और हमारे आत्मविश्वास को चकनाचूर कर दिया, किन्तु अपने इस बूढ़े देश से प्यार करने वाले, इसके एक सामान्य संकेत पर प्राण न्यौछावर करने वाले दीवानों का अभाव न था। एक आवाज उठी और देखते ही देखते राष्ट्र का दबा हुआ आत्माभिमान उन्मत्त हो उठा। इतिहास साक्षी है जाने और अनजाने सहस्रों देशभक्त स्वतंत्रता की अनमोल निधि को पाने के लिए शहीद हो गए।

उपर्युक्त गद्यांश को ध्यानपूर्वक पढ़ें और निम्नलिखित प्रश्नों के उत्तर के लिए सही विकल्प चुनें :

1. **स्वाभिमान** का संधि विच्छेद है:
   - A. स्वा + भिमान
   - B. स्वः + अभिमान
   - C. स्व + अभिमान
   - D. स्वा + अभिमान

2. भारत का राष्ट्रीय स्वाभिमान किस कारण समाप्त हो गया था?
   - A. लम्बे गुलामी से
   - B. निरंकुश शासक से
   - C. स्वार्थी मानव से
   - D. धर्म के विनाश से

3. **आत्मविश्वास** का शब्दार्थ है
   - A. घमण्ड
   - B. गर्व
   - C. अपने पर विश्वास
   - D. अभिमान

4. भारत की अनमोल निधि को पाने के लिए कौन शहीद हो गए?
   - A. देशभक्त
   - B. नेता
   - C. युवा
   - D. युवती

5. **अनमोल निधि** का शब्दार्थ है:
   - A. अनन्त खजाना
   - B. अमूल्य खजाना
   - C. बहुमूल्य
   - D. स्वतंत्रता

गद्यांश 15

दुनिया के विभिन्न देशों के विकास पर विहंगम दृष्टि डालने से यह स्पष्ट हो जाता है कि आज जिस देश ने वैज्ञानिक उपलब्धियों के सहारे अपना औद्योगीकरण कर लिया, उसी को उन्नत देश कहा जाता है। जिस देश में औद्योगीकरण का स्तर नीचा है, वह पिछड़ा हुआ देश कहा जाता है। वैज्ञानिक आविष्कारों और औद्योगीकरण के आधार पर ही किसी देश की प्रगति को आँका जाता रहा है। विज्ञान ने मानव को पूरी तरह बदल दिया है।

उपर्युक्त गद्यांश को ध्यानपूर्वक पढ़ें और निम्नलिखित प्रश्नों के उत्तर के लिए सही विकल्प चुनें :

1. **विहंगम दृष्टि** का क्या अर्थ है?
   - A. एक झलक
   - B. गहन दृष्टि
   - C. गहन चिन्तन
   - D. इनमें से कोई नहीं

2. **विकास** का विपरीत शब्द है :
   - A. उत्थान
   - B. उदय
   - C. पतन
   - D. विनाश

3. **वैज्ञानिक** शब्द में कौन-सा प्रत्यय हैं?
   - A. निक
   - B. वै
   - C. ईक
   - D. इक

4. मानव जीवन को किसने बदल दिया है :
   - A. विकास
   - B. वैज्ञानिक
   - C. विज्ञान
   - D. उद्योग

5. किसी भी देश की स्तर को किससे नापा जाता है?
   - A. उपलब्धियों पर
   - B. औद्योगीकरण से
   - C. वैज्ञानिकों से
   - D. आविष्कारों से

गद्यांश 16

विश्व का वर्तमान उन्नत रूप मानव-श्रम की ही कहानी कह रहा है। गगन चुंबी अट्टालिकाएँ, लंबी-चौड़ी सड़कें, बड़े-बड़े विशाल नगर आकाश में उड़ते वायुयान तथा मानव-जीवन को सुखी और समृद्ध बनाने में योगदान करने वाले ज्ञान-विज्ञान के अनन्त रूप-ये सभी मनुष्य के श्रम का जयघोष करते हैं। स्पष्ट है कि मनुष्य और उसका शरीर विधाता की अनुपम रचना है जो निश्चय ही महान उद्देश्यों की संपूर्ति के

लिए दिया गया है। इस दुर्लभ तन को यदि हम आलस्य, प्रसाद अथवा घटिया कामों में गँवा देते हैं तो उस विधाता के प्रति अन्याय करते हैं।

उपर्युक्त गद्यांश को ध्यानपूर्वक पढ़ें और निम्नलिखित प्रश्नों के उत्तर के लिए सही विकल्प चुनें :

1. विश्व का वर्तमान रूप किसका उद्योतक है?
   A. चिन्तक का   B. नेता का
   C. वैज्ञानिक का   D. मानव श्रम

2. गगन चुंबी अट्टालिकाएँ का अर्थ है :
   A. आकाश में उड़ने वाला   B. आकाश को छूने वाला
   C. बहुमंजिली इमारत   D. इनमें से कोई नहीं

3. आकाश का समानार्थक शब्द है :
   A. वसुन्धरा   B. धरा
   C. पयोद   D. गगन

4. सुखी का विपरीत शब्द है :
   A. प्रसन्न   B. अप्रसन्न
   C. दुखी   D. उदासी

5. विधाता की अनुपम रचना क्या है?
   A. मानव शरीर   B. समुद्र
   C. वन   D. पृथ्वी

गद्यांश 17

हमारे देश में एक ऐसा भी युग था जब नैतिक और आध्यात्मिक विकास ही जीवन का वास्तविक लक्ष्य माना जाता था। अहिंसा की भावना सर्वोपरि थी। आज पूरा जीवन दर्शन ही बदल गया है। सर्वत्र पैसे की हाय-हाय तथा धन का उपार्जन ही मुख्य ध्येय हो गया है, भले ही धन-उपार्जन के तरीके गलत ही क्यों न हों? इन सबका असर मनुष्य के प्रतिदिन के जीवन पर पड़ रहा है। समाज का वातावरण दूषित हो गया है—

बाह्य वातावरण तो दूषित है ही, आज सब जानते हैं पर्यावरण की समस्याएँ कितनी चिन्तनीय हो उठी है। इन सबके कारण मानसिक और शारीरिक तनाव-खिंचाव और व्याधियाँ पैदा हो रही हैं।

उपर्युक्त गद्यांश को ध्यानपूर्वक पढ़ें और निम्नलिखित प्रश्नों के उत्तर के लिए सही विकल्प चुनें :

1. भारत का प्राचीन आदर्श था :
   A. सत्य और अहिंसा   B. नैतिक और आध्यात्मिक विकास
   C. धन उपार्जन   D. इनमें से कोई नहीं

2. अहिंसा का विपरीत शब्द है :
   A. हिंसा   B. सत्याग्रह
   C. विनम्रता   D. नैतिकता

3. जीवन दर्शन क्यों बदल गया है?
   A. हिंसा के कारण   B. अहिंसा के कारण
   C. धन लिप्सा के कारण   D. आध्यात्मिक विकास के कारण

4. समाज का वातावरण दूषित क्यों हो गया है?
   A. शारीरिक तनाव   B. मानसिक व्याधियाँ
   C. पर्यावरण की समस्याएँ D. धन उपार्जन के गलत तरीके

5. पर्यावरण का शब्दार्थ है:
   A. जलमंडल   B. स्थलमंडल
   C. वायुमंडल   D. वातावरण

उत्तरमाला

गद्यांश 1
1. C   2. D   3. B   4. A   5. D

गद्यांश 2
1. A   2. D   3. D   4. C   5. A

गद्यांश 3
1. C   2. D   3. B   4. C   5. B

गद्यांश 4
1. D   2. D   3. C   4. A   5. C

गद्यांश 5
1. B   2. D   3. D   4. C   5. A

गद्यांश 6
1. B   2. B   3. D   4. A   5. C

गद्यांश 7
1. C   2. B   3. D   4. B   5. B

गद्यांश 8
1. D   2. A   3. D   4. D   5. D

गद्यांश 9
1. D   2. B   3. B   4. D   5. C

गद्यांश 10
1. D   2. C   3. B   4. D   5. C

गद्यांश 11
1. A   2. A   3. A   4. A   5. C

गद्यांश 12
1. B   2. D   3. D   4. C   5. C

गद्यांश 13
1. B   2. D   3. D   4. C   5. B

गद्यांश 14
1. C   2. A   3. C   4. A   5. B

गद्यांश 15
1. A   2. D   3. C   4. C   5. C

गद्यांश 16
1. D   2. C   3. D   4. C   5. A

गद्यांश 17
1. B   2. A   3. C   4. D   5. D

English Language

1

Comprehension Passages

ENGLISH LANGUAGE COMPREHENSION

The objective of language comprehension test is to ascertain the ability of the candidates to understand the passage properly.

Therefore candidates are required to take notice of the following points:

1. Read the full passage very attentively and intelligently.
2. Try to comprehend the gist of it.
3. Make a mental note of all the important details and points given in the passage.
4. Read the passage for the second time in case you have not been able to understand it satisfactorily.
5. Divide the time proportionately for all the passages.
6. Answer the questions on the basis of facts, as given in the paragraph.
7. Don't waste much time in answering the questions of any one passage.
8. Check all the answers once again, very carefully, to see whether any question is left unanswered by mistake.

MODEL QUESTIONS (FOR PRACTICE)

Directions: *Each of the following passages is followed by five questions. Read the passage carefully and then answer the questions that follow each. For each question, four probable answers A, B, C and D are given. Only one out of these is correct. Choose the correct answer.*

PASSAGE-1

The use of words like 'welcome', 'thank you', 'please', etc., at the right moment reflects a polite nature. The civic sense also lies within the scope of good manners. We should not shout or talk loudly in public places like hospitals and libraries and create disturbance. We should not cheat people or make fun of them. Cleanliness is also necessary. We must not throw the waste on roads and make use of dustbins. We should not harm the public property as it belongs to all of us. While in a queue, discipline should be maintained. We must give fair chance to others.

1. Expressions like 'welcome' 'thank you' and 'please' reflect
   A. happiness   B. discipline
   C. civic sense   D. polite nature

2. While in a library, we should
   A. respect others   B. avoid arguments
   C. talk in low tone   D. be courteous

3. A public property belongs to
   A. nobody   B. all of us
   C. government   D. one who maintains it

4. Discipline is
   A. the rule of proper conduct or action
   B. the rule of road sense
   C. making use of dustbins
   D. forming a queue

5. The most appropriate title for this passage would be
   A. Polite Nature   B. Courtesy
   C. Good Manners   D. Civic Sense

PASSAGE-2

There is an old proverb 'Early to bed and early to rise makes a man healthy and wise.' I am in the habit of getting up early in the morning and have formed the habit of taking long morning walks in the past two years. It is a light exercise and best for physical fitness. The morning air which is fresh and pure is beneficial for the lungs. The early rays of the rising sun are good for healthy skin. 'Health is wealth' and doctors also recommend morning walk to their patients for gaining sound health and freshness of energy.

1. What is good for lungs?
   A. Sunrays   B. Fresh air
   C. Sound sleep   D. Light exercise

2. What is a light exercise?
   A. Early to bed   B. Early to rise
   C. Morning walk   D. Gaining sound health

3. What is good for skin?
   A. Fresh air   B. Morning air
   C. Morning walk   D. Rising sun's rays

4. What is best for physical fitness?
   A. Light exercise   B. Long morning walk
   C. Early to rise   D. Fresh and pure air

5. Long morning walk
   A. bring sound sleep
   B. ensures physical fitness
   C. ensures healthy skin
   D. keeps healthy, wealthy and wise

PASSAGE-3

Mahatma Gandhi lived a splendid long life and has set great moral standards before us. He showed to the world the true way to peace. He wished to see India prosper but he became a martyr for the noble cause of Hindu-Muslim unity at the time of partition when a religious fanatic, Nathuram Godse, shot him dead on January 30, 1948. His last words were 'Hey Ram'. He lived and died for his country and countryman.

1. Mahatma Gandhi showed the world the true way to
   A. prosperity
   B. love
   C. truth
   D. peace

2. Mahatma Gandhi became a martyr for the noble cause of
   A. truth
   B. non-violence
   C. freedom of India
   D. Hindu-Muslim unity

3. Mahatma Gandhi was shot dead
   A. before India achieved independence
   B. by a mad man
   C. by an intolerant religious person
   D. by a non-religious person

4. Mahatma Gandhi set great moral standards. It means
   A. he was a great religious teacher
   B. he was a great moralist
   C. he made India morally stronger
   D. moral was everything to him

5. Gandhiji lived and died for his country and countryman. It means
   A. he was born in India and died in India
   B. he was a patriot
   C. he was a great moralist
   D. he sacrified his life for India and her people

PASSAGE-4

On one hot day a crow felt very thirsty. He flew from one place to another in search of water. After long hours of labour he found a pitcher. Eagerly, he perched on the mouth of the pitcher. He found that the water was at the bottom of the vessel. He tried his best to dip his beak but did not succeed. He did not know what to do. Suddenly some pebbles lying nearby gave him an idea. One by one he dropped the pebbles with his beak into the pitcher. The level of water slowly came up to the mouth of the pitcher. The crow then drank the water and quenched his thirst.

1. The crow found a pitcher
   A. as it flew
   B. after many hours of labour
   C. full of water
   D. which was empty

2. What is the moral of the passage?
   A. No pains, no gains
   B. God helps those who help themselves
   C. Necessity is the mother of invention
   D. Try and try again, you will succeed at last

3. The crow flew from place to place
   A. in search of pitcher
   B. in search of pebbles
   C. in search of water
   D. in search of a vessel

4. The pitcher, the crow found
   A. was full of water
   B. was dry
   C. had little water in the bottom
   D. had water up to its mouth

5. As the crow dropped pebbles into the pitcher, what happend?
   A. The pitcher broke down
   B. The water leaked one of the pitcher
   C. The level of water into the pitcher rose up slowly
   D. Water level immediately rose to the mouth of the pitcher

PASSAGE-5

Once upon a time a crane and a fox lived in a forest. They were good friend. One day the fox invited the crane to a feast. He made a tasty food and served it before the crane on a plate. The crane could not eat anything because of the long beak. But the fox licked all his food. The crane felt insulted. He decided to teach the fox a lesson. Next day he invited the fox. He prepared the same tasty food and placed it in front of the fox inside a narrow glass. The crane ate easily while the fox looked on. Now, it was the fox's turn to remain hungry.

1. What is the moral of the passage?
   A. Beware of the wicked
   B. One good turn deserves another
   C. Be contented with what you have
   D. Tit for tat

2. The crane could not eat tasty food because the
   A. food was served in a shallow plate
   B. food was very hot
   C. food was served in a long jar
   D. crane was not hungry

3. The fox had to remain hungry because
   A. the food served was not enough in quantity
   B. the food was served inside a narrow glass
   C. the food served was not tasty
   D. the food was all liquid

4. Why did the crane feel insulted?
   A. Because he was invited to feast but he could not eat anything
   B. Because the food was served in a shallow plate and he could not eat
   C. Because the food was too hot
   D. Because the fox gulped all the food quickly

5. The crane successfully taught a lesson to the fox when he invited the fox to a feast and served the food
   A. in a narrow glass
   B. in a large plate
   C. in a broken plate
   D. in a long jar

PASSAGE-6

The family set down at the table and began to talk about the summer holidays. They had to decide a place to visit during the vacation. Should they go to their village or to a hill station? The parents preferred the village while the children wished to go the hill station. After few moments of discussion the elders decided to visit both the places. First they shall go to the village for a week and then stay at the hill station for the remaining days. For the first time the family shall be together during the holidays. The children were happy with the holiday plan.

1. The purpose for which the family set down at the table was
   A. to decide a place to visit during the vacation
   B. to educate the children how to carry articles during a visit to a hill station
   C. to decide the date when they should start their journey
   D. to tell the children that they will visit a hill station during this vacation

2. The final plan was to visit
   A. their village
   B. a hill station
   C. their village as well as a hill station
   D. their home town

3. The final decision was made by
   A. the boys   B. the girls
   C. the women   D. the elders

4. They decided first to go to their village and stay there for
   A. a day   B. a week
   C. ten days   D. a fortnight

5. Why were children happy?
   A. Because a hill station was included in their holiday plan
   B. Because a visit to their village was excluded from their holiday plan
   C. Because their choice prevailed
   D. Because they were going all alone to the hill station

PASSAGE-7

Once Govind intended to go on pilgrimage with his family. He asked Mirind to accompany. But for his trade's reason, he did not go with him. So Govind thought it safe to leave the box of his jewellery with him, as it was dangerous to leave it in a lone house or take it on the journey. So he went to him with the box. He took him to a lonely place under a tree and handed it over to him. He told Mirind, "Keep it safe with you. I shall return from the journey after six month then I shall take it back from you." Mirind said, "Don't worry, I shall keep it as safe as own."

1. Govind intended to go
   A. for a business trip
   B. to a hill station
   C. on a long journey to a sacred place
   D. to his home town for a long period

2. Why did Govind leave his box of jewellery with Mirind?
   A. Because it was not safe to take the box with him on a long journey
   B. Because Mirind was his fast friend
   C. Because the box was very heavy
   D. Because his house was unsafe

3. Why did Govind take Mirind to a lonely place?
   A. To tell him that the box contained valuable jewellery
   B. So that no third person could see box
   C. To show him what was within the box
   D. To tell him that the box will remain with him

4. Where did Govind hand over the box of jewellery to Mirind?
   A. At Mirind's house
   B. At his own house
   C. In a lonely place
   D. In a lonely place under a tree

5. It was not safe to leave the box in a lone house. Here the word 'lone house' means
   A. a house in a deserted place
   B. a house where none lives
   C. a house without door and lock
   D. a house near the forest

PASSAGE-8

Zahir-ud-din Babar was the first Mughal emperor of India. A descendent of Timur on father's side and Changez Khan on his mother's side, Babar was a brave warrior. After defeating Ibrahim Lodhi in the First Battle of Panipat in 1526 he entered Delhi and soon gained control over Agra. After many more battles with Rajputs he extended his empire over Punjab, Uttar Pradesh and north Bihar. He died at a young age of 48 years in 1530 at his capital Agra without getting much time to consolidate his victories.

1. Zahir-ud-din Babar was the first
   A. Muslim ruler of India   B. Mughal ruler of India
   C. Afghan ruler of India   D. Turk ruler of India

2. Babar was born in the years
   A. 1480   B. 1482
   C. 1492   D. 1962

3. Babar first occupied
   A. Punjab   B. Agra
   C. Delhi   D. Panipat

4. Babar was a brave warrior. Here brave warrior means
   A. courageous soldier   B. a kind hearted soldier
   C. a clever fighter   D. a victorious general

5. Babar extended his empire over Punjab and Uttar Pradesh after many more battles with the
   A. Afghans   B. Rajputs
   C. Mughals   D. Lodhies

PASSAGE-9

Our National Flag is tricolour. It has three equal horizontal strips. The strip at the top is saffron, in the middle is white and at the bottom is green. The ratio of width to length of the flag is 2 : 3. In the centre of the white strip is a wheel in navy blue. The wheel represents the *chakra*. Its design is similar to the wheel which appears on the abacus of the Sarnath Lion Capital of Ashoka. Its diameter approximates to the width of the white strip. The wheel has 24 spokes. It was adopted by Constituent Assembly on July 22, 1947. We love our national flag. We respect it. We are ready to sacrifice our life to protect its honour. It represents the nation. So it is a symbol of national honour.

1. In our national flag the wheel is located in the centre of
   A. saffron strip
   B. white strip
   C. green strip
   D. blue strip

2. In our national flag which of the strips is at the bottom in our national flag
   A. blue
   B. white
   C. saffron
   D. green

3. Why do we love our national flag?
   A. Because it is tricolour
   B. Because it has three strips
   C. Because it has a wheel at the centre
   D. Because it is a symbol of national honour

4. Our national flag was approved by
   A. President
   B. Lok Sabha
   C. Parliament
   D. Constituent Assembly

5. The diameter approximates to the width of the white strip. Here the word 'approximates' means
   A. is more or less equal
   B. is exactly equal
   C. is not equal
   D. is related

PASSAGE-10

Distance in large cities are long. All the people do not have their own means of transport. They have to depend upon the state or private buses. The number of bus users is very large. Every bus stop is, therefore, crowded. The number of buses is not adequate. Thus people suffer the torture of long wait at the bus stop. Some bus stops are quite orderly. People form queues and get into the buses turn by turn. However, often this order is forgotten and confusion spreads when the bus comes and the law of jungle prevails.

1. Why are the bus stops crowded?
   A. Because they are small is size
   B. Because the number of passengers is very large
   C. Because they are situated at some busy centre
   D. Because people do not form queues

2. Long wait at the bus stop is the result of
   A. over-crowding in the buses
   B. late running of buses
   C. shortage of buses
   D. slow speed of buses

3. Some bus stops are quite orderly where
   A. there is no crowd
   B. the number of buses is adequate
   C. people do not have to wait for long
   D. people form queues and enter the buses one by one

4. Most of the people who travel by buses are
   A. non-working
   B. do not have their own vehicles
   C. have to go a long distance
   D. live in large cities

5. What happens when people do not have their own transport?
   A. They have to wait for a bus at a bus stop
   B. They have to depend upon the state or private buses
   C. They have to travel long distances
   D. They form queues and get into buses one by one

ANSWERS

Passage 1.	1	2	3	4	5
	D	C	B	A	C

Passage 2.	1	2	3	4	5
	B	C	D	B	B

Passage 3.	1	2	3	4	5
	D	D	C	B	D

Passage 4.	1	2	3	4	5
	B	C	C	C	C

Passage 5.	1	2	3	4	5
	D	A	B	B	A

Passage 6.	1	2	3	4	5
	A	C	D	B	A

Passage 7.	1	2	3	4	5
	C	A	B	D	B

Passage 8.	1	2	3	4	5
	B	B	C	A	B

Passage 9.	1	2	3	4	5
	B	D	D	D	A

Passage 10.	1	2	3	4	5
	B	C	D	B	B

● ● ●

English Grammar

PARTS OF SPEECH

Part of speech	Definition or Function	Examples
Noun	Name of a person, place, animal, quality or thing	Ram, boy, dog pen, sun, Delhi, truth, honesty
Pronoun	Used in place of a noun	I, you, he she, they
Articles & Determiners	Points out indefinite and definite nouns	a, an, the, few, some
Adjective	Describes a noun or pronoun	big, honest, wooden valuable, quiet, deep, soft, narrow
Adverb	Describes a verb, an adjective or another adverb	silently, widely, softly, quietly, very, carefully
Verb	Tells about action or state of something or someone	is, am, was, have, do, like, walk, work, make, throw, tell
Conjuction	Joins words, clauses or sentences	and, but, when, yet, while, else
Preposition	Links a noun or pronoun to another word	at, to, after, on for, under, over, with
Interjection	Expresses sudden feelings or emotions	Ah!, Alas!, oh!, ouch!, hi!, well!, Hurrah!

NOUNS

A word which denotes a person, a thing, an animal or a place is said to be a noun.

There are two noun numbers in English — the *Singular* and the *Plural*.

Singular Numbers : A noun that denotes one person or one thing, is said to be in the Singular number. For example — book, pencil, bird, dog, hen etc. are in singular number.

Plural Number : A noun that denotes more than one person or one thing is said to be in plural number. For example — boys, pens, lions, girls, men etc. are in plural number.

REMEMBER

Singular	Plural	Singular	Plural
Cat	Cats	Book	Books
Pen	Pens	Room	Rooms
Tree	Trees	Bus	Buses
Bush	Bushes	Box	Boxes
Glass	Glasses	Dish	Dishes
Judge	Judges	Tax	Taxes
Watch	Watches	Calf	Calves
Thief	Thieves	Knife	Knives
Scarf	Scarves	Wife	Wives
Leaf	Leaves	Wolf	Wolves
Half	Halves	Monarch	Monarchs
Roof	Roofs	Hoof	Hoofs
Gulf	Gulfs	Staff	Staffs
Radio	Radios	Bamboo	Bamboos
Folio	Folios	Hero	Heroes
Volcano	Volcanoes	Mango	Mangoes
Potato	Potatoes	Photo	Photos
Piano	Pianos	Baby	Babies
Fly	Flies	Country	Countries
Lady	Ladies	Boy	Boys
Monkey	Monkeys	Ox	Oxen
Child	Children	Man	Men
Woman	Women	Tooth	Teeth
Axis	Axes	Basis	Bases
Foot	Feet	Goose	Geese
Englishman	Englishmen	Radius	Radii
Vertex	Vertices	Stimulus	Stimuli

1. Note the plurals of the following nouns:

Singular	Plural	Singular	Plural
copy	copies	cry	cries
baby	babies	duty	duties
body	bodies	country	countries
family	families	diary	diaries
fly	flies	fairy	fairies
city	cities	spy	spies
army	armies	storey	storeys
bay	bays	monkey	monkeys

2. The following nouns do not undergo any change in plural form, in general.

Singular	Plural	Singular	Plural
deer	deer	sheep	sheep
thousand	thousand	pair	pair
hundred	hundred	score	score
dozen	dozen	gross	gross

Note: We can write—

(*a*) thousands of men; (*b*) two pairs of shoes; (*c*) dozens of mangoes; (*d*) scores of people etc. But—
(*a*) two thousand rupees; (*b*) three hundred men; (*c*) five dozen eggs, etc.

3. The following nouns are usually used in plural forms. They take a plural verb after them—

eatables	fetters	surroundings
riches	alms	spectacles
trousers	pants	scissors
premises	thanks	annals
congratulations	goods	shorts
tongs	pains	arms
breeches	(for troubles)	

4. The following are the nouns which are plural in appearance but are usually used in singular number. They are followed by a singular verb—

news	politics	physics
mathematics	economics	ethics
politics	classics	gallows
statistics	athletics	innings
mechanics	summons	mumps

5. Collective nouns often used as plurals—

public	police	cattle
audience	clergy	folk
people	poultry	nation
elite	gentry	glitterati

6. The nouns that are usually used in singular forms—

advice	hair	rice
fuel	alphabet	machinery
offspring	issue	furniture
mischief	stationery	luggage
bedding	information	abuse

7. Material nouns are always used in singular number—

gold	copper	milk
water	silk	wool

Note: They may be used in plural with a different meaning. copper coins (coppers), chains or fetters (irons), cans made of tin (tins).

GENDERS

The difference in sex is denoted by Gender in grammar. The various genders are as follows :

1. **Masculine Gender :** A noun that denotes a male is said to be of the masculine gender, as man, uncle, ox, boy etc.
2. **Feminine Gender :** A noun that denotes a female is said to be of feminine gender, as woman, aunt, princess, cow etc.
3. **Common Gender :** Nouns which denote both males and females are said to be of the common gender, as friend, cousin, person, parent, baby etc.
4. **Neuter Gender :** A noun that denotes the name of object without life is said to be of neuter gender, as file, table, pencil.

REMEMBER

Masculine	*Feminine*
Boy	Girl
Son	Daughter
Brother	Sister
Murderer	Murderess
Sorcerer	Sorceress
Son-in-law	Daughter-in-law
Father-in-law	Mother-in-law
Man-servant	Maid-servant
Land-lord	Land-lady
Bachelor	Maid
Gentleman	Lady
Monk	Nun
Earl	Countess
Lad	Lass
Sir	Madam
Duke	Dutchess
Emperor	Empress
Milk-man	Milk-maid
Pea-cock	Pea-hen
Step-father	Step-mother
Hero	Heroine
Viceroy	Vicerine
Mr.	Mrs.
Governor	Governess
Master	Mistress
Wizard	Witch
Heir	Heiress
Host	Hostess
Lion	Lioness
Mayor	Mayoress
Actor	Actress
Buck	Doe
Colt	Filly
Dog	Bitch
Horse	Mare
Count	Countess
Hunter	Huntress
Prince	Princess
Abbot	Abbess
God	Goddess
Author	Authoress
Ox	Cow
Widower	Widow
Grand-father	Grand-mother
He-goat	She-goat
Milk-man	Milk-woman
Bridegroom	Bride
Tiger	Tigress
Priest	Priestess
Poet	Poetess
Shepherd	Shepherdess
Nephew	Niece
Stag	Hind

PRONOUNS

The repetition of a noun in a sentence or a set of sentences is really boring. So, instead of repeating the noun, we can use a word (for that noun) called the pronoun.

"A pronoun is a word that we use instead of a noun".

Example:

This is *Sachin*. *He* plays cricket.

Note: *He* is the pronoun used in place of *Sachin*.

Kinds of Pronouns

1. **Personal pronouns :** A pronoun which is used instead of the name of a person is known as a 'Personal Pronoun'. A list of the 'Personal pronouns' is listed below :

   I, my, mine, me, we   (First Person)

   You, your, yours   (Second Person)

   He, his, him, she, her, hers, it,

   its, they, their, theirs, them   (Third Person)

2. **Demonstrative, Indefinite and Distributive Pronouns :**

   (a) **Demonstrative Pronouns :** Pronouns used to point out the objects to which they refer are called Demonstrative Pronouns.

   Examples :

   (i) *This* is a present from my uncle.

   (ii) *These* are merely excuses.

   (iii) Bembay mangoes are better than *those* of Bangaluru.

   (b) **Indefinite Pronouns :** All pronouns which refer to persons or things in a general way and do not refer to any particular person or thing are called Indefinite Pronouns

   Examples :

   (i) *Somebody* has stolen my watch.

   (ii) *Few* escaped unhurt.

   (iii) Did you ask *anybody* to come?

   (c) **Distributive Pronouns :** Each, either, neither are called distributive pronouns because they refer to persons or things one at a time. For this reason they are always singular and followed by the verb in singular.

   Examples :

   (i) *Each* of the men received a reward.

   (ii) *These* men received *each* a reward.

   (iii) *Either* of you can go.

3. **Relative Pronouns :** A relative pronoun refers or relates to some noun going before, which is called its Antecedent.

   Examples :

   (i) I met Hari *who* used to live here.

   (ii) I have found the pen *which* I had lost.

   (iii) Here is the book *that* you lent me.

4. **Interrogative Pronouns :** These pronouns, are used for asking questions.

   Examples :

   (i) *Whose* book is this?

   (ii) *What* will all the neighbours say?

   (iii) *Which* do you prefer, tea or coffee?

   Note : Interrogative pronouns can also be used in asking indirect questions. Consider the following examples :

   (i) I asked *who* was speaking.

   (ii) Tell me *what* you have done.

   (iii) Say *which* you would like best.

Behaviour of the Pronouns

1. If three pronouns are used together in the same sentence they are arranged in the following order :

2	+	3	+	1
↓		↓		↓
Second		Third		First
Person		Person		Person

   Examples :

   I, you and he must help *that* poor man.   (Incorrect)

   You, he and I must help *that* poor man.   Correct)

2. When two or more singular nouns are joined by and, the pronoun used for them should be plural.

   Examples :

   Mohan and Sohan are friends. *They* play football. *They* live at Lajpat Nagar.

3. But if these nouns joined by and refer to the same person or thing, the pronoun used should be singular.

   Examples :

   (i) Delhi, the beautiful city and the capital of India, is famous for *its* historical monuments.

   (ii) The manager and owner of the firm expressed *his* views on the demands of the workers.

4. When two nouns are used with as well as, the pronoun agrees with the first subject.

   Examples :

   (a) Mohan as well as his friends is doing *his* work.

   (b) The students as well as their teachers are doing *their* work.

5. When two singular nouns joined by 'and' are preceded by *each* or *every*, the pronoun used must be singular and should agree in gender with the second noun.

   Examples :

   (a) Every man and every woman will do *her* best for the nation.

   (b) Each boy and each girl went to *her* house.

6. When two nouns are joined by using 'with', the pronoun agrees with the noun coming before 'with'.

   Examples :

   (a) The boy with *his* parents has gone to see a movie.

   (b) The children with *their* parents have gone to picnic.

7. When two different nouns are joined by either.......... or; neither .... nor, the pronoun is used according to the number and gender of the second noun.

Examples :
(a) Either your sister or you have done *your* work.
(b) Neither the students nor the teacher was in *his* class.

8. The pronoun coming after '*than*' must be in the same case as that coming before '*than*'.
   Examples :
   (a) She plays better than *me*.   (Incorrect)
       She plays better than *I*.   (Correct)
   (b) His elder brother is more intelligent than *him*.
       (Incorrect)
       His elder brother is more intelligent than *he*.
       (Correct)

9. 'Many a' always takes a singular pronoun and singular verb.
   Example :
   Many a soldier has met *his* death in the battle field.

10. 'Who', 'Whose', 'Whom' are used only for persons.
    Examples :
    (a) *Who* is knocking at the door?
    (b) *Whose* pen is this?
    (c) *What* do you want?

11. 'Which' is used for things.
    Example : *Which* game do you like?

MULTIPLE CHOICE QUESTIONS

Directions: *In the following questions choose the correct options to fill the blanks.*

1. The place was so dirty that ..... wished to run away from there.
   A. everybody   B. anybody
   C. few   D. some

2. ..... was there to help me.
   A. Somebody   B. Anything
   C. Anybody   D. Nobody

3. Is there .... to eat?
   A. some   B. something
   C. any   D. few

4. ..... of the students were making a great noise.
   A. Anyone   B. Somebody
   C. Many   D. Nobody

5. ..... of the students can solve this sum.
   A. Someone   B. Anybody
   C. Somebody   D. None

6. ...... of us should try our best to make India a heaven.
   A. Any   B. Somebody
   C. Anybody   D. All

7. ...... of us do not know the real meaning of our lives.
   A. Any   B. Something
   C. Several   D. Many

8. My .... black.
   A. hairs are   B. hair is
   C. hairs shall   D. hair will

9. She saw two .... on the last Sunday.
   A. thiefs   B. theifs
   C. thieves   D. theives

10. My sister is a ....
    A. bacheloress   B. bachelor
    C. unmaried   D. spinster

11. One is supposed to do ....
    A. our duty   B. their duty
    C. one's duty   D. his duty

12. Take anything .... you want.
    A. that   B. which
    C. than   D. then

13. I cannot tolerate ....
    A. separated you   B. your separation
    C. separation from you D. you separated

14. He is .... faithful partner.
    A. Yours   B. You
    C. Your   D. Your's

15. Ajay is more smart than ....
    A. her   B. hers
    C. herself   D. she

16. Vivek works harder than ....
    A. me   B. I
    C. her   D. his

17. They should help ....
    A. the poor people   B. the poor
    C. the poor persons   D. the poor peoples

18. .... are mad.
    A. All his sons   B. His all sons
    C. Sons all his   D. All sons his

19. The poor fellow .... to fate.
    A. resigned   B. resigned himself
    C. resigned itself   D. resigned themselves

20. Nobody will help you but ....
    A. I   B. me
    C. ours   D. his

21. It is a good chance, You must avail .... this opportunity.
    A. of   B. yourself of
    C. for   D. from

22. The person who is elected .... my relative.
    A. is   B. he is
    C. his   D. him

23. He made ....
    A. yours mention   B. mention of you
    C. mention for you   D. mention about you

24. .... I know, he is quite faithful.
    A. As far as   B. So far as
    C. So far this   D. So far so

25. It is a duty of a person to take .... for his family.
- A. pain
- B. pains
- C. pain-killers
- D. pained

26. She does not love .... husband.
- A. his
- B. her
- C. its
- D. their

27. Let .... work together.
- A. him and me
- B. he and I
- C. he and him
- D. I and me

28. Copper, Silver and Gold ....
- A. each will do
- B. either will do
- C. any one will do
- D. any will do

29. Jessica and Roma are very irregular .... habits.
- A. in her
- B. in their
- C. in its
- D. in every

30. One likes to enjoy .... who was a great poet.
- A. The sonnets of Shakespeare
- B. Shakespeare's sonnets
- C. Sonnets
- D. Shakespeare

ANSWERS

1	2	3	4	5	6	7	8	9	10
A	D	B	C	D	D	D	B	C	D
11	12	13	14	15	16	17	18	19	20
C	A	C	C	D	B	B	A	B	B
21	22	23	24	25	26	27	28	29	30
B	A	B	A	B	B	A	C	B	A

ARTICLES

The family of the articles has only three members. They are : A, An and The. However, they fall under two groups :

(a) Definite Article *(b)* Indefinite Article

'The' is known as definite article whereas 'a' and 'an' are known as indefinite articles.

Use of the Definite Article 'The'

'The' is used before

1. The superlative degree :
   He is the ablest man of the town.
   (ablest is a superlative degree)
2. The name of states, countries etc. having a descriptive name :
   (i) The J & K is a small state. (J & K is a descriptive name)
   (ii) He lives in the U.S.A. (U.S.A. is a descriptive name)
   (But the Delhi and the America are wrong because neither Delhi nor America is a descriptive name)
3. The names of the scriptures :
   The Gita is a holy book. (Gita is a scripture)
4. Name of newspapers :
   The Tribune is published from Chandigarh.
5. Name of rivers, canals, seas, oceans, bays, gulfs, groups of islands etc. :
   (i) The Ganga is a holy river.
   (ii) The Indian Ocean is the deepest ocean.
   (iii) The Persian Gulf is a narrow gulf.
6. The name of famous buildings :
   The Taj is one of the best buildings in India.
7. The names of nationals, sects and communities:
   (i) The English defeated the Germans in the World War.
   (ii) The rich should help the poor.
   (iii) The Hindus believe in the caste system.
8. Proper nouns used as common nouns :
   (i) Kalidas is the Shakespeare of India.
   (ii) Delhi is the London of India.
9. Famous historical events :
   The Industrial Revolution changed the face of England.
10. The directions and the celestial bodies:
    The sun rises in the east.
11. Titles : Akbar, the Great was loved by his subjects.

Do not use 'the'

1. Before languages :
   The English is an international language. (Incorrect)
   English is an international language. (Correct)
2. Before the names of games :
   The hockey is a popular game. (Incorrect)
   Hockey is a popular game. (Correct)

Use of the Indefinite Articles 'A' and 'An'

'A' is used before :

1. All singular common nouns beginning with a consonant :
   (i) A boy sings a song.
   (ii) A black and a white cow were grazing in the field.
2. If a word begins with a vowel but gives the sound of a consonant, 'a' should be used before it :
   (i) He was helped in his work by a European.
   (ii) He is a one-eyed man.
   (iii) It is a useful work.

'An' is used as follows :

1. All singular common nouns beginning with a vowel (*i.e.*, a, e, i, o, u) :
   (i) He is an artist. (ii) He is an old man. (iii) I intend to buy an umbrella.
2. If a word starts with a consonant but gives the sound of a vowel, "an" should be used before it :
   (i) Brutus is an honourable man.
   (ii) He is an honour to his profession.
   (iii) He is an L.L.B.

Demonstratives, that, these and those

1. The demonstrative adjectives and pronouns are for objects nearby the speaker:
   this (singular) those (plural)
   and for objects far away from the speaker.
   That (singular) those (plural)
2. Demonstratives are the only adjectives that agree in number with their nouns.
   That hat is nice.
   Those hats are nice.
3. When there is the idea of selection, the pronoun "one" (or "ones") often follows the demonstrative.
   I want a book. I'll get this (one).
   If the demonstrative is followed by an adjective, "one"(or "ones") must be used.
   I want a book. I'll get this big one.

MULTIPLE CHOICE QUESTIONS

Directions: *In the following questions choose the correct options to fill the blanks.*

1. .... will have to be paid for this material.
   - A. Half rupee
   - B. Half a rupee
   - C. A half rupee
   - D. An half rupee

2. .... is taking keen interest in India.
   - A. The USA
   - B. USA
   - C. An USA
   - D. A USA

3. Only .... can save our country.
   - A. the Hitler
   - B. a Hitler
   - C. Hitler
   - D. an Hitler

4. I can run for ....
   - A. hundred miles
   - B. the hundred miles
   - C. a hundred miles
   - D. an hundred miles.

5. .... man-eater has been killed.
   - A. The
   - B. A
   - C. An
   - D. Either A or B

6. What .... fine idea!
   - A. the
   - B. an
   - C. a
   - D. No article

7. .... earth is moving around the sun.
   - A. An
   - B. A
   - C. The
   - D. No article

8. This is .... first example while I got.
   - A. the
   - B. a
   - C. an
   - D. No article

9. This is .... house which was built during earthquake.
   - A. a
   - B. an
   - C. the
   - D. No article

10. .... America is a rich country.
    - A. The
    - B. An
    - C. A
    - D. No article

11. .... U.S.A. is a developed country.
    - A. A
    - B. An
    - C. The
    - D. No article

12. .... Bible is a holy book.
    - A. A
    - B. The
    - C. An
    - D. No article

13. .... rich should help the poor.
    - A. The
    - B. A
    - C. An
    - D. No article

14. .... Gold is a costly metal.
    - A. The
    - B. A
    - C. An
    - D. No article

15. Kalidas is .... Shakespeare of India.
    - A. a
    - B. an
    - C. the
    - D. No article

16. I cannot do .... difficult work.
    - A. a such
    - B. the such
    - C. such the
    - D. such a

17. How foolish .... plan it is!
    - A. a
    - B. an
    - C. the
    - D. No article

18. An ink is .... useful article.
    - A. an
    - B. a
    - C. the
    - D. No article

19. There are .... husband and wife.
    - A. a
    - B. an
    - C. the
    - D. No article

20. He is learning .... French
    - A. the
    - B. a
    - C. an
    - D. No article

ANSWERS

1	2	3	4	5	6	7	8	9	10
B	A	B	C	D	C	C	A	C	D

11	12	13	14	15	16	17	18	19	20
C	B	A	D	C	D	A	B	D	D

ADJECTIVES & ADVERBS

An Adjective is a word which adds something to the meaning of a noun or a pronoun.

Mridula is an *intelligent* girl. He has a *black* goat.
He is a *brilliant* student. She is a *clever* girl.
It is a *beautiful* picture.

In the sentences given above, the words in italics are adjectives.

An Adverb is a word which qualifies the meaning of a Verb, an Adjective or another Adverb.

(*i*) He talks *slowly*.
(*ii*) He is a *very* good student.
(*iii*) He talks *very* slowly.

In sentence (*i*), *slowly* qualifies the verb *talks*.
In sentence (*ii*), *very* qualifies the adjective *good*.
In sentence (*iii*), *very* qualifies the adverb *slowly*.

Adjectives have three degrees of comparison :

1. **Positive Degree :** It expresses the common form of an adjective.

   Example :
   Ram is a *tall* boy.
   In the above sentence *tall* is an adjective and expresses the common form.

2. **Comparative Degree :** It expresses the more of the same form.

   Example :
   Ram is *taller* than Mahesh.
   In the above sentence *taller* is an adjective that expresses the more of the common form of the adjective *tall*.

   "When and How to Use" Comparative Degree?

   (a) Comparative Degree is used when two persons or two groups of persons or things are compared.

   Examples :
   (a) He is *wiser* than his younger brother.
   (b) This glass is *cleaner* than the other.

   (b) When two different qualities in the same person are compared, more is used instead of 'er' to form the comparative. The formula used in this case should be :

   More + Positive Degree
   She is *fairer* than polite. (Incorrect)
   She is *more fair* than polite. (Correct)

   (c) When selection of one out of two persons or things is meant, the degree of comparison is followed by of and *the* is used before it.

   Example :
   Zia is abler of *the* two sisters.

   (d) If two comparatives are used in the same sentence to impress upon an idea, both should be preceded by the definite article.

   Examples :
   (i) The higher you go, the cooler it is.
   (ii) The more we get, the more we desire.

(e) When one person or thing is compared with another of the same kind, other is used after the comparative degree. In such sentences other is normally preceded by any or all.

Examples :
(i) Kalidas is greater than any dramatist.
   (Incorrect)
   Kalidas is greater than any other dramatist.
   (Correct)
(ii) Lead is heavier than all metals.
   (Incorrect)
   Lead is heavier than all other metals.
   (Correct)

(f) Senior, junior, superior, inferior, prior, anterior (earlier than) and posterior (later than) are always followed by 'to'.

Examples :
(i) Ram is senior *to* Mohan by three years.
(ii) That pen is inferior *to* that.
(iii) He is junior *to* me in rank.
(iv) This event was posterior *to* that.

Note: Never use *than* after the above mentioned adjectives.

Important Information

(a) 'Preferable' is also used as an adjective of the comparative degree. As such, it is always followed by *to* and not *a*.
   Death is preferable than dishonour. (Incorrect)
   Death is preferable *to* dishonour. (Correct)

(b) To intensify the Degree of comparison, we use *far* or *much* before the comparative.

   Examples :
   (i) This book is *far* better than that.
   (ii) His performance was *much* better than Mohan's.
   Warning : Always avoid the use of double comparatives.
   Don't say : Ram is more cleverer than his younger brother.
   Say: Ram is cleverer than his younger brother.

3. **Superlative Degree :** It expresses the most of the common form of an adjective.
   Example :
   He is the ablest man of the town.

How and when to use the Superlative Degree?

(a) The Superlative Degree is used when more than two persons or things are compared.
(b) The Superlative Degree is generally preceded by 'the' and followed by 'of' in most of the cases or otherwise.
(c) When an adjective of the superlative degree is preceded by a Possessive Adjective or a Noun in the Possessive case, 'the' should not be used before it.
   Example :
   Which is Kalidas' best play?

It will be a blunder to use 'the' before the Superlative Degree in such cases.

Don't say : Which is Kalidas' the best play.

(d) To intensify the degree of comparison, *by far* is used before the superlative degree.

Example :

India is *by far* the most beautiful country of the world.

Note: Always avoid the use of double superlatives.

Don't say : He is the most strongest boy in the class.

Say : He is the strongest boy in the class.

Use of some Important Adjectives

1. (a) **'Some'** is used as follows :
   - (i) With countable nouns where it means— a little, a small quantity.
   - (ii) In a question which shows some request.

   Examples :
   - (i) There is some water in the bottle.
   - (ii) Some of the students were absent yesterday.
   - (iii) Will you have some milk?
   - (iv) Will you buy some fruit for me?

   (b) **'Any'** is used as follows :
   - (i) In negative sentences.
   - (ii) In interrogative sentences.
   - (iii) After 'Hardly', 'Scarcely' and 'Barely'.
   - (iv) After 'If'.

   Examples :
   - (i) There is not any sugar in the pot.
   - (ii) We haven't any rice in the house.
   - (iii) I have hardly any money.
   - (iv) There are scarcely any plants in this field.
   - (v) If there is any danger, blow the whistle.

2. (a) **Older :** Older (and oldest) are used for persons animals and things. But 'Older' and 'Oldest' refer to the persons who do not belong to the same family.

   Examples :
   - (i) Radha is older than Shyama.
   - (ii) John is the oldest member of the staff.
     'Older' and 'Oldest' refer to the persons who do not belong to the same family.

   (b) **Elder** (and **eldest**) are used in respect of the members of the same family like sons, daughters, brothers, sisters.

   Examples :
   - (i) My elder sister is a lecturer.
   - (ii) Meenakshi is the eldest of the three sisters.

   Note :
   - (i) 'Elder' is not followed by 'than'.
   - (ii) 'Elder' and 'Eldest' cannot be used for things.

3. (a) **'Few'** is negative and is the opposite of 'Many'. It means 'not many'.

   (b) **'A few'** is positive and means 'some at least'. It is the opposite of 'None'.

   (c) **'The few'** means 'minority' and suggests 'whether there is'.

Examples :
- (i) We have few holidays in school.
- (ii) Only a few boys will fail in the examination.
- (iii) The few poems that he wrote are very popular.

4. (a) **Further** means 'something additional'.

   (b) **Farther** means 'a greater distance'.

   Examples :
   - (i) Further discussion will be held in the office of the principal.
   - (ii) Amritsar is farther from Delhi than Ambala.

5. (a) **Little** is negative. It means, 'not much', or 'hardly any'.

   (b) **A little** is positive. It means 'some quantity'.

   (c) **The little** denotes quantity. It means, 'not much but all that is, or whatever quantity there is'.

   Examples :
   - (i) There is little hope of his success.
   - (ii) He knows a little of everything.
   - (iii) I have spent the little money I had.
   - (iv) The little knowledge of shoe-making proved very useful to me.

6. (a) **'Much'** expresses 'quantity'.

   (b) **'Many'** expresses 'number'.

   (c) **'Many a'**—'Singular noun' and 'Singular verb' are used with 'many a'.

   Examples :
   - (i) There is not *much* water in the jug.
   - (ii) *Many* boys are absent today.
   - (iii) *Many* a battle has been fought on the soil of India.

7. (a) **'Less'** denotes 'in a small degree'.

   (b) **'Fewer'** denotes 'number'.

   Examples :
   - (i) He devotes less time to his studies.
   - (ii) There are no fewer than ten chairs in this room.

8. (a) **'Each'** is used for a single number of 'two persons' or 'things'.

   (b) **'Every'** is used for a single number of 'many persons' or 'things'.

   Examples :
   - (i) Each boy must take part in games.
   - (ii) There are only two poets. Each poet recited his poem.
   - (iii) Every man dies in this world.
   - (iv) Every man is expected to do his duty.

9. (a) **'Either'** means one of the two or both.

   (b) **'Neither'** is negative of the either.

   Examples :
   - (i) You may buy either of these two chairs.
   - (ii) Neither of them could speak on the stage.

10. (a) **'Later'** expresses 'late in time'.

    (b) **'Latter'** means 'second in position or order'.

    Examples :
    - (i) My father reached later than I expected.
    - (ii) The latter position was better than the former.

Use of some Important Adverbs

1. (a) Also, too, enough:
    (i) He taught English. Also, he edited the school magazine
    (ii) He is a writer and also he is a painter.
    (iii) He is too obstinate to listen to any reason.
    (iv) This is too difficult a piece for the junior students.
    (v) Sarla was kind enough to help the poor.
    (vi) He is brave enough to help the truth.
    Note: 'Too' is used in a negative sense, but enough is used in a positive sense.

   (b) Fairly and rather: Both suggest the meaning 'moderately'. But, mainly 'fairly' is used with the words that denote a positive meaning and rather is used with the words that denote a negative meaning:
    (i) Rita did fairly well in that competition, but her performance was rather poor in sports.
    (ii) Mona is fairly rich, but she is rather stingy.
    Note: 'Rather' can also be used in a positive sense.
    (i) This is a rather interesting job.
    (ii) That boy is rather smart.

   (c) Hardly, barely, scarcely: These words mostly convey the negative suggestions and are almost similar.
    (i) I have hardly any strength now.
    (ii) There was barely any supply to the township,
    (iii) There were scarcely a hundred guests present.
    Note: With slight variance in the meaning, the words given above convey the idea of 'very little', 'not enough', 'lack of quantity and number'.

   (d) Yet, Still: These adverbs can often be used to connect the sentence units:
    (i) He has been defeated many times in the contest; still he wants to be a competitor.
    (ii) Mona was sick; yet she went on doing her work.
   (e) Alone:
    (i) He alone (none else) is capable of handling that fire,
    (ii) He hunted all alone in the forest. (not in any company)

Special Note:
   (a) Apart from their conventional positions the adverbs might be used in different positions with different meanings and angles.
    (i) He had only four books.
    (ii) John only contacted his friend in need.
    (iii) He greeted me only.
    (iv) Only he greeted me there.
   (b) Inversion: Some adverbs can be inverted *i.e.* placed in the beginning of the sentence and then be followed by an interrogative form. The most common of these adverb are: so, seldom, never, nowhere, under no circumstances, hardly, scarcely etc.
    (i) So big was the bus that it could not enter the narrow lane.
    (ii) Hardly had he reached the station when he received the message.

MULTIPLE CHOICE QUESTIONS

Directions: *In the following questions choose the correct options to fill the blanks.*

1. The girl whom you met is the .... sister of Ravi.
    A. eldest
    B. elder
    C. older
    D. oldest

2. The historical place is ....
    A. seeing worth
    B. worthy of seeing
    C. worth seeing
    D. worthy seeing

3. These flowers smell ....
    A. sweet
    B. sweetly
    C. more sweetly
    D. sweetest

4. .... aspirant cannot pass the entrance examination.
    A. Each
    B. Every
    C. All
    D. No

5. Harivansh Rai .... second Shakespeare.
    A. is a
    B. is
    C. is the
    D. is an

6. .... student in the class got prizes.
    A. Each and every
    B. Every and each
    C. Every
    D. Never

7. It is .... picture than the one we saw last Monday.
    A. interesting
    B. much interesting
    C. more interesting
    D. most interesting

8. She is clever ....
    A. that her mother is
    B. as her mother is
    C. to her mother is
    D. than her mother is

9. They will get ....
    A. Red, green and black paper
    B. Red, green black paper
    C. Red and green and black paper
    D. Red green black paper

10. Health is .... wealth.
    A. preferable to
    B. more preferable than
    C. more preferable to
    D. most preferable then

11. .... water that was in the jug evaporated.
    A. Little
    B. The little
    C. Small
    D. A small

12. He has not sung .... songs.
    A. much
    B. most
    C. more
    D. many

13. Srishti has searched .... office.
    A. whole the
    B. the whole
    C. a whole
    D. some whole

14. Premchand was .... best and .... famous writer.
    A. a, the most
    B. the, a most
    C. the, more
    D. the, the most

15. William Shakespeare is famous as ....
 A. a poet and a dramatist
 B. a poet and dramatist
 C. the poet and the dramatist
 D. a poet and the dramatist

16. What does .... leader suggest?
 A. other
 B. another
 C. others
 D. anothers

17. He .... money.
 A. has few
 B. have few
 C. has little
 D. have little

18. The .... boys are rewarded.
 A. first two
 B. two first
 C. firsts two
 D. two's first

19. He is .... brave.
 A. stronger than
 B. stronger then
 C. more strong then
 D. more strong than

20. No sooner said ....
 A. so done
 B. and done
 C. then done
 D. but done

21. She returned .... than I had thought.
 A. quickly
 B. more quicker
 C. more quickly
 D. quicker

22. He is .... foolish person.
 A. rather the
 B. a rather
 C. rather a
 D. rather

23. This pen .... rupees.
 A. costs twenty
 B. twenty costs only
 C. costs only twenty
 D. only costs twenty

24. It is .... pride.
 A. nothing else but
 B. nothing else than
 C. else nothing than
 D. but

25. This tea is .... to drink.
 A. too hot
 B. very hot
 C. enough hot
 D. much hot

ANSWERS

1	2	3	4	5	6	7	8	9	10
A	C	A	B	A	C	C	C	A	A
11	**12**	**13**	**14**	**15**	**16**	**17**	**18**	**19**	**20**
B	D	B	D	B	B	C	A	D	C
21	**22**	**23**	**24**	**25**					
C	C	C	A	A					

DETERMINERS

Determiners are actually Adjectives. They are always followed by nouns.

Determiners are of the following kinds:

1. **Demonstrative Determiners :** this, that, these, those
2. **Possessive Determiners :** my, our, your, his, her, its, their
3. **Quantitative Determiners :** some, any, much, enough, sufficient, whole, a little, the little, little, all, both
4. **Numerical Determiners:** a few, some, few, the few, any, several, many, no, etc.

 One, two, three ...   (Cardinals)

 First, second, third ...   (Ordinals)
5. **Distributive Determiners:** either, neither
6. **Articles: Indefinite:** a, an, **Definite:** the

MULTIPLE CHOICE QUESTIONS

Directions: *In the following questions choose the correct options to fill the blanks.*

1. Give me .... rice.
 A. some
 B. few
 C. a few
 D. any

2. ...... sheep grazing on the slope of the hill had gone away.
 A. Any
 B. The few
 C. This
 D. Much

3. Have you got .... magazines to read?
 A. all
 B. much
 C. some
 D. little

4. I have .... money that I want to spend on shares.
 A. any
 B. much
 C. less
 D. some

5. There is .... owl on the branch of the tree.
 A. a
 B. the
 C. an
 D. some

6. My brother is .... MBA.
 A. a
 B. an
 C. the
 D. any

7. Have you got .... cheese?
 A. some
 B. many
 C. a few
 D. few

8. No, I have not got .... cheese.
 A. many
 B. few
 C. any
 D. some

9. There is only .... milk left in the bottle.
   A. enough   B. few
   C. much   D. a little
10. There is .... hope of his recovery.
   A. any   B. little
   C. many   D. few
11. .... dogs were barking at the strangers.
   A. Some   B. Any
   C. Much   D. Less
12. The girl bought her father .... juice.
   A. few   B. some
   C. any   D. many
13. You should take .... honey everyday.
   A. any   B. many
   C. a little   D. a few
14. .... boy was punished by the teacher.
   A. Either   B. All
   C. Any   D. Many
15. .... girl was asked to join the army.
   A. None   B. Neither
   C. All   D. Any
16. .... water in the jug has been drunk by Mohan.
   A. The little   B. The few
   C. A few   D. Few
17. I shall play .... piano at the party.
   A. some   B. any
   C. the   D. few
18. .... labourers were found dead in the mine.
   A. Any   B. Fewer
   C. Many   D. Less
19. Could I borrow .... umbrella?
   A. our   B. your
   C. yours   D. my
20. My brother is standing in the .... row.
   A. any   B. many
   C. some   D. first

ANSWERS

1	2	3	4	5	6	7	8	9	10
A	B	C	D	C	B	A	C	D	B

11	12	13	14	15	16	17	18	19	20
A	B	C	A	B	A	C	C	B	D

THE VERB

A Verb is a word that tells something about the action or state of or happenning to a person or thing.

A Verb tells the following:

1. What a person or thing does.
   Sachin goes to school daily.
   The bell *rang* loudly.
   Many birds fly in the sky.
   She *sang* a song.
2. What a person or thing is.
   India *is* the biggest democracy in the world.
   Ram Mehar *is* very rich.
   They *are* happy.
3. What is done to a person or thing.
   You *are liked* by all.
   Two thieves *were arrested.*
   Four students *were punished* by the teacher.
4. What happens to a person or thing.
   His maternal uncle *died* last week.
   Two ships *sank* yesterday.
   Leaves *turn* yellow in autumn.
5. What a person or thing has, had, and so on.
   I *have* a new car.
   He *had* a scooter last year.
   He *has* several cows and goats.

It goes without saying that a verb is the most important part of a sentence. No sentence is complete without a Verb.

Important Information

1. If two or more singular nouns are joined by 'and' the verb used will be plural.
   Example:
   (i) He and I were going to the market.
   (ii) Ram and Mohan are friends.

2. If two singular nouns joined by 'and' points out to the same thing or person, the verb used must be singular.
   Example:
   (i) Rice and curry is the favourite food of the Punjabis.
   (ii) The Collector and District Magistrate is away.

3. In case two subjects are joined by 'as well as' the verb agrees with the first subject.
   Example :
   (i) Kanta as well as her children is playing.
   (ii) Children as well as their mother are playing.
   In the case of first sentence the verb (is) agrees with Kanta and in the case of second sentence the verb (are) agrees with the children.

4. 'Neither', 'Either', 'Every', 'Each', 'Everyone', and 'Many a' are followed by a singular verb.
   Example :
   (i) Either of the plans is to be adopted.
   (ii) Neither of the two brothers is sure to pass.
   (iii) Every student is expected to be obedient.
   (iv) Everyone of them desires this.
   (v) Many a person is drowned in the sea.

5. If two subjects are joined by 'Either .... or' / 'Neither .... nor', the verb agrees with the subject near to it.

   Example :
   (i) Either my brother or I am to do this work.
   (ii) Neither he nor they are prepared to do this work.

6. 'A great many' is always followed by a 'plural noun' and a 'plural verb'. For example :
   A great many students have been declared successful.

7. Similarly if two subjects are joined by 'with', 'together with', 'no less than', in addition to 'and not', etc. the verb agrees with the first subject.

   Example :
   (i) The boy with his parents has arrived.
   (ii) He, no less than I, is to blame.

8. Nouns, plural in form, but singular in meaning, take a singular verb.

   Example :
   This news was broadcast from television yesterday.

MULTIPLE CHOICE QUESTIONS

Directions: *In the following questions choose the correct options to fill the blanks.*

1. The bus with all its passengers .... lost.
   A. were   B. was
   C. are   D. would

2. You as well as I .... responsible for this work.
   A. am   B. are
   C. was   D. is

3. Raghava like all his companions .... a spoiled child.
   A. are   B. were
   C. is   D. will be

4. Pen and ink .... required for me.
   A. are   B. were
   C. is   D. has required

5. Every girl and every boy .... attended the seminar.
   A. have   B. has
   C. is   D. are

6. Not only she but all her sisters ...... been married.
   A. has   B. have
   C. is   D. are

7. There .... nothing but miseries in life.
   A. is   B. are
   C. were   D. will be

8. Neither prose nor poem .... given.
   A. were   B. was
   C. has   D. have

9. Either he or I .... wrong.
   A. is   B. are
   C. am   D. were

10. Either Sulekha or Rekha .... coming here.
    A. are   B. is
    C. were   D. have

11. .... the child or his parents to blame?
    A. Is   B. Are
    C. Were   D. Has

12. You and I .... neighbours.
    A. am   B. are
    C. was   D. has

13. The house with all its belongings ..... sold away.
    A. were   B. are
    C. was   D. must

14. Either water or juice .... required.
    A. is   B. are
    C. were   D. has

15. There were not as many tables as .... required.
    A. was   B. were
    C. is   D. are

16. They each .... a book.
    A. have   B. are
    C. has   D. is

17. He and I .... class friends.
    A. is   B. am
    C. was   D. are

18. She as well as I .... guilty.
    A. is   B. are
    C. am   D. must be

19. Purushottam .... not read more on this chapter.
    A. needs
    B. has been need
    C. need
    D. had been need

20. He came .... to his aunt.
    A. run   B. running
    C. to run   D. in run

ANSWERS

1	2	3	4	5	6	7	8	9	10
B	B	C	C	B	B	A	B	C	B

11	12	13	14	15	16	17	18	19	20
A	B	C	A	B	A	D	A	C	B

CONJUNCTIONS

A conjunction is a word which connects words, clauses or sentences.

Look at the following sentences.
(i)　He bought apples *and* mangoes.
(ii)　God made the country *and* man made the town.
(iii)　The door was open *but* there was no one in the house.
(iv)　He knows that I am here *and* that I want to see him.

In the sentence (i), *and* connects two words—*apples* and *mangoes.*

In the sentence (ii), *and* connects two sentences—*God made the country* and *man made the town.*

In the sentence (iii), *but* connects two sentences— *The door was open* and *there was no one in the house.*

In the sentence (iv), *and* connects two clauses—*that I am here* and *that I want to see him.*

The main coordinating conjunctions are:
and, but, for, or, nor, also, either ..... or, neither ..... nor.

There are some conjunctions which are used in pairs. They are:
either .... or, ... neither .... nor, both .... and, though .... yet, whether .... or, not only .... but also.

Example: *Either* take it *or* leave it.

It is *neither* useful *nor* ornamental.

They *both* like *and* respect me.

Though he is suffering from high fever, *yet* he does not cry.

He does not care *whether* you go *or* stay.

He is *not only* doltish, *but also* obstinate.

The conjunctions which are used in pairs in this way, are called correlative conjunctions, or merely correlatives.

Use of Important Conjunctions

1. **As soon as :** As soon as denotes simultaneous time.
   Example : As soon as he saw his enemy, he took to his heels.
2. **No sooner .... than :**
   (a)　'No sooner' is always followed by 'than'.
   (b)　Please remember that 'No sooner' is always followed by do/does/did. As such only first form of the verb should be used after the subject.
   Example :
   No sooner did he see his enemy than he took to his heels.
3. **Hardly :** Hardly is followed by when.
   Examples :
   (i)　Hardly had I left the house when it started raining.
   (ii)　We had hardly come into the room when his father began chastising him.
   Note :
   A.　Hardly is never followed by than.
   B.　'Scarcely' can also be used in the sense and manner of 'Hardly'.

4. **Lest :** Lest is used in the sense of so that .... not. It is always followed by should. Lest is negative in sense. Hence 'not' should never be used with it.
   Example :
   Work hard lest you should fail.
   Note : 'Lest' is always followed by 'should' and not 'may'.
5. **Unless :** Unless expresses condition. It is also used in the negative sense. Use of 'not' is not allowed with unless because unless is already in the negative sense.
   Example :
   Unless you labour hard you will not pass.
6. **Until :** 'Until' expresses time. It means 'till not'.
   Example : Wait here until I return.
   Note : Until is in the negative sense. So 'not' should not be used with it. Example :
   Wait here until I do not return.　　(Incorrect)
   Wait here until I return.　　　　(Correct)
7. **As well as :** When two subjects are joined by 'as well as', the verb always agrees with the first subject.
   Examples :
   (i)　The teacher as well as students is playing.
   (ii)　Students as well as the teacher are playing.
   Note : 'Both' and 'as well as' cannot be used together in the same sentence.
   Examples :
   Both Sita as well as Kanta are beautiful.
   (Incorrect)
   Sita as well as Kanta is beautiful.　(Correct)
   Both Sita and Kanta are beautiful.　(Correct)
8. **As if :** 'As if' is used in the sense of pretension. While using 'as if' in a sentence, we should see that even the third person singular subject gets 'were'.
   Example : He talks as if he were mad.
9. **Till :** Till expresses time. Till is always used in the affirmative.
   Example :
   We did not come back till sunset.
10. **Rather than :** 'Rather than' is used in the sense of 'preference'. 'Rather' is always followed by 'than'.
    Example :
    I would rather die than submit.
11. **As long as/so long as :** Both express time during which an action or event takes place.
    Example :
    As long as there is life, there is hope.
12. **However :** It is both a subordinate and co-ordinate clause.
    Examples :
    (a)　Mala worked hard, she however, failed.
    (b)　However hard he may work, he cannot pass.
13. **Such as :** 'Such as' gives us the sense of 'like'. Such is always followed by 'as'.
    Example :
    Life is such a puzzle as cannot be solved.

MULTIPLE CHOICE QUESTIONS

Directions: *In the following questions choose the correct options to fill the blanks.*

1. Neither he .... his friend is good.
   - A. or
   - B. and
   - C. but
   - D. nor

2. The officer asked the peon .... why he was late.
   - A. that
   - B. if
   - C. but
   - D. No word needed

3. Both Ajay .... Vijay are intelligent.
   - A. or
   - B. nor
   - C. and
   - D. No word needed

4. No Sooner did the thief see the public .... he ran away.
   - A. then
   - B. and
   - C. but
   - D. than

5. Abhinav .... his brothers was going to Mumbai.
   - A. but
   - B. yet
   - C. No word needed
   - D. together with

6. He behaves .... he were the captain of the team.
   - A. as if
   - B. as
   - C. No word needed
   - D. that

7. Either Rupali .... Sonali is going to attend the meeting.
   - A. and
   - B. but
   - C. nor
   - D. or

8. Neither Nirmal .... Ashwinee is going to listen the speech.
   - A. and
   - B. but
   - C. nor
   - D. or

9. Ravi .... Prakash are going to Kolkata.
   - A. or
   - B. nor
   - C. but
   - D. and

10. Rice .... curry is my usual breakfast.
    - A. and
    - B. but
    - C. then
    - D. than

11. Hardly had he left .... his brother came.
    - A. then
    - B. than
    - C. when
    - D. that

12. I would rather have a copy .... a book.
    - A. then
    - B. than
    - C. when
    - D. that

13. He is no other .... my friend.
    - A. then
    - B. than
    - C. when
    - D. but

14. He saw a snake ....he awoke.
    - A. then
    - B. when
    - C. than
    - D. No word needed

15. Ten years have passed .... my grandmother died.
    - A. since
    - B. when
    - C. then
    - D. than

16. She is .... good .... bad.
    - A. either, not
    - B. neither, or
    - C. neither, nor
    - D. neither, than

17. The cellphone is both cheap .... best.
    - A. than
    - B. and
    - C. then
    - D. or

18. No sooner did the rogue see the police .... he disappeared.
    - A. then
    - B. than
    - C. so
    - D. because

19. Srishti will go .... Sanju goes.
    - A. if
    - B. than
    - C. then
    - D. although

20. She is wise .... timid.
    - A. and
    - B. yet
    - C. but
    - D. however

21. Make hay .... the sun shines.
    - A. though
    - B. while
    - C. after
    - D. before

22. He is so weak .... he cannot walk.
    - A. but
    - B. that
    - C. then
    - D. so

23. Although he is rich, ... he is unhappy.
    - A. but
    - B. yet
    - C. so
    - D. still

24. Wait here .... I come back.
    - A. till
    - B. until
    - C. before
    - D. after

25. He is my friend .... I shall help him.
    - A. so
    - B. hence
    - C. that is why
    - D. therefore

26. He must go away .... he will be beaten.
    - A. otherwise
    - B. and
    - C. or
    - D. else

27. God loves good men .... good men love God.
    - A. and
    - B. or
    - C. that
    - D. those

28. He was late .... he was not punished.
    - A. but
    - B. yet
    - C. still
    - D. therefore

29. Walk slowly ...., you may fall.
    - A. and
    - B. or
    - C. so
    - D. otherwise

30. Work hard, ... you will fail.
    - A. and
    - B. or
    - C. otherwise
    - D. else

ANSWERS

1	2	3	4	5	6	7	8	9	10
D	D	C	D	D	A	D	C	D	A
11	**12**	**13**	**14**	**15**	**16**	**17**	**18**	**19**	**20**
C	B	B	B	A	C	B	B	A	C
21	**22**	**23**	**24**	**25**	**26**	**27**	**28**	**29**	**30**
B	B	B	A	B	C	A	C	D	D

PREPOSITIONS

A *Preposition* is a word which is placed before a noun or a pronoun to show its relation to some other word in the sentence.

1. I saw a goat *in* the field.
2. I am fond *of* hot coffee.

In sentence 1, the word *in* shows the relation between two things—*goat* and *field*.

In sentence 2, the word *of* shows the relation between the attribute expressed by the adjective *found* and *tea*.

The words *in* and *of* are here used as prepositions.

The noun or pronoun which is used with a preposition is called its object. The noun or pronoun is in the objective case. It is governed by the preposition. Now it is absolutely clear that in sentence 1, the noun *field* is in the objective case. The word *field* is governed by the preposition *in*.

A preposition may have two or more objects.

The road runs over *hill* and *plain*.

Here, the words *hill* and *plain* are used as objects.

Use of Important Prepositions

1. **Among, Between**
   '**Among**' is used for more than two persons or things; '**Between**' is used only for two.
   Examples :
   (i) Distribute these sweets *among* the poor students of the class.
   (ii) Distribute these books *between* Ram and Shyam.

2. **Among, In**
   '**Among**' is used before collective plural nouns. '**In**' is used before collective singular nouns.
   Examples :
   (i) I found him standing *among* the crowd.
   (ii) I saw him in the crowd.

3. **Beside, Besides**
   '**Beside**' means 'by the side of'. '**Besides**' means 'in addition to'.
   Examples :
   (i) The daughter was sitting *beside* her mother.
   (ii) *Besides* his relatives, he invited his friends also.

4. **In, Within**
   '**In**' means at the expiry of a period of time in future, '**Within**' means before the expiry of a period of time in any tense.
   Examples :
   (i) She will return *in* a week.
   (ii) I shall finish my work *within* a weak.

5. **On, Upon**
   '**On**' is used for things at rest; '**Upon**' is used for things in motion.
   Examples :
   (i) He is sitting *on* the floor.
   (ii) The dog sprang *upon* the table.

6. **By, With**
   '**By**' denotes the agent or doer, '**With**' denotes the instrument with which anything is done.
   Examples :
   (i) The bird was killed *by* the hunter with an arrow.
   (ii) He beat the dog *with* a stick.
   (iii) I shall reach here *by* five o'clock.

7. **After, In**
   '**After**' means at the end of a period of time in the past. '**In**' means at the end of a period of time in future.
   Examples :
   (i) I shall return your book *in* a week.
   (ii) He returned the book *after* a week.

8. **For, From, Since**
   '**For**' is used before a noun denoting a period of time with all the tenses. '**From**' is used before a noun or phrase denoting a point of time, it is used in all the tenses. '**Since**' is used before a noun or phrase denoting some point of time and is always produced by a verb in the perfect continuous tense or third form of a verb.
   Examples :
   (i) We have been playing cards *for* two hours.
   (ii) She stayed with her uncle *from* the 15th of March to the 15th of May.
   (iii) I have been reading this book *since* morning.

9. **Above, Over**
   '**Above**' means 'higher from', **Over** is used in the following four senses :
   (i) In the sense of 'above' :
   At noon, the sun is *over* our heads.
   (ii) In the sense of 'beyond' :
   I cannot get *over* my disappointment.
   (iii) In the sense of 'Superiority' :
   God *over* all blesses for ever more.
   (iv) In the sense of 'Conclusion' :
   It is all *over* with me.

10. At, Towards

'**At**' denotes the idea of aim, '**Towards**' denotes the idea of destination.

Examples :

(i) He threw the stone *at* the cat.

(ii) He went *towards* the house.

11. At, In, On

'At' is used as follows :

(i) '**At**' is used with small towns and villages. **Examples:**
(a) He was born *at* Sonepat.
(b) He lives *at* village Bangra. (Bangra is a village)

(ii) '**At**' is used before a noun denoting a definite point of time.

Example :

He called on me *at* 9 p.m. yesterday.

'In' is used as follows :

(iii) '**In**' is used with the names of big cities, provinces and countries.

Examples :
(a) His father lives *in* England.
(b) His younger brother lives *in* Calcutta.

(iv) '**In**' is used before the names of months and years.

Example :

His elder sister was born *in* 1972 *in* the month of May.
'**On**' is used with dates and names of days. **Examples:**
(a) I joined college *on* the 26th April.
(b) He will leave for Kolkata *on* Wednesday next.

Important Information

1. '**In**' is also used in the following phrases :
In the morning; In the evening, In winter, In summer.
2. '**In**' also denotes a place inside anything.
He travelled *in* a crowded bus.
3. '**At**' is used in the following phrases :
At home, *At* the station, *At* work, *At* play.

12. Below, Beneath

Below means 'of lower level in position, dignity and expectation' etc. *Beneath* means 'under'.

Examples :

(i) It is *below* my dignity to talk to her.

(ii) They rested *beneath* the shade of a tree.

13. In, Into, To

'**In**' expresses Rest or Motion inside anything. '**Into**' expresses Motion towards the inside of anything or change from one medium to another. '**To**' denotes motion from one place to another.

Examples :

(i) The boys are *in* the room.

(ii) Translate this passage from English *into* Hindi.

(iii) Every morning he goes *to* the temple.

14. Till, By, Of, Off

- '**Till**' means upto or not earlier than.
- '**By**' means not later than.
- '**Of**' shows cause, source, separation, quality, contents, possession, apposition, point of reference, space in time etc.
- '**Off**' shows separation at a near distance, and detached condition.

Consider the following examples:

(i) I shall work *till* 5 a.m.

(ii) Madhu died *of* cancer.

(iii) The nib *of* the pen is made *of* gold.

(iv) He presented me a bottle *of* perfume.

(v) Our principal is a man *of* principle.

(vi) He lived in the house *of* his friend.

(vii) *By* this time tomorrow, I'll have finished my job.

(viii) My house is *off* the road.

(ix) The book fell *off* the table.

MULTIPLE CHOICE QUESTIONS

Directions: *Tick the correct preposition for the blank in each of the following sentences.*

1. He applied ...... the manager.
A. for B. to
C. with D. by

2. Trust ...... God and do the right.
A. in B. for
C. to D. with

3. She is worthy ...... a prize.
A. with B. for
C. to D. of

4. Mr. Gomes has no taste ...... music.
A. of B. for
C. with D. to

5. You are hard ...... hearing.
A. at B. of
C. with D. for

6. He is sure ...... his success
A. for B. with
C. on D. of

7. Preeti was warned ...... the danger ahead.
A. for B. at
C. of D. about

8. I am thankful ...... you for a good advice.
A. for B. with
C. to D. of

9. Deepak would not surrender ...... the police.
A. with B. to
C. for D. on

10. The small plant in your lawn is very sensitive ...... touch.
A. on B. with
C. to D. about

11. Divya was sure to succeed ..... the examination.
   A. for   B. in
   C. to   D. with

12. Geeta was jealous ...... Ravina's beauty.
   A. to   B. with
   C. for   D. of

13. He was ignorant ..... what was happening there.
   A. for   B. of
   C. to   D. with

14. Your pen is inferior ...... mine.
   A. than   B. with
   C. from   D. to

15. Reenu is no match ...... Meenu.
   A. to   B. for
   C. with   D. upon

16. It is necessary ...... you to apply for this job.
   A. on   B. with
   C. for   D. to

17. Be loyal ...... your country.
   A. for   B. to
   C. on   D. with

18. Mukesh is junior ...... me.
   A. than   B. to
   C. from   D. of

19. Deepika was innocent ...... the crime.
   A. of   B. with
   C. from   D. to

20. I am desirous.... joining the Indian cricket team.
   A. for   B. of
   C. to   D. on

ANSWERS

1	2	3	4	5	6	7	8	9	10
B	A	D	B	B	D	D	D	B	D

11	12	13	14	15	16	17	18	19	20
B	D	B	D	B	D	B	B	A	B

SYNONYMS

A synonym is a word which conveys a meaning similar to the given word.

REMEMBER

Words	Synonyms
Add	Increase
Adequate	Enough
Adjust	Adapt
All	Aggregate
Allow	Permit
Abode	Dwelling
Apt	Proper
Assess	Appraise
Accuse	Calumniate
Abashed	Timid
Annoy	Displease
Ample	Enough, Sufficient
Amplify	Increase
Apathetic	Unenthusiastic
Accost	Address
Authentic	True
Adjust	Fit
Approve	Assent, Allow, Accept
Adapt	Conform
Adversary	Opponent, Rival, Competitor
Beat	Whack
Benign	Kind
Breeze	Zephyr
Baffle	Puzzle
Booty	Spoil

Words	Synonyms
Beauty	Charm
Beast	Animal
Bandit	Robber
Blaze	Shine
Bond	Tie
Bend	Twist
Bate	Diminish
Beg	Plead
Barbaric	Wild, Savage
Bashful	Shy, Reserved
Begin	Start
Blend	Mix, Mingle
Bizarre	Funny
Below	Under
Bedevil	Confuse
Bemoan	Lament
Babble	Nonsense
Blame	Fault
Behaviour	Demeanour
Call	Accost
Copy	Imitate
Close	Shut
Caress	Love
Camp	Stay
Connect	Attach
Cut	Injure, Curtail
Cling	Stick
Conical	Funny
Convey	Carry
Conspicuous	Prominent
Cheerful	Happy, Pleasant

Words	Synonyms
Curtail	Decrease
Cheerless	Sad, Dejected
Curious	Strange
Circumstance	Factor, Situation, Condition
Competent	Capable
Congruent	Overlapping
Cope	Deal, Endure
Confident	Sure
Complex	Intricate
Cajole	Coax, Flatter
Cunning	Crafty
Delectable	Joyful, Delightful
Devilish	Diabolical
Delicate	Soft
Devil	Fiend
Delay	Postpone
Dislike	Repugnance
Destroy	Ruin
Dwell	Live, Dilate
Declare	Pronounce
Drunk	Flushed
Deficient	Lacking
Damn	Condemn, Curse
Decrease	Diminish
Destruction	Devastation
Efficient	Competent
Ethnic	Racial
Enthral	Enslave
Earnest	Serious
Envious	Jealous
Ending	Final
Egg	Incite
Extempore	At once
Extensive	Far-ranging
Extra	Surplus
Existence	Life
Exceed	Overstep
Enormous	Vast
Excessive	Superfluous
Free	Unhindered
Frigid	Cold
Feed	Cater
Fame	Reputation
Frame	Make
First	Initial
Frighten	Terrorise, Intimidate
Fervent	Fervid
Fall	Decline
Feeble	Frail
Fickle	Changeable
Finish	Conclude
Fraud	Deception
Forgiving	Placable

Words	Synonyms
Grow	Develop
Greed	Avidity
Greet	Welcome
Grave	Serious
Group	Constellation
Given	Bestowed
Gratitude	Thankfulness
Have	Possess
Hire	Rent
Hit	Strike
Handsome	Beautiful
Hinder	Prevent
Heap	Pile
Hope	Expect
Hard	Harsh
Help	Aid
Hymn	Song
Henpecked	Enslaved
Hoodwink	Mystify, Cheat
Humble	Polite, Urbane, Modest
Harass	Vex, Trouble
Impart	Instil
Intact	Untouched
Instal	Establish
Indict	Impeach
Imitate	Ape
Instigate	Incite
Initiate	Start, Introduce
Inimical	Unfriendly
Insufferable	Intolerable
Impartiality	Justice
Jolly	Merry
Joyful	Delectable
Join	Conjoin
Kind	Benign
Kill	Murder
Kindred	Similar
Kinship	Relationship
Keen	Sharp
Knowledge	Scholarship
Lazy	Slothful
Large	Substantial, Gargantuan
Listless	Careless, Lackadaisical
Lax	Loose
Little	Small
Lifelike	Realistic
Lofty	High
Lenient	Soft, Gentle
Lacking	Deficient, Wanting
Lessen	Decrease
Middleclass	Bourgeois
Mitigate	Lessen, Abate
Modesty	Humility, Lowliness

Words	Synonyms
Mix	Mingle, Blend
Mixture	Mingling
Mixed	Assorted
Modify	Decrease
Mean	Imply
Multifarious	Varied
Miscarry	Abort
Note	Notice
Noble	Stately
Native	Indigenous
Needful	Necessary
Notify	Declare
Nervous	Shaky, Tremulous, Timid
Natural	Spontaneous
Near	Close
Normal	Natural
Offend	Displease
Oppress	Persecute, Tyrannize
Opponent	Adversary
Obstruct	Hinder, Check
Offence	Fault
Offender	Villain
Overstep	Exceed
Overlapping	Congruent
Occult	Mystic
Profane	Unholy
Patience	Forbearance
Pornographic	Obscene
Plenitude	Abundance
Prominent	Important
Prodigal	Spender
Procrastinate	Postpone
Promote	Develop, Honour
Persecute	Tyrannise
Profess	Claim
Pliant	Flexible
Plebian	Common
Polished	Sophisticated
Quake	Shake
Quit	Leave
Queer	Eccentric
Quell	Suppress
Quantify	Allot
Reply	Answer
Relinquish	Retire
Read	Peruse
Relation	Reference
Render	Do
Remainder	Residuals
Repeat	Reiterate
Repentant	Contrite
Retaliative	Retaliatory
Rumour	Hearsay
Reveal	Divulge

Words	Synonyms
Ritualistic	Ceremonious
Soft	Delicate
Sort	Kind, Choose, Select
Selfish	Egoistic
Sensual	Earthly
Suppress	Quell, Check
Stimulate	Provoke
Tasteless	Insipid
Travel	Journey
True	Authentic, Faithful, Truthful
Turbulence	Turmoil
Tragedy	Calamity
Tasteful	Tasty, Delicious
Touching	Painful
Thankful	Grateful
Tremendous	Great, Huge
Tough	Strong
Terminate	Conclude, End
Theory	Doctrine
Tell	Relate
Tremble	Shake, Shiver
Urge	Spur
Unbeaten	Unsubdued
Use	Utilize, Practise
Underhand	Unfair, Undue
Unfair	Unjust
Unravel	Reveal, Divulge
Unimportant	Common
Unconcerned	Apathetic
Unimitated	Inimitable
Unfortunate	Unlucky
Understand	Perceive, Comprehend
Vain	Proud, Haughty, Conceited, Shameless
Vale	Valley, Dale, Dell
Vice	Fault
Virtue	Quality
Veracity	Reality
Value	Price, Prize
Vex	Tease
Vibrate	Quiver, Shake
Violent	Excessive
Vivid	Clear, Lucid
Victory	Triumph
Vulgar	Indecent
Virtuous	Honest
Variegated	Varied, Multifarious
Well	Good
Yell	Cry, Shout
Yonder	There
Yearn	Wish, Desire
Yoke	Slavery
Zest	Earnestness, Enthusiasm
Zealous	Earnest

ANTONYMS

A antonym is a word which conveys a meaning opposite to the given word.

REMEMBER

Words	Antonyms
Abhor	Love
Abnormal	Normal
Able	Unable
Acceptable	Unacceptable
Adequate	Inadequate
Amusing	Boring
Angry	Calm
Apex	Bottom
Attract	Repel
Bad	Good
Barren	Fertile
Beautiful	Ugly
Bitter	Sweet
Brave	Cowardly
Brief	Lengthy
Bright	Dull
Calm	Violent
Careful	Careless
Clear	Vague, Cloudy
Cold	Hot
Cruel	Kind
Dear	Cheap
Deep	Shallow
Difficult	Easy
Direct	Indirect
Dishonest	Honest
Disobey	Obey
Encourage	Discourage
Enormous	Tiny
Excellent	Bad
Expensive	Cheap
Eat	Fast
Fair	Unfair
Fake	Authentic
False	True
Famous	Notorious
Fool	Genius
Generous	Miserly
Genius	Fool
Genuine	Unauthentic
Gigantic	Tiny
Glad	Depressed
Good	Bad
Great	Little
Happy	Sad
Hard	Soft
Hate	Love
Honest	Dishonest
Idle	Busy

Words	Antonyms
Immoral	Moral
Include	Exclude
Incorrect	Correct
Intelligent	Unintelligent
Kind	Cruel
Like	Dislike
Long	Short
Lucid	Vague
Major	Minor
Naive	Experienced
Nadir	Apex
Neat	Clumsy
Obedient	Disobedient
Obscure	Clear
Oppose	Support
Optimistic	Pessimistic
Out	In
Patience	Impatience
Peaceful	Belligerent
Pious	Impious
Polite	Impolite
Potent	Impotent
Prominent	Unimportant
Proper	Improper
Pure	Impure
Quick	Slow
Quiet	Disturbance
Real	False, Unreal
Reject	Select, Choose
Reliable	Unreliable
Respect	Disrespect
Right	Wrong
Robust	Feeble, Weak
Sad	Happy
Secret	Open
Sensible	Insensible
Severe	Mild
Sharp	Blunt
Simple	Complex
Sociable	Unsociable
Tall	Short
Tidy	Untidy
Uncanny	Canny
Violent	Calm
Vivid	Vague
Strong	Weak
Big	Small
Easy	Difficult
Fast	Slow
High	Low
Catchy	Unattractive
Ugly	Handsome, Beautiful, Tidy
Tasty	Insipid
Sonorous	Harsh

MULTIPLE CHOICE QUESTIONS

Directions (Qs. 1 to 20): *In the following questions choose the word which best expresses the meaning of the given word.*

1. ABSURD
   - A. Foolish
   - B. Simple
   - C. Courageous
   - D. Silly

2. ABANDON
   - A. Lose
   - B. Profit
   - C. Vacate
   - D. Foil

3. CAJOLE
   - A. Pause
   - B. Lenient
   - C. Blast
   - D. Lure

4. COMBAT
   - A. Fight
   - B. Conflict
   - C. Shoot
   - D. Quarrel

5. LAMENT
   - A. Condone
   - B. Console
   - C. Complain
   - D. Contribution

6. DEBACLE
   - A. Disgrace
   - B. Defeat
   - C. Collapse
   - D. Decline

7. SHIVER
   - A. Fear
   - B. Tremble
   - C. Shake
   - D. Ache

8. TORTURE
   - A. Terror
   - B. Harassment
   - C. Torment
   - D. Tranquility

9. LAUDABLE
   - A. Lovable
   - B. Commendable
   - C. Profitable
   - D. Oblivious

10. FIXED
    - A. Sterile
    - B. Static
    - C. Stubborn
    - D. Parennial

11. QUEER
    - A. Unfamiliar
    - B. Cute
    - C. Curious
    - D. Strange

12. SUFFICIENT
    - A. Fit
    - B. Proper
    - C. Adequate
    - D. Vast

13. GLOSS
    - A. Brightness
    - B. Soothing
    - C. Rubbing
    - D. Miracle

14. LONGING
    - A. Prune
    - B. Apathy
    - C. Curtail
    - D. Craving

15. JEER
    - A. Applaud
    - B. Magnanimity
    - C. Avoid
    - D. Scoff

16. ZENITH
    - A. Minimum
    - B. Nadir
    - C. Plant
    - D. Peak

17. GARB
    - A. Distort
    - B. Dress
    - C. Trivial
    - D. Rage

18. ABHOR
    - A. Rude
    - B. Reconcile
    - C. Crave
    - D. Detest

19. YIELD
    - A. Shum
    - B. Incisive
    - C. Retain
    - D. Surrender

20. YOKE
    - A. Twist
    - B. Release
    - C. Link
    - D. Extra

Directions (Qs. 21 to 26): *In the following questions choose the word which best expresses the opposite of the given word.*

21. TRAGIC
    - A. Dramatic
    - B. Strong
    - C. Gentle
    - D. Comic

22. ORAL
    - A. Verbal
    - B. Sane
    - C. Minor
    - D. Written

23. ADMIRE
    - A. Hate
    - B. Unlike
    - C. Dislike
    - D. Enough

24. VIOLENT
    - A. Gentle
    - B. Savage
    - C. Haughty
    - D. Decline

25. ADVERSITY
    - A. Windfall
    - B. Inprosperity
    - C. Prosperity
    - D. Slave

26. GENUINE
    - A. Spurious
    - B. Obscure
    - C. Countless
    - D. Apathetic

ANSWERS

1	2	3	4	5	6	7	8	9	10
D	C	D	A	C	C	B	C	B	B

11	12	13	14	15	16	17	18	19	20
D	C	A	D	D	D	B	D	D	C

21	22	23	24	25	26
D	D	C	A	C	A

●●●

It is such an exercise which starts with the primary schools and continues in the highest level of competitive examinations. One must practise it regularly to score well.

Directions (Qs. 1 to 15): *Pick out the most effective word(s) from the given words to fill in the blanks to make the sentence meaningfully complete.*

1. The student ...... that book from the library to study at home.
   A. issued   B. borrowed
   C. hired   D. lent

2. I wish I ...... a king.
   A. was   B. am
   C. should be   D. were

3. He ...... to listen to my arguments and walked away.
   A. denied   B. disliked
   C. objected   D. refused

4. The flow of blood was so ...... that the patient died.
   A. intense   B. adequate
   C. profuse   D. extensive

5. When I met her yesterday, it was the first time I ...... her since Christmas.
   A. saw   B. have seen
   C. had seen   D. have been seing

6. Can you pay ...... all these articles?
   A. for   B. of
   C. off   D. out

7. I ...... you to be at the party this evening.
   A. expect   B. hope
   C. look forward to   D. desire

8. ...... being a handicapped person, he is very cooperative and self-reliant.
   A. Because   B. Although
   C. Since   D. Despite

9. The child broke ...... from his mother and ran towards the painting.
   A. away   B. after
   C. down   D. with

10. With his ...... income, he finds it difficult to live a comfortable life.
    A. brief
    B. sufficient
    C. meagre
    D. huge

11. He could ...... a lot of money in such a short time by using his intelligence and working hard.
    A. spend
    B. spoil
    C. exchange
    D. accumulate

12. Though the brothers are twins, they look ......
    A. alike   B. handsome
    C. indifferent   D. different

13. Unfavourable weather conditions can ..... illness.
    A. cure   B. detect
    C. treat   D. enhance

14. No sooner did the bell ring, ... the actor started singing.
    A. when   B. than
    C. after   D. before

15. If I ...... realised it, I would not have acted on his advice.
    A. was   B. had
    C. were   D. have

Directions (Qs. 16 to 25): *In each question, an incomplete statement (Stem) followed by four fillers is given. Pick out the best one which can complete the incomplete stem correctly and meaningfully.*

16. Unless you work harder you will fail, means .....
    A. if you fail you will work harder.
    B. you must at least plan well than you will not fail.
    C. hardly you will fail if you do not desire so.
    D. if you do not put more efforts, then you will fail.

17. Even if it rains I shall come, means .....
    A. if I come it will not rain.
    B. if it rains I shall not come.
    C. I will certainly come whether it rains or not.
    D. whenever there is rain I shall come.

18. Dinesh is as stupid as he is lazy means .....
    A. Dinesh is stupid because he is lazy.
    B. Dinesh is lazy because he is stupid.
    C. Dinesh is either stupid or lazy.
    D. Dinesh is equally stupid and lazy.

19. He is so lazy that he .....
    A. cannot depend on others for getting his work done.
    B. cannot delay the schedule of completing the work.
    C. can seldom complete his work on time.
    D. dislike to postpone the work that he undertakes to do.

20. He always stammers in public meetings, but his today's speech .....
- A. was fairly audible to everyone present in the hall.
- B. was not received satisfactorily.
- C. could not be understood properly.
- D. was free from that defect.

21. In order to raise the company's profit, the employees.....
- A. demanded two additional increments.
- B. decided to go on paid holidays.
- C. requested the management to implement new welfare schemes.
- D. offered to work overtime without any compensation.

22. Although, he is reputed for making very candid statements, ...
- A. his today's speech was not fairly audible.
- B. his promises had always been realistic.
- C. his speech was very interesting.
- D. his today's statements were very ambiguous.

23. I felt somewhat more relaxed .....
- A. but tense as compared to earlier.
- B. and tense as compared to earlier.
- C. as there was already no tension at all.
- D. and tension-free as compared to earlier.

24. With great efforts his son succeeded in convincing him not to donate his entire wealth to an orphanage ....
- A. and lead the life of a wealthy merchant.
- B. but to a home for the forsaken children.
- C. and make an orphan of himself.
- D. as the orphanage needed a lot of donations.

25. Even though it is a very large house, ...
- A. there is a lot of space available in it for children.
- B. there is hardly any space available for children.
- C. there is no dearth of space for children.
- D. the servants take a long time to clean it.

ANSWERS

1	2	3	4	5	6	7	8	9	10
B	D	D	C	C	A	A	D	A	C

11	12	13	14	15	16	17	18	19	20
D	D	D	B	B	D	C	D	C	D

21	22	23	24	25
D	D	D	C	B

● ● ●

Spotting Errors

The most common errors in English are of spellings, grammar and usage of words. By regular practice, the errors can be easily spotted and minimised.

MULTIPLE CHOICE QUESTIONS

Directions: *In the following questions some of the sentences have errors and some are correct. Find out which part of a sentence has an error, the number of that part is your answer. If a sentence is free from errors, then your answer is D i.e., No error.*

1. (A) Either Ram or/(B) you is responsible/(C) for this action./(D) No error.

2. (A) The student flatly denied/(B) that he had copied/(C) in the examination hall./(D) No error.

3. (A) By the time you arrive tomorrow/(B) I have finished/(C) my work./(D) No error.

4. (A) The captain with the members of his team/(B) are returning/(C) after a fortnight./(D) No error.

5. (A) After returning from/(B) an all-India tour/(C) I had to describe about it./(D) No error.

6. (A) The teacher asked his students/(B) if they had gone through/(C) either of the three chapters included in the prescribed text./(D) No error.

7. (A) Do you know/(B) how old were you/(C) when you came here?/(D) No error.

8. (A) Beware of/(B) a fair-weather friend/(C) who is neither a friend in need nor a friend indeed./(D) No error.

9. (A) Copernicus proved/(B) that Earth/(C) moves round the Sun./(D) No error.

10. (A) The property/(B) was divided/(C) among the two brothers./(D) No error.

11. (A) I am quite certain/(B) that the lady is not only greedy/(C) but miserly./(D) No error.

12. (A) The brilliant success in the examination/(B) as well as his record in sports/(C) deserves high praise./(D) No error.

13. (A) I cannot find/(B) where has he gone/(C) though I have tried may best./(D) No error.

14. (A) If I was/(B) the Prime Minister of India/(C) I would work wonders/(D) No error.

15. (A) If it weren't/(B) for you,/(C) I wouldn't be alive today./(D) No error.

16. (A) He looked like a lion/(B) baulked from/(C) its prey./(D) No error.

17. (A) Widespread flooding/(B) is affecting/(C) large areas of the villages./(D) No error.

18. (A) If we really set to/(B) we can get the whole house/(C) cleaned in an afternoon./(D) No error.

ANSWERS

1	2	3	4	5	6	7	8	9	10
B	D	B	B	C	C	D	D	B	C
11	**12**	**13**	**14**	**15**	**16**	**17**	**18**	**19**	**20**
C	D	B	A	C	C	C	A	A	C

EXPLANATORY ANSWERS

1. Replace 'is' by 'are'.
2. No error.
3. Replace 'have' by 'would have'.
4. Replace 'are' by 'is'.
5. Replace 'had to describe' by 'described'.
6. Replace 'either' by 'any'.
7. No error.
8. No error.
9. Omit 'that'.
10. Replace 'among' by 'between'.
11. Add 'also'.
12. No error.
13. Replace 'has he' by 'he has'.
14. Replace 'was' by 'were'.
15. Replace 'wouldn't be' by 'would not have been'.
16. Replace 'its' by 'his'.
17. Replace 'areas' by 'area'.
18. Replace 'set to' by 'set on'.

One Word Substitution

There are many single words in English language which can be perfectly used for a number of words. These words help in expressing ideas in a short and correct manner for the right occasion. Such words not only increase the vocabulary but also enable you to economise in the use of words to a great extent.

Multiple Word Expression	*Substitution*
One who always looks towards the bright side of things	Optimist
One who always looks towards the dark side of things	Pessimist
The time when one develops from a child into an adult	Adolescence
The process of growing more plants in order to form a forest.	Afforestation
The science which deals with farming	Agriculture
From some other country or place etc.	Alien
A term, etc. giving more than one meaning	Ambiguous
A vehicle which is used to carry sick persons	Ambulance
An animal which can live both in water and on land	Amphibian
A lawless situation when there is no government	Anarchy
Belonging to the history of thousands of years old	Ancient
Once a year	Annual
A very old object but still valuable	Antique
Words of opposite meanings	Antonyms
Words of similar meanings	Synonyms
Signatures of a famous person	Autograph
A government led by one person with absolute authority	Autocracy
A written work of one's own life history	Autobiography
A person who has never been married	Bachelor
A person usually having no hair on his head	Bald
A place where one can deposit money and get interest	Bank
A person who cuts our hair	Barber
A building/group of buildings where soldiers live	Barracks
A person who makes buns and biscuits	Baker
A person who lives by asking people for food and money without doing any useful job	Beggar
The crime of having married to two persons at the same time	Bigamy
The branch of science which deals with the study of plants	Botany
Able to speak two languages	Bilingual
Able to speak more than two languages	Polyglot
The branch of science which deals with the living organisms	Biology
A powerful snow storm	Blizzard
A great successful book or movie	Blockbuster
A short news on the radio or TV	Bulletin
A system in which the most important works are organised by the government officials	Bureaucracy
A person who has no vision in his eyes	Blind
A page or a series of pages on which the information of days, weeks, months, etc. is given	Calendar
A person who eats human flesh	Cannibal
A complete list of items often arranged alphabetically	Catalogue
A sudden disaster	Catastrophe
A period of 100 years	Century

Multiple Word Expression	Substitution
A branch of science which deals with chemicals	Chemistry
A printed leaf usually issued by banks that we sign to carry certain financial deal	Cheque
A person who makes or mends shoes	Cobbler
A group of people who has been chosen by others to make decisions on their own	Committee
A building in which nuns live	Convent
An animal which feeds on other animals	Carnivorous
A person who does criticism	Critic
A person who cannot hear	Deaf
A condition in which one loses a lot of water from one's body because of vomiting, etc.	Dehydration
A system of government in which the people cast their votes to elect their leaders	Democracy
The study of skin problems	Dermatology
A long piece of land covered with sand	Desert
The art of managing relationships between countries	Diplomacy
A piece of information about the words in a book form	Dictionary
A piece of information about the telephone numbers of the people in a book from	Directory
A person in charge of a newspapers, magazine etc.	Editor
A person who thinks he is better than the others	Egoist
To leave your country and settle in some other country	Emigrate
A book or series of books giving almost all knowledge about an area or some persons etc.	Encyclopaedia
Study of insects	Entomology
Time when day and night are of the same duration	Equinox
To sell things out of the country	Export
To purchase things from some other country	Import
A plant or animal no longer in existence	Extinct
A situation when there is a shortage of food for a long period of time	Famine
An amount of money that we pay for some action or services	Fee
Related to women	Feminine
An animal strong and aggressive	Ferocious
A piece of land where plants grow easily from the soil that is favourable to them	Fertile
A work of literature having some imaginary events	Fiction
A large amount of water covering certain area	Flood
A person who sells flowers	Florist
A religious ceremony for burying or cremating a dead person	Funeral
A substance which kills fungus	Fungicide
A person studying or having studied the diseases and the related things of female reproductive system	Gynaecologist
The murder of the person of the same group race or country	Genocide
A substance which kills germs	Germicide
A situation in which many people die because of fire during war	Holocaust
The act of killing a person deliberately	Homicide
A word having the pronunciation as the other one does but it differs in meaning	Homophone
A word having the same spelling as the other one does but it is pronounced in some other way	Homonym
A person who is attracted towards the person of the same sex	Homosexual
Go across and parallel to the ground	Horizontal
A substance which kills the insects	Insecticide
That cannot be corrected	Incorrigible
That cannot be defeated	Invincible
That cannot be eaten	Inedible
That cannot be seen	Invisible
A place in a school or college where books are kept for the benefit of students, teachers etc.	Library
A place in a school or college where scientific experiments are performed	Laboratory

Multiple Word Expression	*Substitution*
An official who is a judge in the lowest court	Magistrate
A piece of music or a book before it is printed	Manuscript
Related to men	Masculine
One who believes in the existence of God	A theist
One who does not believe in the existence of good	An atheist
That can be believed	Credible
That cannot be believed	Incredible
That which dissolves in a solvent	Soluble
That which does not dissolves in a solvent	Insoluble
Hard writing that can be read	Legible
Hard writing that cannot be read	Illegible
A person who does jobs beneficial to mankind	Philanthropist
A person who goes on foot	Pedestrian
A person who fights for his own country	Patriot
An act of killing oneself	Suicide
A woman whose husband is dead	Widow
A man whose wife is dead	Widower
A person who eats vegetarian and non-vegetarian diets	Omnivorous
Something which is everywhere at the same time	Omnipresent
One who knows everything	Omniscient
A child who does not have parents	Orphan
An award etc. given after the death of the person	Posthumous
The place where animals are kept for amusement and to increase the knowledge of the public	Zoo
The science which deals with the study of animals	Zoology

MULTIPLE CHOICE QUESTIONS

Directions: *In questions given below, out of the four alternatives, choose the one which can be substituted for the given words/sentences.*

1. Something that relates to everyone in the world
A. General
B. Common
C. Usual
D. Universal

2. An expression of mild disapproval
A. Warning
B. Denigration
C. Impertinence
D. Reproof

3. One who is not easily pleased by anything
A. Maiden
B. Medieval
C. Precarious
D. Fastidious

4. Murder of a king
A. Infanticide
B. Matricide
C. Genocide
D. Regicide

5. A remedy for all diseases
A. Stoic
B. Marvel
C. Panacea
D. Recompense

6. A dramatic performance
A. Mask
B. Mosque
C. Masque
D. Mascot

7. Study of birds
A. Orology
B. Optology
C. Ophthalmology
D. Ornithology

8. Ready to believe
A. Credulous
B. Credible
C. Creditable
D. Incredible

9. Incapable of being seen through
A. Ductile
B. Opaque
C. Obsolete
D. Potable

10. One who eats everything
A. Omnivorous
B. Omniscient
C. Irresistible
D. Insolvent

11. A place where bees are kept is called
A. An apiary
B. A mole
C. A hive
D. A sanctuary

12. One who cannot be corrected
A. Incurable
B. Incorrigible
C. Hardened
D. Invulnerable

13. One who is in charge of a museum
A. Curator
B. Supervisor
C. Caretaker
D. Warden

14. Continuing fight between parties, families, clans, etc.
A. Enmity
B. Feud
C. Quarrel
D. Skirmish

15. A voice loud enough to be heard
A. Audible
B. Applaudable
C. Laudable
D. Oral

16. A paper written by hand
 A. Handicraft B. Manuscript
 C. Handiwork D. Thesis

17. Habitually silent or talking little
 A. Serville B. Unequivocal
 C. Taciturn D. Synoptic

18. To slap with a flat object
 A. Chop B. Hew
 C. Gnaw D. Swat

19. A person who speaks many languages
 A. Linguist B. Monolingual
 C. Polyglot D. Bilingual

20. A light sailing-boat built specially for racing
 A. Canoe B. Yacht
 C. Frigate D. Dinghy

21. A fixed orbit in space in relation to earth
 A. Geological B. Geo-synchronous
 C. Geo-centric D. Geo-stationary

22. A style in which a writer makes a display of his knowledge
 A. Pedantic B. Verbose
 C. Pompous D. Ornate

23. A religious discourse
 A. Preach B. Stanza
 C. Sanctorum D. Sermon

24. A place that provides refuge
 A. Asylum B. Sanatorium
 C. Shelter D. Orphanage

25. Detailed plan of a journey
 A. Travelogue B. Travelkit
 C. Schedule D. Itinerary

26. A person who insists on something
 A. Disciplinarian B. Stickler
 C. Instantaneous D. Boaster

27. A drawing on transparent paper
 A. Red print B. Blue print
 C. Negative D. Transparency

28. One who believes that all things and events in life are predetermined is a
 A. Fatalist B. Puritan
 C. Egoist D. Tyrant

29. A school boy who cuts classes frequently is a
 A. Defeatist B. Sycophant
 C. Truant D. Martinet

30. The act of violating the sanctity of the church is
 A. Blasphemy B. Heresy
 C. Sacrilege D. Desecration

31. A place where monks live as a secluded community
 A. Cathedral B. Diocese
 C. Convent D. Monastery

32. One who is fond of fighting
 A. Bellicose B. Aggressive
 C. Belligerent D. Militant

33. Tending to move away from the centre or axis
 A. Centrifugal B. Centripetal
 C. Axiomatic D. Awry

34. Words inscribed on tomb
 A. Epitome B. Epistle
 C. Epilogue D. Epitaph

35. Leave or remove from a place considered dangerous
 A. Evade B. Evacuate
 C. Avoid D. Exterminate

36. Original inhabitants of a country
 A. Abroge B. Aborger
 C. Aborgory D. Aborigins

37. Government by the officials
 A. Theocracy B. Plutocracy
 C. Bureaucracy D. Democracy

38. Incapable of being exhausted
 A. Inexhaustible B. Inaexhaustible
 C. Exhaustable D. Non-tired

39. A person of good understanding, knowledge and reasoning power
 A. Expert B. Intellectual
 C. Snob D. Literate

40. One absorbed in his own thoughts and feelings rather than in things outside
 A. Scholar B. Recluse
 C. Introvert D. Intellectual

ANSWERS

1	2	3	4	5	6	7	8	9	10
D	D	D	D	C	C	D	A	B	A

11	12	13	14	15	16	17	18	19	20
A	B	A	B	A	B	C	D	A	B

21	22	23	24	25	26	27	28	29	30
D	A	D	A	D	B	D	A	C	C

31	32	33	34	35	36	37	38	39	40
D	A	A	D	B	B	C	A	B	C

●●●

Spelling Errors

There are thousands of words in English language. It is difficult to remember the spellings and meanings of all at once. Try to learn as many as you can. Use a dictionary regularly.

Directions: *Find the correctly spelt words.*

1. A. Damage   B. Dammage
   C. Damaige   D. Dammege

2. A. Efficiant   B. Effecient
   C. Efficient   D. Eficient

3. A. Schedule   B. Schdule
   C. Schedale   D. Schedeule

4. A. Occurad   B. Occurred
   C. Ocurred   D. Occured

5. A. Grieff   B. Grief
   C. Grieef   D. Grrief

6. A. Guarantee   B. Garuntee
   C. Guaruntee   D. Gaurantee

7. A. Meddicine   B. Medicine
   C. Medicene   D. Medicinne

8. A. Benefeted   B. Benefitted
   C. Benifited   D. Benefited

9. A. Acommodation   B. Acomodation
   C. Accomodation   D. Accommodation

10. A. Querrelsome   B. Quarrelsame
    C. Quarrelsome   D. Querralsome

11. A. Sympathetic   B. Smypathetic
    C. Sympothetic   D. Sympethetic

12. A. Prograssive   B. Progressive
    C. Progresive   D. Prograsive

13. A. Uncivilized   B. Uncevilized
    C. Uncivillized   D. Uncevelized

14. A. Extravagant   B. Extreragent
    C. Extreregant   D. Extravegent

15. A. Missunderstood   B. Miesunderstood
    C. Misunderstood   D. Misunderstod

16. A. Belligerent   B. Beligirent
    C. Belligarant   D. Belligerrent

17. A. Astonished   B. Astronished
    C. Astoneshed   D. Asstonished

18. A. Sincerely   B. Sencerely
    C. Sincerelly   D. Sincerrely

19. A. Rigourous   B. Rigerous
    C. Rigorous   D. Regerous

20. A. Satellite   B. Sattellite
    C. Satelite   D. Sattelite

21. A. Pesanger   B. Passenger
    C. Pessenger   D. Pasanger

22. A. Humurous   B. Humorous
    C. Humoreus   D. Humorrous

23. A. Exeggerate   B. Exaggerate
    C. Exadgerate   D. Exagerate

24. A. Fariegn   B. Forein
    C. Foriegn   D. Foreign

25. A. Excesive   B. Excessive
    C. Exccessive   D. Exccesive

26. A. Forcaust   B. Forcast
    C. Forecast   D. Forecaste

27. A. Paralleted   B. Paralelled
    C. Parralleled   D. Parallelled

28. A. Ocasion   B. Occassion
    C. Occasion   D. Ocassion

29. A. Boquet   B. Bouquet
    C. Bouquete   D. Bouquette

30. A. Chettering   B. Chaterring
    C. Chattering   D. Chatering

31. A. Discourage   B. Disscourage
    C. Discourege   D. Discaurage

32. A. Curageous   B. Courageous
    C. Courrageous   D. Couregeous

33. A. Abandon   B. Abanddon
    C. Abendon   D. Abbandon

34. A. Embarassment   B. Emberrassement
    C. Embarrassment   D. Embbaresment

35. A. Eccintric   B. Eccentrie
    C. Eccentric   D. Eccintrie

36. A. Occasional   B. Occassional
    C. Occesional   D. Occessional

37. A. Querrel   B. Querral
    C. Quarrel   D. Quarel

38. A. Contrebution   B. Contribution
    C. Contributtion   D. Conterbution

39. A. Desgrace   B. Disgrece
     C. Disgrice   D. Disgrace

40. A. Harassment   B. Herassment
     C. Harasment   D. Harassmient

41. A. Imaginative   B. Imeginative
     C. Imagenative   D. Imaginetive

42. A. Suficient   B. Suficiant
     C. Sufficient   D. Sufficiant

43. A. Adequate   B. Edequate
     C. Adaquete   D. Edaquete

44. A. Exparienced   B. Experianced
     C. Experienced   D. Experrienced

45. A. Flatering   B. Fletering
     C. Flattering   D. Fletaring

46. A. Cuttiveted   B. Culltrivated
     C. Cultivated   D. Caltivated

47. A. Praiceworthy   B. Peiseworthy
     C. Praiseworthy   D. Praisaworthy

48. A. Profesional   B. Professionel
     C. Professional   D. Profissional

49. A. Ameteur   B. Amateur
     C. Amataur   D. Amateor

50. A. Unfevourable   B. Unfevaurable
     C. Unfavourable   D. Unfivourable

ANSWERS

1	2	3	4	5	6	7	8	9	10
A	C	A	B	B	A	B	B	D	C

11	12	13	14	15	16	17	18	19	20
A	B	A	A	C	A	A	A	C	A

21	22	23	24	25	26	27	28	29	30
B	B	B	D	B	C	A	C	B	C

31	32	33	34	35	36	37	38	39	40
A	B	A	C	C	A	C	B	D	A

41	42	43	44	45	46	47	48	49	50
A	C	A	C	A	C	C	C	B	C

•••

REASONING ABILITY

SERIES

Directions : *In each of the following series determine the order of the letters. Then from the given options select the one which will complete the given series.*

1. BMK, DLM, FKO, HJQ, ?
   - A. JIR
   - B. JIT
   - C. JHS
   - D. JIS

2. A, CD, FGH, ?
   - A. IJKL
   - B. KLMN
   - C. JKLM
   - D. LMNO

3. BXJ, ETL, HPN, KLP, ?
   - A. PHR
   - B. NIR
   - C. NHR
   - D. MHR

4. PUF, QVG, RWH, ?
   - A. SXI
   - B. SYZ
   - C. SXJ
   - D. SVI

5. DEF, HIJ, MNO, ?
   - A. RTV
   - B. STU
   - C. PTU
   - D. SRU

Directions : *Which of the following groups of letters will complete the given series?*

6. ab---b-bbaa-
   - A. babba
   - B. abaab
   - C. abbab
   - D. baaab

7. aa-ab--aaa-a
   - A. baaa
   - B. abab
   - C. aaab
   - D. aabb

8. -baa-aab-a-a
   - A. baab
   - B. abab
   - C. aaba
   - D. aabb

9. -a cca-ccca-acccc-aaa
   - A. ccaa
   - B. acca
   - C. caac
   - D. caaa

10. c-bbb--abbbb-abbb-
   - A. abccb
   - B. bacbb
   - C. aabcb
   - D. abacb

Directions : *In the following questions, select the number(s) from the given options for completing the given series.*

11. 3, 9, 27, 81, 243, ?
    - A. 486
    - B. 729
    - C. 972
    - D. 359

12. 1, 6, 12, 19, 27, ?
    - A. 38
    - B. 35
    - C. 36
    - D. 54

13. 2, 6, 14, 30, 62, ?
    - A. 126
    - B. 128
    - C. 120
    - D. 130

14. 8, 48, 16, 96, 32, ?
    - A. 192
    - B. 150
    - C. 64
    - D. 288

15. 2, 8, 14, 24, 34, 48, ?
    - A. 66
    - B. 62
    - C. 58
    - D. 64

Directions : *In the given series find the number which is wrong.*

16. 5, 25, 120, 625, 3125, 15625
    - A. 15625
    - B. 625
    - C. 120
    - D. 5

17. 4, 8, 11, 22, 18, 36, 24, 50
    - A. 8
    - B. 22
    - C. 36
    - D. 24

18. 2, 4, 12, 24, 72, 142, 432
    - A. 432
    - B. 12
    - C. 142
    - D. 72

19. 2, 3, 4, 4, 6, 8, 9, 12, 16
    - A. 3
    - B. 9
    - C. 6
    - D. 12

20. 97, 91, 86, 83, 79, 77, 76, 76
    - A. 86
    - B. 76
    - C. 91
    - D. 83

ANSWERS

1	2	3	4	5	6	7	8	9	10
D	C	C	A	B	D	C	B	D	A

11	12	13	14	15	16	17	18	19	20
B	C	A	A	B	C	D	C	B	D

4

EXPLANATORY ANSWERS

1. The letters in one group correspond to the letters in the next group in the manner +2, −1, +2 respectively.

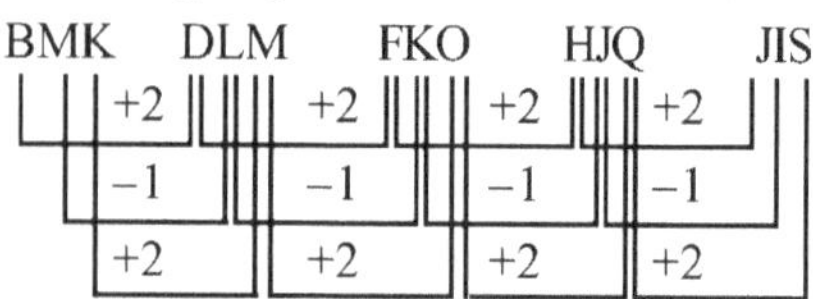

2. The letters are in natural sequence and from one group to the next one letter is dropped. Also the number of letters in groups is increased by one.

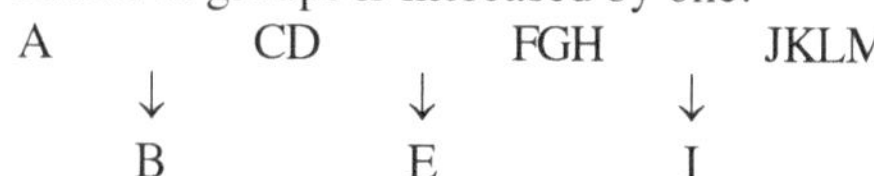

3. The letters in one group correspond to the letters in the next group in the manner +3, −4, +2 respectively, *i.e.,*

BXJ   ETL   HPN   KLP   NHR

+3, −4, +2

4. The three letters in each group are moved one step forward.

PUF   QVG   RWH   SXI

+1, +1, +1

5. The letters are in natural order. The number of letters dropped in between the groups is increased by one at each step.

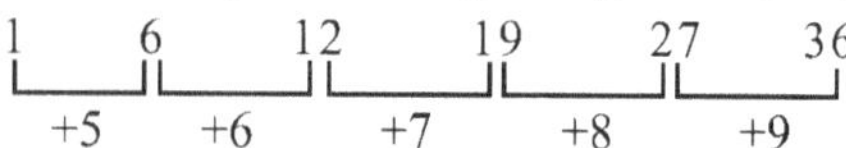

6. The series is abbaab, abbaab

7. The series is aaaaba, aaaaba

8. The series is aba, aba, aba, aba

9. The series is c,a,cc,aa, ccc, aaa, cccc, aaaa

10. The series is cabbbb, cabbbb, cabbbb

11. The numbers in the series are multiplied by 3 to get the next numbers.

12. The difference between the numbers in the series increases by 1, after beginning from 5, *i.e.,*

1   6   12   19   27   36

+5   +6   +7   +8   +9

13. The difference between the numbers in the series doubles each time, after beginning from 4, *i.e.,*

2   6   14   30   62   126

+4   +8   +16   +32   +64

14. *Explanation I* : The sequence in the series is × 6, ÷ 3 which is repeated.

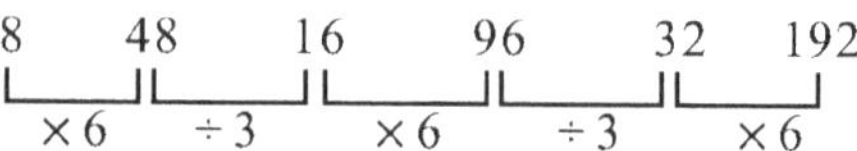

Explanation II : There are two alternate series and the numbers are multiplied by 2.

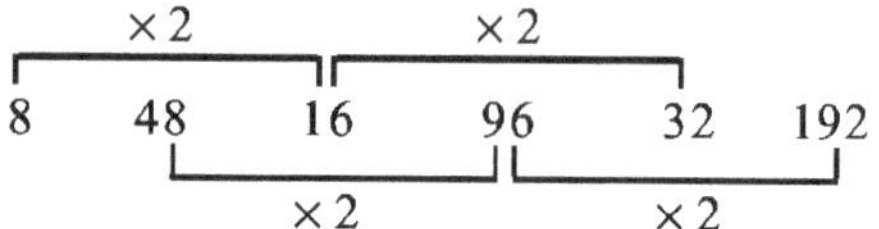

Series I : 8, 16, 32

Series II : 48, 96, 192

15. The sequence in the series is :

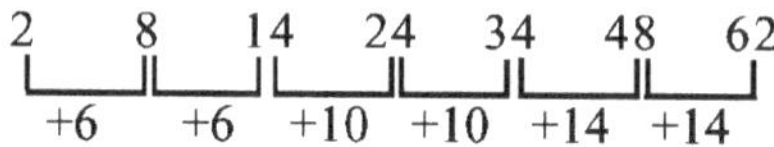

The difference increases by 4 at alternate step.

16. The numbers in the series are multiplied by 5 to get the next number.

∴ 125 should be in place of 120.

17. Two numbers form a pair. The first number increases by 7 for the next pair and the second number is the double of first number.

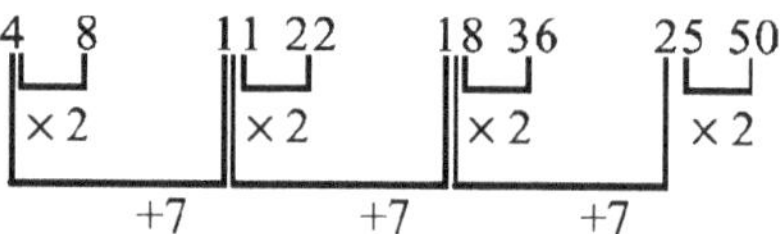

∴ 25 should be in place of 24.

18. There are two alternate series and in each series, the numbers are multiplied by 6 to get the next number.

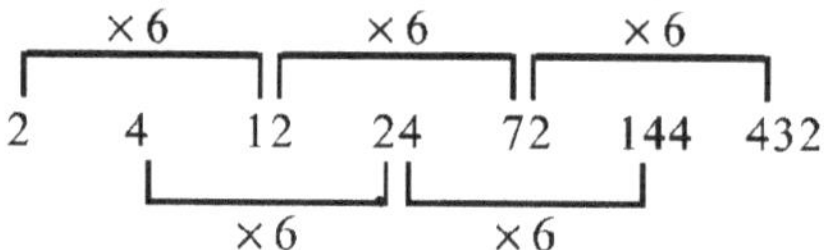

∴ 144 should be in place of 142.

19. There are three alternate series and in each series, the numbers are multiplied by 2 to get the next number.

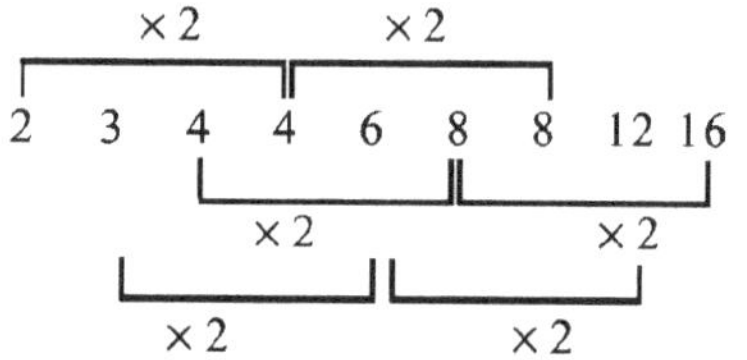

Series I : 2, 4, 8

Series II : 3, 6, 12

Series III : 4, 8, 16

∴ 8 should be in place of 9.

20. The difference between the consecutive numbers in the series decreases by 1 at each step.

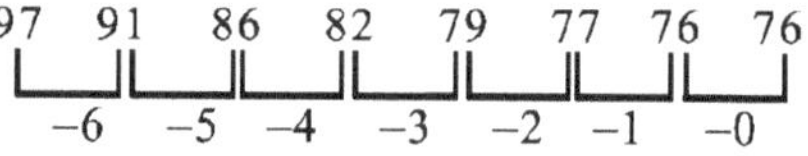

∴ 82 should be in place of 83.

ANALOGIES OR RELATIONSHIPS

Directions : *In the questions given below establish the relationship between the two words. Then from the given options select one which has the same relationship as of the given two words.*

1. ADULT : BABY : : FLOWER : ?
   A. Seed   B. Bud
   C. Fruit   D. Butterfly

2. WRITER : READER : : PRODUCER : ?
   A. Creator   B. Contractor
   C. Creature   D. Consumer

3. ENTRANCE : EXIT : : LOYALTY : ?
   A. Treachery   B. Patriotism
   C. Fidelity   D. Reward

4. MOTHER : MATERNAL : : FATHER : ?
   A. Eternal   B. Detrimental
   C. Paternal   D. Formidable

Directions : *In the questions given below one term is missing. Based on the relationship of the two given words find the missing term from the given options.*

5. GFC : CFG : : RPJ : ?
   A. JRP   B. JPR
   C. PJR   D. RJP

6. BCF : DEG : : MNQ : ?
   A. OPR   B. PQS
   C. OPP   D. QRT

7. NATION : ANITNO : : HUNGRY : ?
   A. HNUGRY   B. UNHGYR
   C. YRNGUH   D. UHGNYR

8. SSTU : MMNO : : AABC : ?
   A. GGHH   B. IJKK
   C. XXYZ   D. NOOP

ANSWERS

1	2	3	4	5	6	7	8
B	D	A	C	B	A	D	C

EXPLANATORY ANSWERS

1. The youngone of an adult is a baby and that of a flower is a bud.
2. A writer aims to please the readers by his writings, a producer aims to please the consumers by his products.
3. The related words are opposites.
4. Relations on the mother's side are maternal and on the father's side paternal.
5. The letters of the first group are reversed.

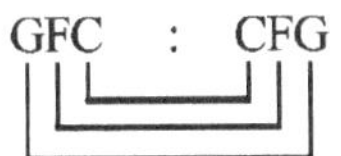 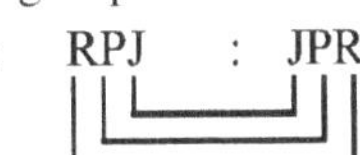

6. The three letters are moved 2, 2 and 1 steps forward respectively.

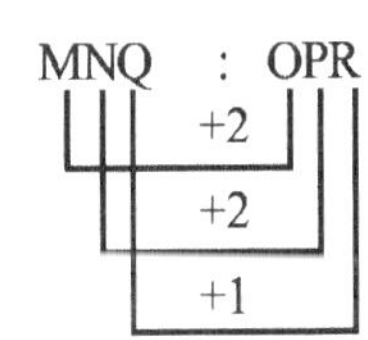

7. The word is divided in sections of two letters and the letters are reversed.

8. The first letter in each group is repeated and followed by two consecutive letters.

ODD ONE OUT

Directions : *Three of the following four in each question are alike in a certain way and so form a group. Select the group of letters that does not belong to that group.*

1. A. ACE   B. LOR
   C. GIK   D. VXZ

2. A. TSR   B. LKJ
   C. PQO   D. HGF

3. A. EF LM   B. KJ SR
   C. XW HG   D. ED YX

4. A. JOPK   B. BOPC
   C. QOPR   D. TOPS

5. A. DfH   B. MoQ
   C. UwY   D. lnO

6. A. JKkL   B. OPpQ
   C. DEEf   D. VWwX

7. A. BdfH   B. FHJL

   C. RTvX   D. uVwX

8. A. DFHEG   B. TWXUV
   C. OQSPR   D. JLNKM

9. A. FEUV   B. DCXW
   C. BAZY   D. HGTS

10. A. UTSR   B. XYZW
   C. ONML   D. IHGF

ANSWERS

1	2	3	4	5	6	7	8	9	10
B	C	A	D	D	C	D	B	A	B

EXPLANATORY ANSWERS

1. The sequence in each group is +2. Only option B has sequence in +3, *i.e.,*

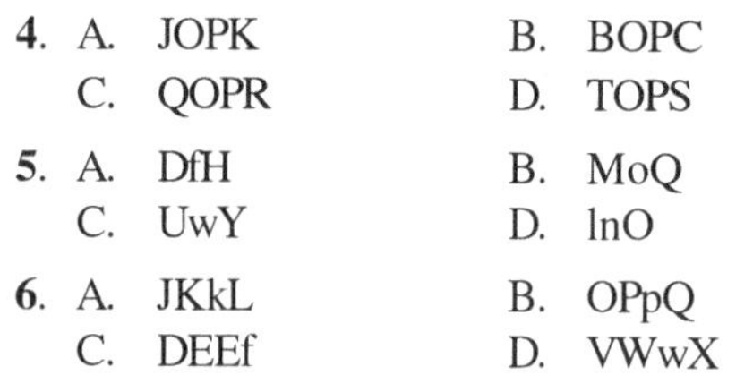

2. The sequence of alphabet in each group is in reverse order. Only option C has sequence in disturbed order.

3. Two consecutive alphabet in each group are in reverse sequence (–1), *i.e.,*

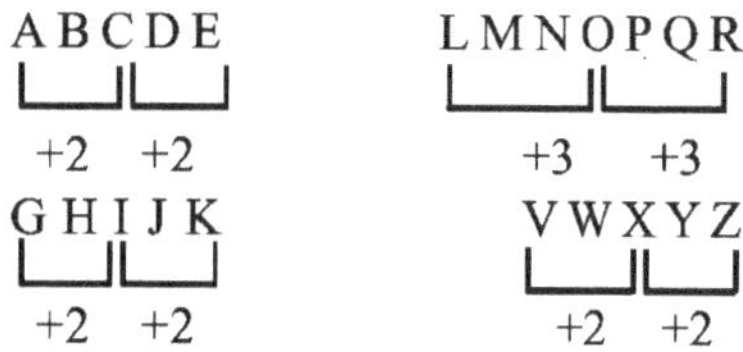

Only in option (A) the sequence is in natural order (+1), *i.e.,*

4. In each group, letters 'OP' are common. The two corner alphabet are in natural order (+1); *i.e.,*

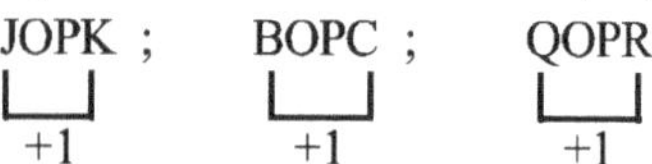

Only in option (D) they are in reverse order (–1); *i.e.,*

TOPS
–1

5. In other groups, only the alphabet in the centre is of lower case. In this option letter 'L' on the left is also in lower case.

6. In other groups, the third letter which is a repeat of the second alphabet is in lower case.

7. In each group, the sequence of the alphabet, irrespective of the case, is +2; *i.e.,*

Only in option (D) the sequence is in natural order (+1), *i.e.,*

uV w X
+1 +1 +1

8. In each group; the alphabet at positions-first, fourth, second, fifth and third, form a natural sequence.

In option (B), the alphabet at positions first, fourth, fifth, second and third, form the natural sequence.

9. In each group, two alphabets in the corner and two alphabets in the centre correspond to their reverse order positioned alphabet. *i.e.,*

natural order → A B C D E F G H I J K L M
reverse order → Z Y X W V U T S R Q P O N
natural order → N O P Q R S T U V W X Y Z
reverse order → M L K J I H G F E D C B A

As such—

D corresponds with W and

C corresponds with X.

B corresponds with Y and

A corresponds with Z.

H corresponds with S and

G corresponds with T.

Similarly,

F should correspond with U and

E should correspond with V;

i.e. letters 'UV' should be written as 'VU'

10. In each group, the alphabet are in reverse order.

In option (B), the order is disturbed.

CODING AND DECODING

Directions : *In the following questions select the right option which indicates the correct code for the word or letter given in the question.*

1. If CHAIR is coded as FKDLU then RAID is coded as:
   A. ULGD   B. ULKG
   C. ULDG   D. UDLG

2. If CONDEMN is coded as CNODMEN, then TEACHER is coded as :
   A. TEACHER   B. TAEECHR
   C. TCAEEHR   D. TAECEHR

3. In a code language COME is written as XLNV and ABLE as ZYOV. How will MOLLY be written in that code?
   A. NLOBO   B. NLBOO
   C. LNOOB   D. NLOOB

4. In a certain code PROFESSION is written as EFORPNOISS. In the same code DICTIONARY will be written as :
   A. YRANOITCID   B. ITCIDYRANO
   C. ITCIDYRNAO   D. ITCDIYARNO

5. JUNE is coded as NXPF, how will STAY be coded in the same manner?
   A. WWCZ   B. WVCZ
   C. WWDB   D. VWZC

Directions : *In the following questions study the coded patterns and then select the right option from the given alternatives.*

6. In a certain language, (a) 'go ju mi' stands for 'plenty of money'; (b) pao ju go nei vu' for 'money creates lots of problems'; (c) 'kol vu nei' for 'problems create tension'; and (d) 'sol tun ju haw' for 'still money is needed'. Which of the following words stand for 'money'?
   A. nei   B. ju
   C. haw   D. go

7. In a certain language, (a) 'FOR' stands for 'old is gold'; (b) 'ROT' stands for 'gold is pure'; (c) 'ROM' stands for 'gold is costly'. How will 'pure old gold is costly' be written?
   A. TFROM   B. FOTRM
   C. FTORM   D. TOMRF

8. In a certain code '415' means 'milk is hot'; '18' means 'hot soup'; and '895' means 'soup is tasty'. What number will indicate the word 'tasty'?
   A. 9   B. 8
   C. 5   D. 4

9. In a certain code '643' means 'she is beautiful', '593' means 'he is handsome', and '567' means 'handsome meets beautiful'. What number will indicate the word 'meets'?
   A. 5   B. 3
   C. 7   D. 6

10. In a certain code language, (a) 'dugo hui mul zo' stands for 'work is very hard'; (b) 'hui dugo ba ki' for 'Bingo is very smart'; (c) 'nano mul dugo' for 'cake is hard', and (d) 'mul ki qu' for 'smart and hard'. Which of the following words stand for 'Bingo'?
    A. jalu   B. dugo
    C. ki   D. ba

ANSWERS

1	2	3	4	5	6	7	8	9	10
D	D	D	B	A	B	A	A	C	D

EXPLANATORY ANSWERS

2. In this word, the second and third letters interchange their places and the fifth and sixth letters do the same. Other letters retain their position.

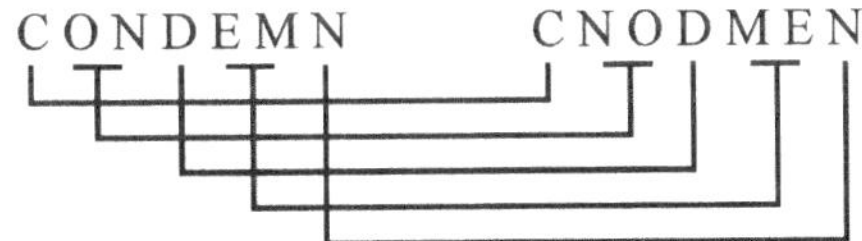

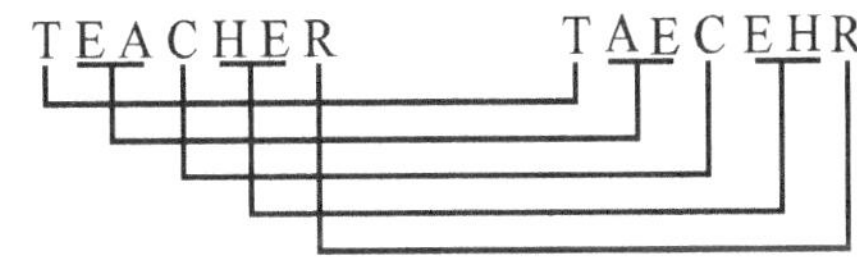

3. The letters of the word are coded by their represented letters in the reverse series.

C	O	M	E	→	letters in natural series
X	L	N	V	→	letters in reverse series
↓	↓	↓	↓		
3rd	15th	13th	5th	→	position of letters
A	B	L	E	→	letters in natural series
Z	Y	O	V	→	letters in reverse series
↓	↓	↓	↓		
1st	2nd	12th	5th	→	position of letters

Similarly,

M	O	L	L	Y	→	letters in natural series
N	L	O	O	B	→	letters in reverse series
↓	↓	↓	↓	↓		
13th	15th	12th	12th	25th	→	position of letters

4. The word is divided into two equal parts and the letters of each part are written backwards.

Similarly,

5. The word is coded by moving the letters +4, +3, +2, and +1 steps respectively.

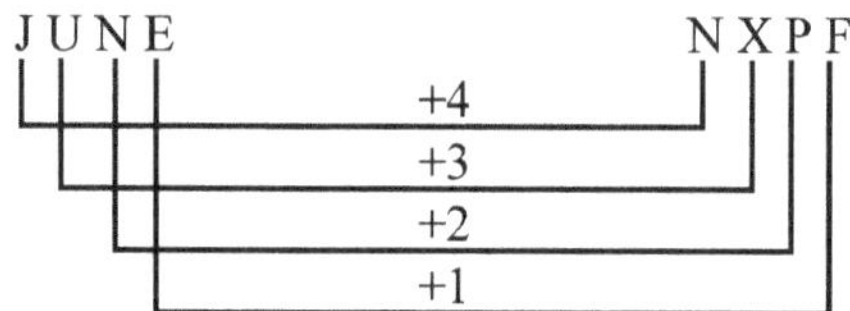

Similarly,

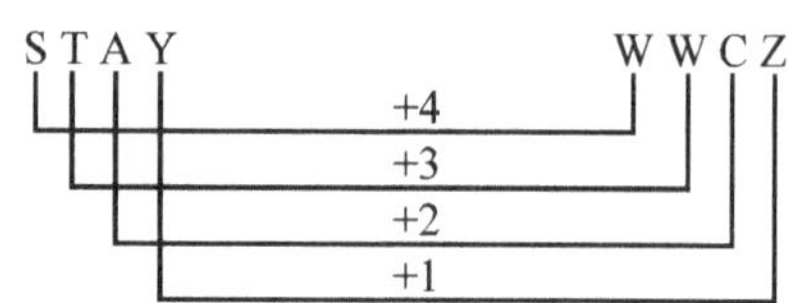

6.

Code	Sentence
1. go *ju* mi	plenty of *money*
2. pao *ju* go nei vu	*money* creates lots of problems
3. kol vu nei	problems create tension
4. sol tun *ju* haw	still *money* is needed

In 1st, 2nd and 4th codes and their sentences the word 'ju' is repeated and so is 'money'.

8.

Code	Sentence
1. 415	milk is hot
2. 18	hot soup
3. 895	soup is *tasty*

From 3rd code and its sentence neither number '9' is repeated nor the word 'tasty'.

9.

Code	Sentence
1. 643	she is beautiful
2. 593	he is handsome
3. 567	handsome *meets* beautiful

From 3rd code and its sentence, neither number '7' nor the word 'meets' is repeated.

10.

Code	Sentence
1. *dugo hui* mul zo	work *is very* hard
2. *hui dugo* **ba** *ki*	**Bingo** *is very smart*
3. nano mul *dugo*	cake *is hard*
4. mul *ki* qu	*smart* and hard

From 2nd code and its sentence, neither 'ba' nor 'Bingo' is repeated.

(Words repeated are in italics)

STATEMENT ANALYSIS

1. Among five friends, A is heavier than B; C is lighter than D; B is lighter than D but heavier than E. Who among them is the heaviest?

   A. B   B. C
   C. A   D. Can't say

2. Pune is bigger than Jhansi, Sitapur is bigger than Chittor. Raigarh is not as big as Jhansi, but is bigger than Sitapur. Chittor is not as big as Sitapur. Which is the smallest?

   A. Jhansi   B. Pune
   C. Chittor   D. Sitapur

3. Ajay works more than Ram. Alok works as much as Raju. Pankaj works less than Alok. Ram works more than Alok. Who works the most of all?

   A. Ajay   B. Ram
   C. Alok   D. Raju

4. Vipul is taller than Hans. Hans is taller than Anand. Alok is taller than Ashok. Ashok is taller than Hans. Who among them is the tallest?

   A. Vipul
   B. Alok
   C. Ashok
   D. Cannot be determined

5. Pramod is taller than Gopal. Gopal is shorter than Madhu. To find out who among them is the tallest, which of the following further informations is necessary?

- A. Madhu is taller than Gopal.
- B. Madhu is shorter than Pramod's brother
- C. Pramod is taller than Madhu.
- D. Pramod is taller than Madhu's brother.

6. Among five friends P, Q, R, S and T, who is the youngest? To arrive at the answer which of the following information given in the statements (*a*) and (*b*) is sufficient?

(*a*) R is younger than P and T.

(*b*) S is younger than Q.

- A. Only (*a*) alone is sufficient
- B. Either (*a*) or (*b*) is sufficient
- C. Both (*a*) and (*b*) together are needed
- D. Both (*a*) and (*b*) together are not sufficient

7. Sushma is richer than Rashmi whereas Anand is richer than Priya. Arun is as rich as Rashmi. Shoba is richer than Sushma.

Which of the following statements is correct according to the above propositions?

- A. Rashmi is poorer than Priya.
- B. Priya is richer than Arun
- C. Arun is poorer than Sushma.
- D. Anand is richer than Rashmi

8. A is elder to B while C and D are elder to E who lies between A and B. If C be elder to B, which one of the following statements is necessarily true?

- A. E is elder to B
- B. A is elder to C
- C. C is elder to D
- D. D is elder to C

9. Vikram is taller than Rajan but shorter than Annie. Jamal is taller than Annie. Sita is taller than Vikram. Rajan is shorter than Sita. Who is the shortest of all in the group?

- A. Sita
- B. Rajan
- C. Vikram
- D. Cannot be determined

10. Suresh is as much older than Kamal as he is younger than Prabodh. Navin is as old as Kamal. Which of the following statements is wrong?

- A. Suresh is older than Navin
- B. Kamal is younger than Suresh
- C. Prabodh is not the oldest
- D. Navin is younger than Prabodh

ANSWERS

1	2	3	4	5	6	7	8	9	10
D	C	A	D	C	D	C	A	B	C

EXPLANATORY ANSWERS

1. The five friends in descending order of weight are : A/D, B/C, E or A/D, B, C/E. Either A or D is the heaviest.

2. The order of cities in descending order of size is : Pune, Jhansi, Raigarh, Sitapur, Chittor.

3. On the basis of doing work, the descending order will be : Ajay, Ram, Alok/Raju, Pankaj.

4. On the basis of height, the descending order will be Vipul/Alok, Ashok, Hans, Anand. Either Vipul or Alok is the tallest.

5. According to the information both Pramod and Madhu are taller than Gopal. Option (c) decides who is the tallest.

6. Statements are not inter-related.

7. On the basis of wealth, the descending order will be :

1. Shobha, Sushma, Rashmi/Arun

2. Anand, *and* Priya

(The two statements are not inter-related.)

8. The order in descending seniority will be : A/C/D, E, B.

9. On the basis of height the descending order will be :

Jamal/Sita, Annie, Vikram, Rajan.

or

Jamal, Sita/Annie, Vikram, Rajan.

10. On the basis of age the descending order will be : Prabodh, Suresh, Kamal/Navin.

PLACE ARRANGEMENT

Directions: *In the following questions, understand the arrangement pattern and then select the right answer from the given options :*

1. Five boys are sitting in a row. Raghu is not adjacent to Shyam or Amit. Ajay is not adjacent to Shyam. Raghu is adjacent to Mayank. If Mayank is at the middle in the row, then Ajay is adjacent to whom out of the following?
   A. Amit   B. Raghu
   C. Mayank   D. Shyam

2. Mini is to the right of Rajni but to the left of Ananta. Saya is to the right of Mini but to the left of Jaya. Who is on the extreme left if all the girls are facing North?
   A. Jaya   B. Mini
   C. Rajni   D. Saya

3. Kittu is in-between Mohan and Sohan. Raju is to the left of Sohan and Shyam is to the right of Mohan. If all of the friends are sitting facing South, then who is on their extreme right?
   A. Mohan   B. Sohan
   C. Kittu   D. Shyam

4. A, B, C, D and E are running one behind the other. C is not near E and A is not near D. B is next to A and E is not near D. Who is in the middle?
   A. B   B. E
   C. A   D. Cannot be said

5. O, P, Q, R, S and T are standing on a bench according to their height. P is taller than O but shorter than S. Only S is taller than T. R is shorter than P but taller than Q. Who is the shortest?
   A. O   B. Q
   C. P   D. Cannot be said

ANSWERS

1	2	3	4	5
B	C	D	A	D

EXPLANATORY ANSWERS

1. The order of sitting is :
   Amit, Shyam, Mayank, Ajay, Raghu
   or
   Ajay, Raghu, Mayank, Amit, Shyam

2. The order in which the girls are positioned is :
   Rajni, Mini, Ananta, Saya, Jaya
   or
   Saya, Jaya, Ananta
   or
   Saya, Ananta, Jaya

3. The order of sitting while facing South is:
   Shyam, Mohan, Kittu, Sohan, Raju.

4. The positions while running behind the other is :

E	E
A	A
B *or*	B
C	D
D	C

5. In descending order of height, the standing positions are :

S	S
T	T
P *or*	P
R	R
O	Q
Q	O

Either O or Q is the shortest. The information given is not enough to clarify the answer.

DIRECTION SENSE

Directions : *In the following questions, select the right answer from the given options to depict the correct direction/distance.*

1. Kittu walks towards East and then towards South. After walking some distance he turns towards West and then turns to his left. In which direction is he walking now?

A. North	B. South
C. East	D. West

2. A person is driving towards West. What sequence of directions should he follow so that he is driving towards South?
A. left, right, right
B. right, right, left
C. left, left, left
D. right, right, right

3. Richa drives 8 km to the South, turns left and drives 5 km. Again, she turns left and drives 8 km. How far is she from her starting point?

A. 3 km	B. 5 km
C. 8 km	D. 13 km

4. Dingi runs 40 km towards North then turns right and runs 50 km. He turns right and runs 30 km, and once again turns right and runs 50 km. How far is he from his starting point?
A. 90 km B. 50 km
C. 10 km D. 5 km

5. Debu walks towards East then towards North and turning 45° right walks for a while and lastly turns towards left. In which direction is he walking now?
A. North B. East
C. South-East D. North-West

ANSWERS

1	2	3	4	5
B	D	B	C	D

EXPLANATORY ANSWERS

1. 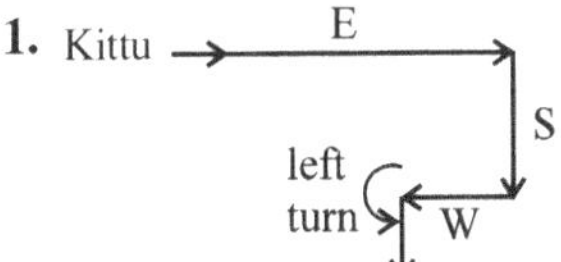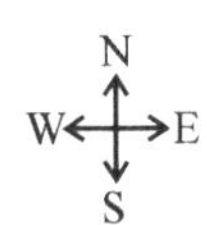

2. 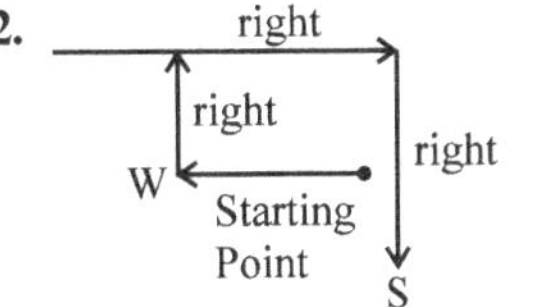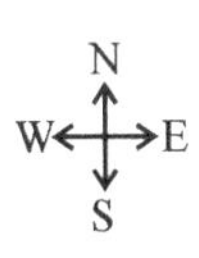

3. 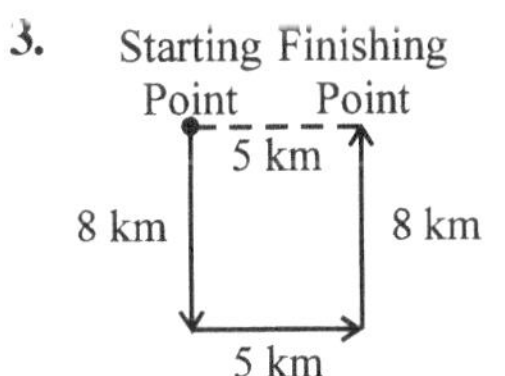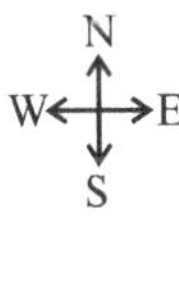

4. 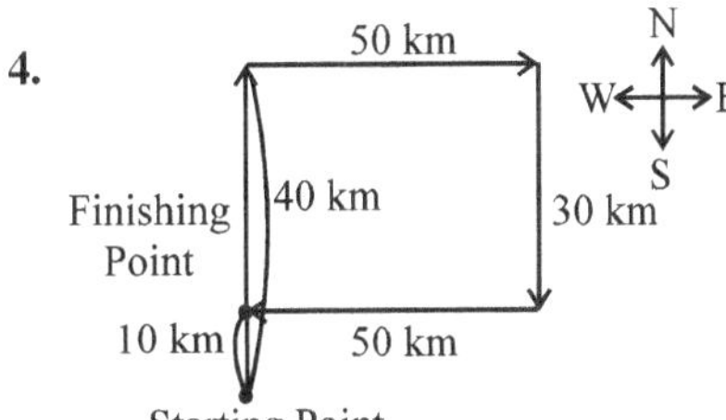

5. 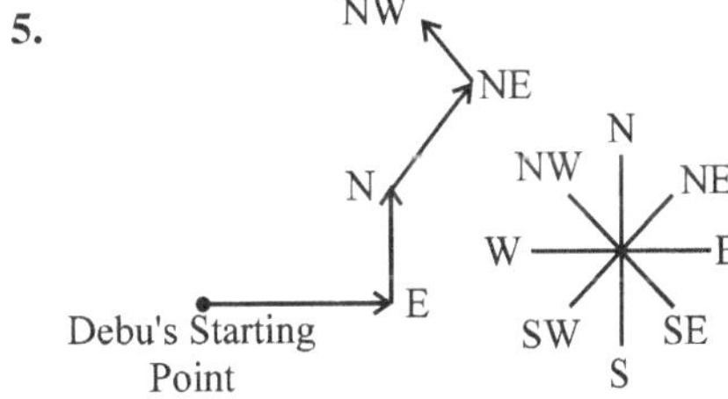

BLOOD RELATIONSHIPS

Directions : *In each of the following questions keenly study the relationship mentioned between the persons, and then from the given options select the right relationship as the answer.*

1. 'A' is the father of 'B' and 'C'. 'B' is the son of 'A' but 'C' is not the son of 'A'. What is 'C's' relation with 'A'?
A. Daughter B. Son
C. Niece D. Nephew

2. A lady said, "The person standing there is my grandfather's only son's daughter". How is the lady related to the standing person?
A. Sister B. Mother
C. Aunt D. Cousin

3. Ravi is the brother of Amit's son's son. What is Amit's relation to Ravi?
A. Cousin B. Father
C. Grandfather D. Son

4. Mayank said, "My mother is the sister of Rajat's brother." What is Rajat's relation with Mayank?
   A. Cousin   B. Maternal uncle
   C. Uncle   D. Brother-in-law

5. Introducing Lily, Raghav said, "Her father is my mother's only son". How is Lily related to Raghav?
   A. Aunt   B. Daughter
   C. Mother   D. Sister

ANSWERS

1	2	3	4	5
A	A	C	B	B

EXPLANATORY ANSWERS

1. 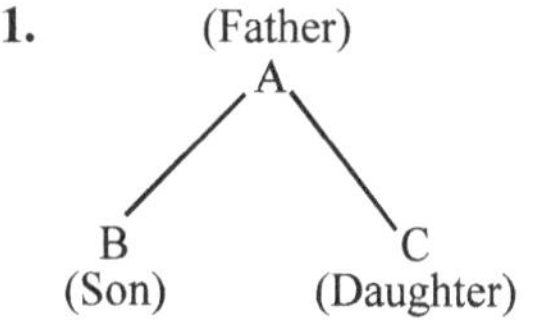

'C' is not the son of 'A', but 'A' is the father of 'C'. So, 'C' is the daughter of 'A'.

2. 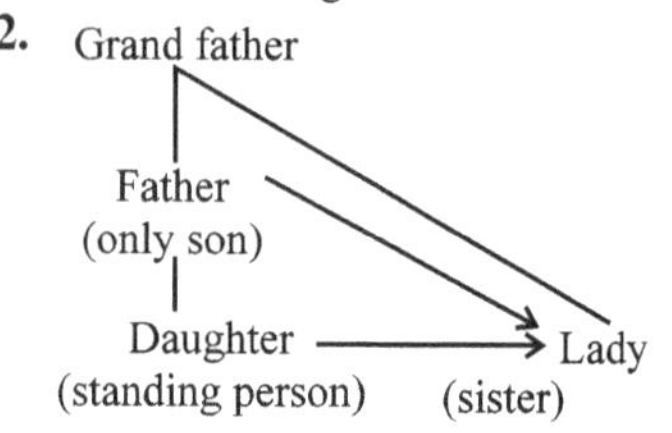

Lady's grandfather's son is lady's father and father's daughter will only be lady's sister.

4. 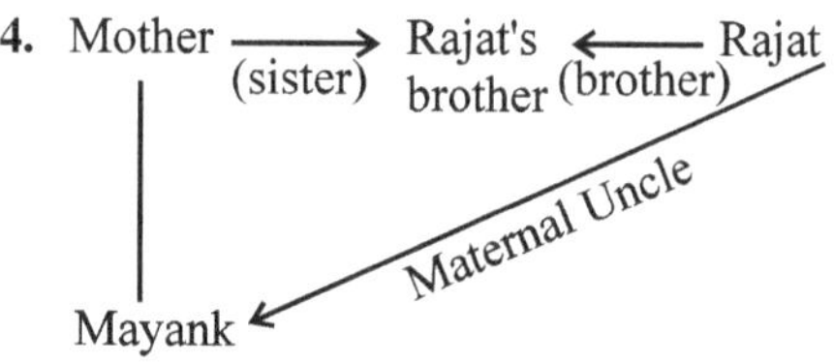

Mayank's mother is the sister of Rajat's brother. So Rajat is also the brother of Mayank's mother. Relation of the brother with his sister's child is maternal. So Rajat is Mayank's maternal uncle.

CALENDAR, CLOCK, TIME, DISTANCE

1. If the day before yesterday was Thursday, when will Sunday be?
   A. Tomorrow   B. Day after tomorrow
   C. Today   D. Two days after today

2. There are twenty people working in an office. The first group of five works between 8:00 A.M. and 2:00 PM. The second group of ten works between 10:00 AM to 4:00 PM. And the third group of five works between 12 noon to 6:00 PM. There are three computers in the office which all the employees frequently use. During which of the following hours the computers are likely to be used most?
   A. 1:00 PM - 3:00 PM
   B. 12 noon - 2:00 PM
   C. 2:00 PM - 4:00 PM
   D. 10:00 AM - 12 noon

3. If the seventh day of a month is three (3) days earlier than Friday, what day will it be on the nineteenth day of the month?

   A. Sunday   B. Monday
   C. Wednesday   D. Friday

4. Radha remembers that her father's birthday is after 16th but before 21st of March, while her brother Mangesh remembers that his father's birthday is before 22nd but after 19th of March. On which date is the birthday of their father?
   A. 19th
   B. 20th
   C. 21st
   D. Cannot be determined

5. A man is three (3) years older than his wife and four (4) times as old as his son. If the son attains an age of fifteen (15) years after three (3) years, what is the present age of the mother?
   A. 45 years   B. 51 years
   C. 48 years   D. 60 years

6. A clock is so placed that at 12 noon its minute hand points towards north-east. In which direction does its

hour hand point at 1.30 P.M.?
A. East   B. West
C. North   D. South

7. If in the above question clock is turned through an angle of 135° in an anticlockwise direction, in which direction will its minute hand point at 8.45 P.M.?
A. East   B. West
C. North   D. South

8. A couple married in 1980 had two children, one in 1982 and the other in 1984. Their combined ages will equal the years of the marriage in?
A. 1986   B. 1985
C. 1987   D. 1988

9. Manoj left home for the bus stop 15 minutes earlier than the usual time. It takes 10 minutes to reach the stop. He reached the stop at 8.40 a.m. What time does he usually leave home for the bus stop?
A. 8.30 a.m.   B. 8.55 a.m.
C. 8.45 p.m.   D. None of these

10. Mamuni went to the movies nine days ago. She goes to the movies only on Thursday. What day of the week is today?
A. Sunday   B. Tuesday
C. Thursday   D. Saturday

11. If Thursday was the day after the day before yesterday five days ago, what is the least number of days ago when Sunday was three days before the day after tomorrow?
A. Two days ago   B. Three days ago
C. Four days ago   D. Five days ago

12. 1.12.91 is the first Sunday. Which is the fourth Tuesday of December 91?
A. 31.12.91   B. 24.12.91
C. 17.12.91   D. 26.12.91

13. If the third day of a month is Monday, which of the following will be the fifth day from 21st of that month?
A. Tuesday   B. Monday
C. Wednesday   D. Thursday

14. Keshav runs a factory in three shifts of eight hours each with 210 employees. In each shift minimum of 80 employees are required to run the factory effectively. No employee can be allowed to work for more than 16 hours a day. At least how many employees will be required to work for 16 hours every day?
A. 30   B. 60
C. Data inadequate   D. None of these

15. If 15 horses eat 15 bags of gram in 15 days, in how many days will one horse eat one bag of grain?
A. 15 days   B. 1/15 days
C. 1 day   D. 30 days

16. A century leap year is divisible by :
A. 4   B. 16
C. 40   D. 400

17. If the fifth day of a month is Friday, which of the following will be the Seventh day from 10th of that month?
A. Tuesday   B. Monday
C. Wednesday   D. Thursday

18. Day after tomorrow is my birthday. On the same day next week falls 'Holi'. Today is Monday. What will be the day after 'Holi'?
A. Wednesday   B. Thursday
C. Friday   D. Saturday

19. A clock shows the time as 3 : 30 p.m. If the minute hand gains 2 minutes every hour, how many minutes will the clock gain by 4 a.m.?
A. 23 Minutes   B. 24 Minutes
C. 25 Minutes   D. 26 Minutes

20. Two brothers were expected to return home on the same day. Rajat returned 3 days earlier but Rohit returned 4 days later. If Rajat returned on Thursday, what was the expected day when both the brothers were to return home and when did Rohit Return?
A. Wednesday, Sunday
B. Thursday, Monday
C. Sunday, Thursday
D. Monday, Friday

ANSWERS

1	2	3	4	5	6	7	8	9	10
A	B	A	B	A	A	D	A	D	D

11	12	13	14	15	16	17	18	19	20
A	B	C	D	A	D	C	B	C	C

EXPLANATORY ANSWERS

1. Thursday —Day-before-yesterday
Friday —Yesterday

Saturday —Today
Sunday — Tomorrow

2. 1. 5 people work between 8 a.m. to 2 p.m.

2. 10 people work between 10 a.m. to 4 p.m.

3. 5 people work between 12 noon to 6 p.m.

So, computers are used most between 12 noon to 2 p.m.

3. 7th day is 3 days earlier than Friday so, 10th day is Friday, so also is 17th.

∴ 19th day will be 2nd day ahead of Friday, *i.e.,* Sunday.

4. Father's birthday

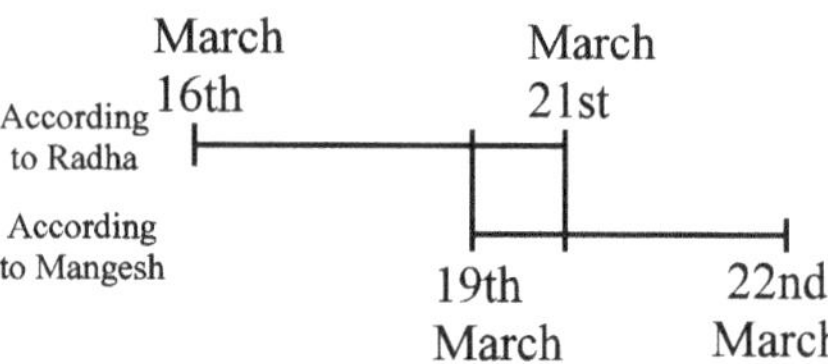

∴ Their father's birthday is on 20th March.

5. Present age of son is 15 – 3 = 12 years. Age of the man is 4 times the age of son, *i.e.,*

12 × 4 = 48 years

Man is 3 years elder to his wife/son's mother.

So Age of the mother is 48 – 3 = 45 years

6.  

At 12 noon

At 1.30 p.m. the hour hand will point towards East.

7. 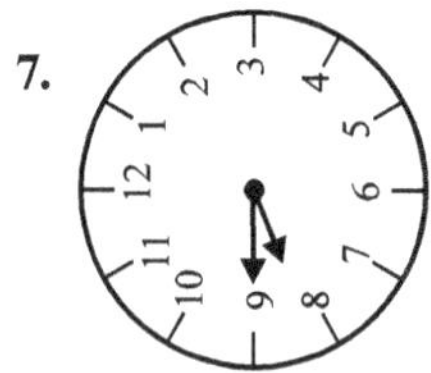

After rotating the clock in earlier question, its minute hand will point towards South at 8:45 p.m.

8. 1982 — 2 years later — 1st child

1984 — 4 years later — 2nd child

Total age of children — 2 years.

1985 — 5 years later — Total age of children: 4 years.

1986 — 6 years later — Total age of children : 6 years.

9. Manoj reached the bus stop at 8.40 a.m. He left his home at 8:40 – 10 minutes = 8:30 a.m. He left 15 minutes earlier than usual, so his actual time of leaving home is 8:30 am + 15 minutes = 8:45 a.m.

10. Mamuni goes to the movies on Thursday, so nine days ago was Thursday.

∴ Two days ago was also Thursday. So, today is Saturday.

11. Day after the day-before-yesterday five days ago is the 6th day which is Thursday. And so, the 3rd day will be Sunday. Three days before the day-after-tomorrow is Yesterday which is the 1st day of the five days. So, two days ago was Sunday.

12. First Sunday is on 1st December

First Tuesday is on 3rd December

3 weeks later, Fourth Tuesday will be on 3 + (7 × 3) = 24th December.

13. 3rd day of the month is Monday

5th day from 21st is 26th

26 – 3 = 23 days

23 days later, 23/7 leaves 2 days.

So, two days ahead of Monday will be Wednesday.

14. 80 employees are required for double shift.

15. 15 horses eat 15 bags of grain in 15 days

15 horses eat 1 bag of grain in 1 day

1 horse eats 1 bag of grain in 15 days

16. A leap year is divisible by 4 and a century leap year is divisible by 400.

17. Seventh day from 10th is 17th.

5th day is Friday. Next Friday is on 12th, 17 – 12 = 5, 5 days ahead of Friday will be Wednesday. So, 17th is Wednesday.

18. Today is Monday

Day-after-tomorrow is Wednesday

Next week 'Holi' is also on Wednesday

So, Day after Holi is Thursday.

19. Hours between 3:30 p.m. and 4 a.m. are — 12½ hours. Number of minutes gained will be 12½ × 2 = 25 minutes.

20. Rajat returned on Thursday. 3 days later was the day of expected return, *i.e.,* Sunday. Rohit returned 4 days after Sunday, *i.e.,* Thursday.

ROWS AND RANKS

1. In a row of trees, one tree is fifth from either end of the row. How many trees are in the row?
   A. 11
   B. 8
   C. 10
   D. 9

2. Jaya ranks 5th in a class of 53. What is her rank from the bottom in the class?
   A. 49th
   B. 48th
   C. 47th
   D. 50th

3. Mohan ranks twenty-first in a class of sixty-five students. What will be his (Mohan's) rank if the lowest candidate is assigned rank 1?
   A. 44th
   B. 45th
   C. 46th
   D. Data inadequate

4. If Rahul finds that he is 12th from the right in a line of boys and 4th from the left, how many boys should be added to the line such that there are 28 boys in the line?
   A. 12
   B. 14
   C. 20
   D. 13

5. In a row of boys, Rajan is tenth from the right and Suraj is tenth from the left. When Rajan and Suraj interchange their positions, Suraj will be twenty-seventh from the left. Which of the following will be Rajan's position from the right?
   A. Tenth
   B. Twenty-sixth
   C. Twenty-ninth
   D. None of these

6. Mahesh and Suresh are ranked 11th and 12th respectively from the top in a class of 41 students. What will be their respective ranks from the bottom?
   A. 32nd and 33rd
   B. 29th and 30th
   C. 30th and 31st
   D. 31st and 30th

7. Uma ranked 8th from the top and 37th from bottom in a class. How many students are there in the class?
   A. 47
   B. 46
   C. 45
   D. None of these

8. In a queue, Sadiq is 14th from the front and Joseph is 17th from the end, while Jane is in between Sadiq and Joseph. If Sadiq be ahead of Joseph and there be 48 persons in the queue, how many persons are there between Sadiq and Jane?
   A. 5
   B. 6
   C. 7
   D. 8

9. Rohan ranked eleventh from the top and twenty-seventh from the bottom among the students who passed the annual examination in a class. If the number of students who failed in the examination was 12, how many students appeared for the examination?
   A. 48
   B. 49
   C. 50
   D. Cannot be determined

10. Some boys are sitting in a row. P is sitting fourteenth from the left and Q is seventh from the right. If there are four boys between P and Q, how many boys are there in the row?
   A. 19
   B. 21
   C. 25
   D. 23

ANSWERS

1	2	3	4	5	6	7	8	9	10
D	A	B	D	D	D	D	C	B	C

EXPLANATORY ANSWERS

1.
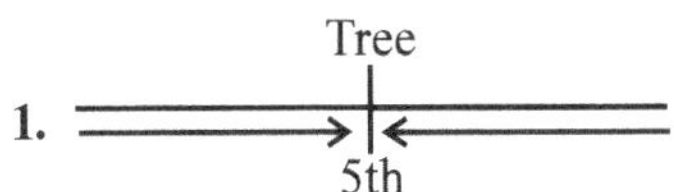

Total number of trees in the row are :
(5 + 5) −1 =9

2.
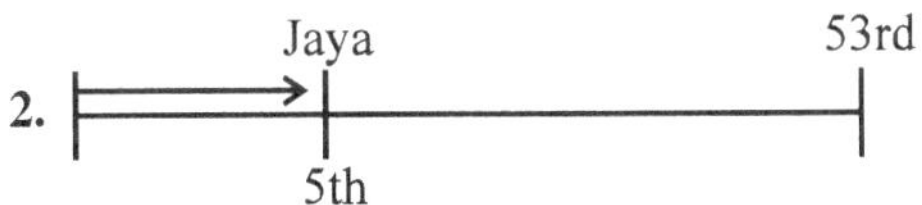

Jaya's rank from the bottom is :
(53 − 5) +1 = 49th.

3.
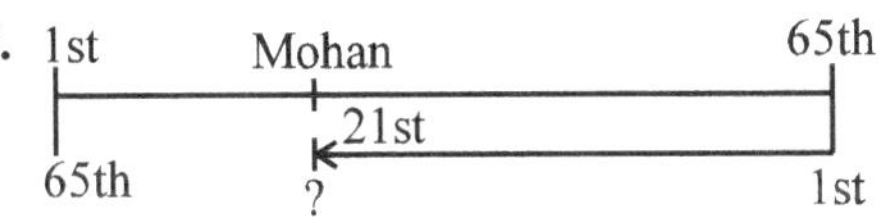

Note : Mohan's rank from the last or the question asked means the same.

Mohan's rank is (65 − 21) +1 = 45th

4. 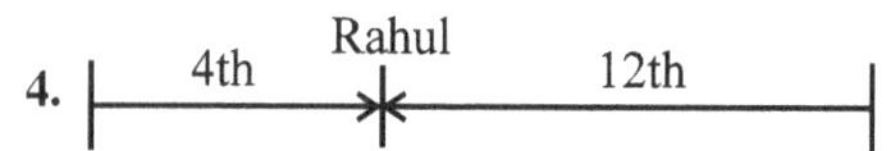

The number of boys in the line are :
(4 + 12) – 1 = 15
To make a line of 28 boys, (28 –15) *i.e.* 13 more boys are needed.

5. 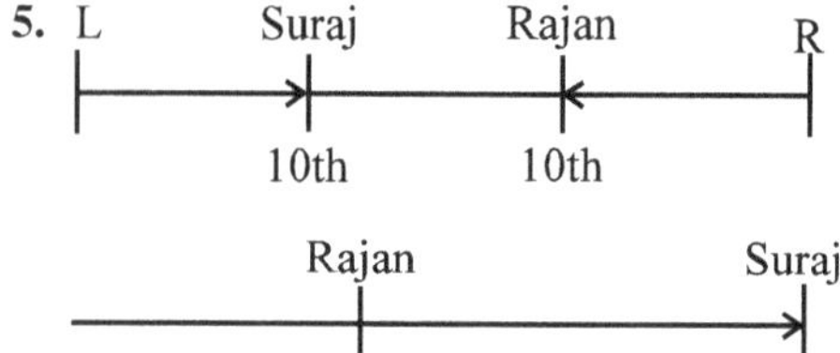

As the position of boys is equal from both ends, Rajan will also be 27th from the right after changing positions.

6. 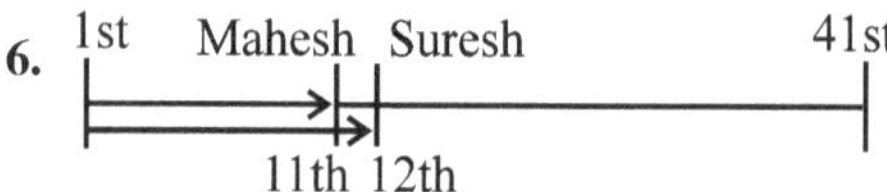

Mahesh's position from bottom is :
(41 – 11) + 1 = 31st
Suresh's position from bottom is :
(41 – 12) +1 = 30th

7. 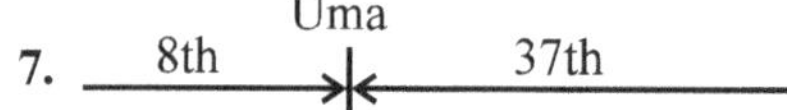

8. Total number of students in the class are :
(8 + 37) – 1 = 44

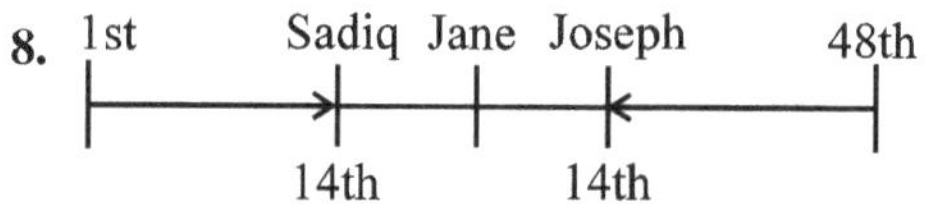

Sadiq's position from last is :
(48 – 14) + 1 = 35th
Number of persons between Sadiq and Joseph are (35 – 17) – 1 = 17
Jane is in-between Sadiq and Joseph *i.e.,* she's at 9th position from both the boys.
∴ there are 8 persons between Sadiq and Jane.
Note : (8 + 8) – 1 = 17

9. 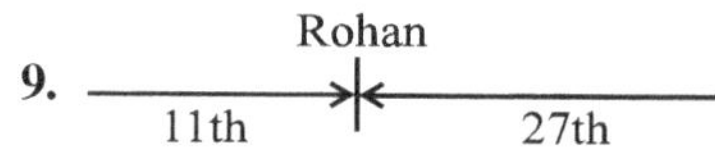

Number of students who passed the examination (11+ 27) – 1 = 37
Those who failed = 12
Total number of students who appeared in the examination = 37 + 12 = 49.

10. 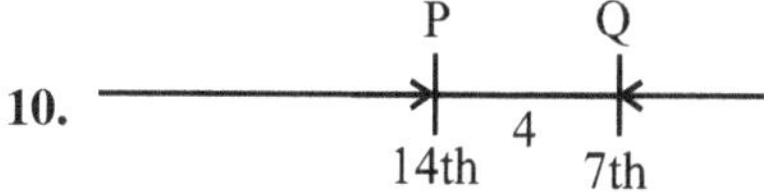

The number of boys in the row are :
(14 + 4 + 7) = 25

NUMBER PROBLEMS

---

1. How many 6's are there in the following series of numbers which are preceded by 7 but not immediately followed by 9?
6 7 9 5 6 9 7 6 8 7 6 7 8 6 9 4 6 7 7 6 9 5 7 6 3
A. One   B. Two
C. Three   D. Four

2. In a chess tournament each of six players will play every other player exactly once. How many matches will be played during the tournament?
A. 12   B. 15
C. 30   D. 36

3. How many 4's are there in the following series which are preceded by 7, but are not preceded by 8?
3 4 5 7 4 3 7 4 8 5 4 3 7 4 9 8 4 7 2 7 4 1 3 6
A. 1   B. 2
C. 3   D. 4

4. How many even numbers are there in the following series of numbers, each of which is immediately preceded by an odd number, but not immediately followed by an even number?
5 3 4 8 9 7 1 6 5 3 2 9 8 4 3 5
A. Nil   B. 1
C. 2   D. 3

5. If all the numbers from 1 to 51 which are exactly divisible by 3 are arranged in descending order, which of the following numbers will come at the seventh and tenth places from the top?
A. 33 & 27   B. 33 & 21
C. 21 & 30   D. 33 & 24

ANSWERS

1	2	3	4	5
C	B	D	C	D

EXPLANATORY ANSWERS

1. 6 7 9 5 6 9 7 6 8 7 6 7 8 6 9 4 6 7 7 6 9 5 7 6 3
<u>　1　</u>　<u>　2　</u>　　　　　　　　　<u>　3　</u>

2. When all the players have to play with each other then the method of calculating the number of matches to be played is $\dfrac{n\,(n-1)}{2}$ where '*n*' is the number of players playing the match. So, the number of matches played will be :
$(6 \times 5) \div 2 = 30 \div 2 = 15$

3. 3 4 5 7 4 3 7 4 8 5 4 3 7 4 9 8 4 7 2 7 4 1 3 6
　　<u>1</u>　<u>2</u>　　　<u>3</u>　　　<u>4</u>

4. 5 3 4 8 9 7 1 6 5 3 2 9 8 4 3 5
　　　　　<u>1</u>　<u>2</u>

5. The numbers divisible by 3 in descending order are :
51, 48, 45, 42, 39, 36, 33, <u>30</u>, 27, <u>24</u>, 21,
　　　　　　　　　　　　7th　　　10th
18, 15, 12, 9, 6, 3.

SYMBOL SUBSTITUTION

1. If "+" means "–"; "–" means "×"; "×"means "÷" and "÷" means "+", then
15 × 5 ÷ 10 + 5 – 3 = ?
A. 9.5　　　　　　　B. 0
C. – 2　　　　　　　D. 24

2. If "+" means "–"; "–" means "×"; "×"means "÷" and "÷" means "+", then
15 × 3 ÷ 15 + 5 – 2 = ?
A. 0　　　　　　　　B. 10
C. 20　　　　　　　D. 6

3. If "+" means "÷"; "×" means "–"; "÷"means "+" and "–" means "×", then
16 ÷ 8 × 6 – 2 + 12 = ?

A. 22　　　　　　　B. 24
C. 23　　　　　　　D. 20

4. If "+" means "×"; "–" means "÷"; "÷"means "+" and "×" means "–", then what will be the value of 20　÷ 40 – 4 × 5 + 6 = ?
A. 60　　　　　　　B. 1.67
C. 150　　　　　　D. 0

5. If "+" means "×"; "–" means "÷"; "×"means "–" and "÷" means "+", then
5 + 8 – 4 × 2 ÷ 9 = ?
A. 15　　　　　　　B. 13
C. 17　　　　　　　D. 11

ANSWERS

1	2	3	4	5
C	B	C	D	C

EXPLANATORY ANSWERS

1. 15 ÷ 5 + 10 – 5 × 3
3 + 10 – 15 = – 2

2. 15 ÷ 3 + 15 – 5 × 2
5 + 15 – 10 = 10

3. 16 + 8 – 6 × 2 ÷ 12
16 + 8 – 1 = 23

4. 20 + 40 ÷ 4 – 5 × 6
20 + 10 – 30 = 0

5. 5 × 8 ÷ 4 – 2 + 9
10 – 2 + 9 = 17

MISSING NUMBERS

Directions: *In each question given below which one number can be placed at the sign of interrogation?*

1. 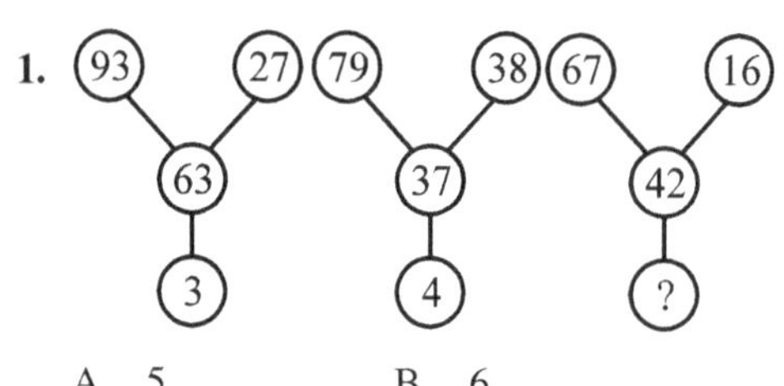

A. 5   B. 6
C. 8   D. 9

2. 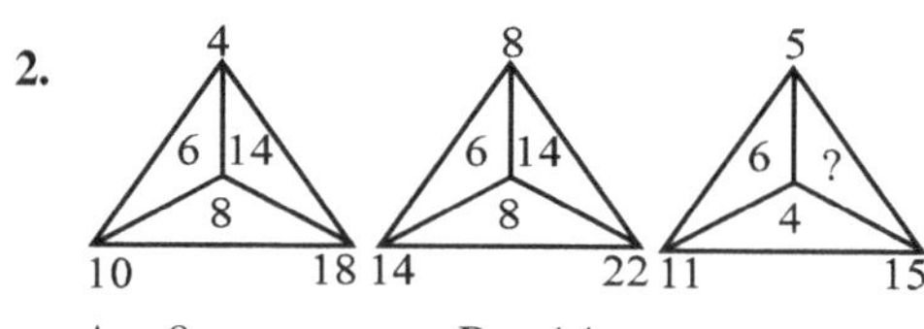

A. 8   B. 14
C. 10   D. 6

3. 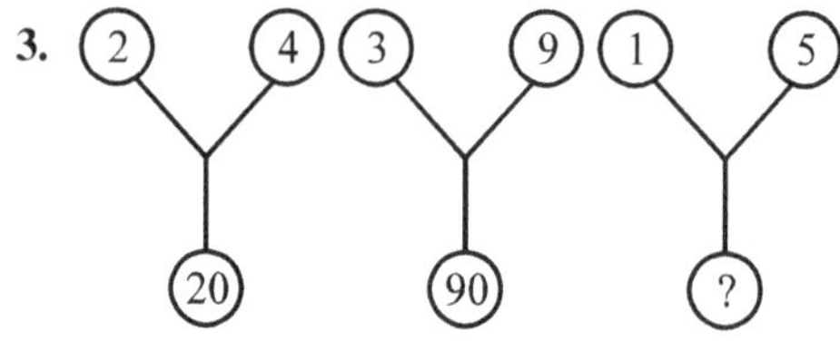

A. 20   B. 25
C. 26   D. 75

4.

27	22	50
13	12	26
9	2	?

A. 12   B. 39
C. 18   D. 24

5.

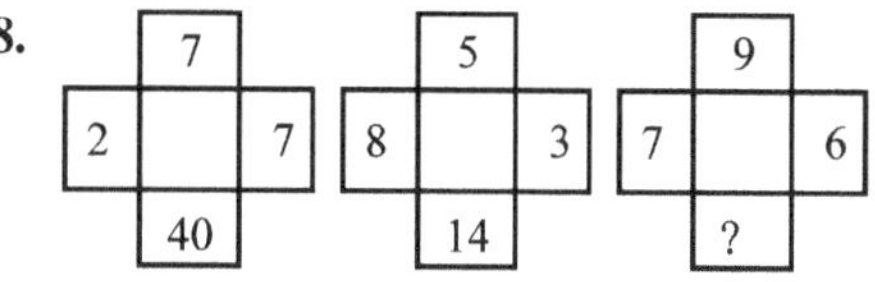

A. 25   B. 47
C. 37   D. 41

6. 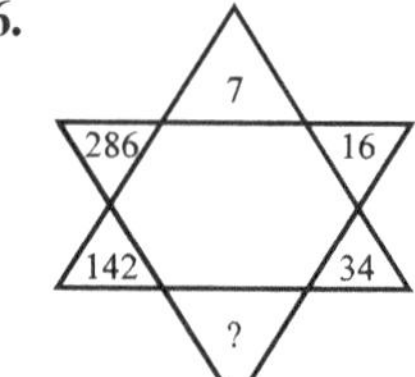

A. 70   B. 68
C. 56   D. 92

7. 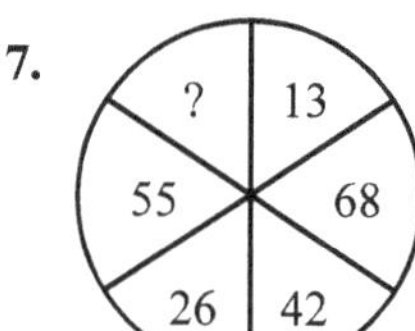

A. 41   B. 37
C. 29   D. 25

8.

A. 72   B. 68
C. 82   D. 96

9.

42	(21)	22
78	(?)	84
162	(18)	99

A. 12   B. 13
C. 60   D. 72

10. 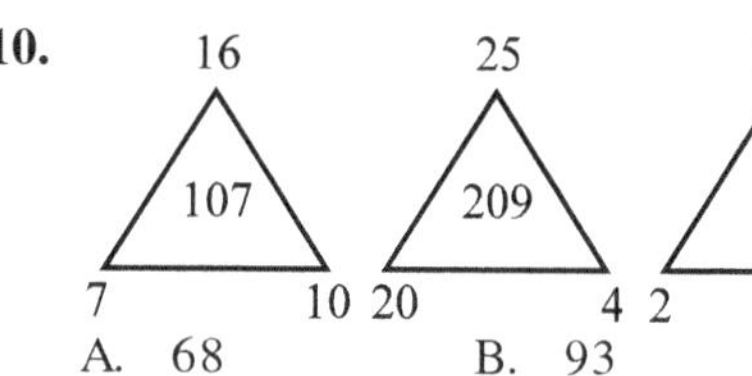

A. 68   B. 93
C. 175   D. 217

ANSWERS

1	2	3	4	5	6	7	8	9	10
D	C	C	A	D	A	C	B	B	A

EXPLANATORY ANSWERS

1. The sum of numbers on right and centre subtracted from the number on the left gives the number at the bottom, *i.e.,*

$$93 - (27 + 63) = 3$$
$$79 - (38 + 37) = 4$$

Similarly,
$67 - (16 + 42) = 9$

2. The number inside each triangle is the difference of the numbers at its base *i.e.*
   $10 - 4 = 6$, $18 - 4 = 14$ and $18 - 10 = 8$
   $14 - 8 = 6$, $22 - 8 = 14$ and $22 - 14 = 8$, similarly
   $11 - 5 = 6$, $15 - 5 = 10$ and $15 - 11 = 4$.

3. The sum of squares of two numbers at the top gives the third number below, *i.e.*,
   $2^2 + 4^2 = 20$
   $3^2 + 9^2 = 90$, similarly
   $1^2 + 5^2 = 26$

4. The sum of numbers in 1st and 2nd column plus 1 is the number in the 3rd column, *i.e.*,
   $27 + 22 + 1 = 50$
   $13 + 12 + 1 = 26$, similarly
   $9 + 2 + 1 = 12$

5. The product of numbers on either side of the triangle plus the number at the base is the number inside the triangle, *i.e.*,
   $(5 \times 3) + 4 = 19$
   $(6 \times 4) + 5 = 29$, similarly
   $(7 \times 5) + 6 = 41$

6. Clockwise starting from number 7, the next number is obtained by doubling the number and adding 2, *i.e.*,
   $(7 \times 2) + 2 = 16$
   $(16 \times 2) + 2 = 34 \ldots$, similarly
   $(34 \times 2) + 2 = 70$

$(70 \times 2) + 2 = 142$
$(142 \times 2) + 2 = 286$

7. The difference between the numbers in opposite sectors is 13, *i.e.*,
   $26 - 13 = 13$
   $68 - 55 = 13$, similarly
   The missing number is $42 - 13 = 29$
   ($42 + 13 = 55$ is not given as option)

8. The number at the bottom is obtained by subtracting the sum of two numbers in the centre grid line from the square of the number at the top, *i.e.*,
   $7^2 - (2 + 7) = 40$
   $5^2 - (8 + 3) = 14$, similarly
   $9^2 - (7 + 6) = 68$

9. The number inside the brackets is obtained by multiplying the number on the left by 2 and then dividing the product by the sum of digits of number on the right, *i.e.*,
   $(42 \times 2) \div (2 + 2) = 21$
   $(162 \times 2) \div (9 + 9) = 18$, similarly
   $(78 \times 2) \div (8 + 4) = 13$

10. Subtracting the sum of squares of two numbers at the base from the square of number at the apex gives the number inside the triangle, *i.e.*,
    $16^2 - (7^2 + 10^2) = 107$
    $25^2 - (20^2 + 4^2) = 209$, similarly
    $19^2 - (2^2 + 17^2) = 68$

ALPHABET PROBLEMS

Directions : *The following questions are based on alphabet series in natural or reverse order and the combinations that can be made by changing the position of alphabet in given words.*

1. Which alphabet comes immediately before the sixth alphabet from the left extreme in alphabetical series?
   A. U   B. E
   C. F   D. V

2. Which letter is midway between G and S?
   A. L   B. N
   C. M   D. No letter

3. Which letter should be ninth letter to the left of ninth letter from the right if the first half of the alphabet is reversed?
   A. I   B. D
   C. F   D. E

4. If the alphabet is in reverse order, which letter will be eighth letter to the left of the seventh letter counting from the right end?
   A. O   B. P
   C. N   D. Q

5. What will be the fifth letter to the right of the thirteenth letter from the right?
   A. R   B. S
   C. I   D. O

ANSWERS

1	2	3	4	5
B	C	D	A	B

EXPLANATORY ANSWERS

1. 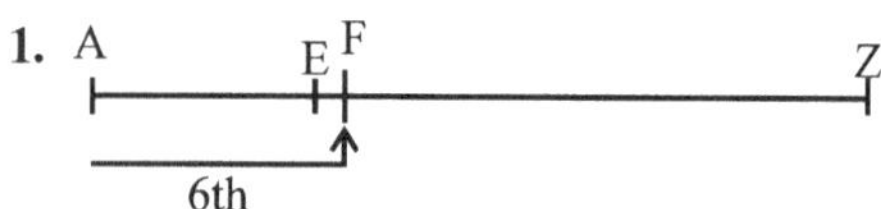

Sixth letter from left is 'F' and letter immediately before 'F' is 'E'.

2. 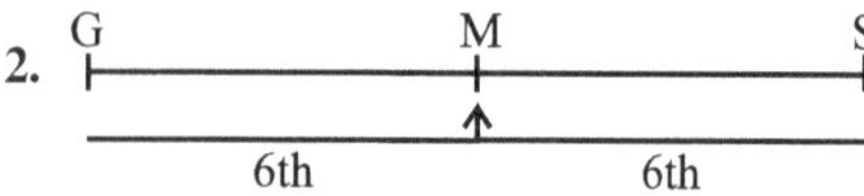

'M' is midway between G and S.

3. 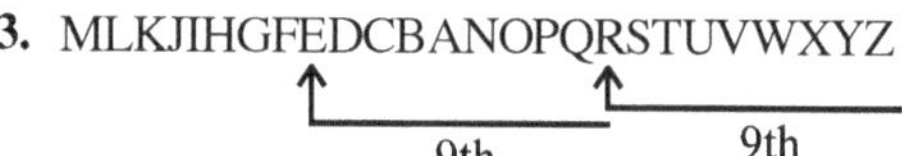

4. 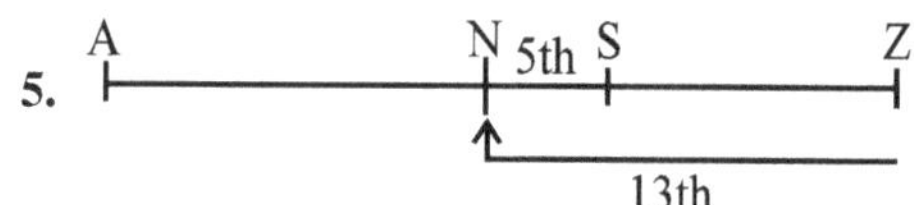

5. A   N 5th S   Z   13th

13th letter from right is 'N' and 5th letter to the right of 'N' is 'S'.

NON-VERBAL SERIES

Directions (Q. 1–10) : *In each of the following questions which one of the five answer figures given below should come after the problem figures if the sequence are continued?*

Problem Figures   Answer Figures

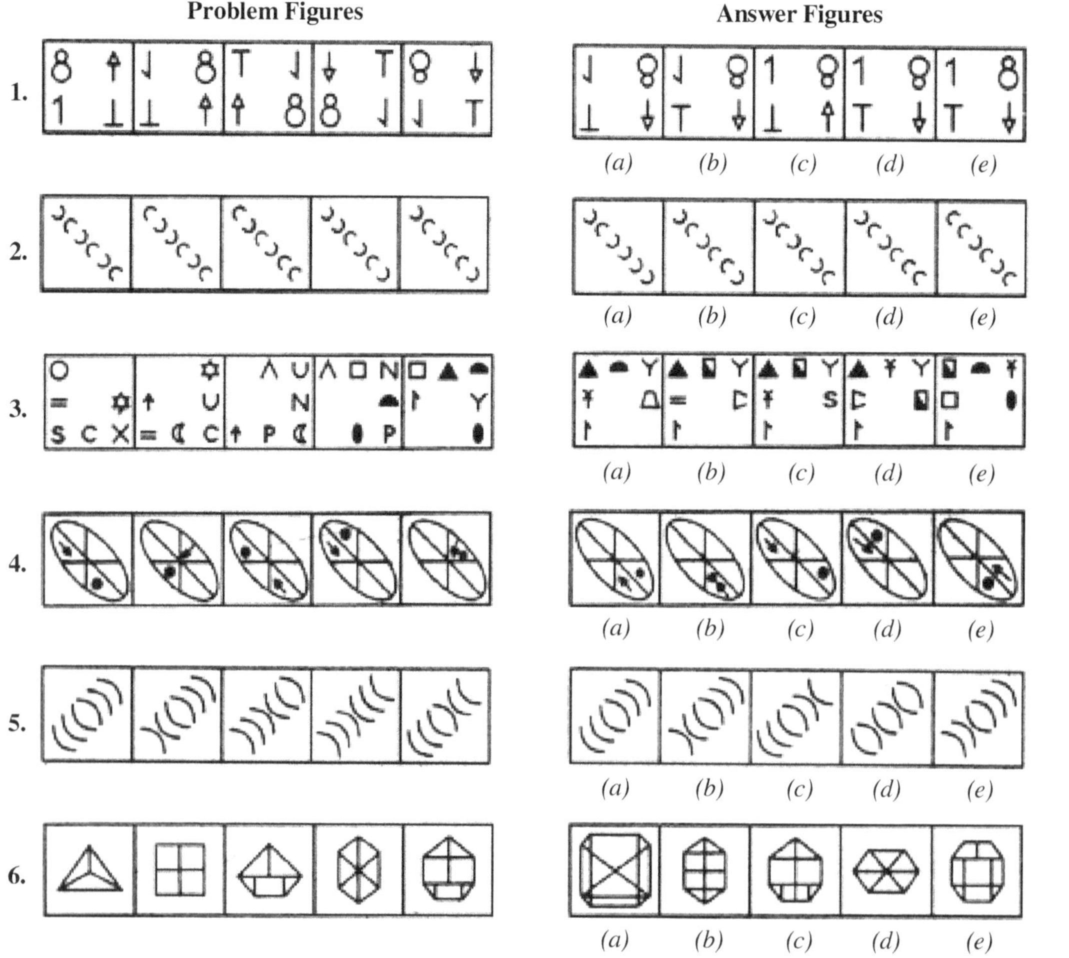

7. 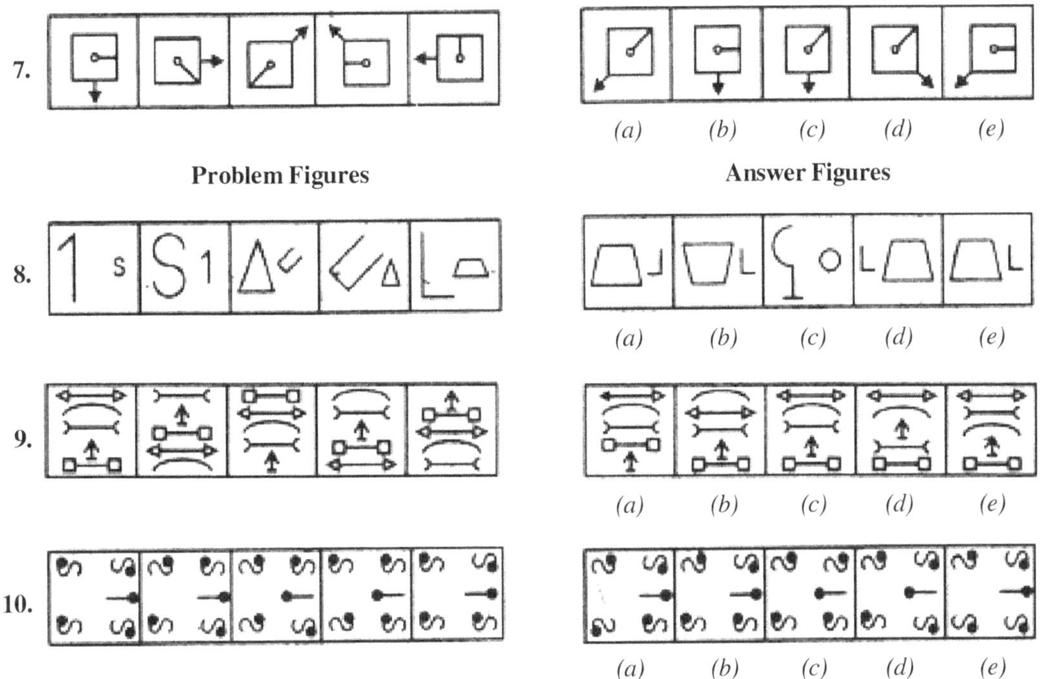

Problem Figures

Answer Figures

(a) (b) (c) (d) (e)

8.

9.

10.

(a) (b) (c) (d) (e)

Directions (Q. 11-20) : *In each of these questions, a series begins with an unmarked figure on the extreme left in the row of figures. One and only one of the five lettered figures in the series does not fit into the series. The two unmarked figures, one on the extreme left and the other on the extreme right fit into the series. Take as many aspects into account as possible of the figures in the series and find out the one and only of the five marked figures which does not fit into the series. The letter of that figure is the answer.*

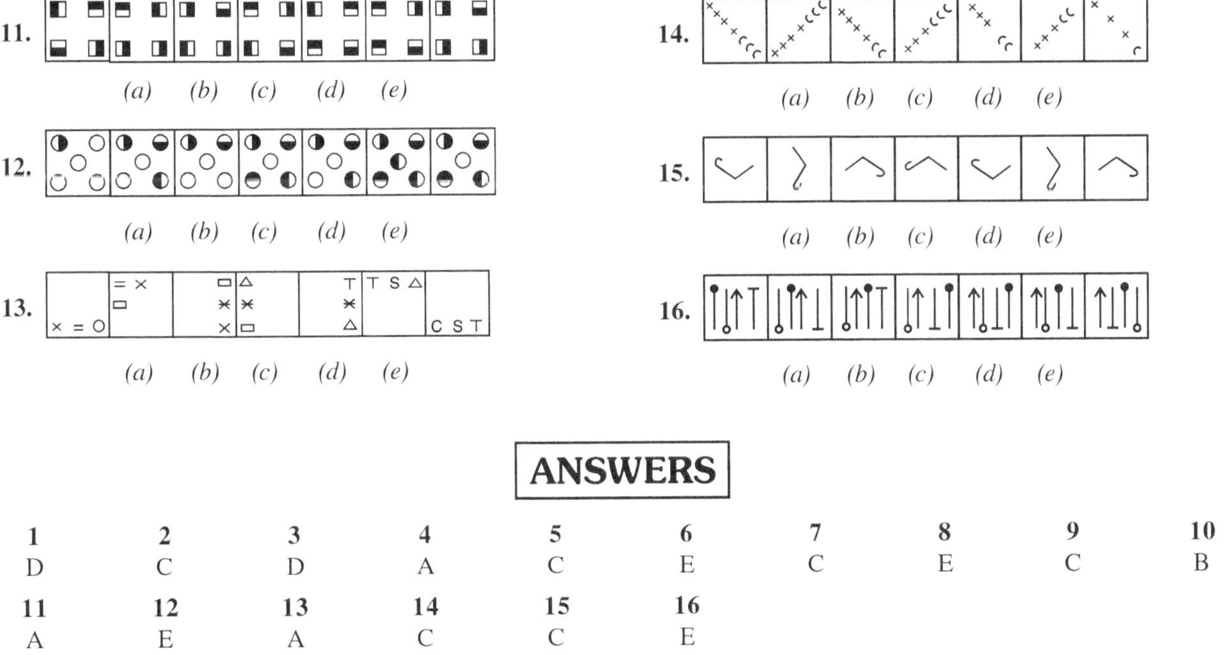

11.   (a) (b) (c) (d) (e)

12.   (a) (b) (c) (d) (e)

13.   (a) (b) (c) (d) (e)

14.   (a) (b) (c) (d) (e)

15.   (a) (b) (c) (d) (e)

16.   (a) (b) (c) (d) (e)

ANSWERS

1	2	3	4	5	6	7	8	9	10
D	C	D	A	C	E	C	E	C	B

11	12	13	14	15	16
A	E	A	C	C	E

EXPLANATORY ANSWERS

1. In each step, all the elements move to the adjacent corner (of the square boundary) in a CW direction and the element that reaches the upper-left corner gets vertically inverted.

2. We can label the arcs as shown . The arcs get inverted in the sequence (1 & 2), (3, 4 & 5), (6 & 1), (2, 3 & 4), (5 & 6), ...

3. All the elements move half-a-side of the square boundary in ACW direction in each step. Also, first, third and fifth elements are replaced by new elements in one step and second, fourth and sixth elements are replaced by new elements in the next step. The two steps are repeated alternately.

4. In each step, the dot moves one space CW and the arrow moves two spaces CW.

5. One arc and four arcs get inverted alternately.

6. The number of parts increases by one along with the number of sides in the figure.

7. The pin rotates 45°CW and 90°CW alternately and moves one space (each space is equal to half-a-side of the square) and two spaces CW alternately. The arrow rotates 90°ACW and 45°ACW alternately and moves two spaces and one space.

8. In one step, the two elements interchange positions and the smaller element gets enlarged while the larger element gets reduced in size. In the next step, the smaller element is replaced by a new small element and the larger element is replaced by a new large element.

9. In each step, the elements move in the order .

10. The upper-left element gets laterally inverted in first, third, fifth. .... steps; the upper-right element gets rotated through 180° is first, fourth, seventh,.... steps; the lower-left element gets laterally inverted in second, fourth, sixth, ... steps; the lower-right element gets rotated through 180° in third, sixth,... steps and the pin at the middle-right position gets laterally inverted in every second step.

11. The shade in the top left square is moved one step clockwise till figure B and then reversed, the process is repeated. The shade in the top right square is moved one step anticlockwise till figure D and then reversed. The shade in the bottom left square is moved one step clockwise in alternate figures and the shade in bottom right square is moved one step clockwise after two figures. In figure 'A' the rule is isolated by the shade in the bottom left square.

12. In alternate figures a new circle is shaded clockwise. The pattern of the shade is also moved clockwise. In figure 'E' right half of the circle in the centre should have been shaded.

13. The three elements are placed either horizontally or vertically. In option 'A' neither of the placements can be applied.

14. The placement of elements is same in alternate figures. The number and type of elements is same in two subsequent figures. In this manner, figure 'C' should have four crosses and two C shapes.

15. *(c)* : The element is moved one step anticlockwise and the arc at one end is turned outside and inside alternately. In figure 'C' the element should be on the right side with the arc turned outside on the top side.

16. The left most element, line segment with the dot is moved one step towards right till figure C where it reaches the extreme right position. This process is repeated from figure D where the element on the extreme left, line segment with a circle, is moved. In figure 'E' the placement of the elements does not follow the rule of the series.

VENN DIAGRAMS

1. What is the number which is common to only two geometrical figures?

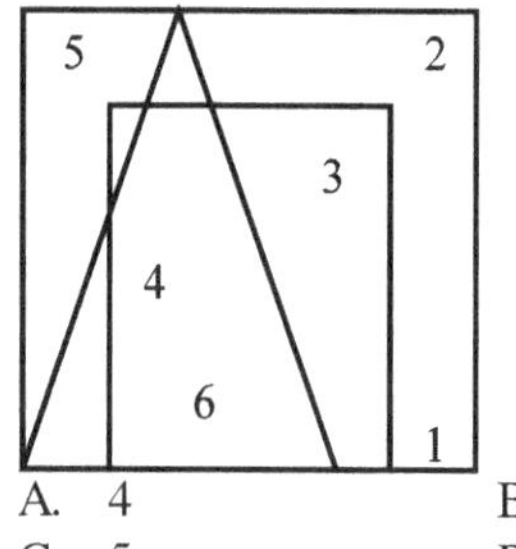

A. 4　　　　B. 3
C. 5　　　　D. 2

Directions (Qs. 2 and 3) : *In the following diagram, rectangle represents Hindi Announcers, circle represents English Announcers, square represents French Announcers, and triangle represents German Announcers.*

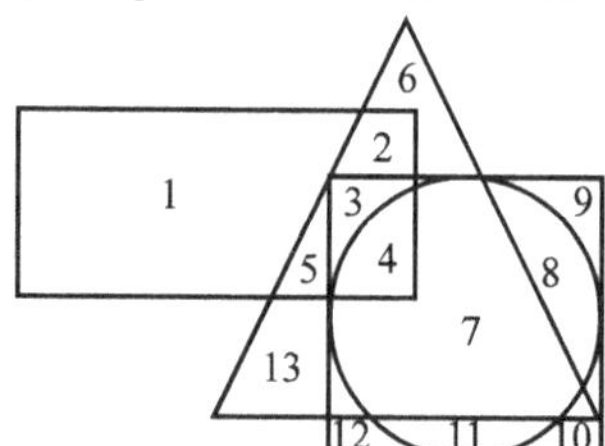

2. Which area represents those announcers who can present programmes in Hindi, French and German only?

A. 1   B. 2
C. 3   D. 4

3 Which area represents those announcers who can present programmes in French and English only?

A. 7   B. 9
C. 11   D. 13

Directions (Qs. 4 and 5) : *Study the diagram to answer these questions.*

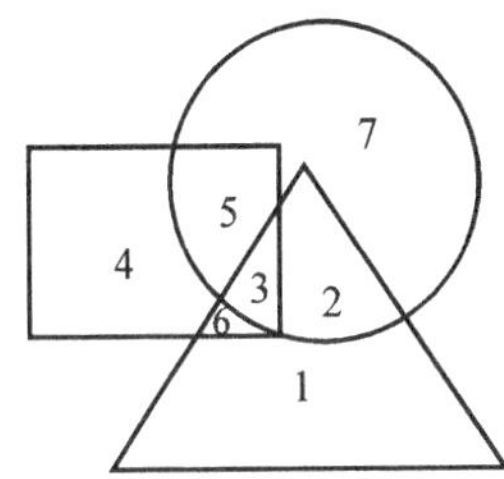

4. Which number is in all the geometrical figures?

A. 5   B. 6
C. 2   D. 3

5. Number 6 is in :

A. Rectangle and triangle
B. Circle and traingle
C. Rectangle and circle
D. Rectangle only

Directions (Qs. 6 to 9) : *In the following diagram*

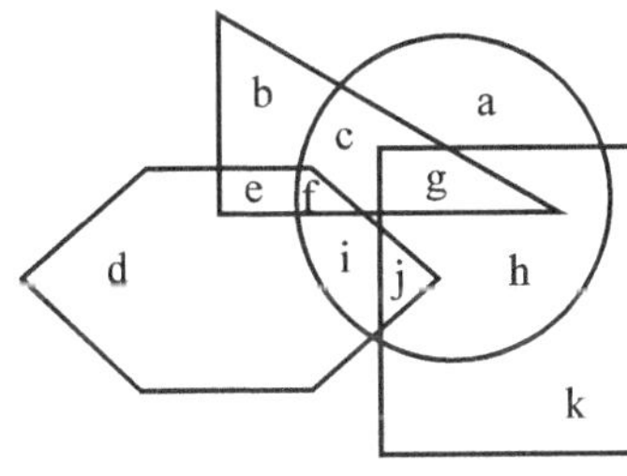

The Circle represents players
The Triangle represents outdoor games
The Hexagon represents indoor games and
The Square represents national level players
Study the diagram and answer the questions given below :

6. The letter in the section representing the players who play indoor games at national level is :

A. f   B. i
C. j   D. g

7. The letter representing the section of outdoor as well as indoor game players who do not play at the national level is :

A. c   B. f
C. e   D. i

8. The section representing national level players who do not play either outdoor or indoor games but still come under the category of players is :

A. k   B. g
C. c   D. h

9. Persons who play outdoor games but do not come under the category of players are represented in the section marked :

A. b   B. c
C. a   D. d

Directions (Qs. 10 to 13) : *Study the diagram given below.*

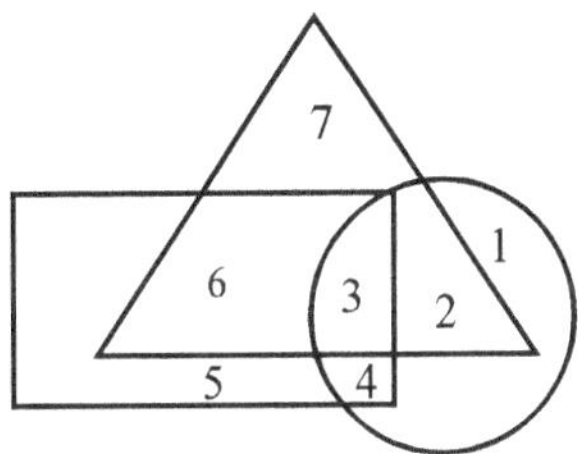

A college provides three different activities, students union represented by triangle, literary society represented by rectangle and social service league represented by circle.

10. Those who take part in both literary society and social service league but not in students union are represented by :

A. 3 & 4   B. 5 & 6
C. 5 & 1   D. 4

11. Those who take part in students union but not in social service league are represented by:

A. 2 & 7   B. 6 & 7
C. 6   D. 7

12. Those students who are members of literary society only and not of any other activity are represented by:

A. 2   B. 5
C. 3 & 4   D. 3

13. Those students who are members of all three groups are represented by :

A. 2   B. 3
C. 4   D. 6

ANSWERS

1	2	3	4	5	6	7	8	9	10
B	C	C	D	A	C	B	D	A	D

11	12	13
B	B	B

EXPLANATORY ANSWERS

1.

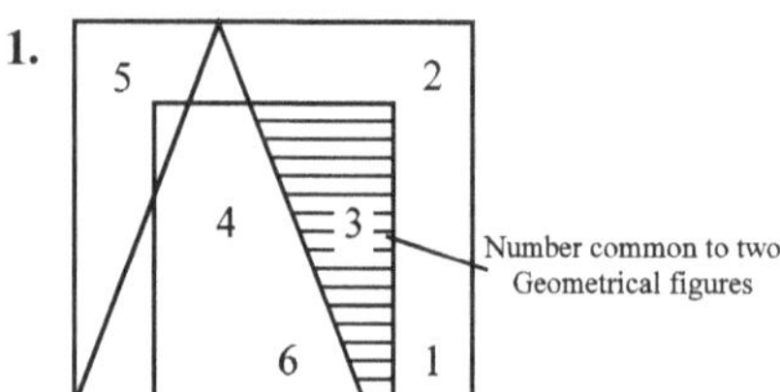

Note : Numbers 4 and 6 are common to all three geometrical figures.

Qs. 2 and 3.

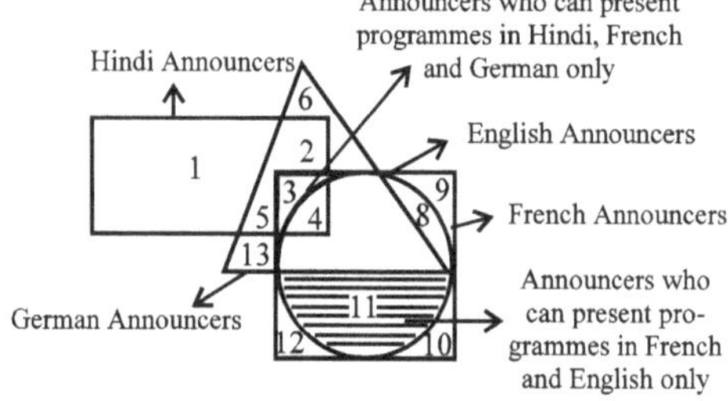

Qs. 4 and 5.

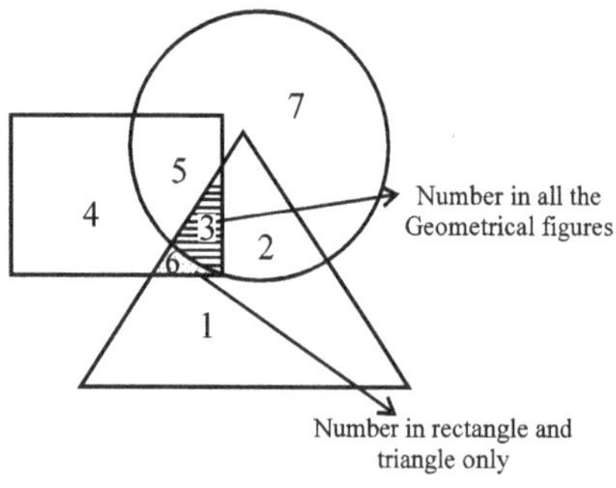

Qs. 6 to 9.

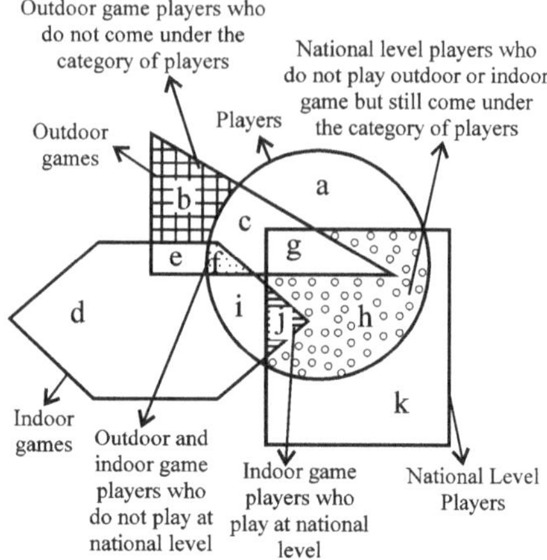

Qs. 10 to 13.

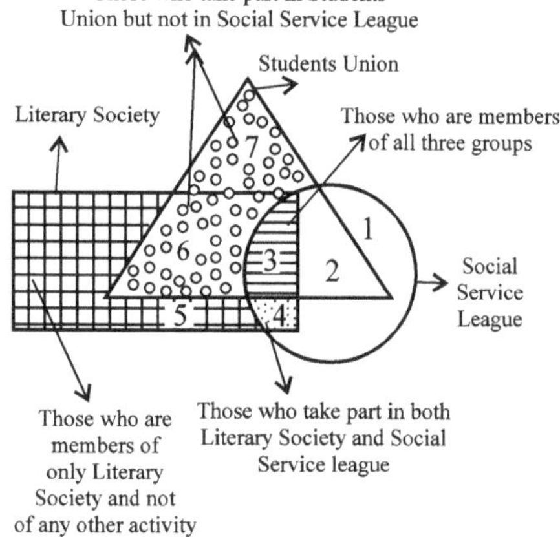

QUANTITATIVE APTITUDE

NUMBER SYSTEM

1. There are four numbers A, B, C and D. Average of the first three *i.e.*, A, B and C is 15 and that of B, C and D is 16. If the last number, *i.e.*, D is 19, then the first number is—
   A. 15   B. 16
   C. 17   D. 18

2. Of the three numbers, the first is twice the second and thrice the third. If the average of three is 22, the three numbers are—
   A. 12, 18, 36
   B. 18, 12, 36
   C. 36, 12, 18
   D. 36, 18, 12

3. If a person is standing on the sixth number in the queue from both the ends, the total persons in the queue are—
   A. 9   B. 11
   C. 12   D. 13

4. A number '*x*' when multiplied by 5 and added to three times its own gives 64, the number is—
   A. 8   B. 12
   C. 14   D. 18

5. A number which when multiplied by 11 is as much above 180 as it was originally below it. The number is—
   A. 25   B. 30
   C. 40   D. 45

6. The sum of a number and its reciprocal is thrice the difference of the number and its reciprocal. Find the number.
   A. $\sqrt{2}$ B. $\sqrt{3}$
   C. $\sqrt{5}$ D. $\sqrt{7}$

7. A boy was asked to find $\dfrac{7}{9}$ of a fraction. He made a mistake of dividing the fraction by $\dfrac{7}{9}$ and so got an answer which exceeded the correct answer by $\dfrac{8}{21}$. Find the correct answer.
   A. $\dfrac{2}{3}$ B. $\dfrac{5}{7}$
   C. $\dfrac{7}{12}$ D. $\dfrac{7}{15}$

8. There are 408 boys and 312 girls in a school, which are to be divided into equal sections of either boys or girls alone. Find the maximum number of boys or girls that can be placed in a section. Also find the total number of sections thus formed.
   A. 10, 20   B. 24, 30
   C. 24, 40   D. 30, 30

9. The sum of all possible two-digit number formed from three different one-digit natural numbers, when divided by the sum of the original three numbers is equal to—
   A. 11   B. 18
   C. 22   D. 36

10. There are four prime numbers written in ascending order. The product of the first three is 385 and that of the last three is 1001. The last number is—
    A. 19   B. 17
    C. 13   D. 11

11. If the number 357 ★ 25 ★ is divisible by both 3 and 5, then the missing digits in the unit's place and thousandth place respectively are—
    A. 0, 4   B. 5, 4
    C. 5, 6   D. 0, 6

12. The difference between two numbers is 1365. When the larger number is divided by the smaller one, the quotient is 6 and the remainder is 15. The smaller number is:
    A. 360   B. 295
    C. 270   D. 240

13. When a number is divided by 31, the remainder is 29. When the same number is divided by 16, what will be the remainder?
    A. 15   B. 13
    C. 11   D. Data inadequate

14. In dividing a number by 585, a student applied the method of short division. He divided the number successively by 5, 9 and 13 (factor of 585) and got the remainders 4, 8 and 12. If he had divided the number by 585, the remainder would have been:
    A. 584   B. 292
    C. 144   D. 24

15. When a number divided by 6 leaves a remainder 3. When the square of the same number is divided by 6, the remainder is:
    A. 3   B. 2
    C. 1   D. zero

ANSWERS

1	2	3	4	5	6	7	8	9	10
B	D	B	A	B	A	C	B	C	C

11	12	13	14	15
C	C	D	A	A

EXPLANATORY ANSWERS

1. $\dfrac{A+B+C}{3} = 15,$

or, $A + B + C = 15 \times 3 = 45$ ... *(i)*

$\dfrac{B+C+D}{3} = 16,$

or $B + C + D = 48$ ... *(ii)*

$D = 19$

$\therefore$ $B + C + 19 = 48$ or, $B + C = 48 - 19 = 29$

But, $A + B + C = 45$

Putting the value of $B + C = 29$ in the above equation *(i)*, we get $A + 29 = 45$

$\therefore A = 45 - 29 = 16.$

2. Let the third number $= x$

$\therefore$ First number $= 3x$

Second number $= \dfrac{3x}{2}$

$\therefore \dfrac{1}{3}\left[x + 3x + \dfrac{3x}{2}\right] = 22 \Rightarrow \dfrac{11}{2} x = 66$

$\Rightarrow x = \dfrac{66 \times 2}{11} = 12 =$ Third number,

$12 \times 3 = 36 =$ First number,

$\dfrac{12 \times 3}{2} = 18 =$ Second number.

3. If the person is standing at sixth number in the queue from both sides, that means there are five persons ahead and five persons behind him. Hence, total number of persons in the queue is $5 + 1 + 5 = 11$.

4. $5 \times x + 3x = 64 \Rightarrow 8x = 64$

$\therefore x = \dfrac{64}{8} = 8.$

5. Let the number is x

$\therefore 180 - x = 11x - 180$

$\Rightarrow 180 + 180 = 11x + x$

$\Rightarrow 360 = 12x,$

$\Rightarrow x = \dfrac{360}{12} = 30.$

6. Let the no. $= x$ then its reciprocal $= \dfrac{1}{x}$

By the question, $\left(x + \dfrac{1}{x}\right) = 3\left(x - \dfrac{1}{x}\right)$

$\Rightarrow \dfrac{x^2 + 1}{x} = \dfrac{3(x^2 - 1)}{x}$

$\Rightarrow x^2 + 1 = 3x^2 - 3$

$\Rightarrow 3x^2 - x^2 = 3 + 1$

$\therefore x = \sqrt{2}.$

7. Let the required fraction $= x$

then, by the question $x \div \dfrac{7}{9} - x \times \dfrac{7}{9} = \dfrac{8}{21}$

$\Rightarrow x \times \dfrac{9}{7} - \dfrac{7x}{9} = \dfrac{8}{21}$

$\Rightarrow \dfrac{32x}{63} = \dfrac{8}{21}$

$\Rightarrow x = \dfrac{8}{21} \times \dfrac{63}{32} = \dfrac{3}{4}$

Hence, the correct answer $= \dfrac{3}{4} \times \dfrac{7}{9} = \dfrac{7}{12}.$

8.
```
312) 408(1
     312
     ───
     96) 312 (3
         288
         ───
         24) 96 (4
             96
             ──
             ×
```

$\therefore$ Maximum number of girls or boys that can be placed in a section $= 24$ and total number of such

section $= \dfrac{408}{24} + \dfrac{312}{24}$

$= 17 + 13 = 30$

9. Let three different one digit natural numbers be x, y and z.

Then, sum of all possible two digits numbers

$= (10x + y) + (10y + x) + (10x + z)$
$\quad\quad + (10z + x) + (10y + z) + (10z + y)$

$= 22x + 22y + 22z = 22 (x + y + z)$

Hence, required number $= 22$.

10. Let four prime numbers be a, b, c and d respectively.

Now, $\dfrac{abc}{bcd} = \dfrac{385}{1001}$

$\Rightarrow \quad \dfrac{c}{d} = \dfrac{5}{13}$

Hence, $a = 5$ and $d = 13$

11. $357 \star 25 \star$

For divisible by 5, the last digit must be either 0 or 5.

If last digit is 0, then other required digit will be 2 or 5 or 8

Hence, the numbers are (0, 2) or (0, 5) or (0, 8)

If last digit is 5, then other required digit will be 0 or 3 or 6 or 9

Hence, the numbers are (5, 0) or (5, 3) or (5, 6) or (5, 9)

So, correct option is (c).

12. Here, $(x + 1365) = 6x + 15$

$\Rightarrow 5x = 1350$

$\therefore \quad x = \dfrac{1350}{5} = 270$

Hence, the smaller number = 270.

13. The number = $31x + 29$.

Here, given data is inadequate.

14.

$$\begin{array}{r|l} 5 & a \\ \hline 9 & b - 4 \\ \hline 13 & c - 8 \\ \hline & 1 - 12 \end{array}$$

Now, $c = 13 \times 1 + 12 = 25$

$b = 9c + 8 = 9 \times 25 + 8 = 233$

$a = 5b + 4 = 5 \times 233 + 4$

$\qquad\qquad = 1165 + 4 = 1169$

$1169 = 585 \times 1 + 584$

Hence, required remainder = 584.

15. The number = $6x + 3$

Now, $(6x + 3)^2 = 36x^2 + 36x + 9$

$\qquad\qquad = (36x^2 + 36x + 6) + 3$

$\qquad\qquad = 6(6x^2 + 6x + 1) + 3$

Hence, required remainder = 3.

LCM AND HCF

1. The L.C.M. and H.C.F. of two numbers are 4284 and 32 respectively. If one of the numbers is 204, the other is

A. 672   B. 576

C. 676   D. 572

2. Two numbers are in the ratio of 8 : 15. If their H.C.F. is 4, the numbers are

A. 32 and 60   B. 16 and 30

C. 80 and 150   D. 64 and 120

3. The greatest number that will divide 366, 513 and 324 leaving the same remainder in each case is

A. 21   B. 18

C. 27   D. 42

4. The L.C.M. of two numbers is 45 times their H.C.F. If the sum of the L.C.M. and the H.C.F. of these two numbers is 1150 and one of the numbers is 125, then the other number is

A. 256   B. 225

C. 250   D. 255

5. The H.C.F. and the L.C.M. of two numbers are 50 and 250 respectively. On dividing one of these numbers by 2, 50 is obtained as quotient. The numbrs are

A. 100, 125   B. 80, 100

C. 125, 100   D. 200, 250

6. Three bells ring respectively at an interval of 15 seconds, 20 seconds and 24 seconds. If they ring continuously for 12 minutes then how many times, during this period, will they ring together?

A. 2 times   B. 6 times

C. 5 times   D. 3 times

7. If the sum of two numbers is 55 and the H.C.F. and L.C.M. of these numbers are 5 and 120 respectively. Find the sum of their reciprocals.

A. $\dfrac{120}{11}$ B. $\dfrac{11}{120}$

C. $\dfrac{601}{55}$ D. $\dfrac{55}{601}$

8. The LCM of two numbers is 48. The numbers are in the ratio of 2 : 3. The sum of the numbers is

A. 64   B. 40

C. 32   D. 28

9. Find the greatest number that will divide 43, 91 and 183 so as to leave the same remainder in each case.

A. 13   B. 9

C. 7   D. 4

10. The greatest possible length which can be used to measure exactly the length 7m, 3m 85cm, 12m 95 cm is

A. 42 cm	B. 35 cm
C. 25 cm	D. 15 cm

11. A, B and C start at the same time in the same direction to run around a circular park. A completes a round in 252 seconds, B in 308 seconds and C in 198 seconds, all starting at the same point. After what time will they meet again at the starting point?
  A. 46 minutes 12 seconds
  B. 45 minutes
  C. 42 minutes 36 seconds
  D. 26 minutes 18 seconds

12. Which of the following has most numbers of divisors?

A. 182	B. 176
C. 101	D. 99

13. Which is of the following is a co-primes?
  A. $(23, 92)$ B. $(21, 35)$
  C. $(18, 25)$ D. $(16, 62)$

14. Let N be the greatest number that will divide 1305, 4665 and 6905, leaving the same remainder in each case. Then find the sum of the digits in N.
  A. 8   B. 6
  C. 5   D. 4

15. The greatest number which one dividing 1657 and 2037 leaves remainder 6 and 5 respectively, is:
  A. 305   B. 235
  C. 127   D. 123

ANSWERS

1	2	3	4	5	6	7	8	9	10
A	A	A	B	A	B	B	B	D	B

11	12	13	14	15
A	B	C	D	C

EXPLANATORY ANSWERS

1. 1st number × 2nd number = LCM × HCF
∴ 204 × 2nd number = 4284 × 32
∴ 2nd number $= \dfrac{4284 \times 32}{204} = 672$
∴ 2nd number = 672

2. Let the numbers be $8x$ and $15x$
$8x = 2 \times 2 \times 2 \times x$
$15x = 3 \times 5 \times x$
∴ LCM of $8x$ and $15x = 2 \times 2 \times 2 \times x \times 3 \times 5$
$= 120x$
Now, 1st number × 2nd number = HCF × LCM
$\Rightarrow 8x \times 15x = 4 \times 120x$
$\Rightarrow 120x^2 = 4 \times 120x$
$\Rightarrow x = 4$
∴ Numbers are $8 \times 4 = 32$ and $15 \times 4 = 60$

3. Difference between 366 and 513 = 513 − 366
$= 147$
and difference between 513 and 324
$= 513 - 324 = 189$
∴ HCF of 147 and 189

```
147) 189 (1
     147
  × 42) 147 (3
       126
    × 21) 42 (2
         42
        ×
```

∴ The required largest number is 21.

4. LCM of the two numbers = 45 × HCF
and LCM + HCF = 1150
$\Rightarrow 45 \times HCF + HCF = 1150$

$\Rightarrow$ HCF(45 + 1) = 1150
$\Rightarrow$ HCF $= \dfrac{1150}{46} = 25$
∴ LCM = 45 × 25 = 1125
∵ 1st number × 2nd number = LCM × HCF
∴ 125 × 2nd number = 1125 × 25
∴ 2nd number $= \dfrac{1125 \times 25}{125} = 225.$

5. According to the condition of the problem, 50 is obtained on dividing one of the numbers by 2
∴ One of the numbers = 50 × 2 = 100
Now, 1st number × 2nd number = LCM × HCF
∴ 100 × 2nd number = 250 × 50
∴ 2nd number $= \dfrac{250 \times 50}{100} = 125$
Hence, numbers are 100 and 125.

6. LCM of 15, 20 and 24

```
5 | 15, 20, 24
4 |  3,  4, 24
3 |  3,  1,  6
  |  1,  1,  2
```

LCM = 5 × 4 × 3 × 2 = 120
∵ 12 minutes = 12 × 60 = 720 seconds
∴ Number of times the bells will ring together during 12 minutes
$= \dfrac{720}{120} = 6$ times.

7. Let the number be x and y.

Then, $x + y = 55$;

$xy = $ HCF $\times$ LCM $= 5 \times 120$

$\therefore$ Sum of their reciprocals

$$= \frac{1}{x} + \frac{1}{y} = \frac{x+y}{xy} = \frac{55}{5 \times 120} = \frac{11}{120}.$$

8. Let the two numbers be $2x$ and $3x$;

their LCM $= 6x$

Now, $\quad 6x = 48 \qquad \therefore \quad x = 8$

Hence, the numbers are $2 \times 8, \quad 3 \times 8 = 16, 24$

Their sum $= 16 + 24 = 40$.

9.
```
  2240) 3360 (1        1120) 5600 (5
        2240                  5600
  1120 ) 2240 (2               ×
         2240
          ×
```

Hence, N = HCF of 3360,

$\qquad$ 2240 and 5600 = 1120

Sum of digits in N = 1 + 1 + 2 + 0 = 4.

10. 7m = 700 cm;

3m 85 = 385 cm;

12m 95cm = 1295 cm

```
  385) 700 (1
       385
       315) 385 (1
            315
             70) 315 (4
                 280
                  35 ) 70 (2
                       70
                        ×
     35) 1295 (37
         105
         245
         245
          ×
```

Hence, required length = HCF of 700 cm, 385 cm, 1295 cm = 35 cm.

11.

```
  2 | 252,  308,  198
  2 | 126,  154,   99
  3 |  63,   77,   99
  3 |  21,   77,   33
  7 |   7,   77,   11
 11 |   1,   11,   11
        1,    1,    1
```

Hence, LCM $= 2 \times 2 \times 3 \times 3 \times 7 \times 11 = 2772$

Hence, A, B, C will meet again at the starting point after 2772 sec. = 46 min 12 sec.

12.

Numbers	*Their divisors*
182	$\rightarrow$ 1, 2, 7, 13, 14, 26, 91 and 182
176	$\rightarrow$ 1, 2, 4, 8, 16, 22, 44, 88 and 176
101	$\rightarrow$ 1 and 101
99	$\rightarrow$ 1, 3, 9, 11, 33 and 99

Therefore, 176 has the most number of divisors.

13. HCF of 23 and 92 = 23

HCF of 21 and 35 = 7

HCF of 18 and 25 = 1

HCF of 16 and 62 = 2

Hence, 18 and 25 are co-prime numbers.

14. N = HCF of (4665 − 1305),

(6905 − 4665) and (6905 − 1305)

= HCF of 3360, 2240 and 5600 = 112

Sum of digit of 1 + 1 + 2 = 4.

15. Required number = HCF of (1657 − 6) and (2037 − 5)

= HCF of 1651 and 2032 = 127.

```
  1651) 2032 (1
        1651
        381) 1651 (4
             1524
             127) 381 (3
                  381
                   ×
```

AVERAGE

1. One-third of a certain journey was covered at the rate of 25 km per hour, one-fourth at the rate of 30 km per hour and the rest at the 50 km per hour. What is the average speed per hour for whole journey?

A. $33\frac{1}{3}$ kmph $\qquad$ B. $44\frac{1}{4}$ kmph

C. $22\frac{1}{2}$ kmph $\qquad$ D. 33 kmph

2. A batsman has a certain average of runs for 16 innings. In the 17th innings, he makes a score of 85 runs thereby increasing his average by 3. What is the average after the 17th inning?

A. 33 runs $\qquad$ B. 34 runs

C. 37 runs $\qquad$ D. 36 runs

3. The average of 6 observations is 12. A new seventh observation is included and the new average is decreased by 1. The seventh observation is

A. 1   B. 3
C. 5   D. 6

4. The average age of 30 students in a class is 12 years. The average age of a group of 5 of the students is 10 years and that of another group of 5 of them is 14 years. The average age of the remaining students is
A. 8 years   B. 10 years
C. 12 years   D. 14 years

5. Out of the three given numbers, the first number is twice the second and thrice the third. If the average of three numbers is 121, what is the difference between the first and third number?
A. 144   B. 77
C. 99   D. 132

6. If the average marks of three batches of 55, 60 and 45 students is 50, 55 and 60, then average marks of all the students is:
A. 55   B. 54
C. 54.68   D. 55.68

7. The average of 8 numbers is 20. The average of first two numbers is $15\frac{1}{2}$ and that of the next three is $21\frac{1}{3}$. If the sixth number is less than the seventh and eighth numbers by 4 and 7 respectively, then the eighth number is:
A. 27   B. 25
C. 22   D. 18

8. A pupil's marks were wrongly entered as 83 instead of 63. Due to that the average marks for the class got increased by half. What is the number of pupils in the class?
A. 73   B. 40
C. 40   D. 10

9. A cricketer whose bowling average is 12.4 runs per wicket takes 5 wickets for 26 runs and thereby decreases his average by 0.4. The number of wickets taken by him till the last match was:
A. 85   B. 80
C. 72   D. 64

10. The average weight of a class of 24 students is 35 kg. If the weight of the teacher is included, the average rises by 400 g. What is the weight of the teacher?
A. 55 kg   B. 53 kg
C. 50 kg   D. 45 kg

11. Nine men went to a hotel. Eight of them spent Rs. 3 for each over their meals and the ninth spent Rs. 2 more than the average expenditure of all the nine. What is the total money spent by them?
A. Rs. 29.25   B. Rs. 29.50
C. Rs. 29   D. Rs. 30

12. The average age of 24 students in a class is 10. If the teacher's age is included, the average increases by one. The age of the teacher is
A. 25   B. 30
C. 35   D. 40

13. The average of 5 consecutive even numbers A, B, C, D and E is 34. What is the product of B and D?
A. 1152   B. 1368
C. 1224   D. 1088

14. The average of 50 numbers is 30. If two numbers, 35 and 40 are discarded, then the average of the remaining numbers is nearly:
A. 29.68   B. 29.27
C. 28.78   D. 28.32

15. The average monthly salary of 20 employees of an organisation is Rs. 1500. If the manager's salary is added, then the average salary increases by Rs. 100. Find the manager's monthly salary?
A. Rs. 4800   B. Rs. 3600
C. Rs. 2400   D. Rs. 2000

ANSWERS

1	2	3	4	5	6	7	8	9	10
A	C	C	C	D	C	B	B	A	D

11	12	13	14	15
A	C	A	A	B

EXPLANATORY ANSWERS

1. Let the total distance covered during journey = 60 km

$\frac{1}{3}$ of the distance covered during journey

$$= 60 \times \frac{1}{3} = 20 \text{ km}$$

$\frac{1}{4}$ of the distance covered during journey

$$= \frac{1}{4} \times 60 = 15 \text{ km}$$

∴ The distance covered during the rest of journey = 60 – (20 + 15) = 25 km

Time taken to cover 20 km at 25 km/h

$$= \frac{20}{25} \text{ hours} = \frac{4}{5} \text{ hour}$$

Time taken to cover 15 km at 30 km/h

$$= \frac{15}{30} \text{ hours} = \frac{1}{2} \text{ hour}$$

Time taken to cover 25 km at 50 km/h

$$= \frac{25}{50} \text{ hours} = \frac{1}{2} \text{ hour}$$

Total time taken $= \dfrac{4}{5} + \dfrac{1}{2} + \dfrac{1}{2}$

$$= \frac{9}{5} \text{ hours}$$

Hence average speed per hour $= 60 \div \dfrac{9}{5}$

$$= \frac{60 \times 5}{9} = \frac{100}{3} \text{ km/h}$$

$$= 33\frac{1}{3} \text{ km/h}$$

2. Average increase in the score of 17 innings
$$= 3 \text{ runs}$$
Total increase in the score of 17 innings
$$= 3 \times 17 = 51 \text{ runs}$$
$\therefore$ His average of 16 innings $= 85 - 51$
$$= 34 \text{ runs}$$
Hence, average after the 17th innings
$$= 34 + 3 = 37 \text{ runs}$$

3. Seventh observation $= (7 \times 11 - 6 \times 12) = 5$

4. Let, the required average age be x
Then, $5 \times 10 + 5 \times 14 + 20 \times x = 30 \times 12$
$\Rightarrow \quad 20x = 360 - 120$
$\Rightarrow \quad 20x = 240$
$\Rightarrow \quad x = 12$

5. Let the three numbers be x, $\dfrac{x}{2}$ and $\dfrac{x}{3}$ respectively,

Now, $\dfrac{1}{3}\left(x + \dfrac{x}{2} + \dfrac{x}{3}\right) = 121$

$\Rightarrow \dfrac{11x}{6} = 121 \times 3$

$\therefore \quad x = \dfrac{121 \times 3 \times 6}{11} = 198$

Hence, required difference $= x - \dfrac{x}{3} = \dfrac{2x}{3}$

$$= \frac{2}{3} \times 198 = 132$$

6. Required average Marks

$$= \frac{55 \times 50 + 60 \times 55 + 45 \times 60}{55 + 60 + 45} = \frac{8750}{160} = 54.68$$

7. Let the sixth, seventh and eighth numbers are x, $x + 4$ and $x + 7$.
Sum of last three numbers

$$= 8 \times 20 - \left(2 \times \frac{31}{2} + 3 \times \frac{64}{3}\right)$$

$\Rightarrow x + x + 4 + x + 7 = 160 - 95$
$\Rightarrow 3x + 11 = 65$
$\Rightarrow 3x = 54 \qquad \therefore \ x = 18$
New eighth number $= x + 7 = 18 + 7 = 25$

8. Let the total number of pupils in the class be x; then,

$$\frac{83 - 63}{x} = \frac{1}{2} \quad \Rightarrow \quad \frac{20}{x} = \frac{1}{2} \qquad \therefore \ x = 40$$

9. Let the number of wickets taken by him be x till the last match.

Then, $\dfrac{x \times 12.4 + 26}{x + 5} = 12$

$\Rightarrow \ 12.4x + 26 = 12x + 60$

$\Rightarrow 0.4x = 34 \quad \therefore \ x = \dfrac{340}{4} = 85$

10. Let the weight of the teacher be x kgs, then

$$\frac{24 \times 35 + x}{25} = 35.4$$

$\Rightarrow \ 840 + x = 885 \qquad \therefore \quad x = 45 \text{ kgs}$

12. Age of the teacher $= (25 \times 11 - 24 \times 10)$ years
$$= 35 \text{ years}$$

13. Let 5 consecutive even numbers A, B, C, D and E be x, $x + 2$, $x + 4$, $x + 6$ and $x + 8$ respectively.

Now, $\dfrac{x + x + 2 + x + 4 + x + 6 + x + 8}{5} = 34$

$\Rightarrow 5x + 20 = 170$
$\Rightarrow 5x = 150 \qquad \therefore \ x = 30$
Then, $\ B = x + 2 = 30 + 2 = 32$;
$D = x + 6 = 30 + 6 = 36$
Hence, their product $= 32 \times 36 = 1152$

14. The average of remaining 48 numbers

$$= \frac{50 \times 30 - (35 + 40)}{48} = \frac{1500 - 75}{48}$$

$$= \frac{1425}{48} = 29.68$$

15. Let manager's salary be Rs. x, then

$$\frac{20 \times 1500 + x}{21} = 1600$$

$\Rightarrow \ 30,000 + x = 33600$
$\therefore \ x = \text{Rs. } 3600$

PROBLEMS BASED ON AGES

1. The ratio of ages of A and B is 3 : 11. After 3 years the ratio becomes 1 : 3. What are the ages of A and B?
   A. 9 years, 33 years
   B. 10 years, 40 years
   C. 9 years, 27 years
   D. None of these

2. Two years ago, the ratio of Ram's and Mohan's age was 3 : 2 and at present 7 : 5. What are their present ages?
   A. 14 years, 10 years
   B. 15 years, 10 years
   C. 13 years, 9 years
   D. None of these

3. The ages of Samir and Saurabh are in the ratio of 8 : 15 respectively. After 9 years the ratio of their ages will be 11 : 18. What is the difference between their ages in years?
   A. 20 years
   B. 21 years
   C. 22 years
   D. 24 years

4. The present age of father is 34 years more than that of his son. 12 years ago, father's age was 18 times the age of his son. The present age of son in years is:
   A. 12
   B. 14
   C. 16
   D. 18

5. A mother is 25 years older than her daughter. Five years ago, the age of the mother was 6 times the age of the daughter. What is the present age of mother?
   A. 25 years
   B. 29 years
   C. 32 years
   D. 35 years

6. The difference between the present ages of P and Q is 4 years. The ratio of their ages after 5 years will be 9 : 8. The present age of P is:
   A. 24 years
   B. 30 years
   C. 32 years
   D. None of these

7. Ten years ago, the age of Divya was half of the age of Namrata. If the ratio of present ages of both is 3 : 4, the sum of their present ages is:
   A. 35 years
   B. 30 years
   C. 25 years
   D. 18 years

8. The ratio between the present ages of A and B is 5 : 3 respectively. The ratio between A's age 4 years ago and B's age 4 years hence is 1 : 1. The ratio between A's age 4 years hence and B's age 4 years ago is:
   A. 4 : 1
   B. 3 : 1
   C. 2 : 1
   D. 1 : 3

9. Ram got married 8 years ago. His present age is $\frac{6}{5}$ times his age at the time of marriage. Ram's sister was 10 years younger to him at the time of his marriage. What is the present age of Ram's sister?
   A. 40 years
   B. 38 years
   C. 36 years
   D. 32 years

10. A father said to his son, "I was as old as you are at present at the time of your birth." If the father's age is 38 years now. Five years ago the age of son was:
    A. 38 years
    B. 33 years
    C. 19 years
    D. 14 years

ANSWERS

1	2	3	4	5	6	7	8	9	10
A	A	B	B	D	D	A	B	B	D

EXPLANATORY ANSWERS

1. Let the ages of A and B be $3x$ and $11x$ years; then
$$\frac{3x+3}{11x+3} = \frac{1}{3} \quad \Rightarrow \quad 9x + 9 = 11x + 3$$
$\Rightarrow 2x = 6 \quad \therefore \quad x = 3$
Hence, their present age, $3x = 3 \times 3 = 9$ years;
$11x = 11 \times 3 = 33$ years

2. Let the present ages of Ram and Mohan are $7x$ and $5x$ years; then
$$\frac{7x-2}{5x-2} = \frac{3}{2} \quad \Rightarrow \quad 14x - 4 = 15x - 6 \quad \therefore \quad x = 2$$
Hence, their present ages : $7 \times 2 = 14$ years and $5 \times 2 = 10$ years

3. Let the present ages of Samir and Saurabh are $8x$ and $15x$ years respectively; then
$$\frac{8x+9}{15x+9} = \frac{11}{18} \quad \Rightarrow \quad 144x + 162 = 165x + 99$$
$\Rightarrow 21x = 63 \quad \therefore \quad x = 3$
Hence, difference of their ages $= 15x - 8x = 7x$
$= 7 \times 3 = 21$ years

4. Let the present ages of father and his son be $x + 34$ and x years respectively; then

$18(x - 12) = x + 34 - 12$

$\Rightarrow 18x - 216 = x + 22$

$\Rightarrow 17x = 238 \qquad \therefore x = 14$

Hence, present age of his son = 14 years

5. Let the present ages of mother and her daughter are $(x + 25)$ and x years respectively; then

$6(x - 5) = x + 25 - 5$

$\Rightarrow \quad 6x - 30 = x + 20$

$\Rightarrow \qquad 5x = 50 \qquad \therefore x = 10$

Hence, the age of the mother = 10 + 25

$= 35$ years

6. Let the present ages of P and Q be $(x + 4)$ and x years; then, $\dfrac{x + 4 + 5}{x + 5} = \dfrac{9}{8} \quad \Rightarrow \quad 8x + 72$

$= 9x + 45 \qquad \therefore x = 27$

Hence, present age of P = 27 + 4 = 31 years

7. Let the present ages of Divya and Namrata are $3x$ and $4x$ years respectively; then

$\dfrac{3x - 10}{4x - 10} = \dfrac{1}{2}$

$\Rightarrow \quad 6x - 20 = 4x - 10$

$\Rightarrow \qquad 2x = 10 \quad \therefore x = 5$

Hence, sum of their ages = $3x + 4x = 7x$

$= 7 \times 5 = 35$ years

8. Let the present ages of A and B are $5x$ and $3x$ years respectively; then,

$\dfrac{5x - 4}{3x + 4} = 1 \qquad \Rightarrow \quad 5x - 4 = 3x + 4$

$\Rightarrow 2x = 8 \quad \therefore \quad x = 4$

Hence, their present ages are 20 years and 12 years.

So, required ratio = $(20 + 4) : (12 - 4)$

$= 24 : 8 = 3 : 1$

9. Let the present age of Ram be x years; then

$\dfrac{x}{x - 8} = \dfrac{6}{5} \qquad \Rightarrow \qquad 5x = 6x - 48$

$\therefore \quad x = 48$

Hence, present age of Ram's sister

$= 48 - 10 = 38$ years.

10. Let the age of father was x years at the time of his son's birth, then present age of father and his son will be $2x$ and x years,

Now, $\qquad 2x = 38 \qquad \therefore \quad x = 19$ years

Hence, 5 years ago the age of son was

$19 - 5 = 14$ years

CHAIN RULE

1. A fort has provision for 50 days. After 15 days a reinforcement of 150 men arrives and the provision now lasts 25 days. How many men were there in the fort?

  A. 300   B. 225

  C. 275   D. 200

2. In a fort there is provisions for 40 days for 275 persons. If after 16 days 125 persons leave the fort for how many more days the provisions will last?

  A. 35 days   B. 44 days

  C. 45 days   D. 53 days

3. 60 men could complete a work in 250 days. They worked together for 200 days. After that the work had to be stopped for 10 days due to bad weather. How many more men should be engaged to complete the work in time?

  A. 20   B. 18

  C. 15   D. 10

4. A contractor undertook to complete a project in 90 days and employed 60 men on it. After 60 days, he found that $\dfrac{3}{4}$ of the work has already been completed. How many men can he discharge so that the project may completed exactly on time?

  A. 15   B. 20

  C. 30   D. 40

5. A flagstaff 17.5 m high casts a shadow of length 40.25 m. The height of the building, which casts a shadow of length 28.75m under similar condition will be:

  A. 21.25 m   B. 17.5 m

  C. 12.5 m   D. 10 m

6. If 5 men or 9 women can do a piece of work in 19 days, then 3 men and 6 women will do the same work in how many days?

  A. 21   B. 18

  C. 15   D. 12

7. A certain number of men can finish a piece of work in 100 days. If there were 10 men less, it will take 10 days more for the work to be finished. How many men were there originally?

  A. 110   B. 100

  C. 82   D. 75

8. Some persons can do a piece of work in 12 days. Two times the number of such persons will do half of that work in:

A. 12 days   B. 3 days
C. 6 days   D. 4 days

9. 2 men and 7 boys can do a piece of work in 14 days; 3 men and 8 boys can do the same in 11 days. Then 8 men and 6 boys can do three times of this work in
A. 30 days   B. 4 days
C. 21 days   D. 18 days

10. If 3 men or 6 boys, working 7 hours a day can do a piece of work in 10 days; how many days will it take to complete a piece of work twice as large with 6 men and 2 boys working together for 8 hours a day?

A. 9   B. $8\dfrac{1}{2}$

C. $7\dfrac{1}{2}$ D. $6\dfrac{1}{2}$

11. If 15 men can do a certain amount of work in 20 days working 8 hours a day, in how many days will 10 men do three times the work working 6 hours a day?
A. 120 days   B. 70 days
C. 100 days   D. None of these

12. 40 men consume 60 kgs of rice in 15 days, then in how many days will 30 men consume 12 kgs of rice?

A. 9 days   B. $6\dfrac{1}{4}$ days

C. 4 days   D. $3\dfrac{1}{4}$ days

13. 56 men can complete a piece of work in 24 days. In how many days can 42 men complete the same piece of work?
A. 48   B. 32
C. 20   D. 16

14. Running at the same constant rate, 6 identical machines can produce a total of 270 bottles per minute. At this rate, how many bottles could 10 such machines produce in 4 minutes?
A. 1400   B. 1600
C. 1800   D. 2000

15. 400 persons, working 9 hours a day complete $\dfrac{1}{4}th$ of the work in 10 days. The number of additional persons, working 8 hours a day, required to complete the remaining work in 20 days, is:
A. 275   B. 250
C. 675   D. 200

ANSWERS

1	2	3	4	5	6	7	8	9	10
B	B	C	B	C	C	A	B	C	C

11	12	13	14	15
A	C	B	C	C

EXPLANATORY ANSWERS

1.

Days	Men
35↑	x ↓
25	$x+150$

$$\Rightarrow \frac{x+150}{x} = \frac{35}{25} \qquad \Rightarrow 1 + \frac{150}{x} = \frac{35}{25}$$

$$\Rightarrow \frac{150}{x} = \frac{10}{25}$$

$$\therefore x = \frac{25}{10} \times 150 = 375$$

Required number of men = 375 – 150 = 225

2.

Persons	Days
275↑	24 ↓
150	x

$$\Rightarrow \frac{x}{24} = \frac{275}{150} \qquad \therefore x = \frac{275}{150} \times 24 = 44 \text{ days}$$

3.

Days	Men
50↑	60 ↓
40	x

$$\Rightarrow \frac{x}{60} = \frac{50}{40} \qquad \therefore x = \frac{50}{40} \times 60 = 75 \text{ men}$$

Hence, number of additional men = 75 – 60
$$= 15$$

4.

Work	Days	Men
$\dfrac{3}{4}$ ↓	60 ↑	60 ↓
$\dfrac{1}{4}$	30	x

$$\Rightarrow \frac{x}{60} = \frac{60}{30} \times \frac{1/4}{3/4}$$

$$\therefore x = \frac{60}{30} \times \frac{1}{3} \times 60 = 40 \text{ days}$$

Hence, number of men to be discharged
$$= 60 - 40 = 20$$

5.

Shadow (m)	Object (m)
40.25	17.5
28.75	x

$$\Rightarrow \quad \frac{x}{17.5} = \frac{28.75}{40.25}$$

$$\therefore \quad x = \frac{28.75 \times 17.5}{40.25} = 12.5 \text{ m}$$

6. 5 men $\equiv$ 9 women

$$\therefore \quad 3 \text{ men} = \frac{9}{5} \times 3 = \frac{27}{5} \text{ women}$$

Hence, 3 men and 6 women $= \dfrac{27}{5} + 6$

$$= \frac{57}{5} \text{ women}$$

Women	Days
9	19
$\frac{57}{5}$	x

$$\Rightarrow \quad \frac{x}{19} = \frac{9 \times 5}{57}$$

$$\therefore \quad x = \frac{9 \times 5}{57} \times 19$$

$$= 15 \text{ days}$$

7.

Days	Men
100	x
110	$x - 10$

$$\Rightarrow \quad \frac{x-10}{x} = \frac{100}{110}$$

$$\Rightarrow \quad 110x - 1100 = 100x$$
$$\Rightarrow \quad 10x = 1100 \qquad \therefore \quad x = 110$$

Hence, initially the number of men = 110

8.

Work	Persons	Days
1	x	12
$\frac{1}{2}$	$2x$	a

$$\Rightarrow \quad \frac{a}{12} = \frac{x}{2x} \times \frac{1}{2} \qquad \therefore \quad a = \frac{1}{4} \times 12 = 3 \text{ days}$$

9. Here, 14×2 men $+ 14 \times 7$ boys $\equiv 11 \times 3$ men $+ 11 \times 8$ boys

$$\Rightarrow 28 \text{ men} + 98 \text{ boys} \equiv 33 \text{ men} + 88 \text{ boys}$$
$$\Rightarrow 5 \text{ men} = 10 \text{ boys}$$
$$\therefore 1 \text{ man} = 2 \text{ boys}$$

Then, 2 men and 7 boys $\equiv$ 4 boys + 7 boys
$$= 11 \text{ boys}$$

& also, 8 men and 6 boys $\equiv$ 16 boys + 6 boys
$$= 22 \text{ boys}$$

Work	Boys	Days
1	11	14
3	22	x

$$\Rightarrow \quad \frac{x}{14} = \frac{11}{22} \times \frac{3}{1}$$

$$\therefore \quad x = \frac{1}{2} \times 3 \times 14$$

$$= 21 \text{ days}$$

12.

Men	Rice (kgs)	Days
40	60	15
30	12	x

$$\Rightarrow \quad \frac{x}{15} = \frac{12}{60} \times \frac{40}{30}$$

$$\therefore \quad x = \frac{12}{60} \times \frac{40}{30} \times 15 = 4 \text{ days}$$

14.

Machines	Time (minutes)	Bottles
6	1	270
10	4	x

$$\Rightarrow \quad \frac{x}{270} = \frac{4}{1} \times \frac{10}{6}$$

$$\therefore \quad x = \frac{4 \times 10}{6} \times 270$$

$$= 1800 \text{ bottles}$$

15.

Work	Hours	Days	Persons
$\frac{1}{4}$	9	10	400
$\frac{3}{4}$	8	20	x

$$\Rightarrow \quad \frac{x}{400} = \frac{10}{20} \times \frac{9}{8} \times \frac{3/4}{1/4}$$

$$\therefore \quad x = \frac{1}{2} \times \frac{9}{8} \times 3 \times 400 = 675$$

Hence, number of additional persons
$$= 675 - 400 = 275$$

TIME AND DISTANCE

1. Starting from a point at a speed of 4 km/hr a man reaches at a cerain place and returns back to the point from where he had started journey on bicycle at the speed of 16 km/hr. His average speed during the entire journey will be :
   A. 6.4 km/h
   B. 8.4 km/h
   C. 5.4 km/h
   D. 10 km/h

2. A motorist covers a certain distance at a average speed of 48 km/h in 45 minutes. What speed in km/h he must maintain to cover the same distance in 30 minutes?
   A. 66 km/h
   B. 79 km/h
   C. 80 km/h
   D. 72 km/h

3. A policeman saw a thief at a distance of 200 m. The policeman and the thief started running at the same time. If the policeman runs at a speed of $4\frac{1}{6}$ m per second and the thief at a speed of $3\frac{1}{3}$ m per second, after what time the policeman will catch the thief?
   A. 12 min
   B. 10 min
   C. 9 min
   D. 4 min

4. A monkey wants to climb up a glazed pole. He climbs 12 metres in 1 minute and then he slips back 3 metres in the next minute. If the pole is 63 metre high, how long does he take to climb at the top of the pole?
   A. $11\frac{1}{4}$ min
   B. $12\frac{1}{2}$ min
   C. $12\frac{3}{4}$ min
   D. $14\frac{3}{4}$ min

5. The distance between two stations A and B is 300 km. A train leaves the station A with a speed of 40 km/hr. At the same time another train departs from the station B with a speed of 50 km/hr. How much time will these two trains take to cross each other?
   A. 3 hrs 40 min
   B. 3 hrs 20 min
   C. 2 hrs 20 min
   D. 3 hrs 45 min

6. Nilesh goes to school from his village at the speed of 4 km/hr and returns from school to village at the speed of 2 km/hr. If he takes 6 hours in all, then what is the distance between the village and the school?
   A. 8 km
   B. 6 km
   C. 5 km
   D. 4 km

7. By increasing the speed of the bus by 10 km/hr the time of journey for 72 km is reduced by 36 minutes. What was the original speed of the bus?
   A. 30 km/hr
   B. 35 km/hr
   C. 40 km/hr
   D. 45 km/hr

8. A train covers a distance in 50 minutes, if it runs at a speed of 48 km/hr on an average. The speed at which the train must run to reduce the time of journey to 40 minutes will be:
   A. 70 km/hr
   B. 60 km/hr
   C. 55 km/hr
   D. 50 km/hr

9. A certain distance is covered by a vehicle at a certain speed. If half of this distance is covered by another vehicle in double the time, the ratio of the speeds of the two vehicles is:
   A. 4 : 1
   B. 1 : 4
   C. 2 : 1
   D. 1 : 2

10. A is faster than B. A and B each walk 24 km. The sum of their speeds is 7 km/hr and sum of times taken by them is 14 hours. What is the speed of A?
    A. 7 km/hr
    B. 5 km/hr
    C. 4 km/hr
    D. 3 km/hr

ANSWERS

1	2	3	4	5	6	7	8	9	10
A	D	D	C	B	A	A	B	A	C

EXPLANATORY ANSWERS

1. Average speed during the entire journey
$$= \frac{2xy}{x+y} = \frac{2 \times 4 \times 16}{4+16} = \frac{8 \times 16}{20} = 6.4 \text{ km/hr.}$$

2. Let required speed be x km/hr; then
$$x \times \frac{1}{2} = 48 \times \frac{3}{4} \quad \therefore \quad x = 48 \times \frac{3}{4} \times 2$$
$$= 72 \text{ km/hr}$$

3. Suppose the policeman will catch the thief after t seconds

then, $\left(\dfrac{25}{6}-\dfrac{10}{3}\right)t = 200 \Rightarrow \dfrac{5}{6}t = 200$

$\therefore\ t = \dfrac{200 \times 6}{5} = 240$ sec $= 4$ min.

4. The monkey climbs 12 metres in 1 minute and then he slips back 3 metres in the next minute
$\therefore$ The monkey climbs in the first 2 minutes
$\qquad = 12 - 3 = 9$ metres
$\therefore$ In the first 12 minutes the monkey climbs
$\qquad = 9 \times 6 = 54$ metres
Remaining height of the pole to be covered by the monkey $= 63 - 54 = 9$ metre
$\therefore$ The monkey will climb the height of 9 metres in the 13th minute
$\because$ The monkey climbs 12 metres in 1 minute
$\therefore$ The monkey will climb 9 metres in $\dfrac{1}{12} \times 9$
$\qquad = \dfrac{3}{4}$ minute
$\therefore$ Time spent in climbing at the top of the pole
$\qquad = \left(12 + \dfrac{3}{4}\right)$ minutes $= 12\dfrac{3}{4}$ minutes

5. The two trains are moving in the opposite directions
$\therefore$ Relative speed $= 40 + 50 = 90$ km/hr.
$\therefore$ Time taken to cross each other $= \dfrac{300}{90} = 3\dfrac{1}{3}$ hours
or, 3 hours 20 minutes.

6. Let x km be the distance between village and the school; then
$$\dfrac{x}{4} + \dfrac{x}{2} = 6 \qquad\qquad \Rightarrow \dfrac{3x}{4} = 6$$
$\therefore\ x = \dfrac{6 \times 4}{3} = 8$ km

8. Let x km/hr be the required speed of the train; then
$$x \times \dfrac{40}{60} = 48 \times \dfrac{50}{60}$$
$\therefore\ x = \dfrac{48 \times 50}{40} = 60$ km/hr

9. Let x km/hr and t hr be the certain speed and certain time.
Then, ratio of their speeds $= \dfrac{x}{t} : \dfrac{x}{2 \times 2t} = 1 : \dfrac{1}{4} = 4 : 1$

10. Let speeds of A and B are x_1 and x_2 km/hr and times taken by them are t_1 and t_2 hrs, then
$$x_1 + x_2 = 7 \text{ km/hr} \qquad\qquad \text{...(i)}$$
$$t_1 + t_2 = 14 \text{ hrs} \qquad\qquad \text{...(ii)}$$
Now, $\dfrac{24}{x_1} + \dfrac{24}{x_2} = 14 \quad \Rightarrow \dfrac{24\left(x_1 + x_2\right)}{x_1 x_2} = 14$
$\therefore\ x_1 x_2 = \dfrac{24 \times 7}{14} = 12$
Then, $x_1 - x_2 = \sqrt{\left(x_1 + x_2\right)^2 - 4 x_1 x_2}$
$$\qquad\qquad = \sqrt{\left(7\right)^2 - 4 \times 12} = 1 \qquad \text{...(iii)}$$
Solving *(i)* and *(iii)* we get $x_1 = 4$ km/hr

TIME AND WORK

1. A and B working together complete a work in 35 days. If A takes 60 days to complete it, how long would B alone take to complete it?
   A. 64 days   B. 72 days
   C. 81 days   D. 84 days

2. A few children working together can do a piece of work in 18 days. If the number of children employed on the work is made double, how long would they take to complete half of the work?
   A. $4\dfrac{1}{2}$ days   B. $2\dfrac{1}{3}$ days
   C. $8\dfrac{3}{4}$ days   D. $6\dfrac{1}{2}$ days

3. 10 men or 18 boys can do a piece of work in 15 days. In how many days would 25 men and 15 boys complete the same work working together?
   A. $5\dfrac{1}{2}$ days   B. $4\dfrac{1}{2}$ days
   C. $6\dfrac{2}{3}$ days   D. $2\dfrac{1}{3}$ days

4. A cistern is filled by a tap in $3\dfrac{1}{2}$ hours. Due to a leak in the bottom of the cistern, it takes half an hour longer to fill the cistern. If the cistern is full, how long will it take the leak to empty it?
   A. 28 hours   B. 29 hours
   C. $31\dfrac{1}{3}$ hours   D. 38 hours

5. A is twice as good a workman as B and thrice as good a workman as C. If C alone can do a piece of work in 24 days, how long would the three persons take to finish the work working together?

A. $3\frac{3}{11}$ days   B. $4\frac{4}{7}$ days

C. $4\frac{4}{11}$ days   D. $3\frac{4}{11}$ days

6. If 3 men and 5 women can do a piece of work in 8 days and 2 men and 7 boys can do the same work in 12 days. Find the number of boys, the work done by whom can equate the work done by 10 women.

A. 19 boys   B. 21 boys
C. 23 boys   D. 15 boys

7. 8 men alone can complete a piece of work in 12 days. 4 women alone can complete the same piece of work in 48 days and 10 children alone can complete the piece of work in 24 days. In how many days can 10 men, 4 women and 10 children together complete the piece of work?

A. 6   B. 8
C. 10   D. 15

8. A works twice as fast as B. If B can complete a piece of work independently in 12 days. Find in how many days A and B together can complete the work?

A. 8 days   B. 6 days
C. 4 days   D. 18 days

9. A contractor undertook to complete a project in 90 days and employed 60 men on it. After 60 days, he found that $\frac{3}{4}$ of the work has already been completed. How many men can he discharge so that the project may be completed exactly on time?

A. 15   B. 20
C. 30   D. 40

10. A can do a piece of work in 25 days and B can do it in 20 days. They work together for 5 days and then A goes away. In how many days will B finish the remaining work?

A. 33 days   B. 20 days
C. 11 days   D. 10 days

ANSWERS

1	2	3	4	5	6	7	8	9	10
D	A	B	A	C	B	A	C	B	C

EXPLANATORY ANSWERS

1. (A + B)'s 1 day's work = $\frac{1}{35}$

and also, A's 1 day's work = $\frac{1}{60}$

Hence, B's 1 day's work = $\frac{1}{35} - \frac{1}{60} = \frac{5}{420} = \frac{1}{84}$

So, B will do the whole work in 84 days.

3. 10 men $\equiv$ 18 boys

25 men $\equiv \frac{18}{10} \times 25 = 45$ boys

Hence, 25 men + 15 boys = 45 + 15 = 60 boys
Now, 18 boys can do a piece of work in 15 days.

Hence, 60 boys will do a piece of work in $\frac{15 \times 18}{60} = \frac{9}{2}$

days = $4\frac{1}{2}$ days.

4. In 1 hour $\frac{2}{7}$ cistern is filled by the tap.

Hence, in $\frac{1}{2}$ hour $\frac{2}{14} = \frac{1}{7}$ cistern is filled by the tap.

So, $\frac{1}{7}$ cistern is emptied by the leakage in 4 hours.

So, 1 cistern will be emptied by the leakage in 28 hours.

6. Here, (3 men + 5 women) × 8
$\equiv$ (2 men + 7 boys) × 12
$\Rightarrow$ 40 women $\equiv$ 84 boys

$\therefore$ 10 women $\equiv \frac{84}{40} \times 10 = 21$ boys

Hence, work done by 10 women
= work done of 21 boys.

7. B's 1 day's work = $\frac{1}{4} - \frac{1}{12} = \frac{2}{12} = \frac{1}{6}$

Hence, B alone will complete the work in 6 days.

8. Ratio of efficiency of A and B = 2 : 1
Then, ratio of their time taking = 1 : 2
Hence, if B can complete the work in 12 days, then A in 6 days.

Now, (A + B)'s 1 day's work = $\frac{1}{6} + \frac{1}{12} = \frac{3}{12} = \frac{1}{4}$

So, A and B together can complete the work in 4 days.

9. After 60 days remaining work $= 1 - \dfrac{3}{4} = \dfrac{1}{4}$

In 60 days $\dfrac{3}{4}$ work has been done by 60 men

In 30 days $\dfrac{1}{4}$ work will be done by $60 \times \dfrac{4}{3} \times \dfrac{1}{4} \times \dfrac{60}{30}$

$= 40$ men.

Hence, required number of men $= 60 - 40 = 20$ (which are to be discharged).

BOATS AND STREAMS

1. A boat goes 6 km upstream and back to the starting point in 2 hours. If the current of the stream runs at the rate of 4 km/hr, find the speed of the boat in still water.
   A. 6 km/hr   B. 8 km/hr
   C. 10 km/hr   D. 12 km/hr

2. A boat covers 24 km upstream and 36 km downstream in 6 hours, while it covers 36 km upstream and 24 km downstream in 6½ horus. Find the speed of the current.
   A. 2 km/hr   B. 4 km/hr
   C. 6 km/hr   D. 8 km/hr

3. A man can row 5 km/hr in still water and the speed of the stream is 1.5 km/hr. He takes an hour when he travels upstream to a place and back again to the starting point. How far is the place from the starting point?
   A. 2.275 km   B. 3.5 km
   C. 1.5 km   D. None of these

4. The speed of a boat in still water is 6 km/hr and the speed of the stream is 1.5 km/hr. A man rows to a place at a distance of 22.5 km and comes back to the starting point. Find the total time taken by him.
   A. 8 hours   B. 10 hours
   C. 12 hours   D. 4 hours

5. A boat covers 20 km downstream and 6 km upstream in 3 hours, while it covers 30 km downstream and 12 km upstream in 5 hours. What is the speed of boat in still water?
   A. 6 km/hr   B. 8 km/hr
   C. 10 km/hr   D. 12 km/hr.

6. Samir can travel 12 miles downstream in a certain river in 6 hours less than it takes him to travel the same distance upstream. But when he could double his rowing rate for his 24-mile round trip, the downstream 12 miles would then take only one hour less than the upstream 12 miles. Find the speed of the current in miles/hour.
   A. $2\dfrac{2}{3}$ B. $2\dfrac{1}{3}$
   C. $1\dfrac{2}{3}$ D. $1\dfrac{1}{3}$

7. A boat takes 6 hours to travel from place M to N downstream and back from N to M upstream. If the speed of the boat in still water is 4 km/hr; what is the distance between two places?
   A. 6 kms   B. 8 kms
   C. 12 kms   D. Data inadequate

8. A man can row upstream at 8 km/hr and downstream at 13 km/hr. The speed of the stream is:
   A. 2.5 km/hr   B. 4.2 km/hr
   C. 5 km/hr   D. 10.5 km/hr

9. A man's speed with the current is 15 km/hr and the speed of the current is 2.5 km/hr. The man's speed against the current is:
   A. 12.5 km/hr   B. 10 km/hr
   C. 9 km/hr   D. 8.5 km/hr

10. A motorboat, whose speed is 15 km/hr in still water goes 30 km downstream and comes back in a total of 4 hours 30 minutes. What is the speed of the stream (in km/hr)?
   A. 10   B. 6
   C. 5   D. 4

ANSWERS

1	2	3	4	5	6	7	8	9	10
B	A	A	A	B	B	D	A	B	C

EXPLANATORY ANSWERS

1. Let the speed of a boat in still water $= x$ km/hr; then

$$\frac{6}{x-4}+\frac{6}{x+4}=2 \quad \Rightarrow \quad \frac{2x}{x^2-16}=\frac{1}{3}$$

$$\Rightarrow x^2 - 6x - 16 = 0$$

$$\Rightarrow (x-8)(x+2) = 0$$

Hence, the speed of the boat = 8 km/hr.

2. Let x km/hr and y km/hr be the speeds of the boat in still water and the speed of the current respectively, then

$$\frac{24}{x-y}+\frac{36}{x+y}=6 \Rightarrow \frac{4}{x-y}+\frac{6}{x+y}=1 \quad ...(i)$$

And, $\quad \dfrac{36}{x-y}+\dfrac{24}{x+y}=\dfrac{13}{2} \qquad ...(ii)$

Solving these two equations, we get

$$x + y = 12; \; x - y = 8$$

Hence, $y = \dfrac{1}{2}(12-8)=2$ km/hr.

3. Let required distance be x km, then

$$\frac{x}{5-1.5}+\frac{x}{5+1.5}=1 \Rightarrow \frac{x \times 2}{7}+\frac{x \times 2}{13}=1$$

$$\Rightarrow 40x = 91 \qquad \therefore x = 91/40 = 2.275 \text{ km}$$

4. Required time period $= \dfrac{22.5}{6+1.5}+\dfrac{22.5}{6-1.5}$

$$= \frac{45}{15}+\frac{45}{9} = 8 \text{ hours.}$$

5. Let x km/hr and y km/hr be the speed of boat in still water and speed of current respectively; then

$$\frac{20}{x+y}+\frac{6}{x-y}=3 \qquad\qquad ...(i)$$

and also, $\quad \dfrac{30}{x+y}+\dfrac{12}{x-y}=5$

$$\Rightarrow \frac{15}{x+y}+\frac{6}{x-y}=\frac{5}{2} \qquad ...(ii)$$

Solving equations *(i)* & *(ii)*, we get $x + y = 10$ and $x - y = 6$

Since, $x = \dfrac{1}{2}(10 + 6) = 8$ km/hr.

6. Let x km/hr and y km/hr be the speed of rowing in still water and speed of the current respectively; then

$$\frac{12}{x-y}-\frac{12}{x+y}=6 \Rightarrow \frac{24y}{x^2-y^2}=6$$

$$\Rightarrow x^2 = y^2 + 4y \qquad\qquad ...(i)$$

Again, $\quad \dfrac{12}{2x-y}-\dfrac{12}{2x+y}=1$

$$\Rightarrow \frac{24y}{4x^2-y^2}=1 \Rightarrow x^2 = \frac{y^2+24y}{4} \qquad ...(ii)$$

From equations (i) and (ii), we get

$$y^2 + 4y = \frac{y^2+24y}{4} \Rightarrow 3y^2 = 8y$$

$$\therefore \; y = \frac{8}{3} = 2\frac{1}{3} \text{ miles/hr.}$$

8. The speed of the stream $= \dfrac{1}{2}(13 - 8) = \dfrac{5}{2}$

$$= 2.5 \text{ km/hr.}$$

9. The man's speed in still water

$$= 15 - 2.5 = 12.5 \text{ km/hr}$$

Hence, the men's speed against the current

$$= 12.5 - 2.5 = 10 \text{ km/hr}$$

10. Let speed of the stream be x km/hr, then

$$\frac{30}{15+x}+\frac{30}{15-x}=4\frac{1}{2} \Rightarrow \frac{30 \times 30}{225-x^2}=\frac{9}{2}$$

$$\Rightarrow \frac{200}{225-x^2}=1 \qquad \Rightarrow x^2 = 225 - 200$$

$$\Rightarrow x^2 = 25 \qquad\qquad \therefore \; x = 5 \text{ km/hr.}$$

ALLIGATION OR MIXTURE

1. A shopkeeper buys 26 kgs of milk @ Rs. 16 per kg. He also buys from another source an inferior quality of milk @ Rs. 10 per kg. How much quantity of the latter should he buy to mix it with the former so that he can sell the mixture @ Rs. 14 per kg without making any loss?

   A. 13 kgs   B. 12 kgs

   C. 14 kgs   D. 16 kgs

2. Two vessels A and B contain mixture of milk and water in the ratio 4 : 1 and 9 : 11 respectively. They are mixed in the ratio of 3 : 2. Find the ratio of milk : water in the resulting mixture.

  A. 34 : 16   B. 33 : 17
  C. 16 : 34   D. 17 : 33

3. A shopkeeper has 50 kgs of rice. He sells a part of it at 20% profit and the rest at 40% profit. If he gains 25% on the whole, find the quantity of each part.

  A. 12.5 kgs and 37.5 kgs
  B. 37.5 kgs and 12.5 kgs
  C. 23.5 kgs and 21.5 kgs
  D. 21.5 kgs and 23.5 kgs

4. A man bought a certain quantity of sugar for Rs. 8000. He sells one-fourth of it at 20% loss. At what per cent profit should he sell the remainder stock so as to make an overall profit of 20%?

  A. 20%   B. 30%
  C. 35%   D. 40%

5. Rs. 675 was divided among 75 boys and girls. Each boy gets Rs. 20 whereas a girl gets Rs. 5. Find the number of boys and girls.

  A. 20, 55   B. 15, 60
  C. 25, 50   D. 30, 45

6. A vessel contains mixture of liquids A and B in the ratio 3 : 2. When 20 litres of the mixture is taken out and replaced by 20 litres of liquid B, the ratio changes to 1 : 4. How many litres of liquid A was there initially present in the vessel?

  A. 12 litres   B. 18 litres
  C. 24 litres   D. 22 litres

7. A container is full of milk. One-third of milk is taken out of it and replaced by same quantity of water. Then again one-third of the mixture is taken out of it and replaced by the same quantity of water. The process is repeated 4 times. If 16 litres of milk is left in the container at the end of 4th operation, find the capacity of the container.

  A. 76 litres   B. 81 litres
  C. 82 litres   D. 85 litres

8. The cost of type-I rice is Rs. 15 per kg and type-II is Rs. 20 per kg. If both type I and type II are mixed in the ratio of 2 : 3, then find the price per kg of the mixed variety.

  A. Rs. 19.50   B. Rs. 19
  C. Rs. 18.50   D. Rs. 18

9. In what ratio must a grocer mix two varieties of tea worth Rs. 60 a kg and Rs. 65 a kg so that by selling the mixture at Rs. 68.20 a kg he may gain 10%?

  A. 4 : 5   B. 3 : 5
  C. 3 : 4   D. 3 : 2

10. A vessel contains 80 litres of milk. 16 litres of milk was taken out of the vessel and replaced by water. Then 16 litres of mixture was withdrawn and again replaced by water. The operation was repeated for third time. How much milk is now left in the vessel?

  A. 96.40 litres
  B. 50.36 litres
  C. 40.96 litres
  D. 32.76 litres

ANSWERS

1	2	3	4	5	6	7	8	9	10
A	B	B	B	A	B	B	D	D	C

EXPLANATORY ANSWERS

1. 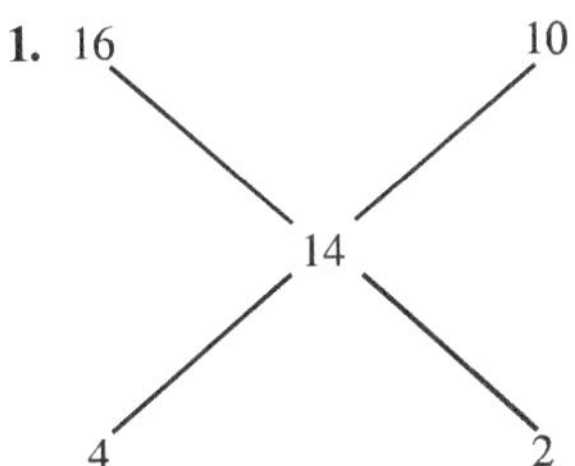

or 2 : 1 $\dfrac{\text{Quantity of milk @ Rs.10 per kg}}{\text{Quantity of milk @ Rs. 16 per kg}} = \dfrac{1}{2}$

So, quantity of milk @ Rs. 10 per kg. $= \dfrac{26}{2} = 13$ kgs.

2. Fraction is

               Milk   *Water*

A : $\dfrac{4}{5}$ $\dfrac{1}{5}$

B : $\dfrac{9}{20}$ $\dfrac{11}{20}$

$(3A + 2B) = A \text{ and } B : \left(\dfrac{12}{5}+\dfrac{9}{10}\right)\left(\dfrac{3}{5}+\dfrac{11}{10}\right)$

                                   $\dfrac{33}{10}$ $\dfrac{17}{10}$

So, Ratio of milk : water in the resulting mixture
                 = 33 : 17.

3. 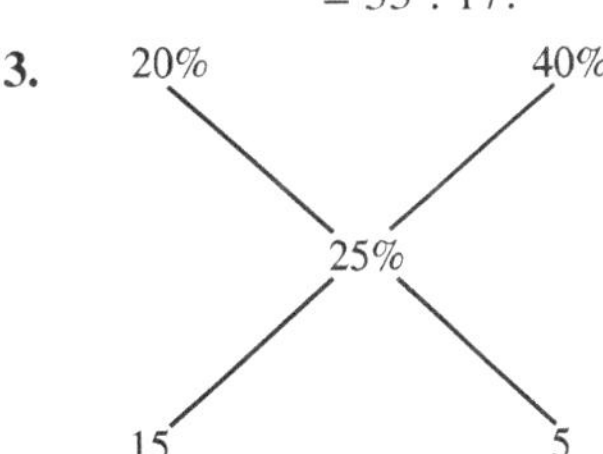

or 3 : 1

$$\text{Quantity sold at 20\% profit} = \frac{3}{3+1} \times 50$$
$$= 37.5 \text{ kgs.}$$
$$\text{Quantity sold at 40\% profit} = (50 - 37.5)$$
$$= 12.5 \text{ kgs.}$$

4. Let the remainder stock be sold at $x\%$ profit.

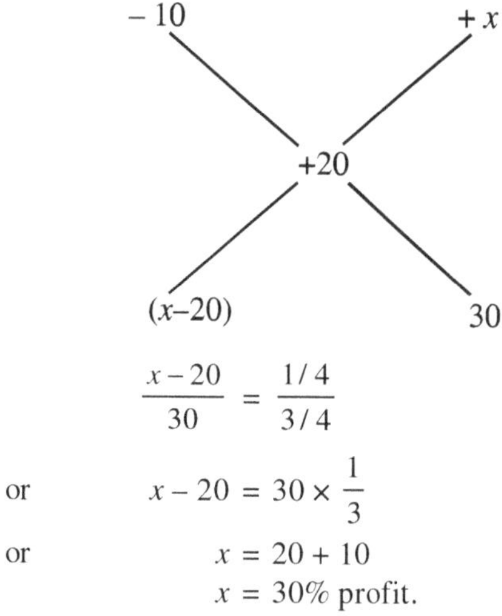

$$\frac{x - 20}{30} = \frac{1/4}{3/4}$$

or $\qquad x - 20 = 30 \times \dfrac{1}{3}$

or $\qquad x = 20 + 10$
$$x = 30\% \text{ profit.}$$

5. Average money per head (boy or girl)
$$= \text{Rs.} \frac{675}{75} = \text{Rs. } 9$$

$$\frac{4}{4+11} \times 75 = 20$$

Number of boys $= \dfrac{4}{4+11} \times 75 = 20$

Number of girls $= \dfrac{11}{4+11} \times 75 = 55.$

6. % of liquid B initially present in the vessel
$$= \frac{2}{3+2} \times 100 = 40\%$$

% of liquid B finally present in the vessel
$$= \frac{4}{1+4} \times 100 = 80\%$$

The second solution is liquid B which is being mixed and it has 100% liquid B.

80% of liquid B present in the resultant mixture may be taken as average percentage. So, using rule of alligation on liquid B per cent, we can write,

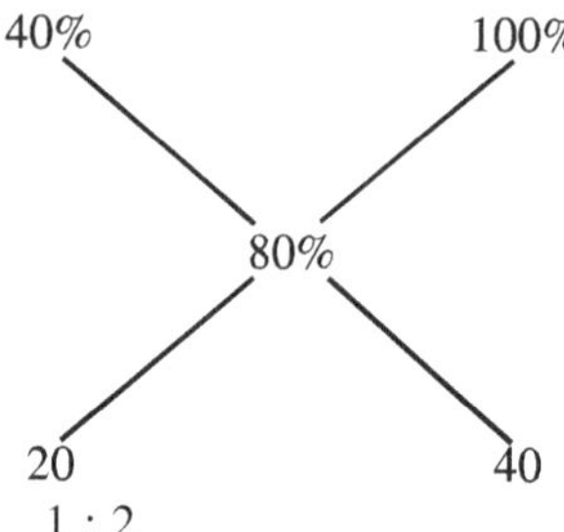

or $\qquad 1 : 2$

The ratio of liquid left in the vessel to liquid B being mixed = 1 : 2

Since the quantity of liquid B being mixed is 20 litres, the quantity of liquid left in the vessel is 10 litres. Therefore, the total quantity of liquid initially present in the vessel
$$= 10 + 20 = 30 \text{ litres}$$

$$\text{Quantity of liquid A} = \frac{3}{2+3} \times 30 = 18 \text{ litres.}$$

7. Let capacity of the container be x litre; then

$$x(1 - 1/3)^4 = 16 \quad \Rightarrow \quad x\left(\frac{2}{3}\right)^4 = 16$$

$$\Rightarrow x \times \frac{16}{81} = 16 \qquad \therefore \ x = 81 \text{ litres}$$

8. Let the price per kg of mixed variety be Rs. x; then

By the rule of alligation,

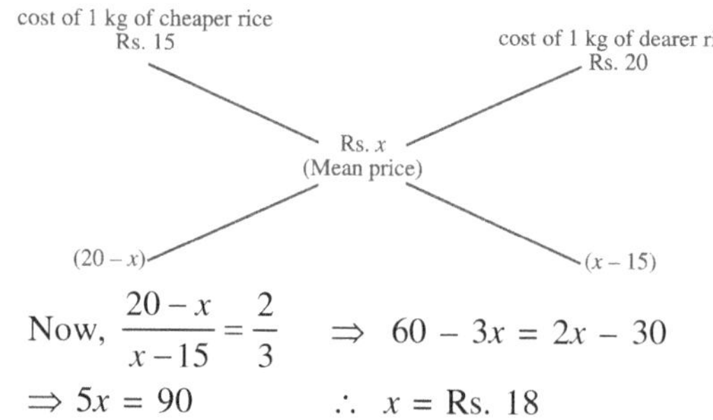

Now, $\dfrac{20 - x}{x - 15} = \dfrac{2}{3} \quad \Rightarrow \quad 60 - 3x = 2x - 30$

$\Rightarrow 5x = 90 \qquad \therefore \ x = \text{Rs. } 18$

9. S.P. of 1 kg mixture = Rs. 68.20, Gain % = 10%

Hence, C.P. of 1 kg mixture $= \dfrac{100}{110} \times \text{Rs. } 68.20$

$$= \text{Rs. } 62$$

By the rule of alligation

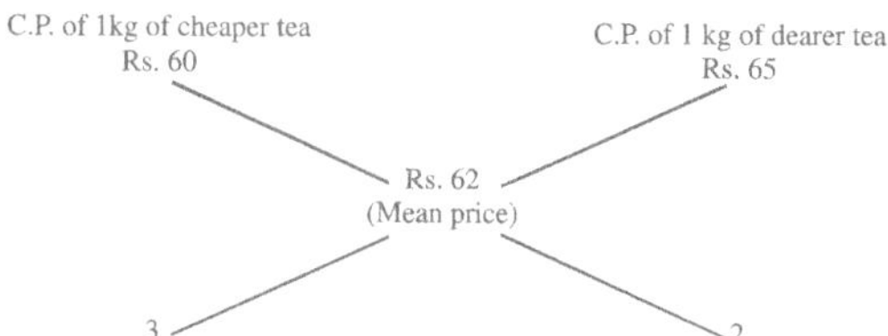

Hence, required ratio = 3 : 2

10. Amount of milk left $= 80 \left(1 - \dfrac{16}{80}\right)^3 = 80 \left(\dfrac{4}{5}\right)^3$

$$80 \times \frac{64}{125} = 40.96 \text{ litres.}$$

PERCENTAGE

1. A student who secures 20% marks in an examination fails by 30 marks. Another student who secures 32% gets 42 marks more than those required to pass. The percentage of marks required to pass is:
   A. 20
   B. 25
   C. 28
   D. 30

2. In a college election, a candidate secured 62% of the votes and is elected by a majority of 144 votes. The total number of votes polled is:
   A. 600
   B. 800
   C. 925
   D. 1200

3. In an organisation, 40% of the employees are matriculates, 50% of the remaining are graduates and the remaining 180 are postgraduates. How many employees are graduates?
   A. 360
   B. 240
   C. 300
   D. 180

4. The population of a village is 4500. $\frac{5}{9}$ th of them are males and rest females. If 40% of the males are married, then the percentage of married female is :
   A. 35
   B. 40
   C. 50
   D. 60

5. A's income is 10% more than B's. How much per cent is B's income is less than A's?
   A. 10%
   B. 7%
   C. $9\frac{1}{11}\%$
   D. $6\frac{1}{2}\%$

6. If the price of a television set is increased by 25%, then by what percentage should the new price be reduced to bring the price back to original level?
   A. 15%
   B. 20%
   C. 25%
   D. 30%

7. In an election one of the two candidates gets 40% votes and loses by 100 votes. Total number of votes is :
   A. 500
   B. 400
   C. 600
   D. 1000

8. The gross income of a person is Rs. 20000. 10% of his income is exempted from income tax and his net income is Rs. 19100. The rate of income tax is :
   A. 3%
   B. 2%
   C. 4%
   D. 5%

9. The owner of a cell phone shop charges his customer 32% more than the cost price. If a customer paid Rs. 6600 for the cell phone, then what was the cost price of the cell phone?
   A. Rs. 5000
   B. Rs. 5500
   C. Rs. 5800
   D. Rs. 6100

10. If the cost of pins reduced by Rs. 4 per dozen, 12 more pins can be purchased for Rs. 48. The cost of pins per dozen after reduction is:
    A. Rs. 8
    B. Rs. 12
    C. Rs. 16
    D. Rs. 20

11. In an examination 80% of the students passed in Mathematics and 70% passed in English, while 10% students failed in both the subjects. If 360 students passed in both the subjects, find the total number of students who appeared in the examination.
    A. 400
    B. 600
    C. 630
    D. 640

12. Electric tax is increased by 20% and its consumption is decreased by 20%. The change in the expenditure is:
    A. 4% decrease
    B. 4% increase
    C. 5% decrease
    D. 5% increase

13. The selling price of certain commodity was reduced by 25%. As a result of it, the sales increased by 30%. What was the effect of it on cash collected by daily sales?
    A. 2.5% decrease
    B. 2.5% increase
    C. 5% decrease
    D. 5% increase

14. The wheat sold by a grocer contained 10% low quality wheat. What quantity of good quality wheat should be added to 150 kgs of wheat so that the percentage of low quality wheat becomes 5%?
    A. 50 kgs
    B. 85 kgs
    C. 135 kgs
    D. 150 kgs

15. Nilam spends 15% of her monthly income on household expenses. She spends 17% of the monthly income in travelling and 6% on medical expenses and saves the rest Rs. 15,500. What is her monthly income?
    A. Rs. 20,000
    B. Rs. 25,000
    C. Rs. 30,000
    D. Rs. 35,000

ANSWERS

1	2	3	4	5	6	7	8	9	10
B	A	D	C	C	B	A	D	A	B

11	12	13	14	15
B	A	A	D	B

22

EXPLANATORY ANSWERS

1. $\quad$ 20% of $x + 30 = 32$% of $x - 42$

$\Rightarrow \qquad$ 12% of $x = 72$

$\Rightarrow \qquad x = \dfrac{72 \times 100}{12} = 600$

Pass Mark $= 20$% of $600 + 30 = 150$

Pass percentage $= \left(\dfrac{150}{600} \times 100\right)\% = 25\%$

2. (62% of $x - 38$% of $x) = 144$

$\Rightarrow$ 24% of $x = 144 \quad \Rightarrow \quad x = \dfrac{144 \times 100}{24} = 600$

3. $\quad$ Matriculates $= \dfrac{40}{100} x = \dfrac{2x}{5}$

Remaining $= \left(x - \dfrac{2x}{5}\right) = \dfrac{3x}{5}$

Graduates $= \dfrac{50}{100} \times \dfrac{3x}{5} = \dfrac{3x}{10}$

Remaining $= \dfrac{3x}{5} - \dfrac{3x}{10} = \dfrac{3x}{10}$

Now, $\dfrac{3x}{10} = 180 \quad \therefore \quad x = \dfrac{10 \times 180}{3} = 600$

$\therefore$ Graduates $= \dfrac{3 \times 600}{10} = 180$.

4. Males $= \left(\dfrac{5}{9} \times 4500\right) = 2500$

Females $= 2000$

$\therefore \quad$ Married males $= \dfrac{40}{100} \times 2500 = 1000$

and married females $= 1000$

$\therefore$ Percentage of married females

$= \left(\dfrac{1000}{2000} \times 100\right)\% = 50\%.$

5. Required percentage $= \left[\dfrac{10}{(100 + 10)} \times 100\right]\% = 9\dfrac{1}{11}\%.$

6. Required reduction $= \dfrac{25}{100 + 25} \times 100 = 20\%.$

7. Out of 100, difference in votes $= (60 - 40) = 20$

20% of $x = 100$

$\therefore x = \dfrac{100 \times 100}{20} = 500$.

8. Gross income $=$ Rs. 20000

Income exempted from income tax $= 10$% of gross income

$\therefore$ Income on which income tax is chargeable

$= (100 - 10\%) = 90$% of gross income

$= 20000 \times \dfrac{90}{100} = $ Rs. 18000

$\therefore$ Total income tax paid on

$= $ Rs. 20000 $-$ Rs. 19100 $= $ Rs. 900

$\therefore$ Rate per cent of income tax $= \dfrac{900}{18000} \times 100 = 5\%$

9. Let cost price of the cell phone be Rs. x; then

$x + \dfrac{32}{100} \times x = 6600 \quad \Rightarrow \dfrac{132x}{100} = 6600$

$\therefore \quad x = \dfrac{100 \times 6600}{132} = $ Rs. 5000.

10. Let reduced price by Rs. x per dozen, then

$\dfrac{48}{x} - \dfrac{48}{x + 4} = 1 \quad \Rightarrow \dfrac{48 \times 4}{x^2 + 4x} = 1$

$\Rightarrow \quad x^2 + 4x - 192 = 0$

$\Rightarrow (x + 16)(x - 12) = 0$

$\therefore \qquad\qquad x = $ Rs. 12.

11. Here, percentage of students failed in Mathematics and English be 30% and 20% respectively.

Percentage of students failed either one or both subjects

$= 30 + 20 - 10 = 40\%$

Hence, percentage of pass students $= 100 - 40 = 60\%$

Now, 60% $= 360$

$\therefore \quad 100\% = \dfrac{360}{60} \times 100 = 600.$

12. Let initially electric tax is Rs. 100 and consumption $= 100$ units

Decrease in consumption

$= 100 \times 100 - 120 \times 80 = $ Rs. 400

Hence, decrease percentage $= \dfrac{400 \times 100}{100 \times 100} = 4\%.$

13. Let the selling price of a commodity be Rs. 100 and number of sales $= 100$ units

Decrease in daily cash $= 100 \times 100 - 75 \times 130$

$= $ Rs. 250

Hence, decrease percentage $= \dfrac{250 \times 100}{100 \times 100} = 2.5\%.$

14. Let x kg of good wheat be added; then

$\dfrac{10}{100} \times 150 = \dfrac{5}{100}(150 + x)$

$\Rightarrow 150 + x = 300 \quad \therefore \quad x = 150$ kg.

15. Let her monthly income be Rs. x; then

$x - \left(\dfrac{15}{100} \times x + \dfrac{17}{100} \times x + \dfrac{6}{100} \times x\right) = 15{,}500$

$\Rightarrow x - \dfrac{38x}{100} = 15500 \quad \Rightarrow \dfrac{62x}{100} = 15500$

$\therefore \quad x = \dfrac{15500 \times 100}{62} = $ Rs. 25000.

PROFIT AND LOSS

1. Ashok bought 25 kg of rice at the rate of Rs. 6 per kg and 35 kg of rice at the rate of Rs. 7 per kg. He mixed the two and sold the mixture at the rate of Rs. 6.75 per kg. What was his gain or loss in the transaction?
   A. Rs. 16 gain   B. Rs. 16 loss
   C. Rs. 10 gain   D. None of these

2. Profit after selling a commodity for Rs. 425 is same as loss after selling it for Rs. 355. The cost of the commodity is :
   A. Rs. 285   B. Rs. 390
   C. Rs. 295   D. Rs. 400

3. Ram bought 4 dozen apples at Rs. 12 per dozen and 2 dozen at Rs. 16 per dozen. He sold all of them to earn 20%. At what price per dozen did he sell the apples?
   A. Rs. 14.40   B. Rs. 16.00
   C. Rs. 16.80   D. Rs. 16.20

4. At what price must Kantilal sell a mixture of 80 kg sugar at Rs. 6.75 per kg with 120 kg at Rs. 8 per kg to gain 20%?
   A. Rs. 7.50 per kg   B. Rs. 8.20 per kg
   C. Rs. 8.35 per kg   D. Rs. 9 per kg

5. A person bought an article and sold it at a loss of 10%. If he had bought it for 20% less and sold it for Rs. 55 more, he would have had a profit of 40%. The C.P. of the article is :
   A. Rs. 200   B. Rs. 225
   C. Rs. 250   D. None of these

6. A dealer sold a machine to a shopkeeper at 20% profit. The shopkeeper sold the machine to a customer so as to get 25% profit for himself. The difference between the selling price of the dealer and that of the shopkeeper was found to be Rs. 129. What is the initial price of the machine?
   A. Rs. 410   B. Rs. 420
   C. Rs. 430   D. Rs. 440

7. A man bought a horse and cart. If he sold the horse at 10% loss and the cart at 20% gain he would not loss anything. If he sold the horse at 5% loss and the cart at 5% gain he would lose Rs. 10 in the bargain. What did he pay for each?
   A. Rs. 400, Rs. 200   B. Rs. 300, Rs. 300
   C. Rs. 250, Rs. 350   D. Rs. 350, Rs. 250

8. The marked price of a radio is 20% more than its cost price. If a discount of 10% is given on the marked price, the gain percentage is:
   A. 8   B. 10
   C. 12   D. 15

9. A dishonest dealer sells his goods at the cost price and still earns a profit of 60% by underweight. What weight does he use for a kg?
   A. 625 gms   B. 750 gms
   C. 800 gms   D. 850 gms

10. A man sells two horses for Rs. 990 each. On one he gains 10% and the other he loses 10%. What is his total percentage of gain or loss in the transaction?
    A. 1% gain   B. 1% loss
    C. 2% gain   D. 2% loss

ANSWERS

1	2	3	4	5	6	7	8	9	10
C	B	B	D	C	C	A	A	A	B

EXPLANATORY ANSWERS

1. C.P. of 60 kg mixture = Rs. $(25 \times 6 + 35 \times 7)$
   = Rs. 395
   S.P. of 60 kg mixtire = Rs. (60×6.75)
   = Rs. 405
   ∴   Gain = Rs. $(405 - 395)$
   = Rs. 10

2. Let   C.P. = Rs. x
   Then, $425 - x = x - 355 \Rightarrow 2x = 780$
   ∴ $x = $ Rs. 390

3. C.P. of 6 dozen apples = Rs. $(12 \times 4 + 16 \times 2)$
   = Rs. 80
   ∴   S.P. = Rs. $\left(\dfrac{120}{100} \times 80\right)$
   = Rs. 96
   ∴   S.P. per dozen = Rs. $\left(\dfrac{96}{6}\right)$ = Rs. 16

4. C.P. of 1 kg sugar $= \dfrac{80 \times 6.75 + 120 \times 8}{200}$

$\qquad\qquad\qquad\quad = $ Rs. 7.50

$\therefore \qquad$ S.P. of 1 kg $= $ Rs. $\left(\dfrac{120}{100} \times 7.50\right)$

$\qquad\qquad\qquad\qquad = $ Rs. 9 per kg

5. Let, $\qquad$ C.P. $= $ Rs. x,

then, $\qquad$ S.P. $= \dfrac{90}{100} \times x = $ Rs. $\dfrac{9x}{10}$

Now, when C.P. $= $ Rs. $\dfrac{80x}{100} = $ Rs. $\dfrac{4x}{5}$;

then, S.P. $= \dfrac{140}{100} \times \dfrac{4x}{5} = $ Rs. $\dfrac{28x}{25}$

But, $\dfrac{28x}{25} - \dfrac{9x}{10} = 55 \;\Rightarrow\; \dfrac{11x}{50} = 55$

$\therefore \qquad\qquad x = $ Rs. 250

6. Let the initial price $= $ Rs. x; then C.P. for dealer

$\qquad\qquad = \dfrac{120}{100} \times x = $ Rs. $\dfrac{6x}{5}$

Again, C.P. for shopkeeper $= \dfrac{125}{100} \times \dfrac{6x}{5}$

$\qquad\qquad\qquad\qquad = $ Rs. $\dfrac{3x}{2}$

Now, $\dfrac{3x}{2} - \dfrac{6x}{5} = 129 \;\Rightarrow\; \dfrac{3x}{10} = 129$

$\therefore \;\; x = \dfrac{10 \times 129}{3} = $ Rs. 430

7. Here, 10% C.P. of horse $= $ 20% C.P. of cart; Hence, C.P. of horse $= 2 \times$ C.P. of cart;
Let C.P. of cart and horse be Rs. x and Rs. $2x$ respectively; then,

$\dfrac{5}{100} \times 2x - \dfrac{5}{100} \times x = 10 \;\Rightarrow\; \dfrac{1}{20}x = 10$

$\therefore x = 200$

Hence, C.P. of a cart $= $ Rs. 200 and C.P. of a horse
$\qquad\qquad = 2 \times 200 = $ Rs. 400

8. Let C.P. be Rs. 100; then marked price
$\qquad\qquad = $ Rs. 120

Since, S.P. $= \dfrac{90}{100} \times 120 = $ Rs. 108

$\therefore$ Profit $= 108 - 100 = $ Rs. 8, Hence, gain $= 8\%$.

9. Required weight $= \dfrac{100}{160} \times 1000 = 625$ gms.

10. Here, loss $\% = \left(\dfrac{10}{10}\right)^2 = 1\%$.

SIMPLE INTEREST

1. A lent a sum of Rs. 1250 to B at a certain rate of interest for 3 years and a sum of Rs. 1500 to C at the same rate of interest for 2 years. If he was paid total Rs. 258.75 as interest in both cases, find the rate of interest at which money was lent by him.

   A. $4\dfrac{1}{6}\%$ B. $6\dfrac{1}{4}\%$

   C. $2\dfrac{1}{7}\%$ D. $3\dfrac{5}{6}\%$

2. A invested Rs. 5000 at a certain rate of simple interest and Rs. 4000 for the same period at 1% higher rate of interest. If the interest in both cases is same, the former rate of interest is :

   A. 3%   B. 4%
   C. 6%   D. 5%

3. If a certain sum of money at simple interest amounts to Rs. 1900 in 3 years and to Rs. 2050 in 5 years, the rate per cent per annum is :

   A. 4½%   B. 3½%
   C. 2½%   D. 5¼%

4. A certain sum of money lent out on simple interest amounts to Rs. 1760 in 2 years and to Rs. 2000 in 5 years. Find the sum.

   A. Rs. 1650   B. Rs. 1500
   C. Rs. 1580   D. Rs. 1600

5. Out of the sum of Rs. 1550, a part was lent out at 5% p.a. simple interest and the remaining at 8% p.a. simple interest. If the total interest in both cases after 3 years is Rs. 300, the sum of money lent out at 8% p.a. simple interest was:

   A. Rs. 760   B. Rs. 775
   C. Rs. 750   D. Rs. 780

6. If simple interest on a certain sum of money for 4 years at 5% p.a. is same as the simple interest on Rs. 840 for 10 years at the rate of 4% p.a., the sum of money is:

   A. Rs. 1780   B. Rs. 1660
   C. Rs. 1680   D. Rs. 1620

7. What equal instalment of annual payment will discharge a debt which is due as Rs. 848 at the end of 4 years at 4% per annum simple interest?

A. Rs. 200 B. Rs. 212
C. Rs. 225 D. Rs. 250

8. Madhavi lent Rs. 5000 to Kamla for 5 years and Rs. 3000 to Vimla for 4 years. Find the rate of interest, if Madhavi gets an interest of Rs. 600 in the end.
A. 1.62% B. 2.5%
C. 3% D. 4%

9. A sum of money doubles itself in 7 years at simple interest. In how many years it will become four fold?

A. 10 years B. 14 years
C. 21 years D. 35 years

10. An amount doubles itself at the end of 8 years with a certain rate of simple interest. What will be the total simple interest on Rs. 8000 at that rate at the end of 4 years?
A. Rs. 2000 B. Rs. 4000
C. Rs. 6000 D. None of these

ANSWERS

1	2	3	4	5	6	7	8	9	10
D	B	A	D	C	C	A	A	C	B

EXPLANATORY ANSWERS

1. $\dfrac{1250 \times R \times 3}{100} + \dfrac{1500 \times R \times 2}{100} = 258.75$

$\Rightarrow 6750\,R = 25875$

$\therefore \quad R = \dfrac{25875}{6750} = \dfrac{23}{6} = 3\dfrac{5}{6}\%$

2. Here, $\dfrac{5000 \times R \times T}{100} = \dfrac{4000 \times (R+1) \times T}{100}$

$\Rightarrow 5R = 4R + 4 \quad \therefore \quad R = 4\%$

3. Simple interest for 2 years
$= $ Rs. 2050 – Rs. 1900 = Rs. 150

$\therefore$ Simple interest for 1 year = Rs. $\dfrac{150}{2}$ = Rs. 75

Since simple interest for 3 years = Rs. 75 × 3
$= $ Rs. 225

$\therefore$ Principal = Rs. 1900 – Rs. 225 = Rs. 1675

Hence, Rate = $\dfrac{75 \times 100}{1675 \times 1}$ = 4½%

4. Interest for 3 years = Rs. 2000 – Rs. 1760
$= $ Rs. 240

$\therefore$ Interest for 1 year = Rs. $\dfrac{240}{3}$ = Rs. 80

And interest for 2 years = Rs. 80 × 2 = Rs. 160
$\therefore$ Principal = Rs. 1760 – Rs. 160 = Rs. 1600

5. Let Rs. x and Rs $(1550 - x)$ were lent out at 8% and 5% respectively; then

$\dfrac{x \times 8 \times 3}{100} + \dfrac{(1550 - x) \times 5 \times 3}{100} = 300$

$\Rightarrow 24x + 23250 - 15x = 30000$

$\Rightarrow 9x = 6750 \quad \therefore \quad x = \dfrac{6750}{9}$ = Rs. 750

6. Here, $\dfrac{P \times 5 \times 4}{100} = \dfrac{840 \times 4 \times 10}{100} \Rightarrow 5P = 8400$

$\therefore \quad P = \dfrac{8400}{5}$ = Rs. 1680

7. Let equal instalment be Rs. x; then

$x + \dfrac{x \times 4 \times 3}{100} + x + \dfrac{x \times 4 \times 2}{100} + x + \dfrac{x \times 4 \times 1}{100} + x = 848$

$\Rightarrow 4x + \dfrac{24x}{100} = 848 \quad \Rightarrow \dfrac{106x}{25} = 848$

$\therefore x = \dfrac{848 \times 25}{106}$ = Rs. 200

8. $\dfrac{5000 \times R \times 5}{100} + \dfrac{3000 \times R \times 4}{100} = 600$

$\Rightarrow \quad 250\,R + 120\,R = 600$
$\Rightarrow \quad\quad\quad\quad 370R = 600$

$\therefore \quad\quad\quad\quad R = \dfrac{600}{370}$ = 1.62%

9. Let principal be Rs. x; then amount = Rs. $2x$, Hence, I = $2x - x$ = Rs. x.

$R = \dfrac{x \times 100}{x \times 7} = \dfrac{100}{7}\%$ p.a.

Now, amount = Rs. $4x$; then I = $4x - x$ = Rs. $3x$

Hence, T = $\dfrac{3x \times 100}{x \times \dfrac{100}{7}} = \dfrac{3 \times 100 \times 7}{100}$ = 21 years

10. Let principal = Rs. x; then amount = Rs. $2x$; I
$= 2x - x$ = Rs. x

$R = \dfrac{x \times 100}{x \times 8} = \dfrac{25}{2}\%$

Again, I = $\dfrac{8000 \times 25 \times 4}{100 \times 2}$ = Rs. 4000

COMPOUND INTEREST

1. The compound interest on a certain sum of money invested for 3 years at 5% per annum is Rs. 1891.50. What will be the simple interest on the same sum at the same rate for 2 years?
   A. Rs. 1700
   B. Rs. 1200
   C. Rs. 1500
   D. Rs. 2100

2. A sum of money lent out at a certain rate of simple interest amounts to Rs. 6600 in 2 years and to Rs. 6900 in 3 years. What will be the compound interest on the same sum of money if lent out at the same rate for 2 years?
   A. Rs. 605
   B. Rs. 715
   C. Rs. 615
   D. Rs. 595

3. A man deposits Rs. 1200 in a bank on the 1st day of each year. If the bank pays 5% per annum compound interest on deposited sum of money, what will be the amount to his credit on the 10th day of the second year?
   A. Rs. 2560
   B. Rs. 2460
   C. Rs. 2370
   D. Rs. 2860

4. If the difference between compound and simple interest on a certain sum of money for 3 years at 5% per annum is Rs. 244, the sum is :
   A. Rs. 40000
   B. Rs. 25000
   C. Rs. 30000
   D. Rs. 32000

5. A man purchased a sewing machine for Rs. 5000. If due to sustained use value of this sewing machine depreciates by 6% annually, find its value after 3 years.
   A. Rs. 3775.67
   B. Rs. 4152.92
   C. Rs. 4250.25
   D. Rs. 4356.25

6. Find the sum on which the difference between compound and simple interest for 3 years at 10% per annum will be Rs. 868.
   A. Rs. 29500
   B. Rs. 27625
   C. Rs. 28500
   D. Rs. 28000

7. Samir invested Rs. 15000 at the rate of interest 10% p.a. for 1 year. If the interest compound six months. What amount will Samir get at the end of the year?
   A. Rs. 16,500
   B. Rs. 16525.50
   C. Rs. 16537.50
   D. Rs. 18,150

8. The compound interest on a certain sum for 2 years at 10% per annum is Rs. 525. The simple interest on the same sum for double the time at half the rate per cent per annum is:
   A. Rs. 800
   B. Rs. 600
   C. Rs. 500
   D. Rs. 400

9. The least number of complete years in which a sum of money put at 20% compound interest will be more than doubled is:
   A. 6
   B. 5
   C. 4
   D. 3

10. On a sum of money, the simple interest for 2 years is Rs. 660, while the compound interest is Rs. 696.30, the rate of interest being the same in both cases. Find the rate of interest.
    A. Rs. 12%
    B. 11%
    C. 10%
    D. 9%

ANSWERS

1	2	3	4	5	6	7	8	9	10
B	C	B	D	B	D	C	C	C	B

EXPLANATORY ANSWERS

1. Here, $1891.50 = P\left[\left(1+\dfrac{5}{100}\right)^3 - 1\right]$

$\Rightarrow 1891.50 = P\left[\left(\dfrac{21}{20}\right)^3 - 1\right]$

$\Rightarrow 1891.50 = P\left(\dfrac{1261}{8000}\right)$

$\therefore P = \dfrac{1891.50 \times 8000}{1261} = $ Rs. 12000

Now, S.I. $= \dfrac{12000 \times 5 \times 2}{100} = $ Rs. 1200

2. Here, 1 year's S.I. = Rs. 6900 – Rs. 6600
   = Rs. 300

$\therefore$ 2 year's S.I. = 300 × 2 = Rs. 600

$\therefore$ Principal = Rs. 6600 – Rs. 600
   = Rs. 6000

Hence, Rate $= \dfrac{600 \times 100}{6000 \times 2} = 5\%$

$$\therefore \quad \text{C.I.} = 6000\left[\left(1+\frac{5}{100}\right)^2 - 1\right]$$

$$= 6000\left[\left(\frac{21}{20}\right)^2 - 1\right] = \frac{6000 \times 41}{400} = \text{Rs. } 615$$

3. Required amount $= 1200\left(1+\frac{5}{100}\right) + 1200$

$$= 1200 \times \frac{21}{20} + 1200 = 1260 + 1200 = \text{Rs. } 2460$$

4. Here, $P\left[\left(1+\frac{5}{100}\right)^3 - 1\right] - \frac{P \times 5 \times 3}{100} = 244$

$$\Rightarrow P \times \frac{1261}{8000} - \frac{3P}{20} = 244 \Rightarrow P \times \frac{61}{8000} = 244$$

$$\therefore \quad P = \frac{244 \times 8000}{61} = \text{Rs. } 32000$$

5. Here, value of the machine after 3 years

$$= 5000\left(1-\frac{6}{100}\right)^3 = 5000 \times \frac{47}{50} \times \frac{47}{50} \times \frac{47}{50}$$

$$= \text{Rs. } 4152.92.$$

6. Here, $P\left[\left(1+\frac{10}{100}\right)^3 - 1\right] - \frac{P \times 10 \times 3}{100} = 868$

$$\Rightarrow P \times \frac{331}{1000} - \frac{3P}{10} = 868$$

$$\Rightarrow P \times \frac{31}{1000} = 868 \quad \therefore \quad P = \frac{868 \times 1000}{31}$$

$$= \text{Rs. } 28000$$

7. $A = 15000\left(1+\frac{5}{100}\right)^2 = 15000 \times \frac{441}{400}$

$$= \text{Rs. } 16537.50$$

8. Here, $P\left[\left(1+\frac{10}{100}\right)^2 - 1\right] = 525$

$$\Rightarrow P\left[\frac{121}{100} - 1\right] = 525 \Rightarrow P \times \frac{21}{100} = 525$$

$$\therefore \quad P = \frac{525 \times 100}{21} = \text{Rs. } 2500$$

Hence, required S.I. $= \frac{2500 \times 5 \times 4}{100} = \text{Rs. } 500$

9. Here, $P\left(1+\frac{20}{100}\right)^n > 2P \Rightarrow \left(\frac{6}{5}\right)^n > 2$

Hence, if $n = 4$ then, $\left(\frac{6}{5}\right)^4 = \frac{1296}{625} > 2$

So, $n = 4$ years

10. Here, S.I. for 1 year = Rs. 330
Since, simple interest of Rs. 330 for 1 year
$= 696.30 - 660 = \text{Rs. } 36.30$

Hence, required rate $= \frac{36.30 \times 100}{330 \times 1} = \frac{3630}{330} = 11\%$

AREA AND PERIMETER

1. If side of a square is reduced by 50%, its area will be reduced by
   A. 50%   B. 75%
   C. 80%   D. 60%

2. If each side of a square is doubled, its area will become
   A. double   B. four times
   C. three times   D. eight times

3. Three sides of a triangle are in the ratio of 17 : 15 : 8. If the perimeter of this triangle is 40 m, find its area
   A. 50 sq. m.   B. 49 sq. m.
   C. 60 sq. m.   D. 69 sq. m.

4. If the length of a rectangle is increased by 20% and width is decreased by 15%, then its area
   A. decreases by 4%   B. increases by 2%
   C. decreases by 2%   D. increases by 3%

5. If the length of a rectangle is increased by 20%, then by how much per cent its breadth must be decreased so as to keep its area unaltered?
   A. 25%   B. $8\frac{1}{3}\%$
   C. $16\frac{2}{3}\%$ D. 20%

6. The ratio of length and breadth of a rectangular plot is 71 : 61 respectively. The area of the plot is 17324 m². What is perimeter of the plot?
   A. 264 m   B. 284 m
   C. 528 m   D. 614 m

7. If the length and breadth of a rectangular field are increased, the area increases by 50%. If the increase in length was 20%, by what percentage was the breadth increased?

A. 20% B. 25%
C. 30% D. 40%

8. The length and breadth of a varandah is 40 m and 15 m respectively. How many stone slabs of size 6 decimetre × 5 decimetre each are needed in flooring it:
A. 1000 B. 2000
C. 3000 D. 4000

9. The circumference of a circular plot is 396 m. What is the area of the circular plot?

A. 9,446 m² B. 9,856 m²
C. 12,474 m² D. 18,634 m²

10. If the sides of an equilateral triangle are increased by 20%, 30% and 50% respectively to form a new triangle, the increase in the perimeter of the equilateral triangle is:

A. 25% B. $33\dfrac{1}{3}\%$
C. 50% D. 100%

ANSWERS

1	2	3	4	5	6	7	8	9	10
B	B	C	B	C	C	B	B	C	B

EXPLANATORY ANSWERS

1. Area of the square $= x^2$ sq. m.

Side of the new square $= x - 50\%$ of $x = \dfrac{x}{2}$ m

$\therefore$ Area of the new square $= \left(\dfrac{x}{2}\right)^2 = \dfrac{x^2}{4}$ sq. m.

$\therefore$ Reduction in area of the square $= x^2 - \dfrac{x^2}{4}$

$$= \dfrac{3x^2}{4} \text{ sq. m.}$$

$\therefore$ Percentage reduction $= \dfrac{3x^2/4}{x^2} \times 100 = 75\%$

2. Area of the square $= x^2$ sq. m
Now, area of the new square $= (2x)^2 = 4x^2$ sq. m
Hence, it is clear that if side of a square is doubled, its area becomes four times.

3. Suppose sides of the triangle are $17x$ m, $15x$ m and $8x$ metres
$\therefore$ Perimeter $= 17x + 15x + 8x = 40x$
Now, $40x = 40$
$\Rightarrow$ $x = 1$ m
Therefore, the sides are $17 \times 1 = 17$ m, $15 \times 1 = 15$ m and $8 \times 1 = 8$ m
$\because$ $(17)^2 = (15)^2 + (8)^2$,
i.e., it is a right angled triangle
$\therefore$ Area of the right angled triangle

$$= \dfrac{1}{2} \times 8 \times 15 = 60 \text{ sq. m.}$$

4. Area of the rectangle $= xy$ sq. metre

Area of the new rectangle $= \dfrac{120}{100}x \times \dfrac{85}{100}y$

$$= 1.020\, xy \text{ sq. metre}$$

$\therefore$ Increase in the area $= 1.02\, xy - xy = .02\, xy$ sq. m.

$\therefore$ Percentage increase $= \dfrac{.02xy}{xy} \times 100 = 2\%$

5. Area of the rectangle $= xy$
On reducing the breadth by A% and increasing the length by 20%

Length of the new rectangle $= \dfrac{120x}{100} x = 1.2x$

Breadth of the new rectangle $= y - A\%$ of $y = y\left(1 - \dfrac{A}{100}\right)$

$\therefore$ Area of the new rectangle $= 1.2x \times y\left(1 - \dfrac{A}{100}\right)$

Now, $xy = 1.2\, xy\left(1 - \dfrac{A}{100}\right) \Rightarrow 1 = 1.2\dfrac{(100 - A)}{100}$

$\Rightarrow$ $1.2\,A = 120 - 100$

$\therefore$ $A = \dfrac{20}{1.2} = 16\dfrac{2}{3}\%$

6. Let length and breadth of a rectangle be $71x$ and $61x$ m; then

$71x \times 61x = 17324 \Rightarrow x^2 = \dfrac{17324}{71 \times 61} = 4$

$\therefore$ $x = 2$
Hence, length $= 71 \times 2 = 142$ m; breadth
$= 61 \times 2 = 122$ m
Since, perimeter $= 2(142 + 122) = 2 \times 264 = 528$ m

7. Here, $20 + x + \dfrac{20 \times x}{100} = 50 \Rightarrow x + \dfrac{x}{5} = 30$

$\Rightarrow \dfrac{6x}{5} = 30$ $\therefore x = \dfrac{5 \times 30}{6} = 25$

Hence, breadth was increased by 25%

8. Required number of stone slabs $= \dfrac{40 \times 15}{\dfrac{6}{10} \times \dfrac{5}{10}}$

$$= \dfrac{40 \times 15 \times 100}{6 \times 5} = 2000$$

VOLUME AND SURFACE AREA

1. If a solid sphere of 3 cm radius is melted and recast into a right circular cone whose base radius is same as that of the sphere, the height of the cone will be
   A. 8 cm
   B. 12 cm
   C. 6 cm
   D. 5 cm

2. Diameter of a roller is 2.4 m and it is 1.68 m long. If it takes 1000 complete revolutions once over to level a field, the area of the field is
   A. 12672 sq. m
   B. 12671 sq. m
   C. 12762 sq. m
   D. 11768 sq. m

3. If each edge of a cube is increased by 10%, then by how much per cent will the surface area of this cube be increased?
   A. 21%
   B. 18%
   C. 15%
   D. 20%

4. Height and base radius of a solid cylinder are 14 m and 4 m respectively. It is melted and recast into a solid cone of the same base radius as that of the cylinder, what will be the height of the cone?
   A. 21 m
   B. 42 m
   C. 48 m
   D. 54 m

5. A room is in the form of a cube of side 10 m. How many bales of cotton can be kept in it if each bale covers 5 cu m space?
   A. 100
   B. 175
   C. 200
   D. 225

6. Three cubes having side 2 cm, 3 cm and 4 cm respectively are melted together to form a new cube. The side of the new cube will be
   A. 3.526 cm
   B. 4.628 cm
   C. 4.626 cm
   D. 4.528 cm

7. If base diameter of a cylinder is increased by 50%, then by how much per cent its height must be decreased so as to keep its volume unaltered?
   A. 45.56%
   B. 55.56%
   C. 50.16%
   D. 62.33%

8. The surface area of a cube is 600 sq. m. Its diagonal is
   A. $10\sqrt{3}$ cm
   B. $5\sqrt{3}$ cm
   C. $4\sqrt{2}$ cm
   D. $10\sqrt{2}$ cm

9. The base diameter of a conical tomb is 28 m and its slant height is 50 m. Find the cost of white washing its curved surface at the rate of 80 paise per sq. m?
   A. Rs. 1860
   B. Rs. 1760
   C. Rs. 1950
   D. Rs. 1875

10. The volume of a cuboid is 1120 cu cm and its height is 5 cm while the length and the breadth of the cuboid are in the ratio 8 : 7. The length of this cylinder exceeds the breadth by
   A. 4 cm
   B. 2 cm
   C. 7 cm
   D. 5 cm

ANSWERS

1	2	3	4	5	6	7	8	9	10
B	A	A	B	C	C	B	A	B	B

EXPLANATORY ANSWERS

1. Volume of the cone = Volume of the sphere

   $\therefore \dfrac{1}{3}\pi(3)^2 \times h = \dfrac{4}{3}\pi \times 3^3 \Rightarrow h = 12$ cm

   Hence, height of the cone = 12 cm.

2. Surface area of the roller = $2\pi rh$

   $= 2 \times \dfrac{22}{7} \times 1.2 \times 1.68 = 12.672$ sq. m

   In one complete revolution, the roller covers 12.672 sq. m.

   $\therefore$ It will cover in 1000 revolutions

   $= 12.672 \times 1000 = 12672$ sq. m

   Hence, area of the field = 12672 sq. m.

3. Percentage increase in the surface area of the cube

   $= \left(x + y + \dfrac{xy}{100}\right)\%$

   $= \left(10 + 10 + \dfrac{10 \times 10}{100}\right)\% = 21\%.$

4. Here,

   volume of the cone = Volume of the cylinder

   $\Rightarrow \dfrac{1}{3}\pi r^2 \times \text{height} = \pi r^2 \times 14$

   $\therefore \qquad \text{Height} = 14 \times 3 = 42$ m

   Thus, height of the cone = 42 m.

5. Volume of the cubical room $= (10)^3$
$$= 1000 \text{ cu m}$$

Number of cotton bales which can be placed in the room

$$= \frac{\text{Volume of the room}}{\text{Volume of each cotton bale}} = \frac{1000}{5} = 200.$$

6. Volume of the new cube $= 2^3 + 3^3 + 4^3$
$$= 8 + 27 + 64 = 99\text{cu cm}$$

$\therefore$ Side of the new cube $= \sqrt[3]{99} = 4.626$ cm.

7. Change in the volume of the cylinder

$$= \left(x + y + (-z) + \frac{xy + y(-z) + (-zx)}{100} + \frac{xy(-z)}{100^2} \right)\%$$

Since volume of the cylinder remains unchanged.

$\therefore \qquad$ Change $= 0\%$

Now, $\left(50 + 50 + (-z) + \frac{50 \times 50 - 50z - 50z}{100} + \frac{50 \times 50 \times (-z)}{100^2} \right) = 0$

$\therefore \quad 100 - z + 25 - z - .25z = 0$

$\Rightarrow 2.25z = 125 \Rightarrow z = \dfrac{125}{2.25} = 55.56$

$\therefore$ Height of the cylinder should be decreased by 55.56%.

8. Here, $\qquad 6 \times (\text{side})^2 = 600$

$\Rightarrow \qquad\qquad \text{side}^2 = 100$

$\Rightarrow \qquad\qquad \text{side} = \sqrt{100} = 10$ cm

$\therefore$ Diagonal of the cube $= \sqrt{3} \times \text{side}$

$$= \sqrt{3} \times 10$$

$$= 10\sqrt{3} \text{ cm.}$$

9. Area of the curved surface of the cone

$$= \frac{22}{7} \times \frac{28}{2} \times 50 = 2200 \text{ sq. m.}$$

$\therefore$ Cost of white washing at 80 paise per sq. m

$$= 2200 \times \frac{80}{100} = \text{Rs. } 1760.$$

10. Suppose the length and the breadth of the cuboid are $8x$ cm and $7x$ cm

$\therefore$ Here, $\quad 8x \times 7x \times 5 = 1120$

$\Rightarrow x^2 = \dfrac{1120}{280} = 4 = (2)^2 \quad \Rightarrow \quad x = 2$

$\therefore$ Length of the cuboid $= 8 \times 2 = 16$ cm
Breadth of the cuboid $= 7 \times 2 = 14$ cm

Hence, it is clear that length of the cuboid exceeds the breadth by 2 cm.

SERIES

Directions (Qs. 1 to 7) : *In the following number series, one of the numbers does not fit into the series. Find the wrong number.*

1. 2, 5, 10, 18, 26, 37, 50
A. 2   B. 5
C. 37   D. 18

2. 3 , 18, 38, 78, 123, 178, 243
A. 123   B. 178
C. 3   D. 38

3. 380, 188, 92, 48, 20, 8, 2
A. 188   B. 92
C. 48   D. 20

4. 5, 11, 23, 47, 96, 191, 383
A. 11   B. 23
C. 47   D. 96

5. 89, 78, 86, 80, 85, 82, 83
A. 78   B. 86
C. 80   D. 85

6. 58, 57, 54, 50, 42, 33, 32
A. 57   B. 54
C. 50   D. 32

7. 2, 20, 27, 44, 64
A. 27   B. 8
C. 20   D. 44

Directions (Qs. 8 to 10) : *Complete the following series.*

8. 1 4 9 16 25 36 49 ....
A. 54   B. 56
C. 64   D. 81

9. 11 13 17 19 23 29 31 37 41 ....
A. 43   B. 47
C. 53   D. 51

10. 3 7 6 5 9 3 12 1 15 ....
A. 18   B. 13
C. −1   D. 3

ANSWERS

1	2	3	4	5	6	7	8	9	10
D	C	C	D	A	C	C	C	A	C

EXPLANATORY ANSWERS

1.

2	5	10	18	26	37	50

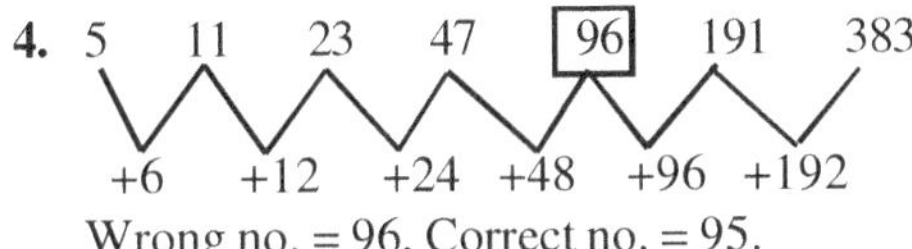

1^2+1 2^2+1 3^2+1 4^2+1 5^2+1 6^2+1 7^2+1

Wrong no. = 18, Correct no. = 17.

2. Only 3 is a prime number.

3. Wrong no. = 48, Correct no. = 44
Each term will be four more than two times the next term.

4. 5   11   23   47   [96]   191   383

$+6$ $+12$ $+24$ $+48$ $+96$ $+192$

Wrong no. = 96, Correct no. = 95.

5. If 87 is written in place of 78 then tens digit of each term will be 8.

6. 58   57   54   [50]   42   33   22

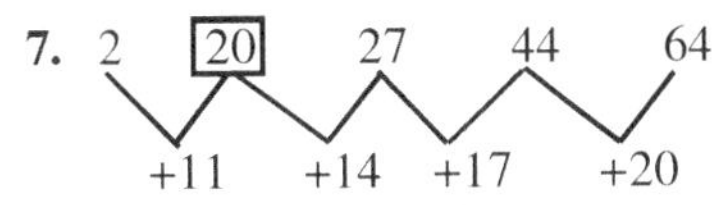

-1 -3 -5 -7 -9 -11

Wrong no. = 50, Correct no. = 49.

7. 2   [20]   27   44   64

$+11$ $+14$ $+17$ $+20$

Wrong no. = 20, Correct no. = 13.

8. Numbers are $1^2, 2^2, 3^2, 4^2, 5^2, 6^2, 7^2$.
So, the next number is $8^2 = 64$.

9. Numbers are all primes. The next prime is 43.

10. There are two series, beginning respectively with 3 and 7. In one 3 is added and in another 2 is subtracted. The next number is $1 - 2 = -1$.

APPROXIMATE VALUES

1. $85432 \div 2106 + 59.5614 = ?$
   (a) 100   (b) 60
   (c) 80   (d) 140

2. $\sqrt{67621} = ?$
   (a) 320   (b) 260
   (c) 200   (d) 280

3. 9.7 % of 5011 + 55.03 % of 4991
   (a) 5500   (b) 7200
   (c) 6000   (d) 4200

4. $730 \times 199 = ?$
   (a) 350000   (b) 335000
   (c) 300000   (d) 34600

5. $.0144 \times 0.36 = ?$
   (a) 0.5   (b) 0.005
   (c) 0.05   (d) 0.005

6. 31% of 1508 + 26% of 2018
   (a) 1500   (b) 2000
   (c) 1000   (d) 1200

7. $3015 + 13594 + 3738 = ?$
   (a) 40000   (b) 36000
   (c) 42000   (d) 46000

8. $6012 \times 119 = ?$
   (a) 560000   (b) 448000
   (c) 900000   (d) 720000

9. $2712.1563 \div 1805.4018 + 3.4982 = ?$
   (a) 9   (b) 8
   (c) 4   (d) 5

10. $4182. 365 \div 20.886 = ?$
   (a) 300   (b) 200
   (c) 150   (d) 250

ANSWERS

1	2	3	4	5	6	7	8	9	10
A	B	D	A	B	C	A	D	D	B

EXPLANATORY ANSWERS

1. $85432 \div 2106 + 60 = 40 + 60 = 100$
Therefore, (B) is the correct answer.

2. $\sqrt{67621} = \sqrt{67600} = 260$
Therefore, (B) is the correct answer.

3. 29.7% of $5011 + 55.03\%$ of 4991
$= 30\%$ of $5000 + 55\%$ of 5000

$= \dfrac{30}{100} \times 5000 + \dfrac{55}{100} \times 5000$

$= 1500 + 2750 = 4250 \Rightarrow 4200$
Therefore, (D) is the correct answer.

4. $1730 \times 199 = 1730 \times 200$
$= 346000 \Rightarrow 350000$
Therefore, (B) is the correct answer.

5. $0.0144 \times 0.36 = 0.0140 \times 0.36 = .005040$
$\Rightarrow .005$
Therefore, (B) is the correct answer.

6. 31% of $1508 + 26\%$ of 2018
$= 30\%$ of $1500 + 25\% \times 2000$

$= \dfrac{30}{100} \times 1500 + \dfrac{25}{100} \times 2000$

$= 450 + 500 = 950 \Rightarrow 1000$
Therefore, (C) is the correct answer.

7. $23015 + 13594 + 3738$
$= 23000 + 13600 + 3700$
$= 40300 \Rightarrow 40000$
Therefore, (A) is the correct answer.

8. $6012 \times 119 = 6000 \times 120 = 720000$
Therefore, (D) is the correct answer.

9. $2712.1563 \div 1805.4018 + 3.4982$
$= 2700 \div 1800 + 3.5 = 1.5 + 3.5 = 5$
Therefore, (D) is the correct answer.

10. $4182.\,365 \div 20.886 = 4200 \div 21 = 200$
Therefore, (B) is the correct answer.

GENERAL AWARENESS

NATIONAL SYMBOLS

NATIONAL EMBLEM

State emblem of India is an adaptation from the Sarnath Lion Capital of Ashoka. It was adopted by the Government of India on January 26, 1950. In the adapted form, only three lions are visible, the fourth being hidden from the view. The wheel (Dharma Chakra) appears in relief in the centre of the abacus with a bull on the right and a horse on the left.

The bell-shaped lotus has been omitted. The words "Satyameva Jayate" meaning "Truth alone triumphs" are inscribed below the Emblem in Devanagari script.

NATIONAL FLAG

The National Flag of India is a horizontal tricolour of deep saffron (Kesari), white and dark green in equal proportion. In the centre of the white band there is a wheel in navy blue colour. It has 24 spokes. The ratio of the length and the breadth of the flag is 3 : 2. Its design was adopted by the Constituent Assembly of India on July 22, 1947.

NATIONAL ANTHEM

Rabindranath Tagore's song 'Jana-gana-mana' was adopted by the Constituent Assembly as the National Anthem of India on January 24, 1950.

Jana-gan-mana-adhinayaka jaya he, Bharata-bhagya-vidhata
Punjab-Sindh-Gujarat-Maratha-Dravida-Utkala-Banga
Vindhya-Himachala-Yamuna-Ganga Uchhala-jaladhi-taranga.
Tava subha name jage, Tava subha asisa mange,
Gahe tava jaya gatha,
Jana-gana-mangala-dayak, jaya he Bharata bhagya vidhata,
Jaya he, jaya he, jaya he, Jaya jaya jaya, jaya he.

NATIONAL SONG

Bankim Chandra Chatterji's 'Vande Mataram' which was a source of inspiration to the people in their struggle for freedom, has been adopted as National Song. It has an equal status with the National Anthem.

Vande Mataram
Sujalam, suphalam, malayaja-shitalam,
Shasya shyamalam, Mataram
Shubhrajyotsna,pulkita yaminim,
Phulla kusumita drumadalashobhinim,
Subhasinim sumadhura—bhashinim,
Sukhadam, Varadam, Mataram.

National Bird and Animal of India: Peacock and Tiger

National Aquatic Animal: Dolphin

National Flower: Lotus; **National Game:** Hockey

National Calendar: It was adopted on March 22, 1957. It has 365 days in the year and the first month of the year is Chaitra.

NATIONAL CALENDAR

It is based on the Saka era with Chaitra as its first month and a normal year of 365 days. It was adopted from March 22, 1957. Dates of the national calendar have a permanent correspondence with dates of Gregorian calendar as Chaitra I falls on March 22 in a normal year and March 21 in a leap year. In official communications, both Saka and Gregorian calendar dates are written. Months of the national calendar are Chaitra, Vaishakha, Jaishtha, Ashada, Shravan, Bhadra, Ashvina, Kartika, Margashirsha, Pausha, Magha and Phalguna.

NATIONAL ANIMAL

The magnificent tiger — Panthera tigris (Linnaeus) is the national animal of India. Tiger is found in several parts of the country and is known for its grace, strength, agility and enormous power. 'Project Tiger' was launched in 1973 to check their dwindling population in India.

NATIONAL BIRD

The Indian Peacock — Pavo Christatus (Linnaeus) is the national bird of India. It is a colourful, swan-sized bird with a fan-shaped crest of feathers on its head and a long-slander neck. The male species is more colourful with blue breast and a spectacular bronze-green train of around 200 elongated feathers.

National Flower—Lotus

National Tree—Banyan

National Fruit—Mango

National Currency—Rupee '₹' (One Rupee = 100 Paise)

National Aquatic Animal—Dolphin

BOOKS AND AUTHORS

Name of Book	Author	Name of Book	Author
Ain-e-Akbari	Abul Fazal	Arthshastra	Kautilya
Anand Math	Bankim Chandra Chatterjee	Coolie	Mulk Raj Anand
An Unknown Indian	Nirad C. Chaudhuri	Das Kapital	Karl Marx

Name of Book	Author	Name of Book	Author
Discovery of India	Jawaharlal Nehru	Neeti Shatak	Bhartrihari
Eternal India	Mrs. Indira Gandhi	Nehru and His Vision	Dr. K.R. Narayanan
Godan	Prem Chand	Old Man and the Sea	Ernest Hemingway
Gitanjali	Rabindranath Tagore	One World	Wendell Wilkie
Gora	Rabindranath Tagore	Panchtantra	Vishnu Sharma
Geet Govinda	Jayadeva	Paradise Lost	John Milton
Harsha Charit	Bana Bhatta	Ramayana	Valmiki (in Sanskrit)
Hindu View of Life	Dr. S. Radhakrishnan	Raghuvansham	Kalidas
India Wins Freedom	Maulana Abul Kalam Azad	Rajtarangini	Kalhan
Jobs of Millions	V.V. Giri	Ram Charit Manas	Tulsi Das
Jungle Book	Rudyard Kipling	Abhijnan Shakuntalam	Kalidas
Kamayani	Jai Shankar Prasad	Satanic Verses	Salman Rushdie
Kadambari	Bana Bhatta	Saket	Maithili Sharan Gupta
Life Divine	Sri Aurobindo	Speed Post	Shobha De
Last days of Netaji	G.D. Khosla	The God of Small Things	Arundhati Roy
Les Miserables	Victor Hugo	Treasure Island	R.L. Stevenson
Mahabharat	Veda Vyas	Twelfth Night	William Shakespeare
Macbeth	William Shakespeare	Train to Pakistan	Khuswant Singh
Mein Kempf	Hitler	Uttara Ram Charitra	Bhava Bhuti
Meghduta	Kalidas	Vanity Fair	W.M. Thackeray
Mother (Maa)	Maxim Gorky	War and Peace	Leo Tolstoy
Mother India	Katherine Mayo	Wealth of Nations	Adam Smith
My Experiments with Truth	Mahatma Gandhi	Wake up India	Annie Besant
My Presidential Years	R. Venkataraman		

INVENTIONS AND DISCOVERIES

Discovery	Discoverer	Discovery	Discoverer
Geographical Discoveries		Printing for the blind	Louis Braille
America	Columbus	Radium	Madame Curie
Brazil	Cabral	Telegraph	Samuel Morse
North Pole	Robert Peary	Television	J.L. Baird
Everest (Conquered)	Tabie Junko	Telephone	Graham Bell
Planetary Motion	Kepler	Wireless	G. Marconi
Hawaiian Islands	Captain Cook	X-rays	W.K. Roentgen
South Pole	Amundsen		
Solar System	Copernicus	**Mechanical**	
		Aeroplane	Wright Brothers
Chemistry and Physics		Bicycle	Macmillan
Atom Bomb	Otto Hahn	Computer	Charles Babbage
Atomic Theory	Dalton	Dynamo	Michal Faraday
Atomic Numbers	Moseley	Diesel Engine	Rudolf Diesel
Cosmic Rays	R.S. Millikan	Engine (Railway)	Stephenson
Dynamite	Alfred Nobel	Fountain Pen	Waterman
Electrons Theory	Bohr	Gramophone	Edison
Electricity (current)	Volta	Locomotive Power of Steam	James Watt
Electric Telegraphy (Code)	S. Morse	Helicopter	Brequet
Gravitation	Newton	Life Boat	Henry Greathead
Gas Light	Murdock	Microscope	Z. Jansen
Oxygen	J. Priestly	Printing Press	Gutenberg
Photography	L. Daguerre	Revolver	Colt

Discovery	Discoverer	Discovery	Discoverer
Sewing Machine	Elias Howe	Homoeopathy (Discovered)	Hahnemann
Thermometer	Fahrenheit	Insulin	F. Banting
Transistor	W. Shockley	Penicillin	Alexander Flemming
Typewriter	Sholes	Malaria Parasite	Dr. Ronald Ross
Telescope	Hans Lippershey	Stethoscope	Laennec
Tank (Military)	Swinton	Vitamins	Funk
Medical		Anti-Rabies Treatment	Pasteur
Antiseptic Surgery	Lord Joseph Lister	**General**	
Bacteria	Leeuwenhock	Nylon	Carouthers
Circulation of Blood	William Harvey	Science of Geometry	Euclids

WORLD'S GEOGRAPHICAL SURNAMES

● City of Sky-scrapers—New York ● City of Seven Hills—Rome ● City of Dreaming Spires—Oxford ● City of Golden Gate—San Francisco ● City of Magnificent Buildings—Washington D.C. ● City of Eternal Springs—Quito (S. America) ● China's Sorrow—Hwang Ho ● Cockpit of Europe—Belgium ● Dark Continent—Africa ● Emerald Isle—Ireland ● Eternal City—Rome ● Empire City—New York ● Forbidden City—Lhasa (Tibet) ● Garden City—Chicago ● Gate of Tears—Strait of Bab-el-Mandeb ● Gift of the Nile—Egypt ● Granite City—Aberdeen (Scotland) ● Hermit Kingdom—Korea ● Herring Pond—Atlantic Ocean ● Holy Land—Jerusalem ● Island Continent—Australia ● Islands of Cloves—Zanzibar ● Isle of Pearls—Bahrein (Persian Gulf) ● Key to the Mediterranean—Gibralter ● Land of Cakes—Scotland ● Land of Golden Fleece—Australia ● Land of Maple Leaf—Canada ● Land of Morning Calm—Korea ● Land of Midnight Sun—Norway ● Land of the Thousand Lakes—Finland ● Land of the Thunderbolt—Bhutan ● Land of White Elephant—Thailand ● Land of Thousand Elephants—Laos ● Land of Rising Sun—Japan ● Loneliest Island—Tristan De Gunha (Mid-Atlantic) ● Manchester of Japan—Osaka ● Pillars of Hercules—Strait of Gibraltar ● Pearl of the Antilles—Cuba ● Playground of Europe—Switzerland ● Quaker City—Philadelphia ● Queen of the Adriatic—Venice ● Roof of the World—The Pamirs, Central Asia ● Sugar bowl of the world—Cuba ● Venice of the North—Stockholm ● Windy City—Chicago ● Whiteman's grave—Guinea Coast of Africa ● Yellow River—Huang Ho (China) ● Sickman of Europe—Turkey

CURRENCIES OF DIFFERENT COUNTRIES

Country	Currency	Country	Currency
Australia	Australian Dollar	Poland	Zloty
Bangladesh	Taka	Spain	Euro
Belgium	Euro	Indonesia	Rupiah
Britain	Pound (Sterling)	Iraq	Dinar
Myanmar	Kyat	Italy	Euro
Canada	Canadian Dollar	Japan	Yen
Germany	Euro	Mexico	Peso
Iran	Rial	Netherland	Euro
India	Rupee	European Union	Euro
Ceylon	Rupee	Sweden	Krone
China	Yuan	Switzerland	Swiss Franc
Czech Republic	Koruna	Turkey	Lira
Denmark	Krone	U.A.E.	Dirham
France	Euro	U.S.A.	Dollar
Pakistan	Rupee	Russia	Rouble

CAPITAL OF COUNTRIES

Country	Capital
Austria	Vienna
Afghanisatan	Kabul
Algeria	Algiers
Angola	Luanda
Australia	Canberra
Argentina	Buenos Aires
Bangladesh	Dhaka
Belgium	Brussels
Bolivia	Lapaz
Bulgaria	Sofia
Bhutan	Thimpu
Brazil	Brasilla
Canada	Ottawa
China	Beijing
Cyprus	Nicosia
Columbia	Bagota
Denmark	Copenhegan
Ethiopia	Addis Ababa
Finland	Helsinki
France	Paris
Germany	Berlin
Greece	Athens
Guatemala	Guatemala City
Hungary	Budapest
Iran	Tehran
India	New Delhi
Indonesia	Jakarta
Iraq	Baghdad
Italy	Rome
Ireland	Dublin
Japan	Tokyo
Kampuchea (Combodia)	Phnom Penh
Korea (North)	Pyong Yang
Korea (South)	Seoul
Kenya	Nairobi
Kuwait	Kuwait
Laos	Vientiane
Lebanon	Beirut
Mexico	Mexico City
Malaysia	Kualalumpur
Morocco	Rabat
Mozambique	Maputo
New Zealand	Welington
Netherlands	Amsterdam
Panama	Panama City
Portugal	Lisbon
Poland	Warsaw
Sri Lanka	Colombo
Sweden	Stockholm
Switzerland	Bern
Sudan	Khartoum
Sierre	Leone
South Africa	Capetown
Saudi Arabia	Riyadh
Spain	Madrid
Thailand	Bangkok
Turkey	Ankara
Russia	Moscow
Azerbaijan	Baku
Armenia	Yerevan
Latvia	Riga
Ukrain	Kiev
U.S.A.	Washington
U.K.	London
U.A.R.	Cairo
Vietnam	Hanoi
Zambia	Lusaka

INDIAN CITIES AND THEIR RIVERS

City	State	River
Agra	U.P.	Yamuna
Ahmedabad	Gujarat	Sabarmati
Allahabad	U.P.	Confluence of the Ganga, Yamuna, and invisible Saraswati
Alwaye	Kerala	Periyar
Kolkata	West Bengal	Hooghly
Cuttack	Odisha	Mahanadi
Delhi	Delhi	Yamuna
Haridwar	Uttarakhand	Ganga
Kanpur	Uttar Pradesh	Ganga
Ludhiana	Punjab	Sutlej
Lucknow	Uttar Pradesh	Gomati
Nasik	Maharashtra	Godavari
Patna	Bihar	Ganga
Srinagar	J & K	Jhelum
Surat	Gujarat	Tapti
Tiruchirapally	Tamil Nadu	Kaveri
Ujjain	Madhya Pradesh	Shipra
Vijayawada	Andhra Pradesh	Krishna
Varanasi	Uttar Pradesh	Ganga

WONDERS OF THE WORLD

Seven Wonders of the Ancient World: (1) the Pyramids of Egypt, built in approximately 2700 BC; (2) the Hanging Gardens at Babylon; (3) the temple of Artemis at Emphesus; (4) the statue of Zeus at Olympia; (5) the tomb of Mausolus at Halicarnassus, built in nearly 350 BC; (6) the Colossus of Rhodes, built in nearly 280 BC; (7) the Pharos Lighthouse at Alexandria.

Seven Wonders of the Medieval World: (1) the Colosseum of Rome; (2) the Great Wall of China; (3) the Porcelain Tower of Nanking; (4) the Mosque at St. Sophia (Constantinople); (5) Stonehenge; (6) the Catacombs of Rome; (7) the Leaning Tower of Pisa.

Seven New Wonders of the World: (1) Taj Mahal of Agra (India); (2) Pyramid at Chichen Itza (Mexico); (3) Machu Picchu (Peru); (4) Statue of Christ The Redeemer (Brazil); (5) Great Wall of China; (6) Roman Colosseum, Italy; (7) Ruins of Petra, Jordan.

STATES OF INDIA (CAPITALS, PRINCIPAL LANGUAGES)

States Principal Languages	Capitals	States Principal Languages	Capitals
■ Andhra Pradesh—*Telgu and Urdu*	Hyderabad	■ Maharashtra—*Marathi*	Mumbai
■ Arunachal Pradesh— *Monpa, Adi, Nissi etc.*	Itanagar	■ Meghalaya—*Khashi, Jayantia and Garo*	Shillong
■ Assam—*Assamese and Bengali*	Dispur	■ Manipur—*Manipuri*	Imphal
■ Bihar—*Hindi and Maithili*	Patna	■ Mizoram—*Mizo and English*	Aizawl
■ Chattishgarh—*Hindi*	Raipur	■ Nagaland—*Naga, Assamese and English*	Kohima
■ Goa—*Konkani*	Panaji		
■ Gujarat—*Gujarati*	GandhiNagar	■ Odisha—*Odiya*	Bhubaneshwar
■ Haryana—*Hindi*	Chandigarh	■ Punjab—*Punjabi*	Chandigarh
■ Himachal Pradesh— *Hindi and Pahari*	Shimla	■ Rajasthan—*Hindi, Rajasthani*	Jaipur
		■ Sikkim—*Sikkimese and Gorkhali*	Gangtok
■ Jammu & Kashmir— *Kashmiri, Dongri, Urdu, Ladakhi, Dardi and Pahari*	Srinagar	■ Tamil Nadu—*Tamil*	Chennai
		■ Tripura—*Bengali, Tripuri and Manipuri*	Agartala
■ Jharkhand—*Hindi*	Ranchi	■ Uttar Pradesh—*Hindi*	Lucknow
■ Kerala—*Malyalam*	Thiruvananthpuram	■ Uttarakhand—*Hindi*	Dehradun
■ Karnataka—*Kannada*	Bengluru	■ West Bengal—*Bengali*	Kolkata
■ Madhya Pradesh—*Hindi*	Bhopal	■ Telangana—*Telgu and Urdu*	Hyderabad

Union Territories Principal Languages	Capitals	Union Territories Principal Languages	Capitals
■ Andaman and Nicobar Islands— *Hindi, Nicobarese, Bengali, Malayalam, Tamil, Telugu*	Port Blair	■ Daman and Diu—*Gujarati*	Daman
		■ Delhi—*Hindi, Punjabi*	Delhi
■ Chandigarh—*Hindi, Punjabi, English*	Chandigarh	■ Lakshadweep—*Malayalam*	Kavaratti
		■ Puducherry—*Tamil, Telugu, Malayalam, English and French*	Puducherry
■ Dadar and Nagar Haveli— *Gujarati, Hindi*	Silvasa		

HIGH COURTS IN INDIA

Name	Year	Territorial Jurisdiction	Seat
Allahabad	1866	Uttar Pradesh	Allahabad (Bench at Lucknow)
Andhra Pradesh	1954	Andhra Pradesh / Telangana	Hyderabad
Bombay	1862	Maharashtra, Goa, Dadar & Nagar Haveli and Daman & Diu	Mumbai (Benches at Nagpur, Panaji and Aurangabad)
Calcutta	1862	West Bengal and Andaman & Nicobar	Kolkata (Circuit Bench at Port Blair)
Chhattisgarh	2000	Chhattisgarh	Bilaspur
Delhi	1966	Delhi	Delhi
Guwahati	1948	Assam, Nagaland, Mizoram and Arunachal Pradesh	Guwahati (Benches at Kohima, Aizawl and Itanagar)
Gujarat	1960	Gujarat	Ahmedabad
Himachal Pradesh	1971	Himachal Pradesh	Shimla
Jammu & Kashmir	1928	Jammu & Kashmir	Srinagar and Jammu
Jharkhand	2000	Jharkhand	Ranchi
Karnataka	1884	Karnataka	Bengaluru (Circuit Benches at Dharwar and Gulbarga)
Kerala	1958	Kerala & Lakshadweep	Ernakulam
Madhya Pradesh	1956	Madhya Pradesh	Jabalpur (Benches at Gwalior and Indore)
Madras	1862	Tamil Nadu & Puducherry	Chennai (Bench at Madurai)
Orissa	1948	Odisha	Cuttack
Patna	1916	Bihar	Patna
Punjab and Haryana	1966	Punjab, Haryana and Chandigarh	Chandigarh
Rajasthan	1949	Rajasthan	Jodhpur (Bench at Jaipur)
Sikkim	1975	Sikkim	Gangtok
Uttarakhand	2000	Uttarakhand	Nainital
Tripura	2013	Tripura	Agartala
Meghalaya	2013	Meghalaya	Shillong
Manipur	2013	Manipur	Imphal

HILL STATION

Station	State
1. Almora, Mussoorie Nainital	: Uttarakhand
2. Cherrapunji (Shillong), Khasi Hills (Shillong)	: Meghalaya
3. Ooty, Kodaikanal Yereaud	: Tamil Nadu
4. Dalhousie, Kassauli	: Himachal Pradesh
5. Darjeeling	: West Bengal
6. Gulmarg, Srinagar	: Kashmir
7. Mahabaleshwar	: Maharashtra
8. Mt. Abu	: Rajasthan
9. Panchmarhi	: Madhya Pradesh
10. Ranchi	: Jharkhand

NATIONAL PARKS

1. Corbett National Park : Nainital, Uttarakhand
2. Dudhwa National Park : Lakhimpur Kheri, UP
3. Kaziranga National Park : Jorhat, Assam
4. Kanha National Park : Jabalpur, Bhedaghat
5. Gir National Park : Rajkot, Junagarh, Gujarat
6. Guindy National Park : Guindy, Chennai, Tamil Nadu
7. Nagairhole National Park : Coorg, Karnataka
8. Bandipur National Park : Mysore, Karnataka

NATIONAL WILDLIFE SANCTUARIES

1. Dachigam Wildlife Sanctuary : Srinagar, Jammu and Kashmir
2. Sariska : Alwar, Rajasthan
3. Hazaribagh Wildlife Sanctuary : Hazaribagh, Jharkhand
4. Tiger Project : Sawai Madhopur, Rajasthan
5. Mudhumali Wildlife Sanctuary : Mudhumalia, Nilgiri, Tamil Nadu
6. Periyar Wildlife Sanctuary : Idukki, Kottayam, Kerala

HOLY PLACES IN INDIA

1.	Amarnath	Kashmir
2.	Ayodhya	Uttar Pradesh
3.	Badrinath	Uttarakhand
4.	Dwarka	Gujarat
5.	Haridwar	Uttarakhand
6.	Kancheepuram	Tamil Nadu
7.	Kedarnath	Uttarakhand
8.	Mathura	Uttar Pradesh
9.	Puri	Odisha
10.	Rameswaram	Tamil Nadu
11.	Tirupati	Andhra Pradesh
12.	Ujjain	Madhya Pradesh
13.	Varanasi	Uttar Pradesh
14.	Bodh Gaya	Bihar

SPORTS

Terms Associated With Sports :

Cricket : Ashes, Bye, Bodyline, Bowling, Break, Cover-point, Creases, Chinaman, Chucker, Drive, Duck, Follow on, Googly, Hit-Wicket, Hat-trick, Leg-before-wicket, Leg break, Leg-bye, Maiden over, No ball, Night-watchman, Runner, Run-out, Stumped, Silly-point, Slip.

Football : Handball, Corner kick, Dribble, Free Kick, Hat-trick, Off-side, Penalty Kick, Try, Throw in, Wembley.

Hockey : Bully, Carry, Corner kick, Corner, Penalty stroke, Off-side, Penalty, Roll in scoop, Sticks, Sudden death, Striking circle, Short Corner, Scoop, Tie-breaker, Under-cutting, Hat-trick.

Tennis : Backhand drive, Deuce, Fault, Half-volley, Net, Let, Volley, Smash, Service.

Billiards : Break, Cannons, Cue, Pot, Jigger, Scratch, In Bauk, In, Off.

Bridge : Dummy, Finesse, Grand-slam, Little Slam, Revoke, Ruff slam, Trump, Tricks, Vulnerable.

Volley Ball : Booster, Love, Service, Volley, Smasher.

Badminton : Smash, Drop, Let.

Chess : Check, Checkmate, Gambit, State-mate.

Golf : Bogy, Caddie, Hole, Links, Stymie, Tee, Put.

Polo : Chukker, Mallet, Bunder.

Baseball : Bunting, Diamond, Pitcher, Put-out, Strike, Home.

Boxing : Knockout, Punch, Upper-cut, Jab, Hook.

FAMOUS TROPHIES

Agha Khan Cup	Hockey
Beighton Cup	Hockey
Corbillion Cup	World Table Tennis (Women)
Davis Cup	Lawn Tennis
Duleep Trophy	Cricket
Durand Cup	Football
Ezra Cup	Polo
I.F.A. Shield	Football
Irani Cup	Cricket (India)
Jayalaxmi Cup	Table Tennis (Women)
Lady Rattan Tata Trophy	Hockey (Women)
Nehru Cup	Hockey (India)
Obaidullah Cup	Hockey
Ranji Trophy	Cricket (India)
Rangaswamy Cup	Hockey (India)
Rovers Cup	Football (India)
Santosh Trophy	Football (India)
Subroto Cup	Football
Thomas Cup	Badminton
Uber Cup	Badminton (Women)
Wellington Trophy	Rowing (India)

BIGGEST, LARGEST, TALLEST OF THE WORLD

Largest Desert	Sahara (Africa)
Biggest Palace	Palace of Parliament (Romania)
Tallest Statue	Statue of Budha (China)
Rainiest Place	Mowsynram near Cherrapunjee (Meghalaya, India)
Biggest Ocean	Pacific Ocean
Deepest Ocean	Pacific Ocean
Largest Telescope (Reflector)	Large Binocular Telescope (Arizona, USA)
Largest Mammal	Whale
Fastest Animal	Cheetah
Lightest Substance	Hydrogen gas
Longest River	Nile
Highest Waterfalls	Salto Angel Falls (Venezuela)
Tallest Animal	Giraffe
Largest Bird (Land)	Ostrich
Hardest Mineral	Diamond
Largest Delta	Sunderbans (W.B. India)
Largest Museum	American Museum of Natural History (New York)
Longest Day	June, 22
Shortest Day	December, 22
Biggest Army	People's Liberation Army, China
Largest Salt Water Lake	Caspian Sea
Highest Mountain Peak	Everest (8848 metre high)
Biggest Dam	Lloyd Dam (U.S.A.)
Longest Wall	Great Wall of China
Largest Peninsula	India
Largest Planet	Jupiter
Coldest Place	Polus Nedostupnosti (Antarctica −58°C)

Smallest Continent	Australia
Largest Lake	Caspian Sea
Deepest Lake	Baikal, 3200 ft.
Finest Harbour	Sydney Harbour
Smallest Planet	Mercury
Largest Continent	Asia
Planet nearest to the Sun	Mercury
Longest Highway Tunnel	Laerdal Tunnel (Norway)
Biggest Bridge	Danyang-Kunshan Grand Bridge (164,800 m), China
Highest Building	Burj Khalifa, Dubai
City largest (Population)	Tokyo
City Biggest in area	Mt. Isa (Australia)
City highest	Wen Chuan (China)
Country Biggest	Russia (17075000 sq. km.)
Electorate, Largest	India (over 80 crores)
Longest Epic	Mahabharat
Island, Biggest in the World	Greenland
Park Biggest	Central Park (New York, USA)
Population, Largest	China
Longest Railway Platform	Gorakhpur (India)
Swimming Course	English Channel

FIRST IN INDIA

Governor General of Independent India	— Lord Mountbatten
Commander-in-chief of free India	— General Roy Bucher
Cosmonaut	— Sq. Ldr. Rakesh Sharma
Field Marshal	— S.H.F.J. Manekshaw
Indian Governor General of Indian Union	— C. Rajagopalachari
Indian I.C.S. Officer	— Satyendra Nath Tagore
Indian to swim across English Channel	— Mihir Sen
Indian Women to swim across English Channel	— Miss Arti Saha
Man to climb Mount Everest	— Tenzing Norgay
Man to climb Mount Everest without Oxygen	— Phu Dorjee
Man to climb Mount Everest twice	— Nwang Gombu
Nobel Prize Winner	— Rabindra Nath Tagore
President of Indian National Congress	— W.C. Banerjee
President of Indian Republic	— Dr. Rajendra Prasad
Talkie Film	— Alam Ara (1931)
Test Tube Baby (Documented)	— Indira
Viceroy of India	— Lord Canning
Woman Minister of Indian Union	— Rajkumari Amrit Kaur
Woman Governor	— Mrs. Sarojini Naidu
Woman President of Indian National Congress	— Dr. Annie Besant
Woman Prime Minister	— Mrs. Indira Gandhi

Woman Speaker of a State Assembly	— Mrs. Shanno Devi
Prime Minister of India	— Pt. Jawaharlal Nehru
Muslim President of Indian Union	— Dr. Zakir Hussain
Speaker of Lok Sabha	— G.V. Mavlankar
Women to Climb Mount Everest	— Bachhendri Pal
Woman Judge in Supreme Court	— Mrs. Meera Sahib Fatima Biwi
Women Chief Justice of a High Court	— Smt. Leela Seth
The First Indian Weightlifter to Win bronze medal in Olympics	— Karnam Malleshwari (Sydney, in 2000)
World Chess Champion	— Vishwanathan Anand
India's First Woman Merchant Navy Officer	— Sonali Banerjee
The First Woman Air Vice-Marshal	— P. Bandopadhyaya
The First Indian to be appointed as United Nations Civilian Police Advisor	— Ms. Kiran Bedi
The First Women to be appointed Deputy Governor of Reserve Bank of India	— K.J. Udeshi
The First Indian Lady to win a medal in World Athletic Championship	— Anju Bobby George
The First Sikh Prime Minister of India	— Dr. Manmohan Singh

IMPORTANT DAYS

* **January**

5-11	Road Safety Week
12	National Youth Day
15	Army Day
23	National Day of Patriotism
26	Republic Day
30	Martyr's Day

* **FEBRUARY**

1-14	Oil Conservation Fortnight
14	Valentine's Day

* **MARCH**

4	National Safety Day
8	International Women's Day
15	Consumers' Day
21	World Forest Day
22	World Day for Water
24	World Meteorological Day

* **APRIL**

7	World Health Day
7-13	Handloom Week
14-20	Fire Service Week
18	World Heritage Day
22	World Earth Day

* **MAY**

1	May Day
5	National Labour Day
8	World Red Cross Day

11	National Technology Day
15	International Day of the Family
17	World Telecommunication Day
24	Commonwealth Day
31	World No-Tobacco Day

✶ **JUNE**

5	World Environment Day
21	International Day of Yoga
26	International Day against Drug Abuse and Illicit Trafficking

✶ **JULY**

11	World Population Day

✶ **AUGUST**

1-7	World Breast feeding Week
10	Sanskrit Divas
15	Independence Day
20	Sadbhavana Divas

✶ **SEPTEMBER**

1-7	National Nutrition Week
5	Teachers' Day
8	International Literary Day
14	Hindi Diwas
23	World Deaf Day
27	World Tourism Day

✶ **OCTOBER**

2	✶ Gandhi Jayanti ✶ International Day of Non Violence ✶ Anti-Leprosy Day
4	World Animal Day
6	World Habitat Day (Ist Monday)
8	Indian Air Force Day
14	World Standard Day
15	International Day of Rural Women
16	World Food Day
24	United Nations Day
27	Infantry Day
28	World Thrift Day
31	Anti-Terrorism Day

✶ **NOVEMBER**

2	All Saints Day
14	Children's Day
15-21	National Cooperative Week
19-25	Quami Ekta Week
20	Child Rights Day
26	Constitution Day

✶ **DECEMBER**

1	World AIDS Day
3	World Day for the Disabled
4	Naval Day
7	Flag Day
8	SMRC Day
10	Human Rights Day
14	National Energy Conservation Day

PARLIAMENTS OF IMPORTANT COUNTRIES

Afghanistan	—	Shora
Britain	—	Parliament House of Commons, House of Lords
Denmark	—	Folketing
The Netherlands	—	States General
India	—	Sansad
Israel	—	Knesset
Iran	—	Majlis
Ireland	—	Airetann
Iceland	—	Althing
Japan	—	Diet
Norway	—	Storting
Russia	—	Supreme Soviet
Spain	—	Cortes
Sweden	—	Riksdag
U.S.A.	—	Congress Senate
Germany	—	Bundestag

MINERAL RESOURCES OF THE WORLD

Articles	Producers	Articles	Producers
Aluminium	China	Asbestos	Russia
Boxide	Australia	Chromium	South Africa
Copper	Chile	Cobalt	Congo (Kinshasa)
Diamonds	Russia	Gold	China
Iron-ore	Australia	Lead	China
Platinum	South Africa	Silver	Mexico
Silicon	China	Sulfur	China
Tin	China	Titanium	China
Tungsten	China		

TEN LARGEST COUNTRIES AND THEIR AREAS

Rank by Area	Country	Area (sq. km.)
1.	Russia	17,075,400
2.	Canada	9,976,139
3.	China	9,561,000
4.	U.S.A.	9,363,123
5.	Brazil	8,511,965
6.	Australia	7,686,848
7.	India	3,287,263
8.	Argentina	2,776,889
9.	Kazakhstan	2,724,900
10.	Algeria	2,381,741

PRESIDENT OF INDIA

He is the constitutional head of the Republic but not the real executive.

Qualifications: (1) Indian citizen; (2) age not less than 35 years; (3) should have qualifications for election to Lok Sabha; (4) should not hold any office of profit; (5) should not be a Member of Parliament or State Legislature.

Election: He is elected by the elected Members of Parliament and State Legislative Assemblies in accordance with the system of proportional representation by means of single transferable vote.

Powers: He makes appointment to all the Constitutional posts. He can address either House of Parliament and send message to them. He can summon and prorogue either House of Parliament and dissolve Lok Sabha. All Bills passed by Parliament must receive his assent to become an Act. He issues Ordinance when Parliament is not in session. No money Bill can be introduced in Lok Sabha without his recommendation. He can grant pardon, reprieve or remit punishment and he can commute death sentences. He can declare national emergency, state emergency and financial emergency.

VICE-PRESIDENT OF INDIA

The Vice-President acts as the ex-officio Chairman of Rajya Sabha and acts as the President when the latter is unable to discharge his functions due to illness, absence or any other reason, or till the election of a new President when a vacancy is caused by the death, resignation or removal of the President.

The Vice-President is elected by an electoral college consisting of the members of both Houses of Parliament in accordance with the system of proportional representation by means of the single transferable vote. He must be a citizen of India, not less than 35 years of age, and should be eligible for election as a member of the Council of States.

COUNCIL OF MINISTERS

Council of Ministers is to aid and advise the President in exercise of his functions. Prime Minister and other ministers are appointed by the President.

Cabinet: Every member of the Council of Ministers is not a Cabinet Minister. Cabinet is a small body consisting of only senior members of Council of Ministers. The Cabinet functions like the executive committee of the Council of Ministers.

PRIME MINISTER OF INDIA

Art. 74(1) of our Constitution states that the Prime Minister shall be at the head of council of ministers. He has the power of selecting and advising the President to dismiss them individually. He is the chairman of the cabinet. Art. 78 provides that it shall be the duty of the Prime minister –

- To communicate to the president all the decisions of the council of ministers relating to the administration of the affairs of the union and proposals for legislation.

- To furnish such information relating to the administration of the affairs of the union and proposals for legislation as the president may call for and

- If the President so requires to submit for the consideration of the council of ministers any matter on which a decision has been take by a minister but which has not been considered by the council.

THE SOLAR SYSTEM: SOME FACTS

Number of Planets: 8—Mercury, Venus, Earth, Mars, Jupiter, Saturn, Uranus and Neptune.

Largest most

Massive planet	Jupiter
Brightest planet	Venus
Brightest star	Sirius
Fastest orbiting planet	Mercury
Longest (Synodic) day	Mercury
Most moons	Jupiter (69)
Planet with largest moon	Jupiter
Greatest average density	Jupiter
Tallest mountain	Earth
Strongest magnetic fields	Jupiter
Most circular orbit	Venus
Shortest (synodic) day	Jupiter
Hottest planet	Venus
No moons	Mercury, Venus
Planet with moon with most eccentric orbit	Neptune
Lowest average density	Saturn
Greatest amount of liquid on the surface	Earth

THE EARTH: FACTS AND DATA

Composition of the Earth: Aluminium (0.4%), Sulphur (2.7%), Silicon (13%), Oxygen (28%), Calcium (1.2%), Nickel (2.7%), Magnesium (17%), Iron (35%)

Surface area	: 510100500 sq km
Land Surface (29.1%)	: 148950800 sq km
Ocean Surface (70.9%)	: 361149700 sq km
Type of water	: 97% salt, 3% fresh
Total area of water	: 382672000 sq km
Equatorial diameter	: 12753 km
Equatorial Circumference	: 40066 km
Polar Circumference	: 39992 km
Polar diameter	: 12710 km
Equatorial radius	: 6376 km
Polar radius	: 6335 km

Mass (estimated weight)	: 594×10^{19} metric tons
Mean distance from the Sun	: 149407000 km
Earth's orbit speed (around sun)	: 107320 kmph
Period of Revolution (round the sun)	: 365 days 5 hrs 48 min. 45.51 seconds
Time of Rotation (on its axis)	: 23 hrs 56 min 4.09 seconds
Inclination of the axis (to the plane of the ecliptic)	: 23°27'

PRINCIPAL MOUNTAIN PEAKS OF THE WORLD

	Mountains	Height in Metres	Range	Date of First Ascent
1.	Mount Everest	8,848	Himalayas	May 29, 1953
2.	K-2 (Godwin Austen)	8,611	Karakoram	July 31, 1954
3.	Kanchenjunga	8,597	Himalayas	May 25, 1955
4.	Lhotse	8,511	Himalayas	May 18, 1956
5.	Makalu I	8,481	Himalayas	May 15, 1955
6.	Dhaulagiri I	8,167	Himalayas	May 13, 1960
7.	Mansalu I	8,156	Himalayas	May 9, 1956
8.	Chollyo	8,153	Himalayas	Oct. 19, 1954
9.	Nanga Parbat	8,124	Himalayas	July 3, 1953
10.	Annapurna I	8,091	Himalayas	June 3, 1950
11.	Gasherbrum I	8,068	Karakoram	July 5, 1958
12.	Broad Peak I	8,047	Karakoram	June 9, 1957
13.	Gasherbrum II	8,034	Karakoram	July 7, 1956
14.	Shisha Pangma (Gosainthan)	8,014	Himalayas	May 2, 1964
15.	Gasherbrum III	7,952	Karakoram	Aug. 11, 1975

POPULAR NICK NAMES OF SOME FAMOUS PERSONALITIES

Andhra Kesari	T. Prakasam
Anna	C.N. Anna Durai
Bang Bandhu	Sheikh Mujibur Rehman
Bapu	Mahatma Gandhi
Bard of Avon	William Shakespeare
Chachaji	Jawaharlal Nehru
Desh Bandhu	C.R. Das
Frontier Gandhi	Khan Abdul Gaffar Khan
Fuhrer	Adolf Hitler
G.B.S.	George Bernard Shaw
Grand Old Man of India	Dadabhai Naoroji
Grand Old Man of Britain	Gladstone
Guru Dev	Rabindra Nath Tagore
Guruji	M.S. Golwalkar
Iron Man of India	Sardar Patel
Lok Nayak	Jayaprakash Narayan
Lady with the Lamp	Florence Nightingale
Lal, Bal, Pal	Lala Lajpat Rai, Bal Gangadhar Tilak, Bipin Chandra Pal
Little Corporal	Napoleon Bonaparte
Lokmanya	Bal Gangadhar Tilak
Mahamana	Pt. Madan Mohan Malaviya
Maid of Orleans	Joan of Arc
Maiden Queen	Queen Elizabeth I
Missile Man	A.P.J. Abdul Kalam

Man of Destiny	Napoleon Bonaparte	Punjab Kesari	Lala Lajpat Rai
Netaji	Subhash Chandra Bose	Shastriji	Lal Bahadur Shastri
Nightingale of India	Sarojini Naidu	Uncle Ho	Ho Chi Minh
Panditji	Jawaharlal Nehru	Wizard of the North	Walter Scott

FAMOUS INTERNATIONAL ORGANISATIONS, HEADQUARTERS AND YEAR OF ESTABLISHMENT

International Organisations	*Headquarters*	*Year of Establishment*
United Nations Organisations (U.N.O.)	New York	1945
International Monetary Fund (I.M.F.)	Washington	1945
World Health Organisation (W.H.O.)	Geneva	1948
Food & Agricultural Organisation (FAO)	Rome	1943
International Labour Organisation (ILO)	Geneva	1919
UNESCO	Paris	1946
International Court of Justice	The Hague	—
Universal Postal Union (UPU)	Berne	1874
International Civil Aviation Organisation (ICAO)	Montreal	1947
UNIDO	Vienna	1967
International Atomic Energy Agency (IAEA)	Vienna	1957
International Finance Corporation (IFC)	Washington	1956
United Nations Development Programme (UNDP)	New York	—
UNICEF	New York	1946
International Maritime Organisation (IMO)	London	1948
World Meteorological Organisation (WMO)	Geneva	1951
International Telecommunication Union (ITU)	Geneva	1947
Arab League	Cairo	1945
Commonwealth of Nations	London	1931
World Trade Organisation (WTO)	Geneva	1995
International Development Association (IDA)	Washington D.C.	1960
International Bank for Reconstruction and Development (IBRD)	Washington D.C.	1946
World Intellectual Property Organisation (WIPO)	Geneva	1967
Organisation of Islamic Conference (OIC)	Jeddah (Saudi Arabia)	1971
European Economic Community (EEC)	Geneva	1957
Red Cross	Geneva	1863
Interpol	Lyons	1923
Asian Development Bank (ADB)	Manila	1966
North Atlantic Treaty Organisation (NATO)	Brussels	1949
Association of South East Asian Nations (ASEAN)	Jakarta	1967

BHARAT RATNA AWARD WINNERS

1. Dr. S. Radhakrishnan	1954		**8.** Dr. D.K. Karve	1958
2. C. Rajagopalachari	1954		**9.** Dr. Bidhan Chandra Roy	1961
3. Dr. C.V. Raman	1954		**10.** Purushottam Das Tandon	1961
4. Dr. Bhagwan Das	1955		**11.** Dr. Rajendra Prasad	1962
5. Dr. M. Visvesvaraya	1955		**12.** Dr. Zakir Hussain	1963
6. Jawaharlal Nehru	1955		**13.** Dr. Pandurang Vaman Kane	1963
7. Govind Ballabh Pant	1957		**14.** Lal Bahadur Shastri	1966

15. Indira Gandhi	1971	
16. V.V. Giri	1975	
17. K. Kamraj	1976	
18. Mother Teresa	1980	
19. Acharya Vinoba Bhave	1983	
20. Khan Abdul Ghaffar Khan	1987	
21. M.G. Ramachandran	1988	
22. Dr. B.R. Ambedkar	1990	
23. Dr. Nelson R. Mandela	1990	
24. Rajiv Gandhi	1991	
25. Sardar Vallabhbhai Patel	1991	
26. Morarji R. Desai	1991	
27. Maulana Abdul Kalam Azad	1992	
28. Jehangir Ratanji Dadabhai Tata	1992	
29. Satyajit Roy	1992	
30. Gulzari Lal Nanda	1997	

31. Mrs. Aruna Asaf Ali	1997
32. Dr. A.P.J. Abdul Kalam	1998
33. M.S. Subbalakshmi	1998
34. C. Subramaniam	1998
35. Jaya Prakash Narayan	1999
36. Prof. Amartya Sen	1999
37. Pt. Ravi Shankar	1999
38. Gopinath Bardoloi	1999
39. Lata Mangeshkar	2001
40. Bismillah Khan	2001
41. Bhimsen Joshi	2008
42. C.N.R. Rao	2014
43. Sachin Tendulkar	2014
44. Madan Mohan Malaviya	2015
45. Atal Bihari Vajpayee	2015

ART AND CULTURE

☞ Classical Dances

Dance	State	Famous Artists
Bharat Natyam	Tamil Nadu	Yamini Krishnamurthy, Rukmini Devi Arundale, Swapna Sundari, Sonal Mansingh, Vaijanti Mala, Mrinalini Sarabhai, Chandralekha, Indrani, Ram Gopal, Bal Saraswati
Kathakali	Kerala	Gopinath, K.K. Nayar, Kunju-Kurup, T.K. Chandu
Kuchipudi	Andhra Pradesh/ Telangana	Sapna Sundari, Raja Reddy, Shobha Nayar, Radha Reddy, Vedantam Satyanarayan, Vimpanti Chinna Satyam.
Kathak	North India	Birju Maharaj, Gopi Krishna, Shambhu Maharaj, Sitara Devi, Vishnu Sharma, Durga Lal, Shobhana Narayan
Odissi	Odisha	Kelucharan Mahapatra, Indrani Rehman, Madhavi Mudgal, Pratima Bedi, Samyukta Panigrahi, Sonal Mansingh, Debudas
Manipuri	Manipur	Uday Shankar, Bipin Singh, Suryamukhi, Darohra Jhaveri

☞ Famous Folk Dances

State	Folk Dance	State	Folk Dance
Andhra Pradesh/ Telangana	Dandari, Banjara	Madhya Pradesh	Lota Nritya, Jawara
Assam	Bihu, Keli Gopal, Sataria	Maharashtra	Tamasha, Dahi Handi, Gof, Deepak Dindi
Bihar	Chhau, Magahi, Durga dance	Manipur	Dhol Cholam
W. Bengal	Kirtan, Kalatri, Asweabadh, Brita, Kalidance	Meghalaya	Nongakarem
Chhattisgarh	Saila, Karama, Bhagoria	Nagaland	Bamboo dance
Gujarat	Garba, Rasalila, Tippani, Dandia,	Odisha	Chhau, Maya Shabari, Dalachai
Haryana	Damyal, Lahoor	Punjab	Gidda, Bhangra, Panihari
Himachal Pradesh	Dussehra dance, Hikat, Notio	Rajasthan	Thumar, Kathaputali, Tera Tali
J&K	Dumhal	Tamil Nadu	Terukalathu, Kabalatam, Kargam, Pulivesham
Jharkhand	Jhau, Ghumakudia, Jadur, Sarhul, Soharai, Karama, Vaima, Loojhari, Jat-Jatin, Vidayat	Tripura	Hazagiri
		Uttar Pradesh	Rasalila, Nautanki, Thali, Dhurang, Jhumela, Huraka, Bol.
Karnataka	Yakshagan, Dolu Kunitha	Uttarakhand	Kajari, Karan
Kerala	Mohini Attam, Padayuni	Goa	Dhode Modini

MUSIC

Main Schools of Classical Music

- There are two main schools of classical music, namely, the Hindustani and the Carnatic. The Hindustani school of classical music is in vogue in north-western India, eastern India and northern parts of the South India.

Musical Instruments

- *They are:* Tabla, Mridangam, Pakhawaj, Chandai, Dholak, Veena, Sitar, Sarod, Gootuvadhyam, Sarangi, Flute, Nadaswaram, Shehnai, Shringi and Turahi.

FAMOUS INTERNATIONAL AIR SERVICES

Air Service	Name of Country	Air Service	Name of Country
Air India	India	K.L.M. Royal Airlines	The Netherlands (Holland)
British Overseas	Britain	Lufthansa Airlines	Germany
Airways Corporation		Iraqi Airways	Iraq
Trans World Airlines	America	National Airlines	Iran
Russian Airlines	Russia	Quantas Airlines	Australia
Japan Airlines	Japan	Hong-Kong Airlines	Hong-Kong
Pakistan International Airlines	Pakistan	Egypt Airlines	Egypt
Malaysia Airlines	Malaysia	Slovak Airlines	Slovakia
Royal Nepal Airlines	Nepal	S.I.A.	Singapore
Swiss Airways	Switzerland	Garuda Airways	Indonesia
Air France	France	Bangladesh Viman Sewa	Bangladesh
Kuwait Airways	Kuwait	Air Lanka	Sri Lanka
Pan American World Airways	America	Elitalia Airlines	Italy
		Air Canada	Canada

FAMOUS RELIGIONS, FOUNDERS, HOLY BOOKS & PLACES OF WORSHIP

Religion	Founder	Holy Books	Place of Worship
Hinduism	Hinduism has no one Founder. (This religion is based upon the religion of original Aryan Settlers)	Ramayan, Vedas, Puranas and Geeta	Temple
Sikh	Guru Nanak Dev	Guru Grantha Sahib	Gurdwara
Christianity	Jesus Christ	Bible	Church
Islam	Prophet Mohammed	Koran (Quran)	Mosque
Parsi	Zoroaster	Zend Avesta	Fire Temple
Jainism	Adinath Rishavdev	Jain Granth	Jain Temple
Buddhism	Gautam Buddha	Tripitaka	Buddha Temple
Jew	Moosa	Torah	Synagogue

INTELLIGENCE AGENCIES OF SOME PROMINENT COUNTRIES

Country	Intelligence Agency	Country	Intelligence Agency
India	Research & Analysis Wing (RAW), Intelligence Bureau (I.B.),Central Bureau of Investigation (C.B.I.)	U.S.A.	Central Intelligence Agency, Federal Bureau of Investigation
Pakistan	Inter Service Intelligence (I.S.I.)	Britain	Military Intelligence (M.I.)-5 and 6, Special Branch, Ultra, Joint Intelligence Organisation

Country	Intelligence Agency	Country	Intelligence Agency
Israel	Mosad	Iran	Sabak
Egypt	Mukhabarat	Iraq	Al-Mukhabarat
Japan	Nicho	Australia	Australian Security and Intelligence Organisation
Russia	K.G.B. (Komitel Gosudars-tvennoy Bezopasnosty) (Committee for State Security)	France	S.D.E.C.E.
Canada	Security Intelligence Service	Spain	C.E.S.I.D.
S. Africa	Bureau of State Security	Cuba	D.G.I.

SOME PROMINENT RACES OF THE WORLD

Races	Country	Races	Country	Races	Country
Veddas	Sri Lanka	Bantu	Central and South Africa	Lapps	European Tundra
Somaid	West Siberia				
Masai	East Africa	Tartars	Siberia	Hausa	Nigeria
Muree	New Zealand	Baddu	Arab's Desert	Kirghiz	Steppes (Russia)
Yakoot	Russian Tundra	Semang	Malaysia	Bushman	Kalahari Desert
Papuans	New Guyana	Eskimo	Canada, Tundra Region		
Pygmy	Congo Basin			Red Indian	North America

FAMOUS STRAITS OF THE WORLD

Strait	Between	Country
Malacca Strait	Andaman Sea and South China Sea	Indonesia
Palk Strait	Mannar and Bay of Bengal	India-Sri Lanka
Magellan Strait	Pacific and South Atlantic Ocean	Chile
Dover Strait	English Channel and North Sea	England-France
Berring Strait	Berring Sea and Chukasi Sea	Alaska-Russia
Sugaroo Strait	Japan Sea and Pacific Ocean	Japan
Sunda Strait	Java and Indian Ocean	Indonesia
Gibralter Strait	Mediterranean Sea and Atlantic Ocean	Spain
Harmuj Strait	Persia and Bay of Oman	Oman-Iran
Hudson Strait	Bay of Hudson and Atlantic Ocean	Canada

FAMOUS NEWSPAPERS OF THE WORLD

Newspaper	Place of Publishing	Language	Newspaper	Place of Publishing	Language
Daily News	New York (America)	English	Hindu, Hindustan, Times of India, Tribune, Statesman, Indian Express, Economic Times	India	English
Guardian	London (Britain)	English			
Pravada	Moscow (Russia)	Russian			
Al-Ahram	Cairo (Egypt)	Arabic			
Merdeca	Jakarta (Indonesia)	Indonesian			
Times	London (Britain)	English	Hindustan, Nav Bharat Times, Dainik Bhaskar, Dainik Jagaran, Punjab Kesari	India	Hindi
People's Daily	Beijing (China)	Chinese			
New Statesman	Britain	English			
Daily Mirror	Britain	English			

IMPORTANT BOUNDARY LINES

Boundary Line	Countries	Boundary Line	Countries
Durand Line	Pakistan and Afghanistan	Seigfrid Line	Germany-France
		24th Parallel	India-Pakistan
Hindenberg Line	Germany-Poland	17th Parallel	The line which defined the boundary between North Vietnam and South Vietnam before the two were united.
Maginot Line	France and Germany		
Mannerhein Line	Russia-Finland		
Mc Mahon Line	India-China		
Order Niesse Line	Germany-Poland	38th Parallel	North Korea and South Korea
Radcliff Line	India-Pakistan	49th Parallel	U.S.A. and Canada

SIGNALS/SIGNS AND MEANING

Signal/Sign	Meaning	Signal/Sign	Meaning
Red Triangle	Family Planning	White Flag	Treaty or Surrender
Red Cross	Medical Help	Yellow Flag	Vehicles with patients of contagious diseases
Red Light	Danger, 'Stop' for the movement of vehicles	Two Bones across with a Skull	Danger of electricity
Green Light	Go		
Olive Branch	Peace	Half mast flown Flag	National mourning
White Pigeon or Dove	Peace	Lotus and culture	Sign of civilization
Black Strip on Arm	(i) Opposition (ii) Sorrow	Wheel (Chakra)	Sign of Progress
		A blind folded woman with	
Black Flag	Opposition	scale in hand	Sign of Justice
Red Flag	(i) Danger (ii) Revolution	Reversed flown	National calamity flag

NATIONAL EMBLEMS OF IMPORTANT COUNTRIES

Country	National Emblem	Country	National Emblem
America	Golden Rod	New Zealand	Kiwi, Fern Southern Cross
Australia	Kangaroo	Norway	Lion
Ireland	Shamrock	Nepal	Kukri
Italy	White Lily	Pakistan	Crescent
Israel	Candelabrum	Poland	Eagle
Iran	Rose	France	Lily
Canada	White Lily	Belgium	Lion
Great Britain	Rose	Bangladesh	Water Lily
Chile	Candor and Huemul	Mongolia	The Soyombo
Germany	Corn Flower	Russia	Double headed eagle
Japan	Chrysanthemum	Lebanon	Cedar Tree
Zimbabwe	Zimbabwe Bird	Sudan	Secretary Bird
Denmark	Beach	Syria	Eagle
Turkey	Crescent and Star	India	Lioned Capital
The Netherlands	Lion		

THE CONTINENTS OF THE WORLD

	Continent (2017)	Population	Yearly Change	Net Change
1.	Asia	4,478,315,164	0.95%	42,090,691
2.	Africa	1,246,504,865	2.5%	30,375,050
3.	Europe	739,207,742	0.05%	358,740
4.	Latin America and the Caribbean	647,565,336	1.02%	6,536,030
5.	Northern America	363,224,006	0.75%	2,694,682
6.	Oceania	40,467,040	1.42%	565,685
	World	**7,515,284,153**	**1.08%**	**82,620,878**

COMPUTER

The computer is the system of that electronic device through which various informations are processed on the basis of a definite set of instructions called program and mathematical (numerical) and non-mathematical both types of informations are processed.

The first mechanical computer was composed or fabricated by Blaise Pascal in 1642 and it is called Pascalene. But in 1833, Charles Babbage first time conceived an automatic calculator or computer. Charles Babbage is called the father of modern computer. Herman made an electronic tabulating machine based on punch cards which operates automatically.

In 1937, first mechanical computer mark-I was fabricated by Howard Akeen. The most outstanding contribution in the development of modern computer goes to John Wan Newmaan who brought the 2nd revolution in the area of computer in 1951. He discovered EDVAC (Electronic Discrete Variable Automatic Computer) and utilised the stored program and the binary number system in the computer.

FUNCTIONS OF COMPUTER

1. Collection and composition (input) of datas;
2. Storage of datas.
3. Processing of datas.
4. Retrieval or output of the proccessed informations and datas.

UNITS OF COMPUTER

1. Input unit.
2. Central processing unit–CPU.
3. External Memory unit.
4. Output unit.

The CPU of the computer is called brain of the computer and sometimes CPU is also called Micro Processor of the computer. The data is entered through the input unit in the computer and through the central processing unit with the help of External Memory Unit datas are arranged and processed. Ultimately by the output unit these datas or informations are issued or released.

PARTS OF COMPUTER

- **Monitor :** The monitor of the computer is like a television in which the picture appears in the form of doted points on the screen and these are called pixcels.
- **Hard Disc and Floppy Disc :** The Hard Disc is the permanent disc in the computers while the Floppy Disc is the disc utilised when datas or informations are to be transferred from one computer to another.
- **Mouse :** The mouse of the computer is like the remote control of TV through which computer is directly regulated or controlled without utilising the key-board.
- **Printer :** The printer is a device which prints any documents or processed informations of the computer.

SOME HIGH LEVEL LANGUAGES

1. **FORTRAN :** This language was developed for solving the mathematical formulae very quickly and conveniently.
2. **COBOL :** This language was developed for the commerical purposes. For the processing of this language a group of sentences is selected called paragraph and all paragraphs composed are called a section, while all sections composed are called a division.
3. **BASIC :** In basic a definite part of the prescribed instruction is only inserted in the computer.
4. **ALGOL :** This was basically fabricated and designed for the complex algebraic calculations.

5. **PASCAL :** It is an amplified and modified form of ALGOL.

6. **COMAL :** This computer language is used for the students of secondary level.

7. **LOGO :** This language is used for children and kids for drawing Graphic line diagrams.

8. **PROLOG :** This language is developed in 1973 in France and this language is used for Artificial Intelligence which is capable and equivalent to the logical program.

9. **FORTH :** This language was invented by Charles Mure which is frequently used in all types of the works in the computer.

COMPUTER VIRUS

The computer virus is an electronic code which is used to abolish or erradicate the inclusive informations or programs of the computer. Some important computer viruses are Micheleanjalo, Dork Avangor, kilo, filip, Macmug, Scores, Casecade, Jeruslem, Date crime, Coloumbs crime, Internet virus, Pachcom, Pach EXE, COM-EXE, Marizuana, C-brain, bloody, Chenge Mungu and Desi etc.

COMPUTER NETWORKING

There are two types of networkings which are usually occur— Local Area Networking (LAN) and Wide Area Networking (WAN). By LAN all the computers of the same buildings are connected like the computers of university premises, computers of offices etc.

By WAN all the comptuers of a large area are connected like the computers of all the offices of a city or town etc. In India a very large computer network namely INDONET has been installing through which all the main towns and cities has to be interlinked.

COMPUTER TERMINOLOGY

- **Bit :** The bit is a unit of measurement of the electronic data. One bit is either 0 or 1 but not both. On composing 8 bits, 1 byte is formed.

- **Bug :** The Bug is the error in the computer program or system and its eradication is called Debug.

- **Byte :** Total eight bits compose a byte. Thus 8 bits = 1 byte.

- **CD-ROM :** A CD like of music CD in which data can be stored substantially called CD-ROM. In a CD with comparison to floppy extremely more datas can be stored but one problem in it is that one time recorded data can not be deleted or modified.

- **Chip :** It is a thin slice on which by a special mechanism a circuit is designed which is normally made from Silicon.

- **Memory System :** The place where computer data and program are temporarily kept is called Memory system. Usually memory is implied from RAM.

- **Modem :** The device which converts digital signals into analogue signals and vice-versa is called Modem.

- **RAM :** It is Random Access Memory (a place) where datas to be processed are kept temporarily and it is unstable memory.

- **ROM :** It is Read Only Memory and it is stable or Non-valatile memory which doesn't ended after power off.

- **Scanner :** It is a device through which graphic image is transformed to digital image and the scanners are of usually two types one desktop and another hand operating.

PROGRAMING

Computers perform phenomenal feats of calculation, but they do not do so in a complicated way. They actually carry out very simple operations, such as addition and subtraction. They achieve their fantastic computing power by carrying out these operations at incredible speed.

The programme, or set of instructions for operating the computer, is therefore written as a sequence of very simple steps. (See box below) Several computer languages have been developed for different applications, including BASIC, COBOL, FORTRAN and PASCAL. Writing programmes is very skilled and time-consuming work. But for most typical computer applications ready-written programmes are available, called "packages".

☞ **How A Programme Works**

Without a programme to tell it what to do and how to do it, a computer is unable to function. If, for example, you wanted to know how many times the word 'the' appears in this paragraph, or in the whole book, it would not be enough merely to put the text into a computer and then ask it how many times the word appears. For the computer to accomplish the calculations it has to be told what to do in simple steps. The instructions might be:

1. Scan the text until a space followed by 'T' or 't' is found.

2. If the next letter is not 'h', go back to step 1.

3. If the letter is 'h', is the next letter 'e'?

4. If not, go back to step 1. If it is, go to step 5.

5. If 'e' is followed by a space, add 1 to the total.

6. Go back to step 1.

A full computer programme for this operation would need to be broken down into even more simple steps, but a series of such programmes could enable a computer to analyse any amount of text in great detail.

DEFENCE

The Supreme Command of the Armed Forces is vested in the hands of the President of the Country. The responsibility for national defence, however, rests with the Cabinet. All important questions having a bearing on defence are decided by the Cabinet Committee on Political Affairs, which is presided over by the Prime Minister. The Defence Minister is responsible to Parliament for all matters concerning the Defence Services. All the administrative and operational control of Armed Forces are exercised by the Ministry of Defence. The three services – Army, Navy and Air Force function through their respective service headquarters headed by the chief of Staff.

COMMISSIONED RANKS IN DEFENCE SERVICES

Army	*Navy*	*Air Force*
General	Admiral	Air Chief Marshal
Lieutenant-General	Vice-Admiral	Air Marshal
Major-General	Rear-Admiral	Air Vice-Marshal
Brigadier	Commodor	Air Commodor
Colonel	Captain	Group Captain
Lieutenant-Colonel	Commander	Wing Commander
Major	Lt.Commander	Squadron Leader
Captain	Lieutenant	Flight Lieutenant
Lieutenant	Sub-Lieutenant	Flying Officer

INTERNAL SECURITY ORGANISATIONS OF INDIA

S. No.	Name of Organisation	Year of Creation	Headquarters
1.	Assam Rifles (A.R.)	1835	Shillong
2.	Central Reserve Police Force (C.R.P.F.)	1939	New Delhi
3.	National Cadet Corps (N.C.C.)	1948	New Delhi
4.	Territorial Army	1948	In different States
5.	Indo-Tibetan Border Police	1962	New Delhi
6.	Home Guard	1962	In different States
7.	Coast Guard	1978	New Delhi
8.	Border Security Force (B.S.F.)	1965	New Delhi
9.	Central Industrial Security Force (C.I.S.F.)	1969	New Delhi
10.	National Security Guard	1984	New Delhi
11.	Police	—	In different States

COMMANDER-IN-CHIEFS OF INDIA

1. General Roy Bucher   Jan. 1, 1948 — Jan. 14, 1949
2. General K. M. Kariappa   Jan. 15, 1949 — Jan. 14, 1953
3. General Maharaj Rajendra Sinhji   Jan. 15, 1953 — March 31, 1955
4. First Marshal of the Indian Air Force — Arjan Singh

FIRST CHIEFS OF STAFF OF INDIAN FORCES

1. General Maharaj Rajendra Sinhji (Army Staff)   April 1, 1955 — May 14, 1955
2. Vice Admiral R.D. Katari (Naval Staff)   April 22, 1958 — June 4, 1962
3. Air Marshal Sri Thomas Elmherst (Air Staff)   Aug. 15, 1947 — Feb. 21, 1950

ARMY INSTITUTES

1.	Sainik Schools upto +2 Level	18 places in India
2.	Rashtriya Indian Military College (prepare for entrance to N.D.A)	Dehradun
3.	National Defence Academy (three services)	Khadakwasla, Pune
4.	Indian Military Academy (Army)	Dehradun
5.	Officers Training Academy (3 services) Short Courses	Chennai
6.	National Defence College	New Delhi
7.	The College of Combat	Mhow
8.	The College of Military Engineering	Kirkee
9.	Military College of Telecommunication Engineering	Mhow
10.	The armoured Corps Centre and School	Ahmed Nagar
11.	The School Artillery	Deolali
12.	The Infantry School	Mhow and Belgaum
13.	College of Material Management	Jabalpur

AIR FORCE INSTITUTIONS

Air Force Academy	Hyderabad
Helicopter Training School	Hakimpet
Flying Instructors School	Tambaram, Chennai
The College of Air Warfare	Secunderabad
Air Force Administrative College	Coimbatore
Air Force Technical College	Jalahalli

DEFENCE PRODUCTION UNITS

1. Bharat Dynamites Ltd.	Hyderabad	8. Mazagaon Dock	Mumbai
2. Praga Tools	Hyderabad	9. Goa Shipyard	Marmugao
3. Mishra Dattu Nigam	Hyderabad	10. Hindustan Shipyard Ltd.	Vishakhapatnam
4. Bharat Electronics Ltd.	Bangalore	11. Hindustan Aeronautics Ltd.	Bangalore, Hyderabad, Nasik, Koraput, Kanpur, Lucknow
5. Bharath Earthmovers Ltd.	Bangalore		
6. Heavy Vehicles Ltd.	Avadi, Chennai		
7. Garden Reach Ship Builders and Engineers Ltd.	Kolkata		

☞ Indian Army Commands

Command	HQ Location	Command	HQ Location
Eastern Command	Kolkata	Western Command	Chandigarh
Northern Command	Udhampur	Southern Command	Pune
Central Command	Lucknow	Training Command	Shimla
South-Western Command	Jaipur		

☞ Indian Air Force Commands

Command	HQ Location	Command	HQ Location
Western Air Command	New Delhi	South-Western Air Command	Gandhinagar
Central Air Command	Allahabad	Eastern Air Command	Shillong
Southern Air Command	Thiruvananthapuram	Training Command	Bengaluru

☞ Indian Navy Commands

Command	HQ Location	Command	HQ Location
Eastern Naval Command	Vishakhapatnam	Western Naval Command	Mumbai
Southern Naval Command	Cochin		

☞ Missile and Other Weapons

Name	Class	Range	Name	Class	Range
✳ Agni I	SRBM	850 km	✳ Brahmos	Supersonic Cruise Missile	290 km
✳ Agni II	MRBM	2500 km			
✳ Agni III	IRBM	3500 km-5500 km			
✳ Agni IV *or* Agni II Prime	IRBM	4000 km	✳ Brahmos 2	Hypersonic Cruise Missile	290 km
✳ Agni V	ICBM	5000 km-6000 km	✳ Prithvi I	SRBM	150 km
✳ Agni VI	ICBM	8000 km-10000 km	✳ Prithvi III	SRBM	350 km
✳ Agni 3SL	ICBM	5200 km-11600 km	✳ Sagarika	SLBM	700 km-2200 km
✳ Dhanush	SRBM	350 km	✳ Shaurya	TBM	700 km-2200 km
✳ Nirbhay	Subsonic Cruise Missile	1000 km	✳ Astra	Air to Air Missile	80 km-100 km

MULTIPLE CHOICE QUESTIONS

1. Match List-I with List-II and select the correct answer from the codes given below the lists:
   List-I
   (*a*) Napoleon Bonaparte
   (*b*) Jean Jacques Rousseau
   (*c*) Croce
   (*d*) Madame Roland
   List-II
   1. 'A history is contemporary history'
   2. 'Liberty what crimes are committed in thy name'
   3. 'Man is born free but everywhere he is in chains.'
   4. 'I am the Child of Revolution'
   Codes :

	(a)	(b)	(c)	(d)
A.	1	2	3	4
B.	4	3	1	2
C.	3	4	2	1
D.	3	4	1	2

2. Abraham Lincon was elected the President of United States in:
   A. 1862   B. 1860
   C. 1875   D. 1855

3. Who was known as the 'Prince of Humanists'?
   A. Francisco Petrarch B. Dante
   C. Boccacio   D. Erasmus

4. D-Day is the day when:
   A. Germany declared war on Britain
   B. US dropped the atom bomb on Hiroshima.
   C. Allied Troops landed in Normandy
   D. Germany surrendered to the allies

5. Whose teachings inspired the French Revolution?
   A. Locke
   B. Rousseau
   C. Hegel
   D. Plato

6. At a time when empires in Europe were crumbling before the might of Napoleon which one of the following Governor-Generals kept the British flag flying high in India?
   A. Warren Hastings   B. Lord Cornwallis
   C. Lord Wellesley   D. Lord Hastings

7. Which one of the following statements regarding Fascism in Italy is *not* true?
   A. The Fascists came to power as a result of popular uprising
   B. In 1926, all political parties except Mussolini's party were banned
   C. The Fascists suppressed the Socialist movement
   D. The Fascists were hostile to the Communists

8. The fall of Czar Nicholas-II is known as:
   A. Bloody Sunday
   B. Bolshevik Revolution
   C. February Revolution
   D. October Revolution

9. Industrial Revolution took place first in:
   A. France   B. Germany
   C. United Kingdom D. Japan

10. The British Prime Minister at the outbreak of World War II was :
    A. Churchill   B. Baldwin
    C. Attlee   D. Chemberlain

11. The 'Great Depression' (1929) economic crisis was met by adopting the policy of
    A. Stimulus   B. Marshall Plan
    C. New Deal   D. Open Door

12. The slogan "No taxation without representation" was raised during the:
    A. American War of Independence
    B. Russian Revolution
    C. French Revolution
    D. Indian Freedom struggle

13. In the nineteenth century the people of Europe started moving from the villages to the cities due to the impact of :
    A. Epidemics
    B. War
    C. Industrialisation
    D. Population explosion in villages

14. The important cause of the Civil War in America was:
    A. Abolition of slavery
    B. Quest for freedom
    C. Industrialisation
    D. Rebellion by the native Americans

15. Industrial Revolution could not have come about without:
    A. Merchant capitalism
    B. The Enclosure Movement
    C. The services of the proletariat class
    D. An agricultural revolution

16. Consider the following statements :
    The French Revolution came about mainly due to the :
    1. Extreme poverty of the people
    2. Impact of the works of great writers
    3. Cruelty of the rulers
    4. Impact of impulsive reaction

Which of the above statements are correct?
A. 1, 2 and 4   B. 2 and 3
C. 1, 3 and 4   D. 1, 2, 3 and 4

17. Asia's oldest and largest Buddhist monastery is situated in :
A. Tawang (Arunachal Pardesh)
B. Lhasa (Tibet)
C. Trincomallee (Sri Lanka)
D. Ulan Bator (Mongolia)

18. Who was the main architect of the Russian Revolution?
A. Karl Marx   B. Lenin
C. Stalin   D. Tolstoy

19. V.I. Lenin is associated with :
A. Russian Revolution of 1917
B. Chinese Revolution of 1949
C. German Revolution
D. French Revolution of 1789

20. Which one of the following statements is *not* correct?
A. Voltaire believed in Natural Religion
B. Rousseau wrote *Social Contract*
C. Montesquieu authored *The Spirit of Laws*
D. Necker believed in 'General Will'

21. 6th April, 1930 is well known in the history of India because this date is associated with...........
A. Dandi March by Mahatma Gandhi
B. Quit India Movement
C. Partition of Bengal
D. Partition of India

22. Which ruler enforced the system of 'Price Control' in India?
A. Mohammad Tughlak
B. Razia Begum
C. Alauddin Khilji
D. Sher Shah Suri

23. The concept of 'Din-e-Elahi' was founded by which king?
A. Dara Shikoh   B. Akbar
C. Sher Shah Suri   D. Shahjahan

24. Who are supposed to be the earliest inhabi-tants of India? Where did they come from?
A. Aryans from Central Asia
B. Dravidians from Mediterranean
C. Negroids from Africa
D. Bhils and the Santhals from West Asia

25. The one chief characteristic of temple architecture of the Gupta Age was :
A. Absence of dome
B. Huge size
C. Beautiful carvings

D. absence of a covered courtyard for the gathering of worshippers

26. The Rigveda consists of :
A. 1000 hymns   B. 2028 hymns
C. 1028 hymns   D. 1038 hymns

27. The central point in Ashoka's dharma was :
A. royalty to kings
B. peace and non-violence
C. respect to elders
D. religious tolerance

28. The social evil which was conspicuously absent during ancient India was :
A. *Sati*-System   B. *Devadasi*-System
C. Polygamy   D. *Purdah*-System

29. Which, among the following, can be accepted as a novelty introduced by Mughal emperors to their buildings?
A. Domes   B. Minarets
C. Arches   D. Attached gardens

30. The first ruler of India who defeated Muhammud of Ghur was :
A. Mularaja II of Gujarat
B. Prithviraja Chauhan of Delhi
C. Jayachand of Kannauj
D. Parmaldeva of Bundelkhand

31. What important event happened in India in 1911?
A. Bengal was partitioned
B. Non-Cooperation movement was launched
C. India's capital was shifted from Calcutta to Delhi
D. Mahatma Gandhi presided over the Congress session

32. The first phase of the Congress Party (1885-1905) was characterized by its efforts to secure:
A. limited independence
B. complete freedom
C. Indianization of services
D. constitutional reforms

33. The Muslim League demanded a separate homeland for the Indian Muslims openly for the first time at its annual session held in Lahore in the year :
A. 1931 A.D.   B. 1936 A.D.
C. 1940 A.D.   D. 1941 A.D.

34. Under whose governorship did the East India Company secure the Diwani Rights in Bengal, Bihar and Odisha from Emperor Shah Alam?
A. Lord Cornwallis
B. Lord William Bentinck
C. Lord Clive
D. Lord Wellesley

35. The Simon Commission was generally boycotted by the Indian political parties. What was the reason for this general non-cooperation?
A. the Commission aimed at dividing the people
B. it was an 'all white' Commission
C. it came after the Jallianwala Bagh carnage
D. it was an eye wash

36. Aligarh Muslim University was founded by :
A. Dr. Saifuddin Kitchlu
B. Mohammad Ali Jinnah
C. Sir Syed Ahmed Khan
D. Maulana Mohammad Ali

37. Ibn Batutah was an African traveller visiting India during the time of :
A. Alivardi Khan
B. Ala-ud-din Khalji
C. Iltutmish
D. Mohammad-bin-Tughlaq

38. The battle of Wandiawash was fought in :
A. 1726   B. 1760
C. 1818   D. 1857

39. The abolition of *Sati* by government regulation was at the time of :
A. Warren Hastings   B. Lord Wellesley
C. Lord Bentinck   D. Lord Ahmerst

40. Pick out the wrong combination :
A. Dilwara Temple : Mt. Abu
B. Pashupati Temple : Kathmandu
C. Padmanabh Temple : Bangalore
D. Minakshi Temple : Madurai

41. Match the following:
(a) Chanhudaro   *(b)* Kalibangan
(c) Lothal   *(d)* Surkotada
1. Alleged discovery of the skeleton of horse.
2. Bead making.
3. Traces of a dock and ship on seal.
4. Evidence of ploughing the fields.
The Correct code is :

	(a)	*(b)*	*(c)*	*(d)*
A.	2	4	3	1
B.	2	1	3	4
C.	1	2	3	4
D.	2	1	4	3

42. Match the Harappan settlements with the banks of rivers on which they were located :
(a) Harappa   1. Ravi
(b) Mohenjodaro   2. Indus
(c) Ropar   3. Sutlej
(d) Kalibangan   4. Ghaggar
(e) Lothal   5. Bhogava

Codes :

	(a)	*(b)*	*(c)*	*(d)*	*(e)*
A.	1	2	3	4	5
B.	1	2	3	5	4
C.	2	1	3	5	4
D.	2	1	4	3	5

43. The Goddess 'Kannagi' whose many temples were erected during the 'Sangam Age' was the goddess of:
A. Chastity   B. Love
C. Prowess   D. Wisdom

44. The Jain goal of life is to attain deliverance from the fetters of mudane existence, the way to which lies through three jewels. Which one of the following was not included among the 'three jewels' of Jainism?
A. Right faith   B. Right action
C. Right knowledge   D. Right conduct

45. The most striking feature of the Ashokan pillar is polish. Name the Ashokan pillar which is considered to be the most graceful of all Ashokan pillars.
A. Sarnath
B. Rampurva
C. Laurya-Nandangarh
D. Rummindei

46. Which are the correct statements?
1. The land grants, started in Satavahana period, paved the way for feudal developments in India.
2. Silk and spices were the Chief Indian export articles of Indo-Roman trade.
3. The Guptas issued the largest number of gold coins in ancient India.
4. The first memorial of a 'SATI' dated 510 A.D. is found at Eran in Madhya Pradesh.
A. 1 and 2   B. 1, 3, and 4
C. 1 and 4   D. 1, 2, 3 and 4

47. Who among the following patronised the 'Gandhara' (Indo-Greek style) School of Art?
A. Ashoka, the Great
B. Harsha Vardhana
C. Kanishka
D. Chandragupta Vikramaditya

48. The Sultanate of Delhi had five ruling dynasties. The dynasty having longest and shortest period were :
A. Ilbari and Khalji
B. Tughlaq and Khalji
C. Tughlaq and Sayyid
D. Ilbari and Lodis

49. Which one of the following events took place at the last during reign of Muhammad-bin-Tughlaq?
A. Introduction of token currency
B. Increase of land-revenue in Doab
C. Transfer of Capital from Delhi to Devagiri.
D. Conquest of Khurasan and Iraq

50. The most learned medieval Muslim ruler who was well versed in various branches of learning including astronomy, mathematics and medicine was :
A. Jalaluddin Khilji
B. Sikander Lodi
C. Ghiyasuddin Tughlaq
D. Muhammad-bin-Tughlaq

51. The 'Sufis' had 12 silsilas. They propounded the idea of Union with God through:
A. Love   B. Rituals
C. Fasts   D. Prayers

52. Match the following:
(*a*) Peshwa   1. Foreign affairs
(*b*) Panditrao   2. Audit and accounts
(*c*) Amatya   3. Providing grants to scholars
(*d*) Sumant   4. General supervision
                 5. Military affairs
Select the correct code :

	(*a*)	(*b*)	(*c*)	(*d*)
A.	2	3	4	5
B.	4	1	2	3
C.	4	3	2	1
D.	3	1	4	2

53. The Regulating Act of 1773 can be regarded as the first measure to :
A. assert the right of British Parliament to legislate for India
B. separate the legislature from the executive
C. separate the judiciary from the executive
D. centralise law-making

54. What was the exact constitutional status of the Indian Republic on 26th January, 1950?
A. A Democratic Republic
B. A Sovereign, Democratic Republic
C. A Sovereign, Secular, Democratic Republic
D. A Sovereign, Socialist, Secular, Democratic Republic

55. When the British obtained the grant of Diwani of Bengal, Bihar and Odisha they acquired the right to :
A. maintain law and order in these territories
B. administer civil justice and collect revenue in these territories
C. collect revenue and establish revenue administration in these territories
D. militarily defend these territories

56. Which of the following were responsible for the growth of nationalism in India during the British rule?
1. Economic exploitation of India.
2. Impact of western education.
3. Role of the Press.

Select the correct answer using the codes given below :
Codes:
A. 1, 2 and 3   B. 1 and 2
C. 2 and 3   D. 1 and 3

57. Which one of the following nationalist leaders has been described as being radical in politics but conservative on social issues?
A. G.K. Gokhale
B. B.G. Tilak
C. Lala Lajpat Rai
D. Madan Mohan Malviya

58. Provincial Autonomy in British India was envisaged by the :
A. Act of 1909   B. Act of 1919
C. Act of 1935   D. Act of 1947

59. Dyarchy means :
A. double government
B. a government in which the centre is very powerful
C. a government based on division of power between centre and provinces
D. None of the above

60. The Indian National Congress observed 'Independence Day' for the first time on 26th January in :
A. 1920   B. 1925
C. 1930   D. 1947

61. ....is situated near the banks of Sabarmati River
A. Bhavnagar   B. Aurangabad
C. Ahmedabad   D. Rajkot

62. Sericulture is:
A. science of the various kinds of serum
B. artificial rearing of fish
C. art of silkworm breeding
D. study of various cultures of a community

63. The most abundant constituents of earth's crust are:
A. Igneous rocks
B. Sedimentary rocks
C. Metamorphic rocks
D. Granite

64. Indian Standard Time is based on:
A. 80°E longitude   B. 82½°E longitude
C. 110°E longitude   D. 25°E longitude

65. Tides in the oceans are caused by :
A. Gravitational pull of the moon on the earth's surface including sea water
B. Gravitational pull of the sun on the earth's surface only and not on the sea water
C. Gravitational pull of the moon and the sun on the earth's surface including the sea water
D. None of these

66. Nagarjunasagar Project is situated on the river:
    A. Tungabhadra
    B. Cauvery
    C. Krishna
    D. Godavari

67. The difference between the Indian Standard Time and the Greenwich Mean Time is:
    A. – 3½ hours
    B. + 3½ hours
    C. – 5½ hours
    D. + 5½ hours

68. Which of the following dams is not on Narmada river?
    A. Indira-Sagar Project
    B. Maheshwar Hydel Power Project
    C. Jobat Project
    D. Koyna Power Project

69. Which of the following statements is **not true** about the availability of water on the earth, the crisis for which is going to increase in the years to come?
    A. About 97.5 per cent of the total volume of water available on the earth is salty
    B. 80 per cent of the water available to us for use comes in bursts as monsoons
    C. About 2.5 per cent of the total water available on the earth is polluted water and cannot be used for human activities
    D. Possibility is that some big glaciers will melt in the coming ten-fifteen years and sea level will rise by 3-4 metres all over the earth

70. Which of the following is **not** a cash crop?
    A. Jute
    B. Paddy
    C. Cashewnut
    D. Sugarcane

71. Through which States does Cauvery River flow?
    A. Gujarat, M.P., Tamil Nadu
    B. Karnataka, Kerala, Tamil Nadu
    C. Karnataka, Kerala, Andhra Pradesh
    D. M.P., Maharashtra, Tamil Nadu

72. Indian Standard Time is the local time of 82½°E which passes through :
    A. Guntur
    B. Delhi
    C. Allahabad
    D. Kolkata

73. The 17th parallel defines the boundary between:
    A. North and South Korea
    B. USA and Canada
    C. North and South Vietnam
    D. China and Russia

74. During the period of south-west monsoon, Tamil Nadu remains dry because:
    A. the winds do not reach this area
    B. there are no mountains in this area
    C. it lies in the rain shadow area
    D. the temperature is too high to let the winds cool down

75. Which country does top in producing cocoa?
    A. Ghana
    B. Brazil
    C. Ivory Coast
    D. Nigeria

76. The biggest reserves of thorium are in :
    A. India
    B. China
    C. The Soviet Union
    D. U.S.A.

77. The Girnar Hills are situated in which of the following states?
    A. Gujarat
    B. Karnataka
    C. Madhya Pradesh
    D. Maharashtra

78. During December 22nd the sun is vertically over:
    A. Tropic of Cancer
    B. Tropic of Capricorn
    C. The Equator
    D. None of the above

79. Photosphere is described as the :
    A. Lower layer of atmosphere
    B. Visible surface of the sun from which radiation emanates
    C. Wavelength of solar spectrum
    D. None of the above

80. Broadly, there are three layers of the earth of the crust, the mantle and the core. The crust forms what percentage of the volume of the earth?
    A. 0.5%
    B. 2.5%
    C. 7.5%
    D. 12.5%

81. The grassland of Argentina is known as :
    A. Pampas
    B. Campos
    C. Savanna
    D. None of the above

82. Different seasons are formed because :
    A. Sun is moving around the earth
    B. of revolution of the earth around the Sun on its orbit
    C. of rotation of the earth around its axis
    D. All of the above

83. Eskers and Drumlins are features formed by:
    A. underground water
    B. running water
    C. the action of wind
    D. glacial action

84. Match List-I and List-II and select the correct answer using the codes given below the Lists :

List-I (Rivers)	List-II (Towns)
(a) Ghaghara	1. Lucknow
(b) Brahmaputra	2. Hoshangabad
(c) Narmada	3. Ahmedabad
(d) Sabarmati	4. Guwahati
	5. Ayodhya

	(*a*)	(*b*)	(*c*)	(*d*)
A.	4	5	1	2
B.	5	4	2	3
C.	5	4	3	1
D.	3	5	2	1

85. Which of the statements as regards the consequences of the movement of the earth is not correct?
   A. Revolution of the earth is the cause of the change of seasons.
   B. Rotation of the earth is the cause of days and nights.
   C. Rotation of the earth causes variation in the duration of days and nights.
   D. Rotation of the earth effects the movement of winds and ocean currents.

86. The world is divided into :
   A. 12 time zones
   B. 20 time zones
   C. 24 time zones
   D. 36 time zones

87. The 'Kiel' canal links the :
   A. Pacific and Atlantic Oceans
   B. Mediterranean Sea and Red Sea
   C. Mediterranean Sea and Black Sea
   D. North Sea and Baltic Sea

88. Match the following :

List-I	**List-II**
(*a*) Himadri	1. Outer Himalayas
(*b*) Shivalik	2. Inner Himalayas
(*c*) Himanchal	3. Middle Himalayas
(*d*) Sahyadri	4. Western Ghats

Codes:

	(*a*)	(*b*)	(*c*)	(*d*)
A.	1	2	3	4
B.	4	2	3	1
C.	2	1	3	4
D.	1	2	3	4

89. The term 'Regur' refers to:
   A. Laterite soils
   B. Black Cotton soils
   C. Red Soils
   D. Deltaic Alluvial Soils

90. Location of sugar industry in India is shifting from north to south because of:
   A. cheap labour
   B. expanding regional market
   C. cheap and abundant supply of power
   D. high yield and high sugar content in sugarcane

91. Consider the following statements :
   1. Ozone is found mostly in the Stratosphere.
   2. Ozone layer lies 55-75 km above the surface of the earth.
   3. Ozone absorbs ultraviolet radiation from the Sun.
   4. Ozone layer has no significance for life on the earth.
   Which of the above statements are correct?
   A. 1 and 3   B. 2 and 4
   C. 2 and 3   D. 1 and 4

92. Match List-I with List-II and select the correct answer using the codes given below the Lists :

List-I (*Crops*)	**List-II** (*Producer*)
(*a*) Banana	1. Colombia
(*b*) Cocoa	2. Ghana
(*c*) Coffee	3. Jamaica
(*d*) Tea	4. Kenya

Codes :

	(*a*)	(*b*)	(*c*)	(*d*)
A.	2	3	1	4
B.	3	2	1	4
C.	3	2	4	1
D.	2	3	4	1

93. Darjeeling and Dharamsala would be the right places to visit if one wanted to get a clear view respectively of :
   A. Kanchanjunga and Dhauladhar ranges
   B. Nandadevi and Dhauladhar ranges
   C. Kanchanjunga and Nandadevi ranges
   D. Nandadevi and Nanga Parvat

94. Atmosphere exists because:
   A. The Gravitational force of the Earth
   B. Revolution of the Earth
   C. Rotation of the Earth
   D. Weight of the gases of atmosphere

95. Victoria lake is located in the continent:
   A. Africa
   B. Asia
   C. North America
   D. South America

96. The famous Lagoon Lake of India is :
   A. Dal Lake   B. Chilka Lake
   C. Pulicat Lake   D. Mansarover

97. Where are most of the earth's active volcanoes concentrated?
   A. Indian Ocean   B. Pacific Ocean
   C. Aral Sea   D. Atlantic Ocean

98. Through which of the following states does the river Chambal flow?
   A. U.P., M.P., Rajasthan
   B. M.P., Gujarat, U.P.
   C. Rajasthan, M.P., Bihar
   D. Gujarat, M.P., U.P.

99. Which country is called the sugar bowl of the world?
A. Cuba   B. India
C. Argentina   D. USA

100. The area covered by forest in India is about:
A. 46%   B. 33%
C. 23%   D. 21.54%

101. A closed economy is the one which :
A. does not permit emigration or immigration
B. permits emigration but no immigration
C. engages in no foreign trade
D. engages in no foreign and domestic trade or transit

102. In a developed economy the major share of employment originates in the :
A. primary sector   B. tertiary sector
C. secondary sector   D. any of the above

103. The Economic and Social Commission for Asia and Pacific (ESCAP) is located at :
A. Bangkok   B. Kuala Lumpur
C. Manila   D. Singapore

104. Commercial vehicles are not produced by which of the following companies in India?
A. TELCO   B. Ashok Leyland
C. DCM Daewoo   D. Birla Yamaha

105. In India, the Public Sector is most dominant in:
A. transport
B. steel production
C. commercial banking
D. organised term-lending financial institutions

106. The main argument advanced in favour of small scale and cottage industries in India is that:
A. cost of production is low
B. they require small capital investment
C. they advance the goal of equitable distribution of wealth
D. they generate a large volume of employment

107. The most serious economic problems of India are:
A. Poverty and unemployment
B. Stagnation, not poverty
C. Unemployment, not poverty
D. Underdevelopment, not poverty

108. Which of the following is not one of the three central problems of an economy?
A. What to produce
B. How to produce
C. When to produce
D. For whom to produce

109. If saving exceeds investment, the national income will:
A. fall   B. rise
C. fluctuate   D. remain constant

110. In which of the following industries in India are the maximum number of workers employed?
A. Sugar   B. Jute
C. Textiles   D. Iron and Steel

111. Terrace Cultivation is practiced mostly:
A. in urban areas
B. on slopes of mountains
C. on tops of hills
D. in undulating tracts

112. Which of the following is a Selective Credit Control method?
A. Bank Rate
B. RBI directives
C. Cash Reserve Ratio
D. Open market operations

113. Which of the following taxes is not shared by the Central Government with the States?
A. Union excise duties
B. Customs duty
C. Income tax
D. Estate duty

114. ICICI is the name of a:
A. Financial Institution
B. Chemical Industry
C. Cotton Industry
D. Chamber of Commerce and Industry

115. Structural Unemployment arises due to
A. Deflationary conditions
B. Heavy industry bias
C. Shortage of raw material
D. Inadequate productive capacity

116. Which of the following is the largest single source of the government's earning from tax revenue?
A. Corporation tax
B. Customs duties
C. Excise duties
D. Income tax

117. The largest public sector bank in India is:
A. Central Bank of India
B. Punjab National Bank
C. State Bank of India
D. Indian Overseas Bank

118. Which of the following statements best explains the term contraband goods?
A. Goods produced only for exports
B. Goods produced in joint sector only
C. Goods for the trading of which licence is not required
D. Goods that are forbidden, from export, import or even possession, by law

119. Price in the market is fixed by:
A. Stock exchange rates
B. The demand and supply ruling in the market at a particular time
C. The Finance Minister
D. None of the above

120. Devaluation of currency helps to promote:
A. National Income
B. Savings
C. Imports at lower cost
D. Exports

121. Balanced economic growth can be achieved only if:
A. All the sectors of economy grow at the same rate
B. Population growth is arrested
C. All the inter dependent sectors grow in harmony
D. Basic and heavy industries are assigned highest priority

122. Which one of the following contributes most to the National Income in India?
A. Agricultural Sector
B. Industrial Sector
C. Foreign Trade Sector
D. Tertiary Sector

123. 'MODVAT' stands for:
A. Ad Valorem tax on output
B. Deduction of cost of inputs from the value of output
C. Reduction in import duties
D. Imposition of tax on professions

124. Largest revenue in India is obtained from:
A. Excise duties
B. Corporation tax
C. Income tax
D. None of the above

125. The term 'devaluation' means:
A. Reducing the value of a currency in terms of another currency
B. Increasing the value of a currency
C. Revising the value of a currency
D. None of the above

126. Per capita net availability of pulses has shown a tendency of:
A. Increase over time
B. Decrease over time
C. Constant over time
D. First increase then decrease

127. National Income is the same as:
A. Net national product at market price
B. Net domestic product at market price
C. Net national product at factor cost
D. Net domestic product at factor cost

128. Which one of the following is not an example of indirect tax?
A. Sales tax
B. Excise duty
C. Customs duty
D. Expenditure tax

129. The major aim of devaluation is to:
A. encourage imports
B. encourage exports
C. encourage both exports and imports
D. discourage both exports and imports

130. Structural unemployment arises due to:
A. deflationary conditions
B. heavy industry bias
C. shortage of raw materials
D. inadequate productive capacity

131. When was the Family Planning Programme officially started in India?
A. 1950
B. 1952
C. 1956
D. 1962

132. When was the Reserve Bank of India nationalised?
A. 1947
B. 1949
C. 1950
D. 1951

133. Which of the following is *not* a feature of the Indian economy?
A. High rate of population growth
B. Disguised unemployment
C. Lowest rate of adult literacy
D. High rate of exports

134. The 'Relative Deprivation' approach for measuring poverty has been adopted by:
A. developing countries
B. developed countries
C. under-developed countries
D. None of the above

135. One of the main factors that led to rapid expansion of Indian exports is:
A. Imposition of import duties
B. Liberalisation of the economy
C. Recession in other countries
D. Diversification of exports

136. Sustainable economic development means an increase in the rate of growth of real:
A. total and per capita product
B. total and per capita product and level of literacy rate
C. total and per capita product and life expectancy at birth
D. total and per capita product, taking into account the cost of degradation of the quality of environment in this process

137. Functional unemployment occurs when:
    A. unemployed have no qualification for job
    B. people frequently change their job
    C. people were thrown out from job due to recession
    D. None of these

138. Which among the following does **not** have a 'free trade zone'?
    A. Kandla
    B. Mumbai
    C. Visakhapatnam
    D. Thiruvanantpuram

139. Sun Belt of USA is important for which one of the following industries?
    A. Cotton textile
    B. Petrochemicals
    C. Hi-tech electronics
    D. Food Processing

140. Commercial banking system in India is
    A. unit banking
    B. branch banking
    C. mixed banking
    D. None of the above

141. Who gives recognition to political parties in India?
    A. Parliament
    B. President
    C. Supreme Court
    D. Election Commission

142. The Quorum of the Legislative Council is :
    A. one-fourth of its total membership
    B. one-third of its membership
    C. one-tenth of its membership
    D. 25

143. The Indian Constitution is:
    A. federal
    B. unitary
    C. a happy mixture of the federal and unitary
    D. federal in normal times and unitary in times of emergency

144. Universal adult franchise implies a right to vote to all:
    A. adult residents of the State
    B. adult male citizens of the State
    C. residents of the State
    D. adult citizens of the State

145. When a resolution prefering a charge against the President has been passed by a specified majority in the House, it is sent to the other House for investigation. If, as a result of such an investigation, a resolution is passed through a specified majority by the other House, declaring that the charge has been sustained, the President shall leave his office. The specified special majority must not be less than :
    A. two-third of the members present and voting
    B. one-third of the members present and voting
    C. three-fourth of the members present and voting and two-third of the total membership

D. two-third of the total membership

146. Which one of the following judicial powers of the President of India has been *wrongly* listed?
    A. he appoints the Chief Justice and other judges of the Supreme Court
    B. he can remove the judges of the Supreme Court on grounds of misconduct
    C. he can consult the Supreme Court on any question of law or fact which is of public importance
    D. he can grant pardon, reprieves and respites to persons punished under Union Law

147. The Vice-president of India can be removed from his office before the expiry of his term if :
    A. the Rajya Sabha passes a resolution by a majority of its members and the Lok Sabha agrees with the resolution
    B. if the Supreme Court of India recommends his removal
    C. the President so desires
    D. None of the above

148. The Chief Justice of a High Court in India is appointed by the :
    A. Governor of the State
    B. Prime Minister of India
    C. Chief Justice of the Supreme Court
    D. President of India

149. Which of the following statements is constitu-tionally not true about the passing of the Union Budgets, Railway Budgets and Finance Bill in India?
    1. Under the law, Finance Bill should be adopted by both the Houses of the Parliament within 45 days of its introduction.
    2. If the Finance Bill is not adopted within specified period, the government loses its authority to levy the taxes proposed in the budgets.
    3. In the absence of full budget, a vote-on-account gives the power to the government to spend.
    4. Government cannot raise revenues without a proper approval of the Finance Bill
    A. Only 2
    B. Only 3
    C. Only 4
    D. Only 1, 2 and 3

150. Normally, on whose advice the President's Rule is imposed in a State?
    A. Chief Minister
    B. Legislative Assembly
    C. Governor
    D. Chief Justice of High Court

151. Which Article of the Indian Constitution deals with Amendment procedure?
    A. Article 368
    B. Article 358
    C. Article 367
    D. All of these

152. Government is the agency through which the will of:
A. the state is expressed
B. the people is expressed
C. the head of the state is expressed
D. the majority is expressed

153. In a unitary system of government :
A. The centre is all powerful
B. The centre is weaker than the states
C. The centre and states stand at par
D. The states and centre are supreme in their respective spheres

154. In Cabinet System of Government the real executive authority rests with :
A. The Council of Ministers
B. The Prime Minister
C. The Constitution
D. The Parliament

155. The Head of the State under a parliamentary government:
A. is an elected representative
B. is a hereditary person
C. is a nominated person
D. may be any one of the above

156. In the event of a ministerial proposal being defeated on the floor of the legislature, under the parliamentary system :
A. the government waits for a general no-confidence motion
B. the minister concerned is taken to task by the Prime Minister
C. the minister is forced to resign
D. the whole Council of Ministers resign

157. The "due process of law" is an essential characteristic of the judicial system of:
A. UK   B. France
C. USA   D. India

158. Under the Constitution it is :
A. obligatory for the President to accept the advice of the Council of Ministers but is not obliged to follow it
B. obligatory for the President to accept the advice of the Council of Ministers
C. not obligatory for the President to seek or accept the advice of the Council of Ministers
D. obligatory for the President to seek the advice of the Council of Ministers if his own party is in power

159. Which one of the following statements is correct?
A. the Presiding Officer of Rajya Sabha is elected every year

B. the Presiding Officer of Rajya Sabha is elected for a term of two years at a time
C. the Presiding Officer of Rajya Sabha is elected for a term of six years
D. the Vice-President of India is the ex-officio Presiding Officer of Rajya Sabha

160. The introduction of "no confidence" motion in the Lok Sabha requires the support of at least:
A. 50 members   B. 70 members
C. 60 members   D. 80 members

161. The High Court comes under :
A. State List   B. Union List
C. Concurrent List   D. None of the above

162. Which one of the following has been wrongly listed as a Fundamental Duty of the Indian citizens?
A. to develop scientific temper, humanism and spirit of inquiry and reform
B. to work for raising the prestige of the country in the international sphere
C. to protect and improve the natural environment
D. to strive towards excellence in all spheres of individual and collective activity

163. Which one of the following is not a Fundamental Duty as outlined in Article 51A of the Constitution?
A. to abide by the Constitution and respect its ideals
B. to defend the country and render national service when called upon to do so
C. to work for the moral upliftment of the weaker sections of society
D. to preserve the rich heritage

164. The main characteristics of the Directive Principles of State Policy given in the Indian Constitution are :
A. not enforceable by any court
B. fundamental in the governance of the country
C. 'Like instruments, instructions, political manifesto and a code of moral precepts which have to guide governors of the country'
D. no law can be passed, which is opposed to these principles

165. Of the following which are true?
A. In a State, the Legislative Council is dominant with regard to non-financial bills and the Legislative Assembly with regard to financial (money) bills
B. Vidhan Parishad can virtually block legisla-tion even if the same is passed by the Vidhan Sabha
C. In case of a tie between the two Houses, the Governor is duty-bound to call a joint session of the two Houses to have the issue settled on a majority verdict

D. If a Bill is twice approved by the Vidhan Sabha, it becomes law even if rejected by the Vidhan Parishad

166. Which one of the following types of emergency can be declared by the President?
A. Emergency due to threat of war and external aggresion
B. Emergency due to break-down of constitu-tional machinery in a State
C. Financial emergency on account of threat to the financial credit of India
D. all the three emergencies

167. The chairman of which of the following parliamentary committees is invariably from the members of ruling party?
A. Committee on public undertakings
B. Public accounts committee
C. Estimates committee
D. Committee on delegated legislation

168. Which of the following is not a formally prescribed device available to the members of parliament?
A. Question hour
B. Zero hour
C. Half-an-hour discussion
D. Short duration discussion

169. Which of the following is not a tool of executive control over public administration?
A. Power of appointment and removal
B. Line agencies
C. Appeal to public opinion
D. Civil services code

170. If the Speaker of the State Legislative Assembly decides to resign, he should submit his resignation to the:
A. Judges of the High Court
B. Deputy Speaker
C. Chief Minister
D. Finance Minister

171. The Constitution of India provides for the nomination of two members of Lok Sabha by the President to represent:
A. the Parsis
B. men of eminence
C. the business community
D. the Anglo-Indian community

172. India is a Federal State because of:
A. dual judiciary
B. dual citizenship prevalent here
C. share of power between the Centre and the States
D. rigid Constitution

173. Residuary Subjects are those subjects which are:
A. contained in the State list
B. contained in the Union list
C. contained in the Concurrent list
D. not covered by any of the three lists

174. Which of the following writs can be issued, by the Supreme Court, to enforce Fundamental Rights?
A. Writ of Habeas Corpus
B. Writ of Mandamus
C. Writ of Quo Warranto
D. All of these

175. When the offices of both the President and the Vice-President of India are vacant, who will discharge their functions?
A. Prime Minister
B. Home Minister
C. Chief Justice of India
D. The Speaker

176. The Supreme Court tenders advice to the President of India on a matter of law or fact:
A. on its own
B. only when such advice is sought
C. only if the matter relates to some basic issue
D. only if the issue poses a threat to the unity and integrity of the country

177. Six months shall **not** intervene between two sessions of the Indian Parliament because :
A. it is the customary practice
B. it is the British convention followed in India
C. it is an obligation under the Constitution of India
D. None of the above

178. The States of the Indian Union can be recognised or their boundaries altered by:
A. the Union Parliament by a simple majority in the ordinary process of legislation
B. two-thirds majority of both the Houses of Parliament
C. two-thirds majority of both the Houses of Parliament and the consent of the legisla-tures of concerned States
D. an executive order of the Union government with the consent of the concerned State governments

179. The Basic Feature theory of the Constitution of India was propounded by the Supreme Court in the case of :
A. Minerva Mills Vs. Union of India
B. Golaknath Vs. State of Punjab
C. Maneka Gandhi Vs. Union of India
D. Keshavananda Vs. State of Kerala

180. Which one of the following writs is issued by a court in case of illegal detention of a person?
A. Habeas corpus   B. Mandamus
C. Certiorari   D. Quo-warranto

181. Name the instrument with the help of which a sailor in a submarine can see the objects on the surface of the sea.
A. Telescope
B. Periscope
C. Gycroscope
D. Stereoscope

182. 'HEMOPHILLIA' is the disease of ....
A. liver
B. blood
C. brain
D. bones

183. Vitamin A is abundantly found in ....
A. Brinjal
B. Tomato
C. Carrot
D. Cabbage

184. .... is not soluble in water.
A. Vitamin A
B. Vitamin B
C. Vitamin C
D. None of these

185. The blood vessels with the smallest diameter are called ....
A. capillaries
B. arterioles
C. venules
D. lymphatics

186. Out of the following .... has the greatest elasticity.
A. steel
B. rubber
C. aluminium
D. annealed copper

187. Cooking gas is a mixture of which of the following two gases?
A. Carbon Dioxide and Oxygen
B. Butane and Propane
C. Carbon Monoxide and Carbon Dioxide
D. Methane and Ethylene

188. The substance most commonly used as a food preservative is:
A. sodium carbonate
B. tartaric acid
C. acetic acid
D. benzoic acid

189. Normally, the substances that fight against diseases in human systems are known as:
A. dioxyribonucleic acids
B. carbohydrates
C. enzymes
D. antibodies

190. The SI unit of temperature is ....
A. Kelvin
B. Celsius
C. Fahrenheit
D. None of the above

191. One of the common fungal diseases of man is :
A. plague
B. ringworm
C. cholera
D. typhoid

192. A clear sky is blue because:
A. red light is scattered more than blue
B. ultraviolet light has been absorbed
C. blue light is scattered more than red
D. blue light has been absorbed

193. Jenner introduced the method of making people immune to :
A. small pox
B. rabies
C. cholera
D. polio

194. The largest cell in the human body is :
A. Nerve cell
B. Live cell
C. Muscle cell
D. Kidney cell

195. What is the device that steps up or steps down the voltage?
A. Dynamo
B. Conductor
C. Inductor
D. Transformer

196. The protein deficiency disease is known as :
A. Kwashiorker
B. Cirrhosis
C. Eczema
D. Clycoses

197. Iron deficiency causes :
A. rickets
B. anaemia
C. cirrhosis
D. goitre

198. Blood group of an individual is controlled by :
A. Haemoglobin
B. Shape of RBC
C. Shape of WBC
D. Genes

199. In a normal man the amount of blood pumped out by the heart per minute is about :
A. 1 litre
B. 3 litres
C. 4 litres
D. 5 litres

200. Red/green colour blindness in man is known as :
A. Protanopia
B. Deutetanopia
C. Both A and B above
D. Marfan's syndrome

201. The blue colour of the water in the sea is due to :
A. Reflection of the blue light by the impurities in sea water
B. Reflection of the blue sky by sea water and scattering of blue light by water molecules
C. Absorption of other colours by water molecules
D. None of the above

202. The image formed on the retina of the eye is:
A. upright and real
B. larger than the object
C. small and inverted
D. enlarged and real

203. Unit of loudness of sound is:
A. bel
B. decibel
C. phon
D. none of these

204. Oil rises up the wick in a lamp :
A. because oil is volatile
B. due to the capillary action phenomenon
C. due to the surface tension phenomenon
D. because oil is very light

205. The 'stones' formed in human kidney consist mostly of :
A. calcium oxalate
B. sodium acetate
C. magnesium sulphate
D. calcium

206. We hear the sound later, while the light is seen earlier:
A. because light's speed is more than that of sound
B. because lights travel in a straight direction while sound in a zigzag direction
C. because sound's frequency is lower than light
D. All of the above

207. Which part of an eye is transplanted?
A. Cornea   B. Retina
C. Iris   D. Sciera

208. The Universal donor group of blood is:
A. O   B. A
C. B   D. AB

209. The green colour of the leaf is due to :
A. Presence of Chloroplast
B. Presence of Chromium
C. Presence of Nicoplast
D. Presence of excess of oxygen

210. Voice of a child is more shrill than that of an elderly person because:
A. the pitch of the child's voice is higher than that of the person
B. the pitch is lower
C. the child is more energetic
D. None of the above

ANSWERS

1	2	3	4	5	6	7	8	9	10
B	C	D	C	B	C	A	C	C	D

11	12	13	14	15	16	17	18	19	20
C	A	C	A	A	D	A	B	A	D

21	22	23	24	25	26	27	28	29	30
A	C	B	C	D	C	B	D	D	B

31	32	33	34	35	36	37	38	39	40
C	D	C	C	B	C	D	B	C	C

41	42	43	44	45	46	47	48	49	50
A	A	A	B	C	D	C	B	B	D

51	52	53	54	55	56	57	58	59	60
A	C	A	B	B	A	B	C	A	C

61	62	63	64	65	66	67	68	69	70
C	C	B	B	C	C	D	D	D	B

71	72	73	74	75	76	77	78	79	80
B	C	C	C	A	A	A	B	B	A

81	82	83	84	85	86	87	88	89	90
A	B	D	B	C	C	D	C	B	D

91	92	93	94	95	96	97	98	99	100
A	B	A	A	A	B	B	A	A	D

101	102	103	104	105	106	107	108	109	110
C	B	A	D	D	D	A	C	D	C

111	112	113	114	115	116	117	118	119	120
B	B	B	A	D	A	C	D	B	D

121	122	123	124	125	126	127	128	129	130
C	A	A	B	A	D	C	D	B	D

131	132	133	134	135	136	137	138	139	140
B	B	D	A	B	D	B	D	D	C

141	142	143	144	145	146	147	148	149	150
D	C	D	D	D	B	A	D	C	C

151	152	153	154	155	156	157	158	159	160
A	B	A	A	A	D	C	B	D	A

161	162	163	164	165	166	167	168	169	170
B	B	C	B	D	D	C	B	B	B

171	172	173	174	175	176	177	178	179	180
D	C	D	D	C	B	C	A	D	A

181	182	183	184	185	186	187	188	189	190
B	B	C	A	A	A	B	D	D	A

191	192	193	194	195	196	197	198	199	200
B	C	A	A	D	A	B	D	D	A

201	202	203	204	205	206	207	208	209	210
B	B	B	B	A	A	A	A	A	A

1809

MADHYA PRADESH

General Knowledge

1. 'Ujjaini and Mahishmati' were important towns of:
   A. Eastern Malwa   B. Western Malwa
   C. Northern Malwa   D. Southern Malwa

2. Sunil Kewat is related to which sports?
   A. Kayaking canoeing   B. Cricket
   C. Hockey   D. Football

3. In which city is the Rani Durgawati museum situated?
   A. Bhopal   B. Jabalpur
   C. Mandsaur   D. Khargon

4. News print factory in India is at:
   A. Nepanagar   B. Hoshangabad
   C. Mandla   D. Indore

5. Where is the Saket Ramayan Kala Sangrahalay situated?
   A. Chanderi   B. Orchha
   C. Ujjain   D. Maihar

6. Phen Wildlife Sanctuary is located in which district?
   A. Mandla   B. Jhabua
   C. Jabalpur   D. Dhar

7. Where is the Gajrath Mahotsav celebrated?
   A. Bhopal   B. Guna
   C. Sagar   D. Dewas

8. Mahi project is in which district?
   A. Indore   B. Dhar
   C. Shahdol   D. Bhopal

9. 'Raneh waterfall' is on the river:
   A. Narmada   B. Ken
   C. Betwa   D. Sone

10. Which of the following is famous as Energy Capital of Madhya Pradesh?
    A. Jabalpur   B. Chhindwara
    C. Ujjain   D. Singrauli

11. Madhya Pradesh Electricity Regulatory authority office is famous as:
    A. Urja Bhavan   B. Yatayat Bhavan
    C. Saur Bhavan   D. Vidhyut Bhavan

12. Which one is not located on National Highway-3?
    A. Indore   B. Shivpuri
    C. Jhansi   D. Gwalior

13. Which of the following cities is famous as Manganese Capital of Madhya Pradesh?
    A. Balaghat   B. Singrouli
    C. Sidhi   D. Anuppur

14. Where was the first spice park of Madhya Pradesh established?
    A. Vidisha   B. Bhopal
    C. Chindwara   D. Raisen

15. Who was the first Lokayukt of Madhya Pradesh?
    A. P.C. Sethi   B. P.V. Dixit
    C. N.V. Lohani   D. None of these

16. In which year was the 51st District Agar Malwa formed?
    A. 2011   B. 2013
    C. 1998   D. 2000

17. The birth place of Chandra Shekhar Azad 'Bhabra' is in:
    A. Madhya Pradesh   B. Rajasthan
    C. Punjab   D. Uttar Pradesh

18. Where is the High Court of Madhya Pradesh situated?
    A. Bhopal   B. Jabalpur
    C. Gwalior   D. Indore

19. In which of the following districts of Madhya Pradesh is the Ramlila Fair held?
    A. Chhindwara   B. Gwalior
    C. Anuppur   D. Jabalpur

20. To which tribe does the Lehangi Dance belong?
    A. Gonds   B. Bhils
    C. Saharias   D. Korku

21. Where is the 'Indira Gandhi Rashtriya Manav Sangrahalaya' located?
    A. Gwalior   B. Bhopal
    C. Sanchi   D. Jabalpur

22. In which year was the Tansen Award founded?
    A. 1979   B. 1980
    C. 1981   D. 1982

23. The maximum rain in Madhya Pradesh occurs at:
    A. Pachmarhi   B. Bhind
    C. Gwalior   D. Betul

24. Which of the following cities is Headquarters of west Central Railway Zone?
    A. Gwalior   B. Jabalpur
    C. Rewa   D. Ratlam

25. Pandav Caves, a famous Tourist spot is situated in:
    A. Raisen   B. Pachmarhi
    C. Sagar   D. None of these

26. In which city is the tourism spot Ashrafi Palace situated?
    A. Chanderi   B. Mandu
    C. Gwalior   D. Orcha

27. Which of the following states has the largest number of people belonging to Scheduled Tribe (According to Census 2011)?
    A. Bihar   B. West Bengal
    C. Madhya Pradesh   D. Punjab

28. Which of the projects is a joint venture of Uttar Pradesh, Madhya Pradesh and Bihar?
    A. Ban Sagar   B. Laxmibai
    C. Barona   D. Tava

29. The Madhya Pradesh Development Day is celebrated on which data?
    A. 1st April 2013   B. 6th April 2013
    C. 15th April 2013   D. 12th April 2013

30. Marble is found in which district?
    A. Jhabua   B. Hoshangabad
    C. Betul   D. Jabalpur

31. What is the number of Zila Panchayats in Madhya Pradesh?
    A. 49   B. 51
    C. 16   D. 21

32. Who was the first woman Chief Minister of Madhya Pradesh?
    A. Meera Kumar   B. Sushma Swaraj
    C. Uma Bharti   D. Sarla Grewal

33. The 'Baiga tribe' is majorly found in:
    A. Shivpuri, Jhabua, Dhar
    B. Shahdol, Sidhi, Dhar
    C. Mandala, Shahdol, Balaghat
    D. Sidhi, Jhabua, Balaghat

34. Where is the Railway Coach factory in Madhya Pradesh?
    A. Beena   B. Morena
    C. Bhopal   D. Hoshangabad

35. Which religion is the predominant religion of the state Madhya Pradesh?
    A. Muslim   B. Hinduism
    C. Sikhism   D. Buddhism

36. Which is the first district of Madhya Pradesh to produce energy from biomass?
    A. Betul   B. Morena
    C. Gwalior   D. Mandsaur

37. In which city is the Thankur Ranmat Singh stadium situated?
    A. Itarsi   B. Rewa
    C. Satna   D. Bhopal

38. When was the 'Lok Vaniki' programme launched by the Government of Madhya Pradesh?
    A. 1998   B. 1999
    C. 1997   D. 1992

39. Kapildhara waterfall is situated on which river?
    A. Narmada   B. Son
    C. Tapti   D. Shipra

40. Gas released during Bhopal Gas Tragedy was:
    A. Methyl Isothicoynate   B. Ethyl Isothicoynate
    C. Methyl Isocyanate   D. Ethyl Isocyanate

41. Which leader of Madhya Pradesh became the country's third Home Minister and then Defence Minister in Nehru's cabinet?
    A. Prakash Chandra Sethi
    B. Ravi Shankar Shukla
    C. Kailash Nath Katju
    D. Dwarka Nath Mishra

42. State foundation day is celebrated in Madhya Pradesh on:
    A. 1st November   B. 1st June
    C. 23rd September   D. 31st December

43. Maheshwar is famous for:
    A. Saree Industry
    B. Ahilya Ghat
    C. Mahamrityunjaya Rath Yatra
    D. All of these

44. Which flower is famous as the state flower of Madhya Pradesh?
    A. Rose   B. White Lily
    C. Marigold   D. Lotus

45. Where does the 'Chandi Devi' mela occur?
    A. Sidhi   B. Shahdol
    C. Rewa   D. Satna

46. Iqbal Award is given in the field of:
    A. Classical music
    B. For film direction
    C. Creative Urdu writing
    D. Hindi literature

47. The ancient city of Madhya Pradesh "Dashpur" is now famous as:
    A. Bhopal   B. Jhabua
    C. Vidisha   D. Mandsaur

48. Which of the following states is to the south of Madhya Pradesh?
    A. Rajasthan   B. Uttar Pradesh
    C. Maharashtra   D. Gujarat

49. According to size (geographical area) Madhya Pradesh is the .... largest state in India.
    A. Third   B. Second
    C. Fourth   D. Fifth

50. Which of the following cities is famous as musical capital of Madhya Pradesh?

A. Indore   B. Maihar
C. Bhopal   D. None of these

51. Which city is the Ginnorgarh fort situated near to?
A. Dewas   B. Dhar
C. Bhopal   D. Rewa

52. In Ho and Bunda tribes the youth homes are called:
A. Gayataru   B. Kalav
C. Gitiora   D. Korku

53. 'Narmada Bachao Andolan' is associated with:
A. J.P. Narayan   B. Medha Patkar
C. P. Chidambaram   D. H.N. Bahuguna

54. Old name of Gwalior is:
A. Gopagiri   B. Rewanchal
C. Geetanjali   D. Gwadar

55. In which fort was Peshwa Bajirao II born?
A. Gwalior fort   B. Raisen fort
C. Aseergarh fort   D. Fort of Dhar

56. Which is the most sacred river of Madhya Pradesh?
A. Ganga   B. Yamuna
C. Narmada   D. Chambal

57. Vikram Award is given to:
A. Senior coach
B. Senior player of the state
C. Coach
D. Young players

58. Female literacy of Madhya Pradesh according to census 2011 is:
A. 78%   B. 61%
C. 59.8%   D. 80%

59. Balaghat city is situated on which river?
A. Narmada   B. Wainganga
C. Pench   D. Tapti

60. In which of the following cities is the Madhya Pradesh Biodiversity Board located?
A. Bhopal   B. Indore
C. Gwalior   D. Jabalpur

61. Which district of Madhya Pradesh has the highest percentage of Scheduled Caste population?
A. Datia   B. Ujjain
C. Tikamgarh   D. Jhabua

62. Cotton Research Centre of Madhya Pradesh is situated in:
A. Khandwa   B. Khargon
C. Jabalpur   D. Indore

63. Which of the following Sanskrit poets was not related to Madhya Pradesh?
A. Kalhan   B. Bhavabhuti
C. Mandan Misra   D. Kalidas

64. The other name of Devi Ahilyabai Holkar Airport is:
A. Gwalior Airport   B. Indore Airport
C. Ujjain Airport   D. Bhopal Airport

65. Where is the SAI Central Regional Centre located?
A. Indore   B. Jhansi
C. Gwalior   D. Bhopal

66. Bargi Project is also named by:
A. Rani Avanti Bai Lodhi Sagar Project
B. Rani Durgavati Sagar Project
C. Rani Karnavati Sagar Project
D. Indira Gandhi Sagar

67. Which of the following districts does not belong to the Chambal division?
A. Morena   B. Bhind
C. Alirajpur   D. Sheopur

68. How many seats are reserved for scheduled tribe members in Legislative assembly of Madhya Pradesh?
A. 51   B. 47
C. 39   D. 10

69. Which of the following months are known as the second summer of Madhya Pradesh?
A. September-October   B. August-September
C. May-June   D. June-July

70. Who among the following established 'Hoshangabad' city?
A. Krishnaraj   B. Nannuk
C. Hoshangshah   D. Vakpati Munj

71. Panna city is famous in Madhya Pradesh due to / which reason?
A. For old needle craft   B. For diamond mines
C. For beautiful palace   D. For paper mill

72. Abdul Latif Khan from Bhopal is a renowned:
A. Urdu Poet   B. Author
C. Classical Singer   D. Sarangi Player

73. Which of the following tourism places isn't situated at Gwalior?
A. Gujari Palace   B. Jai Vilas Mahal
C. Jahaz Mahal   D. Man Singh Palace

74. Asirgarh Fort is situated in which of the following districts of Madhya Pradesh?
A. Betul   B. Khandwa
C. Burhanpur   D. Panna

75. Which of the following forests is found in most abundance in Madhya Pradesh?
A. Tropical Moist Deciduous Forests
B. Tropical Dry Deciduous Forests
C. Tropical Thorn Forests
D. Tropical Rain Forests

76. Which of the following regions of India was known as 'Avantika'?
A. Bundelkhand   B. Dandkaranya
C. Ujjain   D. Nimar

77. Who among the following ladies is famous as "Lokmata"?

    A. Rani Laxmi Bai   B. Ahilyabai Holkar
    C. Avantibai   D. None of these

78. Which is the Antimony producing district of Madhya Pradesh?
    A. Jabalpur   B. Jhabua
    C. Mandsaur   D. Bhopal

79. In Ujjain which of the following ceremonies is celebrated by Government of Madhya Pradesh?
    A. Kalidas Ceremony   B. Malwa Ceremony
    C. Bhoj Ceremony   D. None of these

80. The only tribal sports school of Madhya Pradesh is situated at:
    A. Sehore   B. Jhabua
    C. Alirajpur   D. Indore

81. In which city Abhay Khel Prashal is situated?
    A. Bhopal   B. Indore
    C. Jabalpur   D. Gwalior

82. Which Nobel Laureate's birth place is in Madhya Pradesh?
    A. Rabindra Nath Tagore B. Mother Teresa
    C. Kailash Satyarthi   D. Amartya Sen

83. According to census 2011 child sex ratio of Madhya Pradesh is:
    A. 918   B. 948
    C. 950   D. 960

84. Which is the second largest tribe in Madhya Pradesh according to census 2011?
    A. Gond   B. Bhil
    C. Dindori   D. Barwani

85. Who became the first speaker of Legislative Assembly of Madhya Pradesh?
    A. V R Dave   B. Kunjilal Dubey
    C. Nandan Sahu   D. Jamuna Devi

86. 'Tulsi Award' is given in the field of folk and traditional tribal art. It was founded in:
    A. 1983-84   B. 1984-85
    C. 1985-86   D. 1986-87

87. Which of the following rivers does not fall into the river Yamuna?
    A. Ken   B. Betwa
    C. Son   D. Chambal

88. Where is "Bharat Bhavan" situated?
    A. Bhopal   B. Jabalpur
    C. Indore   D. Sagar

89. Who became the first non-Congress Chief Minister of Madhya Pradesh?
    A. Govind Narayan Singh
    B. V P Dubey
    C. Digvijay Singh
    D. Babulal Gour

90. In which of the following years was Bhopal district carved out from Sehore district?

91. 'Navjeevan' was started from 1915 in Indore. It was:
    A. First Hindi newspaper
    B. First newspaper of Madhya Pradesh
    C. Weekly newspaper
    D. Monthly magazine

92. The Lakshmibai National Institute of Physical Educations is at:
    A. Bhopal   B. Gwalior
    C. Indore   D. Jabalpur

93. Which district of Madhya Pradesh produces the maximum wheat?
    A. Vidisha   B. Hoshangabad
    C. Mandla   D. Ujjain

94. Which of the following is the smallest district of Madhya Pradesh?
    A. Harda   B. Mandsaur
    C. Jabalpur district   D. Betul district

95. What is the main attraction of the Archaeological Museum of Sanchi?
    A. Mauryan period artifacts
    B. Birla Museum
    C. Sculptures, terracotta and paintings
    D. The lion capital, Ashokan pillar of the Mauryan Period

96. Where are the Security Paper Mills located in Madhya Pradesh?
    A. Hoshangabad   B. Dewas
    C. Gwalior   D. Dhar

97. Sardar Sarovar Dam is a downstream project of the ....
    A. Gandhi Sagar Dam
    B. Indira Sagar Dam
    C. Rana Pratap Sagar Dam
    D. Sanjay Sagar Dam

98. The Khajuraho dance festival is held every year. This celebration is usually held in the month of ....
    A. December   B. June
    C. February   D. September

99. The Tawa Reservoir is nestled between the ....
    A. Satpura National Park and the Bani Sanctuary
    B. Kolar and the Halali dam
    C. Rani Avantibai Sagar and the Sukta Sagar
    D. Vyarma and Barna rivers

100. Which of the following Prime Ministers was born in Madhya Pradesh?
    A. Inder Kumar Gujral
    B. Atal Behari Vajpayee
    C. H.D. Deve Gowda
    D. Manmohan Singh

    A. 1970   B. 1971
    C. 1972   D. 1973

101. .... Airport is the busiest airport in Madhya Pradesh.
A. Devi Ahilyabai Holkar
B. Raja Bhoj
C. Jabalpur
D. Gwalior

102. Madhya Pradesh has a Special Economic Zone in ....
A. Jabalpur
B. Bhopal
C. Bhojpur
D. Ujjain

103. The name of airport in Bhopal is ....
A. Devi Ahilyabai Holkar Airport
B. Dumna Airport
C. Panna Airport
D. Raja Bhoj International Airport

104. .... has the largest reserves of diamond in India.
A. Maharashtra
B. Uttar Pradesh
C. Madhya Pradesh
D. Rajasthan

105. Bhoja was an Indian King from the .... dynasty.
A. Paramara
B. Mughul
C. Nanda
D. Maurya

106. Which one of these Chief Ministers has not served a second term?
A. Bhagwantrao Mandloi
B. Sunderlal Patwa
C. Arjun Singh
D. Uma Bharti

107. .... is the state flower of Madhya Pradesh.
A. White Lily
B. Rose
C. Lotus
D. Jasmine

108. .... National Park is one of the 18 biosphere reserves of India.
A. Panna
B. Kanha
C. Madhav
D. Sanjay

109. ...., a town in Dhar district of Madhya Pradesh is also known as Detroit of India.
A. Manawar
B. Badnawar
C. Pithampur
D. Mandu

110. .... is called "Heart of India".
A. Maharashtra
B. Chattisgarh
C. Rajasthan
D. Madhya Pradesh

111. One of the 12 Jyotirlingas in India is present in .... in Madhya Pradesh.
A. Rewa
B. Ujjain
C. Sagar
D. Indore

112. Indian Institute of Forest Management is located in ....
A. Indore
B. Jabalpur
C. Bhopal
D. Gwalior

113. Sharad Joshi Samman is given by Government of Madhya Pradesh for achievement in the field of ....
A. Sports
B. Writing
C. Music
D. Dance

114. .... award is presented by the Government of Madhya Pradesh in the field of Hindustani classical music.
A. Lata Mangeshkar
B. Iqbal
C. Kabir
D. Tansen

115. Ujjain is located at the eastern bank of .... river.
A. Son
B. Narmada
C. Tapti
D. Shipra

116. .... is the state tree of Madhya Pradesh.
A. Teak
B. Sal
C. Banyan
D. Bamboo

117. Malwa Utsav is held in .... in Madhya Pradesh.
A. Ujjain
B. Bhopal
C. Gwalior
D. Jabalpur

118. Tomb of Tansen is located in ....
A. Gwalior
B. Indore
C. Ujjain
D. Morena

119. The Central Institute of Agricultural Engineering is situated in ....
A. Indore
B. Bhopal
C. Jabalpur
D. Rewa

120. The famous Bagh Caves are situated in .... district of Madhya Pradesh.
A. Satna
B. Dhar
C. Bhopal
D. Gwalior

121. Nehru stadium is located in ....
A. Gwalior
B. Bhopal
C. Jabalpur
D. Indore

122. Which of the rivers of Madhya Pradesh is Bargi Dam situated on?
A. Narmada
B. Chambal
C. Tapti
D. Betwa

123. Which one of these National Parks is not in Madhya Pradesh?
A. Kanha National Park
B. Guindy National Park
C. Satpura National Park
D. Sanjay National Park

124. Which one of these is not a tribe of Madhya Pradesh?
A. Gond
B. Bhil
C. Kom
D. Baiga

125. Gatha falls is in .... district of Madhya Pradesh.
A. Panna
B. Rewa
C. Dhar
D. Bhind

126. Which famous playback singer was born in Khandwa, Madhya Pradesh?
A. Kishore Kumar
B. Mohammed Rafi
C. Mahendra Kapoor
D. Kundan Lal Saigal

127. Chachai falls is in .... district of Madhya Pradesh.
    A. Dhar   B. Rewa
    C. Bhind   D. Katni

128. .... cricket stadium in Indore was earlier known as Maharani Usharaje Trust cricket ground.
    A. Roop Singh   B. Holkar
    C. Nehru   D. Colliery

129. .... is the biggest tributary of the river Narmada.
    A. Tawa   B. Sher
    C. Shakkar   D. Dudhi

130. The headquarters of Indian Institute of Tourism and Travel Management is based in ....
    A. Lucknow   B. Kolkata
    C. Delhi   D. Gwalior

131. Nimar Utsav is rejoiced on the banks of .... river.
    A. Chambal   B. Tapti
    C. Mahanadi   D. Narmada

132. Gujari Mahal in Gwalior fort was built by ....
    A. Anangapala
    B. Raja Man Singh Tomar
    C. Prithviraj Chauhan
    D. Jayapala

133. ...., a poet, writer, journalist, was awarded the first Sahitya Akademi Award in Hindi for his work "Him Tarangini".
    A. Harivansh Rai Bachchan
    B. Munshi Premchand
    C. Suryakant Tripathi Nirala
    D. Pandit Makhanlal Chaturvedi

134. There are .... districts in Madhya Pradesh.
    A. 51   B. 42
    C. 66   D. 59

135. Which of these National Parks is not in Madhya Pradesh?
    A. Bandhavgarh National Park
    B. Sanjay National Park
    C. Madhav National Park
    D. Nagzira National Park

136. .... is called Paris of Nimar.
    A. Bhopal   B. Barwani
    C. Burhanpur   D. Bhind

137. The first Chief Minister of Madhya Pradesh was ....
    A. Bhagwantrao Mandloi
    B. Kailash Nath Katju
    C. Dwarka Prasad Mishra
    D. Ravishankar Shukla

138. Khajuraho is famous for ....
    A. Hindu and Jain temples
    B. Exotic architecture
    C. World renowned dance festival
    D. All of these

139. The recipient of which one of the following awards given by Madhya Pradesh Government gets the highest cash prize?
    A. Mahatma Gandhi Award
    B. Kishore Kumar Award
    C. Shikar Award
    D. Sharad Joshi Award

140. Bhopal became the capital of Madhya Pradesh in the year ....
    A. 1956   B. 1965
    C. 1947   D. 1974

141. .... is the highest peak of Madhya Pradesh.
    A. Arma Konda   B. K2
    C. Doddabetta   D. Dhupgarh

142. The largest district in Madhya Pradesh by population is ....
    A. Bhopal   B. Chhindwara
    C. Indore   D. Dhar

143. In 1818, the capital was shifted from Maheshwar to Indore by ....
    A. Madhav Rao Holkar   B. Peshwa Rao
    C. Raju Scindia   D. Maharaja of Rewa

144. States located to the north of Madhya Pradesh are:
    A. Rajasthan and Gujarat
    B. Rajasthan and Uttar Pradesh
    C. Uttar Pradesh and Chhattisgarh
    D. Chhattisgarh and Rajasthan

145. Madhya Pradesh was formerly known as:
    A. Bewar   B. Nizam Dominions
    C. Central Provinces   D. United Provinces

146. The capital of Madhya Pradesh before 1st November 1956 was:
    A. Bhopal   B. Nagpur
    C. Ujjain   D. Gwalior

147. Satpura Wildlife Sanctuary is located at:
    A. Hoshangabad   B. Sindh
    C. Chhindwara   D. Khajuraho

148. Bagdara Sanctuary was established in the year:
    A. 1978   B. 1992
    C. 1981   D. 1975

149. Wildlife Sanctuary near Khajuraho is:
    A. Pench   B. Bagdara
    C. Kanha   D. Panpatha

150. The Black Buck is a unique attraction in:
    A. Bagdara Sanctuary   B. Pench National Park
    C. Satpura Sanctuary   D. Sanjay Dubri

151. Who constructed the Chaturbhuj Temple of Orchha?
    A. Satpura Kings   B. Bundela Rajputs
    C. Raja Bhoj   D. King Vikramaditya

152. The Indian Bison found in Satpura is also called:
    A. Gaur   B. Bail
    C. Mahua   D. Swamp Bison

153. The National Park which was declared as a tiger reserve in 1983 is .... National Park.
- A. Pench
- B. Kanha
- C. Sanjay Dubri
- D. Panpatha

154. The river that flows parallel to the Narmada is:
- A. Denwa
- B. Tawa
- C. Shipra
- D. Tapti

155. The river that DOES NOT join the Yamuna is:
- A. Chambal
- B. Betwa
- C. Sindh
- D. Son

156. Where is the major industry, BHEL located in Madhya Pradesh?
- A. Gwalior
- B. Indore
- C. Ujjain
- D. Bhopal

157. Ganga basin DOES NOT extend to:
- A. Mandsaur
- B. Ujjain
- C. Shajapur
- D. Chhindwara

158. The river that makes a boundary between Madhya Pradesh and Rajasthan is:
- A. Chambal
- B. Sindh
- C. Yamuna
- D. Son

159. The Bagh Irrigation Project benefits the .... district.
- A. Jabalpur
- B. Balaghat
- C. Hoshanpur
- D. Sholapur

160. The Awda dam is located in .... district.
- A. Shivpuri
- B. Morena
- C. Morgura
- D. Jabalpur

161. Bargi is a tributary of the river ....
- A. Narmada
- B. Yamuna
- C. Chambal
- D. Banjar

162. Rani Avanti Bai Lodhi Sagar is located in the river basin of the river ....
- A. Narmada
- B. Tapti
- C. Ganga
- D. Chambal

163. The Choral Irrigation Project benefits the .... district:
- A. Gwalior
- B. Indore
- C. Bhopal
- D. Shivpuri

164. Amarkantak is located in the .... district.
- A. Anuppur
- B. Shahpura
- C. Bhojpur
- D. Itarsi

165. Orchha is a royal town located at the river bank of:
- A. Betwa
- B. Tawa
- C. Barna
- D. Son

166. International cricket stadiums are located in:
- A. Gwalior and Bhopal
- B. Gwalior and Indore
- C. Indore and Bhopal
- D. Jabalpur and Bhopal

167. "Tirthraj" is the name given to:
- A. Khajuraho
- B. Kanha National Park
- C. Orchha township
- D. Amarkantak

168. Gujari Mahal and Gwalior Mahal in Gwalior are built by:
- A. Raja Bhoj
- B. Man Singh Tomar
- C. Raja Dumana
- D. Scindia Devi

169. Khajuraho was the capital to the .... Rulers.
- A. Chandela
- B. Satavahana
- C. Mauryian
- D. Kanha

170. Bhimbetka are rock shelters. These are archeological sites of the .... Period.
- A. Neolithic
- B. Paleolithic
- C. Chalcolithic
- D. Mesolithic

171. The temples of Ujjain are an example of:
- A. Mathura School of Art
- B. Gandhara School of Art
- C. The Chandela Art
- D. The Bundela Art

172. Rajya Sabha member and bollywood actress born in Jabalpur is:
- A. Rekha
- B. Jaya Bachchan
- C. Hema Malini
- D. Asha Parekh

173. The immortal poet Kalidasa belonged to the town of:
- A. Ujjain
- B. Bhojpur
- C. Hoshangabad
- D. Indore

174. According to history, who established Gwalior?
- A. Suraj Sen
- B. Rana Singh
- C. King Vikramaditya
- D. Samrat Ashok

175. Madhya Pradesh is predominantly a:
- A. Valley
- B. Mountain
- C. Plain
- D. Plateau

176. Which of the following cities is a limestone hub and contributes more than 10% to India's total cement production?
- A. Bhopal
- B. Satna
- C. Indore
- D. Jabalpur

177. Atal Behari Vajpayee Park is more popularly called as:
- A. Kanha Park
- B. Indore Regional Park
- C. Gwalior Regional Park
- D. Project Tiger Park

178. Madhya Pradesh Forest Project is aided by:
- A. European Union
- B. USA
- C. World Bank
- D. Reserve Bank of India

179. Chitrakoot is a popular name from the epic period of the Ramayana. Chitrakoot is located in the district:
- A. Satna
- B. Panna
- C. Rewa
- D. Sidhi

180. River that flows in the eastern part of Madhya Pradesh and drains into Bay of Bengal near Odisha is:
- A. Denwa
- B. Mahanadi
- C. Shipra
- D. Chambal

181. Shipra is a river that takes its origin from a hill called:
    A. Mizo Hills
    B. Kakri Bardi Hills
    C. Amarkantak Hills
    D. Kewai Hills

182. Saraswati and Khar are tributaries of the river:
    A. Yamuna
    B. Narmada
    C. Shipra
    D. Chambal

183. The district that lies between Saraswati and Khan rivers is:
    A. Betul
    B. Indore
    C. Dhar
    D. Rewa

184. Yashwant is a lake that supplies water to:
    A. Gwalior
    B. Indore
    C. Bhopal
    D. Shahpura

185. Pagara is a dam located in:
    A. Gwalior
    B. Balaghat
    C. Ujjain
    D. Sholapur

186. Dam in India known for the largest storage capacity is:
    A. Govind Sagar Dam
    B. Indira Sagar Dam
    C. Sardar Sarovar Dam
    D. Pagara Dam

187. Palakmati, the first irrigation tank of the erstwhile Bhopal State, is located in:
    A. Raisen
    B. Shahpura
    C. Urmara
    D. Bhopal

188. Ujjain was the capital of ancient Avanti and was ruled by:
    A. King Vikramaditya
    B. Rana Pratap
    C. Queen Durgavati
    D. King Ashoka

189. Sihoniya is a holy place in Morena. It is known for:
    A. Holy shrine of Jains
    B. A Hindu temple
    C. Meditation centre
    D. A religious discourse centre

190. A monolithic statue of Adinatha is located near:
    A. Barwani Town
    B. Bhagoria
    C. Chaturbhuj
    D. Khandwa

191. Tallest residential building in Madhya Pradesh is the:
    A. Rajawada Palace
    B. Bombay Hospital
    C. Radisson Square
    D. Pinnacle Dreams

192. Sanchi Stupa has inscriptions which are written in this Script.
    A. Brahmi
    B. Prakrit
    C. Bhojtal
    D. Holkar

193. Kandariya Mahadeva temple is located in:
    A. Ujjain
    B. Khajuraho
    C. Bhimbetka Caves
    D. Cave temple in Margi

194. Pahargarh cave paintings are found in rocks near the:
    A. Chambal River
    B. Son River
    C. Asana River (Ashan to Asana)
    D. Barwani Town

195. A marble replica of the Eiffel tower is located in:
    A. Museum in Gwalior
    B. Adinatha Temple
    C. All India Radio Campus at Indore
    D. Cell phone tower in Bhopal

196. Holkars are basically
    A. Marathas
    B. Rajputs
    C. Mauryans
    D. Scindias

197. The name of the last Holkar is:
    A. Yashwant Rao
    B. Shankar Kumar
    C. Deepak Chaurasia
    D. Shivaji Rao

198. Name of the famous cricketer who hailed from Madhya Pradesh.
    A. Mansaur Ali Khan Pataudi
    B. Kapil Dev
    C. Salim Durani
    D. Vinoo Mankad

199. The last Maharaja of Gwalior was:
    A. Madhav Rao Scindia
    B. Peshwa Rao
    C. Bhairavnath
    D. Devi Holkar

200. Founder of Bachpan Bachao Aandolan and Nobel Prize winner who was born in Vidisha is:
    A. Atal Behari Vajpayee
    B. Shankar Dayal Sharma
    C. Kailash Satyarthi
    D. Iswar Pandey

201. Born in Indore and a long time member of the Rajya Sabha, he was the CM of Maharashtra and then resigned. His name is:
    A. Madhav Rao Scindia
    B. Kalyan Kumar
    C. Pramod Mahajan
    D. Prithviraj Chauhan

202. The war that brought erstwhile states like Indore, Nagpur and Rewa under the British was the:
    A. III Battle of Panipat
    B. Battle of Chausa
    C. III Anglo Maratha war
    D. II Battle of Khanwa

203. The three regions that were merged as Madhya Pradesh were ....
    A. The Central Provinces, Berar and Central India
    B. The Kaimur, Satpura and Vindhyan Plateau
    C. The Malwa, Satpura and the Vindhya Plateau
    D. The Madhya Bharath, Vindhya Pradesh and Bhopal

204. The two most important minerals of Madhya Pradesh are ....
    A. Copper and Iron ore
    B. Iron Ore and Coal
    C. Zinc and Manganese
    D. Gold and Diamond

205. Golden triangle of Madhya Pradesh are the regions of ....
    A. Dhar, Singurali and Chhindwara
    B. Singurali, Vidisha and Rewa
    C. Gwalior, Jhansi and Khajuraho
    D. Vidisha, Gwalior and Ujjain

206. .... in Madhya Pradesh is famous for its tigers.
   A. Chitrakoot   B. Jabalpur
   C. Datia   D. Bandhavgarh

207. What is common among the following?
   Badhai, Saira, Jawara, Kalsa.
   A. All are names of crops grown in Madhya Pradesh.
   B. All are types of dance forms in Madhya Pradesh.
   C. All are food types that is common in Madhya Pradesh.
   D. All are different festivals celebrated in Madhya Pradesh.

208. The Sanctuary that is located in Bhind is the ....
   A. Bhind Sanctuary
   B. Kanha Sanctuary
   C. Chambal Gharial Sanctuary
   D. Shivpuri Sanctuary

209. The Dindori district is a part of ....
   A. Satpura Sanctuary
   B. Kanha National Park
   C. Bori Sanctuary
   D. Sanjay Dubri Sanctuary

210. Most of Madhya Pradesh has Sal and Teak trees. Which among the following are the closest features exhibited by these trees?
   A. They have broad leaves
   B. They are very tall trees
   C. They have cone shaped leaves
   D. They have breathing roots

211. Naurendhi sanctuary covers the districts of ....
   A. Sagar, Damoh, Narasinghpur and Raisen
   B. Ratlam, Dhar and Siddhi
   C. Only Sagar
   D. Raisen and Ratlam

212. Which of the following was known as the summer capital of Scindia rulers of Gwalior?
   A. Ranikhet   B. Shivpuri
   C. Jabalpur   D. Chitrakoot

213. Sardarpur Sanctuary is managed for protection of ....
   A. Kharmor   B. Chausingha
   C. Nilgai   D. Gharial

214. Bina Refinery is located in the ....
   A. Chanderi   B. Sagar
   C. Satna   D. Ujjain

215. River Banas is a tributary of the ....
   A. Chambal   B. Narmada
   C. Tapti   D. Betwa

216. When you visit the Ajaigarh fort, the river that you can see is the ....
   A. Tapti and Narmada   B. Yamuna
   C. Ken   D. Khuddar

217. Kwari river flows through the district of ....
   A. Morena   B. Gwalior
   C. Rewa   D. Indore

218. Sunar is a tributary of ....
   A. Narmada   B. Chambal
   C. Son   D. Tapti

219. In which of the following districts is manganese found in abundance?
   A. Balaghat and Chhindwara
   B. Anuppur and Bhind
   C. Sehore and Vidisha
   D. Harda and Gwalior

220. Welspun Solar Project is located in ....
   A. Vidisha   B. Siddhi
   C. Neemuch   D. Dhar

221. Priyadharshini Park is located in ....
   A. Bhopal   B. Indore
   C. Gwalior   D. Ujjain

222. Fresh water reservoir on the Sank river near Gwalior is the ....
   A. Tigra Dam   B. Bansagar Dam
   C. Bargi Dam   D. Dhuty Dam

223. Sanjay Sagar irrigation project benefits the district of ....
   A. Gwalior   B. Ratlam
   C. Indore   D. Vidisha

224. Dhuty dam is located over the ....
   A. Wainganga   B. Barna
   C. Chambal   D. Son

225. Apsara falls in Pachmarhi is also called the ....
   A. Fairy Falls   B. Kabni Falls
   C. Silver Falls   D. Kapil Waterfall

226. The most impressive and largest group of temples in Khajuraho is the ....
   A. Northern group   B. Southern group
   C. Western group   D. Eastern group

227. Roopnath is one of the ....
   A. Temples in Omkareshwar
   B. Vishnu temples in Ujjain
   C. Jain temples in Khajuraho
   D. Jyothirlingams

228. Which fort is known as the "Pearl among forts in India"?
   A. Indore Fort   B. Gwalior Fort
   C. Maharaja Fort   D. Rana Sanga Fort

229. The Geographical centre of India is the village of ....
   A. Karondi near Jabalpur
   B. Bagli in Dewar
   C. Amla in Betul
   D. Shahpur in Betul

230. Pick the CORRECT pair:
   A. Udayagiri caves — Bhojpur
   B. Bhartrihari caves — Vidisha
   C. Pandav caves — Pachmarhi
   D. Bhimbetka caves — Ujjain

231. The place/district in Madhya Pradesh where Krishna and Balarama are said to have received their eduction.
    A. Ratlam
    B. Avanti
    C. Ujjain
    D. Mandu

232. Who among the following called the town of Gwalior the "Key to Hindustan"?
    A. Warren Hastings
    B. Lord Mountbatten
    C. Wellesley
    D. Cornwallis

233. Khajuraho was mentioned as the capital during Mohammad Ghazni's raid and conquest by ....
    A. Fa Hien
    B. Tansen
    C. Pushyamitra
    D. Albiruni

234. Man who was called the "Lion of Chambal" is ....
    A. Daku Man Singh
    B. Dash Mohammad Khan
    C. Tomar Mohammad
    D. Ali Akbar Tomar

235. Moroccan traveller who mentions the Khajuraho temple in his works on India is ....
    A. Albiruni
    B. Fa Hien
    C. Ibn Battuta
    D. Sher Shah Suri

236. Ajaigarh was founded by ....
    A. Man Singh
    B. Guman Singh
    C. Misra Singh
    D. Devilal Gaur

237. Dewas was founded by ....
    A. Tukoji Rao and Jivaji Rao
    B. Prasad Misra and Aji Misra
    C. The Paramaras
    D. Scindia

238. Who among the following was awarded the first Sahitya Academy Award in 1955 for his contribution to Hindi Literature?
    A. Makhanlal Chaturvedi
    B. Mahadevi Verma
    C. Raghuveer Sahay
    D. Vishnu Prabhakar

239. Fertile valley and rolling hills in the north of Madhya Pradesh are called ....
    A. Malwa
    B. Chhota Nagpur
    C. Bundelkhand
    D. Angara

240. The eastern part of Madhya Pradesh was originally ruled by the ....
    A. Gonds
    B. Marathas
    C. Rajputs
    D. Muriyas

241. The district in Madhya Pradesh, whose name means "Place of Peacock"
    A. Ratlam
    B. Rewa
    C. Dhar
    D. Morena

242. The eastern edge of the Narmada and the eastern edge of the Satpura meet at ....
    A. Mitai hills
    B. Mahakaushal
    C. Amarkantak
    D. Kapil Dharma

243. Fossil Park is located in ....
    A. Seoni
    B. Katni
    C. Ratlam
    D. Satna

244. Bandhavgarh Sanctuary was declared as National Park in ....
    A. 2015
    B. 1968
    C. 2005
    D. 1990

245. Phen Sanctuary is in ....
    A. Mandla
    B. Rewa
    C. Sidhi
    D. Jabalpur

246. Ken Gharial Sanctuary is located at ....
    A. Sagar
    B. Chhatarpur
    C. Rewa
    D. Banjar

247. Ancient name of the river Chambal is ....
    A. Sabarmati
    B. Charmawati
    C. Jamadagni
    D. Chitrakoot

248. Madhya Pradesh is the home to the largest reserves of .... in India.
    A. Copper
    B. Gold
    C. Coal
    D. Iron Ore

249. Beniganj is an irrigation canal in the .... district.
    A. Chhatarpur
    B. Rewa
    C. Betul
    D. Dewas

250. One of the finest Teak forests of the state of Madhya Pradesh is found in:
    A. Satpura Sanctuary
    B. Ratapani Tiger reserve
    C. Sanjay Sanctuary
    D. Kanha Sanctuary

251. Largest Watershed Mission in Madhya Pradesh is the .... Watershed Mission.
    A. Indira Gandhi
    B. Rajiv Gandhi
    C. Ganga basin
    D. Ganga - Yamuna

252. Upper Tiwara canal project is located in the ....
    A. Seoni District
    B. Neemuch District
    C. Ratlam District
    D. Guna District

253. Narmada exhibits a different drainage pattern because ....
    A. It passes through a rift valley
    B. It flows to the west
    C. It does not have too many tributaries
    D. It is a short river

254. It you visit Kareva, the nearest tourist spots are ....
    A. Gwalior, Shivpuri and Morena
    B. Ujjain, Ratlam and Dhar
    C. Singrauli, Siddhi and Rewa
    D. Bhopal, Vidisha and Raigarh

255. Bada Mahadev and Chhota Mahadev are temples located near:
    A. Ujjain
    B. Mandu
    C. Narsinghgarh
    D. Bhojpur

256. Swing Palace is also called ....
A. Hindola Mahal
B. Jhula Mahal
C. Hawa Mahal
D. Somnath Mahal

257. Maheshwar is a temple town and it is located on the banks of the river ....
A. Chambal
B. Narmada
C. Betwa
D. Tapti

258. It you are seeing the Dutchess falls, Mahadev hill, Apsara Vihar and the Pandava caves, then you are in:
A. Ujjain
B. Mandu
C. Bhojpur
D. Pachmarhi

259. The High Court of Madhya Pradesh is situated at ....
A. Bhopal
B. Sanchi
C. Nagda
D. Jabalpur

260. Indian Institute of Information Technology and Management is located in .... of Madhya Pradesh.
A. Gwalior
B. Sagar
C. Sanchi
D. Maheshwar

261. Two states located to the east of Madhya Pradesh are:
A. Rajasthan and Uttar Pradesh
B. Andhra Pradesh and Maharashtra
C. Uttar Pradesh and Gujarat
D. Chhattisgarh and Jharkhand

262. The name of 'Madhya Pradesh' was given to the state by:
A. Mahatma Gandhi
B. Peshwa Baji Rao
C. Jawaharlal Nehru
D. Jyotiba Phule

263. Which National Park has one of the highest densities of Bengal tigers known in the world?
A. Madhav National Park
B. Sanjay National Park
C. Bandhavgarh National Park
D. Van Vihar National Park

264. The state symbol of Madhya Pradesh is a:
A. Square with a tiger
B. Circle with a Sal tree
C. Circle with a Banyan tree
D. Square with a Banyan tree

265. The districts in which the Tropic of Cancer DOES NOT pass through are:
A. Ratlam and Ujjain
B. Shahpur and Rajgarh
C. Bhopal and Jabalpur
D. Indore and Balaghat

266. The total number of projects in Madhya Pradesh that are declared as "Project Tiger" reserves are:
A. 6
B. 7
C. 9
D. 25

267. Which of the following wildlife sanctuaries is in Hoshangabad?
A. Chambal National Park
B. Bori Wildlife Sanctuary
C. Dindori National Park
D. Bandhavgarh Wildlife Sanctuary

268. Sanctuary that is known to preserve the Great Indian Bustard is:
A. Kanha
B. Ghatigaon
C. Chambal
D. Gharial

269. The largest National Park in Madhya Pradesh is:
A. Kanha
B. Chambal
C. Sanjay Sagar
D. Sardarpur

270. Dolphins are found in the rivers in the Sanctuary of:
A. Chambal
B. Gharial
C. Sadarpur
D. Shivpuri

271. Teak and Sal are predominantly found in all the National Parks of Madhya Pradesh. These trees are:
A. Evergreen
B. Deciduous
C. Coniferous
D. Alpine

272. Breeding grounds of Gharials are the .... Sanctuary.
A. Son
B. Kanha
C. Ghatigaon
D. Kunwari

273. Which of the following districts is known for production of opium?
A. Shivpuri
B. Mandsaur
C. Sheopur
D. Sidhi

274. The river that has rare species of Turtles is:
A. Chambal
B. Son
C. Jamni
D. Kunwari

275. River that makes a boundary between Madhya Pradesh and Uttar Pradesh are:
A. Jamni
B. Chambal
C. Betwa
D. Gambhir

276. The average length of river Narmada is about:
A. 1000 Kilometers
B. 1300 Kilometers
C. 515 Kilometers
D. 3200 Kilometers

277. What do these have in common—Kapil, Dhara, Mandhar, Dunwadhar?
A. All are tributaries
B. All are estuaries
C. All are waterfalls
D. All are deltas

278. The second longest river in Madhya Pradesh is:
A. Tapti
B. Chambal
C. Rewa
D. Sone

279. Halali reservoir is on the river that was formerly called:
A. Thal
B. Rewa
C. Tawa
D. Jamni

280. The largest dam on river Narmada is:
A. Bargi
B. Sardar Sarovar
C. Tigra dam
D. Barna dam

281. Halali is located at:
A. Raisen
B. Barwani
C. Dindori
D. Ashoknagar

282. Bargi project is on river .... :
A. Narmada
B. Mahanadi
C. Sone
D. Chambal

283. Bank Note Press is located in:
A. Satna
B. Jawad
C. Dewas
D. Umedpura

284. Which region specializes in Jali works (patterns)?
A. Gwalior
B. Ujjain
C. Tikamgarh
D. Chitrakoot

285. The chief deity in Chaturbhuj temple is:
A. Lord Shiva
B. Lord Vishnu
C. Lord Rama
D. Lord Chaturvedi

286. Sundar Mahal is a tourist place located in:
A. Orchha
B. Mandu
C. Khajuraho
D. Kandariya

287. Match Making and Holi festival that is common in Madhya Pradesh is called:
A. Deokothar
B. Bhagoria
C. Phag
D. Lokrang

288. A template on which the Taj Mahal was made is the:
A. Hoshang Shah's Tomb in Mandu
B. Kapil Dharwasa in Rewa
C. Dharana in Shahpura
D. Sanchi Stupa

289. Tansen Sangeeth Samaroh is a common musical festival in:
A. Indore
B. Bhopal
C. Ujjain
D. Gwalior

290. The famous Hindu festival in Ujjain is:
A. Bhagoria
B. Lota and Phag
C. Kumbh Mela
D. Match making and Holi festival

291. The pig sacrifice of the Gonds is popularly called ....
A. Laru Kaj
B. Jhabua
C. Hallali
D. Margi

292. Name the tribe that actively participated in the revolt of 1857.
A. Bhils
B. Gonds
C. Korku
D. Bhaiga

293. Village which was popular as Azadpura was earlier called as:
A. Dhimpura
B. Indore
C. Rewa
D. Mandla

294. First Chief Minister of Madhya Pradesh state between 1950-56 was:
A. Dwarka Prasad Mishra
B. Ravishankar Shukla
C. Kailash Nath Katju
D. Shivaji Rao

295. Name the famous sitarist of Madhya Pradesh.
A. Pt. Nikhil Banerjee
B. Pandit Ravi Shankar
C. Annapurna Devi
D. Ustad Shahi Parwez Khan

296. The community of Bhil tribes are basically:
A. Agriculturists
B. Hunters and Warriors
C. Traders
D. Nomadic herders

297. Who established the original Archaeological Museum on the hilltop of Sanchi?
A. Charles Correa
B. Sir John Marshall
C. Marshall Durand
D. Sir Thomas Roe

298. Rewa Kund lies in:
A. Ujjain
B. Indore
C. Chanderi
D. Mandu

299. An artist known for his nail painting, who was awarded 3 times by APJ Abdul Kalam is:
A. Sumitra Mahajan
B. Wajid Khan
C. Aditya Joshi
D. Meera Kumar

300. The Nawab of Pataudi who was born in Bhopal was:
A. Mansur Ali Khan
B. Muhammed Abdul Ali
C. Wajid Ali
D. Jahangir Muhammad Khan

301. Western part of the Narmada Valley and the southern part of the Vindhya is a region that is called:
A. Nimar
B. Vihdhmar
C. Japar
D. Narmad

302. Common tribes in Madhya Pradesh for whom tattooing is an integral part of the lifestyle are:
A. Gonds
B. Baigas
C. Kikars
D. Bhils

303. The state that ranks number one in population of Special Tribes is:
A. Rajasthan
B. Chhattisgarh
C. Madhya Pradesh
D. Uttarakhand

304. The tribes who have got their names from the older part of the peninsular India are:
A. Gonds
B. Bhils
C. Kakaris
D. Angas

305. The standard meridian of India passes through:
A. Bhopal
B. Durg
C. Ujjain
D. Singrauli

306. The game reserve of Maharaja of Rewa has now been converted into ....:
A. Mahadev Sanctuary
B. Bandipur Sanctuary
C. Bandhavgarh Sanctuary
D. Panna Reserve

307. The oldest forest preserve in India is found in ....
A. Bori Wildlife Sanctuary
B. Kanha National Park
C. Van Vihar Park
D. Bandhvagarh National Park

308. Acchnakamar is a sanctuary. This is located in the district ....
A. Rewa
B. Annuppur
C. Ratlam
D. Morena

309. The Gandhi Sagar Sanctuary is located at ....
A. Mandsaur
B. Son
C. Rewa
D. Jabalpur

310. The Sanctuary that has many rock shelters is:
A. Ken Gharial
B. Shivpuri
C. Narsinghgarh
D. Kanha

311. Nauradhi is a sanctuary that is located in ....
A. Sagar
B. Morena
C. Rewa
D. Banjar

312. Sanctuary that is located in Morena is ....
A. Son Sanctuary
B. Kuno Sanctuary
C. Ghatigaon Sanctuary
D. Bandhavgarh Sanctuary

313. Chambal Originates from ....
A. Sagar District
B. Rewa District
C. Janapav Hills
D. Mikkai Ranges

314. Bina and Dhasaan are tributaries of ....
A. Chambal
B. Tapti
C. Narmada
D. Betwa

315. Kshipra is a river that merges into ....
A. Chambal
B. Narmada
C. Son
D. Swarna

316. The major city that Kshipra passes through is ....
A. Ujjain
B. Morena
C. Gwalior
D. Sagar

317. Largest road bridge of Madhya Pradesh is located across .... river.
A. Narmada
B. Tapti
C. Chambal
D. Tawa

318. Which river is called the "Ganga of Madhya Pradesh"?
A. Narmada
B. Chambal
C. Betwa
D. Tapti

319. Mandhar is a waterfall that is formed by the confluence of ....
A. Narmada and Tapti
B. Narmada and Tawa
C. Chambal and Narmada
D. Chambal and Tapti

320. The district of Guna is divided by .... river:
A. Tawa
B. Tamsa
C. Sindh
D. Jamni

321. Who of the following revolted after the 'Treaty of Durlabh' with British?
A. Jawahar Singh
B. Vinay Singh
C. Pratap Singh
D. None of these

322. Hunas attacked central India during the reign of
A. Samudragupta
B. Skandagupta
C. Chandragupta II
D. Chandragupta Maurya

323. Rudradaman was a ruler of which of the following dynasties?
A. Satavahana
B. Chandella
C. Kalchuri
D. Sakas

324. Which of the following rulers made Orcha the capital of Bundelkhand?
A. Bundela
B. Chandella
C. Mughal
D. Scindia

325. Before independence which of these rulers ruled at Indore?
A. Holkar
B. Maratha
C. Scindia
D. Malwa

326. Bharhut stupa is situated at
A. Chhatarpur
B. Sidhi
C. Satna
D. Vidisha

327. Parmars were the rulers of
A. Kalinga
B. Madhya Pradesh
C. Bengal
D. Andhra

328. In the Mahajanapad yug the Ujjain was capital of
A. Matsya
B. Avanti
C. Ashok
D. Vajji

329. At which of the following places the stone paintings of early man have been found?
A. Bhartrihari caves
B. Udaygiri caves
C. Bagh caves
D. Bhimbetka caves

330. Under the region of which rulers the famous Khajuraho temples were built?
A. Chola
B. Chandella
C. Chalukya
D. Chera

331. The historical place Chitrakoot is situated in
A. Satna
B. Sidhi
C. Dindori
D. Mandala

332. In the ancient India the proofs of the aestone of 'sati' are found at which of the following sites?
A. Sanchi
B. Vidisha
C. Eran
D. Tigwan

333. Which of the following regions of India was known as 'Avantika'?
A. Bundelkhand
B. Dandkaranya
C. Malwa
D. Nimarh

334. Among the following which one was not an active centre of rebel during the first freedom struggle for independence in 1857?
A. Mahu
B. Neemuch
C. Murar
D. Nagda

335. Which of the following freedom fighters is not related to Rewa?
A. Dinesh Chandra Pandey
B. Tribhuvan Nath Tiwari
C. Bhairav Prasad
D. Veer Narayan Pandey

336. The 'Jhanda Satyagraha' started from Jabalpur, which later spread in the whole state was in
A. 1907   B. 1923
C. 1917   D. 1919

337. Pt Nehru inaugurated the Central India State on
A. 1st November, 1956   B. 26th January, 1950
C. 28th May, 1948   D. 15th August, 1947

338. At which of the following places, the British did not make a cantonment for better control?
A. Agra   B. Neemuch
C. Mahu   D. Satna

339. The mighty ruler of Vidarbha, Bheemrath, married her daughter .... with Nala—the king of Nalpur.
A. Kalawati   B. Rajvasanti
C. Damyanti   D. Durgavati

340. The Gupta ruler Samudragupta who is often known as the Napoleon of India ruled on the Northern part of which river?
A. Narmada   B. Mahanadi
C. Tapti   D. Chambal

341. The highest peak of Madhya Pradesh 'Dhupgarh' is in
A. Hoshangabad   B. Satna
C. Rewa   D. Mandsaur

342. Which division of Madhya Pradesh has the maximum number of districts?
A. Indore   B. Jabalpur
C. Bhopal   D. Ujjain

343. The height of the highest point of Malwa Plateau Sigar is:
A. 881 m   B. 870 m
C. 860 m   D. 877 m

344. The height of the highest peak of Madhya Pradesh, Dhupgarh of Satpura Range is
A. 1250 m   B. 1350 m
C. 1450 m   D. 1650 m

345. Vindhya range is made up of
A. Quartz   B. Sand
C. Granite   D. A and B

346. Satpura range is made up of
A. Graphite   B. Basalt
C. Quartz   D. A and B

347. Which of the following states does not share its boundary with Madhya Pradesh?
A. Uttar Pradesh   B. Bihar
C. Chhattisgarh   D. Maharashtra

348. Match the following

List-I	List-II
(Rocks)	*(Region)*
(a) Archaean Times	1. Narmada Valley
(b) Dharwar	2. Gwalior
(c) Cuddapah	3. Balaghat
(d) Tertiary Rock	4. Bundelkhand

Codes:

	(a)	(b)	(c)	(d)
A.	4	3	2	1
B.	3	4	2	1
C.	4	1	2	3
D.	3	2	1	4

349. Which one of the following is not a part of the central highlands of the State of Madhya Pradesh?
A. Bundelkhand plateau
B. Satpura maikal range
C. Malwa plateau
D. Narmada-Son valley

350. Chhindwara, Khandwa, Betul are major towns of which of the following regions of the state?
A. Central highland   B. Satpura-Maikal range
C. Baghelkhand plateau   D. None of the above

351. Narmada originates at
A. Amarkantak   B. Mandsaur
C. Mahu   D. Shahdol

352. The longest river of Madhya Pradesh is
A. Narmada   B. Chambal
C. Sone   D. Betwa

353. The highest waterfall of Madhya Pradesh is
A. Bahuti   B. Dhuandhar
C. Kapildhara   D. Chalia

354. Ujjain is situated on the bank of
A. Khan river   B. Bichia river
C. Parvati river   D. Kshipra river

355. The longest dam in Madhya Pradesh has been built at
A. Betwa   B. Tawa
C. Narmada   D. Chambal

356. Chachai fall is on river ....
A. Narmada   B. Chambal
C. Beehad   D. Ken

357. Which rivers emerge from Amarkantak?
A. Chambal – Sone   B. Betwa – Tawa
C. Narmada – Sone   D. Sone – Tawa

358. Which of the following rivers forms ravines due to erosion?
A. Chambal   B. Narmada
C. Sone   D. Ken

359. Which of the following rivers form estuary?
A. Narmada – Tapti   B. Narmada – Sone
C. Narmada – Ken   D. Narmada – Chambal

360. Which is the second longest river of the state?
A. Chambal   B. Kshipra
C. Betwa   D. Tapti

361. The maximum rain in Madhya Pradesh occurs at
A. Panchmarhi   B. Bhind
C. Hoshangabad   D. Betul

362. Which of the following months is also known as the second summer in Madhya Pradesh?
A. September – October
B. August – September
C. May – June
D. June – July

363. 'Maawath' are
A. rain caused by Western disturbances
B. rain with snow fall and thunderstorm
C. summer rain
D. landslide

364. How many climatic zones are found in Madhya Pradesh?
A. 5
B. 6
C. 4
D. 2

365. The climate of the state of Madhya Pradesh is generally characterised as
A. Tropical
B. Sub-tropical
C. Continental
D. None of these

366. The average weather conditions of a place for a longer period of time refers to as
A. Monsoon
B. Climate
C. Humidity
D. Weather

367. Which part of Madhya Pradesh has a moderate climate?
A. Northern Plains
B. Malwa Plateau
C. Vindhyan Hills
D. Narmada Valley

368. Which among the following districts gains more than average rainfall?
A. Betul
B. Shivni
C. Chhindwara
D. All of these

369. Panchmarhi receives an average annual rainfall of ....
A. 200 cm
B. 212 cm
C. 185 cm
D. 228 cm

370. Which district of Madhya Pradesh receives maximum temperature during summer?
A. Gwalior
B. Morena
C. Datia
D. All of these

371. Which of the following districts is affected mostly by soil erosion?
A. Morena
B. Bhind
C. Guna
D. Shivpuri

372. The parent material of black soil is
A. Basalt rocks
B. Sedimentary rocks
C. Aplite rocks
D. Andesite rocks

373. Madhya Pradesh soils can broadly be classified into
A. 9 categories
B. 5 categories
C. 8 categories
D. 16 categories

374. Black soil lacks minerals like
A. iron and nitrogen
B. phosphorus and iron
C. nitrogen and phosphorus
D. iron

375. Which of the following soils is the most abundant soil type in the Madhya Pradesh?
A. Normal black soil
B. Layered black soil
C. Dark black soil
D. None of these

376. The pH of black soil is
A. 7.5–8.5
B. 6.5–8.5
C. 6.5–7.5
D. 7.5–9.5

377. Match the following

List I	List II
(a) Dark Black soil	1. Mandala
(b) Calcareous Soil	2. Balaghat
(c) Layered Black Soil	3. Hoshangabad
(d) Black Yellow Soil	4. Chhindwara

Codes:

	(a)	(b)	(c)	(d)
A.	1	2	3	4
B.	3	2	1	4
C.	4	3	2	1
D.	3	1	4	2

378. Mixed soils are majorly used in cultivation of
A. cash crops
B. cotton
C. coarse grains
D. sugarcane

379. Laterite soil is
A. found in Gwalior, Bhind and Morena district
B. found in the areas of Chambal valley
C. lacking in phosphorus and nitrogen
D. acidic in nature

380. Match the following

List-I	List-II
(a) Alluvial Soil	1 Humus
(b) Red Yellow Soil	2. Nitrogen
(c) Black Soil	3. Phosphorus and Humus
(d) Laterite Soil	4. Phosphorus and Nitrogen

Codes:

	(a)	(b)	(c)	(d)
A.	1	2	3	4
B.	4	3	2	1
C.	3	1	4	2
D.	2	4	1	3

381. Indian Forest Management Institute is located at
A. Bhopal
B. Indore
C. Gwalior
D. Jabalpur

382. What is the primary role of Sanjivani Sansthan established in Bhopal?
A. Conservation and development of forests
B. To develop eco-tourism
C. Trade of forest herbs development
D. Forest related training

383. When was the forest policy for Madhya Pradesh constituted?
A. 1963   B. 1950
C. 2005   D. 1951

384. Match the following

	List-I	**List-II**
(a)	Sanjivani Sansthan	1. Betul
(b)	Van Rajik Mahavidyalaya	2. Bhopal
(c)	Indian Forest Management Institution	3. Jabalpur
(d)	Bhartiya Van Anusandhan Sansthan	4. Bhopal

Codes:

	(a)	(b)	(c)	(d)
A.	1	3	2	4
B.	1	4	3	2
C.	4	3	2	1
D.	2	1	4	3

385. Consider the following statements
1. The main goal of Forest Policy, 2005 is to use the environmental and financial resources of the state.
2. The new Forest Policy was declared on 4 April, 2005.

Which of the statements given above is/are correct?
A. Only 1   B. Only 2
C. Both 1 and 2   D. None of these

386. When was the 'Lok Vaniki' programme launched by Government of Madhya Pradesh?
A. 1998   B. 1999
C. 1997   D. 1992

387. Bori Wildlife Sanctuary is in which district?
A. Jhabua   B. Rajgarh
C. Hoshangabad   D. Dhar

388. Ghatigaon Wildlife Sanctuary is located in district ....
A. Sidhi   B. Gwalior
C. Jhabua   D. Bhopal

389. Phen Wildlife Sanctuary is located in which district?
A. Mandla   B. Jhabua
C. Jabalpur   D. Dhar

390. National Chambal Wildlife Sanctuary is located in which district?
A. Morena   B. Jhabua
C. Raisen   D. Sidhi

391. Match the following

	List I (Sanctuary)	**List II** (District)
(a)	Panchmarhi	1. Jabalpur
(b)	Ratapani	2. Tikamgarh
(c)	Orchha	3. Hoshangabad
(d)	Durgawati	4. Raisen

392. How many national parks are there in Madhya Pradesh?
A. 3   B. 10
C. 8   D. 4

393. How many sanctuaries are there in Madhya Pradesh?
A. 16   B. 20
C. 22   D. 25

394. "Mandla Plant Fossils" is a
A. Biological Park
B. Sanctuary
C. National Park
D. Tiger Reproduction Centre

395. When was the Madhav National park established?
A. 1959   B. 1969
C. 1971   D. 1974

396. Match the following

	List-I	**List-II**
(a)	Panna National Park	1. 1981
(b)	Kanha National Park	2. 1995
(c)	Van Vihar National Park	3. 1983
(d)	Satpura National Park	4. 1981

Codes:

	(a)	(b)	(c)	(d)
A.	3	2	4	1
B.	1	2	3	4
C.	1	4	2	3
D.	2	3	4	1

397. The state animal of Madhya Pradesh is
A. Musk deer   B. Swamp deer
C. Tiger   D. Crocodile

398. When was the 'Project Tiger' launched?
A. 1973   B. 1985
C. 1995   D. 1972

399. How many parks of Madhya Pradesh are under project tiger?
A. 4   B. 5
C. 6   D. 7

400. Which of the following is the only biosphere reserve located in Madhya Pradesh?
A. Panchmarhi   B. Betul
C. Panna   D. Madhavgarh

401. Highest percentage of land holdings in Madhya Pradesh lies in
A. less than 1 hectare
B. 1-2 hectares
C. more than 2 hectares
D. None of these

402. Highest percentage of land occupied in Madhya Pradesh by
A. cereals   B. pulses
C. oilseeds   D. vegetables

403. *Sujat, Kalawal* and *Malavraj* are varieties of which crops produced in Madhya Pradesh?
A. Jowar   B. Wheat
C. Bajra   D. Rice

404. *Laloo* is a variety of
A. small grain rice   B. medium grain rice
C. long grain rice   D. Both B and C

405. Balaghat district in Madhya Pradesh lies in agro-climatic regions of
A. Wheat zone   B. Rice zone
C. Wheat-Rice zone   D. Wheat-Jowar zone

406. Khandwa and Rajgarh are main producers of
A. Lime   B. Orange
C. Banana   D. Papaya

407. Turmeric in Madhya Pradesh is mainly produced in
A. Khandwa, Badwani   B. Guna, Mandsaur
C. Ujjain, Shajapur   D. Rajgarh, Chhindwara

408. The Madhya Pradesh state Agro-Industries Development Corporation Ltd. is headquartered at
A. Jabalpur   B. Bhopal
C. Satna   D. Indore

409. Madhya Pradesh Seed Certification Agency was established in
A. 1963   B. 1972
C. 1980   D. 1985

410. Madhya Pradesh State Livestock and Poultry Development Corporation was established in
A. 1871   B. 1975
C. 1978   D. 1982

411. The Net irrigated area in Madhya Pradesh is
A. 33 per cent   B. 60.9 per cent
C. 42 per cent   D. 47 per cent

412. The maximum irrigated area in Madhya Pradesh is under the district of
A. Dindori   B. Umaria
C. Shahdol   D. Hoshangabad

413. The minimum irrigated area in Madhya Pradesh is under district of
A. Panna   B. Katni
C. Dindori   D. Shivni

414. Which among the following is the major sources of irrigation in Madhya Pradesh?
A. Canals   B. Wells and Tubewells
C. Ponds   D. Other sources

415. Which among the following districts of Madhya Pradesh is not benefitted from Wainganga canal?
A. Balaghat   B. Morena
C. Gwalior   D. Both B and C

416. Halali canal in Madhya Pradesh emerges from river
A. Chambal   B. Barna
C. Halali   D. Wainganga

417. Gandhi Sagar Dam is located on the river
A. Wainganga   B. Chambal
C. Betwa   D. Barna

418. Samrat Ashok Sagar is constructed across the river
A. Halali   B. Chambal
C. Narmada   D. Barna

419. Which among the following is not a part of Narmada Valley Project?
A. Tawa Reservoir
B. Maan Dam
C. Rani Avanti Bai Lodhi Sagar Project
D. Omkareshwar Dam

420. Baansagar project is located on river
A. Peuch   B. Sone
C. Bargi   D. Betwa

421. Copper is mainly found in ....
A. Balaghat   B. Satna
C. Rewa   D. Betul

422. In which district of Madhya Pradesh, antimony is found?
A. Balaghat   B. Jabalpur
C. Datia   D. Morena

423. The only diamond producing state of India is
A. Madhya Pradesh   B. Andhra Pradesh
C. Rajasthan   D. Bihar

424. Diamond is found in the district of ....
A. Dewas   B. Panna
C. Jhabua   D. Shivni

425. Platinum is found in
A. Jhabua   B. Balaghat
C. Betul   D. Mandsaur

426. Tungsten is found in the Agargaon region of
A. Betul   B. Hoshangabad
C. Jhabua   D. Jabalpur

427. Gondwana group of rocks are rich in ....
A. sandstone and coal   B. granite
C. diamonds and coal   D. limestone

428. Sidhi, Katni and Shahdol are famous for
A. diamond   B. platinum
C. gold   D. nickel

429. Which of the following rocks in the State of Madhya Pradesh are devoid of any fossils?
A. Dharwar
B. Archaean
C. Cuddapah
D. Vindhyan system of rocks

430. Which region of Madhya Pradesh is called Gondwana?
A. Narmada Valley   B. Chambal Valley
C. Northern Region   D. South-East Region

431. The Madhya Pradesh State Industrial Corporation was founded on
A. April, 1965
B. September, 1965
C. October, 1965
D. December, 1965

432. The railway sleepers in Madhya Pradesh are manufactured at
A. Bhopal
B. Budhani
C. Indore
D. Dindori

433. Maheshwar is famous for
A. Silk Saree Industry
B. Ahilya Ghat
C. Ahilya Museum
D. All of the above

434. The note printing press in Madhya Pradesh is located at
A. Hoshangabad
B. Nepanagar
C. Dewas
D. Ujjain

435. Leather complex in Madhya Pradesh is located at
A. Dewas
B. Ujjain
C. Chhindwara
D. Shajapur

436. Which chemical fertilizer is mostly used in Madhya Pradesh?
A. Nitrogen
B. Potash
C. Phosphate
D. Sulphur

437. The biggest undertaking of Madhya Pradesh Government is
A. Madhya Pradesh Finance Corporation
B. Madhya Pradesh Electricity Corporation
C. Madhya Pradesh Transportation Corporation
D. Madhya Pradesh Small Industries Corporation

438. The air cargo complex, Indo-German tool room and dry sea-port in Madhya Pradesh are located at ....
A. Mandideep
B. Pithampur
C. Ujjain
D. Korba

439. Malanpur Industrial Centre is located in
A. Bhind
B. Morena
C. Gwalior
D. Shivpuri

440. A new oil processing unit in Madhya Pradesh is proposed at
A. Malanpur
B. Pithampur
C. Aagasaud
D. Mandideep

441. Software Technology Park is located at
A. Ratlam
B. Gwalior
C. Indore
D. All of these

442. The Cement Corporation of India is in which district of Madhya Pradesh?
A. Jabalpur
B. Durg
C. Katni
D. Raisen

443. The first gem purifying centre in Madhya Pradesh is established at
A. Jabalpur
B. Sidhi
C. Shivni
D. Indore

444. The largest cotton textile producing district of Madhya Pradesh is
A. Indore
B. Jabalpur
C. Raigarh
D. Shivpuri

445. The HMT factory in Madhya Pradesh is established at
A. Bhopal
B. Dewas
C. Betul
D. Datia

446. Which among the following thermal power stations is located in Umaria district of Madhya Pradesh?
A. Satpura
B. Sanjay Gandhi
C. Chandani
D. Vindhyachal

447. Which thermal station is a joint venture of Madhya Pradesh and Rajasthan?
A. Birsinghpur-II
B. Pench
C. Malwa
D. Satpura

448. Nepanagar is getting electricity from
A. Chandani Thermal
B. Vindhyachal
C. Amarkantak
D. Birsinghpur

449. How many hydroelectric power stations are there in Madhya Pradesh?
A. Nine
B. Eleven
C. Three
D. Eight

450. Jawaharsagar hydropower project is on river
A. Pench
B. Baansagar
C. Chambal
D. Sone

451. Gandhi Sagar hydel power project has an installed capacity of ....
A. 280 MW
B. 310 MW
C. 115 MW
D. 210 MW

452. In Madhya Pradesh electricity was first produced in
A. Sohagpur
B. Gwalior
C. Umaria
D. Jabalpur

453. The energy capital of Madhya Pradesh is
A. Shivni
B. Korba
C. Rajgarh
D. Singrauli

454. The first solar village (district) of Madhya Pradesh is
A. Itarasi
B. Sehore
C. Indore
D. Panchmarhi

455. Which of the districts is known as energy district of Madhya Pradesh?
A. Datia
B. Singrauli
C. Chhindwara
D. Panchmarhi

456. Gandhi Sagar Power Station is located in
A. Mandsaur district
B. Ujjain
C. Jhabua
D. Umaria

457. When was the first bio gas plant established in Bhopal?
A. 1980
B. 1983
C. 1984
D. 1985

458. Indira Sagar Vidyut Kendra is located at
A. Punasa
B. Khandwa
C. Omkareshwar
D. Maheshwar

459. Which of the following cities is not covered under JNURM?
A. Indore
B. Jabalpur
C. Gwalior
D. Ujjain

460. MP Urja Vikas Nigam was established in—
A. 1982
B. 1984
C. 1972
D. 1965

ANSWERS

1	2	3	4	5	6	7	8	9	10
B	A	B	A	B	A	B	B	B	D

11	12	13	14	15	16	17	18	19	20
A	C	A	C	B	B	A	B	B	C

21	22	23	24	25	26	27	28	29	30
B	B	A	B	B	B	C	A	B	D

31	32	33	34	35	36	37	38	39	40
B	C	C	C	B	A	B	B	A	C

41	42	43	44	45	46	47	48	49	50
C	A	D	B	A	C	D	C	B	B

51	52	53	54	55	56	57	58	59	60
C	C	B	A	D	C	B	C	B	A

61	62	63	64	65	66	67	68	69	70
A	A	A	B	D	A	C	B	A	C

71	72	73	74	75	76	77	78	79	80
B	D	C	C	B	C	B	A	A	B

81	82	83	84	85	86	87	88	89	90
B	C	A	A	B	A	C	A	A	C

91	92	93	94	95	96	97	98	99	100
D	B	B	A	D	A	B	C	A	B

101	102	103	104	105	106	107	108	109	110
A	A	D	C	A	D	A	A	C	D

111	112	113	114	115	116	117	118	119	120
B	C	B	D	D	C	A	A	B	B

121	122	123	124	125	126	127	128	129	130
D	A	B	C	A	A	B	B	A	D

131	132	133	134	135	136	137	138	139	140
D	B	D	A	D	B	D	D	A	A

141	142	143	144	145	146	147	148	149	150
D	C	A	B	C	B	A	A	D	C

151	152	153	154	155	156	157	158	159	160
B	A	A	D	D	D	D	A	B	B

161	162	163	164	165	166	167	168	169	170
A	A	B	A	A	B	D	B	A	B

171	172	173	174	175	176	177	178	179	180
D	B	A	A	D	B	B	C	A	B

181	182	183	184	185	186	187	188	189	190
B	C	B	B	A	B	A	A	A	A

191	192	193	194	195	196	197	198	199	200
D	A	B	C	C	A	A	A	A	C

201	202	203	204	205	206	207	208	209	210
D	C	D	B	C	D	B	C	B	A

211	212	213	214	215	216	217	218	219	220
A	B	A	B	A	C	A	A	A	C

221	222	223	224	225	226	227	228	229	230
A	A	D	A	A	C	D	B	A	C

231	232	233	234	235	236	237	238	239	240
C	A	D	A	C	B	A	A	C	A

241	242	243	244	245	246	247	248	249	250
D	B	B	B	A	B	B	A	A	B

251	**252**	**253**	**254**	**255**	**256**	**257**	**258**	**259**	**260**
B	A	A	A	C	A	B	D	D	A
261	**262**	**263**	**264**	**265**	**266**	**267**	**268**	**269**	**270**
D	C	C	C	D	A	B	D	A	A
271	**272**	**273**	**274**	**275**	**276**	**277**	**278**	**279**	**280**
B	A	B	B	A	B	C	B	A	B
281	**282**	**283**	**284**	**285**	**286**	**287**	**288**	**289**	**290**
A	A	C	A	B	A	B	B	D	C
291	**292**	**293**	**294**	**295**	**296**	**297**	**298**	**299**	**300**
A	A	A	B	B	B	B	D	B	A
301	**302**	**303**	**304**	**305**	**306**	**307**	**308**	**309**	**310**
A	B	C	A	D	C	A	B	A	C
311	**312**	**313**	**314**	**315**	**316**	**317**	**318**	**319**	**320**
A	B	C	D	A	A	D	C	A	C
321	**322**	**323**	**324**	**325**	**326**	**327**	**328**	**329**	**330**
A	B	D	A	A	C	B	B	D	B
331	**332**	**333**	**334**	**335**	**336**	**337**	**338**	**339**	**340**
A	C	C	D	D	B	B	D	C	A
341	**342**	**343**	**344**	**345**	**346**	**347**	**348**	**349**	**350**
A	A	A	B	D	D	B	A	B	B
351	**352**	**353**	**354**	**355**	**356**	**357**	**358**	**359**	**360**
A	A	A	D	A	C	C	A	A	A
361	**362**	**363**	**364**	**365**	**366**	**367**	**368**	**369**	**370**
A	A	A	A	B	B	C	D	B	D
371	**372**	**373**	**374**	**375**	**376**	**377**	**378**	**379**	**380**
A	A	B	C	A	A	D	C	A	C
381	**382**	**383**	**384**	**385**	**386**	**387**	**388**	**389**	**390**
A	C	C	D	C	B	C	B	A	A
391	**392**	**393**	**394**	**395**	**396**	**397**	**398**	**399**	**400**
A	B	D	C	A	B	B	A	C	A
401	**402**	**403**	**404**	**405**	**406**	**407**	**408**	**409**	**410**
A	A	B	C	B	C	A	B	C	D
411	**412**	**413**	**414**	**415**	**416**	**417**	**418**	**419**	**420**
B	D	C	B	D	C	B	A	D	B
421	**422**	**423**	**424**	**425**	**426**	**427**	**428**	**429**	**430**
A	B	A	B	C	B	A	C	B	D
431	**432**	**433**	**434**	**435**	**436**	**437**	**438**	**439**	**440**
B	A	D	C	A	A	B	B	C	C
441	**442**	**443**	**444**	**445**	**446**	**447**	**448**	**449**	**450**
A	C	A	A	C	B	D	A	B	C
451	**452**	**453**	**454**	**455**	**456**	**457**	**458**	**459**	**460**
C	B	D	A	B	A	C	A	C	A

❏ ❏ ❏

1810

www.ingramcontent.com/pod-product-compliance
Lightning Source LLC
Chambersburg PA
CBHW060112120726
48003CB00009B/2599